ANIMALS IN THE INTERNATIONAL LAW OF ARMED CONFLICT

Animals are the unknown victims of armed conflicts. Wildlife populations usually decline during warfare, with disastrous repercussions on the food chain, on fragile ecosystems and precarious habitats. Armed forces and groups take advantage of the chaos raised by war to engage in the poaching and trafficking of expensive animal products. Livestock, companion and zoo animals, highly dependent on human care, are slaughtered, looted, bombed or starved on a massive scale. Some animals also serve in the military around the world in various capacities and are regularly exposed to the dangers of war. The book is the first legal analysis of these issues. It examines how the concepts and rationales of international humanitarian law can be applied for a better protection of animals. The contributions inter alia discuss the protection of animals as objects, as part of the environment, as combatants or as prisoners of war, a specific status for veterinarian personnel, the recognition of biodiversity hotspots as specially protected zones and the potential of enforcement mechanisms. The concluding chapter draws together novel interpretations and reform proposals.

Anne Peters is Director at the Max Planck Institute for Comparative Public Law and International Law, Heidelberg. She is a member of the Permanent Court of Arbitration and an associate member of the Institut de Droit International. She is currently President of the German Society of International Law and a past president of the European Society of International Law.

Jérôme de Hemptinne is a lecturer in international humanitarian law and international criminal law at the Universities of Utrecht and Louvain. He also teaches at the Geneva Academy of International Humanitarian Law and Human Rights, Sciences-Po and Lille Catholic University. He has previously worked at the Special Tribunal for Lebanon, the Office of Legal Counsel of the United Nations and the International Criminal Tribunal for the former Yugoslavia.

Robert Kolb is Professor of Public International Law at the University of Geneva. He has worked as legal advisor for the International Committee of the Red Cross and the Swiss Federal Department of Foreign Affairs.

Animals in the International Law of Armed Conflict

Edited by

ANNE PETERS

Max Planck Institute for Comparative Public Law and International Law

JÉRÔME DE HEMPTINNE

Geneva Academy of International Humanitarian Law and Human Rights

ROBERT KOLB

University of Geneva

CAMBRIDGE
UNIVERSITY PRESS

CAMBRIDGE
UNIVERSITY PRESS

Shaftesbury Road, Cambridge CB2 8EA, United Kingdom

One Liberty Plaza, 20th Floor, New York, NY 10006, USA

477 Williamstown Road, Port Melbourne, VIC 3207, Australia

314–321, 3rd Floor, Plot 3, Splendor Forum, Jasola District Centre, New Delhi – 110025, India

103 Penang Road, #05–06/07, Visioncrest Commercial, Singapore 238467

Cambridge University Press is part of Cambridge University Press & Assessment, a department of the University of Cambridge.

We share the University's mission to contribute to society through the pursuit of education, learning and research at the highest international levels of excellence.

www.cambridge.org
Information on this title: www.cambridge.org/9781009060271

DOI: 10.1017/9781009057301

First published 2022
First paperback edition 2026

A catalogue record for this publication is available from the British Library

ISBN 978-1-316-51204-3 Hardback
ISBN 978-1-009-06027-1 Paperback

Contents

Contributors

EDITORS

Anne Peters is a director at the Max Planck Institute for Comparative Public Law and International Law (Heidelberg) (Max Planck Institute), a professor at the Universities of Heidelberg, Freie Universität Berlin and Basel and an L. Bates Lea Global Law Professor at the University of Michigan. She holds an honorary doctorate of the University of Lausanne. She was a member (substitute) of the European Commission for Democracy through Law (Venice Commission) in respect of Germany (2011–14) and a legal expert for the Independent International Fact-Finding Mission on the Conflict in Georgia (2009). She was the President of the European Society of International Law (2010–12) and has served on the governance board of various learned societies such as the German Association of Constitutional Law (VDStRL) and the Society of International Constitutional Law (ICON-S). She is currently president of the German Association of International Law (DGIR).

Jérôme de Hemptinne is a lecturer at Utrecht University. He is also teaching IHL and international criminal law at the University of Louvain, at the Catholic University of Lille, at the Institut d'études politiques (Paris) and at the Geneva Academy. He worked for more than a decade at the International Criminal Tribunal for the Former Yugoslavia (ICTY). He also worked at the Office of the United Nations Legal Counsel in New York and at the Special Tribunal for Lebanon (STL). Jérôme de Hemptinne is a member of the editorial committee of the *Journal of International Criminal Justice*.

Robert Kolb is Professor of Public International Law at the University of Geneva. He has worked as a legal advisor for the International Committee of the Red Cross (ICRC) (1998–9) and sporadically for the Swiss Federal Department of Foreign Affairs (since 2000). He was a secretary of the Institut de Droit International (1999–2003) and was a member of the Board of Directors of the Geneva Academy of International Humanitarian Law and Human Rights (Geneva Academy). In 2008, he was the director of studies for The Hague Academy of International Law

(Francophone stream). In 2011, he acted as a counsel for the German Government in the *Jurisdictional Immunities* case (*Germany* v. *Italy*) at the International Court of Justice (ICJ). He acted as legal counsel (*avis de droit*) in several dozens of cases. Robert Kolb was a lecturer in public international law at the Graduate Institute of International Studies (Graduate Institute) (1999–2002), and later an associate professor at the University of Bern (2002–7), as well as adjunct professor at the University of Neuchâtel (2003–8). He has also taught at the Geneva Academy (and its predecessor institute), as well as at the Catholic University of Milan, in 2002.

AUTHORS

Giulio Bartolini is Associate Professor of International Law at the Department of Law, Roma Tre University, where he is also responsible for the Roma Tre International Humanitarian Law Legal Clinic. He is editor-in-chief of the *Yearbook of International Disaster Law* (Brill), director of the summer courses on international disaster law managed in cooperation with the International Federation of Red Cross and Red Crescent Societies and the San Remo International Institute of Humanitarian Law. He is also responsible for the EU Jean Monnet Activity 'Disseminating Disaster Law for Europe'.

Veronika Bílková is the head of the Centre for International Law at the Institute of International Relations in Prague and Associate Professor of Public International Law at the Faculty of Law of the Charles University in Prague. She is a member of the European Commission for Democracy through Law (Venice Commission) of the Council of Europe, a member of the Managerial Board of the EU Fundamental Rights Agency and Vice-President of the European Society of International Law. Her fields of research include public international law, human rights, the use of force, international humanitarian law and foreign policy issues. She has authored five books and many articles published in Czech, English and French.

Ayşe-Martina Böhringer is an assistant professor at the chair of Public Law and International Law (Professor Thilo Marauhn)/Franz von Liszt Institute for International and Comparative Law, Justus Liebig University Giessen. She is a member of the Chamber of Lawyers Frankfurt am Main. Her current research interests relate to German constitutional law, the sociology of law and public international law, with a special focus on international environmental law, international institutional law, the law of armed conflict and the sociology of public international law.

Joshua H. Daskin is the Director of Conservation at Archbold Biological Station in central Florida. Previously, he was a biologist at the United States Fish and Wildlife Service, responsible for assessing the conservation status of international (non-US) species. He completed his doctorate in ecology and evolutionary biology at Princeton University and was a postdoctoral fellow at Yale University. His research focused on the effects of war on the conservation and restoration of wildlife and ecosystems. He also held a Fulbright Scholarship in Australia and worked in land management and restoration ecology for two biodiversity conservation organisations.

Katharine Fortin is an associate professor at Utrecht University where she teaches international humanitarian law, international human rights law and public international law. She is the author of *The Accountability of Armed Groups under Human Rights Law* (Oxford: Oxford University Press 2017) which won the 2018 Lieber Prize. Katharine Fortin has written widely about the framework of law that applies to armed groups in non-international armed conflicts and is an editor of the Armed Groups and International Law blog.

Matthew Gillett is an associate professor (senior lecturer) at the University of Essex. He previously served as a senior legal officer at the Organisation for the Prohibition of Chemical Weapons, as a trial lawyer in the Office of the Prosecutor of the International Criminal Court (ICC), as a human rights officer with the United Nations Assistance Mission in Afghanistan and as a trial lawyer and appeals counsel at the ICTY. He was a member of the New Zealand delegation at the ICC review conference in Kampala in 2010. He teaches and writes on issues including crimes against humanity, international humanitarian law (IHL), terrorism, environmental law and criminal procedure, and has received several awards for his academic work. His book entitled *Prosecuting Environmental Harm before the International Criminal Court* (Cambridge: Cambridge University Press 2022) builds on his doctorate from Leiden University on the same subject.

Etienne Henry is an associate legal officer at the ICJ and a lecturer at the University of Neuchâtel. Prior to this experience, he has held visiting research positions, including at the Geneva Academy of International Humanitarian Law and Human Rights, the Université libre de Bruxelles, the Australian National University, the Diplomatic Academy of the Russian Ministry of Foreign Affairs and the Max Planck Institute for Comparative Public Law and International Law (Heidelberg). His research touches on general international law, especially the law of armed conflict, international law on the use of force and their historical development. His book entitled *Le principe de nécessité militaire: Histoire et actualité d'une norme fondamentale du droit international humanitaire* (Paris: Pedone 2017) was awarded the Francis Durieux prize by the Institut de France and the Professor Walther-Hug prize.

Chris Jenks is a professor of law at the SMU Dedman School of Law in Dallas, Texas. His research agenda focuses on emerging technology's impact on accountability norms. In 2015, he received a Fulbright Senior Scholars Grant to research autonomous weapons. In 2016, he presented on autonomous weapons at the UN Convention on Certain Conventional Weapons Group of Governmental Experts (GGE) meetings in Geneva. In 2017–18, while serving as the Special Counsel to the

General Counsel for the US Department of Defense, he participated in similar meetings as a member of the US delegation.

Tadesse M. Kebebew is a teaching assistant at the Geneva Academy of International Humanitarian Law and Human Rights and a researcher for the Platform for International Water Law at the Geneva Water Hub. He previously served as a research and technology interchange director of Dire Dawa University (Ethiopia) and as a lecturer in law at the College of Law, Dire Dawa.

Sandra Krähenmann is a senior legal and policy adviser at Geneva Call, a Swiss non-governmental organisation that works on the implementation of IHL through the humanitarian engagement of armed non-state actors. She is also teaching at the Geneva Academy. Her current research interests relate to IHL, in particular its interplay with the legal regime governing terrorism and human rights law, transitional justice and positive obligations in human rights law.

Heike Krieger is Professor of Public Law and International Law at Freie Universität Berlin and was Max Planck Fellow at the Max Planck Institute between 2017 and 2021. She is co-chair of the Berlin Potsdam Research Group on 'The International Rule of Law: Rise or Decline?' and editor-in-chief of the *Yearbook of International Humanitarian Law* (T. M. C. Asser Press and Springer). She is also a member of the editorial board of the *Journal of Conflict and Security Law*. Her recent publications include the edited volume *Law-making and Legitimacy in International Humanitarian Law* (Cheltenham: Edward Elgar 2021).

Marco Longobardo is a senior lecturer in international law at the University of Westminster, where he teaches public international law, IHL, international criminal law and other related subjects. He undertook his doctoral studies at the Sapienza University of Rome and previously lectured at the University of Messina and in the context of IHL courses for the personnel of the Italian armed forces. He has published extensively on public international law issues and he is the author of *The Use of Armed Force in Occupied Territory* (Cambridge: Cambridge University Press 2018), for which he was awarded the 2021 Paul Reuter Prize. He is the reviews editor of the *Journal of International Humanitarian Legal Studies* and sits on the advisory board of the *International Community Law Review*.

Marina Lostal is a senior lecturer at the University of Essex and Deputy Director of its Human Rights Centre Clinic. Between 2018 and 2020 she worked as a reparations expert for the Trust Fund for Victims of the ICC. In 2017, she served as an ICC-appointed expert in the reparations phase of the *Al Mahdi* case. She holds an LLM from the University of Cambridge (2009), another from the European University Institute (2010) and a master's in Animal Law & Society from the University Autónoma of Barcelona (2020). She earned a doctorate from the European University Institute (2013). She is the author of *International Cultural Heritage*

Law in Armed Conflict (New York: Cambridge University Press 2017) and is a member of the ILA Participation in Global Cultural Heritage Governance. Her current research interests relate to reparations for victims of international crimes and the treatment of animals under international law.

Thilo Marauhn is Professor of Public Law and International Law at Justus Liebig University Giessen, Extraordinary Professor of International Arms Control Law, Asser Institute/University of Amsterdam, head of the Public International Law Research Group at the Peace Research Institute Frankfurt, permanent Visiting Professor at the University of Lucerne and Adjunct Professor at the University of Wisconsin-Madison. He chairs the German National IHL Committee and serves as president of the International Humanitarian Fact-Finding Commission. His current research interests relate to public international law, focusing on international environmental law, UN law, the law of armed conflict and the sociology of public international law.

José Martínez Soria is Professor of Public Law and Agricultural Law at the Faculty of Law of the Georg-August-University Göttingen and managing director of the Institute for Agricultural Law of the University of Göttingen. He is also a member of the Scientific Advisory Board on Agricultural Policy, Food and Consumer Health Protection of the Federal Ministry of Food and Agriculture, and vice president of the European Council for Rural Law. He conducts research in the fields of constitutional law, administrative law, European law and comparative law. He has published widely on animal welfare law.

Makane Moïse Mbengue is Professor of International Law at the Faculty of Law of the University of Geneva and Director of the Department of International Law and International Organisation. He is also an affiliate professor at Sciences Po Paris (School of Law). Since 2017, he has been the president of the African Society of International Law (AfSIL). Makane Mbengue acts as counsel in disputes before international courts and tribunals (in particular, before the ICJ and in investment cases) and as advisor for governments. He is the author of several publications in the field of international law and a member of the Curatorium of The Hague Academy of International Law and an associate member of the Institut de Droit International.

Joshua Joseph Niyo is a visiting researcher at UCLA School of Law (funded by the Swiss National Science Foundation), a PhD candidate at the Graduate Institute and an assistant lecturer at Uganda Christian University. Until recently, he has been a teaching assistant at the Geneva Academy. He has previously worked for private law firms in Uganda, as well as national and international non-governmental organisations (Chapter Four Uganda, Human Rights Watch, the ICRC and International Justice Mission). He has assisted members of UN treaty and charter-based bodies and has also clerked for both the Ugandan Principal Judge and the Directorate of Public Prosecutions in Kampala (Uganda).

André Nollkaemper is Professor of Public International Law of the Faculty of Law of the University of Amsterdam. He is a member of the Royal Netherlands Academy of Arts and Sciences and the Institut de Droit International, was external Legal Advisor to the Minister of Foreign Affairs of the Netherlands (2010–20) and president of the European Society of International Law (2014–17). He has published widely on questions of international environmental law, protection of species and animal welfare as well as on general international law themes (notably international responsibility) that are relevant to protection of animals in international law.

Karsten Nowrot is a Professor of public law, EU law and international economic law, director of the Research Institute for Economic Law and Labour Law, as well as the current head of the Department of Law at the School of Socio-Economics of the Faculty of Business, Economics and Social Sciences at Hamburg University. He is also an affiliated professor at the Faculty of Law at Hamburg University and serves as deputy director of the Master Programme 'European and European Legal Studies' at the Institute for European Integration of the Europa-Kolleg in Hamburg.

Robert M. Pringle is Professor of Ecology and Evolutionary Biology at Princeton University. His research focuses on understanding how local interactions between species, including humans, scale up to determine the diversity, robustness and resilience of ecosystems. Much of his current research is conducted and applied in Gorongosa National Park (Mozambique), where wildlife was nearly eliminated during the Mozambican Civil War but is now recovering. He serves as a scientific advisor to the Gorongosa Project, which oversees this pioneering restoration effort.

Marco Roscini is Professor of International Law at the University of Westminster and the Swiss Chair of International Humanitarian Law at the Geneva Academy of International Humanitarian Law and Human Rights. He has a doctorate in international law from Sapienza University of Rome and has published widely in the field of international law, including two monographs (*Le zone denuclearizzate* (Turin: Giappichelli 2003) and *Cyber Operations and the Use of Force in International Law* (Oxford: Oxford University Press 2014)). His current research interests relate to the legal regulation of foreign intervention in civil wars, including its history, the law of armed conflict, nuclear disarmament law and international cyber security law.

Britta Sjöstedt is a senior lecturer at the Faculty of Law of Lund University. She is researching and teaching public international law and environmental law. Her current research interests include environmental protection, armed conflict and environmental peacebuilding and she has published widely within this field, including a monograph (*The Role of Multilateral Environmental Agreements: A Reconciliatory Approach to Environmental Protection in Armed Conflict* (Oxford: Hart 2020)). She is a founding board director of the Environmental Peacebuilding Association and the co-chair of its Law Interest Group. She is also a member of the International Law Association's

Committee on the Role of International Law in Sustainable Natural Resource Management for Development.

Manuel J. Ventura is a legal consultant for the Organisation for the Prohibition of Chemical Weapons, an adjunct fellow/lecturer at the School of Law at Western Sydney University, an external lecturer in international law at The Hague University of Applied Sciences and a director of The Peace and Justice Initiative. He has previously served in chambers at the STL, in the Office of the Prosecutor at the ICTY and the International Residual Mechanism for Criminal Tribunals, in Defence at the ICC, and was a law clerk to Chief Justice Mogoeng Mogoeng at the Constitutional Court of South Africa and President Antonio Cassese at the STL. He is an editor of *Modes of Liability in International Criminal Law* (Cambridge: Cambridge University Press 2019) and of *International Humanitarian Law and Non-State Actors: Debates, Law and Practice* (The Hague/Berlin: T. M. C. Asser Press/ Springer 2020). Manuel J. Ventura has an LLM(Hons) in IHL and Human Rights from the Geneva Academy and publishes regularly on topics related to international criminal law and justice.

Clemens Wischermann is Professor Emeritus of Economic and Social History at the University of Konstanz. His books include *Animal History in the Modern City: Exploring Liminality* (London: Bloomsbury Academic 2019) (edited with Aline Steinbrecher and Philip Howell). His current research interests relate to animate history and history of childhood, both in the nineteenth and twentieth centuries.

Forewords

ROBERT KOLB

History is evolutionary; human conscience is evolutionary; perceptions are evolutionary. The fate of animals in their relationships with humans (the 'other' animal) illustrates the point very well. For centuries, in the mould of Roman law, animals were considered simple objects. In the nineteenth century, in many European states, some protective legislation was envisioned or realised in order to spare these living creatures from cruel treatment. But 'cruel' treatment was defined in a very narrow manner. Appalling conditions in industrial contexts and in the holding of animals in farms or by the Church continued undisturbed. Some authors applauded this however modest protective legislation. For them, the main point was that animals are able to suffer and that for that fact, they must be protected. The visionary Jeremy Bentham was amongst these persons.[1] Others cautioned against these legislations and combated them with full and fierce energy. For some Catholic churchmen, always prone to know the ultimate truth, all protection of animals against suffering is an aberration based on a perversion of the natural Divine order of creation. To them, animals are abysmally inferior to humanity. If they were to be protected, compassion would be extended to them, and thus they would heretically be raised to the level of mankind. Luigi Taparelli wrote on these lines.[2] Still today, protection of animals is a theme in Europe but not in many other parts of the world. The treatment of animals, for example in China, continues to be monstrous.

Let us jump to more recent times. When I was in school, in the 1970s–1980s, the common doxa was that animals have no intelligence, no reasoning and no individualised feeling. They were driven merely by instincts. Some dumb conscience was accessible to them, but not more. Again, today most of us would not subscribe to such views. My mother had more than one dog in her life. With these remarkable

[1] Jeremy Bentham, *An Introduction to the Principles of Morals and Legislation* (Oxford: Clarendon 1789), chapter VIII, § 1.

[2] Luigi Taparelli, *Saggio teoritico di diritto naturale* (6th ed., Palermo 1857), 59–60.

creatures, I had experiences which directly contradicted the merely instinct theory. In one situation I walked to a place where I had not been for more than one year. The dog immediately ran to a sort of hole in a fence and robustly smelled around. I was first puzzled by the attitude, but then remembered that the last time I had been there, the dog had seen a cat disappearing through that hole. Unless there were new smells, there is much to make us believe that the dog had a memory of the past event. And that event was more than one year old. Other situations. The same dog, apparently adoring cats, one day saw one trying to escape. Instead of running behind it, the dog changed direction and ran through another way, which I quickly determined to be a short cut. I concluded that the dog had reasoning. I shall not speak of all the other analytical qualities of these animals, spanning from feeling imminent earthquakes to anticipating epileptic crises.

Let us jump to some remote future. What will be the collective thinking on that question? May I guess that our successors might judge us very severely for a great blind spot in our perceptions? Might they not think that the way in which we continue to treat so many animals in the world (who of us would like to be treated thus?) was akin to a silent 'zoocide'? Might they not condemn our pharisaic and hypocritical stance in moralising about innumerable subjects and forgetting so many living creatures in their plight? However that may be, Max Planck, the great physician, was right to suggest that science advances from one burial (of a theory) to the next. The same can be said of human perceptions. New ideas can gain ground only when the tenants of the older schools retire and younger colleagues bring fresh winds. That may not always be a 'progress' but sometimes it is – as it will probably continue to be in the extension of respect and protection for animals. It has sometimes been said that life is a process in which one learns a great lesson of modesty. From childhood, formatted by almost endless narcissism, the human being progressively lives complexity and reduces its importance to an infinitesimal grain in a huge machine. This process is utterly necessary in the context of animals. The arrogance of human superiority perorations has to give way to a more nuanced and modest view. Nature is not beneath us, it is above us.

The present book, with its many particular studies, attempts to be a modest contribution in the direction of framing a new mental setting. It addresses a blind spot in the context of animal protection, namely the place of animals in the context of armed conflicts. At first sight this is an odd subject matter. In armed conflicts, violence – so the argument goes – wreaks havoc everywhere; animals are not here the priority, to say the least. We believe that this view, as for the ones mentioned above, is short-sighted. The question is intriguing, the legal regulation defective, the usefulness of some reflection not manifestly absent. Moreover, the reader will not be wearied for the hundredth time with child soldiers or the definition of combatant. They will rather break new ground, feel perhaps like an explorer of new continents. I wish a pleasant journey!

MAKANE MOÏSE MBENGUE

On 15 August 1893, an arbitral tribunal established by the United States and Her Majesty the Queen of the UK rendered an award in the dispute commonly known as the *Bering Fur Seals* case. The dispute arose between the two countries – including Canada on the UK side – due to an attempt by the United States to control the hunting of seals off the Alaskan coast following its claimed authority over all the Bering Sea waters in 1881. Despite the UK's refusal to recognise the US claim, the United States still ordered in 1886 the seizure of all vessels found sealing in the Bering Sea. Most of the vessels which were seized were Canadian ships sailing from British Columbia and manned by British subjects. In the *Compromis d'arbitrage*, the United States and the UK asked the tribunal to deal, inter alia, with the following question: 'Has the United States any right, and if so, what right of protection or property in the fur-seals frequenting the islands of the United States in Behring Sea when such seals are found outside the ordinary three-mile limit?'

The divergences between the United States and the UK regarding the appropriate answer(s) to this question were revealing of the legal uncertainty that characterised the status of animals under the international law applicable at that time. The United States, which was inviting the tribunal to engage in judicial legislation, considered that it had a right of property over the fur seals under international law. The UK adopted a more conservative approach and invited the tribunal to be deferential to customary international law and to guarantee the freedom of nations to kill wild animals. Two learned observers provided a more detailed account of those divergences in articles published right after the tribunal rendered its award: Russel Duane[3] and J. Stanley Brown.[4]

Duane, an American citizen, explained that:

> Since no wild animal at all similar to the fur-seal ever figured before in an international dispute, it became necessary for our Government, in the absence of precedents of this character, to turn to the common law for some principle which would sustain our claim to ownership in the sea herds. Accordingly, it was argued in our behalf that seals in international law were analogous to such animals as bees, or carrier pigeons, at the common law, which, as Blackstone said, continued to be the property of their custodian even when flying at a great distance from home (*animus revertendi*).[5]

Brown, also an American citizen, went further and remarked that:

> The able representatives of the United States took the position that the Tribunal was bound by no precedents and possessed, by virtue of its origin, a creative as well as

3 Russell Duane, 'The Decision of the Behring Sea Arbitrators', *The American Law Register and Review* (October 1893), 901–21.

4 J. Stanley Brown, 'Fur Seals and the Bering Sea Arbitration', *Journal of the American Geographical Society*, vol. 26, No. 1 (1894), pp. 326–72.

5 Duane, 'The Decision' (n. 3), 910.

> a judicial function. They urged upon the Tribunal the taking of high ground and the settlement of the question upon broad and comprehensive principles. They pointed out that man by means of invention was rapidly extending his dominion over the water as he had over the land, and by employing methods which were not even dreamed of when many existing municipal and international laws were enacted, threatened the very existence of many creatures useful to man.[6]

As already indicated, the UK considered that the tribunal possessed but one function – that its duty was to declare the law and not to make it, but that, whatever its function might be as an international body, it was not vested with the power to make international law. Brown, with vivid passion (and hidden disagreement), depicted the UK position as follows:

> They demanded that the question of property right be settled from the standpoint that the seals were wild animals – *ferae naturae* – which man could only reduce to possession by killing. They insisted that the law relating to wild animals, regardless of its origin, had been accepted by nations as the years ran on; it was very old law, and very good law, but whether good or bad it was the law, and from its teachings as enunciated by them the Tribunal must not allow itself to be enticed away by the seductive citations and insidious argument of learned counsel on the other side. There must be no making of laws to suit new conditions; the old standbys must be adhered to rigidly whether applicable or not. They urged that the seals were wild animals . . . and if the world, or a part of it, desired to turn out in boats and to destroy the industry by shooting the seals in the water, they had a perfect right to do so, for a wild animal was free to all. No matter if seal mothers roaming the sea for food did fall before the guns and spears of the pelagic hunters and their helpless pups starve on the rookeries, the hand of the slaughterer must not be stayed, for the United States had no rights any one was bound legally to respect when the seals were three miles off-shore, while, as for humanitarian considerations, they had no place in the controversy[7].

Despite the progressive nature of the US arguments – and its pioneer concerns for the right of future generations to have the fur-seals being preserved – the majority of the tribunal decided and determined that the United States had not any right of protection or property in the fur-seals frequenting the US islands in the Behring Sea, when such seals were found outside the ordinary three-mile limit of the territorial sea (this was of course long before the development and codification of the law of the sea as reflected in the UNCLOS which extends the territorial sea to twelve nautical miles). Brown criticised in a subtle manner the solution retained by the tribunal as being 'true to the conservatism of the Old World'[8] and as adhering to 'the potency of venerable legal relics'.[9]

6 Brown, 'Fur Seals' (n. 4), 361.
7 Ibid., 363–4.
8 Ibid., 364.
9 Ibid.

This being said, while the tribunal rejected the US contention, it is rather difficult to conclude that the tribunal was so conservative. Indeed, the tribunal enacted some conservation regulations to preserve the fur-seals – perhaps some of the first conservation measures in the history of international law. In particular, the tribunal ruled that '[t]he Governments of the United States and of Great Britain shall forbid their citizens and subjects respectively to kill, capture or pursue at any time and in any manner whatever, the animals commonly called fur seals, within a zone of sixty miles around the Pribilov Islands, inclusive of the territorial waters' (Article 1) and that '[t]he use of nets, fire arms and explosives shall be forbidden in the fur seal fishing' (Article 6).

And this is why the story of the *Bering Fur Seals* case still deserves to be told today – it reveals that the international law relating to the protection of animals has started to be crafted since the end of the nineteenth century. At the same time, it highlights how modern international law has developed and progressed to better encompass the protection and conservation of animals within the 'elementary considerations of humanity'[10] that are applicable in times of peace. Indeed, the protection of animals can no longer be guided by purely commercial and utilitarian (not to say Benthamian) purposes, as it was in reality the case in the *Bering Fur Seals* case. Animals are part of life and every form of life is unique. They warrant respect regardless of their worth to human beings. They deserve even more that respect in times of armed conflicts where human barbarism might endanger their very existence and survival. This is where the progressive development of international law is needed. The recipes for such a development are offered in this beautiful volume.

ANDRÉ NOLLKAEMPER

The protection of animals in armed conflict may not for all appear to be a topic that is high on the shortlist of the most pressing problems of our time. In 2020, attention and research efforts are drawn towards grander themes such as climate change, global pandemics and global inequality. Yet, the protection of animals in armed conflict is a topic for all times. Whoever takes the time to study images, stories and historical accounts of warfare will soon realise that the suffering of animals during armed conflicts is a constant and disturbing phenomenon that occurs in all wars. There is little doubt that in a few generations from now, observers will look back to how animals were treated in those circumstances and wonder how we collectively enacted, maintained and applied laws that so fundamentally disregarded the suffering of animals in times of peace and war.

When looking at the treatment of animals during wartime from the perspective of international law, a superficial assessment could lead one to conclude that there is no shortage of laws that can be relied upon for articulating standards of conduct

[10] To paraphrase the ICJ, *Corfu Channel* case, judgment of 9 April 1949, ICJ Reports 1949, 22.

relevant to the protection of animals in these circumstances. Relevant rules are not only to be found in the laws specifically drafted for armed conflicts – IHL – but also in the wide-ranging body of law relating to the protection of wildlife, species and more generally the environment as it applies in times of peace. We can recall in this regard that the ILC in Article 3 of its Draft Articles on the Effects of Armed Conflicts on Treaties (Draft Articles), drawing on the earlier work of the *Institut de Droit International*, recognised that '[t]he existence of an armed conflict does not *ipso facto* terminate or suspend the operation of a treaties (a) as between States parties to the conflict; [and] (b) as and between a State party to the conflict and a State that is not'.[11] There thus is a general principle of continuity. In particular, in the Annex to the Draft Articles, the ILC expressly identified treaties relating to the protection of the environment as treaties that are not susceptible of termination, withdrawal or suspension of operation in the event of an armed conflict.[12] To the continued applicability of treaties drafted for peacetimes, we can add a wide-ranging body of authorities that recognise the obligations of states in times of armed conflict relating to the protection of the environment, that – at least implicitly – includes the protection of animals. Thus, Principle 24 of the 1992 Rio Declaration provides that '[w]arfare is inherently destructive of sustainable development. States shall therefore respect international law providing protection for the environment in times of armed conflict and cooperate in its further development, as necessary.'[13] And the ILC Draft Principle 3(4)(1) on the Protection of the Environment in Relation to Armed Conflicts stipulates that 'States shall, pursuant to their obligations under international law, take effective legislative, administrative, judicial and other measures to enhance the protection of the environment in relation to armed conflict.'[14]

However, saying that the 'international law of peace' applies in times of armed conflict, does not, in itself, significantly help animals. The question is to what extent international law provides actual protection. One can recall in this context that the ICJ in its advisory opinion on the *Legality of the Threat or Use of Nuclear Weapons* noted that 'the issue is not whether the treaties relating to the protection of the environment are or are not applicable during an armed conflict, but rather whether the obligations stemming from these treaties were intended to be obligations of total restraint during military conflict'.[15] The answer to the latter question clearly was in the negative, as the ICJ added that it 'does not consider that the treaties in question

[11] ILC, Effects of Armed Conflicts on Treaties. Titles and texts of the draft articles on the effects of armed conflicts on treaties adopted by the drafting committee on second reading, 11 May 2011, A/CN.4/L.777, Art. 3.

[12] Ibid., Annex (g).

[13] Declaration on Environment and Development (Rio Declaration), A/CONF.151/26 (1992).

[14] ILC, Draft Principles on the Protection of the Environment in Relation to Armed Conflict (2019), reproduced in UN General Assembly, Report of the ILC, seventy-first session (29 April–7 June and 8 July–9 August 2019), A/74/10, Chap. VI, Draft Principle, 3(4)(a).

[15] ICJ, *Legality of the Use or Threat of Nuclear Weapons*, advisory opinion of 8 July 1996, ICJ Reports 1996, para. 30.

could have intended to deprive a State of the exercise of its right of self-defence under international law because of its obligations to protect the environment'. Building on this, we can observe that the well-documented shortcomings of international law in relation to the protection of animals in peacetime simply will perpetuate themselves in times of war. To mention only one example: the bias towards the protection of endangered species in a wide variety of treaties may be well justified on scientific (biodiversity) grounds. But it is odd to suggest that an animal that happens to belong to a particular species is somehow intrinsically worth more than animals that happen to be part of another (more common) species. In any case, this does nothing to protect cattles that are so often war victims and would not have done anything to protect those horses whose suffering can be observed in footages of World War I. Above all, thinking about international law on the protection of animals in times of armed conflict highlights the emptiness and the undeveloped nature of international law on the protection of animals in times of peace.

Three further observations can be made that shape, and to some extent limit, the actual protection offered by international law to animals. The first is that whatever body of international law that does apply to the protection of animals in armed conflict often hides animals within larger concepts that may obscure them from sight and recognition. This is particularly true when animals are only incidentally protected by provisions of international law which focus on the environment in general rather than on animals per se. Therefore, for example, in the aforementioned 2019 ILC Draft Principles, the obligation to take effective legislative, administrative, judicial and other measures to enhance the protection of the environment in relation to armed conflicts does in some form apply to animals. Indeed, the ILC Special Rapporteur on the subject defined 'environment' in this context as including 'natural resources, both abiotic and biotic, such as air, water, soil, fauna and flora and the interaction between the same factors, and the characteristics of the landscape'.[16] Likewise, the ICJ's pronouncement, in its advisory opinion on the *Legality of the Threat or Use of Nuclear Weapons*, that '[r]espect for the environment is one of the elements that go to assessing whether an action is in conformity with the principles of necessity and proportionality',[17] would seem to apply also to animals.

From one angle, seeing animals as part of the wider concept of environment is significant. It forces us to think about the broader scope of, and the many elements that make up, the environment in their interconnectedness. At the same time, talking about the protection of animals in terms of safeguarding the environment is an abstraction. The obligation to protect the environment does not easily or clearly translate into an obligation that is helpful for individual horses or cows that suffer in warfare. Thus, I strongly believe that any progress in the legal protection of animals – whether in times of peace or war – requires that they be explicitly recognised and

16 ILC, Preliminary Report on the Protection of the Environment in Relation to Armed Conflicts by Marie G. Jacobsson, Special Rapporteur, 30 May 2014, A/CN.4/674, para. 86.

17 ICJ, *Nuclear Weapons* (n. 15), para. 30.

protected for what they are: as individual animals and as species. Accordingly, the initiative to conceptualise, systematise and develop international law applicable to animals into a 'global animal law', deserves much support.

My second point is that the familiar critique of IHL as a body of law that both protects and legitimises, applies fully to the plight of animals in armed conflicts. The ICJ's statements, in the mentioned advisory opinion, on necessity and proportionality in the pursuit of legitimate military objectives,[18] can be read in two ways. While from one angle international law does in principle offer protection to animals, the reverse is also true. When harmful activity is necessary and proportionate, international law shields it and offers a relatively free space for states to act towards animals in ways that would not be permissible in peacetime. This of course is not a novel insight, but it does drive home the point that the protection of animals in armed conflict will be limited and determined by considerations that will pull in quite different directions.

The third and final point relates to compliance with IHL. The larger issue here is how difficult it is to transpose a body of law written for the protection of human beings to the protection of animals. Implementation of, and compliance with, this body of law is largely driven by considerations of reciprocity and self-interest. That may often (though certainly not always) work for protecting individual human beings, but it is not obvious at all when we attempt to extend this shield to animals. How does reciprocity work when the interests at stake are not interests that affect humans directly? Indeed, we do not – as a whole – tend to concede animals' interests much weight in our daily lives. The protection of animals during armed conflict will inevitably be shaped and limited by the protection we accord to animals in peacetime.

This leads to the larger point that in order to understand how international law protects animals in war, we will have to move beyond questions of applicability and interpretation, and examine how this body of law is applied in actual practice and consider the underlying driving mechanisms. It seems to me that it is from this angle that the present study has a lot to offer for advancing our understanding, and thereby paving the way for a strengthening of this body of law that is long overdue. The editors of this volume are therefore to be commended for putting the topic of the protection of animals during warfare on the agenda and for seeking to advance our understanding of the limits and the promise of law in offering such protection.

18 Ibid.

Acknowledgements

The research has been conducted under the auspices of the Law Faculty of the University of Geneva and the Max Planck Institute. It has been directed by Anne Peters and Robert Kolb, coordinated by Jérôme de Hemptinne and financed by the Swiss National Fund (FNS).

The editors are extremely grateful to all the participants in this collective endeavour. Their diligence and expertise have significantly contributed to the writing of a rich set of chapters devoted to a topic that has never before been considered so comprehensively. They benefited from the expertise and advice of many colleagues, especially Annyssa Bellal (Senior Research Fellow at the Geneva Academy), André Nollkaemper and Makane Mbengue, who participated in workshops organised online on 11 and 26 June 2020 in order to discuss important issues that required clarification and further analysis. The editors were extremely fortunate to be able to count on the outstanding commitment of Anette Kreutzfeld, personal assistant to Anne Peters. She provided all necessary editorial and logistic support to the editors throughout the entire life of the project and ensured its smooth and efficient running. The editors are deeply indebted to Matthew J. Milbourne for his skilful editing of several chapters. Finally, they would like to thank warmly Finola O'Sullivan and Tom Randall from Cambridge University Press for their kind and valuable cooperation at the various stages of the preparation and bringing to fruition of this collective book.

Abbreviations

AP I	Protocol Additional to the Geneva Conventions of 12 August 1949, and Relating to the Protection of Victims of International Armed Conflicts of 8 June 1977, 1125 UNTS 3
AP I Commentary	Yves Sandoz, Christophe Swinarski and Bruno Zimmermann (eds.), *Commentary on the Additional Protocols of* 8 *June* 1977 *to the Geneva Conventions of* 12 *August* 1949 (Geneva: ICRC 1987)
AP II	Protocol Additional to the Geneva Conventions of 12 August 1949, and Relating to the Protection of Victims of Non-International Armed Conflicts of 8 June 1977, 1125 UNTS 609
APs	AP I and AP II
CITES	Convention on International Trade in Endangered Species of Wild Fauna and Flora of 3 March 1973, 993 UNTS 243
ECCC	Extraordinary Chambers in the Courts of Cambodia
ECCC Law	Law on the Establishment of the Extraordinary Chambers in the Courts of Cambodia of 27 October 2004
ENMOD	Convention on the Prohibition of Military or any Hostile Use of Environmental Modification Techniques of 10 December 1976, 1108 UNTS 151
EU	European Union

FAO	United Nations Food and Agriculture Organisation
GC I	Convention for the Amelioration of the Condition of the Wounded and Sick in Armed Forces in the Field of 12 August 1949, 75 UNTS 31
GC II	Convention for the Amelioration of the Condition of the Wounded, Sick and Shipwrecked Members of Armed Forces at Sea of 12 August 1949, 75 UNTS 85
GC III	Convention Relative to the Treatment of Prisoners of War of 12 August 1949, 75 UNTS 135
GC IV	Convention Relative to the Protection of Civilian Persons in Time of War of 12 August 1949, 75 UNTS 287
GCs	GC I, GC II, GC III and GC IV
1907 Hague Convention (IV)	Hague Convention (IV) Respecting the Laws and Customs of War on Land of 18 October 1907
Hague Regulations	Regulations Respecting the Laws and Customs of War on Land annexed to the 1907 Hague Convention (IV)
ICC	International Criminal Court
ICC Statute	ICC Statute of 17 July 1998, 2187 UNTS 90
ICJ	International Court of Justice
ICL	International criminal law
ICRC	International Committee of the Red Cross
ICRC Commentary GC I (2016)	ICRC, *Commentary on Geneva Convention (I) for the Amelioration of the Condition of the Wounded and Sick in Armed Forces in the Field* (Geneva: ICRC 2016), available at https://ihl-databases.icrc.org/ihl/full/GCI-commentary
ICRC Commentary GC III (2020)	ICRC, *Commentary on Geneva Convention (III) Relative to the Treatment of Prisoners of War* (Geneva: ICRC 2020), available at https://ihl-databases.icrc.org/ihl/full/GCI-commentary
ICRC Customary Law Database	ICRC Customary International Law Database, available at https://ihl-databases.icrc.org/customary-ihl/eng/docs/home

ICRC Environmental Guidelines	ICRC, *Guidelines on the Protection of the Environment in Armed Conflict: Rules and Recommendations Relating to the Protection of the Natural Environment under International Humanitarian Law, with Commentary* (Geneva: ICRC 2020), available at https://bit.ly/3zwb64D
ICTR	International Criminal Tribunal for Rwanda
ICTR Statute	Statute of the ICTR adopted by United Nations Security Council Resolution 955 on 8 November 1993 and lastly modified by Resolution 1901 on 16 December 2009
ICTY	International Criminal Tribunal for the Former Yugoslavia
ICTY Statute	Statute of the ICTY adopted by United Nations Security Council Resolution 827 on 25 May 1993 and lastly modified by Resolution 1877 on 7 July 2009
IHL	International humanitarian law
ILC	International Law Commission
NATO	North Atlantic Treaty Organisation
NGO	Non-governmental organisation
Pictet Commentary on GC I	Jean Pictet (ed.), *Geneva Convention (I) for the Amelioration of the condition of the Wounded and Sick in Armed Forces in the Field: Commentary* (Geneva: ICRC 1952)
Pictet Commentary on GC III	Jean Pictet (ed.), *Geneva Convention (III) Relative to the Treatment of Prisoners of War: Commentary* (Geneva: ICRC 1960)
Pictet Commentary on GC IV	Jean Pictet (ed.), *Geneva Convention (IV) Relative to the Protection of Civilian Persons in Time of War: Commentary* (Geneva: ICRC 1958)
SCSL	Special Court for Sierra Leone
SCSL Statute	Statute of the SCSL of 16 January 2002, 2178 UNTS 145
UN	United Nations
UN Charter	Charter of the UN of 26 June 1945, 1 UNTS XVI
UNCLOS	UN Convention on the Law of the Sea of 10 December 1982, 1833 UNTS 397
UNEP	UN Environmental Programme

UNESCO	UN Educational, Scientific and Cultural Organisation
UNTS	UN Treaty Series
Vienna Convention on the Law of Treaties	Vienna Convention on the Law of Treaties of 23 May 1969, 1155 UNTS
World Heritage Convention	Convention for the Protection of the World Cultural and Natural Heritage of 16 November 1972, 1037 UNTS 151
WTO	World Trade Organisation
WWF	World Wildlife Fund

PART I

The Need for Protecting Animals in Wartime

Part I of the book lays out historical and ecological foundations for the legal protection of animals during warfare and the main difficulties. It is divided into four chapters. After recalling cross-cutting issues (Chapter 1), it considers the topic from historical (Chapter 2) and ecological (Chapter 3) perspectives. Part I finally introduces the main rationales for, and challenges in, the protection of animals in wartime (Chapter 4).

1

Animals in Wartime

A Legal Research Agenda

Anne Peters and Jérôme de Hemptinne

1 CONTEXT AND PURPOSES OF THE RESEARCH

Wildlife populations remain the unknown victims of armed conflicts throughout the world.[1] Although they rarely disappear completely, these populations usually decline, often significantly, during warfare.[2] Over the last fifty years, a number of species have been vanishing at a particularly rapid rate in this context, with disastrous repercussions on the food chain and the ecological balance of fragile ecosystems and protected areas such as national parks.[3] This is not surprising since 80 per cent of armed conflicts occurring during this period have taken place in countries such as Afghanistan, Burundi, the Central African Republic, Colombia, the Democratic Republic of the Congo, Iraq, Kenya, Mozambique, Nepal, Rwanda, Uganda or Vietnam, all of which contain areas of high global species diversity,[4] where the maintenance of wildlife habitats is precarious. A few figures drawn by the International Committee of the Red Cross (ICRC) from the situation in Mozambique illustrate this tendency. During the fifteen-year civil war in this country, '[t]he Gorongosa National Park lost more than 90% of its animals. The African buffalo went down from 14,000 to 100 individuals, and the hippo population from 3,500 to 100. The elephant population declined from 2,000 to 200.'[5] Moreover, belligerents have taken advantage of the chaos raised by war in order to poach protected species and to engage in the trafficking of expensive animal products. While generating billions of dollars each year – which are in part reinvested into warfare and the acquisition of weapons – such poaching and trafficking activities allow armed groups to grow and reinforce their authority over local populations and

[1] See ICRC, 'Natural Environment: Neglected Victim of Armed Conflict' (5 June 2019), available at https://bit.ly/3HDUcWk, accessed 22 February 2022.

[2] See, for example, Joshua H. Daskin and Robert M. Pringle, 'Warfare and Wildlife Declines in Africa's Protected Areas', *Nature* 553 (2018), 328–32. These authors emphasise that 'war can also relax pressure on wildlife when people avoid combat zones or are tactically disarmed, or when extractive industries decline' (ibid., at 328).

[3] Thor Hanson et al., 'Warfare in Biodiversity Hotspots', *Conservation Biology* 23 (2009), 578–87, at 578.

[4] Ibid.

[5] ICRC, 'Natural Environment' (n. 1).

disputed territories.[6] Sometimes government forces are themselves responsible for poaching and trafficking, complicating the issue further.[7] All this fuels a cycle of violence and ultimately threatens peace and security in the concerned areas.[8]

Livestock and companion animals, which are highly dependent on human care, are also direct victims of hostilities. They are regularly confined and left to starve or let loose without the ability to feed themselves.[9] Often they are pre-emptively eliminated by their owners or wantonly killed by the enemy 'in order to deprive populations presumed to be loyal to the opposing party of their livelihood'.[10] For instance, during the Iraqi occupation of Kuwait in the early 1990s, more than 80 per cent of Kuwaiti livestock (cattle, sheep, and goats) died.[11] Zoo animals are also particularly vulnerable; they are slaughtered, looted, bombed, or starved on a massive scale.[12]

On a different front, certain armed forces have trained, and continue to train, some animals – principally marine mammals such as bottlenose dolphins and California sea lions – to perform military tasks like ship and harbour protection or mine detection and clearance.[13] They also use animals as tools in military research and experiments to develop sophisticated weapons, to improve surgical techniques employed for the treatment of wounded soldiers, or to test resistance to physical assaults and adverse warfare conditions.[14] Millions of horses, mules, donkeys, camels, dogs, elephants, oxen, and birds serve in various other ways – either as means of medical transport, in search and rescue operations, or as communication and logistics tools – thereby becoming particularly vulnerable targets.[15] Companion animals and mascots are also valued for their contribution in lifting the morale of the troops, and in so doing become exposed to the dangers of war.

6 See James McDonald, 'How War Affects Wildlife', *JSTOR Daily* (23 January 2018), available at https://daily.jstor.org/how-war-affects-wildlife/, accessed 22 February 2022.

7 Ibid.

8 Anne Peters, 'Elephant Poaching and Ivory Trafficking as a Threat to the Peace', *American Journal of International Law Unbound* 108 (2014), 162–5.

9 Anne Peters, 'Animals in International Law', *Collected Courses of The Hague Academy of International Law: Recueil des Cours* Vol. 410 (Leiden: Brill 2020), 95–544, at 339.

10 Ibid.

11 John Loretz, 'The Animal Victims of the Gulf War', *Physicians for Social Responsibility Quarterly* 1 (1991), 221–5, at 224.

12 Peters, 'Animals' (n. 9), 339, with references.

13 Terrill Ceiridwen, 'Romancing the Bomb: Marine Animals in Naval Strategic Defense', *Organization & Environment* 14 (2001), 105–13. See also John M. Kistler, *Animals in the Military: From Hannibal's Elephants to the Dolphins of the US Navy* (Santa Barbara: ABC-CLIO 2011), 311–26.

14 Ian Murnaghan, 'Animal Tests in Military Defence', *About Animal Testing* (14 November 2017), available at www.aboutanimaltesting.co.uk/animal-tests-military-defence.html, accessed 22 February 2022. See Bílková, Chapter 17, 'Military Experimentation', in this volume.

15 See generally Jilly Cooper, *Animals in War* (London: Corgi 2000); Rainer Pöppinghege (ed.), *Tiere im Krieg: Von der Antike bis zur Gegenwart* (Leiden: Brill 2009); Eric Baratay, *Bêtes de tranchées: Des vécus oubliés* (Paris: CNRS éditions 2013); Ryan Hediger (ed.), *Animals and War: Studies of Europe and North America* (Leiden: Brill 2013). See de Hemptinne, Chapter 11, 'Medical Transport, Search and Rescue', in this volume.

In view of the foregoing, shielding animals and the ecosystems in which they live from the direct and indirect effects of warfare should be a matter of great concern. However, international humanitarian law (IHL), being deeply anthropocentric, largely ignores this preoccupation. Such silence raises significant questions that can no longer be left unanswered. For instance, does IHL's focus on humans mean that animals are not legally protected in armed conflicts? Or should they be treated as objects[16] and thus governed by the principles of distinction,[17] proportionality,[18] and precaution[19] that commanders and soldiers alike must respect when launching on-the-ground attacks against military objectives? To which animals should these principles apply? Do they apply differently to living creatures rather than inanimate objects? Could animals be treated like those specially protected objects that already receive additional protection by IHL norms, such as means of medical transport and those used in search and rescue operations,[20] or as objects that are indispensable for the survival of civilian populations?[21] Or could animals even be regarded as a part of civilian populations? And, if so, how do these legal regimes reinforce their protection? When used for military purposes, could animals be treated as combatants and legitimately targeted by adversaries? If yes, when and under what conditions and principles? How could the prohibition on unnecessary suffering or the Martens clause play out? In the case of unjustified attacks against protected species, what sanctions could be imposed? Are these sanctions enough? Should the poaching and trafficking of endangered species during armed conflicts be qualified as war crimes or as crimes against humanity? In the last scenario, would the ICC have jurisdiction over these crimes? And how could the cooperation of states prosecuting and trying the authors of such crimes be improved?

More fundamentally, the protection of animals must be examined in light of the fact that the dividing line between humans and animals has been significantly eroded on biological and ethical grounds over the last decades. The next logical question is thus how to determine whether both humans and animals could be protected in a similar manner against superfluous injury or unnecessary suffering.[22] Consequently, should domestic laws that prohibit and punish cruelty to animals influence their treatment under IHL? Would conferring some rights and/or legal personality to animals – as opposed to merely imposing duties upon belligerents – strengthen their protection in the context of IHL?[23] In that case, which animals

[16] See, for example, Art. 52(3) of AP I.

[17] See, for example, Art. 52 of AP I.

[18] See, for example, Art. 51(5)(b) and 57(2)(a)(iii) of AP I.

[19] Art. 57 of AP I.

[20] See, for example, Art. 8(h) of AP I; Art. 11 of AP II.

[21] Art. 54 of AP I; Art. 14 of AP II.

[22] Art. 35(2) of AP I. For an extensive analysis of the application of such a prohibition to animals, see Marco Roscini, 'Animals and the Law of Armed Conflict', *Israel Yearbook on Human Rights* 47 (2017), 35–67, at 51–6.

[23] Anne Peters, 'Rights of Human and Nonhuman Animals: Complementing the Universal Declaration of Human Rights', *American Journal of International Law Unbound* 111 (2018), 255–360, at 356.

deserve legal personality and/or rights and what types of rights should be granted to them?

Furthermore, animals seem to be collectively protected by the general legal framework on the preservation of the environment against 'widespread, long-term and severe' damages caused by war.[24] But how should this regime concretely apply to animals? Do these meagre rules offer sufficient protection, especially in non-international armed conflicts? How do the several existing international treaties that protect the environment, such as the Convention on International Trade in Endangered Species of Wild Fauna and Flora (CITES), the Convention on the Conservation of Migratory Species of Wild Animals,[25] and the Convention on Biological Diversity[26] apply during hostilities? Are they compatible with the core legal norms governing armed conflicts, namely the GCs and their APs? Do these conventions apply extraterritorially, for instance, when states conduct military operations abroad? Do they impose environmental legal obligations upon non-state armed groups? In so doing, under what conditions? Should certain areas of high biodiversity be spared from the conduct of hostilities as part of the cultural heritage of humanity and thus be protected by the World Heritage Convention?

Despite (or because of) the fundamental, operational, and theoretical challenges that the protection of animals raises, such questions have never been thoroughly studied.[27] Most of the work in this area consists of general publications related to the protection of the environment in armed conflict[28] – which sometimes indirectly address certain issues related to the protection of animals – and specific studies on the safeguarding of endangered species. The current state of research in this field is in sharp contrast to the increasing level of legal analysis and domestic litigation actively being conducted concerning the status and protection of animals in peace-time. As a result, a clear lacuna exists in the academic literature.

To fill this gap, our book aims at achieving the following four goals. First, it seeks to create an inventory of the international legal framework available for the

[24] Art. 35(3) and 55(1) of AP I.

[25] Convention on the Conservation of Migratory Species of 23 June 1979, 1651 UNTS 333.

[26] Convention on Biological Diversity of 5 June 1992, 1760 UNTS 79.

[27] Among the rare publications in this domain, see, for example, Karsten Nowrot, 'Animals at War: The Status of "Animal Soldiers" under International Humanitarian Law', *Historical Social Research* 40 (2015), 128–50; Roscini, 'Animals' (n. 22), 35–67; Jérôme de Hemptinne, 'Challenges Regarding the Protection of Animals During Warfare', in Anne Peters (ed.), *Studies in Global Animal Law* (Heidelberg: Springer 2020), 173–83.

[28] See, for example, Michael Schmitt, 'Green War: An Assessment of the Environmental Law of Armed Conflict', *Yale Law Journal* 22 (1997), 1–110; Yoram Dinstein, 'Protection of the Environment in International Armed Conflict', *Max Planck Yearbook of United Nations Law* 5 (2001), 523–49; UNEP, *Protecting the Environment during Armed Conflict: An Inventory and Analysis of International Law* (Geneva: UNEP 2009); ICRC, *Strengthening Legal Protection for Victims of Armed Conflict*, 31st International Conference of the Red Cross and Red Crescent (Geneva: ICRC 2011). See also the ICRC Environmental Guidelines.

protection of animals in armed conflict. Second, our research examines to what extent this legal regime is adequate in specific situations (in occupied territories, protected zones, sea warfare and disaster situations) or in specific practices (when animals are used as tools in medical experiments). Third, the book evaluates to what extent the enforcement of the current legal framework adequately protects animals in terms of the repression of illegal conduct, reparation and rehabilitation. A special emphasis is placed on the regime established for wildlife trafficking and on the enforcement powers of the UN Security Council in this regard. Fourth, the research outlines several measures aiming at increasing the protection of animals during warfare and the enforcement available in this situation.

2 MAIN CHALLENGES

Delicate cross-cutting challenges need to be briefly addressed at the outset. They revolve around the following issues: the silence of IHL on the protection of animals (Section 2.1), the difficulty in identifying animals that are protected in times of war (Section 2.2), the inaptitude of IHL to adequately protect animals (Section 2.3), and the ambivalent nature of the violence inflicted upon animals in wartime (Section 2.4).

2.1 *The Silence of International Humanitarian Law*

Despite the fact that animals are among those affected by armed conflicts, IHL does not clearly and explicitly protect them. As will be discussed in Parts II and III of the book, animals are only indirectly addressed as objects, specially protected objects, weapons of war, means of medical transport and rescue or as part of the environment. A historical reason for IHL's silence on the welfare of animals is that the conventions regulating armed conflicts were adopted at a time when legal entitlements for animals did not attract significant attention. Enacted in response to World War II and during the period of decolonisation, IHL has been essentially geared towards the safeguarding of human beings. The conventions continue to represent an overwhelmingly anthropocentric body of law that has 'a strong utilitarian flavour'.[29] Even the few provisions restricting attacks against the environment were designed with a view to preserving the interests of human beings instead of the environment per se.[30] The Christian roots of IHL might also explain this anthropocentric attitude and the difficulty that this body of law has in conceptualising the protection of the environment and animals independently of human interests.[31] Against this background, three related objections might be voiced against our proposal to improve the legal protection of animals by means of IHL. The first

[29] Schmitt, 'Green War' (n. 28), 6.
[30] Ibid., 69.
[31] See the references in n. 63.

fundamental question is why lawmakers and law-appliers should at all be concerned about the silence of IHL on animals? Why *should* IHL deal with this issue? Animals are killed on a massive scale in peacetime, for human use and consumption under full protection of the law. Would it not be absurd to protect animals in war while upholding the lawfulness of constantly and severely harming animals, for example in factory farming? Second, it is often argued that alleviating the extreme suffering of human beings during hostilities would be impaired should animal protection be put at the forefront. Devoting time, energy and money to protect animals would therefore prevent these resources being used for worthier, human-focused causes.[32] A third, connected criticism is often raised: promoting animal welfare or even rights during armed conflicts would devalue the rights of human beings in these circumstances.[33]

Let us briefly respond to these three objections.[34] First, we wish to point out that the severe shortcomings of the legal regimes governing food and agriculture should not be allowed to stimy a legal evolution in other fields. International humanitarian law can no longer ignore the evolution that the status and protection of animals has undergone in some jurisdictions around the world.[35] In the same way that the rise of human rights and increased awareness of environmental challenges after World War II have influenced and shaped the development of IHL, the increasing concern for animal welfare during the last decades should also progressively impose limits on belligerents' actions. This should apply even more so when it is considered that wars have disastrous effects on wildlife and, in particular, on protected species whose numbers significantly decrease because of hostilities.

Second, and contrary to what is often claimed, safeguarding animals does not necessarily interfere with, or run contrary to, the protection of human beings; the two often run in parallel without impacting negatively on each other. In any case, it will be shown that certain IHL principles – such as the principle of proportionality – are flexible enough to guarantee that human interests prevail over animal interests if one is forced to choose between the two. In other words, when human concerns conflict with those of animals, these principles allow human matters to take precedence.

Third, care for animals in no way inevitably downgrades the rights of humans.[36] On the contrary, promoting animal welfare may increase respect

32 This argument is recalled in Anne Peters, 'Liberté, Egalité, Animalité: Human-Animal Comparisons in Law', *Transnational Environmental Law* 5 (2016), 25–53, at 35.

33 Ibid.

34 This response builds on de Hemptinne, 'Challenges' (n. 27), 175–6.

35 See Global Animal Law Database, available at www.globalanimallaw.org/database/national/index.html, accessed 22 February 2022.

36 Peters, 'Liberté, Egalité, Animalité' (n. 32), 36.

for all life.[37] Indeed, in practice, leaders of animal protection movements have been typically active in combating other forms of social injustice (such as child abuse and violence against women).[38] An alignment (as opposed to a competition) of concerns is also possible in attempts to denounce injustices that occur in war zones.

2.2 *The Identification of Protected Animals*

Which animals should be cared for in times of war? In principle, all living creatures that are not human beings should receive some sort of protection under IHL. However, the level, type and nature of the protection these creatures receive vary widely from one animal to another, depending on a multitude of factors. These factors include the roles animals play during warfare (for example as weapons of war, means of medical transportation and rescue, or as objects of medical experimentation); the circumstances in which they are placed (for example when they are targeted or detained); the areas in which they live (for example in invaded or occupied territories, land or sea, protected or unprotected zones); or the animals' specific nature (for example whether they are endangered or considered vermin). Some safeguards – such as those protecting the environment as a whole – apply generally to the entire wildlife population. In light of this variety of contexts, our introductory chapter will not provide a general legal definition of animal that could apply in each and every situation in war. This issue is left to the individual authors, as such definitions depend on the specific legal question and protective regime examined.

2.3 *The Inaptitude of International Humanitarian Law to Protect Animals*

International humanitarian law neither explicitly addresses animals nor is it particularly well equipped to protect their interests. Indeed, the Geneva Conventions (GCs) and their additional protocols (APs) presuppose temporal and spatial boundaries between war and peace that are not easy to draw when the protection of animals is at stake. These legal instruments assume a world in which dividing lines are clear. In contrast, effective safeguards for animals would need to follow a different logic. Wildlife is usually not confined to the territories of the belligerents and its destruction generally affects the ecological balance on a wider scale. Thus, measures to ensure their protection should potentially extend beyond the territorial borders of the parties to the conflict. Furthermore, the negative impact of war on animals does not necessarily stop with the end of active hostilities. However, IHL conventions do not contain reasonable standards for ensuring long-term measures in the interest of animals.

Moreover, most of the provisions regulating the protection of individuals and the conduct of hostilities are aimed at achieving a compromise between two diverging or

[37] Gary Francione, *Introduction to Animal Rights: Your Child or the Dog?* (Philadelphia: Temple University Press 2000), 174.

[38] Peters, 'Liberté, Egalité, Animalité' (n. 32), 12.

even antagonist interests, considerations of military necessity on the one hand and humanitarian preoccupations on the other. This balancing exercise is particularly complex when animals are at stake. Indeed, the status of animals varies widely from one culture to another (also within belligerent factions) and inevitably changes over time. A proper assessment requires the kind of environmental knowledge that even well-equipped state forces often do not possess, given that the damage inflicted on animals tends to manifest itself in the long run and is often the indirect result of the destruction of certain habitats.[39]

Furthermore, IHL's protective regime cannot be easily transposed to animals. For instance, the rules governing the protection of objects in the GCs and APs[40] are mainly designed for inanimate objects. Even if this regime were extended to animals, assimilating them with pure objects is far from ideal in many respects; it does not properly take into account that animals are sentient beings that experience pain and distress, and it does not accommodate the many different functions that animals can serve during warfare and the rights and duties that such functions normally entail. In this context, applying the rules designed for the protection of individual persons remains a valid option. But this regime is also ill-structured for duly safeguarding the interests of non-human living creatures. The various categories of 'protected persons' – combatants *hors de combat* and prisoners of war on the one side and civilians on the other – cannot, as such, be opened up so as to comprise animals. For reasons that will be further explored throughout the book, animals do not easily fit into this rigid system.[41] As pointed out by Marco Roscini, 'if they were considered combatants, animals would have not only the rights, but also the obligations associated with this status'.[42] Clearly animals are not able to respect these obligations autonomously, which, among other things, require the capacity to identify persons who directly participate in hostilities – and are therefore targetable – or to make proportionality calculations.[43] Moreover, the definition of 'civilians' mentioned in Article 50(1) of AP I only refers to 'persons'.[44] This term is normally, though not compellingly, understood to comprise only humans and thereby excludes other living creatures.

Lastly, it should be noted that the special rules on the protection of the environment per Articles 35(3) and 55(1) of AP I – which encompasses wildlife[45] – have no parallel in the written rules governing non-international armed conflicts, be they common Article 3 of the four GCs or AP II. Moreover, this protection is subject to particularly strict requirements; the damage forbidden under IHL must be cumulatively 'widespread, long-term and severe'. Reflecting the reluctance of governments

39 de Hemptinne, 'Challenges' (n. 27), 179. For an extensive analysis of the concept of proportionality in the context of the protection of the environment, see Schmitt, 'Green War' (n. 28), 55–61.

40 See, for example, Art. 52(2), 51(5)(b), and 57 of AP I.

41 See de Hemptinne, Kebebew and Niyo, Chapter 10, 'Combatants and Prisoners of War?', in this volume.

42 Roscini, 'Animals' (n. 22), 44–5.

43 Nowrot, 'Animals at War' (n. 27), 140.

44 Roscini, 'Animals' (n. 22), 45.

45 Ibid., 61.

to accept tight constraints on their military conduct against rebel groups, the narrow scope of the rules creates a significant gap in protection. Nonetheless, special safeguards offered by IHL to the environment would be essential for a comprehensive protection of animals and the ecosystem in which they live.

2.4 *The Ambivalent Nature of the Violence on Animals*

In peacetime, while acts of violence against human beings are in principle forbidden, the slaughter of animals – in conformity with certain methods and procedures – is widely accepted and practised throughout the world. It might therefore appear paradoxical that in situations of armed conflict, where acts of violence against certain individuals (mainly combatants and civilians who directly participate in the hostilities) are admitted and expected, acts of violence against animals should be strictly constrained.[46] This apparent 'paradox of violence' must be evaluated in light of the following factors which all point to similarities (rather than to a contrast) in the legal regimes of peace and of war for animals. Due to the increased human sensibility about animal welfare, acts of cruelty against animals (as opposed to 'normal' killing) are now increasingly prohibited and sanctioned in peacetime.[47] In other words, the peacetime regime knows lawful and unlawful violence against animals. The same could be said for wartimes: acts of violence against animals during warfare can be lawfully committed when animals become military targets or when the harm inflicted on them constitutes a proportionate collateral damage. A modified wartime regime on animals would form a parallel dual regime with a distinction between lawful and unlawful killing.

The situations of peace and of war are similar also with regard to the forms of violence against animals. Only superficially, the violence allowed in peacetime is of a different nature than violence authorised during armed conflicts. The former aims at satisfying specific economic needs – for instance, food production, or medical, pharmaceutical, and chemical testing. In contrast, the latter is in principle dictated by military considerations, whereby animals are targeted for military purposes. Nevertheless, this delineation between different types of violence is not that straightforward; the slaughtering of animals for human uses also occurs in wartime, while certain forms of violence, which are usually committed in the chaotic circumstances of war (such as poaching and the trafficking of species) can also take place during peacetime.[48] More fundamentally, as Saskia Stucki has demonstrated, the regulation of both forms of violence (by IHL on the one hand and by the laws promoting animal welfare on the other) share the common objective to 'humanise' a violent situation.[49] While the former aims at reducing the

46 de Hemptinne, 'Challenges' (n. 27), 175–6.
47 See above n. 35.
48 de Hemptinne, 'Challenges' (n. 27), 175–6.
49 Saskia Stucki, '(Certified) Human Violence? Animal Welfare Labels, The Ambivalence of Humanizing the Inhumane, and What International Humanitarian Law Has to Do with It', in Anne Peters (ed.), *Studies in Global Animal Law* (n. 27), 121–31, at 127.

suffering of humans caused by armed conflicts, the latter is designed to minimise the suffering of animals resulting from economic exploitation; and both bodies of law start from the same premise: putting an end to these types of violence by completely prohibiting them would be unrealistic since they are both part of the human condition.[50] All mentioned resemblances should facilitate extending the scope of IHL also to (non-human) animals. And if we want to avoid that rules seeking to 'humanise' innately inhumane situations become purely cynical, we should do the utmost to design them in a way that facilitates their application and enforcement.

3 NORMATIVE BACKGROUND

The legal approaches towards animals fall into three paradigms: animal species conservation regimes (Section 3.1), animal welfare norms (Section 3.2), and animal rights (Section 3.3). Current 'hard' international treaties mainly apply the first paradigm, as they are almost exclusively concerned with the conservation of a small subset of animal species.[51] In contrast, animal welfare – defined as 'the physical and mental state of an animal in relation to the conditions in which it lives and dies'[52] – pertains to the individual animal. Thus far, animal welfare is directly addressed only in 'soft' international law, and only very rarely in an ancillary fashion in conservation regimes.[53] Animal rights are the legal entitlements of animals protecting their fundamental interests against encroachment, as opposed to merely benefitting animals in their quality as objects of protective rules. As a groundwork for the detailed doctrinal work done in the following chapters, the three paradigms will now be briefly introduced in turn.

3.1 *Animal Species Conservation*

The conservation of species seeks 'the safeguarding of ecological processes and genetic diversity besides management of natural resources in order to ensure their maintenance by sustainable utilization'.[54] The point of departure for all wildlife conservation treaties

50 Compare Theodor Meron, 'The Humanization of Humanitarian Law', *American Journal of International Law* 94 (2000), 239–78, at 240.

51 'Conservation' is the most frequent term in the international treaties, used interchangeably with 'preservation' and 'protection'. The main reference work is Michael Bowman, Peter Davies, and Catherine Redgwell, *Lyster's International Wildlife Law* (2nd ed., Cambridge: Cambridge University Press 2010). For more on international conservation law, see Rosalind Reeve, *Policing International Trade in Endangered Species: The CITES Treaty and Compliance* (London: Earthscan 2002); Ed Couzens, *Whales and Elephants in International Conservation Law and Politics: A Comparative Study* (London: Routledge 2014).

52 Organisation Internationale des Epizooties (OIE) terrestrial code, Sec. 7 'Animal Welfare' (29th ed., 2021), chapter 7.1. 'Introduction to the Recommendations for Animal Welfare', Art. 7.1.1. 'General Considerations'. The meaning and measurement of animal welfare is controversial and depends, inter alia, on the disciplinary approach.

53 Peters, 'Animals' (n. 9), 503–5.

54 Pieter van Heijnsbergen, *International Legal Protection of Wild Fauna and Flora* (Amsterdam: IOS Press 1997), 52.

(and indeed their rationale) is the value of wildlife *for humans* 'from aesthetic, scientific, cultural, recreational and economic points of view', as the preamble of CITES puts it. Moreover, from an international law (and sovereignty-oriented) perspective, terrestrial wild animals are natural resources.[55] The qualification of 'resource' manifests the purely economic perspective espoused by international lawmakers and law-appliers. As natural resources, wild animals form part of a state's 'permanent sovereignty over natural resources'.[56] Wildlife also falls under a people's right to self-determination over natural resources.[57] This status as a resource under the sovereignty of the territorial or range state and for the disposal of its people is only mitigated – but not eliminated – for those few species covered by conservation treaties. Even under the purview of these regimes, the tension between conservation and human interests constantly comes up in the regular meetings or conferences of the parties to these treaties.

In this context, scholars have suggested classifying wild animals as a 'common concern',[58] a 'global resource',[59] or a 'global public good'.[60] These concepts are valuable as answers to problems of global distributive justice and intergenerational fairness; however, the aspiration of justice is still limited to humans and not directed toward the animals themselves. The principal legal consequence of all these categories remains identical: states are (at most) obliged to manage the animals (as

55 See Principle 2 of the Declaration of the UN Conference on the Human Environment (Stockholm) of 16 June 1972, 11 ILM 1416. According to this principle, '[t]he natural resources of the earth, including the air, water, land, flora, and *fauna* and especially representative samples of natural ecosystems, must be safeguarded *for the benefit of present and future generations* through careful planning or management, as appropriate' (emphases added). In treaty law, see Art. XX(g) of the General Agreement on Tariffs and Trade (GATT), 55 UNTS 194. It states that 'nothing in this Agreement shall be construed to prevent the adoption or enforcement by any contracting party of measures: … (g) relating to the conservation of exhaustible natural resources if such measures are made effective in conjunction with restrictions on domestic production or consumption.' This provision has been interpreted by the WTO appellate body to cover live animals (WTO AB, *United States – Import Prohibition of Certain Shrimp and Shrimp Products*, Report of the Appellate Body of 12 October 1998, WT/DS58/AB/R, para. 131). See also Art. V(1) of the Revised African Convention on the Conservation of Nature and Natural Resources of 11 July 2003, 1001 UNTS 3. It states that: '"Natural Resources" means renewable resources … including soil, water, flora, and fauna.' See also Art. 77(4) of the UNCLOS: according to this provision, '[t]he natural resources referred to in this Part consist of … *living organisms belonging to sedentary species*, that is to say, organisms which, at the harvestable stage, are immobile on or under the seabed or are unable to move except in constant physical contact with the seabed or the subsoil' (emphasis added).

56 UN General Assembly Resolution 1803 (XVII) of 14 December 1962, 'Permanent Sovereignty over Natural Resources'. This principle has the status of customary law. See ICJ, *Armed Activities on the Territory of the Congo (DRC* v. *Uganda)*, judgment of 19 December 2005, ICJ Reports 2005, para. 244.

57 Common Art. 1(2) of the International Covenant on Civil and Political Rights of 19 December 1966, 99 UNTS 171; Art. 21 of the African Charter on Human and Peoples' Rights of 27 June 1981, 1520 UNTS 217.

58 Kemal Baslar, *The Concept of the Common Heritage of Mankind in International Law* (Leiden: Martinus Nijhoff 1998), 313; Patricia Birnie, 'UNCED and Mammals', *Marine Policy* 17 (1993), 501–14, at 514.

59 Michael Glennon, 'Has International Law Failed the Elephant?', *American Journal of International Law* 84 (1990), 1–43, at 34.

60 See, for biodiversity as a global public good, Edith Brown Weiss, 'Establishing Norms in a Kaleidoscopic World: General Course on Public International Law', *Recueil des Cours de l'Académie de droit international de La Haye* 396 (2018), 37–415, at 112.

living resources) in a cooperative and sustainable way. Importantly, even that novel legal status does not prevent the killing of animals as long as it is sustainable. Moreover, the focus is still almost exclusively on the protection of species as collective groups and not on the welfare of animals as suffering individuals.[61] Finally, all legal labels treat animals as things as opposed to persons.

3.2 *Animal Welfare*

The second paradigm is animal welfare (or animal protection). The objective of animal welfare is pursued by the laws of many countries (and some international law), which recognise humans' legal duties towards animals.[62] The underlying ethical ideas of responsibility, care, and compassion in human–animal relationships are rooted in a gamut of belief systems, ranging from animist creeds in hunter-gatherer communities to scientific insights about the interdependence of all forms of life in fragile ecosystems. They are fleshed out in various philosophical and religious traditions encompassing Christian thought,[63] the feminist ethics of care,[64] and others. Duties of care towards nature or natural resources are embodied in various juridic concepts anchored in the legal traditions of the world, ranging from 'commons' to 'public trust'.[65] Humans are conceived as 'trustees', 'stewards', 'custodians', or 'guardians' over nature and natural resources, including animals – as animals are here conceptualised within the category of nature. The commonality is that all these juridic institutions impose

61 Sophie Riley, 'Wildlife Law and Animal Welfare: Competing Interests and Ethics', in Werner Scholtz (ed.), *Animal Welfare and International Environmental Law* (Cheltenham: Edward Elgar 2019), 148–79.

62 See, besides the literature mentioned in the following footnotes, David Favre, *Animal Law, Welfare, Interests, and Rights* (3rd ed., New York: Wolters Kluwer 2019); Thomas G. Kelch, *Globalization and Animal Law: Comparative Law, International Law and International Trade* (2nd ed., Alphen aan den Rijn: Kluwer Law International 2017); Margot Michel, Daniela Kühne, and Julia Hänni (eds.), *Animal Law – Tier und Recht: Developments and Perspectives in the 21st Century* (Zürich: Dike 2012); Anne Peters, Saskia Stucki, and Livia Boscardin (eds.), *Animal Law: Reform or Revolution?* (Zürich: Schulthess 2015).

63 New Christian thinking attempts to reinterpret the 'dominion' of man over nature and animals (Genesis 1:28) in the direction of stewardship. See the Encyclical Letter *Laudato Sì* of the Holy Father Francis 'On Care for Our Common Home' (2015). For scholarship on this issue, see Frank Pasquale (ed.), *Care for the World: Laudato Sì and Catholic Social Thought in an Era of Climate Crisis* (Cambridge: Cambridge University Press 2019). On animals specifically, see Matthew Scully, *Dominion: The Power of Man, the Suffering of Animals, and the Call to Mercy* (New York: St Martin's Griffin 2002); Mark Somos and Anne Peters, 'Christianity, Global Environmental Protection, and Animal Law', in Rafael Domingo and John Witte, Jr. (eds.), *Christianity and Global Law* (London: Routledge 2020), 365–83.

64 Carol Gilligan, *In a Different Voice* (Cambridge: Harvard University Press 1982); Josephine Donovan and Carol J. Adams (eds.), *The Feminist Care Tradition in Animal Ethics* (New York: Columbia University Press 2007).

65 See, for the United States, Joseph L. Sax, 'The Public Trust Doctrine in Natural Resource Law: Effective Judicial Intervention', *Michigan Law Review* 68 (1970), 475–566.

legal obligations (duties) on humans and on states but do not give rise to corresponding animal rights.

The paradigm of guardianship and not of animal rights also underlies constitutional law as it stands.[66] While post–World War II constitutions typically mention the ecological task of the state, only ten constitutions prescribe animal protection, call for compassion, or prohibit animal cruelty: India (1976), Brazil (1988), Slovenia (1991), Switzerland (1992), Luxembourg (1999), Germany (2002), Ecuador (2008), Austria (2013), Egypt (2014) and Russia (2020).[67] To conclude, human stewardship and functional equivalents prevent humans from treating animals with wanton cruelty but do not acknowledge animal rights. Stewardship and care are thus a corollary to animal thinghood.

This thinghood is prevalent in the domestic laws of most countries which explicitly or implicitly qualify animals as things. This category was inherited from Roman private law (*ius civile*), which drew a fundamental distinction between *personae* (persons) and *res* (things). Things can be possessed by persons as property.[68] It can thus be said that animals have been legally coded into property.[69] Moreover, things/objects/property – and thus also animals in the traditional legal framework – can (in law) only be the beneficiaries of protective rules. Such protective rules create duties for their addressees but do not generate rights for the beneficiaries.

In the past decades, the civil law codes of several states have modified the traditional legal status of animals into two variations. The historically first variant is the purely negative statement that animals are not things, which has been articulated in various European states ranging from Austria (1988) to the Netherlands (2013). The second and more progressive legal variant is the positive qualification of animals as 'sentient beings'. The EU coined this concept in 1992. Since 2008, Article 13 of the Treaty on the Functioning of the EU requires that 'the Union and the Member States shall, since animals are sentient beings, pay full regard to the welfare requirements of animals'.[70]

The new legal labels of 'not things' or 'sentient beings' have so far hardly generated tangible legal consequences. In the end, what matters is not the status but the legal

66 See Jessica Eisen, 'Animals in the Constitutional State', *International Journal of Constitutional Law* 15 (2017), 909–54. For the suggestion of the further development of a constitutional principle of care for animals, see ibid., 941.

67 Jessica Eisen and Kristen Stilt, 'Protection and Status of Animals', in Rainer Grote, Frauke Lachenmann, and Rüdiger Wolfrum (eds.), *Max Planck Encyclopedia of Comparative Constitutional Law* (Oxford: Oxford University Press 2017), with further references.

68 The legal concepts of 'thing' and 'property' are not identical but their application to animals amounts to the same result, their commodification and rightlessness. The US-American debate revolves more around the term 'property'.

69 To use Katharina Pistor's phrase in *The Code of Capital: How the Law Creates Wealth and Inequality* (Princeton: Princeton University Press 2019). It is legal coding which turns the animal, a living being, into capital and gives it the capacity to generate wealth for its owner.

70 Treaty on the Functioning of the EU of 26 October 2012.

rules that subsequently apply. The recent trend to remove animals from the category of things does not in itself improve their legal protection. Appreciable and clear legal effects result only from an explicit statement that animal sentience forms a legal limit to subjecting animals to the regime of things, such as in the civil codes of the Czech Republic,[71] Portugal,[72] and Spain.[73]

3.3 *Animal Rights*

The third paradigm of animal rights as entitlements does not form part of international law. Animal rights are also largely unknown in domestic law. They have been acknowledged only by some courts in India, Argentina, Colombia, and most recently in Pakistan and Ecuador.[74]

Importantly, the discussion on the *legal* rights of animals is informed but also confused by the philosophical controversy about the *moral* rights of animals.[75] Legal and moral rights are overlapping categories: distinct but frequently intertwined. In moral and ethical debates, the animal rights position is opposed to animal welfarism. Welfarism is the paradigm that favours incremental reforms in order to improve the conditions in which animals are kept and used.[76] Roughly speaking, this idea builds on utilitarian philosophical tenets.[77]

71 Czech Republic: Civil Code, section 494. According to this provision, '[a] living animal has a special significance and value as a living creature endowed with senses. A living animal is not a thing, and the provisions on things apply, by analogy, to a living animal only to the extent in which they are not contrary to its nature' (official translation by the Ministry of Justice).

72 Portugal: Portuguese Código Civil Portuguese Código Civil, Decreto-Lei n.° 47344, Diário do Governo No. 274/1966, Série I de 1966-11-25, Consolidado, Versão à data de 2018-11-05: 'Livro I PARTE GERAL, Título II Das relações jurídicas, SUBTÍTULO I-A – Dos animais.' Art. 201.-B 'Animais': 'The animals are living beings endowed with sentience and object of legal protection due to their nature'; Art. 201-D: 'Subsidiary Regime: 'In the absence of special rules, the rules applicable to things are applied to animals to the extent that they are not incompatible with their nature.' (our translation).

73 Art. 333*bis*, inserted into the Spanish Civil Code by Law 17/2021 of 15 December 2021 'BOE' núm. 300 of 16 Dec. 2021 (BOE-A-2021-20727, available at www.boe.es/eli/es/l/2021/12/15/17/con).

74 Islamabad High Court, *Islamabad Wildlife Management Board* v. *Metropolitan Corporation Islamabad*, judgment of 21 May 2020, WP No. 1155/2019; Const. Court of Ecuador, *Mona Estrellita*, Sentencia No. 253-20-JH/22, 27 January 2022.

75 See Paola Cavalieri, *The Animal Question: Why Nonhuman Animals Deserve Human Rights* (Oxford: OUP 2001); Cass R. Sunstein and Martha C. Nussbaum (eds.), *Animal Rights: Current Debates and New Directions* (Oxford: Oxford University Press 2004); Sue Donaldson and Will Kymlicka, *Zoopolis* (Oxford: Oxford University Press 2011); Christine Koorsgard, *Fellow Creatures* (Oxford: Oxford University Press 2019).

76 Robert Garner, *Animals, Politics, and Morality* (2nd ed., Manchester: Manchester University Press 2004); Robert Garner, 'Animal Welfare: A Political Defense', *Journal of Animal Law and Ethics* 1 (2006), 161–70.

77 See the famous footnote in Jeremy Bentham, *An Introduction to the Principles of Morals and Legislation* (Oxford: Clarendon 1789), 310–11, fn. 1 entitled 'Interests of the inferior animals improperly neglected in legislation'. Seminally in the twentieth century, Peter Singer, *Animal Liberation: Towards an End to Man's Inhumanity to Animals* (Wellingborough: Thorsons 1975).

Political scientist Robert Garner characterises welfarists as 'those who accept human moral superiority',[78] and he defines their ethics as the position that although animals should not suffer, they nevertheless have no right to life.[79] Concomitantly, 'animal welfare does not challenge the property status of animals'.[80] Key concepts for welfarists are therefore not 'rights' but 'the principle of animal welfare and the associated idea of unnecessary suffering'.[81] The practical consequence is that '[u]sing animals, per se, therefore, is not the problem. It is what they are used for that is the key'.[82]

Moral philosophers in the opposing camp more or less hold that animals ought not only to be treated well but moreover that they ought to be accorded rights.[83] In consequence, 'the rights view challenges the very conception of animals as legal property'.[84] The quest for the abolition of the property status of animals ('abolitionism') has been notably developed by Gary Francione.[85] Abolitionists disparage the welfarists as at best merely accommodating longer chains for their slaves.[86] In the end, the philosophical debate over moral rights for animals has somewhat stalemated. Mainstream philosophy still resides where Robert Nozick characterised it more than forty years ago: 'utilitarianism for animals, Kantianism for people'.[87] The legal debate on animal rights mirrors this philosophical divide, but it remains as yet underdeveloped and has only recently percolated to the level of international law.[88]

To sum up, these three paradigms (animal conservation, animal welfare, and animal rights) could theoretically be employed on the various regulatory levels (national, regional, and international governance). In practice however, international law is almost exclusively concerned with the first approach, with species conservation. We now turn specifically to international law and identify the problems created by its focus on species conservation.

78 Robert Garner, 'A Defense of a Broad Animal Protectionism', in Gary Francione and Robert Garner, *The Animal Rights Debate: Abolition or Regulation?* (New York: Columbia University Press 2010), 103–73, at 112.

79 Ibid., 120.

80 Ibid., 168.

81 Ibid.

82 Ibid., 129.

83 Tom Regan, *The Case for Animal Rights* (updated with a new preface, Berkeley: University of California Press 2004, 1983), 329.

84 Ibid., 394.

85 Gary Francione has elaborated and defended this position since 1995 (*Animals, Property, and the Law* (Philadelphia: Temple University Press 1995)). See, for a good summary, Gary Francione, *Animals as Persons: Essays on the Abolition of Animal Exploitation* (New York: Columbia University Press 2008): 'Animals: Property or Persons?', 25–66.

86 See, for a middle position, Alasdair Cochrane, *Animal Rights Without Liberation: Applied Ethics and Human Obligations* (New York: Columbia University Press 2012), 210.

87 Robert Nozick, *Anarchy, State, and Utopia* (New York: Basic Books 1974), 39.

88 Anne Peters, 'Toward International Animal Rights', in Anne Peters (ed.), *Studies in Global Animal Law* (n. 27), 109–20.

3.4 Three Problems of International Law

The current state of 'hard' international law poses three specific problems for animals. The first problem is the animal welfare gap in international law.[89] A range of international treaties regulate the conservation of certain animal species and their habitats. Extant international law instruments have so far not addressed the welfare of wild animals in their purview, or at best have done so in an incidental, ancillary, and fragmented fashion.[90] In contrast to wildlife, agricultural animals have been directly addressed only in 'soft' international law and by EU law. The result of the focus of 'hard' international law on wildlife is a 'disconnect' between animal welfare and international regulation because animal welfare is not part of the 'sustainable use narrative' of wild animals as natural resources.[91]

The second related problem is worse than a mere lack of regulation. 'Hard' international law's concentration on species protection, namely the 'good-of-its kind' as opposed to the individual animal's 'good-of-its-own',[92] has not only neglected but even undermined the welfare efforts for wild animals. The reason is that species conservation is often antagonistic to the concern for individual animal welfare. In conservation science, the interests of individuals are frequently traded off against perceived benefits that accrue to higher levels of organisation (populations, species, and ecosystems); and 'the conservation of species and populations often trumps all other values, including the welfare of individuals.'[93] This focus on species (and even more the focus on ecosystems) is holistic and anti-individualist. It has therefore been denounced as 'environmental fascism'.[94]

Thirdly, a number of international rules have so far rather stymied animal welfare and protection efforts. The best-known examples of the pernicious effects of international law, applied both by international institutions and states, are in international trade law and international financial law. The 'dark side' of the law has been addressed by critical animal studies,[95] but detailed and critical legal analysis of

89 We owe this term to Guillaume Futhazar, 'Biodiversity, Species Protection, and Animal Welfare under International Law', in Anne Peters (ed.), *Studies in Global Animal Law* (n. 27), 95–108, at 104.

90 See, for international animal law beyond a merely conservationist perspective, Katie Sykes, '"Nations Like unto Yourselves": An Inquiry into the Status of a General Principle of International Law on Animal Welfare', *The Canadian Yearbook of International Law* 49 (2011), 3–49; Sabine Brels, *Le Droit du bien-être animal dans le monde: évolution et universalisation* (Paris:L'Harmattan 2017); Peters (ed.), *Studies in Global Animal Law* (n. 27); Peters, 'Animals' (n. 9).

91 Riley, 'Wildlife Law and Animal Welfare' (n. 61), 159, 171.

92 See, for these terms, Bowman, Davies, and Redgwell, *Wildlife Law* (n. 51), 74.

93 Paul C. Paquet and Chris T. Darimont, 'Wildlife Conservation and Animal Welfare: Two Sides of the Same Coin', *Animal Welfare* 19 (2010), 177–90, at 184.

94 Regan, *Animal Rights* (n. 83), 362.

95 See, for a critical theory of animal liberation specifically in the tradition of the Frankfurt school, Susann Witt-Stahl (ed.), *Das steinerne Herz der Unendlichkeit erweichen: Beiträge zu einer kritischen Theorie für die Befreiung der Tiere* (Aschaffenburg: Alibri 2007); John Sanbonmatsu (ed.), *Critical Theory and Animal Liberation* (Lanham: Rowman & Littlefield 2011). See for other strands of critical approaches to the animal issue, the Brill book series *Critical Animal Studies*, edited by Helena

the negative impact of international law on animals is largely missing. Especially, the rules of IHL have so far not been scrutinised from a critical perspective. But IHL is no different from all man-made law, which has up to now been, and will probably always be, profoundly ambivalent regarding animals. As a standard introduction to the field puts it: 'Individual instances of gratuitous intentional cruelty against certain animals are banned, while institutionalized abuse of animals is allowed and often promoted under the law.'[96] Under cover of law, humans have waged what Dinesh Wadiwel has called a 'war against animals'.[97]

4 STRATEGIES FOR DEVELOPING THE LAW

To face the above-mentioned challenges while making best use of the legal strategies available within the existing normative framework, several options will be explored throughout this book. Potential new directions for developing international law on armed conflict will now be identified (Section 4.1). Strategies that are already underway and which could – and should – be reinforced will also be examined (Section 4.2). That said, developing IHL to increase animal protection requires a critical sensibility (Section 4.3).

4.1 *Available Legal Forms*

As a matter of principle, the development of international law on the protection of animals in armed conflict could come about through treaty, secondary treaty law, custom, and 'soft' law. A first approach could be to enrich this legal framework by new norms specifically tailored to the needs of animals. In this vein, scientists have recently proposed a fifth Geneva Convention incorporating special wildlife safeguards.[98] There are strong arguments in favour of adopting such a new IHL instrument. However, this strategy appears to be unrealistic since, as emphasised above in this chapter, states will not be in a position to reach a consensus any time soon on a topic that is not at the forefront of their agendas.

Another, more modest, solution to enhance the protection of animals would be to turn towards existing international instruments beyond IHL at both regional and international levels. These instruments, which were designed for peacetime, could

Pedersen and Vasile Stănescu. See also *The Journal for Critical Animal Studies* (which since 2003 has been available at http://journalforcriticalanimalstudies.org/, accessed 22 February 2022); Anthony J. Nocella II, John Sorenson, Kim Socha, and Atsuko Matsuoka (eds.), *Defining Critical Animal Studies: An Intersectional Social Justice Approach for Liberation* (New York: Peter Lang 2014). See, for critical legal animal studies, Yoriko Otomo and Edward Mussawir, *Law and the Animal: A Critical Jurisprudence* (London: Routledge 2013).

96 Joan E. Shaffner, *An Introduction to Animals and the Law* (London: Palgrave Macmillan 2011), 192.

97 Dinesh J. Wadiwel, *The War Against Animals* (Leiden: Brill 2015).

98 See, for example, Sarah M. Durant and José C. Brito, 'Protect Environment from Armed Conflicts', *Nature* 571 (2019), 478.

be activated by demonstrating that they are – as a matter of principle – applicable also during armed conflict. They could also be interpreted in a dynamic fashion. In the same manner that international human rights law has gradually improved and expanded the protection for human beings in armed conflicts (and has shaped the interpretation of IHL rules),[99] international environmental law could progressively reinforce certain safeguards provided by IHL or influence the interpretation of existing IHL norms when applied to animals. However, the exact applicability of the conventions governing the protection of the environment and in particular wildlife in international and non-international armed conflicts should be tested first. Potential normative conflicts between this regime and IHL norms need to be tackled. Indeed, when two bodies of law deal with the same issue, they could 'either converge and apply harmoniously, or one or more of their norms could conflict with one another'.[100] Concretely, the needs of animals and of those of human individuals who may also be harmed by the injuries inflicted on animals will need to be balanced against the military interests of the belligerents, who may gain an advantage by conducting attacks in areas where these animals are located.[101] However, as already stated in Section 2.3, this balancing exercise is not an easy task when animals are involved. It must also be kept in mind that some of the most sophisticated provisions contained in environmental conventions impose heavy duties upon belligerents, which might be difficult for poorly organised armed groups to abide by.

An alternative solution could be to develop environmental and wildlife regimes through secondary lawmaking by the relevant treaty bodies. This pathway seems more accessible because it does not require the formal unanimity of the state parties but could proceed by consensus (the absence of formal votes) or majority voting. That being said, the bodies must avoid *ultra vires* action which would trigger a backlash against the concerned regime.

Another option is to rely on international customary norms and general principles of law. Generally speaking, a customary norm and a general principle of law on animal welfare seem to be evolving, building on the recognition that 'animal welfare is a globally recognised issue', as a WTO panel famously found in the *Seal Products* case.[102] Such general norms are particularly relevant in the situation of armed conflicts, especially in non-international armed conflicts, which lack codified principles, for instance on the protection of the environment. In this context, it is necessary to investigate whether the rules that potentially provide protection to

[99] See, for example, Louise Doswald-Beck, *Human Rights in Times of Conflict and Terrorism* (Oxford: Oxford University Press 2012).

[100] Jeanique Pretorius, 'Protecting the Environment in Non-international Armed Conflicts Means Looking Beyond International Humanitarian Law Alone', *Conflict and Environment Observatory* (15 March 2019), available at https://bit.ly/3zqpWeu, accessed 22 February 2022.

[101] Ibid.

[102] WTO, Panel Reports, European Communities: Measures Prohibiting the Importation and Marketing of Seal Products, WT/DS400/R and WT/DS401/R (25 November 2013), para. 7.420.

animals in international armed conflicts can be transposed to non-international armed conflicts via customary international law.

Finally, it is important to keep in mind that the body of 'hard' law governing animal protection at the international level remains fragmented and fairly thin. Therefore, it should be explored to what extent memoranda, principles, declarations, resolutions, recommendations, or codes of practice issued by international organisations, states, or non-governmental organisations and which possess no legally binding force are relevant for establishing new standards applicable to animals during warfare.

4.2 *Exploiting the Available Paradigms*

Making use of all applicable legal forms or 'sources', the three paradigms mentioned in Section 3 could be activated for wartime. The general concepts of conservation and sustainable development, animal welfare considerations, and even animal rights could form parameters for the interpretation, application, and reinforcement of the current international normative framework that directly or indirectly protect animals.

First, an overarching conservation approach enshrined in many international conventions that protect the environment could be followed. Although they are significantly tainted by anthropocentric values, these conventions are useful for reinforcing the protection of animals during armed conflicts. Thanks to them animals are protected, not only directly and individually as 'civilian objects' or as 'property' but also indirectly and globally as components of the environment in which they live. As we will see in Chapter 7, combining such a direct and indirect approach to the protection of animals is all the more justified during warfare given that military operations usually affect the ecosystem in its entirety, with general repercussions on all its elements, including wildlife.[103]

Second, the welfarist approach might help to safeguard the interests of certain groups of animals. For instance, the preoccupation with avoiding unnecessary suffering being inflicted on animals is particularly relevant for the protection of animals used by armed forces for specific purposes, such as weapons of war, means of medical transport, in search and rescue operations and for medical experiments. Animal welfare considerations should also be duly taken into account when defining adequate standards for the protection of endangered or captive animals, especially those located in occupied territories or in protected zones. These considerations will need to be adapted to the specific needs of belligerents and the imperatives of military necessity.

The third mentioned paradigm, animal rights, could reinforce the protection of all groups of animals afflicted by war, be they wild, livestock, or militarised animals.

[103] de Hemptinne, Chapter 7, 'Part of the Environment', in this volume.

This paradigm is currently more theoretical than practical. Already hotly contested for peacetime, its application in the context of war, which is generally more hostile towards rights-based paradigms (even for humans), is unlikely in the near future.

4.3 *Critical Sensibility*

The development of an animal-friendly IHL demands a critical sensibility. Thus, with regard to improving the fate of animals, we acknowledge that a number of '[c]entral dilemmas [persist] in the use of law by humans'.[104] But we submit that these dilemmas do not condemn legal scholars and practitioners to resignation. Legal analysis can contribute to identifying animal suffering and can make normative proposals for legal reform. International law is not only a 'hollow hope'[105] but can be turned into a force for the good of animals.

Although human interests, human indifference, and human complacency have worked together to harm animals on a large (even global) scale, the insight that human and animal interests are often aligned is growing and actively promoted – for example by the African Union.[106] Moreover, various arguments of global justice, both for deprived groups of humans and for animals, are gaining ground and bolster attempts at transforming animal use practices.[107]

The proactive promotion of more demanding animal welfare standards needs to be wary of legal imperialism and of the imposition of western preferences on the rest of the world. This is all the more important as the overwhelming number of armed conflicts take place outside Europe and the western hemisphere. Norm entrepreneurship must therefore proceed in a respectful and culture-sensitive way, without licencing and reifying a collection of cruelties as representative of a 'culture' not worth protecting.[108]

Our overall claim is that we can – and should – pursue a 'realistic utopia' for animals afflicted by war, proceeding 'from the international political world as we see it' and extending 'what are ordinarily thought to be the limits of practicable political possibility'.[109] Treating animals well, in recognition of their value as fellow sentient beings, potentially acknowledging fundamental animal rights (or even animal citizenship), is no longer an individual moral choice but 'a societal issue that has to be resolved politically by legislative means'.[110] Triggering a new legal policy on

104 Catharine A. Mac Of Mice and Men: innon, 'A Feminist Fragment on Animal Rights', in Sunstein and Nussbaum (eds.) (n. 75), 263–276, at 272.

105 Gerald N. Rosenberg, *The Hollow Hope: Can Courts Bring About Social Change?* (2nd ed., Chicago: The University of Chicago Press 2008).

106 African Union: Inter-African Bureau for Animal Resources, *Animal Welfare Strategy for Africa* (AWSA) (2017).

107 Oscar Horta, 'Expanding Global Justice: The Case for the International Protection of Animals', *Global Policy* 4 (2013), 371–80.

108 Paula Casal, 'Is Multiculturalism Bad for Animals?', *Journal of Political Philosophy* 11 (2003), 1–22.

109 John Rawls, *The Law of Peoples* (Cambridge: Harvard University Press 1999), §1, 83 and 11. See also Antonio Cassese, *Realizing Utopia* (Oxford: Oxford University Press 2012), xvii–xxii.

110 Garner, 'Broad Animal Protectionism' (n. 78), 169.

animals in armed conflict is the overarching objective of this research. With this objective, the book examines how the emerging global consensus on animal welfare can be stabilised by appealing to legal, economic, and ethical arguments. To this end, it is not necessary that all authors work in exactly the same paradigm.

5 OVERVIEW OF THE BOOK

The outcomes of the research, mainly conducted by specialists in the fields of public international law, IHL, international criminal law, and animal law, is divided into five main parts that are sub-divided into twenty-two chapters. Having evoked (in this chapter) the context, purposes, structure, methods, challenges, and scope of the research, Part I addresses the rationale for the protection of animals in times of war from historical and ecological perspectives as well as the numerous challenges that the task of protection raises. Parts II, III, and IV constitute the core of the research. Divided into sixteen chapters, they map, analyse, and evaluate the protective and enforcement regimes applicable to animals during warfare as they currently exist. These parts also make recommendations for improving these regimes so as to satisfy the main goals of the research identified in Section 1 of this chapter.

In order to guarantee the coherence of the analysis, to facilitate the readability of the book, and to ultimately reinforce its utility, all chapters in Parts II, III, and IV follow a similar pattern of analysis where it was feasible. First, an introduction briefly presents the specific context in which the protection of animals is addressed. Second, the scope of application of each legal regime is studied. This comprises a critical examination of the applicability of the regime's rules, notably the legal arguments allowing or precluding their 'transfer' to animals. Third, the contents and limits of the relevant legal regime, as applied to animals, are critically presented. Fourth, a general examination of the consequences that may flow from the violation of each and every regime is undertaken. Each chapter's fifth and final section makes recommendations adapted to the specific needs of animals in the context analysed. A short bibliography concludes each chapter.

Part I lays out the historical and ecological foundations for the protection of animals during warfare. Clemens Wischermann (Chapter 2) considers this topic from a *historical perspective*. He focusses on the twentieth century, with special consideration paid to the two World Wars. The author advocates a new type of historiography which integrates perspectives of human–animal studies. This includes a novel appreciation of animal war memorials. Ultimately, the question whether the war experience has the potential to transform human–animal relations cannot yet be answered. In Chapter 3, Joshua Daskin and Robert Pringle analyse the topic from an *ecological angle*. They formulate the broad hypothesis that armed conflicts generally slow down rates of habitat conversion (clearcutting, agriculture, extractive industry, development, etc.) and thus negatively impact wildlife and exacerbate exploitative harvesting (poaching, bushmeat hunting, wildlife trafficking, etc.). To conclude Part I, Heike

Krieger and José Martínez Soria (Chapter 4) present the *rationale and challenges for* the protection of animals in wartime. They demonstrate that the protection of animals in this context is based on diverse, even contradictory assumptions, which prompt diverging regulatory approaches (namely economic considerations versus a political theory of animal rights). These contradictions and divergences create challenges and limits for effective protection measures that may further be aggravated by practical and political obstacles.

Part II concentrates on the many different forms of protection that could be granted to animals in international and non-international armed conflicts. Marco Roscini (Chapter 5) first explores whether animals can qualify as *property* or as *objects* for the purpose of IHL. The author shows that leaving animals outside the legal categories of IHL persons and objects has undesirable normative consequences. The extant criteria to determine whether animals would be targetable or not would be inapplicable to animals. This legal situation would leave animals unprotected. Sandra Krähenmann (Chapter 6) concentrates her attention on IHL's *specially protected objects* regimes from which animals could gain some safety. She examines the rules on 'cultural property' and on 'objects indispensable to the survival of the civilian population'. She critically analyses the safeguards offered to these items by IHL and discusses whether animals can be fitted into the said legal categories. In Chapter 7, Jérôme de Hemptinne shows that animals, as part of the *environment*, benefit from the protection afforded by IHL principles and provisions that provide direct and indirect environmental safeguards. He also reveals that these principles and provisions remain weak and largely unclear, especially in the context of non-international armed conflicts. For this reason, the author argues that they need to be read in conjunction with the growing body of international norms, standards, and mechanisms that prevent and redress environmental harm during peacetime. Ayşe-Martina Böhringer and Thilo Marauhn (Chapter 8) ask to what extent the peacetime labelling of animals as *endangered species* can be relevant in times of armed conflict in light of CITES, other treaty-based instruments, and UN Security Council resolutions dealing with wildlife trafficking. They examine the main problems emerging from armed conflict situations for nature conservation and, in particular, for the protection of fauna and their habitat. Chapter 9, by Chris Jenks, proposes a study of animals as *war weapons*. It emphasises that, while the historical use of animals as weapons and weapons platforms has generally been disastrous for these animals, it is still not expressly prohibited by IHL. In light of this, the author argues that an international instrument whereby states agree not to use animals in this manner is needed. Chris Jenks also considers that the use of animals as weapons should be factored into the current autonomous weapons discussion so that states are naturally incentivised to discontinue using weapons that do not yield the desired results. Jérôme de Hemptinne, Tadesse Kebebew, and Joshua Niyo (Chapter 10) examine to what extent 'animal soldiers' could obtain *combatant status* when involved in hostilities *and prisoner of war* status when falling into enemy hands and, thus, be protected by AP I and GC III. They show that, while these status have not been envisaged to apply to animals, elements of the protection provided by these conventions could help design by analogy a protective regime for 'animal soldiers'. In Chapter 11, Jérôme de Hemptinne emphasises that some general principles enshrined in IHL conventions regarding the protection of *medical transports, equipment, and personnel* could potentially provide minimum safeguards for animals used as a means of medical transportation or for search and rescue operations. He also demonstrates that this regime is in many respects inappropriate for the protection of animals. The application of *sui generis* principles, tailored to the specific needs of sentient beings, should thus be conceived in light of recent developments on the welfare and rights of animals in peacetime. Chapter 12 by Katharine Fortin addresses the role and status of *veterinary personnel*. Her chapter shows that unlike medical personnel, veterinary personnel do not generally have a special status under IHL. As a result, veterinary personnel belonging to armed forces are often considered as combatants and do not usually benefit from any special protections, in stark contrast to their medical colleagues. The author argues that veterinary personnel only exceptionally fall within the scope of Article 24 of GC I, namely when de facto used as medical personnel and dealing exclusively with the care of the wounded and sick in war. For non-international armed conflicts, the author analyses the circumstances in which veterinary personnel fall within the concept of a 'fighter' and when they are deemed to directly participate in hostilities.

Part III is devoted to specific situations in which animals may find themselves during hostilities and to which a special regime is attached. Marco Longobardo (Chapter 13) deals with the legal framework applicable to animals in *occupied territories*. The law of occupation is not exclusive and allows the concurrent application of other rules. Thus, the chapter examines three legal 'strata': the specific IHL of occupation, the local legislation of the occupied territory, and other applicable rules binding upon the occupying power. The assessment whether animals are effectively protected in situations of occupation must take note of all three strata, also in their interplay. In Chapter 14, Matthew Gillett recalls how, and under what conditions, certain *zones are protected* in both international and non-international armed conflicts. He then determines to what extent animals can directly and indirectly benefit from this protection. As the prohibition on attacking protected zones encompasses the zones as a whole, animals located in these zones will generally be incidentally protected due to the reduced likelihood of harm through collateral damage, and from the rehabilitation and flourishing of the environment in such zones. Etienne Henry (Chapter 15), examines the fate of animals in *sea warfare*: animals can be injured or killed either when they take part in hostilities or when they suffer the random consequences of attacks on military objectives. Additionally, some animals have historically been treated as objects susceptible to appropriation (as 'absolute contraband') in prize law. With a few exceptions, the law applicable to naval warfare is silent on the treatment of animal life. The state of the law is uncertain because publicly available state practice in this area is scarce. But recent doctrinal and domestic legal trends point towards a greater recognition of the life and dignity of animals in sea warfare as well. In Chapter 16, Giulio Bartolini examines international law related to animals in *disaster situations*. He tackles two main issues, namely the international regulation of certain categories of animals that might support international relief activities (i.e. rescue dogs), and the integration of animal concerns in national and international disaster management perspectives. Veronika Bílková (Chapter 17) emphasises that despite the increasing number of animals employed in *military defence experimentation* each year, this aspect of animal involvement in armed conflicts is unregulated and largely secret. She then explores to what extent the usual national and EU laws on laboratory animals can apply during situations of armed conflict. She argues that these laws would need to be adapted to the particular vulnerability of animals in wartime, notably for protecting them against unnecessary suffering.

Part IV deals with the enforcement regime. It starts with a contribution by Manuel J. Ventura (Chapter 18) on the *repression of international crimes* which analyses all cases before the various international criminal tribunals in which criminal activity concerning animals have featured as part of the factual allegations or findings. To date, international criminal law has not paid any real attention to international crimes that affect the animal population. The contemporary animal rights movement and domestic court judgments granting legal personality to certain animals raise the question whether existing crimes sufficiently encapsulate and penalise harmful acts against animals. Marina Lostal (Chapter 19) examines enforcement regimes from the perspective of *reparation and rehabilitation measures*. While animals cannot receive reparation, they have already featured in some programmes as reparation assets. The chapter argues that animals could become indirect beneficiaries of reparation. In Chapter 20, Karsten Nowrot analyses the special regime for *wildlife trafficking* and gives an overview of the international treaty-based framework. He then addresses the challenges for the enforcement of these treaties, with a particular emphasis on the additional problems created by ongoing armed conflict. Finally, he suggests some responses with a view to making the overall normative framework more effective in the interests of the animals concerned. In Chapter 21, Britta Sjöstedt focuses on the multiple *roles played by the UN* in preserving animal interests. She examines the measures of the UN Security Council on targeted sanctions against poachers and wildlife product traffickers, commodity sanctions, and the illegal exploitation of natural resources. She also reviews the 'greening practice' of the UN Security Council and the securitisation of the environment and wildlife.

In Part V, the editors summarise the rules and legal instruments identified *de lege lata* and the principles and mechanisms *de lege ferenda* as outlined in the preceding chapters. They conclude by proposing building blocks for a more comprehensive legal regime that adequately protects animals in wartime.

SELECT BIBLIOGRAPHY

Cooper, Jilly, *Animals in War* (London: Corgi 2000).

Nowrot, Karsten, 'Animals at War: The Status of "Animal Soldiers" under International Humanitarian Law', *Historical Social Research* 40 (2015), 128–50.

Peters, Anne, 'Animals in International Law', *Collected Courses of The Hague Academy of International Law: Recueil des Cours* Vol. 410 (Leiden: Brill 2020), 95–544.

Roscini, Marco, 'Animals and the Law of Armed Conflict', *Israel Yearbook on Human Rights* 47 (2017), 51–6.

Schmitt, Michael, 'Green War: An Assessment of the Environmental Law of Armed Conflict', *Yale Law Journal* 22 (1997), 1–110.

Stucki, Saskia, '(Certified) Human Violence? Animal Welfare Labels, the Ambivalence of Humanizing the Inhumane, and What International Humanitarian Law Has to Do With It', in Anne Peters (ed.), *Studies in Global Animal Law* (Heidelberg: Springer 2020), 121–31.

2

Historical Perspectives on Animal Involvement in Wartime

Clemens Wischermann

1 INTRODUCTION

In recent years, the outline of a field of research has emerged that deals with the history of humans and animals in war. So far, historical perspectives on warfare have focused primarily on the twentieth century, with special consideration given to the two World Wars. However, they have largely overlooked the multiple and complex roles played by animals. Recent studies on the history of World War I, for example, allocated no significant role to animals. Moreover, the pictorial representations of the war included in a number of these studies contain almost no animals, though sometimes images of horses are included.[1] This lacuna is curious. Until the beginning of the last century, wars had been grounded on human corporeal engagements, with the two main exceptions being animal energy for logistical support and cavalry horses. The technologisation of warfare during the twentieth century with the help of railways, tanks, and motor vehicles only occurred gradually over a number of decades. Thus, the dependence on animals in conflict remained an important factor even during World War II.

In historical research, animals appear only as resources essential to the war effort. Only a few recent contributions have overcome this reductionist perspective and provide a framework for prospective research. Foremost among them are Rainer Pöppinghege's anthology on the long-durée history of animals in war (which primarily focuses on German military history),[2] Ryan Hediger's anthology *Animals and War: Studies of Europe and North Amerika*,[3] and the work of Éric Baratay, especially his recent monograph on France's World War I experience.[4] Pöppinghege's further book, a (cultural) history of animals in World War I, is written for a general

[1] Paul Gerhard, *Bilder des Krieges, Krieg der Bilder: Die Visualisierung des modernen Krieges* (Paderborn: Schöningh 2004).

[2] Rainer Pöppinghege (ed.), *Tiere im Krieg: Von der Antike bis zur Gegenwart* (Paderborn: Schöningh 2009).

[3] Ryan Hediger (ed.), *Animals and War: Studies of Europe and North America* (Leiden, Brill 2013).

[4] Éric Baratay, *Bêtes des tranchées: Des vécus oubliés* (CNRS éditions: Paris 2013).

readership, and contains not only anecdotes and myths but a wealth of accurate observations on the everyday reality of animals in warfare.[5]

Beyond these important anthologies, the most developed contemporary research approaches bring together research on war and violence with a new approach to historical research: human–animal studies.[6] This chapter's approach, therefore, is what I call 'animate history', which postulates that the fabric of history is made up of the intertwining of multiple living creatures and their different types and degrees of (factual) agency. This new perspective changes our historiography of warfare by including animals within the tableau of historically meaningful actors and actions. Writing a history of humans and animals in wartime, this chapter develops the question of interspecies relationships during and after periods of war, inter alia by suggesting a specific reading of the role of animals in war memorials.

2 ANIMALS IN WAR THROUGH THE AGES

Historian Reinhart Koselleck based his concept of epochs on animals and is famous for the now overused 'horse age'[7] periodisation – or more precisely the tripartite pre-horse age, the horse age, and today's post-horse age. One might object that there have never been more horses in central Europe as today. The more important objection is that Koselleck does not allow horses to *participate* in historical processes. In line with Koselleck, one could also characterise the human epochs by their connection to the primary energy motor of pre-industrial agriculture: the ox.

Éric Baratay's alternative periodisation of European history with a view to the use of animals comprises three major phases.[8] The first period is the 'traditional' era prior the late eighteenth century. During this period, relatively few animals existed in fixed relationships with humans since resources were scarcely sufficient to feed both humans and animals. This was especially true for wars that quickly depleted the food base. The second phase stretched from the end of the eighteenth century through to the middle of the twentieth century. This period was shaped by an

[5] Rainer Pöppinghege, *Tiere im Ersten Weltkrieg: Eine Kulturgeschichte* (Berlin: Rotbuch, 2014).

[6] Mieke Roscher, 'Tiere sind Akteure: Konzeptionen tierlichen Handelns in den Human-Animal Studies', in Kristian Köchy, Martin Böhnert, and Matthias Wunsch (eds.), *Philosophie der Tierforschung Vol. 3: Milieus und Akteure* (Freiburg: Karl Alber 2018), 93–120; Mieke Roscher, 'Actors or Agents? Defining the Concept of Relational Agency in (Historical) Wildlife Encounters', in Alexandra Böhm and Jessica Ullrich (eds.), *Animal Encounters* (Stuttgart: Metzler 2019), 149–70; Aline Steinbrecher, '"In der Geschichte ist viel zu wenig von Tieren die Rede" (Elias Canetti): Die Geschichtswissenschaft und ihre Auseinandersetzung mit den Tieren', in Carola Otterstedt and Michael Rosenberger (eds.), *Gefährten, Konkurrenten, Verwandte: Die Mensch-Tier-Beziehung im wissenschaftlichen Diskurs* (Göttingen: Vandenhoeck 2009), 264–86; Gesine Krüger, Aline Steinbrecher, and Clemens Wischermann (eds.), *Tiere und Geschichte: Konturen einer Animate History* (Stuttgart: Steiner 2014).

[7] Reinhart Koselleck, 'Der Aufbruch in die Moderne oder das Ende des Pferdezeitalters', in Berthold Tillmann (ed.), *Historikerpreis der Stadt Münster* (Münster: LIT 2005), 159–74.

[8] Éric Baratay, *Bêtes de somme: Des animaux au service des hommes* (Paris: Points histoire 2008).

enormous increase in the number and function of animals in human spaces, be it in the agricultural and food industry or as an energy supplier in the manufacturing sector. The number of animals utilised in the great wars rose even more steeply. The extent and form of these wars was possible only through the use of millions of animals. After around 1950, the number of animals in Europe and North America declined rapidly in both everyday activities and in wartime.

These epochal models of animals in wars remain committed to an anthropocentric view of human–animal history. Although Baratay's model improves Koselleck's periodisation, both are inadequate. By contrast, Mieke Roscher and Aline Steinbrecher's work constitutes a significant theoretical and methodological turning point. They conceptualise specific 'animal times': the central criterion for a new historical period are the animals themselves, or more accurately the structure of animal-human relationships.[9] This chapter is inspired by this conceptual shift. Roscher and Steinbrecher take up Susan Nance's sharp critique of the (mainstream) concept of modernity and modernisation, both of which are thought of anthropocentrically. According to Nance, '[w]e need to think about a broader global population – one that explicitly includes nonhumans as historicized beings'.[10] Nance's narrative of *animal modernity* is based on the fact that animals during the past 200 years existed as part of consumer societies. For the purposes of this chapter, I enlarge her perspective to establish 'époques' according to the fate of animals and the development of human–animal relations, at a given time. In the twentieth century, human and animal lives depended directly on modern warfare, and the development of new and destructive technologies changed the path of human–animal relations in wars. Based on the state of historical research, this chapter focuses on dogs, horses, and pigeons and demonstrates how humans embraced them as companions in both world wars, and have continued to commemorate them in war memorials until today.

3 WORLD WAR I

3.1 *Historical Context*

I will focus on animals as companions, not on the use of animals as mere objects and resources in warfare, even if that use was enormous. Baratay estimates that in World War I a total of ten million Equidae and several hundred thousand dogs and racing pigeons were utilised.[11] Gervase Phillips provides a further snapshot of the sheer

[9] Mieke Roscher and Aline Steinbrecher, *Tiere und ihre (Eigen)Zeit: Eine historiographische Herausforderung*, unpublished paper 2017, 21.

[10] Susan Nance, *Animal Modernity: Jumbo the Elephant and the Human Dilemma* (Basingstoke: Palgrave Macmillan 2015), 3.

[11] Éric Baratay, 'Geschichtsschreibung von Seiten der Tiere: Leben und Sterben im Ersten Weltkrieg', *Tierstudien* 5 (2014), 30–43, at 31.

scale of the phenomena during the final months of the war: '[a]t the close of the First World War, the British Empire counted 791,696 draught and riding animals with its armies in all theatres: 510,000 horses; 225,311 mules; 36,834 camels; 8,425 bullocks; 11,028 donkeys and 100,000 carrier pigeons'.[12] As there is a lack of research on other animals, I will focus on dogs, horses, and pigeons.

3.1.1 Dogs

In the twentieth century dogs performed militarily relevant functions in all armies and in all wars. According to Chris Pearson, '[i]n 1917 and 1918 France alone enlisted 15,000 dogs, of which 5,321 died'.[13] For the year 1917 alone, the number of dogs utilised in the German, French, and British armies is estimated at 50,000. Éric Baratay has recently drawn attention to the fact that this close interaction between soldiers and dogs was linked to national upbringing, which varied significantly amongst the European powers and had an important impact on the way each military trained their dogs to deliver messages at the front and during combat operations. Baratay emphasises the particularly close individual bond between a dog and its handler in the British army, such that the dog, once 'brought to the front line, tries to reach the dog handler further back, delivering a message'.[14] Moreover, 'these dogs quickly make their way from the front row of the front by taking the initiative and being able to find their master even if he has changed places in the meantime'.[15] In contrast, the French dog training followed a general conditioning model. Every dog received a basic behaviourist treatment, as if the dogs were nothing more than envelopes to be filled:

> The animal learns to walk from one flag to another in an automated manner, and there is hardly any connection to the dog handler, which is therefore easily exchanged, since the animal is not looking for its master, but a flag. This leads to more frequent failures than in the UK, but the dogs who accept this conditioning well can even walk there and back, which the English dogs are unable to do.[16]

Baratay has identified a third type of dog training in the German-speaking countries which emphasises the character of the animal-human relationship. The German approach was to habituate the dog to several handlers from the outset, which was a military advantage given the high death rates of dog handlers. The education and training techniques of the European countries in World War I, therefore, differed in their basic behavioural assumptions regarding dogs. This consequently shaped their

[12] Gervase Phillips, 'Animals in and at War', in Hilda Kean and Philip Howell (eds.), *The Routledge Companion to Animal-Human History* (London: Routledge 2018), 422–45, at 425.

[13] Chris Pearson, 'Dogs, History, and Agency', *History and Theory* 52 (2013), 128–45, at 140.

[14] Baratay, 'Geschichtsschreibung von Seiten der Tiere' (n. 11), 42; see further Baratay, *Bêtes des tranchées* (n. 4).

[15] Baratay, 'Geschichtsschreibung von Seiten der Tiere' (n. 11), 42.

[16] Ibid.

military application options. But beyond that, the varied national traditions most likely led to different cooperation patterns among dogs and people. One would like to know more about these patterns.

3.1.2 Horses

Pearson reconstructed the British situation during the summer of 1917: 'British numbers reached a peak in August 1917 when the British Expeditionary Force (BEF) had 368,000 horses and 82,000 mules on the Western Front alone.'[17] Most of these horses were not members of the cavalry. Nevertheless, the widespread public perception of human-horse relations in war was nourished predominately by the cavalry, which till today has a very specific relationship with its horses: '[t]he soldiers viewed the animals as "comrades" and projected onto them ideals that could hardly be achieved in total war – namely the chivalrous, selfless and above all individual struggle'.[18] Noble rider-soldiers held onto this picture until the time of the French campaign in the 1940s.

3.1.3 Pigeons

Pigeons were used in large numbers by all armies to transmit messages when telecommunication lines were interrupted, or when troops were encircled by enemy forces. In fact, their longstanding importance to warfare has even led to a few noteworthy pigeons being singled out for praise. For example, the last and most famous pigeon on the French side during World War I was pigeon 787-15: 'This pigeon is the last released by the garrison of Fort de Vaux before surrender on June 7, 1916. It arrives at Verdun with much delay, rendering its message useless. Nevertheless, after the war, he is promoted French hero, so much so that his memory is still alive.'[19] Baratay identifies the pigeon's history, including the reconstruction of the military situation at that time, the presumed flight route, and the weather conditions and combat actions at the time.

One of the most prominent pigeons of the twentieth century was Cher Ami, a 'pigeon soldier' in the US Army that was put into action in France during World War I. Her heroic fame, which continues to this day, is based primarily on the message shown in Figure 2.1.

Some American troops had made a quick advance behind German lines but inexplicably came under fire from their own artillery. Cher Ami is said to have delivered her message, despite suffering a gunshot wound, which saved the soldiers' lives and earned her multiple honours and awards. Upon her death in 1919, the

17 Pearson, 'Dogs, History, and Agency' (n. 13), 139.

18 Rainer Pöppinghege, 'Abgesattelt!: Die publizistischen Rückzugsgefechte der deutschen Kavallerie seit 1918', in Pöppinghege, *Tiere im Krieg* (n. 2), 235–50, at 237.

19 Éric Baratay, 'Héros malgré lui: Le pigeon 787-15 (dit Vaillant) à Verdun', *L'Entre-deux* 3 (2018), 1–22.

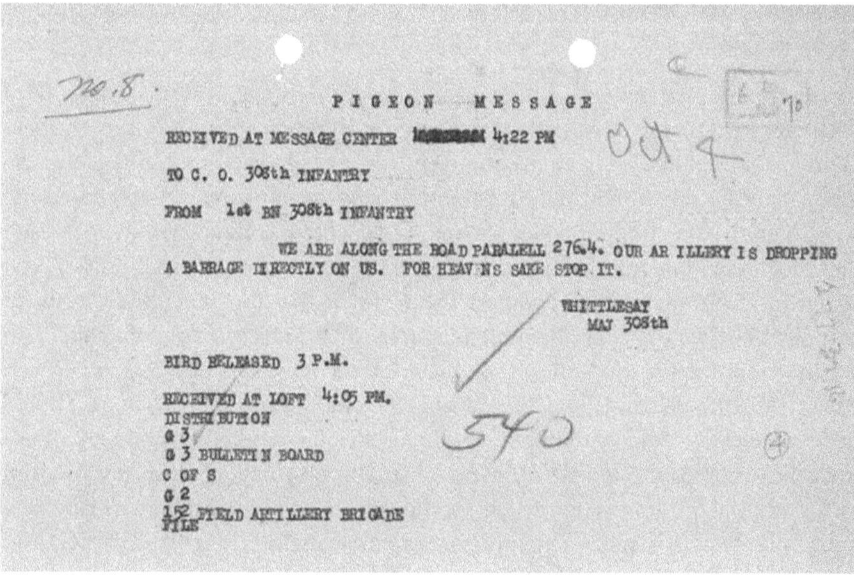

no. 8.

PIGEON MESSAGE

RECEIVED AT MESSAGE CENTER [redacted] 4:22 PM

TO C. O. 308th INFANTRY

FROM 1st BN 308th INFANTRY

WE ARE ALONG THE ROAD PARALELL 276.4. OUR AR ILLERY IS DROPPING A BARRAGE DIRECTLY ON US. FOR HEAV NS SAKE STOP IT.

WHITTLESAY
MAJ 308th

BIRD RELEASED 3 P.M.

RECEIVED AT LOFT 4:05 PM.
DISTRIBUTION
G 3
G 3 BULLETIN BOARD
C OF S
G 2
152 FIELD ARTILLERY BRIGADE
FILE

540

FIGURE 2.1 A pigeon message from Major Whittlesey to the Commanding Officer of the 308th Infantry (US National Archives and Records Administration (NARA)), Identifier 595541, available at http://research.archives.gov/description/595541.

corpse was stuffed, prepared, and then put on display at the Smithsonian Institute where it remains to this day. Comparable heroic narratives of pigeons saving lives at the cost of their own were also circulated on the German side, in both written and visual form.

3.2 *New Historiographical Approaches to the Use of Dogs and Horses*

In an article that considers 'the agency of militarized dogs, especially those of the Western Front (1914–1918)', Chris Pearson suggests one way that 'historians can use primary sources to uncover how individuals in the past have treated dogs as capable creatures and to capture some sense of dogs' embodied and purposeful agency'.[20] Pearson uses training manuals as his primary sources because:

> [they] give some sense of dogs' physical agency. They provide glimpses, however slight and imperfect, of how dogs were capable agents whose attributes dog trainers had to work with and engage to create army dogs. Human trainers had to try to understand dogs in order to harness their capabilities and recognized that particular breeds and individual dogs were more suited for this work than others. The militarized dog, therefore, was not a product of humans imposing their

[20] Pearson, 'Dogs, History, and Agency' (n. 13), 128.

> intentions on the animal object. Instead, it was a mixture of human and canine abilities.[21]

Dogs exemplify one pattern of human–animal relationships in wars, a network of relationships that could be called 'co-socialisation'. Building on findings from the field of human–animal studies, reference should be made to Donna Haraway who uses 'co-socialisation' as a description of the relationship between humans and their (domestic) animals, namely to emphasise how the behaviour of both mutually influences each other.[22] Questions along that line may be asked about the relationship between humans and horses. Baratay counters the myth of the almost endlessly resilient comrade, believing that the 'daily performance of Equidae is overestimated'.[23] In fact: 'in the summer of 1914 and even on the occasion of the attacks of 1918, 60 or even 90 kilometres are demanded on them during the day, although 30 kilometres should not be exceeded – which multiplies the number of exhausted, abandoned, [and] ruined horses.'[24] As the reports on these horses are now being collected and taken seriously for the first time in current research, elements of the comrade myth are now empirically checked. Baratay certainly gives us a more realistic idea of the life of horses under war conditions. He also does not forget the people who previously lived and worked with these horses and had a common agricultural relationship with them up to the moment they were forcibly requisitioned for war:

> Sources mention the excitement of the farmers when they hand over their animals and their recommendations for the treatment of the horses. This indicates the privileged position of these animals in western society, the 'comfort' they enjoy and the close relationship that has developed between these people and these animals. Now, however, the requisitioned horses find themselves treated harshly by unknown people, crammed together with unknown animal comrades, and exposed to the cold and damp of night and rain. They experience great stress, the effects of which (difficulties in adapting and a high mortality rate) are perceptible since the autumn of the same year.[25]

4 WORLD WAR II

4.1 *Historical Context*

The historical account of World War II should start with information on the number of horses, dogs, and pigeons used throughout the conflict. Actual research delivers

21 Ibid., 142.

22 Donna Haraway, *The Companion Species Manifesto: Dogs, People, and Significant Otherness* (Chicago: Prickly 2003); Donna Haraway, *When Species Meet* (Minneapolis: University of Minnesota Press 2008).

23 Baratay, 'Geschichtsschreibung' (n. 11), 41.

24 Ibid. (translation by the author).

25 Ibid., 37 (translation by the author).

only fragmented statistical data. General questions about the relations between animals and humans are comparable to those asked about World War I.

4.1.1 Horses

The facts on the use of horses are aptly summarised by Philipps:

> When Hitler's forces invaded the Soviet Union in June 1941 during Operation Barbarossa, they were logistically dependent upon the 750,000 horses that hauled the artillery, supply wagons, field kitchen and ambulances that accompanied them. As the scale of the war grew, so did their demand for beasts of burden. By early 1945 the Wehrmacht deployed some 1,198,724 horses (a further 1,500,000 had, by then, died in their service).[26]

The German Wehrmacht was not a fully motorised force in World War II. A total of 2.5–3 million horses are said to have been deployed. This was by no means only in the remaining cavalry regiments, as horses were imperative for the mobility of the war effort for almost all troops. The endeavours of Germany's military leaders to keep their precious horses as fit for war as possible were correspondingly great:

> In September 1939 the German army counted just 18 cavalry regiments in its order of battle (each with [an] authorised strength of 1,440 troopers). Yet over the course of the next six years the Third Reich expanded its mounted arm and ultimately deployed no less than eight full cavalry divisions, each with a nominal strength of 11,000–15,000 troopers (only one of these, the 1st Cavalry Division, was mechanised, becoming the 24th Panzer Division in late 1941). The German cavalry arm was, however, dwarfed by its Soviet counterpart. Over the course of the war the Red Army deployed as many as 50 cavalry divisions. Horse-mounted units proved able to travers terrain impassable to other arms, such as the Pripet marshes, and were capable of operating in environmental conditions, such as deep snow or mud, that would render motor vehicles immobile.[27]

4.1.2 Dogs

In addition to the image that humans had given dogs during World War I, a new facet of the human-dog exploitation emerged in World War II, namely the myth of the 'faithful friend'. This myth supposedly allowed dogs to fulfil the will of their masters, and also explained the dogs' seemingly inconsistent behaviour. An exemplary moment in the emergence of this new facet was the Pacific war:

> American forces had suffered severe casualties when confronted by Japanese pill-boxes and fortified bunker complexes. In November 1943 the New Development

[26] Phillips, 'Animals in and at War' (n. 12), 425.
[27] Ibid.

> Division, a research and development unit, began training dogs to run into bunkers with satchels full of explosives, detonated by a timer, attached to their backs. Problems immediately surfaced during training: dogs would turn around when released and return to their handlers. Nor could they reliably be trained to distinguish between a Japanese bunker still in enemy hands and one captured and occupied by American troops.[28]

A traditional interpretation would read this as an example of the unreliability of animal behaviour. In contrast, a detailed analysis that attributes agency to animals would consider the dogs' active part and their behavioural choices in the interaction between humans and dogs.

4.1.3 Pigeons

In the course of the nineteenth century, professional pigeon breeding was well established. Carrier pigeons could fly hundreds of kilometres back to their home crates. As a result, the military use of pigeons was developed during the same time period. Although by the twentieth century pigeons seemed to have become technologically obsolete for the transmission of messages, new technologies were often not yet fit for war purposes. Pigeons, therefore, were used on all fronts. Hundreds of thousands of pigeons were said to have been used on all sides of the conflict, each flying between 500 and 700 km in total.[29] Military interest in carrier pigeons remained high even at the beginning of World War II, as can be shown by a 1939 German directive concerning 'Carrier pigeon material':

> Holland, Luxembourg, and in particular Belgium have valuable private carrier pigeon material and some carefully flown carrier pigeon lines. As far as the population behaves loyally and does not participate in the resistance, carrier pigeon cots found must be safeguarded (possibly placing in collective cots), free flight must be prohibited. The pigeon material is to be reported to OKH Chef HNW. In the event of resistance by the population, the cots have to be confiscated and the animals have to be killed.[30]

4.2 *New Historiographic Approaches to the Use of Horses*

At the core of the idea of comradeship is the imperative not to eat your comrades. But under the realities of war, the comradeship between humans and horses stopped when the latter became the former's food. At first, this is not particularly surprising when one thinks of the disposition prevalent in the nineteenth and twentieth century

28 Ibid., 436.
29 Rainer Pöppinghege and Tammy Proctor, '"Außerordentlicher Bedarf für das Feldheer": Brieftauben im Ersten Weltkrieg', in Pöppinghege, *Tiere im Krieg* (n. 2), 103–17, at 108.
30 Source: Bundes-/Militärarchiv Freiburg, Signatur: RH/ 6/ 3; Oberkommando des Heeres, H.Qu. 10.11.39.

that made it legitimate for humans to rule over animal life. However, the myth of the battlefield[31] would seem to prohibit the eating of horses that were unfit for mobilisation. The contradiction between that myth and the bloody reality of war has yet to be sufficiently investigated. Donna Haraway has got to the heart of what this companionship precisely consists of: 'Companion animals can be horses, dogs, cats, or a range of other beings willing to make the leap to the biosociality of service dogs, family members, or team members in cross-species sports. Generally speaking, one does not eat one's companion animals (nor get eaten by them).'[32] In this analysis, the animal comrade's social characteristics are brought closer to those governing human relationships until the two types of social relationships are congruent. Haraway defines a companion animal by a prohibition on their being eaten. We know that in different cultures – as well as different time periods – the consumption of certain animals is banned. We also know that these bans can have religious, hygiene, or other explanations. Following Haraway, these commandments and prohibitions become a characteristic of biosociality, that is, the way in which biologically different beings live together socially. However, the contemporary predominant perception and interpretation of human-horse relationships in war remains dominated by comrade myth, as opposed to the idea of biosociality

5 POST-WAR PERIODS: COMMEMORATION

The Animals in War Memorial, which was unveiled in 2004 in London, depicts life-size sculptures of mules, dogs, and horses; alongside several other animals, pigeons are present as reliefs. The inscription on the memorial is dedicated to all animals: 'Many and various animals were employed to support British and Allied forces in wars and campaigns over the centuries and as a result millions died. From the pigeon to the elephant they all played a vital role in every region of the world in the cause of human freedom. Their contribution must not be forgotten.'[33] The scholarly examination of the motives and goals of such memorials – as well as the way in which they are socially and politically utilised – has barely begun. Hilda Kean's comparison of memorials in London and Canberra is particularly noteworthy from a human–animal studies perspective. She asks whether they are in fact designed primarily for displaying humanity's power over animals, given that most memorial sites under examination show animals as subordinate to human agendas. This fact is visualised by the London Animals in War Memorial with its animal sculptures and inscriptions: Even if no humans are depicted, service, duty, and sacrifice are ascribed to the animals.

[31] Herbert Franze, *Kriegskamerad Pferd: Sie dienten treu, litten und starben – wofür?* (Berlin: Frieling 2001).

[32] Haraway, *The Companion Species Manifesto* (n. 22), 14.

[33] Hilda Kean, 'Animals and War Memorials: Different Approaches to Commemorating the Human-Animal Relationship', in Hediger, *Animals* (n. 3), 237–62, at 240.

Based on the current state of research and the availability of sources, a second characteristic pattern of human–animal relationships in wars during the twentieth century can be identified alongside the comrade myth. This feature is the heroisation of individual animals, as illustrated by the carrier pigeon. The most important mechanism in this heroising process is the award of military honours, similar to the ones awarded to human soldiers: 'Silent Heroes involves animals that have been awarded the Dickin Medal for Valour, that have received awards from other nations including the American Purple Heart and the French Légion d'Honneur, and those who received none. In the end the telling of their stories is my tribute to the undaunted spirit of them all.'[34] An episode that had been hardly noticed or described by contemporaries, the flight of pigeon 787-15 to the French city of Verdun later received a very detailed description. In the interwar period, the myth of this avian war hero was given complete expression, nourished in important ways by European nationalism. On a plaque on the Fort de Vaux, in a presentation at the Musée du pigeon et de la colombophilie on Mont-Valérien near Paris, and in books and exhibitions, a legend was born which in many ways does not stand up to scientific examination.[35] Nevertheless, this myth lives on even today in controversial commemorative books on World War I in France.[36]

Do only victorious nations build memorial sites for their animal 'soldiers'? Pöppinghege argues that in Germany after World War I, 'pigeons were not worshiped as war heroes. The defeat was apparently not adequate to transfer the victim role from ordinary soldiers to the pigeons.'[37] However, looking at the twentieth century from a more globalised perspective complicates this (national) picture: the dogs lost to the United States during the Vietnam War are probably the most frequently remembered animals in the world. A very common manifestation of animal war memorial culture in the United States are the war dog memorials. They exist in many places, new ones are continually being established, and they appear to be popular among US Army soldiers and veterans. The United States War Dog Association, which has been around since 2000, awards medals (exclusively) to war dogs. This practice can be traced back to Vietnam veterans who set up memorials, established associations, and published countless magazines and books. New memorials related to Afghanistan have also been built.[38]

Commemoration practices started in many countries shortly after the end of World War I and are still an integral part of European and North American

34 Evelyn Le Chêne, *Silent Heroes: The Bravery and Devotion of Animals in War* (London: Souvenir Press 1994), 9.

35 Pigeon 787-15 was neither the only pigeon nor the last creature to leave the fort, and the message it carried arrived long after the surrender of the fort, which rendered the message worthless.

36 Baratay, 'Héros malgré lui' (n. 19), 15.

37 Pöppinghege and Proctor, 'Außerordentlicher Bedarf für das Feldheer' (n. 29), 116.

38 Birgit Schwelling, 'On History, Memory, and Identity: The Vietnam Veterans Memorial as a Lieu de Mémoire', in Walter W. Hölbling, Klaus Rieser, and Susanne Rieser (eds.), *US Icons and Iconicity* (Vienna: Lit 2006), 21–39.

World War I and II memory cultures. Surprisingly, they reached their peak during the last fifteen years, especially in the English- and French-speaking world:

> Take the example of Treo, a black Labrador who made headlines in the United Kingdom in 2010 when Princess Alexandra presented him with a Dickin Medal, the animal equivalent of the Victoria Cross, during a ceremony at the Imperial War Museum. As a member of the 104 Military Working Dog Support Unit, Treo had located various improvised explosive devices in Afghanistan between 2008 and 2010. If reports are to be believed, the pairing of Treo and his handler, Sergeant Dave Heyhoe, was a highly effective amalgamation of human and nonhuman agencies. Heyhoe claims that there was a 'rapport' between himself and Treo; during operations 'you have to understand each other, [and] recognise the slightest change in each other'.[39]

6 CONCLUSION: HUMAN–ANIMAL RELATIONS IN WARTIME

Did human–animal relationships in times of war change the traditional distinctions between humans and animals? To what extent did the empathy of humans for animals that developed during wartime interactions result in social transgressions? These are unanswerable research questions. Rainer Pöppinghege and Tammy Procot extract from the war narratives an animal-centred understanding of dignity comparable to that of human soldiers in suffering and innocence:

> In contrast to the brutal fighting in the trenches, the care of animals such as horses, dogs or pigeons was an almost filigree refuge. The soldiers saw the animals as comrades and emotional retreats. Names like 'four-legged comrades' or 'feathered friends' indicate the warm-hearted relationships with the animals. They admired and pitied them equally because the innocent animals were just as little responsible for the war as the ordinary soldier.[40]

Sociologists Janet M. Alger and Steven F. Alger have raised the cardinal question regarding the relevance of changing traditional inter-species demarcations in wartime: whether – and if so to what extent – have 'ethical concerns regarding the use of animals in wartime . . . altered the moral boundaries between humans and animals'?[41] To this end, they have investigated the US Army's military handling of dogs deployed in World War II, the Vietnam War, and the wars in Iraq and Afghanistan. At the end of World War II, attempts to repatriate the surviving dogs, which were regarded as a valued part of the military's social world, were made. At the end of the Vietnam War, dogs were simply left behind as if they were mere

39 Pearson, 'Dogs, History, and Agency' (n. 13), 144.

40 Pöppinghege and Proctor (n. 2), 114.

41 Janet M. Alger and Steven F. Alger, 'Canine Soldiers, Mascots, and Stray Dogs in US Wars: Ethical Considerations', in Hediger *Animals* (n. 3), 77–104, at 78.

equipment. The situation during the Iraq and Afghan wars, however, is completely different:

> With the wars in Iraq and Afghanistan significant progress was made in the direction of inclusiveness and canine soldiers are currently treated much like human soldiers in many ways. In training methods, medical care and, since the year 2000, in repatriation and retirement, the situation of the MWD (Military War Dog, C.W.) is exemplary, and the dogs are a long way from being defined as 'equipment'.[42]

Still, it remains doubtful whether the animals' experience of violence in wars has been reduced lately. Much research remains to be done.

SELECT BIBLIOGRAPHY

Baratay, Éric, *Bêtes de tranchées: Des vécus oubliés* (Paris: CNRS éditions 2013).

Pearson, Chris, 'Dogs, History, and Agency', *History and Theory* 52 (2013), 128–45.

Phillips, Gervase, 'Animals in and at War', in Hilda Kean and Philip Howell (eds.), *The Routledge Companion to Animal-Human History* (London: Routledge 2018), 422–45.

Pöppinghege, Rainer (ed.), *Tiere im Krieg: Von der Antike bis zur Gegenwart* (Paderborn: Schöningh 2009).

Hediger, Ryan (ed.), *Animals and War: Studies of Europe and North America* (Leiden: Brill 2013).

[42] Ibid., 100.

3

Ecological Effects of Warfare on Wildlife

Joshua H. Daskin and Robert M. Pringle[*]

1 INTRODUCTION

Wildlife – individuals, populations, and communities of animals and other organisms – can be either positively or negatively affected by the military, political, and socio-economic correlates of armed conflict.[1] However, a clear understanding of the conditions under which we can expect one outcome or the other has not emerged. Such clarity would be valuable for evaluating the extent to which wild animals require legal protection in wartime, for designing legal mechanisms to confer such protection, and for prioritising scarce conservation resources.[2]

As a point of departure for this chapter, we consider the intuitive hypothesis that armed conflict may generally (i) exacerbate exploitative harvesting (e.g., bushmeat hunting, wildlife trafficking) owing to food insecurity and the relaxation of law enforcement and social norms, but (ii) reduce habitat conversion (e.g., forest clearing for agriculture, extractive industry, and development) as economies slow and people emigrate from contested areas. Below, we review the evidence available for a first-level assessment of this idea. The few large-scale quantitative analyses conducted to date suggest that, on average, conflict tends to intensify both direct exploitation (Section 2) and habitat conversion (Section 3). However, there are notable local exceptions to this general pattern, as well as a persistent shortage of hard data about exactly how and why conflict affects wildlife. We discuss several major data deficiencies and biases that currently hinder a fuller understanding of the

* We thank Kaitlyn Gaynor for helpful conversations about these issues. We gratefully acknowledge research funding from the US National Science Foundation (IOS-1656527), the Greg Carr Foundation, the Cameron Schrier Foundation, and the Grand Challenges Program of the High Meadows Environmental Institute.

1 Joseph P. Dudley et al., 'Effects of War and Civil Strife on Wildlife and Wildlife Habitats', *Conservation Biology* 16 (2002), 319–29; Thor Hanson et al., 'Warfare in Biodiversity Hotspots', *Conservation Biology* 23 (2009), 578–87; Kaitlyn M. Gaynor et al., 'War and Wildlife: Linking Armed Conflict to Conservation', *Frontiers in Ecology and the Environment* 14 (2016), 533–42.

2 Edd Hammill et al., 'Factoring Attitudes Towards Armed Conflict Risk into Selection of Protected Areas for Conservation', *Nature Communications* 7 (2016) 1–9; Joshua H. Daskin and Robert M. Pringle, 'Warfare and Wildlife Declines in Africa's Protected Areas', *Nature* 553 (2018), 328–32.

ecological effects of warfare, and we identify opportunities to rectify some of these problems (Section 4). Last, we briefly survey emerging evidence that post-war interventions can rehabilitate wildlife populations and ecosystems on relatively rapid timescales (Section 5).

2 EXPLOITATIVE WILDLIFE HARVESTING DURING ARMED CONFLICT

Violence is often accompanied and aggravated by poverty and food insecurity.[3] Accordingly, animals that represent potential sources of food or income may be harvested at higher rates during a conflict. Ungulates and other large mammalian herbivores are highly desired as bushmeat, can feed many people, and are therefore frequently targeted by hunters for local consumption or local/regional trade. In places, firearms and especially automatic weapons become more available during conflicts, which increases the efficiency and scale of hunting.[4] Certain species are exploited both for meat and for the lucrative international trade in tusks, horns, skins, and other body parts, which makes them especially vulnerable. Many wars in Africa have been interwoven with illicit ivory trafficking, although the details of these clandestine actions and transactions are poorly documented.[5] Indeed, there is a paucity of information about the effects of war on wildlife populations in general.

To our knowledge, there have been only two large-scale quantitative assessments of the impacts of warfare on wildlife trends. The first was our own 2018 study, which analysed the population trajectories of 36 large mammalian herbivore species from 126 protected areas in 19 African countries between 1946 and 2010.[6] We found that populations generally declined in the presence of even a modest amount of armed conflict – and that the declines were greatest in areas with the highest frequencies of conflict. We expect that conflict-associated population declines are even more pronounced for mammals that occur outside of formally protected areas, but data to test this conjecture are scarce. The other was a global analysis showing that

3 Ellen Messer and Marc J. Cohen, 'Conflict, Food Insecurity and Globalization', *Food, Culture & Society* 10 (2007), 297–315; Henk-Jan Brinkman and Cullen S. Hendrix, *Food Insecurity and Violent Conflict: Causes, Consequences, and Addressing the Challenges*, Occasional Paper No. 24 (Rome: World Food Programme 2001), 1–32.

4 Franciany Braga-Pereira, Juliano André Bogoni, and Rômulo Romeu Nóbrega Alves, 'From Spears to Automatic Rifles: The Shift in Hunting Techniques as a Mammal Depletion Driver During the Angolan Civil War', *Biological Conservation* 249 (2020), 108744.

5 Ross Reeve and Stephen Ellis, 'An Insider's Account of the South African Security Forces' Role in the Ivory Trade', *Journal of Contemporary African Studies* 13 (1995), 227–43; Robin Thomas Naylor, 'The Underworld of Ivory', *Crime, Law & Social Change* 42 (2005), 261–95; Varun Vira and Thomas Ewing, *Ivory's Curse: The Militarization & Professionalization of Poaching in Africa* (Washington, DC: Born Free USA 2014); Shane C. Campbell-Staton et al., 'Ivory Poaching and the Rapid Evolution of Tusklessness in African Elephants', *Science* 374 (2021), 483–7.

6 Daskin and Pringle, 'Warfare and Wildlife' (n. 2), 328–32.

roughly 80 per cent of all terrestrial mammal and bird species overlapped with a conflict between 1989 and 2018, and that these overlaps were associated with population declines among threatened species.[7]

Most published anecdotes and case studies are in line with this general trend. The Democratic Republic of Congo (DRC) – part of the biodiversity-rich but conflict-plagued Congo Basin – provides several noteworthy examples. In eastern DRC, rebels killed hundreds of hippos (*Hippopotamus amphibius*) around Virunga National Park in the mid-2000s.[8] In central DRC, endangered bonobos (*Pan paniscus*) were hunted at higher rates during conflicts between 1990 and 2010.[9] In north-eastern DRC, the last surviving population of northern white rhino (*Ceratotherium cottoni*) was extinguished from Garamba National Park after anti-poaching efforts broke down during conflicts in the 1990s.[10] The final two northern white rhinos, Najin and Fatu, are living out their days in captivity in Kenya; both are females, meaning that they are the last of their kind.

Declines of large-mammal populations in wartime are thought to stem from a combination of subsistence hunting and commercial wildlife trafficking,[11] abetted by slackened law enforcement[12] and not infrequently by the active involvement of military forces and government officials in poaching and trafficking.[13] The fog of war provides cover for all manner of illicit activities, as evidenced by the literature on conflict ivory.[14] The same fog obstructs scholars' ability to reconstruct the tangled involvement of combatants, civilians, governments, and profiteers in wildlife harvest and sale. Brian Huntley's (2017) account of the Angolan Civil War provides an unusually in-depth portrait of how conflict-associated corruption, poverty, and chaos nearly exhausted that country's wildlife.[15] Sometimes animals are sacrificed as political pawns. In the DRC, charcoal producers controlled by local militias killed endangered mountain gorillas (*Gorilla beringei beringei*) in a gambit to destabilise

7 Uttara Mendiratta, Anand M. Osuri, Sarthak J. Shetty, and Abishek Harihar, 'Mammal and Bird Species Ranges Overlap with Armed Conflict and Associated Conservation Threats', *Conservation Letters* 14 (2021), e12815.

8 Joe Bavier, 'Congo Militia Threaten to Kill Rare Gorillas', *Reuters* (21 May 2007), available at https://reut.rs/3HaGWaW, accessed 22 February 2022.

9 Janet Nackoney et al., 'Impacts of Civil Conflict on Primary Forest Habitat in Northern Democratic Republic of the Congo, 1990–2010', *Biological Conservation* 170 (2014), 321–8.

10 Kes H. Smith, 'Status of Northern White Rhinos and Elephants in Garamba National Park, Democratic Republic of Congo, During the Wars', *Pachyderm* 31 (2001), 79–81.

11 Gaynor et al., 'War and Wildlife' (n. 1), 534.

12 Peter Zahler and Peter Graham, 'War and Wildlife: The Afghanistan Conflict and Its Effects on the Environment', *International Snow Leopard Trust Special Report* (2001), 1–3.

13 Jeffrey A. McNeely, 'Conserving Forest Biodiversity in Times of Violent Conflict', *Oryx* 37 (2003), 142–52; Peter Smallwood, Chris Shank, Alex Dehgan, and Peter Zahler, 'Wildlife Conservation . . . in Afghanistan?', *BioScience* 61 (2011), 506–11.

14 Patience Akumu, 'Illegal Ivory Trade Funding Lord's Resistance Army Rebels', *Independent* (7 June 2013), available at https://bit.ly/3G3rbTl, accessed 22 February 2022; Rene L. Beyers et al., 'Resource Wars and Conflict Ivory: The Impact of Civil Conflict on Elephants in the Democratic Republic of Congo – the Case of the Okapi Reserve', *PLoS One* 6 (2011), e27129.

15 Brian J. Huntley, *Wildlife at War in Angola* (Pretoria: Protea Book House 2017), 533–42.

and dismantle Virunga National Park.[16] Over 150 wildlife rangers in eastern DRC have been killed on the job since 1980, illustrating how efforts to enforce environmental laws can become conflicts within conflicts.[17]

Carnivores are rarely hunted for food, but they are hunted for skins, suffer from the depletion of their prey, and are often killed as bycatch in snares and traps set for other targets. Predators are inherently rarer than their prey – an area with 1,000 kilograms of prey will generally support only about 15 kilograms of carnivore[18] – and their populations are susceptible to total collapse. During the Mozambican Civil War (1977–92), large-herbivore populations declined by more than 90 per cent in Gorongosa National Park, but the populations nonetheless persisted.[19] In contrast, several species of top carnivores were locally eliminated and have only recently begun to recover with the aid of intensive management, extensive snare removal, and the translocation of individuals from other parts of Africa.[20]

Although most of the best-documented examples come from Africa, there are indications that populations of large animals have declined in response to conflicts elsewhere. The poaching of Indian rhino (*Rhinoceros unicornis*), tiger (*Panthera tigris*), and Himalayan blue sheep (*Pseudois nayaur*) spiked during the Nepalese Civil War (1996–2006), in concert with the diminished enforcement of conservation laws and international treaties such as the CITES.[21] In Cambodia, international demand for bushmeat and wildlife products fuelled intense hunting; endangered Asian elephants (*Elephas maximus*), Eld's deer (*Panolia eldii*), and hog deer (*Axis porcinus*), along with critically endangered kouprey (*Bos sauveli*) and Siamese crocodile (*Crocodylus siamensis*), were extirpated from habitats in the eastern part of the country during decades of conflict.[22] The intense poverty and lack of conservation programming throughout Afghanistan's long series of conflicts have left the country's snow leopards (*Panthera uncia*) and their prey vulnerable to being killed and sold by military and civilian hunters.[23] In Pakistan's Balochistan Province, screw-horned goat (*Capra falconeri*) and urial sheep (*Ovis orientalis vignei*) populations declined sharply as automatic weapons became widely available during the

16 Stefan Lovgren, 'Congo Gorilla Killings Fueled by Illegal Charcoal Trade', *National Geographic* (16 August 2007), https://on.natgeo.com/3t3gqg3, accessed 22 February 2022.

17 Bavier, 'Militia Threatens Gorillas' (n. 8).

18 Ian A. Hatton et al., 'The Predator-Prey Power Law: Biomass Scaling across Terrestrial and Aquatic Biomes', *Science* 349 (2015), aac6284.

19 Marc E. Stalmans et al., 'War-induced Collapse and Asymmetric Recovery of Large-Mammal Populations in Gorongosa National Park, Mozambique', *PloS One* 14 (2019), 1–18.

20 Paola Bouley et al., 'Post-war Recovery of the African Lion in Response to Large-Scale Ecosystem Restoration', *Biological Conservation* 227 (2018), 233–42; David Quammen, 'How One of Africa's Great Parks Is Rebounding from War', *National Geographic* (May 2019), available at https://on.natgeo.com/3F2q05n, accessed 22 February 2022.

21 Nabin Baral and Joel T. Heinen, 'The Maoist People's War and Conservation in Nepal', *Politics and the Life Sciences* 24 (2005), 2–11.

22 Colby Loucks et al., 'Wildlife Decline in Cambodia, 1953–2005: Exploring the Legacy of Armed Conflict', *Conservation Letters* 2 (2009), 82–92.

23 Zahler and Graham, 'War and Wildlife in Afghanistan' (n. 12), 1–13.

Soviet-Afghan War (1979–89); snow leopards were later hunted to local extinction when the depletion of their wild prey caused them to switch to eating livestock, prompting retaliation from herders[24] – an illustration of how human-human conflict can translate into human-wildlife conflict.

Other case studies, however, show that alternative outcomes are possible. For example, the 1970s Bush War in Zimbabwe was associated with prodigious growth of elephant populations, allegedly because the bush was too dangerous even for ivory poachers.[25] Are such exceptions as rare as they seem, or are they simply under-reported by scholars and journalists? The record is too sparse and fragmentary to provide a conclusive answer to this question.

3 HABITAT CONVERSION DURING ARMED CONFLICT

Impacts of conflict on animals that are not routinely hunted for food or body parts (which include most birds, reptiles, amphibians, and invertebrates) are more likely to result from changes in the availability and quality of habitat. The conversion of an ecosystem into concrete buildings or intensive agriculture annihilates the resident animal biodiversity of that ecosystem, and even less-intensive land uses can significantly erode the abundance and diversity of animal species. For example, selective logging of valuable timber species can eliminate the specialised birds, butterflies, and bees that eat and pollinate those trees, the specialised predators and parasites of those animals, and so on, with ripple effects throughout the food web – a phenomenon known as coextinction.[26]

It has been proposed that the reduction of human economic activity in conflict zones can decrease rates of habitat conversion.[27] Evaluating this proposition is easiest for forested regions, because deforestation is a relatively straightforward form of habitat conversion to quantify over large areas using aerial and satellite imagery. Contrary to this hypothesis, a recent analysis of deforestation throughout the tropics between 1992 and 2015 found that the rate of forest loss was twofold-to-fourfold greater in areas where conflicts occurred than in peaceful locations.[28] Although informative and pioneering in its scope, this study did not control for potentially confounding variables such as

24 Javed Ahmed, Naseer Tareen, and Paind Khan, 'Conservation of Sulaiman Markhor and Afghan Urial by Local Tribesmen in Torghar, Pakistan', *International Union for the Conservation of Nature* (2001), 1–12.

25 John B. Hallagan, 'Elephants and the War in Zimbabwe', *Oryx* 16 (1981), 161–4.

26 Lian Pin Koh et al. 'Species Coextinctions and the Biodiversity Crisis', *Science* 305 (2004), 1632–4.

27 McNeely, 'Forest Biodiversity in Conflict' (n. 13); Elsa M. Ordway, 'Political Shifts and Changing Forests: Effects of Armed Conflict on Forest Conservation in Rwanda', *Global Ecology and Conservation* 3 (2015), 448–60; Pablo Jose Negret et al., 'Need for Conservation Planning in Postconflict Colombia', *Conservation Biology* 31 (2017), 499–500; Dolores Armenteras, Laura Schneider, and Liliana María Dávalos, 'Fires in Protected Areas Reveal Unforeseen Costs of Colombian Peace', *Nature Ecology & Evolution* 3 (2019), 20–3.

28 David M. Landholm, Prajal Pradhan, and Juergen P. Kropp, 'Diverging Forest Land Use Dynamics Induced by Armed Conflict Across the Tropics', *Global Environmental Change* 56 (2019), 86–94.

human population density and accessibility; additional continental- and global-scale studies are needed to address lingering uncertainties.

Many other studies have focused on the relationship between conflict and deforestation at sub-continental scales. This topic has recently garnered particular attention in Colombia after the signing of a peace accord to end five decades of hostilities.[29] During the Colombian conflict, forced migration of millions of people, mostly from rural to urban areas, created large swaths of abandoned land.[30] Some smaller municipalities experienced net forest regrowth on these disused farms.[31] Moreover, militias required that up to 30 per cent of forests be spared from clearing to limit access, conceal the position of the militants, and provide cover for coca cultivation and weapons trafficking.[32] Nonetheless, many regions rich in mineral resources or suitable for cattle ranching and coca production were deforested during the conflict.[33] Thus, in Colombia, the evidence suggests that conflict had locally variable but overall negative effects on forest cover.

Subsequently, the movement towards peace in Colombia has brought new threats. From 2017 to 2018, fires increased by 600 per cent inside formerly rebel-controlled protected areas, and overall forest disturbance surged – in part because provisions of the peace agreement granted lands for agricultural clearing, commercial development, the harvest of natural resources, and the return of displaced persons in forests that were previously under de facto protection by militants.[34] Thus, researchers analyzing the effects of armed conflict on wildlife must also consider the aftermath, a point to which we return in Section 5.

Conflict-driven habitat degradation is also well-documented in African and Asian regions. Displaced persons in the central DRC fled into and cleared protected forests at twice the peacetime rate,[35] while those fleeing the Rwandan civil war, genocide, and aftermath deforested parts of Nyungwe National Park and much of Giswahiti Forest Reserve.[36] In Afghanistan, conflict has hindered the development

29 Brigitte Baptiste et al., 'Greening Peace in Colombia', *Nature Ecology & Evolution* 1 (2017), 1–3.

30 Negret et al., 'Planning Postconflict Colombia' (n. 27), 499–500.

31 Landholm et al., 'Forest Land Use and Armed Conflict' (n. 28), 86–94.

32 Paulo J. Murillo-Sandoval et al., 'The End of Gunpoint Conservation: Forest Disturbance After the Colombian Peace Agreement', *Environmental Research Letters* 15 (2020), 1–12, available at https://iopscience.iop.org/article/10.1088/1748-9326/ab6ae3, accessed 22 February 2022.

33 Ana María Sánchez-Cuervo and T. Mitchell Aide, 'Consequences of the Armed Conflict, Forced Human Displacement, and Land Abandonment on Forest Cover Change in Colombia: A Multi-scaled Analysis', *Ecosystems* 16 (2013), 1052–70; Negret et al., 'Planning Postconflict Colombia' (n. 27), 499–500; Armenteras et al., 'Fires in Colombian Protected Areas' (n. 27), 20–3; Landholm et al., 'Forest Land Use and Armed Conflict' (n. 31), 86–94.

34 Armenteras et al., 'Fires in Colombian Protected Areas' (n. 27), 20–3; Murillo-Sandoval et al., 'The End of Gunpoint Conservation: Forest Disturbance after the Colombian Peace Agreement' (n. 32), 1–12.

35 Janet Nackoney et al., 'Impacts of Civil Conflict on Primary Forest Habitat in Northern Democratic Republic of the Congo, 1990–2010', *Biological Conservation* 170 (2014), 321–8.

36 Samuel Kanyamibwa, 'Impact of War on Conservation: Rwandan Environment and Wildlife in Agony', *Biodiversity and Conservation* 7 (1998), 1399–406; Ordway, 'Political Shifts and Forests' (n. 27), 448–60.

of sustainable economies as the country's human population has grown enormously;[37] in turn, livestock have overgrazed grasslands and trees have been cleared for fuel and timber, diminishing habitat quality for wild ungulates and reducing their availability as prey for snow leopards and other threatened carnivores.[38] In southeast Asia, the application of defoliants and herbicides such as Agent Orange by the US military in the 1960s and 1970s damaged forests and polluted soils and wetlands.[39] Iraq destroyed 600 oil fields in retribution for attacks by US troops during the First Gulf War in 1991, which contaminated habitats hundreds of kilometres south into the Persian Gulf and killed seabirds, fish, and other marine animals.[40]

Yet, again, there are conspicuous exceptions to the general pattern of conflict-associated degradation. One of the most famous positive side effects of conflict for wildlife is the de facto protected area created by the Korean Demilitarized Zone, which is now home to many at-risk species, including white-naped cranes (*Grus vipio*), Asiatic black bears (*Ursus thibetanus*), and Amur goral (*Naemorhedus caudatus*).[41] In Malaysia, the Royal Belum State Park was recently created in areas that were previously closed to civilians and industrial activity during hostilities with neighbouring Thailand.[42] In Sierra Leone, rebel army bases and combat events were both associated with reduced deforestation rates between 1990 and 2000.[43] An economic downturn during the civil war in El Salvador reportedly slowed agricultural development and forest clearing in the 1980s.[44]

In sum, the available evidence suggests broad similarities between impacts of war on hunting and habitats. Negative effects predominate, but more neutral or even positive outcomes for wildlife sometimes emerge. That conflict can at least occasionally provide a shield for wildlife and their habitats speaks volumes about the reference state: humankind has many ways of destroying, and biodiversity needs protection in both war and peace. Further progress in our understanding of these issues will require both (i) additional large-scale quantitative assessments that build on recent continental and global analyses[45] and (ii) additional finer-scale assessments that capture the kinds of context-specific information that larger-scale syntheses inevitably

37 Smallwood et al., 'Wildlife Conservation in Afghanistan' (n. 13), 506–11.

38 Ibid. See also Zahler and Graham, 'War and Wildlife in Afghanistan' (n. 12), 11–13.

39 Arthur H. Westing, 'Ecological Effects of Military Defoliation on the Forests of South Vietnam', *Bioscience* 21 (1971) 893–8.

40 Severin Carrell, 'Gulf States Fear Iraqi Oil Sabotage', *Independent* (9 February 2003), available at https://bit.ly/3n2phLo, accessed 22 February 2022.

41 Ke Chung Kim, 'Preserving Biodiversity in Korea's Demilitarized Zone', *Science* 278 (1997) 242–3.

42 McNeely, 'Forest Biodiversity in Conflict' (n. 13), 142–52.

43 Robin Burgess, Edward Miguel, and Charlotte Stanton, 'War and Deforestation in Sierra Leone', *Environmental Research Letters* 10 (2015), 1–10.

44 Susanna B. Hecht and Sassan S. Saatchi, 'Globalization and Forest Resurgence: Changes in Forest Cover in El Salvador,' *BioScience* 57 (2007), 663–72.

45 Landholm et al., 'Forest Land Use and Armed Conflict' (n. 28), 86–94; Daskin and Pringle, 'Warfare and Wildlife' (n. 6) 328–32.

obscure. Such situational knowledge is necessary to understand when and where conflict will endanger wildlife, to predict when and where exceptions are likely, and to untangle which agents and what proximate causes (e.g., food insecurity, governance issues, military activities, forced migration) determine the direction and magnitude of war's impact on wildlife. An essential raw ingredient for such studies is greater knowledge about the diversity and abundance of wildlife in warzones.

4 DATA DEFICIENCIES: GEOGRAPHIC AND TAXONOMIC BIASES

A major limitation of the presently available data is the heavy geographic skew in biological field studies. Biodiversity data are generally scarcer and of lower quality in tropical countries than temperate ones, in poorer countries than richer ones, and in conflict-prone regions than peaceful ones.[46] In part, these knowledge gaps reflect the predilections of Northern/Western biologists, who gravitate towards localities that are safe, comfortable, and well-equipped.[47] They likewise reflect the systematic underdevelopment of local capacity and expertise in the Global South, which tends to be especially pronounced in countries with histories of conflict, instability, and poverty.[48]

These data deficiencies are pronounced even for charismatic large mammals, which attract disproportionate attention and funding and are comparatively easy to count (Figure 3.1(A)). They are undoubtedly much worse for other types of animals, (e.g., invertebrates, reptiles, fishes). The Living Planet Index – a global metric of vertebrate species abundance[49] – is the basis for many studies that examine patterns of wildlife population trajectories.[50] In this database, 81 per cent of the data on African large herbivores, carnivores, and primates come from just five countries: South Africa, Tanzania, Kenya, Zimbabwe, and Uganda. A similar bias is present in published studies

46 Laura J. Martin, Bernd Blossey, and Erle Ellis, 'Mapping Where Ecologists Work: Biases in the Global Distribution of Terrestrial Ecological Observations', *Frontiers in Ecology and the Environment* 10 (2012), 195–201; Kerrie A. Wilson et al., 'Conservation Research is Not Happening Where it is Most Needed', *PLoS Biology* 14 (2016), e1002413; James T. Stroud and Kenneth J. Feeley, 'Neglect of the Tropics is Widespread in Ecology and Evolution: A Comment on Clarke et al.', *Trends in Ecology & Evolution* 32 (2017), 626–8.

47 Tatsuya Amano and William J. Sutherland, 'Four Barriers to the Global Understanding of Biodiversity Conservation: Wealth, Language, Geographical Location and Security', *Proceedings of the Royal Society B* 2013 280, 1–7; Ana L Reboredo Segovia, Donato Romano, and Paul R., Armsworth, 'Who Studies Where? Boosting Tropical Conservation Research Where it is Most Needed', *Frontiers in Ecology and the Environment*, 6 January 2020. The latter authors report that 'US scientists still respond negatively to safety concerns,' echoing the findings of the former authors that conflict-prone regions are less-well represented in biodiversity databases.

48 Wilson et al., 'Conservation Research' (n. 46), e1002413.

49 Ben Collen et al., 'Monitoring Change in Vertebrate Abundance: The Living Planet Index', *Conservation Biology* 23 (2009), 317–27.

50 David Vačkář et al., 'Review of Multispecies Indices for Monitoring Human Impacts on Biodiversity', *Ecological Indicators* 17 (2012), 58–67; Megan D. Barnes et al., 'Wildlife Population Trends in Protected Areas Predicted by National Socio-economic Metrics and Body Size', *Nature Communications* 7 (2016), 12747.

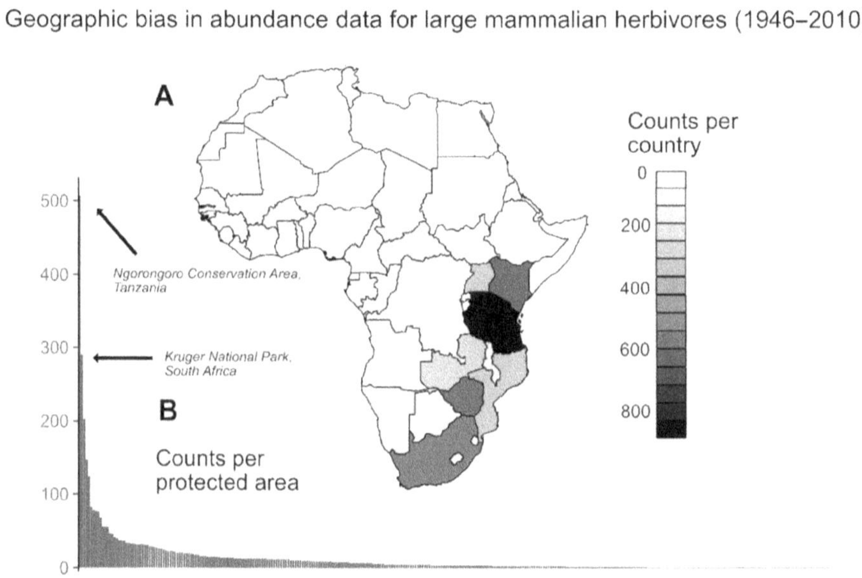

FIGURE 3.1 The number of times large mammalian herbivore populations were counted in (A) each African country and (B) 322 African protected areas between 1946 and 2010. Data from Daskin and Pringle (2018), 2.

that have compiled data from primary sources; in one landmark study of large mammal population trajectories in African protected areas, 76 per cent of the data came from four of the best-studied countries (South Africa, Tanzania, Kenya, and Uganda).[51] Throughout the rest of the continent, there are few if any reliable quantitative data on mammal abundances – notably so for large swaths of West Africa, the mega-diverse Congo Basin, and adjoining countries such as Gabon and South Sudan that are rich in wildlife (at least historically). Even within the few comparatively well-studied countries, a handful of protected areas receive the vast majority of attention. There have been hundreds of wildlife counts in renowned conservancies such as Ngorongoro Crater in Tanzania and Kruger National Park in South Africa, whereas many lesser-known, lesser-staffed, and less-visited protected areas remain essentially unstudied (Figure 3.1(B)).

Given the risk and hardship of working in conflict zones, addressing these data deficiencies to better understand and mitigate the effects of war on wildlife will be challenging. There is an urgent need to couple emerging wildlife-monitoring technologies – which can help to offset the physical risks of conducting research in active warzones – with the cultivation of local capacity where it has been stifled by poverty, underdevelopment, and the tendency of Northern scientists and NGOs to

51 Ian D. Craigie et al., 'Large Mammal Population Declines in Africa's Protected Areas', *Biological Conservation* 143 (2010), 2221–8.

collect data in the tropics without contributing meaningfully to a foundation of local expertise. Technologies with rapidly advancing capabilities for wildlife monitoring include unmanned aerial vehicles (drones) and thermal sensors.[52] Motion-triggered camera traps and audio recorders can be placed in dangerous or inaccessible habitats to document wildlife activity.[53] A major logjam in the use of camera traps for wildlife monitoring is the immense effort required to extract data from hundreds of thousands of images, but multiple efforts are underway to process these data using machine-learning algorithms.[54] It is increasingly easy to envision a future in which the collection, analysis, and satellite transmission of sensor data are all fully automated,[55] requiring minimal human presence in dangerous environments. Similarly, the analysis of environmental DNA shed by organisms is an increasingly well-validated method for biomonitoring, and this approach too is on the path towards automation.[56] There are also many steps that can be taken before conflicts begin to facilitate subsequent analysis of the effects of war on wildlife,[57] such as investing in systematic large-scale surveys to generate baseline data (e.g., The Great Elephant Census).[58]

5 POST-WAR REHABILITATION AND REWILDING

Alongside the evidence that armed conflict generally has negative effects on wildlife and their habitats, there is evidence that natural systems are remarkably resilient in the wake of war – if given the chance. The post-war rehabilitation of Mozambique's Gorongosa National Park is perhaps the most dramatic example. Populations of elephant, hippo, buffalo, and diverse antelope species have all recovered dramatically since 2007 under the aegis of a pioneering public-private conservation

[52] Tracey Hollings et al., 'How Do you Find the Green Sheep? A Critical Review of the Use of Remotely Sensed Imagery to Detect and Count Animals', *Methods in Ecology and Evolution* 9 (2018), 881–92.

[53] J. Marcus Rowcliffe et al., 'Estimating Animal Density Using Camera Traps Without the Need for Individual Recognition', *Journal of Applied Ecology* 45 (2008), 1228–36; Zuzana Burivalova et al., 'Using Soundscapes to Investigate Homogenization of Tropical Forest Diversity in Selectively Logged Forests', *Journal of Applied Ecology* 56 (2019), 1365–2664.

[54] Mohammad S. Norouzzadeh et al., 'Automatically Identifying, Counting, and Describing Wild Animals in Camera-Trap Images with Deep Learning', *Proceedings of the National Academy of Sciences* 115 (2018), E5716–E5725.

[55] Sajid Nazir, Gorry Fairhurst, and Fabio Verdicchio, 'WiSE: A Satellite-Based System for Remote Monitoring', *International Journal of Satellite Communications and Networking* 35 (2017), 201–14; Paul Glover-Kapfer, Carolina A. Soto-Navarro, and Oliver R. Wearn, 'Camera-Trapping Version 3.0: Current Constraints and Future Priorities for Development', *Remote Sensing in Ecology and Conservation* 5 (2019), 209–23.

[56] David A. Bohan et al., 'Next-Generation Biomonitoring: Large-Scale, Automated Reconstruction of Ecological Networks', *Trends in Ecology & Evolution* 32 (2017), 477–87.

[57] Judy Oglethorpe et al, 'Overview C: Conservation in Times of War', in Richard Matthew, Mark Halle, and Jason Switzer (eds.), *Conserving the Peace: Resources, Livelihoods, and Security* (Winnipeg: International Institute for Sustainable Development 2002), 361–84.

[58] Michael Chase et al., 'Continent-Wide Survey Reveals Massive Decline in African Savannah Elephants', *PeerJ* 4 (2016), e2354.

initiative.[59] The precipitous decline of these species in the wake of the Mozambican Civil War had various knock-on effects for the ecosystem. Trees and invasive plant species became more abundant,[60] and the absence of top carnivores altered the behaviour of herbivores and their impacts on plants.[61] Yet the rapid recovery of large herbivores has already begun to reverse this habitat degradation; the abundance of a major invasive plant species has already been reduced to pre-war levels.[62] African wild dogs (*Lycaon pictus*) have recently been reintroduced; leopards appear to have recolonised the ecosystem on their own, and their numbers have since been augmented with translocated individuals.[63] These carnivores are re-establishing the predator-prey interactions that ecologists consider to be essential for the stability of eco systems. Similar efforts to 'rewild' conflict-impacted ecosystems are underway throughout Mozambique,[64] in Rwanda's Akagera National Park,[65] and elsewhere.

The most obvious lesson of success stories like Gorongosa is that an ecosystem degraded by long-term conflict is not lost. This capacity for resilience suggests that efforts to secure protection for wildlife in wartime should consider not just the present and recent past, but also the post-conflict future. In Gorongosa, the park exists not only for wildlife management, but also as an engine of human development.[66] Educational, economic, medical, agricultural, and disaster-relief programming by the national park aims to support the region's populace, reducing their reliance on wildlife as food while bolstering their trust in and cooperation with the park. We believe that similar efforts elsewhere can help to create opportunities for coupled human-natural systems to recover and persist in perpetuity. Because the well-being of people and wildlife are joined in a feedback loop, we suggest that post-war relief efforts should incorporate environmental rehabilitation in addition to traditional human-oriented objectives. The Gorongosa Project provides one model that can be tailored to other circumstances.

59 Robert M. Pringle, 'Upgrading Protected Areas to Conserve Wild Biodiversity', *Nature* 546 (2017), 91–9.

60 Joshua H. Daskin, Marc E. Stalmans, and Robert M. Pringle, 'Ecological Legacies of Civil War: 35-Year Increase in Savanna Tree Cover Following Wholesale Large-Mammal Declines', *Journal of Ecology* 104 (2016), 79–89; Jennifer A. Guyton et al., 'Trophic Rewilding Revives Biotic Resistance to Shrub Invasion', *Nature Ecology & Evolution* 4 (2020), 712–24.

61 Justine L. Atkins et al. 'Cascading Impacts of Large-Carnivore Extirpation in an African Ecosystem', *Science* 364 (12 April 2019), 173–7.

62 Guyton et al., 'Trophic Rewilding' (n. 60), 1–13.

63 Natalie Angier, 'Mozambique is Using Science to Save One of Its National Parks from Destruction', *Independent* (25 July 2018); Natalie Angier, 'How This Spot (in Mozambique) Got Its Leopard', *New York Times* (10 January 2021). https://nyti.ms/3IrQcZT, accessed 22 February 2022.

64 Peace Parks Foundation, 'Conservation Triumphs' (2 December 2019) available at www.peaceparks.org/conservation-triumphs, accessed 22 February 2022.

65 Benedict Moran, 'Rwanda's War Nearly Destroyed This Park. Now It's Coming Back', *National Geographic* (5 May 2019), available at https://on.natgeo.com/3nohZYq, accessed 22 February 2022.

66 Pringle, 'Upgrading Protected Areas' (n. 59), 91–9.

The time needed for ecosystems and wildlife to recover can vary. Habitats recover slowly, but they do recover; tropical forests can regenerate substantially within the span of a few decades.[67] Among animals, time lags are longer for carnivores than for herbivores, but again the timescales are measured in years-to-decades – shorter than the span of a human career. In turn, recovering habitats and wildlife populations can rapidly revive ecosystem services, such as water provision, crop pollination, invasive-species control, and the employment of local people (including former combatants) in environmental management. International collaboration tied to local capacity-building is a key ingredient. With the collaborative assistance of the US Fish and Wildlife Service, urial and screw-horned sheep populations have rebounded in Baluchistan, Pakistan, in part because their conservation provided employment for game rangers and economic benefits from regulated trophy hunting.[68]

6 CONCLUSION

The accumulated evidence suggests that war generally exacerbates both intensive hunting and habitat conversion and is detrimental for individual animals and the populations, communities, and ecosystems of which the individuals are a part. Apparent exceptions to this general pattern are intriguing, and a fuller understanding of the circumstances that lead to exceptional outcomes may ultimately illuminate ways to mitigate the impacts of conflict on wildlife. We believe that the available data clearly suggest a need to consider mechanisms – legal and otherwise – to protect animals and their habitats in wartime. But the present state of knowledge about the ecological impacts of warfare is insufficient to precisely forecast the mechanisms by which conflicts will affect different aspects of biodiversity. Alleviating the current geographic and taxonomic biases in wildlife data is a challenging but crucial step that can be attacked progressively with the aid of emerging technologies. Understanding the social, economic, and political pathways through which war affects wildlife is equally important, and even more challenging. Figuring out how to design and justly enforce wildlife-protection laws in times when people are at their most vulnerable and desperate is undoubtedly most challenging of all.

Despite these hurdles, there is enormous unrealised potential to act in ways that resuscitate conflict-diminished wildlife populations, rehabilitate conflict-degraded ecosystems, advance human well-being, and enrich human experience. Access to a vibrant and intellectually stimulating natural environment is, we believe, a fundamental human right. It is rarely explicitly articulated as such. And yet it is an inextricable component of many widely accepted fundamental rights – to education, to mental and physical health, to participation in cultural life, to contemplation and creative activity, to an adequate standard of living. Many writers have

[67] Ibid.

[68] Ahmed et al., 'Conservation of Urial and Markhor' (n. 24), 1–12.

depicted wildlife conservation as a unique prerogative of the West and the North. It is hardly that. The thrill of safely observing an elephant or a tiger, the serenity of a walk in the forest – these things transcend culture. It is primarily the *access* to such pleasures that is concentrated in wealthy countries. By recognising the indispensability of non-human life to healthy human lives, it may be possible to link protections for people with protections for wildlife, both during and after armed conflicts.

SELECT BIBLIOGRAPHY

Armenteras, Dolores, Laura Schneider, and Liliana María Dávalos, 'Fires in Protected Areas Reveal Unforeseen Costs of Colombian Peace', *Nature Ecology & Evolution* 3 (2019), 20–3.

Baptiste, Brigitte et al., 'Greening Peace in Colombia', *Nature Ecology & Evolution* 1 (2017), 1–3.

Daskin, Joshua H. and Robert M. Pringle, 'Warfare and Wildlife Declines in Africa's Protected Areas', *Nature* 553 (2018), 328–32.

Dudley, Joseph P. et al., 'Effects of War and Civil Strife on Wildlife and Wildlife Habitats, *Conservation Biology* 16 (2002), 319–29.

Gaynor, Kaitlyn M. et al., 'War and Wildlife: Linking Armed Conflict to Conservation', *Frontiers in Ecology and the Environment* 14 (2016), 533–42.

Hanson, Thor et al., 'Warfare in Biodiversity Hotspots', *Conservation Biology* 23 (2009), 578–87.

Huntley, Brian J., *Wildlife at War in Angola* (Pretoria: Protea Book House 2017).

Jennifer A. Guyton et al., 'Trophic Rewilding Revives Biotic Resistance to Shrub Invasion', Nature Ecology & Evolution 4 (2020), 712–24.

Joshua H. Daskin, Marc E. Stalmans, and Robert M. Pringle, 'Ecological Legacies of Civil War: 35-Year Increase in Savanna Tree Cover Following Wholesale Large-Mammal Declines', Journal of Ecology 104 (2016), 79–89.

Justine L. Atkins et al. 'Cascading Impacts of Large-Carnivore Extirpation in an African Ecosystem', Science 364 (12 April 2019), 173–7.

Kim, Ke Chung, 'Preserving Biodiversity in Korea's Demilitarized Zone', *Science* (1997), 242–3.

Martin, Laura, Bernd Blossey, and Ellis Erle, 'Mapping Where Ecologists Work: Biases in the Global Distribution of Terrestrial Ecological Observations', *Frontiers in Ecology and the Environment* 10 (2012), 195–201.

Negret, Pablo Jose et al., 'Need for Conservation Planning in Postconflict Colombia', *Conservation Biology* 31 (2017), 499–500.

Oglethorpe, Judy et al., 'Overview C: Conservation in Times of War', in Richard Matthew, Mark Halle, and Jason Switzer (eds.), *Conserving the Peace: Resources, Livelihoods, and Security* (Winnipeg: International Institute for Sustainable Development 2002), 361–84.

Pringle, Robert M., 'Upgrading Protected Areas to Conserve Wild Biodiversity', *Nature* 546 (2017), 91–9.

Shane C. Campbell-Staton et al., 'Ivory Poaching and the Rapid Evolution of Tusklessness in African Elephants', Science 374 (2021) 483–7.

Stalmans, Marc E. et al., 'War-Induced Collapse and Asymmetric Recovery of Large-Mammal Populations in Gorongosa National Park, Mozambique', *PloS One* 14 (2019), 1–18.

4

The Protection of Animals in Wartime

Rationale and Challenges

Heike Krieger and José Martínez Soria

1 INTRODUCTION

When inquiring into the rationale for the protection of animals in wartime, the reader is immediately confronted with the central challenge that anyone interested in increasing this protection faces: that progressive philosophical approaches on strengthening the position of animals in (human) societies are at odds with the human-centred nature of international humanitarian law (IHL). Therefore, the endeavour to improve the protection of animals in wartime scratches along and often transgresses the limits of *lex lata*. To what extent one is prepared to test these limits by way of interpretation is both influenced by one's approach to the motives for legally protecting animals in wartime and dependent on one's attitude towards the mechanisms of legal change. In the face of a lack of political will, is it preferable to push for progressive interpretations of the law? Or, by accepting that *lex lata* only grants limited protection to certain beings, goods, or values, is it better to continue advocating for new regulatory efforts? The inquiry into the rationale for animal protection is intertwined with the limits of legal methodology and the prospects of legal change.

The protection rationale of legal rules fulfils diverging functions. First, for the purposes of any teleological interpretation, lawyers need to define the object and purpose of a treaty or a rule – a necessarily interdisciplinary undertaking. The object and purpose of a treaty opens the law to external considerations, namely policy arguments based on political or ethical and philosophical perspectives – the last of which will be a central engagement of this chapter. Second, where the protection of IHL shall be extended to animals beyond *lex lata*, analogies come into play. In dealing with analogies, the protection rationale becomes essential for identifying both the gap within the law and the appropriate regulation that ought to fill it.[1] Third, the protection rationale is not always directly integrated into legal analysis. Where it is in no way reflected in the wording or broader structure of a legal text, it

[1] Silja Vöneky, 'Analogy in International Law', in Anne Peters and Rüdiger Wolfrum (eds.), *Max Planck Encyclopedia of Public International Law* (Oxford: Oxford University Press 2008), paras. 16–17.

does not exert any direct impact on legal interpretation at all. Still, in such cases, the protection rationale informs policy arguments for political efforts to change the law.

Against this background, this chapter will critically engage with major approaches to the rationales of animal protection in wartime: Anthropocentrism, speciesism, anthropomorphism, and a rights-based approach (Section 2). In particular, we will analyse how far these approaches are reflected both in *lex lata* and in claims *de lege ferenda* and can be aligned with the general rationale of IHL. We will also deal with the challenges that arise from such an alignment (Section 3). To conclude, the chapter will argue in favour of a straightforward reform approach that aims at a specific convention for the protection of animal rights in wartime (Section 4).

2 BETWEEN LAW AND ETHICS: DIFFERENT RATIONALES FOR ANIMAL PROTECTION

Starting from the perspective of *lex lata*, we broadly distinguish between two major approaches: an anthropocentric approach (Section 2.1 and Section 2.2) and an approach that sees animals as autonomous beings that ought to be considered beyond their utility for humans (Section 2.3).

2.1 *Utilitarian Anthropocentric Approaches*

The currently dominant *lex lata* rationale for the protection of animals in wartime is essentially anthropocentric and informed by utilitarian considerations. Like all law,[2] IHL regulates only human behaviour and predominantly aims to protect human beings.[3] The protection of other goods or values can be granted but primarily in order to serve broader human – including economic and humanitarian – interests. Accordingly, animals are protected, inter alia, as a commodity because they represent an economic resource.[4] They can alleviate human suffering in their function as livestock or when utilised in medical services, and the use of animals for the purposes of alimentation can guarantee human survival in times of war. Since most legal orders equate animals with tangible objects of which private property or public ownership is possible, animals are covered by the rules on military or civilian objects, prohibitions on pillaging and plunder, and other property related rules.[5] Irrespective of the underlying motives, in legal terms the protection is granted unconditionally, even if animals or civilian objects do not fulfil any direct purpose at all.

[2] Hans Kelsen, *The Principles of International Law* (New York: Rinehart & Co. 1952), 97. The statement is used in a different context in order to explain why states and juristic persons are bound by law.

[3] See Peters and de Hemptinne, Chapter 1, 'Wartime', in this volume.

[4] Anne Peters, 'Animals in International Law', *Collected Courses of The Hague Academy of International Law: Recueil des Cours* Vol. 410 (Leiden: Brill 2020), 344–9.

[5] Ibid. See Roscini, Chapter 5, 'Property and Objects'; Krähenmann, Chapter 6, 'Specially Protected Objects', in this volume.

Under international environmental law the anthropocentric approach persists. In the advisory opinion on the *Legality of the Threat or Use of Nuclear Weapons*, the International Court of Justice (ICJ) held: 'The Court also recognizes that the environment is not an abstraction but represents the living space, the quality of life and the very health of human beings, including generations unborn.'[6] Likewise, International Law Commission (ILC) Draft Principles on Protection of the Environment in Relation to Armed Conflicts are apparently grounded on an anthropocentric rationale.[7] While the text itself does not contain any statement on the underlying rationale, there is a refence in the commentary to 'the notion of intergenerational equity as an important part of the ethical basis of international environmental law'.[8] Predominantly, the environment and the animals belonging to it are protected with a view to their benefiting human economy, culture, identity, and aesthetic perception.[9] Yet, the dichotomy between ecocentric and anthropocentric approaches in international environmental law that dominated debates in the 1990s has lost most of its relevance.[10] Any informed anthropocentric approach will be aware of and protect the interdependencies and complexities of ecological systems and therefore will protect the environment as an end in itself and not only those elements that are directly relevant to human interests.[11]

This development also affects the impact of environmental concerns on IHL. In the past, it has been argued that the '"cognitive prism" (of either anthropocentrism or ecocentrism) determines the relative weight accorded to competing interests'.[12] It may be assumed that an anthropocentric viewpoint would imply, for example, that in the balancing exercise required under Article 51 (5)(b) of Additional Protocol (AP) I the environment would be accorded a lesser value.[13] But this perspective has been overcome because of advances in scientific knowledge. Thus, the ILC Draft Principles treat the protection of the environment as equally valuable to other human interests protected by the prohibition against causing excessive damage: 'If the rules relating to proportionality are applied in relation to the protection of the natural environment, it means that attacks against legitimate military objectives

6 ICJ, *Legality of the Threat or Use of Nuclear Weapons*, advisory opinion of 8 July 1996, ICJ Reports 1996, para. 29.

7 UN General Assembly, Report of the ILC, Seventy-first session (29 April–7 June and 8 July–9 August 2019), A/74/10, 211.

8 Ibid., 250.

9 See CITES preamble: 'from aesthetic, scientific, cultural, recreational and economic points of view'. See also Peters and de Hemptinne, Chapter 1, 'Wartime', in this volume.

10 See, for example, Michael Schmitt, 'Green War: An Assessment of the Environmental Law of Armed Conflict', *Yale Law Journal* 22 (1997), 1–110, at 6.

11 Astrid Epiney, 'Gegenstand, Entwicklung, Quellen und Akteure des internationalen Umweltrechts', in Alexander Proelß (ed.), *Internationales Umweltrecht* (Berlin: De Gruyter 2017), Part 1, para. 13.

12 Schmitt, 'Green War' (n. 10), 6.

13 Compare Ibid.

must be refrained from if such an attack would have incidental environmental effects that exceed the value of the military objective in question.'[14]

2.2 *Idealistic Anthropocentric Approaches*

Alongside such predominantly utilitarian approaches, anthropocentrism may also unfold into more idealistic strands that are grounded in moral philosophy and relate to ideas of speciesism. In such understandings, animals may have a moral status or relevance[15] but they do not enjoy specific rights as individuals, and correspondingly there are no direct duties owed to animals beyond those owed to their private owners or the state in whose jurisdiction the animals live.[16]

One idealistic strand is based on a *scala naturae* according to which all forms of life and matter are part of a hierarchical chain. In principle, such forms of speciesism attribute moral value to all beings but accord different values to different species. Thus, speciesism discriminates living entities on moral grounds. Such an approach probably corresponds best with widespread intuitive views on how to conceptualise the relationship between humans and animals: animals deserve compassion and, as part of nature, they possess an intrinsic value but their protection is confined to species conservation efforts or animal welfare projects based on a rationale of human stewardship.[17]

An axiological variant to this rationale starts from the assumption that human beings, unlike animals, are endowed with dignity which justifies conceiving of them as persons with an intrinsic value in their own right and thus seeing them as being categorically different from animals.[18] Possibly the most well-known articulation of this distinction comes from Immanuel Kant. For Kant, the decisive criterion is the capacity to act and make decisions on moral grounds. In this sense only human beings are rational beings who can understand their moral duties and conceive of their lives as ends in themselves. Therefore, humans are unique in possessing dignity as an absolute intrinsic value. Animals, on the other hand, are not rational beings and therefore enjoy neither dignity nor moral rights.[19] Still, there is a specific protection rationale involved in this approach.

14 ILC, Seventy-first session (n. 7), 255.

15 Moral status refers to the idea that animals are morally relevant to human beings and will therefore be protected. Animal rights connotates moral rights for animals, which may encompass hugely varying claims for the improvement of animal welfare. To conceive of animals as bearers of legal rights means to call for certain legal positions that are conferred to animals under legal regimes and may be claimed by 'human advocates' in the interest of animals. (Philipp Bode, *Einführung in die Tierethik* (Stuttgart: utb 2018), 43 and 46.)

16 Ibid., 46.

17 As summarised by Bernd Ladwig, *Politische Philosophie der Tierrechte* (Berlin: Suhrkamp Verlag 2020), 53–4, with reference to Ludwig Siep, *Konkrete Ethik, Grundlagen der Natur- und Kulturethik* (Frankfurt am Main: Suhrkamp Verlag 2004) 226–31; and John Rawls, *A Theory of Justice* (2nd ed., Harvard: Harvard University Press 1999).

18 Ladwig, *Tierrechte* (n. 17), 71.

19 Immanuel Kant, *Die Metaphysik der Sitten, Werkausgabe Band VIII* (Frankfurt am Main: Suhrkamp Verlag 1989), A 93–4 (568–9). It is open to debate whether Kant's approach represents a form of speciesism. Ladwig, *Tierrechte* (n. 17), 74–5.

Kant rejects discretionary uses of violence and brutality against animals because such action directed against sentient beings stupefies human compassion, which fulfils a beneficial moral purpose in relations between fellow human beings.[20]

The Kantian approach permeates legal orders. Historically, it was reflected in national legal prohibitions on the abuse of animals, insofar as such delicts were considered to be directed against the public order.[21] The assumption that harming animals runs counter to the obligations humans have towards themselves can also be used to broaden animal protection under existing IHL. The idea permeates the principle of humanity, which to some extent is increasingly fulfilling the function of a public order clause under progressive interpretations of international law. For example, Anne Peters argues that the principle of humanity in IHL and international criminal law could offer broader protection for animals if understood to cover crimes that 'violate human feelings and shock the conscience of humankind as a whole'.[22] Such an approach is ultimately grounded in Kantian thinking: there are certain things that 'humans must not do [because] the type of crimes … are intuitively recognised as inherently and plainly wrong by all members of the human community'.[23] If humans were to tolerate such behaviour, inter-human morality would be negatively affected.

Both the informed and the idealistic anthropocentric approach translate either into the paradigm of species conservation or animal welfare based on a rationale of human stewardship. Thus, they continue to approach the protection of animals on the basis 'that animals have been legally coded into property'.[24] According to animal rights theories, such an approach is morally and legally flawed and any decisive step to further animal welfare would require a categorical change.

2.3 *Animal Rights Approaches*

Animal rights theories based on considerations of equality and justice advocate for such a categorical change. In pursuing this path, one needs to be aware of potential

20 Kant, *Metaphysik* (n. 19), A 108 (578–9):

> *In Ansehung des Schönen, obgleich Leblosen in der Natur ist ein Hang zum bloßen Zerstören* (spiritus destructionis) *der Pflicht des Menschen gegen sich selbst zuwider: … In Ansehung des lebenden, obgleich vernunftlosen Theils der Geschöpfe ist die Pflicht der Enthaltung von gewaltsamer und zugleich grausamer Behandlung der Thiere der Pflicht des Menschen gegen sich selbst weit inniglicher entgegengesetzt, weil dadurch das Mitgefühl an ihrem Leiden im Menschen abgestumpft und dadurch eine der Moralität im Verhältnisse zu anderen Menschen sehr diensame natürliche Anlage geschwächt und nach und nach ausgetilgt wird … Selbst die Dankbarkeit für lang geleistete Dienste eines alten Pferdes oder Hundes (gleich als ob sie Hausgenossen wären) gehört indirect zur Pflicht des Menschen, nämlich in Ansehung dieser Thiere, direct aber betrachtet ist sie immer nur Pflicht des Menschen gegen sich selbst.*

21 Sabine Lennkh, *Die Kodifikation des Tierschutzrechtes* (Baden-Baden: Nomos 2012), 42.

22 Peters, 'Animals' (n. 4), 365.

23 Ibid., 369.

24 See Peters and de Hemptinne, Chapter 1, 'Wartime', in this volume with reference to Katharina Pistor, *The Code of Capital: How the Law Creates Wealth and Inequality* (Princeton: Princeton University Press 2019).

argumentative fallacies that any animal rights-based protection rationales should avoid. One such fallacy lies in emotion-based sentimental forms of anthropomorphism.

2.3.1 Anthropomorphism as a Limit to and a Basis for Animal Rights

Anthropomorphism offers an ambiguous basis for conceptualising animals as rights-bearers. The concept refers to the attribution of human emotions, characteristics, and behaviour to non-human entities like divine beings, animals, or inanimate objects.[25] In its sentimental variant, anthropomorphism is closely linked to the literary term 'pathetic fallacy', which was originally introduced to the lexicon by John Ruskin[26] and later on transferred to a flawed reasoning or flawed use of an analogy within the life sciences. The pathetic fallacy relies on human emotions. In as much as humans kill and slaughter animals they love and admire them. These emotions tend to prompt attitudes which project human characteristics and virtues into animals.[27]

The extreme nature of war seems to provide fertile ground for the pathetic fallacy. In wartime, love of animals appears to offer humans a 'civilising refuge' nourished by sentimentalism.[28] Both popular literature and academic publications on animals and war are full of pathetic fallacies, and older texts dealing with the subject commonly represent animals as part of the 'heroic' ideals of warfare and thus were a 'projection screen for human emotions'.[29] In more recent times, the huge success of Michael Morpurgo's novel *War Horse*, which was later adapted for both stage and screen to much critical and popular acclaim,[30] is a telling example in this regard. The enduring friendship between a horse, Joey, and a young man during World War I can be read as a metaphor for the capacity of human virtues to persist despite the cruelties of battle. As Morpurgo himself explained: 'I wanted to write the story of the universal suffering of that dreadful war, seen through the eyes of a horse.'[31] *War Horse* and novels like it[32] are based on the parallels that exist between humans and animals with regard to their vulnerability, because both are exposed to the atrocities

25 Philipp von Gall, *Tierschutz als Agrarpolitik* (Bielefeld: transcript 2016), 169–170.

26 John Ruskin, *Modern Painters Vol.* 3 (London: George Routledge and Sons 1843), 152 and 155. Ruskin criticises phrases such as 'They rowed her in across the rolling foam – the cruel, crawling foam'.

27 Von Gall, *Tierschutz* (n. 25), 170.

28 See Rainer Pöppinghege, "Einleitung", in Rainer Pöppinghege (ed.), *Tiere im Krieg: Von der Antike bis zur Gegenwart* (Paderborn: Friedrich Schöningh 2009), 7.

29 Pöppinghege, 'Einleitung' (n. 28), 8.

30 Michael Morpurgo, *War Horse* (London: Kaye and Ward 1982), adapted to stage by Nick Stafford in 2007 and for the big screen by Steven Spielberg (director/co-producer) in 2011.

31 Michael Morpurgo, 'Once Upon a Life: Michael Morpurgo', *Guardian* (11 July 2010), available at https://bit.ly/3HFXtnN, accessed 22 February 2022.

32 On the challenges of conceiving animals as subjects in their own rights within a wartime novel, see Paul Huebener, 'Recognizing and Resisting Animal Subjectivity in Timothy Findlay's *The Wars*', in Ryan Hediger (ed.), *Animals and War* (Leiden: Brill 2013), 177–95, at 193.

of war. Animals are seen as helpless suffering victims of human violence which are subjected to human power in a comparable way to the soldier who conceives of himself not as an actor but an object without agency.[33]

A similar observation concerns war memorials dedicated to animals. Such memorials have been criticised because they 'represent animals only in order to represent human power over animals'.[34] Other authors have emphasised that 'animal representation tells us about humans, rather than animals'.[35] The controversy surrounding the Animals in War Memorial in London[36] exemplifies the negative effects related to anthropomorphism and the sentimentality it often involves.[37] While one may be tempted to interpret the memorial as an effort to acknowledge the autonomous role and status of animals, Hilda Kean argues:

> the over-arching sentiment is the importance of *humans* with the explicit statement that animals played their part in obtaining 'human freedom'. Further, this is not a memorial to all animals who have died in war but only those who 'served and died' alongside 'British and allied forces'. This suggests some commonality of perspective across a human-animal divide, or allegiance to a particular cause rather than a comment on the role of all animals in relation to human warfare.[38]

Indeed, in determining the role of animals in war, there is an inherent risk of instrumentalising animals for human purposes instead of defining their own status. The claim that animals have no choice carries with it an undertone of sentimentality. This wording suggests that, if they were to act freely, animals would make the same decisions as humans do. While this framing suggests some form of animal agency, this agency expresses itself through loyalty to humans and even to their warring causes as if humans and animals share the same motives.[39] Any attempt to conceptualise animals as rights-bearers will need to refrain from such an equation when defining where and how animals and humans are sufficiently similar to accord them the same types of rights. The British environmental campaigner and journalist

33 Ibid., 188–9.

34 Erica Fudge, *Animal* (London: Reaktion Books 2001), 152. See also Nigel Rothfelds, *Representing Animals* (Bloomington: Indiana University Press 2002).

35 Hilda Kean, 'Animals and War Memorials: Different Approaches to Commemorating the Human-Animal Relationship', in Hediger (ed.), *Animals* (n. 32), 237–62, at 239.

36 For a different and more convincing approach, see the Animals in War Memorial in Canberra, Australia; Kean, 'War Memorials' (n. 35), 257–9.

37 The text on the monument runs:

> Animals in War: This monument is dedicated to all the animals that served and died alongside British and allied forces in wars and campaigns throughout time. They had no choice. Many and various animals were employed to support British and Allied Forces in wars and campaigns over the centuries and as a result millions died. From the pigeon to the elephant they all played a vital role in every region of the world in the cause of human freedom. Their contribution must never be forgotten.

38 Kean, 'War Memorials' (n. 35), 240.

39 Marc Bekoff and Jessica Pierce, *Wild Justice: The Moral Lives of Animals* (Chicago: University of Chicago Press 2010), 148–50; Kean, 'War Memorials' (n. 35), 241.

George Monbiot pointedly describes the pathetic fallacy as a 'disneyfication of warfare'.[40]

Nonetheless, sentimental forms of anthropomorphism have also made their way into legal arguments. The sentimental equation of animals and humans provides one possible rationale for calls to treat animals as combatants. In particular, calls to classify military dogs as 'canine members of the armed forces' under US law are based on such sentimental approaches:

> At the heart of the American military is the concept of 'family.' For a military unit to succeed, '[s]oldiers of all ranks must feel they belong to the "family" . . . Building the "family" requires treating one another with dignity and respect.' . . . Over nearly two centuries of military service in the United States, MWDs have become more than just fellow soldiers; they have become family.[41]

For various reasons, such an approach is problematic. It prompts the creation of false analogies, such as the prominent example of the assumption that a grinning chimpanzee is laughing although the animal is actually showing aggressive behaviour.[42] Well known as a problem in debates about livestock-farming, tendencies to humanise animals often prompt severe misunderstandings and misinterpretations about what animal welfare actually means.[43] Moreover, emotional bonds and the humanisation of animals depend considerably on the cultural context.[44] However, IHL's effectiveness and legitimacy depend to a high degree on its claim to enshrine universal values and to operate in a neutral way. Thus, any protection rationale to be integrated into the existing regime should be based on considerations that represent universal values agreed upon by all relevant actors in line with IHL's overall objective and purpose and should not rely on arguments that differ across diverging cultural contexts.[45]

40 George Monbiot, 'The Disneyfication of War Allows Us to Ignore Its Real Savagery', *Guardian* (24 October 2006), available at www.theguardian.com/commentisfree/2006/oct/24/comment.iraq, accessed 22 February 2022.

41 Michael Kranzler, 'Don't Let Slip the Dogs of War: An Argument for Reclassifying Military Working Dogs as "Canine Members of the Armed Forces"', *University of Miami National Security & Armed Conflict Law Review* 4 (2013), 268–94, at 276.

42 On the deeper methodological complexities of anthropomorphism and 'anthropodenialism', see Kristin Andrews, 'Beyond Anthropomorphism: Attributing Psychological Properties to Animals', in Tom Beauchamp and Raymond Frey (eds.), *The Oxford Handbook of Animal Ethics* (Oxford: Oxford University Press 2011), 469–94. See also, for a comparable methodological criticism of anthropomorphism in artificial intelligence, David Watson, 'The Rhetoric and Reality of Anthropomorphism in Artificial Intelligence', *Minds and Machines* 29 (2019), 417–40.

43 José Martínez Soria, 'Paradigmenwechsel in der landwirtschaftlichen Nutztierhaltung', *Rechtswissenschaft* (2016), 441–67.

44 James Serpell, 'Pet-Keeping in Non-western Societies: Some Popular Misconceptions', *Anthrozoös* 1 (1987), 166–74, at 169 and 171.

45 See, on the problem of cultural contingency, Peters and de Hemptinne, Chapter 1, 'Wartime', in this volume with reference to Paula Casal, 'Is Multiculturalism Bad for Animals?', *Journal of Political Philosophy* 11 (2003), 1–22.

On the other hand, anthropomorphism and even some forms of emotional sentimentalism have an important role to play in prompting favourable public perceptions of animal protection and related value shifts as empirical studies prove.[46] Above all, criticism of anthropomorphism should never go so far as to reject that animals are sentient beings.[47]

2.3.2 Egalitarian Theories as a Basis for Moral and Legal Animal Rights

In view of increasing scientific knowledge, the realisation that (at least certain groups of) animals are sentient beings forms the starting point for most ethical theories arguing in favour of animals as moral rights-bearers. The most normatively ambitious rationale views animals as part of a moral community with human beings for the reason that animals suffer and feel pain in comparable ways. The approach emphasising the perception of animals as sentient beings is often characterised as a pathocentric approach. Not the ability to think rationally is decisive but the ability to feel is morally relevant.[48] These theories may be utilitarian,[49] contractual,[50] capacity-based,[51] or, inter alia, based on considerations of justice and equality.[52] Regardless of diverging deductions and justifications, however, these approaches culminate in the claim that animals possess an inherent value and enjoy corresponding moral rights. The principle of justice covers all beings on equal grounds. According to Bernd Ladwig: '[a]s a consequence of the moral principle of equal treatment of equal cases, animals are endowed with rights in those constellations where they are sufficiently similar to human beings and their rights'.[53]

The huge variety of such approaches should not give rise to the impression that the animal rights paradigm would dominate legal practice. Anthropocentrism is still the prevailing rationale from the perspective of *lex lata*. Within this rationale, IHL offers protection for animals in particular through the rules on civilian objects.[54] If protection for animals shall be increased, remaining protection gaps need to be

46 See, for example, Max Butterfield, Sarah E. Hill and Charles G. Lord, 'Mangy Mutt or Furry Friend? Anthropomorphism Promotes Animal Welfare', *Journal of Experimental Social Psychology* 48 (2012), 957–60; Michael J. Manfredo, Esmeralda G. Urquiza-Haas, Andrew W. Don Carlos, Jeremy T. Bruskotter, and Alia M. Dietsch, 'How Anthropomorphism Is Changing the Social Context of Modern Wildlife Conservation', *Biological Conservation* 241 (January 2020).

47 See, for a critique on the reproach of anthropomorphism, von Gall, *Tierschutz* (n. 25), 170–71.

48 See, for an overview, Bode, *Tierethik* (n. 16), 20–1.

49 See, in particular, Peter Singer, *Practical Ethics* (3rd ed., Cambridge: Cambridge University Press 2011); Peter Singer, *Animal Liberation* (London: Harper Collins Reissue 2009).

50 Mark Rowlands, *Animal Rights: Moral Theory and Practice* (2nd ed., New York: Palgrave Macmillan 2009).

51 Martha Nussbaum, *Frontiers of Justice: Disability, Nationality, Species Membership* (Harvard: Harvard University Press 2006).

52 Ladwig, *Tierrechte* (n. 17).

53 Ibid., 26 (authors' translation).

54 Marco Sassòli, *International Humanitarian Law, Rules, Controversies, and Solutions to Problems Arising in Warfare* (Cheltenham: Edward Elgar 2019), 10.187.

identified[55] and addressed within existing law-making processes, such as the ones by the International Committee of the Red Cross (ICRC) or the ILC. If one aims to operationalise an animal rights approach in IHL *lex ferenda*, however, several challenges will need to be overcome.

3 FROM MORAL RIGHTS TO LEGAL RIGHTS?

To conceive of animals as bearers of moral rights does not automatically imply that they are bearers of legal rights. To conceive of animals as bearers of legal rights and to integrate them into concepts like civilian or combatant would require the deliberate transgression of long-established, traditional categories. For this purpose, three methodological steps need to be taken. First, a clear legal case must be made for the similarities that justify placing animals somewhat counterintuitively into the same category as human beings. Second, it must be ascertained that the consequences attached to new categories correspond with animals' specific characteristics. Third, the system and the underlying rationale of IHL itself must not be impaired. While ethical approaches to animal rights may help us in affirmatively answering the first question, the example of animal combatants demonstrates that to completely equate animals with humans does not necessarily benefit the former. Still, the third step remains the most problematic. Such a transformation from ethics to law requires a deliberate act to integrate the extra-legal rationale into IHL, either through the creation of a new treaty or by way of interpretation. Particularly in the latter case, the rationale must be aligned with the wording, the systematic structure, and the objectives and purposes of IHL; otherwise, frictions may arise that could weaken the compliance pull of IHL and its concerted objective to provide protection to humans (see Section 4).

Even if one is prepared to accept that the concepts of combatant, civilian, and protected person are not necessarily confined to human beings despite the obvious original intention of state parties[56] and common linguistic usages and understandings, systemic challenges persist. Conceiving of animals as rights-bearers will be systematically flawed if IHL does not grant rights to individuals. In this regard, opinions range from traditional perspectives that claim IHL does not bestow any subjective rights on individuals[57] over those claims that distinguish according to

55 Ibid.

56 See, for more on this argument, Peters, 'Animals' (n. 4), 374–85.

57 Rene Provost, *International Human Rights and Humanitarian Law* (Cambridge: Cambridge University Press 2002), 16–56; Silja Vöneky, 'Implementation and Enforcement of International Humanitarian Law', in Dieter Fleck (ed.), *Handbook of International Humanitarian Law* (4th ed., Oxford: Oxford University Press 2021), 21.19, paras. 5–6: observing 'a notable trend towards recognizing an individual right to reparation'; ICJ, *Jurisdictional Immunities of the State (Germany* v. *Italy; Greece Intervening)*, reply of the Federal Republic of Germany of 5 October 2010, paras. 45, 39–49; ICJ, *Jurisdictional Immunities of the State (Germany* v. *Italy; Greece Intervening)*, judgement of 3 February 2012, ICJ Reports 2012, separate opinion of Judge Koroma, ibid., para. 9; separate opinion of Judge Keith, ibid., paras. 18–19.

specific provisions[58] to broad claims that IHL contains individual subjective rights in view of its progressive humanisation.[59] While the latter approach is backed by calls 'for a more morally informed and individually focused law of war',[60] it still struggles to prove that it is backed by state practice.[61] If the nature of IHL is still appropriately described as an objective legal regime that includes 'objective rules of behavior addressed to states', of which individuals are only beneficiaries and not subjective individual rights-bearers,[62] animal rights do not fit.

However, if one conceives of IHL as including subjective rights, animals would not necessarily benefit. Such an approach would introduce into IHL the debate on the extent to which the possession of legal rights presupposes that a rights-bearer holds certain qualities and capacities.[63] In particular through the prism of law, the philosophical critique raised by Carl Cohen against the concept of animal rights resonates. According to his hierarchical approach, rights depend on the human capability for rational choice and are therefore necessarily human. For categorical reason, rights cannot be of any relevance for animals since they cannot understand, exercise, or respond to moral claims and rights. Human beings can create and defend their own moral principles as well as behave in accordance with these rules. According to Cohen, 'human[s] … confront choices that are purely moral', but the 'capacity for moral judgment does not arise in the animal world' so that as a matter of logic the idea of animal rights should be rejected.[64] While transferring the idea of moral rights for animals to the sphere of legal rights would thus face considerable argumentative and conceptual challenges, anthropocentric approaches to protecting the welfare of animals are in line with IHL's traditional

58 Yoram Dinstein, *The Conduct of Hostilities under the Law of Armed Conflict* (3rd ed., Cambridge: Cambridge University Press 2016), 28–9.

59 Lawrence Hill-Cawthorne, 'Rights under International Humanitarian Law', *European Journal of International Law* 28 (2017), 1187–215, at 1211–12; Frédéric Mégret, 'Theorizing the Laws of War', in Anne Orford and Florian Hoffmann (eds.), *The Oxford Handbook to the Theory of International Law* (Oxford: Oxford University Press 2016), 762–78, at 775.

60 Hill-Cawthorne, 'Rights' (n. 59), 1195. See, on arguments in favour of such an approach, Anne Peters, 'Direct Rights of Individuals in the International Law of Armed Conflict', *Max Planck Institute for Comparative Public Law & International Law Research Paper* No. 2019-23. See, for counterarguments, Ziv Bohrer, 'Divisions over Distinctions in Wartime', in Ziv Bohrer, Janina Dill, and Helen Duffy (eds.), *Law Applicable to Armed Conflict* (Cambridge: Cambridge University Press 2020), 106–96, at 182–95; Heike Krieger, 'Addressing the Accountability Gap in Peacekeeping: Law-Making by Domestic Courts as a Way to Avoid UN Reform?', *Netherlands International Law Review* 62 (2015), 259–77, part 3.2.

61 Cases where states recognise rights of individuals in armed conflict predominantly concern international human rights law. See, for example, ECtHR, *Hanan* v. *Germany*, Grand Chamber, appl. No. 4871/16; ECtHR, *Armenia* v. *Azerbaijan*, appl. No. 42521/20.

62 Sassòli, *International Humanitarian Law* (n. 54), 9.05.

63 On this debate, see Peters, 'Animals' (n. 4), 403–10.

64 Carl Cohen, 'Why Animals Do Not Have Rights', in Carl Cohen and Tom Regan (eds.), *The Animal Rights Debate* (Lanham: Rowman and Littlefield 2001), 27–40, at 35. Such approaches, however, face the problem of explaining 'non-paradigmatic cases' in human beings. See Bode, *Tierethik* (n. 16), 239–243 and 243–4.

nature as an objective protection regime: they reduce many of the philosophical and legal complexities associated with a rights-based approach because such approaches refrain from advocating interpretative paradigm shifts. Thereby, they allow a focus on the actual gaps in protection.

Moreover, such an anthropocentric animal welfare approach can be appropriately reconciled with approaches from just war theory, which look into moral justifications for the choices embedded in IHL. From the perspective of animal welfare in wartime, the just war theory of Jeff McMahan offers a way to explain the protection rationale because it relies on the individual moral liability of combatants, which animals lack. According to McMahan, one should differentiate between combatants who fight a just war in line with the applicable *jus ad bellum* and therefore receive combatant immunity and those who participate in an unjust war and therefore must be seen to engage moral responsibility, which results in a loss of immunity.[65] McMahan aims to 'make a person morally liable to force or violence' based on his or her 'moral responsibility for initiating or sustaining' an unjust threat.[66] Since animals do not take the decision to participate in war and are not responsible in moral and legal terms for their conduct, it may be argued that – as a consequence of the decisiveness of the choice for supporting a just or an unjust war – animals should not be subjected to any harm.

However, most international humanitarian lawyers will strongly disagree with McMahan's approach since his concept provides an ethical justification that decouples existing law from its moral foundations, which thereby either reduces it to a utilitarian instrument[67] or creates considerable dangers for the practical application of IHL. To fulfil its fundamental humanitarian objectives, IHL needs to operate neutrally and be applied equally to all parties of a conflict irrespective of whether a party has illegally commenced an armed conflict.[68] This requires the strict separation of *jus ad bellum* and *jus in bello* to be upheld.

A more appropriate way of morally explaining the laws of war that still allows them to be aligned with concerns for animal welfare has been offered by Janina Dill and Henry Shue. Their argument relies on considerations of necessity for morally explaining the laws of war: 'In the morally tainted environment that is war, the best available rules center on allowing only violence that is necessary for a war to be waged. The military necessity of individuals' engagement in the fighting, not their moral status, should determine whether or not they are immune from

65 Jeff McMahan, 'The Ethics of Killing in War', *Ethics* 114 (2004), 693–733, at 696–8.

66 Ibid., 721. See also Jeff McMahan, *Killing in War* (Oxford: Oxford University Press 2009).

67 Mutatis mutandis Ian Clark, 'Taking "Justness" Seriously in Just War: Who Are the "Miserable Comforters" now?', *International Affairs* (2017), 327–41, at 330.

68 Christopher Greenwood, 'Historical Development and Legal Basis', in Fleck, *Handbook* (n. 57), 1–43, at note 101. Accordingly, the preamble to AP I stresses that 'the provisions of the Geneva Conventions of 12 August 1949 and of this Protocol must be fully applied in all circumstances to all persons who are protected by those instruments, without any adverse distinction based on the nature or origin of the armed conflict or on the causes espoused by or attributed to the Parties to the conflict.'

attack.'[69] This approach explains why the distinction between combatants and civilians needs to be drawn and is deeply rooted in the structure and logic of IHL. The legal principle of military necessity offers the required interface.

According to the principle of military necessity, which goes back to the Saint Petersburg Declaration of 1868, measures are permitted that are actually necessary to overpower or weaken the military capacity of an adversary subject to all further legal restrictions included in IHL.[70] While this definition already includes elements of a proportionality test, modern approaches suggest that military necessity must be understood as a proper balancing exercise. Thus, a military measure that fulfils the military's needs better than any other option will not be regarded as militarily necessary if one of the other options offers better protection to civilians while only slightly disadvantaging the military.[71] Such an evolving understanding of military necessity justifies and limits the use of military force and offers a rationale that informs the rules operating on the basis of considerations of military necessity, such as the principle of proportionality or the duty to take precautionary measures according to Article 57(2)(a)(ii) of API I.[72] As Yishai Beer explains: '[m]ilitary force in general, [and] targeting in particular, should be lawful only to the extent that it is effectively necessary for achieving a given military advantage'.[73] Such rationale also allows for the far-reaching protection of animals. In modern warfare the use and killing of animals will hardly prove to be a military necessity. Based on this understanding, for example, precautionary duties require parties to a conflict to take all feasible precautions in the choice of means and methods of attack with a view to avoiding or minimising incidental loss of animal life.

Admittedly, necessity fulfils an ambivalent legal function because it entails both enabling and constraining effects.[74] Thus, such an approach allows for humans to be killed in certain circumstances and would apply also, within certain parameters, to the killing of animals. But as long as the protection of animals in wartime can only be achieved on the basis of existing rules of IHL, necessity offers a workable rationale. Even though such an approach relies on an evolutive understanding of military

69 Janina Dill and Henry Shue, 'Limiting the Killing in War: Military Necessity and the St. Petersburg Assumption', *Ethics and International Affairs* 26 (2012), 311–33, at 312; Janina Dill, 'Should International Law Ensure the Moral Acceptability of War?', *Leiden Journal of International Law* 26 (2013), 253–70; Henry Shue, 'Laws of War, Morality, and International Politics: Compliance, Stringency, and Limits', *Leiden Journal of International Law* 26 (2013), 271–92.

70 American Military Tribunal at Nuremberg, *US* v. *List*, judgment of 19 February 1948, 11 NMT 1230, 1253: 'Military necessity permits a belligerent, subject to the laws of war, to apply any amount and kind of force to compel the complete submission of the enemy with the least possible expenditure of time, life, and money.' See, on the evolving meanings of military necessity, Davis Luban, 'Military Necessity and the Cultures of Military Law', *Leiden Journal of International Law* 26 (2013), 315–49, at 339–47.

71 Luban, 'Military Necessity' (n. 70), 344.

72 Yishai Beer, 'Humanity Considerations Cannot Reduce War's Hazards Alone: Revitalizing the Concept of Military Necessity', *European Journal of International Law* 26 (2016), 801–28, at 818.

73 Beer, 'Humanity' (n. 72), 814.

74 Ibid., 802.

necessity, it implies only a small interpretative step and not a substantive paradigm change. Any such paradigm shift would require an explicit political act.

4 A CATEGORICAL CHALLENGE

On a methodological or heuristic level, law faces problems of categorisation in dealing with animals as sentient beings. As a social construct, law needs to rely on constructed terms and categories. In general, categorisation serves to identify differences between distinct phenomena through comparison and helps in analysing and explaining these differences.[75] Categorisation also allows for diverging legal consequences to be attached to diverging phenomena. Different categories are often constructed on a binary basis by relying on traditionally established dichotomies, including dead/alive, nature/culture, and human/animal. While such binary thinking can be criticised for oversimplifying, ignoring grey areas, perpetuating biases, and providing a foil for discrimination,[76] dichotomy-based processes of categorisation remain essential for reducing complexities in order to explain social phenomena and make law workable. Law, especially IHL, needs simple and plain categories to be identified easily in times of conflict under the fogs of war. Therefore, existing categories should be left unimpaired.

Moreover, any attempt to introduce animal rights into IHL needs to rely on dynamic interpretations that are, however, currently not backed by corresponding state practice.[77] If it 'appears to be unrealistic [to adopt a new IHL agreement] since … states will not be in [a] position to reach a consensus any time soon on a topic which is not at the forefront of their agendas',[78] why is it realistic to assume that they consent to a dynamic interpretation that categorically changes the law as it stands? A dynamic interpretation is not an instrument for circumventing (the lack of) state consent.

Moreover, tensions between ethical coherence, practical attainability, and existing legal regulations risk undermining the legitimacy and thus the effectiveness of

75 See, on differences and similarities between terms and categories from a legal perspective, Heinrich Honsell and Theo Mayer-Maly, *Rechtswissenschaft: Die Grundlagen des Rechts* (Berlin: Stämpfli, Nomos, Manz 2017), 162–4.

76 See, for a critic of the effects of categorisation from a perspective of gender and race, Evelyn Nakano Glenn, 'The Social Construction and Institutionalization of Gender and Race', in Beth Hess, Judith Lorber, and Myra Marx Ferree (eds.), *ReVisioning Gender* (Thousand Oaks: Sage 1999), 3–43.

77 So far, the pertinent case law predominantly concerns decisions under national or international human rights law. While courts in Argentina and Colombia have granted animals the status of rights-holders, in many other cases standing or jurisdiction *ratione personae* was denied. See Tom Sparks, 'Protection of Animals Through Human Rights: The Case-Law of the European Court of Human Rights', in Anne Peters (ed.), *Studies in Global Animal Law* (Heidelberg: Springer 2020), 153–71, at 166 note 89. See also, on the interdependencies between dynamic interpretation and subsequent state practice, UN, *Yearbook of the ILC 2018*, Vol. II, Part Two, A/73/10, conclusions 7 and 8.

78 Peters and de Hemptinne, Chapter 1, 'Wartime', in this volume.

IHL. There is an inherent danger that morally based claims for the legal rights of animals will detach existing law from ethics and thereby put additional strain on IHL's legitimacy:

> The key concern is that the laws of war currently do not reflect a coherent or compelling moral position. For many international lawyers and political theorists, on the other hand, the problem is instead what to do about the challenge to law, and the worry is that these proposed ethical revisions do not lend themselves at all to effective application in a practical legal system. If we accept these ethical principles, we further diminish the prospects for law. . . . [L]aw faces an unpalatable choice of deficits, either in ethical coherence or in practical attainability.[79]

Such an unpalatable choice between a deficit in ethical coherence or practical attainability constitutes a particularly grave concern for IHL in view of 'discourses about its effectiveness and a tendency to question its impact', as well as the currently widespread perception that IHL 'is more often violated than respected'.[80] If lawyers argue in favour of paradigmatic shifts within *lex lata* that are neither covered by state consent nor seem to be practically attainable anytime soon, they contribute to perceptions of international law as an empty promise.[81] An approach that aims to integrate ethics, politics, and law in order to avoid unpalatable choices and to reduce such tensions may be seen to serve IHL's overall objectives and the likelihood of appropriately attaining them. International humanitarian law remains 'a profoundly pragmatic branch of international law'.[82]

Instead of interpretative moves to bring moral rights into the legal sphere, explicit protection regimes in the form of new international legal agreements should be pursued as the appropriate way forward. Any conceptual transfer of animals from the categories of property and tangible objects to combatants or civilians, or any attempt to completely ban the use of animals in war, is eventually a political value decision that should not be brought about incrementally through interpretative processes but should instead result from transparent and open political discussions. Obviously one may wonder whether it is at all realistic to generate momentum for such a political act, both in general and in relation to our current conjuncture.[83] Nevertheless, creating such a momentum should be a high priority for animal rights activists.

79 Clark, 'Just War' (n. 67), 330.

80 ICRC, 'International Humanitarian Law and the Challenges of Contemporary Armed Conflicts: Recommitting to Protection in Armed Conflict on the 70th Anniversary of the Geneva Conventions' (Geneva: ICRC 2019), 76, available at https://bit.ly/32VfAY7, accessed 22 February 2022.

81 See Sassòli, *International Humanitarian Law* (n. 54), 4.79–4.80.

82 Ibid., 4.79.

83 On current challenges for the adoption of new IHL treaties, see ibid., 4.29–4.33. For treaties on animal protection in wartime, see Peters and de Hemptinne, Chapter 1, 'Wartime', in this volume.

SELECT BIBLIOGRAPHY

Cohen, Carl and Tom Regan (eds.), *The Animal Rights Debate* (Lanham: Rowman and Littlefield 2001).
Dill, Janina and Henry Shue, 'Limiting the Killing in War: Military Necessity and the St. Petersburg Assumption', *Ethics and International Affairs* 26 (2012), 311–33.
Hediger, Ryan (ed.), *Animals and War* (Leiden: Brill 2013).
Ladwig, Bernd, *Politische Philosophie der Tierrechte* (Berlin: Suhrkamp Verlag 2020).
Nussbaum, Martha, *Frontiers of Justice: Disability, Nationality, Species Membership* (Harvard: Harvard University Press 2006).
Peters, Anne, 'Animals in International Law', *Collected Courses of The Hague Academy of International Law: Recueil des Cours* Vol. 410 (Leiden: Brill 2020).
Rowlands, Mark, *Animal Rights: Moral Theory and Practice* (2nd ed., New York: Palgrave Macmillan 2009).
Singer, Peter, *Animal Liberation* (London: Harper Collins Reissue 2009).

PART II

The Protection of Animals in International and Non-international Armed Conflicts

Part II is devoted to the many different aspects of protection that could be granted to animals in international and non-international armed conflicts given:

- Their characteristics as property and as objects (Chapter 5), specially protected objects (Chapter 6), and endangered species (Chapter 8);
- the environment in which they reside (Chapter 7); and
- the functions that can be assigned to them as weapons of war (Chapter 9), as combatants and prisoners of war (Chapter 10), and as means of medical transport, search and rescue (Chapter 11).

Part II also addresses the status and protection of veterinary personnel in international and non-international armed conflicts (Chapter 12).

5

Animals as Property and as Objects

Marco Roscini

1 INTRODUCTION

This chapter explores whether animals can be considered as 'property' and 'objects' under the law of armed conflict, in particular under Article 23(g) of the Hague Regulations and under the law of targeting codified in Additional Protocol (AP) I. The purpose is to verify whether these rules apply to animals and, if so, to discuss to what extent they protect them from destruction, seizure and attack in the conduct of hostilities.

Although references to it will be made when necessary, the present chapter does not discuss the protection of animals as property under the law of occupation, as this forms the object of a separate chapter.[1] It also does not address the targeting provisions granting special protection to certain objects or to the natural environment, as these topics are examined elsewhere in this book.[2]

2 SCOPE OF APPLICATION OF THE LAWS THE CONDUCT OF HOSTILITIES PROTECTING PROPERTY AND OBJECTS

2.1 *Animals as 'Property' under Article 23(g) of the Hague Regulations*

Article 23(g) of the Hague Regulations provides that it is prohibited '[t]o destroy or seize the enemy's property, unless such destruction or seizure be imperatively demanded by the necessities of war'. There is consensus that this rule reflects customary international law in both international and non-international armed conflicts, at least as far as the prohibition of destruction is concerned.[3] While Article 23(g) of the Hague Regulations qua treaty law applies only to land warfare,

[1] See Longobardo, Chapter 13, 'Occupied Territory', in this volume.

[2] See Krähenmann, Chapter 6, 'Specially Protected Objects'; de Hemptinne, Chapter 7, 'Part of the Environment'; de Hemptinne, Chapter 11, 'Medical Transport, Search and Rescue', in this volume.

[3] Jean-Marie Henckaerts and Dana Constantin, 'Protection of the Natural Environment', in Andrew Clapham and Paola Gaeta (eds.), *The Oxford Handbook of International Law in Armed Conflict* (Oxford: Oxford University Press 2014), 469–91, at 472; ICRC Customary Law Database,

as a customary provision it extends to all other domains of warfare (sea, air, space and cyberspace).[4]

What Article 23(g) protects is 'enemy's property', be it private or public.[5] Whether or not animals constitute 'property' has been the subject of debate in animal law scholarship.[6] If 'welfarist' scholars maintain that it is ethically acceptable to continue to see animals as 'property' but advocate for a more humane treatment, others (the 'abolitionists') argue for the elimination of property status and for classifying at least some animals as legal persons entitled to certain rights.[7] Among the former group, David Favre has suggested that a fourth category of property, living property, should be added to the traditional ones – real property, personal property and intellectual property – so to include vertebrate animals.[8] According to Favre, 'some animals, but not all animals, should possess some but not all possible legal rights' and, therefore, can continue to be classified as 'property'.[9] These views are challenged by Gary Francione, a leading abolitionist scholar, who argues that 'the liberal theory of property assumes that animals have no interests, or, at least, no interests that will prevail against human interests' and that 'to classify something as property in the legal sense is to say that the thing is to be regarded solely as a means to the end to be determined by human property owners.'[10] For Francione, therefore, animals, as sentient beings, should not be considered as property, but right holders.

If this view was accepted and animals ceased to qualify as 'property', Article 23(g) would not apply to them. In the context of the law of armed conflict, however, some state practice and case-law suggest that animals fall under the scope of the provisions protecting private and public property. The United States, for instance, classifies

Rule 50. The customary character of the prohibition to seize private property in non-international armed conflict, however, is controversial (Yutaka Arai-Takahashi, 'Protection of Private Property', in Andrew Clapham, Paola Gaeta and Marco Sassòli (eds.), *The 1949 Geneva Conventions: A Commentary* (Oxford: Oxford University Press 2015), 1515–34, at 1529).

4 Sigrid Redse Johansen, *The Military Commander's Necessity: The Law of Armed Conflict and Its Limits* (Cambridge: Cambridge University Press 2019), 342.

5 Arai-Takahashi, 'Protection' (n. 3), 1517; Yoram Dinstein, *The Conduct of Hostilities under the Law of International Armed Conflict* (3rd ed., Cambridge: Cambridge University Press 2016), 287; UK Ministry of Defence, *The Joint Service Manual of the Law of Armed Conflict* (Oxford: Oxford University Press 2004), 393.

6 For an in-depth analysis of the different approaches to animal rights and the law, see Malgosia Fitzmaurice, *Whaling and International Law* (Cambridge: Cambridge University Press 2015), 153–83.

7 See David Favre, 'Living Property: A New Status for Animals within the Legal System', *Marquette Law Review* 93 (2009–10), 1021–72, at 1023. See also Taimie L. Bryant, 'Similarity or Difference as a Basis for Justice: Must Animals Be Like Humans to Be Legally Protected from Humans?', *Law & Contemporary Problems* 70 (2007), 207–354, at 209; Katie Sykes, '"Nations Like unto Yourselves": An Inquiry into the Status of a General Principle of International Law on Animal Welfare', *Canadian Yearbook of International Law* 49 (2011), 3–50, at 9.

8 See Favre, 'Living Property' (n. 7), 1042–7.

9 Ibid., 1032.

10 Gary L. Francione, *Animals, Property, and the Law* (Philadelphia, PA: Temple University Press 2005), 46.

military working dogs as 'equipment': A 2012 legislative proposal submitted to the US Congress reclassified them as 'canine members of the armed forces', but the bill lapsed without being turned into law.[11] In *Gotovina, Čermak and Markač*, the International Criminal Tribunal for the former Yugoslavia (ICTY) qualified animals as property the appropriation of which was, in the case before the tribunal, not justified by military necessity.[12] Addressing the issue of 'property loss', the Eritrea-Ethiopia Claims Commission (EECC) also found 'extensive evidence of [the] gratuitous, and patently unlawful, slaughter and burning of the goats, sheep, donkeys and cattle so critical to the survival of rural civilians' and, consequently, held Ethiopia in violation of its obligations under applicable international humanitarian law (IHL).[13] In the final award, the EECC referred to livestock as 'property',[14] as did the International Criminal Court (ICC).[15]

The question, however, is whether *wildlife* and *stray* animals can also qualify as 'enemy's property' under Article 23(g). While the expression is broad enough to include both public and private enemy property, the ordinary meaning of 'property' is 'a thing or things belonging to someone'.[16] If 'property' is interpreted according to its ordinary meaning, then, it would at best include farm and zoo animals as well as pets and other domestic animals, but not wild, stray or unowned animals. As has been noted, '[t]hat a living being lives upon or crosses over the real property of a human does not constitute possession of that living being [...]. Wild beings within natural ecosystems are not personal property. While governments assert the right to control access to wild animals, they do not have possessory rights or ownership of wild animals.'[17] An interpretation of Article 23(g) limited to domestic animals, however, is not consistent with the object and purpose of the provision, which arguably is to protect a belligerent and its nationals from unnecessary economic damage.[18] Indeed, wildlife can be subject to different forms of exploitation, such as hunting and fishing, and its destruction can cause significant economic losses: if Article 23(g) applies to it, the causation of these economic losses

11 H.R. 4103 and S. 2134.

12 ICTY, *Prosecutor* v. *Ante Gotovina, Ivan Čermak and Mladen Markač*, trial judgment of 15 April 2011, IT-06-90-T, para. 1783.

13 EECC, *Partial Award, Western Front, Aerial Bombardment and Related Claims – Eritrea's Claims* 1, 3, 5, 9–13, 14, 21, 25 and 26, decision of 19 December 2005, paras. 29–30.

14 EECC, *Final Award, Ethiopia's Damages Claims*, decision of 17 August 2009, para. 4.

15 ICC, *The Prosecutor* v. *Germain Katanga*, order for reparations pursuant to Article 75 of the Statute of 24 March 2017, ICC-01/04-01/07-3728-tENG, para. 95 ff.

16 Catherine Soanes (ed.), *The Oxford Compact English Dictionary* (2nd ed., Oxford: Oxford University Press 2003), 907.

17 Favre, 'Living Property' (n. 7), 1044. See also Anthony Leibler, 'Deliberate Wartime Environmental Damage: New Challenges for International Law', *California Western International Law Journal* 23 (1992–3), 67–138, at 105–6. A peculiar case is that of unmarked mute swans swimming in open waters in England, over which the British monarch retains the right to claim ownership, although this right is mainly exercised only on certain stretches of the River Thames.

18 Article 31(1) of the Vienna Convention on the Law of Treaties. This provision includes, among the main criteria for interpretation, not only the literal one, but also those which take into account (a) the context and (b) the object and purpose of the provision.

will need to be justified by imperative considerations of military necessity. This conclusion finds support in the US Law of War Manual, which defines 'enemy property' as '[a]ll property located in enemy territory . . . regardless of its ownership'.[19] If this is correct, then, Article 23(g) covers all animals that are present in enemy territory, regardless of whether they are domesticated, migratory, liminal, wild or stray.[20]

The destruction of property by the occupying power 'except where such destruction is rendered absolutely necessary by military operations' is also prohibited by Article 53 of Geneva Convention (GC) IV. Unlike Article 23(g) of the Hague Regulations, which applies to the entire territory of the belligerent parties, Article 53 only protects property in occupied territory.[21] In particular, it protects animals 'belonging individually or collectively to private persons, or to the State, or to other public authorities, or to social or cooperative organizations'. The considerations with regard to the qualification of wild and stray animals as enemy's property made above in relation to Article 23(g) can be extended, *mutatis mutandis*, to Article 53.[22]

2.2 *Animals as 'Objects' under the Law of Targeting*

2.2.1 The Principle of Distinction

Article 48 of Additional Protocol (AP) I provides for the obligation of the parties to the armed conflict to 'at all times distinguish between the civilian population and combatants and between civilian objects and military objectives and accordingly [to] direct their operations only against military objectives'. Article 52(1) of AP I reiterates that '[c]ivilian objects shall not be the object of attack or of reprisals' and, in the following paragraph, specifies that '[i]n so far as objects are concerned, military objectives are limited to those objects which by their nature, location, purpose or use make an effective contribution to military action and whose total or partial destruction, capture or neutralization, in the circumstances ruling at the time, offers a definite military advantage'. The customary status of the principle of distinction is well established.[23] On 19 December 1969, the UN General Assembly

19 US Department of Defense, *Law of War Manual* (Washington, DC: Office of General Counsel, US Department of Defense 2016), 286.

20 Boothby also maintains that 'property' in the context of Article 23(g) of the Hague Regulations includes both domestic and wild animals (William H. Boothby, *The Law of Targeting* (Oxford: Oxford University Press 2012), 197).

21 Pictet Commentary on GC IV, 301. The ICJ controversially found that Article 23(g) is 'not pertinent' in situations of belligerent occupation (ICJ, *Legal Consequences of the Construction of a Wall in the Occupied Palestinian Territory*, advisory opinion of 9 July 2004, ICJ Reports 2004, para. 124). See the critical comments of Dinstein, *The Conduct* (n. 5), 195–6; Arai-Takahashi, 'Protection' (n. 3), 1519–20.

22 For a more detailed discussion of Article 53, see Longobardo, Chapter 13, 'Occupied Territory', in this volume.

23 ICRC Customary Law Database, Rule 14. See also Christopher Greenwood, 'Customary Law Status of the 1977 Additional Protocols', in Astrid J. M. Delissen and Gerard J. Tanja (eds.), *Humanitarian Law of Armed Conflict: Challenges Ahead* (Dordrecht, Boston and London: Martinus Nijhoff

by unanimous vote adopted Resolution 2444, which expressly recognised the principle of civilian immunity and its corollary requiring the parties to an armed conflict to distinguish civilians from combatants at all times.[24] The customary nature of the principle of distinction has also been upheld by the International Committee of the Red Cross (ICRC)[25] and by national and international courts: In particular, according to the International Court of Justice (ICJ)'s advisory opinion on the *Legality of the Threat or Use of Nuclear Weapons*, the obligation to distinguish between combatants and non-combatants is an 'intransgressible [principle] of international customary law' which is 'to be observed by all States whether or not they have ratified the conventions that contain' it.[26] According to the ICTY, 'it is now a universally recognized principle … that deliberate attacks on civilians or civilian objects are absolutely prohibited by international humanitarian law.'[27]

The obligation of distinction also applies in non-international armed conflicts, as can be inferred from common Article 3(1) of the GCs, which prohibits violence on those 'taking no active part in hostilities',[28] and more explicitly from Article 13(2) of AP II.[29] Although these provisions only refer to civilians and the civilian population, and not to civilian objects, the ICRC's position is that the customary protection of civilian objects against attack applies regardless of the type of armed conflict.[30] The ICTY also reached the same conclusion in several cases.[31]

I have argued elsewhere that animals do not fit in the dichotomy civilians/combatants for the purposes of the application of the principle of distinction because those notions appear to refer to 'persons' and because, if they were considered combatants, animals would necessarily possess not only the rights, but also the obligations associated with this status, and it can be doubted that they have an autonomous capacity to understand and apply the law.[32] The question, therefore, is

Publishers 1991), 93–114, at 108; US Department of Defense, Conduct of the Persian Gulf War: Final Report to Congress (1992), *International Legal Materials* 31 (1992), 615–44, at 621–2.

24 UN General Assembly Resolution 2444 (XXIII) of 19 December 1968, A/RES/2444. The Preamble to this resolution states that these fundamental humanitarian law principles apply 'in all armed conflicts', both international and non-international. The United States acknowledged that Resolution 2444 is declaratory of customary international law (Arthur W. Rovine, 'Contemporary Practice of the United States Relating to International Law', *American Journal of International Law* 67 (1973), 118–26, at 122).

25 ICRC Customary Law Database, Rules 1 and 7.

26 ICJ, *Legality of the Use or Threat of Nuclear Weapons*, advisory opinion of 8 July 1996, ICJ Reports 1996, paras. 78–9.

27 ICTY, *Prosecutor* v. *Zoran Kupreškić et al.*, trial judgment of 14 January 2000, IT-95-16-T, para. 521. See also EECC, *Partial Award* (n. 13), para. 95.

28 A. P. V. Rogers, *Law on the Battlefield* (3rd ed., Manchester: Manchester University Press 2012), 305.

29 Under Article 13(2) of AP II, '[t]he civilian population as such, as well as individual civilians, shall not be the object of attack'.

30 ICRC Customary Law Database, Rule 10.

31 See, for example, ICTY, *Prosecutor* v. *Tadić*, decision on the defence motion on jurisdiction of 10 August 1995, IT-94-1, para. 127.

32 Marco Roscini, 'Animals and the Law of Armed Conflict', *Israel Yearbook on Human Rights* 47 (2017), 35–67, at 44–5.

whether they at least qualify as 'civilian objects', so that attacks, as defined in Article 49(1) of AP I,[33] cannot be directed against them. The ordinary meaning of the word 'object' encompasses only inanimate things.[34] This conclusion seems to find support in the AP I Commentary, which defines 'objects' as 'tangible and visible *things*'.[35] The *travaux préparatoires* of Article 52(2) of AP I also suggest that the notion of 'object' is limited to non-living things.[36]

If we resort to contextual interpretation, however, we will find that Article 54(2) of AP I refers to livestock animals as 'objects'.[37] Furthermore, the French and Spanish versions of Articles 48, 52(1) and 52(2) employ the expressions '*biens*'/'*bienes*', which translate into English as 'assets', 'goods', 'possession' or 'property'.[38] All these expressions have a broader meaning than 'object' and are not limited to inanimate things, but also include living beings that are susceptible of appropriation and ownership. The AP I Commentary is also more ambiguous than it would seem at first sight. The reference to 'tangible and visible things' was made to exclude 'the general objective (in the sense of aim or purpose) of a military operation',[39] and not to differentiate between living and inanimate targets.

Alternatively, animals could be considered a third category of military objectives, distinct from both human beings and objects. Yoram Dinstein, for instance, appears to see 'other living creatures' like animals as a separate category of possible lawful targets, in addition to objects, combatants and civilians taking direct part in hostilities.[40] This

33 Article 49(1) of AP I defines 'attacks' as 'acts of violence against the adversary, whether in offence or in defence'.

34 *The Oxford Compact English Dictionary* defines 'object' as a 'material thing that can be seen and touched' (Soanes (ed.), *The Oxford Compact English Dictionary* (n. 16), 775). The AP I Commentary quotes the definition contained in the 1970 edition of *The Oxford Dictionary*: 'something placed before the eyes, or presented to the sight or other sense, an individual thing seen, or perceived, or that may be seen or perceived; a material thing' (AP I Commentary, para. 2007).

35 AP I Commentary, para. 2010 (emphasis added).

36 Statement of the US representative, in Official Records of the Diplomatic Conference on the Reaffirmation and Development of International Humanitarian Law Applicable in Armed Conflicts, Geneva, 7 February 1975, CDDH/III/SR.15, vol. XIV, 119, para. 11.

37 Article 54(2) of AP I. This provision reads as follows:

> [i]t is prohibited to attack, destroy, remove or render useless objects indispensable to the survival of the civilian population, such as foodstuffs, agricultural areas for the production of foodstuffs, crops, livestock, drinking water installations and supplies and irrigation works, for the specific purpose of denying them for their sustenance value to the civilian population or to the adverse Party, whatever the motive, whether in order to starve out civilians, to cause them to move away, or for any other motive.

38 Beryl T. Atkins et al. (eds.), *Collins-Robert French-English English-French Dictionary* (2nd ed., London, Glasgow and Toronto: Collins 1987), 73; Henry Saint Dahl (ed.), *Dahl's Law Dictionary* (5th ed., Buffalo, NY: William S. Hein 2010), 46. A *bien* as a French legal notion is defined as '*[t]oute chose matérielle susceptible d'appropriation*' (Gérard Cornu (ed.), *Vocabulaire juridique* (10th ed., Paris: PUF 2014), 127), while *bienes* in Spanish are '*[c]osas materiales y derechos sujetos al dominio*' (Ignacio Rivera García (ed.), *Diccionario de términos jurídicos* (Orford, NH: Equity Publishing Corporation 1985), 27).

39 AP I Commentary, para. 2010.

40 Dinstein, *The Conduct* (n. 5), 106. In Dinstein's view, the definition of 'military objective' contained in Article 52(2) of AP I 'must be regarded as confined to inanimate objects' (ibid., 105).

interpretation, which implicitly limits 'objects' to inanimate things, is, however, inconsistent with the object and purpose of AP I, and of Article 52(2) in particular. The object and purpose of AP I is to 'improve the protection provided by the [Geneva] Conventions to the victims of international armed conflicts',[41] and the specific object and purpose of the definition of 'military objective' contained in Article 52(2) is to facilitate the application of the principle of distinction in attacks contained in Articles 48 and 52(1). Under Article 31(1) of the Vienna Convention on the Law of Treaties, between two or more possible interpretations, we must choose the one most consonant with this object and purpose. If animals amounted to a third category falling outside the scope of Articles 43 and 52(2) of AP I,[42] the undesirable normative consequence – *de lege lata* – would be that both the criteria to determine whether a person is a combatant and, therefore, targetable *and* those to establish whether an object is a military objective would be inapplicable to animals. As a result, we would be left without any agreed criterion to establish their targetability. This is clearly an unreasonable interpretive result, which is at odds with the object and purpose of both AP I in general and its Article 52(2) in particular.

For all the above reasons, the preferable interpretation of the law as it currently stands is to consider animals as 'objects' for the purposes of the principle of distinction. This ensures that animals are protected from attack whenever they are of a civilian character. As Francione has observed, '[c]ommon-law and civil-law traditions are dualistic in that there are two primary normative entities in these systems: persons and things. Animals are treated as things, and, more specifically, as the property of persons'.[43] The law of armed conflict, including AP I, incorporates this traditional dualistic construction. This conclusion finds explicit confirmation in the 2006 Danish Military Manual, according to which '[u]nder IHL, objects may consist of smaller components, larger terrain objects, areas (which may be point targets* or area targets*), animals (alive or dead), and corpses'.[44] Marco Sassòli also maintains that 'the natural environment consists of civilian objects because everything that is not a military objective is a civilian object and only objects determined to satisfy the necessary elements turn into military objectives. In IHL terms, therefore, each element of the flora, fauna and stones as well as the earth's surface, water and air are "civilian objects".'[45]

[41] AP I Commentary, para. 3685.

[42] According to Article 43(2) of AP I, '[m]embers of the armed forces of a Party to a conflict (other than medical personnel and chaplains covered by Article 33 of the Third [Geneva] Convention) are combatants, that is to say, they have the right to participate directly in hostilities'. Paragraph 1 of the same provision clarifies who can be considered a member of the armed forces of a Party to a conflict.

[43] Francione, *Animals* (n. 10), ii (emphasis in the original). It appears that most legal systems consider animals as 'moveable objects' (Jérôme de Hemptinne, 'The Protection of Animals During Warfare', *American Journal of International Law Unbound* 111 (2017), 272–6, at 274–5).

[44] Danish Ministry of Defence/Defence Command Denmark, *Military Manual on International Law Relevant to Danish Armed Forces in International Operations* (Copenhagen 2016), 292 (emphasis in the original).

[45] Marco Sassòli, *International Humanitarian Law, Rules, Controversies, and Solutions to Problems Arising in Warfare* (Cheltenham: Edward Elgar 2019), 569–70. Another commentator has suggested that animals that contribute to the belligerents' military effort are 'matériel' falling under the scope of

It is worth noting that 'object' is broader than 'property' and applies irrespectively of considerations of ownership. Unlike in Article 23(g) of the Hague Regulations, then, no interpretive doubt can arise in relation to wild and stray animals: they are also covered by Articles 48, 52(1) and 52(2), regardless of who owns them.

2.2.2 The Principle of Proportionality

Another reason to consider animals as 'objects' under the current law of targeting is that this allows their inclusion in the proportionality calculation of damage incidental to an attack on a military objective. Indeed, Article 51(5)(b) of AP I provides that an attack is indiscriminate, and thus prohibited, if it 'may be expected to cause incidental loss of civilian life, injury to civilians, damage to civilian objects, or a combination thereof, which would be excessive in relation to the concrete and direct military advantage anticipated'.[46] This provision, commonly referred to as the principle of proportionality,[47] has been incorporated in several military manuals, including the US Law of War Manual,[48] the German Military Manual,[49] the UK Military Manual,[50] and the French Manuel de droit des conflits armés.[51] It reflects customary international law and, although it does not appear expressly in AP II, it is generally accepted that it also applies to attacks in non-international armed conflicts.[52]

The same reasons for qualifying animals as objects from the perspective of the principle of distinction apply in the context of the principle of proportionality. Of course, if animals were considered as sentient beings or as having legal personality, they would carry heavier weight in the proportionality calculation of incidental damage,[53] but the letter and spirit of existing law simply do not allow such interpretation. The fact that civilian animals are 'objects', damage to which needs to be factored in when calculating the proportionality of an attack on a military objective, finds support in the ICJ's advisory opinion on the *Legality of the Threat or Use of*

Article 52(2) of AP I (Agnieszka Jachec-Neale, *The Concept of Military Objective in International Law and Targeting Practice* (London: Routledge 2015), 27).

46 The same language appears in Articles 57(2)(a)(iii) and 57(2)(b) of AP I in relation to the duty to take precautions in attack.

47 The expression is used, for instance, in the British Manual of the Law of Armed Conflict (UK Ministry of Defence, *The Joint Service Manual of the Law of Armed Conflict* (Oxford: Oxford University Press 2004), 68).

48 US Department of Defense, *Law of War Manual* (n. 19), 241.

49 German Federal Ministry of Defence, *Law of Armed Conflict Manual*, Joint Service Regulation (ZDv) 15/2 (Berlin: Ministry of Defence May 2013), Section 512.

50 UK Ministry of Defence, *The Joint Service Manual of the Law of Armed Conflict* (n. 5), 86.

51 Ministère de la Défense, *Manuel de droit des conflits armés*, Définition of 'Proportionnalité (principe de)', available at https://bit.ly/34vqsMY, accessed 22 February 2022.

52 See ICRC Customary Law Database, Rule 14. See also High Court of Justice, *Public Committee Against Torture in Israel* v. *Government of Israel*, 14 December 2006, 769/02, para. 42 (per President Barak).

53 de Hemptinne, 'The Protection' (n. 43), 276.

Nuclear Weapons, where the court held that 'States must take environmental considerations into account when assessing what is necessary and proportionate in the pursuit of legitimate military objectives. Respect for the environment is one of the elements that go to assessing whether an action is in conformity with the principles of necessity and proportionality' (the natural environment includes the fauna).[54] Draft Principle 15 of the International Law Commission (ILC)'s Draft Principles on the Protection of the Environment in Relation to Armed Conflicts also provides that '[e]nvironmental considerations shall be taken into account when applying the principle of proportionality and the rules on military necessity'.[55] The same position was taken in the Final Report to the Prosecutor by the Committee Established to Review the NATO Bombing Campaign Against the Federal Republic of Yugoslavia,[56] and several states have invoked the applicability of the principle of proportionality to environmental damage.[57] The fact that the destruction of livestock can be lawful damage incidental to an attack on a military objective is also expressly acknowledged by the ICTY Trial Chamber in the *Kupreškić* case, although the court found that, in the case before it, the damage was not 'collateral', but rather 'it was the primary purpose of the attack'.[58]

3 CONTENTS AND LIMITS OF THE LAWS ON THE CONDUCT OF HOSTILITIES PROTECTING PROPERTY AND OBJECTS

3.1 *Article 23(g) of the Hague Regulations*

If Article 23(g) of the Hague Regulations applies to animals as argued above, then they cannot be destroyed or seized 'unless such destruction or seizure be imperatively

54 ICJ, Nuclear Weapons (n. 26), para. 30.

55 ILC, Draft Principles on the Protection of the Environment in Relation to Armed Conflict (2019), reproduced in UN General Assembly, Report of the ILC, Seventy-first session (29 April–7 June and 8 July–9 August 2019), A/74/10, Draft Principle 15.

56 ICTY, Final Report to the Prosecutor by the Committee Established to Review the NATO Bombing Campaign Against the Federal Republic of Yugoslavia, para. 18 (text in *International Legal Materials* 39 (2000), 1257–83, at 1263).

57 See, for example, Australia (ICRC Customary Law Database, Rule 43, footnote 19), Austria (ibid.), Canada (ibid.), Colombia (ibid.), Iran (ibid.), Jordan (ibid.), Romania (ibid.), US (ibid.). Marco Sassòli also argues that

> IHL prohibits any attack directed against the natural environment unless a certain part of it constitutes a military objective and that part is attacked. All of the natural environment's component parts . . . benefit from the proportionality rule and the duty of both an attacker as well a defender to take feasible precautionary measures to avoid or minimize incidental effects on civilian objects. All of this taken together offers a good framework that protects the natural environment during armed conflicts.

(Sassòli, *International Humanitarian Law* (n. 45), 570)

58 ICTY, *Kupreškić* trial judgment (n. 27), para. 762. See also EECC, *Final Award* (n. 14), para. 124 ('many animals were lost to starvation, shelling or other causes unrelated to looting. Much property was lost to shelling or other battle damage, for which there is no *jus in bello* liability').

demanded by the necessities of war'. Note that Article 23(g) applies regardless of the amount of damage caused. The protection granted to animals by this provision is at the same time broader and narrower than that arising from the law of targeting. It is broader because Article 23(g) applies not only to 'attacks' as defined in Article 49(1) of AP I, but to seizure, destruction or damage that is the consequence of any military operations, including military movements and manoeuvres.[59] It is narrower because, if attacks may only be directed against military objectives under the principle of distinction, Article 23(g) permits to destroy and seize enemy property that does not qualify as a military objective, so long as this is justified by imperative military necessity and unless this is limited by specific regulations. As has been observed, '[a]s long as the movement or manoeuvre does not amount to an act of violence (which for example would be the case with "show of force" manoeuvres), the right to destroy or seize enemy property has a wider scope than the right to attack military objectives'.[60] Furthermore, as the principle of proportionality only applies to attacks, in the case of other military operations that lead to incidental damage to animals the legality test will be whether or not such incidental destruction is justified by considerations of imperative military necessity, and not the more restrictive one provided in Article 51(5)(b) of AP I.[61]

Military necessity must be real and not hypothetical and must be assessed reasonably by a commander on the basis of the information available at the moment of the decision. 'Imperatively' aims at emphasising 'that military necessity has to be mulled over attentively and not acted upon flippantly'.[62] In the *Hostage* case, the US Military Tribunal clarified that 'imperative necessities of war' require that there is 'some reasonable connection between the destruction of property and the overcoming of the enemy forces'.[63] Acts of sheer vandalism against animals or their seizure or destruction motivated by private gains, therefore, would be wanton and thus prohibited under Article 23(g). The same conclusion would apply to 'speeding in open terrain, just for the rush of it, without thought for the stress and danger imposed on grazing livestock nearby'.[64] The killing of infected animals in order to protect the health of troops, on the other hand, would arguably be consistent with the rule under examination, as would the destruction

59 Attacks do not encompass 'military movement or manoeuvre as such' (Michael Bothe, Karl J. Partsch and Waldemar Solf, *New Rules for Victims of Armed Conflicts* (1st ed., Dordrecht, Boston and London: Martinus Nijhoff Publishers 1982), 289).

60 Redse Johansen, *The Military Commander's Necessity* (n. 4), 346–7. The US Law of War Manual confirms that '[i]f imperative military necessity justifies the seizure or destruction of an object, that object does not necessarily satisfy the definition of a military objective' (US Department of Defense, *Law of War Manual* (n. 19), 286). However, if property qualifies as a military objective, the destruction under Article 23(g) is ipso facto justified by imperative necessities of war.

61 Bothe, Partsch and Solf, *New Rules* (n. 59), 320; US Department of Defense, *Law of War Manual* (n. 19), 288.

62 Dinstein, *The Conduct* (n. 5), 12.

63 *United States* v. *W. List and Others (Hostage Case)*, 8 *Trials of War Criminals* 34, 66 (1949). This language has been incorporated in US Department of Defense, *Law of War Manual* (n. 19), 286. The reasonable connection with military ends can exist both in attack and in defence (Dinstein, *The Conduct* (n. 5), 288).

64 Redse Johansen, *The Military Commander's Necessity* (n. 4), 345.

of burrows resulting from digging trenches. Low overflights that cause stress-related damage to animals could also turn into a military necessity 'as the circumstances may point out the chosen route as the only feasible alternative in order to avoid enemy anti-access aerial denial systems'.[65] Similarly, the absence of alternative feasible routes could require armoured vehicles to drive through enemy territory inhabited by wild animals, which could be killed or injured as a consequence.[66] This would, in principle, not be a violation of Article 23(g), but if the armoured vehicles are driven at unnecessarily excessive speed with increased risks for animals, the resulting destruction might be considered wanton and thus unlawful. It should also be recalled that, under Article 57(1) of AP I, 'constant care shall be taken to spare ... civilian objects' in all military operations, not only in attacks.[67]

As military operations qualifying as attacks under Article 49(1) of AP I are subject to the specific rules provided therein,[68] the practical relevance of Article 23(g) of the Hague Regulations is now limited to the *destruction or damage* of enemy property resulting from military operations short of attack.[69] Even though destruction of enemy civilian property has often been carried out by retreating armies in order to deny its use to the enemy armed forces, in most cases such destruction would amount to an attack and would therefore be regulated by the relevant rules of AP I.[70] Article 23(g) retains its separate significance when it comes to the *seizure* of enemy property in the conduct of hostilities. While seizure mainly refers to taking possession of property, it can also be extended to its use.[71] The seizure or use of civilian horses to be employed as means of transportation by combatants, for instance, would be entirely permissible under this rule.[72] In the *High Command* case, the tribunal also found that the order to seize cattle, horses and chickens in villages 'used by the partisans as a base of operations' but leaving a small amount of food for the population was not unlawful.[73]

65 Ibid., 358. As a consequence of stress induced by military manoeuvres, for instance, reindeer could abort their calves, fox mothers could eat their kits, and minks could escape (ibid.).

66 I have borrowed the example, and applied it to animals, from Redse Johansen, *The Military Commander's Necessity* (n. 4), 345.

67 Military operations include 'all movements and acts related to hostilities that are undertaken by armed forces' (AP I Commentary, para. 1875).

68 The US Law of War Manual, for instance, expressly states that the rules on the seizure and destruction of enemy property apply '[o]utside the context of attacks' (US Department of Defense, *Law of War Manual* (n. 19), 285).

69 Redse Johansen, *The Military Commander's Necessity* (n. 4), 357.

70 Ibid., 352. Before the codification of the targeting rules in AP I, the Nuremberg war crimes tribunals found that even extensive destruction by retreating armies may be justified by the imperative necessities of war under Article 23(g) of the Hague Regulations (*The High Command Case (US v. von Lebb)*, 12 *Trials of War Criminals* 1, 125 (1949); *The Hostage Case* (n. 63), 69).

71 Redse Johansen, *The Military Commander's Necessity* (n. 4), 360.

72 Bothe, Partsch and Solf, *New Rules* (n. 59), 320. It should also be noted that, under Article 4 of the Hague Regulations and Article 18(1) of GC III, horses may be confiscated from prisoners of war even if they are their personal property.

73 *High Command* case (n. 70), 48.

3.2 *The Law of Targeting*

If they are considered 'objects' as suggested above, animals may be targeted consistently with the principle of distinction only if they meet the two-pronged test spelled out in Article 52(2) of AP I, that is, when they 'by their nature, location, purpose or use make an effective contribution to military action and whose total or partial destruction, capture or neutralization, in the circumstances ruling at the time, offers a definite military advantage'.[74] Animals will constitute military objectives mostly because of their use, as in the case of horse cavalry, mine-sweeping dolphins and pigeons carrying military communications.[75] Some could be dual-use objects, for instance pack mules which carry water or food destined to both combatants and civilians. The fact that an object is *also* used for civilian purposes does not affect its qualification under the principle of distinction: if the two requirements provided in Article 52(2) are present, the object is a military objective, but the neutralisation of its civilian component needs to be taken into account when assessing the incidental damage on civilians and civilian objects under the principle of proportionality. What is prohibited is to attack the dual-use object *because* of its civilian function or to attack a dual-use object where the anticipated military value of the attack is outweighed by the expected civilian damage. It should also be recalled that, under Article 52(3) of AP I, '[i]n case of doubt whether an object which is normally dedicated to civilian purposes ... is being used to make an effective contribution to military action, it shall be presumed not to be so used'.[76] Unlike its counterpart with regard to persons (Article 50(1) of AP I), however, the customary status of this provision is dubious.[77]

A belligerent could be tempted to attack animals in order to deprive the enemy of an important economic resource, as in the case of fisheries. To meet the definition of 'military objective' under Article 52(2) of AP I, however, the object's effective contribution must be to 'military action', which corresponds to the 'general prosecution of the war'.[78] It should be recalled that, for the US, '[i]t is not necessary that the

[74] For an in-depth analysis of this provision, see Robert Kolb, *Advanced Introduction to International Humanitarian Law* (Cheltenham: Edward Elgar 2014), 159–63; Dinstein, *The Conduct* (n. 5), 106–17; Boothby, *The Law of Targeting* (n. 20), 98–107. The two requirements are cumulative. As Boothby notes, '[w]hile in the overwhelming majority of cases, an object which is military in character will also constitute a military objective, the two tests must still be applied because circumstances might arise in which a military object nevertheless does not satisfy the two tests' (ibid., 103).

[75] It has been reported, for instance, that white beluga whales have been trained, allegedly by Russia, for military purposes in polar waters (Hannah Ellis-Petersen, 'Whale with Harness Could Be Russia Weapon, Say Norwegian Experts', *Guardian* (29 April 2019) available at https://bit.ly/3eWcE01, accessed 22 February 2022). An interesting question is whether certain animals, because of their inherent characteristics, their incorporation in the armed forces or their training, could be considered military objectives by nature.

[76] The provision only applies when doubt concerns the use of the object, not its nature, location or purpose (Boothby, *The Law of Targeting* (n. 20), 71).

[77] Dinstein, *The Conduct* (n. 5), 113.

[78] Rogers, *Law on the Battlefield* (n. 28), 67.

object provide immediate tactical or operational gains or that the object make an effective contribution to a specific military operation. Rather, the object's effective contribution to the war-fighting or war-sustaining capability of an opposing force is sufficient.'[79] If 'war fighting' can be considered equivalent to 'military action', 'war sustaining' is much broader and includes activities not directly connected to the hostilities, which would allow attacks aimed at incapacitating political and economic targets in order to 'persuade' the enemy to stop fighting. This expanded notion of military objective is at odds with the definition contained in Article 52(2) of AP I as 'the causal linkage between damage to or destruction of financial or commercial facilities not otherwise linked to the military war effort and military advantage is insufficiently direct'.[80]

Animals could also be the collateral victims of an attack on a lawful military objective. As has been seen, the principle of proportionality under Article 51(5)(b) of AP I prohibits incidental damage to civilian animals which may be expected to be excessive in relation to the concrete and direct military advantage anticipated from the attack.[81] The Final Report by the Committee established to Review the NATO Bombing Campaign Against the Federal Republic of Yugoslavia noted that '[t]he main problem with the principle of proportionality is not whether or not it exists but what it means and how it is to be applied'.[82] This is because '[t]he intellectual process of balancing the various elements is so complicated, [and] needs to take into account such a huge amount of data and so many factors, that any attempt to design a formula which is both comprehensive and precise would be ridiculous'.[83] To make things worse, under Article 51(5)(b) it is not the incidental damage that actually occurs or the military advantage that is effectively gained from the attack that count, but the 'expected' damage and the 'anticipated' military advantage. These complexities are even more evident when the incidental damage involves animals. Indeed, the value that different military actors will attribute to them will greatly vary: the approach of different societies and individuals to animals is so diverse that any evaluation of proportionality in this context will be driven by many more variables (of a cultural, economic, religious, ideological, philosophical, educational nature) than in its application to human beings and inanimate objects. As a consequence, belligerents will likely 'arrive at disparate conclusions as to the normative boundaries within which [they] must

79 US Department of Defense, *Law of War Manual* (n. 19), 214.

80 Boothby, *The Law of Targeting* (n. 20), 106. Of the same opinion Dinstein, *The Conduct* (n. 5), 109–10; Giulio Bartolini, 'Air Operations Against Iraq (1991 and 2003)', in Natalino Ronzitti and Gabriella Venturini (eds.), *The Law of Air Warfare: Contemporary Issues* (Utrecht: Eleven Publishing 2006), 227–72, at 235–6.

81 For an analysis of this provision, see Kolb, *Advanced Introduction* (n. 74), 172–5; Dinstein, *The Conduct* (n. 5), 149–64.

82 ICTY, Final Report to the Prosecutor by the Committee Established to Review the NATO Bombing Campaign Against the Federal Republic of Yugoslavia (n. 56), para. 48.

83 Stefan Oeter, 'Methods and Means of Combat', in Dieter Fleck (ed.), *The Handbook of International Humanitarian Law* (3rd ed., Oxford: Oxford University Press 2013), 115–230, at 191.

operate'.[84] Those following a utilitarian approach will value animals taking into account only their relevance for human well-being and will only include their usefulness to humans in the proportionality calculation (for example, the killing of animals will be considered relevant *because and when* it deprives the civilian population of food).[85] The opposite approach will consider animals as having intrinsic value, regardless of their usefulness for humans.[86] Between these two extremes, there can be intermediate positions where the utilitarian and the intrinsic value approaches are reconciled in different ways, giving prevalence to the one or the other depending on the circumstances of the case or the type of animal concerned.[87] Incidental damage to animals at risk of extinction, for instance, could be given more weight in the proportionality calculation regardless of its immediate consequences on humans.[88]

Whatever the preferred approach may be, it should be recalled that the principle of proportionality allows even extensive damage to animals if the concrete and direct military advantage anticipated from an attack justifies it. Reverberating and long-term effects arising from an attack on a military objective must be considered when calculating proportionality to the extent that they can be reasonably foreseen.[89] This is of particular relevance for attacks that might contribute to the extinction of species indispensable for the good functioning of the ecosystem where these animals live.

An interesting question that has been raised is whether soldiers should assume an increased risk in order to protect civilian animals located around a military target when conducting an attack.[90] Only a 'concrete and direct' military advantage is relevant in the calculation of the proportionality of the attack, and not 'abstract protectiveness of the means and methods used to attack'.[91] A belligerent 'cannot justify higher numbers of civilian casualties for the sole reason that it has opted for a more secure . . . operation instead of a less secure . . . operation'.[92] If the security of the attacking forces cannot be a determinant factor in the calculation of proportionality, however, it could be relevant in the context of the duty to take

84 Michael N. Schmitt, 'War and the Environment: Fault Lines in the Prescriptive Landscape', *Archiv des Völkerrechts* 37 (1999), 25–67, at 51.

85 The utilitarian approach was for instance adopted by the EECC where it noted that there is not necessarily a clear separation between losses of property and deaths or personal injury, because '[i]n poor countries like Ethiopia and Eritrea, with low incomes and life expectancies, security of property often is vital to survival. Property such as livestock . . . has a direct impact on one's possibility to survive. Thus, awards of compensation for loss or destruction of property frequently stem from serious threats to physical integrity' (EECC, *Final Award* (n. 14), para. 4).

86 Schmitt has identified these approaches in relation to the application of the principle of proportionality to the environment in general (Schmitt, 'War and the Environment' (n. 84), 52).

87 Schmitt, 'War and the Environment' (n. 84), 52–3.

88 de Hemptinne, 'The Protection' (n. 43), 275.

89 Boothby, *The Law of Targeting* (n. 20), 105.

90 de Hemptinne, 'The Protection' (n. 43), 275.

91 Robin Geiß, 'The Principle of Proportionality: "Force Protection" as a Military Advantage', *Israel Law Review* 45 (2012), 71–89, at 85.

92 Ibid., 87.

precautions.[93] Indeed, Article 57(2)(a)(ii) of AP I requires the belligerents to 'take all feasible precautions in the choice of means and methods of attack with a view to avoiding, and in any event to minimizing, incidental loss of civilian life, injury to civilians and damage to civilian objects'. It is clear that the determination of what is a 'feasible' precaution will consider the additional risks encountered by the attacking forces, which are under no obligation to sacrifice themselves. That this is the correct relevance of the security of the attacking forces in the framework of the law of targeting is confirmed in the UK Military Manual, which includes the 'risks to his own troops' among the factors that a commander needs to evaluate in the context of the duty to take precautions when choosing means or methods of attack.[94] A targeteer, then, *may* go for a certain means or method of warfare that minimises the risk for the attacking forces (even if it is at the cost of reducing the military advantage he or she anticipates) providing that this does not increase the expected incidental damage on civilians or civilian objects, including animals.

4 CONSEQUENCES OF VIOLATIONS OF THE LAWS ON THE CONDUCT OF HOSTILITIES PROTECTING PROPERTY AND OBJECTS

Violations of Article 23(g) of the Hague Regulations entail not only state responsibility, with consequent obligation on the responsible state, 'if the case demands', to provide compensation,[95] but also trigger individual criminal liability. Indeed, the language of Article 23(g) is reproduced in the list of war crimes under the jurisdiction of the ICC contained in Article 8 of the ICC Statute. Individuals, thus, can be prosecuted by the court for the destruction and seizure of the enemy's or adversary's property not justified by imperative considerations of military necessity both in international and non-international armed conflicts.[96]

The destruction and appropriation of property, including animals, not justified by military necessity also constitutes a grave breach of the GCs as provided in Article 147 of GC IV, which is linked to Article 53 of the same convention.[97] Under Article 146 of GC IV, the contracting states are under an obligation either to prosecute the accused of such grave breach, regardless of his/her nationality, or to extradite him/her to another concerned contracting party if such a party 'has made out a prima facie case'. Article 147, however, requires the destruction and appropriation to be

93 Oeter, 'Methods and Means' (n. 83), 201.

94 UK Ministry of Defence, *The Joint Service Manual of the Law of Armed Conflict* (n. 5), 84. The Final Report to Congress on the Conduct of the Persian Gulf War also recalls that coalition forces took the 'risk to aircraft and aircrews' into account when choosing means of warfare for attacks on targets in populated areas (US Department of Defense, Conduct of the Persian Gulf War (n. 23), 622).

95 Article 3 of the 1907 Hague Convention (IV).

96 Article 8(2)(b)(xiii) and 8(2)(e)(xii) of ICC Statute.

97 Yoram Dinstein, *The International Law of Belligerent Occupation* (Cambridge: Cambridge University Press 2009), 197. Unlike Article 53, however, Article 147 does not require military necessity to be 'absolute'.

'extensive' for it to qualify as a grave breach. This adjective is also contained in the corresponding provision of the ICC Statute.[98] While the killing of animals in the conduct of hostilities which is not justified by military necessity under Article 23(g) and the corresponding customary rule triggers individual criminal liability as a war crime regardless of the extent of the damage caused, therefore, prosecution of the same conduct as a grave breach of GC IV 'committed against persons or property protected by the present Convention' in occupied territory has a higher threshold, since it requires demonstration of its extensive character. Having said that, in *Blaškić* the ICTY found that '[t]he notion of "extensive" is evaluated according to the facts of the case – a single act . . . may suffice to characterize an offence under this count'.[99]

The killing of animals could be not only a war crime, but also an element of the crime against humanity of persecution. In the *Kupreškić* case, the ICTY trial chamber found that the Muslim population's livestock, which were killed by military units of the Hrvatsko Vijeće Obrane (HVO) and members of the Jokers during the attack on Ahmici on 16 April 1993, 'had for their owners not only economic value, but also and probably even more importantly, emotional, psychological and cultural significance'.[100] The trial chamber further noted that the attack

> was not a combat operation. Rather, it was a well-planned and well-organized killing of civilian members of an ethnic group, the Muslims, by the military of another ethnic group, the Croats. The primary purpose of the massacre was to expel the Muslims from the village, by killing many of them, by burning their houses and their livestock, and by illegally detaining and deporting the survivors to another area. The ultimate goal of these acts was to spread terror among the population so as to deter the members of that particular ethnic group from ever returning to their homes.[101]

The point is reiterated in *Prosecutor* v. *Dario Kordić and Mario Čerkez*: 'when the cumulative effect of such property destruction is the removal of civilians from their homes on discriminatory grounds, the "wanton and extensive destruction and/or plundering of . . . livestock" may constitute the crime of persecution'.[102]

Individual criminal liability also arises, in addition to state responsibility,[103] from attacking, damaging or destroying objects in violation of the principles of distinction and proportionality, which constitute well-established war crimes.[104] It is worth

98 Article 8(2)(a)(iv) of ICC Statute.

99 ICTY, *Prosecutor* v. *Blaškić*, trial judgment of 3 March 2000, IT-95-14-T, para. 157.

100 ICTY, *Prosecutor* v. *Zoran Kupreškić and others*, trial judgment of 14 January 2000, IT-95-16-T, para. 336.

101 Ibid., para. 749.

102 ICTY, *Prosecutor* v. *Dario Kordić and Mario Čerkez*, trial judgment of 26 February 2001, IT-95-14/2-T, para. 205.

103 Article 91 of AP I.

104 Articles 8(2)(b)(ii) and 8(2)(b)(iv) of the ICC Statute. For the ICRC, the customary protection of civilian objects against attack applies regardless of the type of armed conflict (Henckaerts and Doswald-Beck (eds.), *Customary International Humanitarian Law* (n. 3), vol. I, 34.

recalling, however, that only serious infringements of an IHL rule protecting important values, entailing grave consequences for the victim, have been considered subject to prosecution before the ICTY.[105] Article 8(1) of the ICC Statute also limits the court's jurisdiction to 'war crimes in particular when committed as part of a plan or policy or as part of a *large-scale* commission of such crimes'.[106] The Office of the Prosecutor has acknowledged this 'as statutory guidance indicating that the Court should focus on war crimes meeting these requirements'.[107] In addition, gravity is an admissibility threshold for the ICC to have jurisdiction: Article 17(1)(d) of the ICC Statute provides that a case is inadmissible, and must then be rejected, if it 'is not of sufficient gravity to justify further action by the Court', and Article 53 provides that the Prosecutor may not initiate an investigation or, after an investigation, proceed to a prosecution if he or she considers the case inadmissible under Article 17.[108] All in all, it is unlikely that the killing of a very limited number of animals which do not constitute a military objective, with modest negative consequences on human beings, will be prosecuted by the ICC, at least as a violation of the principles of distinction and proportionality.

5 CONCLUDING RECOMMENDATIONS

Article 23(g) of the Hague Regulations and the law of targeting as codified in AP I apply to animals considered, respectively, as 'property' and as 'objects': animals, therefore, enjoy the protection provided by those rules. This entails that animals can only be attacked when they qualify as military objectives or when they constitute proportionate incidental damage resulting from an attack on a military objective. In military operations short of attack, they can only be destroyed or seized if military

105 ICTY, *Prosecutor* v. *Tadić*, decision on the defence motion for interlocutory appeal on jurisdiction of 2 October 1995, IT-94-1, para. 94.

106 Article 8(1) of the ICC Statute (emphasis added).

107 ICC, situation on registered vessels of Comoros, Greece and Cambodia, Article 53(1) report of 6 November 2014, ICC-01/13-6-AnxA, para. 137. The pre-trial chamber, however, found that 'the term "in particular" in article 8(1) implies that the existence of a plan, policy or large-scale commission is not a condition for the Court's jurisdiction, contrary to what is provided for in article 7 with regard to crimes against humanity' (ICC, decision pursuant to Article 15 of the Rome Statute on the authorisation of an investigation into the Situation in the Islamic Republic of Afghanistan of 12 April 2019, ICC-02/17, para. 65).

108 The decision of the office of the Prosecutor not to initiate the investigation of situations because of insufficient gravity has so far occurred only twice: Iraq and Mavi Marmara, and only in the latter case was the decision challenged by the referring party (see ICC, OTP Response to Communications Received Concerning Iraq of 9 February 2006, pp. 8–9, available at https://bit.ly/3n7srNR, accessed 22 February 2022; Situation on Registered Vessels of Comoros, Greece and Cambodia, Article 53(1) Report (n. 107), paras. 133–48). On gravity and the ICC, see William A. Schabas, *An Introduction to the International Criminal Court* (5th ed., Cambridge: Cambridge University Press 2017), 182–6; Kai Ambos, *Treatise on International Criminal Law, Vol. III: International Criminal Procedure* (Oxford: Oxford University Press 2016), 284–95; Margaret M. DeGuzman, 'Gravity and the Legitimacy of the International Criminal Court', *Fordham International Law Journal* 32 (2009), 1400–65.

necessity 'imperatively' dictates it. The violation of these rules triggers not only state responsibility, but also the criminal liability of the responsible individual(s).

Existing law, as applicable to animals, raises however two concerns. First, the language used is inadequate: when it categorises them as 'property' or 'objects', the *jus in bello* objectifies animals even though, unlike inanimate things, they are living creatures with their own interests, which can take independent actions and are capable of subjective perception and suffering. Indeed, the classification of animals as 'objects' under the law of targeting is at odds with their increasing recognition as sentient beings, for instance in the Treaty on the Functioning of the EU.[109] Secondly, the law of armed conflict adopts an anthropocentric approach and primarily aims to protect the interests of humans, not the welfare of animals: animals, therefore, are granted protection to the extent that this is motivated by human interests, and not as separate entities worthy of protection per se.

These problems could be solved by adopting specific norms devoted to the protection of animals in the conduct of hostilities, norms which consider them as sentient beings capable of emotions and not as 'objects' or 'property'. This could occur in different ways. The parties to the conflict could conclude special agreements 'at any time' during an armed conflict in relation to 'all matters concerning which they may deem it suitable to make separate provision'.[110] States could also make unilateral declarations during or outside the context of an armed conflict where they commit to confer certain specific protection to animals in warfare. Multilateral norms would not necessarily have to take the form of treaties, as the normative process could start from the adoption of commonly agreed principles for animal welfare in armed conflict. In the adoption of these multilateral norms, the ICRC, together with environmentalist NGOs, could play an important role. Finally, customary international law rules specifically protecting animals in armed conflict could eventually sediment. However, it has been observed that 'compelling evidence for the existence of any *customary* principle concerning welfare should probably not be expected, since state practice regarding the protection of animals is almost invariably attributable to *domestic* standards and sensibilities rather than to

109 EU: Treaty on the Functioning of the EU, 26 October 2012, Art. 13.

> In formulating and implementing the Union's agriculture, fisheries, transport, internal market, research and technological development and space policies, the Union and the Member States shall, since animals are sentient beings, pay full regard to the welfare requirements of animals, while respecting the legislative or administrative provisions and customs of the Member States relating in particular to religious rites, cultural traditions and regional heritage.

It is acknowledged, however, that 'the only achievable standard appears to be within the realm of animal welfare (reduction of suffering and pain). The animal rights approach is not widely accepted (or followed), as it is less compromising than the animal welfare approach' (Fitzmaurice, *Whaling* (n. 6), 182).

110 See Article 6 of GC I, GC II and GC III; Article 7 of GC IV.

any sense of *international legal obligation*, rendering proof of *opinio juris* extremely difficult'.[111]

One of the most challenging issues for the negotiation of animal-specific norms applicable in the conduct of hostilities, however, is likely to be the identification of their subjective scope of application, that is, what categories of animals they should encompass.[112] Domestic animals like dogs and cats as well as the so-called charismatic megafauna[113] (e.g., elephants, dolphins, whales, lions, orangutans), and perhaps mammals in general, would probably be relatively uncontroversial candidates for inclusion. More debatable would be their extension to all vertebrates, not to mention smaller creatures like insects. It is to be expected, therefore, that different species will be assigned different levels of protection under the law of armed conflict.

SELECT BIBLIOGRAPHY

Boothby, William H., *The Law of Targeting* (Oxford: Oxford University Press 2012).

Dinstein, Yoram, *The Conduct of Hostilities under the Law of International Armed Conflict* (3rd ed., Cambridge: Cambridge University Press 2016).

Fitzmaurice, Malgosia, *Whaling and International Law* (Cambridge: Cambridge University Press 2015).

de Hemptinne, Jérôme, 'The Protection of Animals During Warfare', *American Journal of International Law Unbound* 111 (2017), 272–6.

Jachec-Neale, Agnieszka, *The Concept of Military Objective in International Law and Targeting Practice* (London: Routledge 2015).

Nowrot, Karsten, 'Animals at War: The Status of "Animal Soldiers" under International Humanitarian Law', *Historical Social Research* 40 (2015), 128–50.

Peters, Anne, 'Global Animal Law: What It Is and Why We Need It', *Transnational Environmental Law* 5 (2016), 9–23.

Redse Johansen, Sigrid, *The Military Commander's Necessity: The Law of Armed Conflict and Its Limits* (Cambridge: Cambridge University Press 2019).

Roscini, Marco, 'Animals and the Law of Armed Conflict', *Israel Yearbook on Human Rights* 47 (2017), 35–67.

Schmitt, Michael N., 'War and the Environment: Fault Lines in the Prescriptive Landscape', *Archiv des Völkerrechts* 37 (1999), 25–67.

111 Michael Bowman, Peter Davies and Catherine Redgwell, *Lyster's International Wildlife Law* (2nd ed., Cambridge: Cambridge University Press 2010), 673 (emphasis in the original).

112 Karsten Nowrot, 'Animals at War: The Status of "Animal Soldiers" under International Humanitarian Law', *Historical Social Research* 40 (2015), 128–150, at 139.

113 Fitzmaurice, *Whaling* (n. 6), 167.

6

Animals as Specially Protected Objects

Sandra Krähenmann

1 INTRODUCTION

In addition to the general protection afforded to civilian objects under the rules governing targeting, international humanitarian law (IHL) also provides special protection to particular categories of objects. It identifies these objects and grants them additional layers of protection against attacks as well as some restrictions on their use for military purposes which could turn them into military objectives. This chapter addresses whether animals could be covered by two particular categories of specially protected objects, namely cultural property and objects indispensable to the survival of the population. Other categories of specially protected objects are covered in different chapters, principally animals as part of the environment[1] and animals as means of medical transport, search and rescue[2]. Moreover, this chapter does not discuss again the question whether animals could be 'objects', a question extensively covered in Chapter 5.[3] Instead, this chapter focuses on the question whether animals could be protected as cultural property or objects indispensable to the survival of the population in light of the scope of application of the relevant rules (Section 2) and their content and limitations (Section 3). After outlining the consequences of violations of these rules (Section 4), the chapter will conclude with some recommendations (Section 5).

2 SCOPE OF APPLICATION OF THE LAWS ON SPECIALLY PROTECTED OBJECTS

This section devoted to the scope of application of the laws on specially protected objects will treat separately cultural property (Section 2.1) from objects indispensable to the survival of the population (Section 2.2).

[1] See de Hemptinne, Chapter 7, 'Part of the Environment', in this volume.
[2] See de Hemptinne, Chapter 11, 'Medical Transport, Search and Rescue', in this volume.
[3] See Roscini, Chapter 5, 'Property and Objects', in this volume.

2.1 Animals as 'Cultural Property'

Detailed and multi-layered rules of IHL provide for the protection of cultural property,[4] recognising that cultural property has an intrinsic value that deserves protection in addition to the general protection provided to cultural property as normally civilian objects. The Hague Convention for the Protection of Cultural Property in the Event of Armed Conflict (1954 Hague Convention)[5] and the 1999 Second Protocol to the 1954 Hague Convention (1999 Second Protocol)[6] contain detailed rules to safeguard cultural property from the effects of hostilities. Pursuant to Article 1 of the 1954 Hague Convention, 'cultural property' includes, irrespective of 'origin or ownership':

> movable or immovable property of great importance to the cultural heritage of every people, such as monuments of architecture, art or history, whether religious or secular; archaeological sites; groups of buildings which, as a whole, are of historical or artistic interest; works of art; manuscripts, books and other objects of artistic, historical or archaeological interest; as well as scientific collections and important collections of books or archives or of reproductions of the property defined above.[7]

The 1999 Second Protocol refers back to the same definition. In contrast, Additional Protocol (AP) I and AP II do not use the notion of 'cultural property' and simply refer to 'historic monuments, works of art or places of worship which constitute the cultural or spiritual heritage of peoples,' though without prejudice to the 1954 Convention, and, for AP I, other relevant instruments.[8]

Before assessing if animals could constitute cultural property, it must be preliminarily determined whether the scope of the definition under the 1954 Hague Convention is substantially the same as in AP I and AP II despite the differences in drafting. While the 1954 Hague Convention refers to the 'cultural heritage of every people', both AP I and AP II make reference to the 'cultural and spiritual heritage of peoples'. 'Spiritual' was included in order to clarify that only places of worship of particular importance would be afforded special protection rather than all places of worship,[9] and thus is irrelevant for the definition of cultural property. While there is

4 For a thorough analysis, see Roger O'Keefe, *The Protection of Cultural Property in Armed Conflict* (Cambridge: Cambridge University Press 2006).

5 Hague Convention for the Protection of Cultural Property in the Event of Armed Conflict of 14 May 1954, 249 UNTS 240.

6 Second Protocol to the 1954 Hague Convention of 26 March 1999, 2253 UNTS 172. The First Protocol to the 1954 Hague Convention of 14 May 1954 focuses on the protection of cultural property during occupation. It contains the same definition of cultural property as the 1954 Hague Convention and will not be analysed for the purposes of the present chapter. On the protection of animals in occupied territory, see Longobardo, Chapter 13, 'Occupied Territory', in this volume.

7 Art. 1 of the 1954 Hague Convention (n. 5). The definition also covers buildings that preserve or exhibit such cultural property as well as refuges for movable cultural property in times of armed conflict.

8 See Art. 54 of AP I and Art. 16 of AP II on 'Cultural Objects Places of Worship'.

9 See AP I Commentary, paras. 2042–4 and AP II Commentary, paras. 4843–4. See also O'Keefe, *The Protection* (n. 4), 212–13.

an ongoing debate whether AP I and AP II encompass a narrower category of cultural property because of the reference to 'peoples' in the sense of mankind rather than 'every people' as in the 1954 Hague Convention,[10] this debate is immaterial for present purposes. The International Committee of the Red Cross (ICRC) Customary Law Database recognises that, under customary IHL, in international and non-international armed conflicts, cultural property must be respected and that the cultural heritage of every people is protected against attack unless required by imperative military reasons.[11] Any difference in scope relates to applicable treaty law rules and the level of protection granted. In particular, part of the debate seems animated by the lack of an explicit reference to a waiver of protection against attack in case of imperative military necessity in AP I and AP II,[12] rather than the notion of cultural property itself.

The questions and difficulties associated with considering animals as property in terms of ownership and animals as civilian objects are analysed elsewhere,[13] but for present purposes it deserves to be underlined that the notions of cultural property and cultural objects are substantially the same because cultural property is protected irrespective of ownership.[14] Tangible cultural heritage is largely used as a synonym for cultural property.[15] An important limitation of the concept of cultural property in IHL is that it focuses on tangible cultural heritage, to the exclusion of intangible cultural heritage. Tangible cultural property can be immovable and movable.[16]

On a first glance, there seems to be little room to consider animals as cultural property considering the categories of cultural property provided in IHL treaties. The focus is overwhelmingly on human-made objects, such as buildings and other monuments of historic or architectural signification, archaeological sites, and works of art. Indeed, there are no references to animals or anything non-human made in AP I and AP II Commentaries, the 2003 UNESCO Declaration on the Intentional Destruction of Cultural Heritage, the 2016 Military Manual for the Protection of Cultural Property authored under the auspices of UNESCO,[17] or major treatises on the protection of cultural property under IHL.[18] Moreover, none of the international

10 For a detailed analysis, see O'Keefe, *The Protection* (n. 4), 207–18. He argues that the definition is substantially the same. In the same sense, see also Roger O'Keefe et al., *Protection of Cultural Property: Military Manual* (Paris: UNESCO 2016).

11 Rule 38 of the ICRC Customary Law Database.

12 In particular, in its explanation of the customary law rule, the ICRC contrasts the notion of cultural property under the 1954 Hague Convention (n. 5) which includes such a waiver with the 'limited amount of very important cultural property' under AP I and AP II which does not include such a waiver. See commentary to Rule 38 of the ICRC Customary Law Database.

13 See Roscini, Chapter 5, 'Property and Objects', in this volume.

14 Art. 1 of 1954 Hague Convention (n. 5).

15 Roger O'Keefe, 'Cultural Heritage and International Humanitarian Law', in Francesco Francioni and Ana Filipa Vrdoljak (eds.), *The Oxford Handbook of International Cultural Heritage Law* (Oxford: Oxford University Press 2020), 43–74, at 43.

16 Ibid.

17 O'Keefe et al., *Protection of Cultural Property: Military Manual* (n. 10).

18 See for example O'Keefe, *The Protection* (n. 4); O'Keefe, 'Cultural Heritage' (n. 15).

registries for cultural property under special protection or enhanced protection during armed conflict include any references to animals or the habitat of animals.[19]

However, on a second glance, animals may benefit in various ways from the protection afforded to cultural property. First, animals may be protected indirectly through the protection afforded to cultural heritage sites, namely when they inhabit the surrounding areas. For example, numerous insects, birds, and mammals inhabit Angkor Archaeological Park, which is a cultural property granted enhanced protection in times of armed conflict under the 1999 Second Protocol.

Second, the notion of cultural heritage may be interpreted as including some categories of animals, in particular endangered and endemic species. From its origins in IHL with a focus on the protection during times of armed conflict, the protection of cultural heritage has evolved into a much broader body of law on cultural heritage that increasingly recognises the intrinsic links between cultural and natural heritage, including the flora and fauna. In particular, the World Heritage Convention encompasses both cultural and natural heritage. The definition of natural heritage includes 'geological and physiographical formations and precisely delineated areas which constitute the habitat of threatened species of animals and plants of outstanding universal value from the point of view of science or conservation'.[20] In other words, through the conservation of their natural habitat, threatened species as well as other species of universal value are to be protected. Though maintaining the distinction between natural and cultural heritage,[21] at least to some extent the World Cultural Heritage Convention also recognises the linkages between the two with cultural heritage sites that include 'the combined works of nature and man'.[22] An example of such cultural heritage sites are cultural landscapes, reflecting the interaction between people and their environment, officially recognised in 1992.[23] Moreover, the World Heritage List maintained by UNESCO envisages both cultural and natural heritage sites.[24] Along the same lines, the 2001 Underwater Cultural Heritage Convention englobes in its definition of cultural heritage underwater traces of human existence such as sites or vessels 'together with

[19] For the regimes on special protection and enhanced protection, see below Section 3.1.

[20] Art. 1 of the World Heritage Convention. The UNESCO Operational Guidelines further elucidate the criteria for outstanding universal value, which includes broader considerations of biodiversity, including the presence of endemic species. See 2019 UNESCO Operational Guidelines, UNESCO Doc. 43 COM 11A.

[21] For a discussion of the 'dualistic' approach, see Ben Boer, 'The Environment and Cultural Heritage', in *The Oxford Handbook* (n. 15), 318–46, at 329.

[22] Art. 1 of the World Heritage Convention.

[23] World Heritage Committee, Report, 16th session, 1992, UNESCO Doc. WHC-92/CONF.002/12, 55. The committee stressed the need for interdisciplinary assessments, in light of the 'relationship of many cultural landscapes to the maintenance of ecosystem processed and biological diversity'. More generally on the notion of cultural landscape as cultural heritage, see Amy Strecker, 'Landscape as Cultural Heritage', in *The Oxford Handbook* (n. 15), 272–94.

[24] The list is available at https://whc.unesco.org/en/list/, accessed 22 February 2022.

their archaeological and natural context'.[25] To the extent that animal wildlife is an integral part of such a natural context, animals would be protected as part of mixed cultural heritage. For example, in the case of underwater cultural heritage, marine life species flourishing around such sites would be part of the cultural heritage to be safeguarded.

Hence, the interpretation of IHL rules on the protection of cultural heritage could take into account the developing broader notion of cultural heritage under general international law. Several arguments support this approach. The 1972 World Heritage Convention, including the designation of natural heritage sites, does not cease to apply in times of armed conflict. In addition, the AP I Commentary lists the World Heritage Convention as part of 'other relevant instruments' whose provisions on protection are supposed to be confirmed and not modified by the rule on cultural property.[26] The threat posed by armed conflict is a criterion to include both cultural and natural heritage sites on the World Heritage in Danger List.[27] Amongst others, the World Heritage in Danger List includes the five natural heritage sites in the Democratic Republic of the Congo (DRC), inhabited by many endangered species, and threatened by the protracted armed conflicts in the country. Finally, there are undoubtedly linkages between the World Heritage listing and the notion of cultural property, though World Heritage listing is limited to immovable cultural property. In particular, the 2016 Military Manual for the Protection of Cultural Property argues that compliance with IHL rules on the protection of cultural property 'guarantees compliance with the World Cultural Heritage Convention' and that the designation and marking of a site as cultural heritage are 'in practice conclusive indicators that the site is of sufficient importance to the cultural heritage of the state concerned to be considered "cultural property"'[28] for the purposes of the relevant IHL rules. Arguably, affording the same level of protection to natural heritage sites, including the animals that inhabit them, would serve the same purpose. Moreover, the World Heritage Emblem is used to mark both natural and cultural heritage sites on the World Heritage List, without any distinction between the two. Additionally, for the purposes of whether cultural heritage should be granted 'enhanced protection' under the 1999 Second Protocol, World Heritage listing satisfies the criteria of 'greatest importance to humanity'.[29]

[25] Art. 1 of the Convention on the Protection of the Underwater Cultural Heritage of 2 November 2001, 2562 UNTS 3.

[26] See AP I Commentary, para. 2062. Art. 16 of AP II does not contain the same reference, but according to the AP II Commentary, '[t]hese omissions [including the World Cultural Heritage Convention] have no material consequences for protection', para. 4837.

[27] Art. 11(4) of the World Heritage Convention. The World Heritage List in Danger is available at https://whc.unesco.org/en/danger/, accessed 22 February 2022.

[28] O'Keefe et al., *Protection of Cultural Property: Military Manual* (n. 10), 7. Note that the designation as a World Cultural Heritage has also served as factor before international criminal tribunals, see below Section 4.1.

[29] Art. 10(a) of the 1999 Second Protocol (n. 6). Pursuant to the guidelines for the implementation of the 1999 Second Protocol, '[i]t is presumed that the Committee, subject to other relevant considerations,

The enhanced protection regime also illustrates how cultural heritage law could influence and broaden the notion of cultural property under IHL. On a first glance, the notion of cultural landscape does not easily fit with the definition of cultural property under IHL as discussed above. Yet, the granting of enhanced protection to the World Cultural Heritage Globustan Rock Art Cultural Landscape[30] as an archaeological site under the 1999 Second Protocol illustrates that such landscape may fit within the notion of cultural property under IHL.[31]

However, reference to the World Heritage List will not protect animals per se, but only animals as part of a heritage site. This approach leaves open the question whether animals or some categories of animals – namely endangered species – could be considered movable cultural property, protected even when their habitat is not a protected site. Though it may seem a stretch, arguably the evolution of cultural heritage law to progressively recognise the interrelationship between humanity and nature could inform the interpretation of the notion of cultural property under IHL in the sense that endangered animals may be cultural property, namely objects of 'historical or archaeological interests', similarly to cultural landscapes that have been included as archaeological sites.

Finally, it deserves to be underlined that the designation of cultural property for the purposes of IHL is left to each individual state. In order to comply with their obligations under the World Heritage Convention, as well as other international law treaties governing endangered species,[32] states could indeed designate endangered species and their habitat as cultural property for the purposes of IHL.

A challenge associated with the approach outlined above is that cultural heritage international instruments bind states parties, but do not address armed non-state actors, contrary to the relevant IHL treaties. That said, various theories are advanced to argue that armed non-state actors are bound by human rights obligations, whether under customary international law or as a matter of treaty law, namely when they control territory and exercise governmental functions,[33] in particular in the absence of the official state authorities.[34] By analogy, a similar theory may be developed for

will consider that immovable cultural property inscribed on the World Heritage List satisfies the condition of greatest importance for humanity' (UNESCO, Guidelines for the Implementation of the 1999 Second Protocol to the Hague Convention of 1954 on the Protection of Cultural Property in the Event of Armed Conflict (Paris: UNESCO 2018), para. 36).

30 See its entry on the World Heritage List, available at https://whc.unesco.org/en/list/1076, accessed 22 February 2022.

31 UNESCO, International List of Cultural Property under Enhanced Protection, 2019, available at https://bit.ly/3F6vUm6, accessed 22 February 2022.

32 On endangered species and relevant international instruments, see Böhringer and Marauhn, Chapter 8, 'Endangered Species', in this volume.

33 Katharine Fortin, *The Accountability of Armed Groups under Human Rights Law* (Oxford: Oxford University Press 2017), 19.

34 Ibid., in particular chapters 8–9. Fortin argues that an armed group may 'acquire obligations under international human rights law, not only through its own functionality, but also through the absence of the *de jure* government' (283).

the purposes of cultural heritage law. Moreover, the relationships between the protection of cultural heritage and human rights law, namely cultural rights, could also be advance in favour of such an approach.[35] Indeed, the 2016 Strategy for Reinforcing UNESCO's Action for the Protection of Culture and the Promotion of Cultural Pluralism in the Event of Armed Conflict expands the traditional IHL focus on tangible cultural property by explicitly referring to intangible cultural heritage and cultural rights.[36] A final challenge may be the question of the capacity of an armed group to comply with cultural heritage law, in particular in respect of positive measures to be taken. Yet, this issue is not unique to cultural heritage law. For example, for the purposes of human rights law, a theory of gradated human rights obligations depending on the capacity of a group has been proposed,[37] and may be adapted for the purposes of cultural heritage law. Finally, the same argument could also be made for the precautionary measures to be taken by armed non-state actors for the protection of cultural property in times of armed conflict in the traditional sense, in particular because contrary to states, armed non-state actors do not have access to UNESCO for technical assistance.[38]

A final argument in favour of including at least endangered or endemic species under the notion of cultural heritage for IHL purposes is that the distinction between natural and cultural heritage has been criticised as artificial, as at least immovable cultural heritage sites are part and parcel of a natural context, that includes the flora and fauna as well.[39] The concept of cultural biodiversity embodies this approach.[40] In this respect, the apparent limitation of IHL to cultural property to the exclusion of natural heritage is another example of how an inadequate legal framework for times of peace is prolonged in times of armed conflict.[41] Perhaps quite revealingly, the one area of international law where the term cultural heritage is used holistically is in the context of indigenous peoples' rights.[42] The cultural heritage of indigenous peoples to be protected includes not only the traditional uses of animals, but more generally indigenous peoples' particular relationship with the land and its flora and fauna. Hence, during an armed conflict, arguably indigenous lands, flora and fauna would deserve special protection as way to preserve indigenous peoples' cultural heritage.

35 See also the discussion in de Hemptinne, Chapter 7, 'Part of the Environment', in this volume.

36 2016 Strategy for Reinforcing UNESCO's Action for the Protection of Culture and the Promotion of Cultural Pluralism in the Event of Armed Conflict, adopted by the General Conference of UNESCO, UNESCO Doc. 38C/49, 2 November 2015.

37 Daragh Murray, *Human Rights Obligations of Non-state Armed Groups* (Oxford: Hart Publishing 2016), 172–201.

38 Kristine Hausler et al., '20 Years of the Second Protocol to the Hague Convention for the Protection of Cultural Property in Armed Conflict: Have all the Gaps Been Filled?', *EJIL Talk! Blog* (20 May 2019), available at https://bit.ly/3HGP7MT, accessed 22 February 2022.

39 Boer, 'The Environment and Cultural Heritage' (n. 21), 319.

40 Ibid., 319.

41 See Peters and de Hemptinne, Chapter 1, 'Wartime', in this volume.

42 For a detailed analysis, see Dalee Sambo Dorough and Siegfried Wiessner, 'Indigenous Peoples and Cultural Heritage', in *The Oxford Handbook* (n. 15), 407–30.

In sum, despite the apparent limitations in the notion of cultural property in IHL, a progressive interpretation in light of other international law instruments relating to the protection of both cultural and natural heritage would allow to include some categories of animals, namely endangered species and species endemic to particular areas under the notion of cultural property. The category of animals potentially covered by the notion of cultural property is limited to wildlife, namely endangered or endemic species. Domesticated animals, in particular livestock, may benefit from special protection as a good indispensable to the survival of the population, addressed in the following subsection.

2.2 *Objects Indispensable to the Survival of the Civilian Population*

Animals are clearly protected under the prohibition to attack, destroy or otherwise rendering useless objects[43] to the survival of the civilian population in both international and non-international armed conflicts.[44] The illustrative list of such objects in both AP I[45] and AP II[46] specifically includes livestock as an example. The prohibition to destroy such objects is also linked to the prohibition of starvation as a method of warfare.[47]

However, there are two important limitations that come with the inclusion of livestock as objects indispensable to the survival of the civilian population. First, animals are not protected as such, but rather as 'a means of sustenance'[48] for the civilian population, or in other words from a purely utilitarian perspective.[49] Second, only animals that are indispensable to the survival of the population are covered. Livestock is provided as an illustrative example, but potentially other animals, such as game, could also be covered.[50] Some argue that not all livestock is protected, 'but only those indispensable to the survival of the civilian population',[51] depending on context, for example whether there are large food reserves. Yet, for livestock, arguably it is only in exceptional circumstances that they are not objects indispensable to the survival of the civilian population. On the one hand, objects indispensable to the survival 'means objects which are of basic importance for the population from the point of view of providing the means of

43 On animals as objects for the purposes of the conduct of hostilities, see Roscini, Chapter 5, 'Property and Objects', in this volume; Marco Roscini, 'Animal and the Law of Armed Conflict', *Israel Yearbook of Human Rights* 47 (2017), 35–66, at 42–8.

44 According to the ICRC Customary Law Database, this is also a customary international law rule during both international and non-international armed conflicts (see Rule 54).

45 Art. 54(2) of AP I.

46 Art. 14 of AP II.

47 Art. 54(1) of AP I and Art. 14 of AP II. See also Rule 53 of ICRC Customary Law Database.

48 AP II Commentary, para. 4791.

49 Roscini, 'Animals' (n. 43), 59.

50 Ibid.

51 Ibid.

existence'.[52] On the other hand, a reverberating effect of the destruction of livestock is its negative effect of food security more generally in armed conflict. The destruction of livestock, as well as looting, has been identified as a major source of food insecurity in armed conflict.[53] Accordingly, attacks against livestock as well as more generally the impact of armed conflict on livestock are generally addressed from the perspective of food security, including in the context of UN Security Council Resolution 2417 (2018).[54] Recognising the linkages between armed conflict and food insecurity, UN Security Council Resolution 2417 reaffirms the prohibition of starvation and destruction of objects indispensable to the survival of the civilian population, such as livestock.[55]

3 CONTENTS AND LIMITS OF THE LEGAL REGIME GOVERNING SPECIALLY PROTECTED OBJECTS

As specially protected objects, animals would benefit from further protection against the effects of armed conflict than as civilian objects, with a different regime for cultural property (Section 3.1) and goods indispensable to the survival of the civilian population (Section 3.2).

3.1 *Cultural Property*

The general special protection regime strives to protect cultural property against the effects of armed conflicts with two fundamental and intertwined obligations, namely the prohibition to attack except in cases of imperative military necessity and the obligation to avoid the use of cultural property for military purposes.

International humanitarian law prohibits attacking cultural property other than in the exceptional situation when such an attack is required by 'imperative military necessity'.[56] According to Article 6 of the 1999 Second Protocol such imperative military necessity may be invoked when 'cultural property has, by its function, been made into a military objective; and there is no feasible alternative available to obtain

52 AP I Commentary, para. 4802.

53 See, for example, Food Security Information Network, *2020 Global Report on Food Crises* which highlights, amongst others, the attacks and thefts of livestock by armed groups in Nigeria (70) and the Central African Republic (74); UN Office of the Coordinator for Humanitarian Affairs, *Factsheet Hunger and Armed Conflict*, no date, available at https://bit.ly/3zzppaj, accessed 22 February 2022; Special Rapporteur on the Right to Food, *Interim Report of the Special Rapporteur on the Right to Food in Conflict Situations*, 23 October 2017, A/72/188, 2017.

54 See, in particular, the periodic updates of UN Food and Agriculture Organisation (FAO)/World Food Program (WFP) for the UN Security Council on food security in countries with conflict situations. See for example FAO/WFP, *Monitoring Food Security in Countries with Conflict Situations*, Issue No. 7, January 2020, annexed to S/2020/62.

55 UN Security Council Resolution 2417 of 28 May 2018, S/RES/2417, para. 1.

56 Art. 4 of 1954 Hague Convention (n. 5); Rule 38 of ICRC Customary Law Database.

a similar military advantage to that offered by directing an act of hostility against that objective'.[57] Moreover, even in the case of such an imperative military necessity, the intrinsic cultural value of the property needs to be part of the proportionality analysis and 'special care must be taken in military operations to avoid damage'.[58] Under these rules, directing attacks against cultural property will only be very rarely justified under IHL.[59]

Animals that could be included under the notion of cultural property, in particularly endemic or endangered animals that form part of world cultural heritage, would thus enjoy a high level of protection against attack under this regime. However, application of the rules may be very challenging because under this approach, cultural property includes potentially very large areas. For example, Parc Virunga in the DRC, a world natural heritage site home to, amongst others, mountain gorillas and hippopotamuses, covers 800,000 hectares,[60] considerably larger than for example Angkor with 40,100 hectares or the cultural landscape of Globustan with 537 hectares, both registered as cultural property under enhanced protection under the 1999 Second Protocol.[61] In addition, though they may be concentrated in particular locations, animals would also be moving around. Weighting the military advantage to be gained from an attack justified by imperative military necessity with the potential harm done to animals and their habitat may be very difficult to assess in such circumstances. Yet, at least part of these concerns may be addressed by the prohibition to use of cultural property for military purposes unless required by military necessity[62] and avoid locating military objectives near cultural property.[63] In principle, the situation that cultural property may become the target of an attack should not arise as its use for military purposes is prohibited outside the exceptional circumstance of imperative military necessity.

International humanitarian law governing the protection of cultural property also sets up two specialised regimes for the protection of particularly important cultural property. First, under the 1954 Hague Convention, cultural property may be granted so-called special protection,[64] providing a slightly higher degree of protection. The special protection regime has barely been used, mostly due to the stringent eligibility conditions and cumbersome designation process[65] and has largely been replaced by

[57] Art. 6(a) of 1999 Second Protocol (n. 6).
[58] Rule 38 of ICRC Customary Law Database. See also Art. 7 of 1999 Second Protocol (n. 6).
[59] O'Keefe, 'Cultural Heritage' (n. 15), 55.
[60] See its entry on the World Cultural Heritage in Danger List, available at https://whc.unesco.org/en/list/63, accessed 22 February 2022.
[61] See UNESCO, International List of Cultural Property under Enhanced Protection (2019), available at https://bit.ly/3F6vUm6, accessed 22 February 2022.
[62] Art. 4(1) of 1954 Hague Convention (n. 5); Art. 39 of ICRC Customary Law Database.
[63] Art. 8 of 1999 Second Protocol (n. 6).
[64] Art. 8 of 1954 Hague Convention (n. 5). The Register for Cultural Property under Special Protection is available at https://bit.ly/3t7dr6G, accessed 22 February 2022.
[65] O'Keefe, *The Protection* (n. 4), 141.

the enhanced protection regime set up by the 1999 Second Protocol.[66] Cultural property granted enhanced protection shall never be used for military purposes.[67] Its protection from attack is increased as such cultural property may only be attacked when its use transformed it into a military objective.[68] In contrast, cultural property, as any other civilian object, may be transformed into a military objective through its nature, location and purpose as well pursuant to the general definition of military objective under IHL.[69] Animals protected because they inhabit a cultural heritage site granted enhanced protection, such as for example Angkor, would benefit from this regime indirectly.

Outside the conduct of hostilities, the protection of animals as cultural property could also contribute to their protection against trafficking and poaching in times of armed conflict through the prohibition of theft, pillage, misappropriation and acts of vandalism of cultural property.[70] In addition, parties to the conflict have a due diligence obligation to prevent theft, pillage, misappropriation and acts of vandalism on the territory under their control.[71]

Admittedly, applying the rules designed to protect cultural property in armed conflict with a view to protecting endangered species would require specialised scientific knowledge on wildlife protection and conservation. Yet, the protection of cultural property in its traditional understanding presents similar challenges and requires expertise in the identification, monitoring, preservation and management of cultural property as well as preparatory measures taken during times of peace with a view to ensuring protection in times of armed conflict. Indeed, the specialised regime for the protection of cultural property acknowledges this need. State parties to the 1954 Convention are required to establish services or specialists within their armed forces for the protection of cultural property.[72] Additionally, the 1999 Second Protocol provides for measures to be taken in times of peace, including preparing inventories, planning in-situ protection or removal of movable cultural property.[73] A similar approach could be adopted to protect endangered species.

3.2 *Objects Indispensable to the Survival of the Civilian Population*

Animals as livestock are protected by two distinct obligations. First, attacking livestock with the purpose of deliberately depriving civilians of food is

66 For a detailed discussion, see O'Keefe, *The Protection* (n. 4), 263–74. The List of Cultural Property under Enhanced Protection is available at https://bit.ly/3f1kozg, accessed 22 February 2022.
67 Art. 12 of 1999 Second Protocol (n. 6).
68 Art. 13(b)(2) of 1999 Second Protocol (n. 6).
69 Art. 52(1) of AP I; Rule 8 of ICRC Customary Law Database.
70 Art. 4(3) of 1954 Hague Convention (n. 5); Rule 40 of ICRC Customary Law Database.
71 Ibid. See also O'Keefe, 'Cultural Heritage' (n. 15), 57.
72 Art. 7(2) of 1954 Hague Convention (n. 5).
73 Art. 5 of 1999 Second Protocol (n. 6).

prohibited as a method of warfare.[74] Second, livestock is protected by the prohibition to attack, destroy, remove or otherwise rendering useless objects indispensable to the survival 'for the specific purpose of denying them for their sustenance value to the civilian population or the adverse Party, whether in order to starve out civilians, cause them to move away or any other motive'.[75] Livestock is thus not generally protected against attacks, but only against attacks with the 'specific purpose of denying them for their sustenance value', though the motive for such attacks is not limited to cause starvation, but can be 'any other'. However, even without such a specific purpose, livestock would remain protected as civilian object, unless transformed into a military objective.[76] This possibility is also foreseen in Article 53(1), which specifies that objects indispensable to the survival of the civilian population, such as livestock, is not protected if used by an adverse party 'as sustenance solely for the members of its armed forces' or 'in direct support of military action'.[77] Therefore, in addition to the reduction of animals to a means of sustenance, an additional limitation is that such animals are primarily protected due to their use to the civilian population. Accordingly, livestock that is only used for armed forces would not be protected.[78] Similarly, harm to livestock is lawful if it is the proportionate incidental effect of an attack against a military objective, provided that the result is not incidental starvation. Some read the rules governing the protection of objects indispensable to the survival of the civilian population in a narrow way that would only prohibit deliberate harm to livestock with the purpose of causing starvation. However, it has been argued persuasively that the prohibition to attack objects indispensable to the survival of the civilian population encompasses a broader obligation that also covers incidental starvation.[79] Under such an approach, the incidental harm to livestock during military operations leading to starvation may also be prohibited. Arguably, this could not only apply to direct harm to livestock, but also indirect harm, for example when as a result of military operations, livestock is deprived of water, which in turn would cause the starvation of the civilian population. Finally, in one respect livestock enjoys a higher level of protection in non-international armed conflicts than in international armed conflicts: while during international armed conflicts, a belligerent party could kill livestock for imperative military necessity in its

[74] Art. 54(1) of AP I and Art. 14 of AP II. See also Rule 53 ICRC Customary Law Database.

[75] Art. 54(2) of AP I.

[76] Roscini, Chapter 5, 'Property and Objects', in this volume.

[77] Art. 54(3) of AP I. See also the commentary to Rule 54 of ICRC Customary Law Database on the customary law nature of this exception.

[78] AP I Commentary, paras. 2110–12.

[79] Gloria Gaggioli, 'Joint Blog Series on International Law and Armed Conflict: Are Sieges Prohibited Under Contemporary IHL?' *EJIL: Talk! Blog* (30 January 2019), available at https://bit.ly/3HGsTdS, accessed 22 February 2022.

own territory in defence against an invasion,[80] there is no such exception for non-international armed conflicts as it was considered unworkable.[81]

4 CONSEQUENCES OF VIOLATIONS OF THE LEGAL REGIME GOVERNING SPECIALLY PROTECTED OBJECTS

4.1 *Violations of the Legal Regime Governing Cultural Property*

In addition to triggering state responsibility, there may also be penal consequences for the violation of the rules governing the protection of cultural property. The 1954 Hague Convention includes a limited and rather weak obligation for states to punish breaches of the convention by both disciplinary and penal sanctions.[82] In order to reinforce the penal consequences,[83] the 1999 Second Protocol introduced a differentiated approach depending on the importance of the cultural property in what has been called the 'cultural value'[84] approach that is applicable to both international and non-international armed conflicts.[85] The first category are serious violations constituted by attacking cultural property under enhanced protection; using cultural property under enhanced protection or its vicinity for military purposes; or the extensive destruction or appropriation of cultural property.[86] For these serious violations, state parties are required to make them punishable offences and establish jurisdiction over such offences on the basis on territoriality, nationality of the perpetrator and universality.[87] Moreover, for this category of offences, states have a duty to extradite or prosecute.[88] For a second category of serious violations, namely attacking cultural property and the theft, pillage, misappropriation or acts of vandalism of cultural property, the 1999 Second Protocol provides for more limited consequences: states parties only have to establish jurisdiction on the basis of territoriality and passive nationality.[89] If animals were protected as cultural property, either as part of a heritage site, including one under enhanced protection, or as

80 Art. 54(4); see also Roscini (n. 43), 60.
81 Sivakumaran, *The Law of Non-International Armed Conflict* (n. 103), 425–6.
82 Art. 28 of 1954 Hague Convention (n. 5). See also Micaela Frulli, 'International Criminal Law and the Protection of Cultural Heritage', in *The Oxford Handbook* (n. 15), 100–20, at 102.
83 O'Keefe, *The Protection* (n. 4), 274.
84 Frulli, 'International Criminal Law' (n. 82), 106.
85 O'Keefe, *The Protection* (n. 4), 275.
86 Art. 15(1)(a–c) of 1999 Second Protocol (n. 6). For a detailed discussion on serious violations, see O'Keefe, *The Protection* (n. 4), 277–80.
87 Arts 16(1)(a–c) and 17(a) of 1999 Second Protocol (n. 6). Universality is here used in the sense that states have to exercise jurisdiction when the alleged offender is present on their territory coupled with the obligation to extradite or prosecute. See also the discussion in Frulli, 'International Criminal Law' (n. 82), 105.
88 Art. 17(a) of 1999 Second Protocol (n. 6).
89 Art. 16(1)(a)(b) of 1999 Second Protocol (n. 6).

a category of cultural property apart, there would thus be the possibility to penalise harm to animals on this basis under national law.

In contrast, the definition of the international crime of attacking cultural property subject to the jurisdiction of the International Criminal Court (ICC) is considerably narrower. Without referring to the term cultural property, the ICC Statute includes the war crime of deliberately directing attacks against buildings dedicated to religion, education, art, science, or charitable purposes and historic monuments,[90] provided that they are not military objectives during both international[91] and non-international armed conflicts.[92] Under this definition, it is difficultly to conceive that attacks directed against animals that inhabit a cultural or natural heritage sites are covered. Another significant gap is that the definition does not include movable cultural property,[93] thus leaving no room for including animals as movable cultural property. Not surprisingly, the jurisprudence of international courts, namely the ICC and the International Criminal Tribunal for the former Yugoslavia (ICTY) have focused on clearly identifiable buildings of historic and religious values,[94] though they have also acknowledged their cultural value, namely by referencing their status as a World Heritage.[95] Yet despite the limitation of the definition of the war crime, the reparations order in the case of *Al Mahdi* suggests that the ICC may take into account more broadly the importance of protecting cultural heritage, including in its relationship with communities, for the purposes of reparations.[96] As part of a lengthy discussion on 'the importance of international cultural heritage', the chamber adopts a broad understanding of cultural heritage

> as encompassing the sources enabling cultural identification and development processes of individuals and groups, which they, implicitly or explicitly, wish to transmit to future generations. It includes tangible heritage composed of sites, structures and remains of archaeological, historical, religious, cultural or aesthetic value, as well as intangible heritage comprising traditions, customs and practices,

[90] Moreover, the same provision also includes a reference to hospitals, illustrating what Frulli calls the 'civilian-use' centered approach, based on the normally civilian use of cultural property rather than inherent cultural value, an approach that can be traced back to general IHL. She also points out that the ICTY Statute included a similar narrow definition, but marginally better as it did not include the reference to hospitals. See Frulli, 'International Criminal Law' (n. 82), 104–6.

[91] Art. 8(2)(b)(ix) of ICC Statute.

[92] Art. 8(2)(e)(iv) of ICC Statute.

[93] Micaela Frulli, 'The Criminalization of Offences Against Cultural Heritage in Times of Armed Conflict: The Quest for Consistency', *European Journal of International Law* 22 (2011), 203–17, at 212–13.

[94] For a detailed discussion, see Frulli, 'International Criminal Law' (n. 82), 106–9; Frulli, 'The Criminalization' (n. 93), 209–10.

[95] ICTY, *Prosecutor* v. *Jokić*, trial judgment of 18 May 2004, IT-01-42/1, paras. 23 and 49; ICTY, *Prosecutor* v. *Strugar*, trial judgment of 31 January 2005, IT-01-42, paras. 183 and 279; ICC, *Prosecutor* v. *Al Mahdi*, judgment and sentence of 27 September 2016, ICC-01/12-01/15, paras. 39 and 46.

[96] ICC, *Prosecutor* v. *Al Mahdi*, Reparations Order of 17 August 2017, ICC-01/12-01/15.

knowledge, vernacular or other languages, forms of artistic expression and folklore.[97]

Such a notion of cultural heritage is reminiscent of the definition of cultural heritage used for indigenous communities[98] and may allow the chamber to take into account harm done to animals or their habitat, in particular when part of a natural heritage site, in the reparations stage of proceedings. Additionally, the chamber highlighted the important role played by the World Heritage Convention, 'created for the protection of cultural and natural heritage of outstanding value'[99] and concluded that: 'The destruction of international cultural heritage thus carries a message of terror and helplessness; it destroys part of humanity's shared memory and collective consciousness; and it renders humanity unable to transmit its values and knowledge to future generations. It is an irreplaceable loss that negates humanity.'[100] Arguably, the destruction of natural heritage sites, including the animals that inhabit them, would be an equally irreplaceable loss.

4.2 *Violations of the Rules Governing Objects Indispensable to the Survival of the Civilian Population*

The prohibition to attack objects indispensable to the survival of the civilian population is not in itself a war crime. However, the ICC Statute included, for the first time on an international level, the crime of starvation as a method of warfare, though only for international armed conflicts.[101] This 'glaring'[102] gap in the ICC Statute has been severely criticised[103] and was remedied in 2019 when the Assembly of State Parties unanimously accepted a Swiss proposal[104] to include the crime of starving civilians during non-international armed conflicts.[105] However, criminalising starvation only offers a very limited avenue to hold those responsible for harm against animals accountable, reflecting the limitations of the IHL regime for the protection of objects indispensable to the survival of the civilian population.

97 Ibid., para. 15.

98 See above, Section 2.1.

99 *Prosecutor* v. *Al Mahdi* (n. 96), para. 20.

100 Ibid., para. 22.

101 Art. 8(2)(b)(xxv) of the ICC statute.

102 War Crimes Committee of the International Bar Association, *Report on the Swiss Proposal to Amend the Rome Statute to Include the War Crime of Starvation in Non-International Armed Conflicts* (2019), 6, available at https://bit.ly/3t6ZLsg, accessed 22 February 2022.

103 Sandesh Sivakumaran, *The Law of Non-international Armed Conflict* (Oxford: Oxford University Press 2018), 423; Rogier Bartels, 'Time to Fix the Rome Statute and Add the Crime of Starvation in Non-international Armed Conflicts!', *EJIL: Talk! Blog* (3 December 2019), available at https://bit.ly/3G5APVH, accessed 22 February 2022.

104 For the Swiss Proposal, see *Report of the Working Group on Amendments*, Annex IV, Assembly of State Parties, ICC Doc. ICC-ASP/17/35, 2018.

105 Resolution ICC-ASP/18/Res. 5, 2019.

Additionally, the amendment will only apply to the states who ratify it.[106] As of April 2022, only 8 states ratified it.[107]

5 CONCLUDING RECOMMENDATIONS

In the absence of a special protection regime for animals, some categories of animals may be protected to some extent under the existing concept of specially protected objects. On the one hand, in a paradigmatic illustration of the anthropocentric nature of IHL, livestock is protected as an object indispensable to the survival of the civilian population, reducing animals to a means of sustenance. On the other hand, under a progressive interpretation taking into account broader cultural heritage law, endangered or endemic species may be protected as cultural property, including when their natural habitat is a protected natural or cultural site.

Additionally, the very existence of specially protected objects illustrates that it is possible to provide for a differentiated regime of protection for different categories of objects, if such objects require special protection either due to their particular vulnerability or particular importance. Undoubtedly, endangered species may require such special protection due to their particular importance. Similarly, animals more generally could be considered as particularly vulnerable during armed conflict, thus deserving special protection. In particular the detailed rules on the protection of cultural property could also serve as an example of how to design and implement a regime that assigns different levels of protection to various categories of animals. Finally, the regime governing cultural property shows that complex protection challenges during armed conflict that require specialised expertise may be addressed. This can be done by requiring states to include such expertise within their armed forces, and by the institutional embedding of such a regime to build up the required expertise and capacity.

SELECT BIBLIOGRAPHY

Boer, Ben, 'The Environment and Cultural Heritage', in Francesco Francioni and Ana Filipa Vrdoljak (eds.), *The Oxford Handbook of International Cultural Heritage Law* (Oxford: Oxford University Press 2020), 318–46.

Dorough, Dalee Sambo and Siegfried Wiessner, 'Indigenous Peoples and Cultural Heritage', in Francesco Francioni and Ana Filipa Vrdoljak (eds.), *The Oxford Handbook of International Cultural Heritage Law* (Oxford: Oxford University Press 2020), 407–30.

106 For a critical discussion of the amendment regime for the ICC Statute, see Kevin Jon Heller, 'The Rome Statute's Flawed Amendment Regime: Starvation in NIAC Edition', *Opinio Juris Blog* (7 December 2019), available at https://bit.ly/3eZ3YWq, accessed 22 February 2022.

107 For the status of the amendment, see UNTS, Amendment to Article 8 of the ICC Statute (Intentionally Using Starvation of Civilians) C.N. 394.2020. Treaties-XVIII.10.g. of 15 September 2020, available at https://bit.ly/3F5Q3sz, accessed 22 February 2022.

Fortin, Katharine, *The Accountability of Armed Groups under Human Rights Law* (Oxford: Oxford University Press 2017).
Frulli, Micaela, 'International Criminal Law and the Protection of Cultural Heritage', in Francesco Francioni and Ana Filipa Vrdoljak (eds.), *The Oxford Handbook of International Cultural Heritage Law* (Oxford: Oxford University Press 2020), 100–20.
Gaggioli, Gloria, 'Joint Blog Series on International Law and Armed Conflict: Are Sieges Prohibited Under Contemporary IHL?' *EJIL: Talk!* Blog (30 January 2019).
Heller, Kevin Jon, 'The Rome Statute's Flawed Amendment Regime: Starvation in NIAC Edition', *Opinio Juris Blog* (7 December 2019).
Murray, Darragh, *Human Rights Obligations of Non-State Armed Groups* (Oxford: Hart Publishing 2016).
O'Keefe, Patrick, J., 'Underwater Cultural Heritage', in Francesco Francioni and Ana Filipa Vrdoljak (eds.), *The Oxford Handbook of International Cultural Heritage Law* (Oxford: Oxford University Press 2020), 295–317.
O'Keefe, Roger, *The Protection of Cultural Property in Armed Conflict* (Cambridge: Cambridge University Press 2006).
O'Keefe, Roger et al., *Protection of Cultural Property: Military Manuel* (Paris: UNESCO 2016).
O'Keefe, Roger, 'Cultural Heritage and International Humanitarian Law', in Francesco Francioni and Ana Filipa Vrdoljak (eds.), *The Oxford Handbook of International Cultural Heritage Law* (Oxford: Oxford University Press 2020), 43–74.
Strecker, Amy, 'Landscape as Cultural Heritage', in Francesco Francioni and Ana Filipa Vrdoljak (eds.), *The Oxford Handbook of International Cultural Heritage Law* (Oxford: Oxford University Press 2020), 272–94.
Sivakumaran, Sandesh, *The Law of Non-International Armed Conflict* (Oxford: Oxford University Press 2018).

7

Animals as Part of the Environment

Jérôme de Hemptinne[*]

1 INTRODUCTION

As part of the environment, animals benefit from the protection of international humanitarian law (IHL) principles and provisions which provide direct and indirect environmental safeguards.[1] However, these principles and provisions remain weak, and largely unclear,[2] especially in the context of non-international armed conflicts. For this reason, they need to be read in conjunction with the growing body of international norms, standards, and mechanisms preventing and redressing environmental harm during peacetime.[3] This regime offers significant protection to animals suffering from the general deterioration of natural habitats and ecosystems caused by mankind. That said, the extent to which international environmental law (IEL) continues to apply during warfare, thereby reinforcing the protection of animals, is debated.[4] Moreover, it is often argued that the 'macro perspective' offered by IEL is at odds with the 'micro preoccupation' of the protection of animals which prioritises the aim of guaranteeing their individual welfare.[5] Indeed, many general environmental instruments remain guided by underlying anthropocentric values and principles – such that governing 'sustainable development' – which treat animals more as commodities to be exploited than as living creatures that experience pain and distress.[6] At the same time, it should be recognised at the outset that the few

* I am indebted to Makane Mbengue for his helpful comments on an earlier draft.

1 See Art. 35(3) and 55 of AP I. See also ICRC Environmental Guidelines, para. 24.

2 Michael Bothe, Carl Bruch, Jordan Diamond, David Jensen, 'International Law Protecting the Environment during Armed Conflict: Gaps and Opportunities', *International Review of the Red Cross* 92 (2010), 569–92, at 570.

3 Ibid.

4 Ibid.

5 Sabrina Tremblay-Huet, 'Should Environmental Law Learn from Animal Law? Compassion as a Guiding Principle for International Environmental Law Instead of Sustainable Development', *Revue québécoise de droit international* 1(1) (2018) 125–44, at 128; Thomas G. Kelch, 'CITES, Globalization, and the Future of Animal Law', in Randal Abate (ed.), *What Can Animal Law Learn from Environmental Law?* (Washington, DC: Environmental Law Institute 2006), 269–80, at 270.

6 Ibid. See Krieger and Martínez Soria, Chapter 4, 'Rationale and Challenges', this volume.

IHL provisions and principles protecting the environment were also originally designed with the objective of preserving and protecting the interests of human beings, instead of the environment and wildlife per se.[7] Furthermore, while they might be grounded on diverging considerations during peacetime, the norms protecting the environment and those safeguarding animals usually pursue a similar overall goal when they apply in the context of warfare: preserving the environment as a whole from the destructive effect of hostilities, by imposing meaningful constraints on belligerents, which are compatible with military imperatives.

Following the pattern of analysis developed in the other parts of this research, I will examine in this chapter the main issues stemming from the application to animals of the legal regimes protecting the environment in international and non-international armed conflicts, in light of the above issues. To do so, I will consider the scope of application (Section 2), as well as the content and limits (Section 3) of these legal regimes. I will then analyse the legal consequences that flow from violating their fundamental norms (Section 4). All of this is with a view to proposing recommendations in order to ameliorate the fate of animals during warfare (Section 5).

2 SCOPE OF APPLICATION OF THE LEGAL REGIMES PROTECTING THE ENVIRONMENT

For the convenience of the reader, the scope of application of IHL (Section 2.1) will be examined separately from that of IEL (Section 2.2). Under IHL, the norms protecting the environment are succinct and subject to strict conditions of application, while, under IEL, environmental treaties are comprehensive and diverse, but their material, personal, and territorial scopes of application in wartime remain unclear.

2.1 *International Humanitarian Law*

The environment is safeguarded by IHL in three ways.[8] First, the general principles governing the conduct of hostilities that are addressed to civilian objects – that is, the principles of distinction,[9] proportionality,[10] and precaution[11] – are applicable to the environment.[12] Second, restrictive rules protect the environment as such. Contained

[7] Michael Schmitt, 'Green War: An Assessment of the Environmental Law of Armed Conflict', *Yale Law Journal* 22 (1997), 1–110, at 69.

[8] For a recent detailed analysis of the protection of the environment under IHL, see ICRC Environmental Guidelines. See also the debates and their evolution between those who are in favour of an 'anthropocentric approach' to the protection of the environment – the environment should only be safeguarded if it affects the civilian population – and those who promote an 'intrinsic value' conception of the environment – the environment should be protected as such, even if damages caused to it by war would not impact humans (ibid., para. 19).

[9] Art. 48, 51(2) and 52(2) of AP I; Art. 13(2) of AP II.

[10] Art. 51(5)(b) and 57 of AP I.

[11] Art. 57 and 58 of AP I.

[12] ICRC Environmental Guidelines, para. 23.

in Articles 35(3) and 55 of Additional Protocol (AP) I, these rules envisage the prohibition against using means and methods of warfare that are intended, or may be expected, to cause long-term, widespread, and severe damage to the natural environment, as well as the interdiction of attacking the environment in reprisal. Third, other IHL rules that seek to prevent or limit certain damage, or to regulate the usage of specific weapons or combat techniques, also play a role in this context. They include rules on specially protected objects such as works and installations containing dangerous forces[13] and objects indispensable to the survival of the civilian population,[14] rules on pillage[15] and on enemy property,[16] as well as provisions prohibiting incendiary weapons or the use of herbicides as a method of warfare.[17] In the same vein, IHL also prohibits in a specific convention the destruction of the environment as a form of weapon.[18]

I will limit myself to making three main observations regarding the scope of application of this legal regime. First, there is no agreed definition of the term 'environment' under IHL.[19] It is, however, of note that Articles 35(3) and 55 of AP I refer to the 'natural environment' which, according to the AP I Commentary to Article 35(3), must be differentiated from the 'human environment'.[20] The natural environment usually encompasses 'everything that exists or occurs naturally and is therefore not man-made, such as the general hydrosphere, biosphere, geosphere, and atmosphere (including fauna, flora, oceans and other bodies of water, oil, and rocks)'.[21] However, distinguishing the 'natural environment' from the 'human environment' is rather artificial: both of them are usually intimately linked. This explains why it is now generally admitted that the environment also includes 'natural elements that are or may be the product of human intervention, such as foodstuffs, agricultural areas, drinking water, and livestock'.[22] In light of this evolution, the International Committee of the Red Cross (ICRC) understands today the 'natural environment to constitute the natural world together with the system of inextricable interrelations between living organisms and their inanimate environment, in the widest sense possible'.[23] Accordingly, this notion encompasses all animals

13 Art. 56 of AP I and Art. 15 of AP II.
14 Art. 54 of AP I and Art. 14 of AP II.
15 Art. 33(2) of GC IV.
16 Art. 53 of GC IV.
17 Protocol on Prohibitions or Restrictions on the Use of Incendiary Weapons (Protocol III) of 10 October 1980, 1342 UNTS 171.
18 See ENMOD Convention.
19 ICRC Environmental Guidelines, para. 15. See also *International Humanitarian Law and the Challenges of Contemporary Armed Conflicts: Recommitting to Protection in Armed Conflicts on the 70th Anniversary of the Geneva Conventions* (Geneva: ICRC 2019), 67.
20 AP I Commentary, para. 1451.
21 ICRC Environmental Guidelines, para. 16; ICRC, *Challenges of Contemporary Armed Conflicts* (n. 19), 67.
22 Ibid.
23 ICRC Environmental Guidelines, para. 16

(including farm or companion animals) and, in particular, wildlife and its habitats, as well as the relationship that these elements entertain with the ecological system in which they exist, and that this interconnected system is protected as a whole.[24] Thereby, the entire population of animals located in a given natural area or site, as well as its habitat, is duly safeguarded from the effects of hostilities. This means that these animals are protected by IHL, not only directly and individually as 'civilian objects' or as 'properties', but also indirectly and globally as general components of the environment in which they live.[25] Combining such a direct and indirect approach to the protection of animals is all the more justified during warfare given that military operations usually affect the ecosystem in its entirety, with general repercussions on all its components, including wildlife. Moreover, when conducting military operations, commanders and their subordinates will often lack the necessary means and resources to plan, prepare, and take measures that aim at protecting each and every animal individually.

Second, as we will see below, Articles 35(3) and 55 of AP I prohibit causing damage to the environment even when it constitutes a legitimate military target.[26] However, the scope of application of these provisions is limited by the fact that the damage that is forbidden must be cumulatively 'widespread, long-term and severe'.[27] Although the *travaux préparatoires* of Articles 35(3) and 55 indicate that each condition was extensively discussed during the negotiations of AP I, only the word 'long-term' was clarified as meaning 'years' or 'decades'.[28] There is no indication of what 'widespread' and 'severe' signify. Traditionally, widespread is understood to refer to 'several hundred square kilometres' and severe means 'serious disruption of the ecosystem'.[29] Article 55 of AP I suggests an additional requirement: the damage to the environment should cause 'prejudice the health or survival of the population'. Even if '(t)his should be read as a mere illustration of the seriousness of the damage, thereby underlying the purpose of the norm',[30] it shows the overwhelmingly anthropocentric nature of Article 55.

When interpreted in light of the negotiating history of AP I, the threshold imposed by IHL for the protection of the environment seems very high, if not impossible to

24 Cordula Droege, Marie-Louise Tougas, 'The Protection of the Natural Environment in Armed Conflict: Existing Rules and Need for Further Legal Protection', *Nordic Journal of International Law* 82 (2013), 21–52, at 25.

25 Marco Roscini, 'Animals and the Law of Armed Conflict', *Israel Yearbook of Human Rights* 47 (2017), 35–67, at 61–2.

26 Michael Bothe, 'The Protection of the Environment in Times of Armed Conflict', *German Yearbook of International Law* 34 (1991), 54–62, at 56.

27 ICRC Customary Law Database, Rule 45.

28 AP I Commentary, para. 1452.

29 Droege, Tougas, 'The Protection of the Natural Environment' (n. 24), 32.

30 Liesbeth Lijnzaad, Gerard J. Tanja, 'Protection of the Environment in Times of Armed Conflict: The Iraq-Kuwait War', *Netherlands International Law Review* 40 (1993), 169–99, at 181. See also Yoram Dinstein, 'Protection of the Environment in International Armed Conflict', *Max Planck Yearbook of United Nations Law* 5 (2001), 523–49, at 531–2; Schmitt, 'Green War' (n. 7), 69.

meet in practice.[31] That said, the terminology used is imprecise and ambiguous, leaving a wide margin for interpretation. Furthermore, it 'reflects a kind of thinking prevailing at a time when environmental consciousness in connection with armed conflict had just begun to develop, in the aftermath of the Vietnam War'.[32] Today, the importance of environmental values, the progressive understanding that the environment must be protected as such, and the awareness of the dramatic consequences that wars have on the whole ecosystem, and wildlife in particular, should impact the way Articles 35(3) and 55 are interpreted.[33] What might not have appeared to be widespread, long-term, and severe damage forty years ago may be considered as such nowadays.[34] For instance, it is increasingly accepted by scientists that harming an essential component of the ecosystem – for instance, a particular species – can seriously disrupt its balance on a wide scale.[35] Destroying biodiversity spots or area known to be populated by endangered species, or by a great diversity of fauna and flora, can also entail serious repercussions for the environment as a whole, even if the area concerned is relatively small.[36] In fact, widespread, long-term, and severe damage is a relative notion, the significance of which is contingent upon several factors, including the environmental awareness available to military commanders and soldiers, when planning and conducting military operations, as well as the nature and type of all types of foreseeable effect – including cumulative and indirect (reverberating) effect – of the potential harm that may be caused to the environment by their operations.[37] As recently emphasised by the ICRC,

> There is . . . increasing and more sophisticated knowledge of and scientific data on the connectedness and interrelationships between the different parts of the natural environment, as well as of the interdependent nature of environmental processes. For instance, marshlands in southern Iraq were devastated as a result of drainage works and damming, which in turn led to massive loss and environmental degradation, such as desertification and depletion of biodiversity, including the extinction of certain species. There is also more knowledge of the effects of the harm caused, including cumulative and indirect effects. When assessing whether damage meets

31 Bothe, Bruch, Diamond, Jensen, 'International Law Protecting the Environment' (n. 2), 576.

32 Wil D. Verwey, 'Protection of the Environment in Armed Conflict: In Search of a New Legal Perspective', *Leiden Journal of International Law* 8 (1995), 7–40, at 14.

33 Djamchid Montaz, 'Les règles relatives à la protection de l'environnement au cours des conflits armés à l'épreuve du conflit entre l'Irak et le Koweït', *Annuaire français de droit inernational* XXXVII (1991), 203–19, at 209–10; Bothe, Bruch, Diamond, Jensen, 'International Law Protecting the Environment' (n. 2), 576.

34 Bothe, 'The Protection of the Environment' (n. 26), 57. See also ICRC Environmental Guidelines, para. 54.

35 Daniella Dam-de Jong, *International Law and Governance of Natural Resources in Conflict and Post-Conflict Situations* (Cambridge: Cambridge University Press 2015), 230.

36 ICRC Environmental Guidelines, para. 58.

37 Bothe, 'The Protection of the Environment' (n. 26), 57; Géza Herczegh, 'La protection de l'environnement naturel et le droit humanitaire' in Christophe Swinarski (ed.), *Studies and Essays on International Humanitarian Law and Red Cross Principles in Honour of Jean Pictet* (Geneva/La Haye: Martinus Nijhoff Publishers 1984), 725–33, at 732.

> the widespread, long-term and severe threshold, cumulative effects are another factor to consider in addition to individual effects; for example, in considering whether the oil spills during the 1990–1991 Gulf War met the threshold, these separate events were considered as a single operation. Finally, as climate risks and shocks increase, the natural environment, particularly where it is already degraded, may become less capable of absorbing the effects of this damage.[38]

In this regard, it should be observed that new standards are progressively emerging from IEL that reflects the level of scientific knowledge currently available and the environmental priorities that must be taken into account when evaluating the potentially harmful character of a given military operation.[39] I will come back to this issue below when analysing the relationship between IEL and IHL.

Third, specific norms of IHL governing the protection of the environment are limited not only by strict conditions of their application, but also by the fact that they do not formally apply in the context of non-international armed conflicts. Neither common Article 3 of the four Geneva Conventions (GCs), nor AP II, encompass any provision dealing specifically with the environment. Moreover, the ICRC considers that only general principles on the conduct of hostilities – which are applicable to all civilian objects and hence to the environment – have attained customary law status in the context of non-international armed conflicts.[40] Indeed, the customary rule prohibiting widespread, long-term, and severe damage to the natural environment in international armed conflicts[41] is, according to the ICRC, only 'likely to become customary in due course' in non-international armed conflict.[42] Reflecting the reluctance of states to accept heavy constraints on the way they conduct hostilities against rebels on their national territories, such a restricted scope of application of the norms specifically protecting the environment creates an unjustified lacuna. International humanitarian law still assumes a world in which dividing lines between international and non-international armed conflicts are clear. In contrast, the safeguarding of the environment is grounded in theoretical and practical assumptions that differ from IHL. From a theoretical perspective, the environment is progressively ascribed a universal normative value, which is incompatible with the constraints imposed by the sovereignty of states.[43] Indeed, it is increasingly recognised that environmental concerns exceed the mere domestic affairs of individual states, which entails, amongst other things, that certain essential or rare natural resources, including species, receive an absolute protection in all circumstances, wherever

38 ICRC Environmental Guidelines, para. 54.

39 Bothe, 'The Protection of the Environment' (n. 26), 57. See also ICRC Environmental Guidelines, para. 54.

40 ICRC Customary Law Database, Rule 43.

41 Roscini, 'Animals' (n. 25), 62–4.

42 ICRC Customary Law Database, Rule 45.

43 Markus Vordermayer, 'The Extraterritorial Application of Multilateral Environmental Agreements', *Harvard International Law Review* 59 (2018), 60–124, at 110.

they are.[44] On a more pragmatic level, belligerents in non-international armed conflicts – be they governmental forces or armed groups – can damage natural resources like any other belligerents with general repercussions on wildlife. As also observed by the ICRC, 'major damage to the environment rarely respects international frontiers'.[45] Even when they are caused within the boundaries of a non-international armed conflict, such damage usually affects the ecological balance on a wide scale. This is even more so given that protected areas, habitats and, more generally, interconnected ecosystems often extend beyond the frontiers of a single state. Accordingly, protection of the environment should transcend the territorial and political boundaries on which IHL is grounded. As a matter of fact, when drafting its Draft Principles on Protection of the Environment in Relation to Armed Conflicts, the International Law Commission (ILC) seemingly endorsed this approach by affirming that 'care shall be taken to protect the natural environment against widespread, long-term and severe damage' in all armed conflicts, international or non-international.[46]

2.2 *International Environmental Law*

Animals could also benefit from the protections offered by a growing number of multilateral environmental conventions which concern them directly – such as the Convention on International trade in Endangered Species of Wild Fauna and Flora (CITES), or the Convention on the Conservation of Migratory Species of Wild Animals[47] – or more specific agreements that deal with certain animals – such as the Agreement on the Conservation of Albatrosses and Petrels,[48] or the International Convention on the Regulation of Whaling.[49] Other conventions of a more global nature – such as the Convention on Biological Diversity,[50] the UN Framework Convention on Climate Change,[51] the African Convention on the Conservation of Nature and Natural Resources (revised),[52] the Convention on Wetlands of International Importance, Especially as Waterfowl Habitat,[53] the Convention on

44 Ibid.

45 ICRC Customary Law Database, Rule 45.

46 ILC, Draft Principles on the Protection of the Environment in Relation to Armed Conflict (2019), reproduced in UN General Assembly, Report of the ILC, Seventy-first Session (29 April–7 June and 8 July–9 August 2019), A/74/10, Draft Principle 15.

47 Convention on the Conservation of Migratory Species of Wild Animals (Convention on Migratory Species) of 23 June 1979, 1651 UNTS 333.

48 Agreement on the Conservation of Albatrosses and Petrels of 19 June 2001, 2258 UNTS 257.

49 International Convention on the Regulation of Whaling of 2 December 1946, 161 UNTS 72.

50 Convention on Biological Diversity of 5 June 1992, 1760 UNTS 79.

51 UN Framework on Climate Change (Framework on Climate Change) of 9 May 1992, 1771 UNTS 107.

52 African Convention on the Conservation of Nature and Natural Resources (African Convention) signed on 15 September 1968 and revised on 11 July 2003.

53 Convention on Wetlands of International Importance, Especially as Waterfowl Habitat (Ramsar Convention) of 3 December 1982, 996 UNTS 245.

Persistent Organic Pollutants,[54] or the World Heritage Convention – provide indirect protection to animals. Relevant norms of customary international law – such as the prohibition against states using or permitting the use of their territory in such manner as to cause injury in or to the territory of states (the so-called Trail Smelter Principle)[55] – and soft law instruments – such as the Declaration of the UN Conference on the Human Environment,[56] the World Charter of Nature,[57] or the Declaration on Environment and Development[58] – could also play a role in addressing some of the IHL deficiencies and gaps raised above and, therefore, in reinforcing wildlife protection.[59] That said, these conventions, instruments, and principles are subject to numerous constraints imposed by their narrow substantive, personal, and territorial scopes of application. Let's briefly examine these constraints in turn.

Substantive scope of application. It should first be determined whether a given multilateral environmental convention applies during armed conflict and, if so, to what extent it grants direct or indirect protection to animals. While certain agreements provide for their total or partial application,[60] suspension or derogation in this context,[61] most are silent, or are ambiguous on the matter.[62] It is interesting to note in this regard that the ILC presumes that the existence of an armed conflict does not ipso facto terminate or suspend the operation of environmental treaties.[63] This presumption seems particularly justified for multilateral treaties protecting common environmental goods (such as biodiversity), shared natural resources (such as rivers

[54] Convention on Persistent Organic Pollutants (Stockholm Convention) of 22 May 2001, 2256 UNTS 119.

[55] Trail Smelter case, *United States* v. *Canada*, Award, Reports of International Arbitral Awards, 16 April 1938 and 11 March 1941, vol. III, 1905–82.

[56] Declaration of the UN Conference on the Human Environment, A/Conf.48/14/Rev. 1 (1973).

[57] World Charter of Nature, UN General Assembly Resolution 37/7 of 28 October 1982.

[58] Declaration on Environment and Development (Rio Declaration), A/CONF.151/26 (1992).

[59] For a study of the applicability of these conventions during armed conflicts, see UNEP, *Protecting the Environment during Armed Conflicts: An Inventory Analysis of International Law* (Nairobi: UNEP 2009), 40–3. As stated by the ICRC, 'as far as rules of customary international environmental law are concerned, the applicability of any such rules in the context of armed conflict will depend on whether there is "a general practice accepted as law" (*opinio juris*) in this regard'. See ICRC Environmental Guidelines, para. 34.

[60] See, for instance, World Heritage Convention; Ramsar Convention (n. 53); African Convention (n. 52). See also UNEP, Protecting the Environment (n. 59), 37.

[61] See, for instance, Vienna Convention on Civil Liability for Nuclear Damage of 21 May 1963, 1063 UNTS 265.

[62] See, for instance, CITES; Convention on Migratory Species (n. 47); Convention on Biological Diversity (n. 50); Framework on Climate Change (n. 51); Convention of Stockholm (n. 54); Agreement on the Conservation of Albatrosses and Petrels (n. 48). See also, in this regard, Philippe Sands, Jacqueline Peel, *Principles of International Environmental Law* (Cambridge: Cambridge University Press 2018), 830.

[63] ILC, Effects of Armed Conflicts on Treaties. Titles and Texts of the Draft Articles on the Effects of Armed Conflicts on Treaties Adopted by the Drafting Committee on Second Reading, 11 May 2011, A/CN.4/L.777, Art. 3, 6 and 7.

or lakes) or endangered species (such as rhinos or elephants).[64] That being said, even if most environmental treaties should remain applicable during warfare, certain provisions that are contained in these treaties – such as those creating obligations that are driven by the principle of 'good neighbourliness' – might be incompatible with a state of war and thus inapplicable in this circumstance.[65] As far as soft law instruments are concerned, notwithstanding their potential importance for the protection of animals, they are not legally binding, unless they amount to customary international law. Some of these instruments expressly apply in the context of armed conflicts.[66] Most of them are laconic on their scope of application.[67] The practice of states might clarify matters. Nevertheless, state authorities will often be reluctant to express any views on sensitive environmental issues that may directly affect their sovereign powers to conduct warfare.

Personal scope of application. In international and non-international armed conflicts, state armed forces are, in principle, bound by international environmental law (IEL), except if the concerned state can obtain derogation from its treaty obligations or if grounds of necessity or *force majeure* can be invoked. In non-international armed conflicts, the question whether armed groups must comply with environmental norms is controversial. Indeed, in contrast to rights and duties contained in IHL conventions, those enshrined in environmental treaties are not directly addressed to armed groups, but only to state authorities. Nonetheless, it is increasingly accepted that non-state actors – which control part of the national territory and exercise quasi-governmental functions – are also bound by human rights obligations.[68] This acceptance could be extended to basic environmental obligations given the fact that environmental damage caused by warfare usually also violates the fundamental rights of local populations, such as the right to life, the right to a standard of leaving adequate for health and well-being, the right of individuals not to be deprived of their own means of subsistence, the right of all peoples to freely dispose of their natural wealth and resources, or the right to access to a healthy environment.[69] Since IHL of non-international armed conflicts – as opposed to IHL governing occupation – does not provide any rules on the exploitation and administration of natural resources, imposing basic environmental duties and responsibilities on armed groups drawn from IEL is essential in order, for instance, that natural resources are used in a manner that ensures their long-term

64 See Silja Vöneky, 'Armed Conflict, Effect on Treaties' (1 January 2012), para. 10, available at SSRN: https://ssrn.com/abstract=3369609 or http://dx.doi.org/10.2139/ssrn.3369609, accessed 22 February 2022.

65 For an in-depth analysis of the applicability of IEL in armed conflicts, see Raphael van Steenberghe, 'Interactions between International Environmental Law and International Humanitarian Law regarding the Protection of the Environment during Warfare', *Journal of International Criminal Justice* (forthcoming 2022).

66 See World Charter of Nature (n. 57).

67 See Stockholm Declaration (n. 54); Rio Declaration (n. 58) (except the elusive principle 24).

68 Marco Sassòli, *International Humanitarian Law: Rules, Controversies, and Solutions to Problems Arising in Warfare* (Cheltenham: Edward Elgar 2019), 490.

69 Sands, Peel, *Principles of International Environmental Law* (n. 62), 815.

availability, or does not exceed their capacity of regeneration. This is even more so that protecting these resources would ultimately serve the interests of animals. It is true that most states would reluctantly accept that non-state actors should play such a role, as it would appear to give them a formal right to exploit and administer natural resources that do not formally belong to them. Having said that, it might also be in the interest of states that armed groups be obliged to avoid causing harm to their own resources by refraining taking certain actions ('negative obligations'). In contrast, imposing positive obligations upon non-state actors to preserve the environment by improving a particular regime would certainly be less acceptable as it would necessitate exercising state-like responsibilities. In any event, implementing these positive obligations might often exceed limited capabilities of armed groups.[70]

Territorial scope of application. When confronted with an international or a non-international armed conflict within their own territory, states are, in principle, obliged to comply with the obligations contained in environmental treaties identified above. But do they have also extraterritorial environmental duties when they carry out military operations in the territory of third states? This question has rarely been addressed.[71] The customary 'no-harm rule' – according to which a state has the 'responsibility to ensure that activities within their jurisdiction or control do not cause damage to the environment of other States or of areas beyond the limits of national jurisdiction'[72] – could be invoked as providing 'a sufficient normative response to all instances of extraterritorial environmental harm'.[73] Moreover, it has been emphasised that environmental concerns are usually not confined territorially, as illustrated by the fact that many multilateral conventions protecting the environment and, in particular, wildlife – such as the Convention on Migratory Species,[74] the Ramsar Convention (which sought to protect wetlands primarily as the habitat of waterfowl),[75] the World Heritage Convention,[76] or the European Convention on the Conservation of European Wildlife and Natural Habitats[77] – contain 'traces of extraterritorial application'.[78] But preventing damages from impacting third states does not mean that belligerents are bound to respect IEL when conducting military operations in the territories of these states. In this case, it should be recalled that human rights apply extraterritorially when the concerned state exercises effective control of an area outside its own territory. As we have seen, environmental norms

70 Sassòli, *International Humanitarian Law* (n. 68), 490.

71 See Vordermayer, 'Extraterritorial Application' (n. 43), 60–124.

72 Principle 2 of the Rio Declaration (n. 58).

73 Vordermayer, 'Extraterritorial Application' (n. 43), 85. There is no total overlap between the no-harm customary rule and the principle of extraterritorial application of IEL. (ibid., 85–7).

74 Ibid., 100–2.

75 Art. 2(2) of the Ramsar Convention (n. 53).

76 Vordermayer, 'Extraterritorial Application' (n. 43), 96–9.

77 European Convention on the Conservation of European Wildlife and Natural Habitats of 19 September 1979, Eur. T.S. No 104.

78 Vordermayer, 'Extraterritorial Application' (n. 43), 87–106. This is not surprising given that vulnerable habitats and ecosystems often extend beyond national territories.

often possess a human rights component justifying that these norms and rights apply to non-state entities. The application of environmental norms beyond national boundaries could be justified on the same basis.

This would mean that environmental resources – such as the habitats of wildlife – be protected extraterritorially when the following conditions are met: (i) If these resources fall within the substantial scope of application of the convention at stake; and (ii) if they are placed under the effective control of belligerents (for instance, in case of occupation). Two important diverging considerations must however be raised. On the one hand, fully respecting obligations on the conservation, utilisation, and development of natural resources, as required under the terms of many multilateral treaties, especially outside the jurisdiction of the territorial state, will often impose an excessive burden on belligerents, in the extreme circumstances of war. On the other hand, during certain phases of an armed conflict, if no control can yet be exercised over the territory of the other belligerent state, there would be a justifiable expectation that environmental resources, in particular wildlife, be conserved and protected as such, even when the strict conditions imposed by Articles 35(3) and 55 of AP I are not met.

3 CONTENTS AND LIMITS OF THE LEGAL REGIMES PROTECTING THE ENVIRONMENT

While IHL provisions contain minimal environmental safeguards (Section 3.1), IEL not only significantly reinforces these guarantees, but also provides an 'overall context of interpretation' of vague IHL provisions which allows them to be read and applied to animals in an effective and meaningful manner (Section 3.2).

3.1 *International Humanitarian Law*

Under IHL, the natural environment is usually considered to be a civilian object.[79] As such, the environment is a complete entity protected against military attacks which occur in both international and non-international armed conflicts.[80] However, this general protection is not absolute. Specific elements of the

[79] ICRC Environmental Guidelines, paras. 18–19. ICRC, *Challenges of Contemporary Armed Conflicts* (n. 19), 67. See also Droege, Tougas, 'The Protection of the Natural Environment' (n. 24), 25–7; Tara Smith, 'Critical Perspectives on Environmental Protection in Non-international Armed Conflict: Developing the Principles of Distinction, Proportionality and Necessity', *Leiden Journal of International Law* 32 (2019), 759–79, at 764–5. As the ICRC noted, '[t]here is, however, some debate as to whether all parts of the natural environment that do not qualify as military objectives are necessarily civilian objects'. Indeed, for some, the natural environment is only protected by IHL if it affects the civilian population while, for others, the environment must be safeguarded as such, 'even if damage to it would not necessarily harm humans in a reasonably foreseeable way for the purposes of IHL assessment' (ICRC Environmental Guidelines, para. 19).

[80] ICRC Environmental Guidelines, para. 18; ICRC Customary Law Database, Rule 43. See also Smith, 'Critical Perspectives on Environmental Protection' (n. 79), 763–5.

environment can become military objectives if, by their strategic location (for instance, when these elements provide soldiers with a vantage point over their adversary's location), use or purpose (for instance, when these elements are utilised for concealment), they make an effective contribution to military action and if their total or partial destruction, capture or neutralisation, in the circumstances prevailing at the time, offers a definite military advantage.[81] In principle, no component of the natural environment is a military objective by its nature.[82] Moreover, wildlife can never be treated as a military objective by virtue of its use or purpose, even if the trading of endangered species might contribute to sustaining military activities.[83] However, animals could well become legitimate indirect targets of military attacks conducted in areas in which they are located and which, themselves, constitute military objectives.

That said, as noted by the ICRC, 'the concept of an "area" must not be interpreted so broadly that a large expanse of forest is deemed a military objective simply because combatants are located in a small portion of it'.[84] Furthermore, the natural environment always remains protected against excessive collateral damage. Indeed, according to the principle of proportionality,[85] it is prohibited to launch any attack against a military objective which may be expected to cause damage to parts of the natural environment constituting civilian objects (such as wildlife) which would be excessive in relation to the military advantage anticipated.[86] Given the importance that the protection of the environment (and animals which form part of it) has acquired over the last four decades – as reflected by the numerous multilateral conventions and soft law initiatives on the matter – the environment (and animals) should benefit from a particularly heavy weight in the proportionality calculation. Moreover, causing disproportionate damage to wildlife may ipso facto violate the principle of proportionality since it can never constitute, by itself, a military objective.

It should be noted that such damage could be the result, not only of direct effects of an attack conducted against a particular group of animals or against a part of the environment in which they live, but also of indirect effects of military operations launched against an area which does not contain many animals, but the destruction of which affects the ecological balance on a wide scale and, consequently, causes the disappearance of animals situated elsewhere.[87] In all these circumstances, however, the damage must be foreseeable. It is true that assessing the foreseeability of such damage, especially when it is indirect, requires environmental awareness that even

81 Art. 52(2) of AP I. See also ICRC, *Challenges of Contemporary Armed Conflicts* (n. 19), 68.
82 Droege, Tougas, 'The Protection of the Natural Environment' (n. 24), 28.
83 Ibid., 29.
84 ICRC, *Challenges of Contemporary Armed Conflicts* (n. 19), 68.
85 Art. 57 of AP I.
86 ICRC Customary Law Database, Rule 43.
87 ICRC, *Challenges of Contemporary Armed Conflicts* (n. 19), 68. See also CRC Environmental Guidelines, para. 18.

well-equipped state armed forces may not possess. At the same time, such 'knowledge . . . is constantly increasing, and there is a growing understanding of long-term risks attendant to disruption of ecosystems'.[88] In any event, when planning and conducting concrete military operations, both commanders and soldiers have a duty to reasonably value environmental objects and assess potential damage that may be caused to them by using all necessary means and resources at their disposal.[89]

Accordingly, wildlife should be fully brought into the proportionality equation. Of course, the importance that animals carry in this equation will depend on the value attributed to them. In most societies, 'such a value judgement is contingent upon what animals offer to humankind as working tools, food, clothing, etc. It is, however, increasingly accepted that animals also have value in their own right and, as a consequence, that their interests should not be automatically subordinated to the military interests of humans.'[90] In other words, the fact that animals are no longer seen as inanimate objects but as living beings, experiencing emotions, should be duly taken into consideration when undertaking a proportionality assessment of a pending attack impacting on the environment. This could be done in four concrete ways. First, before launching an attack on the natural environment, belligerents should take all the necessary precautions to determine whether, and to what extent, animals are present in the specific areas being targeted. Second, areas which are densely populated by animals should carry heavier weight in the proportionality calculation than areas in which no – or very few – animals are present. The diversity of species living in these areas should also be taken into account. Third, all reasonable measures should be taken to avoid any collateral damage to endangered species.[91] This rule is based on the absolute necessity of sparing vulnerable animals from hostilities and other human activities that threaten them, as illustrated by the CITES, which prohibits unpermitted trading. Fourth, all reasonable measures should be taken to avoid collateral harm to animals that are necessary for the survival of the civilian population.[92] This rule flows from Articles 54 of AP I and 14 of AP II that grant special protections to these types of objects.

As we know, the natural environment is also specifically safeguarded by Articles 35(3) and 55 of AP I. The difference between this form of protection and the general protection as a civilian object is that the specific safeguard is absolute.[93] If

88 Yoram Dinstein, *The Conduct of the Hostilities Under the Law of International Armed Conflict* (Cambridge: Cambridge University Press 2004), 177; Droege, Tougas, 'The Protection of the Natural Environment' (n. 24), 79; Smith, 'Critical Perspectives on Environmental Protection' (n. 79), 773.

89 Smith, 'Critical Perspectives on Environmental Protection' (n. 79), 774.

90 Jérôme de Hemptinne, 'The Protection of Animals During Warfare', *American Journal of International Law Unbound* 111 (2017), 272–6, at 275.

91 ICRC, *Challenges of Contemporary Armed Conflicts* (n. 19), 68.

92 Ibid.

93 ICRC Customary Law Database, Rule 45; ICRC Environmental Guidelines, para. 49.

widespread, long-term, and severe damage is inflicted, an inquiry into whether this behaviour or result could be justified on the basis of military necessity or whether incidental damage was excessive is not necessary.[94] Moreover, the damage does not need to be intentional, as long as it is accepted and foreseeable.[95] It is precisely for these reasons that the expression 'widespread, long-term, and severe' sets such a high threshold.[96] When examining the scope of application of these provisions, we have however seen that this expression should be interpreted with flexibility, consistent with modern environmental concerns, values, and realities that derive from the standards imposed by numerous environmental instruments.

Finally, according to the ICRC Customary Law Database, 'all feasible precautions must be taken to avoid, and in any event to minimize, incidental damage to the environment',[97] including, for instance, avoiding locating military objectives within or near areas of high species richness – especially when these species are in danger – or clearly delineating and designating these areas as demilitarised zones before an armed conflict occurs.[98] Indeed, as recently noted by the ICRC,

> Hostilities may have particularly disastrous consequences when they occur in zones of major ecological importance or particular fragility. Taking all feasible precautions to protect the natural environment against the effects of attacks is therefore particularly pertinent for parties to conflicts who control territory featuring such areas; special consideration should be given to the protection of those parts of the natural environment that are especially vulnerable to the adverse consequences of hostilities. Such areas include groundwater aquifers, national parks and endangered species habitats. For example, the consequences of conflict in the Democratic Republic of the Congo on Virunga National Park, which contains some of the richest biodiversity in Africa, are well documented, and include the destruction of unique ecosystems and threats to species.[99]

This customary principle – which is envisaged as applying in both international and non-international armed conflicts[100] – is perfectly compatible with IHL if it were understood as an expression of the traditional obligation to take *precautionary* measures before undertaking military operations, as enshrined in Articles 57 and 58 of AP I. However, the ICRC reads such principle in a much more progressive and innovative manner, as encompassing the requirement to take *preventive* actions in order to avoid environmental damage. Indeed, it stated in this regard that '[l]ack of scientific certainty as to the effects on the environment of certain military operations does not absolve a party to the conflict from taking such precautions'.[101] This duty – which is

94 Ibid.
95 UNEP, Protecting the Environment (n. 59), 11.
96 ICRC Customary Law Database, Rule 45.
97 ICRC Customary Law Database, Rule 44.
98 See also ICRC Environmental Guidelines, paras. 144–6.
99 Ibid., para. 144.
100 Ibid.
101 Ibid. See also ICRC Environmental Guidelines, paras. 129–46.

currently only formally envisaged by IHL conventions when new weapons are tested[102] – has to be exercised with due regard to the fact that animals are no longer treated in most systems as inanimate objects, but as living beings experiencing pain and distress.[103] As we will see below, this ICRC approach once again illustrates the influence that IEL exercises over IHL when applying general principles governing the conduct of hostilities to the environment.[104]

3.2 *International Environmental Law*

There are many hundreds of environmental treaties currently in force. As shown above, their content and nature vary widely from one convention to the other. Some propose a sectorial approach which aim at protecting particular species or areas. Others are more holistic in nature: they focus not only on environmental protection and conservation, but more broadly on issues of common interest for humanity, such as sustainable development and the impact of climate change on ecosystems or biological diversity. Some are multilateral agreements; others are regional or bilateral treaties. These conventions have also to be read in conjunction with environmental soft law instruments.

It is beyond the scope of this section to study in detail these conventions and instruments. It is sufficient to note that they could all potentially play a role in increasing the protection and the conservation of wildlife. For that to happen, however, the concrete application of an IEL norm or principle must not be displaced by IHL. Yet, whether specific norms or principles coming from these two regimes apply simultaneously, or whether one of these norms or principles will prevail over the other remains unclear. Few legal articles and judgments have been devoted to this issue.[105] This can be explained by the fact that, a priori, these two special regimes do not overlap much and, thus, do not seem to contradict each other.[106] Being complementary and mutually reinforcing in many respects, they can both apply harmoniously without generating normative conflicts. Indeed, we have seen above that IHL contains rudimentary provisions on the environment. Beyond certain general principles governing the conduct of hostilities that potentially apply to natural resources and animals, and the few provisions that specifically protect them, IHL does not address any other environmental matters, for instance, those

102 See Art. 36 of AP I.

103 With regard to the distinction between precautionary measures and preventive actions, see Böhringer and Marauhn, Chapter 8, 'Endangered Species', this volume.

104 Sassòli, *International Humanitarian Law* (n. 68), 572–3.

105 See on this issue Mara Tignino, 'Droit international de l'environnement', in Raphael Van Steenberghe (ed.), *Droit international humanitaire: un régime spécial de droit international?* (Brussels: Bruylant 2013), 267–99, at 292–6; Jorge E. Viñuales, 'Le concept de "régime special" dans les rapports entre droit humanitaire et droit de l'environnement', *Research Paper* 12 (Geneva: The Graduate Institute Center for International Environmental Studies 2012), 1–20.

106 Tignino, 'Droit international de l'environnement' 2013 (n. 105), 292.

relating to the conservation and the preservation of wildlife. This lacuna offers much scope to IEL to fill the remaining gaps by playing a *complementary role*.

Moreover, IHL provisions and customary principles are themselves rather broad and vague. They allow an important amount of discretion on how to read and apply them concretely. In this respect, IEL could also play an *interpretative role* by giving a meaning and substance to these provisions and principles in order that they be read in accordance with fundamental environmental standards, as they progressively emerge from the numerous international conventions and soft law instruments adopted since 1977.[107] This means that, through a 'harmonious interpretation' or a 'systemic approach' (as enshrined in Article 31(3)(c) of the Vienna Convention on the Law of Treaties), relevant IHL provisions and principles could be interpreted and applied[108] by reference to the normative context, as provided by IEL, in which they operate.[109] All this should be done with a view to modernising old IHL norms and principles governing the conduct of hostilities with current environmental norms and fostering consistency and complementarity between these two bodies of law. Such an approach, based on the principle of 'mutual supportiveness'[110] or the principle of 'harmonisation', could lead to a form of 'environmentalisation' of warfare and IHL through the application of reasonable standards drawn from IEL, in light of contemporary concerns expressed by most states about the protection and the conservation of the fauna and flora.

Two observations must be made regarding this suggested approach. First, as recalled above, when IEL plays a complementary role, a normative conflict between specific norms belonging to IEL and to IHL could occur in practice. As recently noted by the ICRC, '[the] potential incompatibility between a rule of international environmental law and IHL must be considered on a rule-by-rule basis, but where a rule of international environmental law is more protective of the natural environment than the parallel rule of IHL, this difference should be interpreted as incompatibility only if there are clear reasons for doing so'.[111] If such an incompatibility between specific norms were to arise in practice, one would have to determine which norm concretely displaces the other, because it 'is either more precise or has ... a narrower material or personal scope of

107 Viñuales, 'Le concept de régime spécial' (n. 105), 13.

108 This approach seems to be endorsed by the ICJ when stating that: 'while the existing international law relating to the protection and the safeguarding of the environment does not specifically prohibit the use of nuclear weapons, it indicates important environmental factors that are properly to be taken into account in the context of the implementation of the principles and rules of the law applicable in armed conflict' (ICJ, *Legality of the Threat or Use of Nuclear Weapons*, advisory opinion of 8 July 1996, ICJ Reports 1996, para. 33).

109 Viñuales, 'Le concept de régime spécial' (n. 105), 14; Tignino, 'Droit international de l'environnement' (n. 105), 293.

110 See, in this regard, Riccardo Pavoni, 'Mutual Supportiveness as a Principe of Interpretation and Law-Making: A Watershed for the "WTO-and-Competing-Regimes" Debate?', *European Journal of International Law* 21 (2010), 649–79.

111 ICRC Environmental Guidelines, para. 33.

application'.[112] This determination should be made on a case-by-case basis in function of the norms and the concrete factual situation at stake.[113] However, we have already stated that, in many instances, IEL will be the only applicable regime because of its inherent aptitude to regulate precisely and explicitly matters relating to the conservation and preservation of the environment and, in particular, wildlife and certain protected species, on which IHL remains silent. In this case, there will not be any normative conflict strictly speaking. In other concrete situations, the application of a specific rule governing the conduct of hostilities might not be compatible with the application of an IEL principle or norm that is not adjusted to the needs of warfare and that does not take into consideration military imperatives.

Second, our understanding of the natural system, including wildlife, and of its relationship with human beings, has been constantly advancing over the last decades. Accordingly, IEL has evolved rapidly and continues to do so. Such constant transformation does not aid in identifying concrete and firm environmental standards that can serve as stable points of reference and, ultimately, that can be applied and respected by belligerents. It has however been shown above that certain IHL principles, such as the principles of distinction and proportionality, the notion of 'environment' itself, the 'long-term, widespread, and severe damage' criteria, or the concept of precautionary measures can be 'tainted' by widely recognised IEL standards in such a way that the laws of armed conflicts can be adjusted to – or interpreted in light of – modern environmental challenges, including those affecting animals.

4 LEGAL CONSEQUENCES OF VIOLATIONS OF THE LEGAL REGIMES PROTECTING THE ENVIRONMENT

In its Draft Principles on Protection of the Environment in Relation to Armed Conflicts, the ILC acknowledges that, under the existing rules of international law on responsibility and liability of states, states shall incur responsibility for their internationally wrongful acts, in relation to an armed conflict, that cause damage to the environment.[114] It further underlines that '[w]hen the source of environmental damage in armed conflict is unidentified, or reparation from the liable party unavailable, states should take appropriate measures to ensure that the damage does not remain unrepaired or uncompensated'.[115] In this regard, the ILC proposes pragmatic solutions, such as establishing special compensation funds or other mechanisms of collective reparation for that purpose,[116] in light of the UN

112 Sassòli, *International Humanitarian Law* (n. 68), 439.
113 Ibid.
114 Principle 13 *quater* of the ILC Draft Principles on the Protection of the Environment in Relation to Armed Conflicts (n. 46).
115 Ibid.
116 Ibid.

Compensation Commission established in the aftermath of the Iraqi invasion and occupation of Kuwait in the early 1990s. The ILC further considers that damage to the ecosystem services should be considered in reparation measures.[117]

Despite the rise of ecological concerns, neither IHL nor international criminal law is equipped to deal with the criminal responsibility of those who violate the fundamental norms governing the protection of the environment per se.[118] Indeed, under IHL, violations of Articles 35 and 55 of AP I do not constitute grave breaches. Nonetheless, it should be noted that other criminal acts that may cause environmental harm – such as launching indiscriminate attacks affecting the civilian population or civilian objects[119] – fall under the 'grave breaches regime'. Moreover, as we know, neither common Article 3 of the GCs, nor AP II, contain any provisions on grave breaches.

It is true that, in the context of international armed conflicts, launching an attack with the knowledge that such attack will cause widespread, long-term, and severe damage to the natural environment is increasingly recognised as constituting a war crime.[120] However, the International Criminal Court (ICC) Statute – which, for the first time, criminalises this act – is particularly restrictive in this regard.[121] For instance, it requires that such an attack be 'clearly excessive in relation to the concrete and direct military advantage anticipated'. Needless to say, this requirement is at odds with the texts of Articles 35(3) and 55 of AP I, which, as noted previously, are not conditioned by a proportionality test. Should the widespread, long-term, and severe criteria be met, these provisions will be automatically breached even if the military operation is 'clearly proportional'.[122] Moreover, reflecting IHL, the ICC Statute does not extend this prohibition to non-international armed conflicts, which is a serious omission. Finally, it should be emphasised that, despite numerous attempts to make ecocide an international crime under the ICC jurisdiction,[123] criminal actions conducted against the environment to date have not formally been listed in the statutes of international courts and tribunals as among the underlying criminal conducts that may constitute crimes against humanity or acts of genocide.

5 CONCLUDING RECOMMENDATIONS

In light of the above analysis, the following fourteen general guidelines are proposed. First, animals should be protected, not only directly and individually as civilian

117 Ibid.

118 For a general analysis of this question, see UNEP, Protecting the Environment (n. 59), 29–33.

119 Art. 85(3)(b) of AP I.

120 UNEP, Protecting the Environment (n. 59), 30.

121 Art. 8(2)(b)(iv) of ICC Statute.

122 Dinstein, 'Protection of the Environment' (n. 30), 536.

123 See Anastacia Greene, 'The Campaign to Make Ecocide an International Crime: Quixotic Quest or Moral Imperative?', *Fordham Environmental Law Review* 30 (2019), 1–48.

objects or as properties, but also indirectly and globally as general components of the environment in which they live. Second, the conditions of application of Articles 35(3) and 55 of AP I, which protect the environment and wildlife per se, should be read with flexibility in order to accommodate progressively emerging environmental standards. Third, the protection of the environment should transcend territorial and political boundaries in order to apply, in the same manner, both in international and non-international armed conflicts. Fourth, during wartime, animals should benefit from the protections offered by a growing number of multilateral conventions, as well as by fundamental customary principles which ensure conservation and protection of the environment in peacetime. Fifth, environmental conventions should be presumed to apply during armed conflict provided that their obligations are consistent with IHL. Sixth, fundamental provisions of IEL should be deemed to bind armed groups which control part of the national territory and exercise quasi-governmental functions. Seventh, fundamental provisions of IEL should apply extraterritorially when the natural resources concerned – including certain zones or areas in which animals are located – are placed under the effective control of belligerents. Eighth, wildlife should never be considered, as such, a military objective by nature, use, or purpose. Ninth, animals could become a legitimate target of a military attack conducted against the environment in which they are situated as long as the attack does not create excessive collateral damage. Tenth, the environment and wildlife should carry a heavy weight in the proportionality calculation that reflects the increasing importance attached to these elements in modern societies. Eleventh, IEL should play a complementary role in filling gaps left by IHL where it does not provide for a comprehensive regime of protection and conservation of the environment and wildlife in armed conflicts. Twelfth, environmental standards, as they emerge from international conventions and the practice of states, should serve as points of reference when interpreting unclear IHL provisions and principles. Thirteenth, the restrictive standards imposed by the ICC provisions protecting the environment should not be considered as reflective of customary international law and should therefore not be reproduced in other international instruments. Fourteenth, the criminalisation of acts committed against the environment per se in non-international armed conflicts should be recognised.

SELECT BIBLIOGRAPHY

Bothe, Michael et al., 'International Law Protecting the Environment During Armed Conflict: Gaps and Opportunities', *International Review of the Red Cross* 92 (2010), 569–92.

Dinstein, Yoran, 'Protection of the Environment in International Armed Conflict', *Max Planck Yearbook of United Nations Law* 5 (2001), 523–49.

Droege, Cordula and Marie-Louise Tougas, 'The Protection of the Natural Environment in Armed Conflict: Existing Rules and Need for Further Legal Protection', *Nordic Journal of International Law* 82 (2013), 21–52.

Montaz, Djamchid, 'Les règles relatives à la protection de l'environnement au cours des conflits armés à l'épreuve du conflit entre l'Irak et le Koweït', *Annuaire français de droit inernational* XXXVII (1991), 203–19.
Sands, Philippe and Jacqueline Peel, *Principles of International Environmental Law* (Cambridge: Cambridge University Press 2018).
Schmitt, Michael, 'Green War: An Assessment of the Environmental Law of Armed Conflict', *Yale Law Journal* 22 (1997), 1–110.
Smith, Tara, 'Critical Perspectives on Environmental Protection in Non-International Armed Conflict: Developing the Principles of Distinction, Proportionality and Necessity', *Leiden Journal of International Law* 32 (2019), 759–79.
Tignino, Mara, 'Droit international de l'environnement', in Raphael Van Steenberghe (ed.), *Droit international humanitaire: un régime spécial de droit international?* (Brussels: Bruylant 2013), 267–99.
Tremblay-Huet, Sabrina, 'Should Environmental Law Learn from Animal Law? Compassion as a Guiding Principle for International Environmental Law Instead of Sustainable Development', *Revue québécoise de droit international* 1–1 (2018), 125–44.
Viñuales, Jorge E., 'Le concept de "régime special" dans les rapports entre droit humanitaire et droit de l'environnement', *Research Paper* 12 (Geneva: The Graduate Institute Center for International Environmental Studies 2012), 1–20.
Vordermayer, Markus, 'The Extraterritorial Application of Multilateral Environmental Agreements', *Harvard International Law* Review 59 (2018), 60–124.

8

Animals as Endangered Species

Ayşe-Martina Böhringer and Thilo Marauhn

1 INTRODUCTION

'Endangered species' may be a politico-ethical label, a descriptive, extra-legal notion or a precisely defined concept. This depends on the context to which it is applied. Its normative power results mainly from other factors than the law. There is no proper treatment of the notion of endangered species in international law. One might expect it to be included among the definitions of a treaty referring thereto in its name, the Convention on International Trade in Endangered Species of Wild Fauna and Flora (CITES). However, Article I of the CITES does not. Indeed, the term is only taken up by Article II(1) of the CITES, the second sentence of which reads: 'Trade in specimens of these species must be subject to particularly strict regulation in order not to *endanger* further their survival and must only be authorized in exceptional circumstances.'[1] It can be taken from this provision that the verb 'to endanger' points to the rationale of the provision, even of the treaty as a whole, which aims at 'not to endanger ... [the] survival' of species protected by the convention. It is noteworthy that the primary objective of the CITES is not explicitly stated in the convention, it must be taken from Article II(1) of the CITES by way of interpretation.[2]

At first sight the protection of species from extinction, and measures taken to ensure the survival of species, suggest the inclusion of a broad range of threats and the adoption of a variety of approaches to protect endangered species. Such prima facie considerations invite creative thinking in the context of efforts to enhance the protection of animals in wartime. As the editors point out in their introductory chapter, the notion of endangered species might form part of an 'inventory of the international legal framework available for the protection of animals in armed conflicts'.[3] It could allow insights into the link between the form of protection and

[1] Emphasis added.

[2] On CITES, see Rosalind Reeve, 'Wildlife Trade, Sanctions and Compliance: Lessons from the CITES Regime', *International Affairs* 82 (2006), 881–97.

[3] See Peters and de Heptinne, Chapter 1, 'Wartime'.

specific characteristics of animals.[4] The notion might even be integrated into international humanitarian law (IHL), as the editors suggest.[5]

This chapter will raise the question to what extent the peacetime labelling of animals as endangered species can be relevant in times of armed conflict, whether international or non-international. This requires stocktaking of such peacetime labelling as well as illustrating the relevance of categorising animals as endangered species in international environmental law (IEL) (Section 2). Subsequently, we will provide an analysis of the applicability of pertinent treaties during hostilities and raise the question to what extent the notion and the regulatory approaches to their protection can be made use of to protect animals in wartime (Section 3). This chapter will then briefly discuss the consequences that may flow from the violation of the principles established previously (Section 4). This will be followed by recommendations (Section 5).

2 THE CONCEPT OF ENDANGERED SPECIES

The notion 'endangered species' has been developed in the context of peacetime IEL. The assumption of its relevance for the legal protection of animals in times of armed conflict necessitates a closer analysis of its background and legal implications before reflecting upon its transferability to IHL. The International Union for the Conservation of Nature and Natural Resources' (IUCN's) central role for the development of the endangered species concept[6] invites considerations of the organisation's international law status and of the so-called Red List for Threatened Species™ (Red List),[7] in particular its making, normative quality, and overall regulatory impact on the conservation of nature.

2.1 *The International Union's Role in Conceptualising Endangered Species*

For its part, the IUCN has played a decisive role in fostering the concept of 'endangered species'. Its predecessor, the International Union for the Protection of Nature (IUPN) was formally established in 1948 in the framework of an international conference dedicated to the protection of species and their habitats.[8] The IUPN's work was characterised by a combination of risk assessment through technical

4 Ibid.

5 Ibid.

6 With regard to the term 'concept', see Thilo Marauhn, 'General Principles and Fragmentation of International Environmental Law', in Peter Reiff et al. (eds.), *Protecting the Environment for Future Generations: Principles and Actors in International Environmental Law* (Berlin: Erich Schmidt Verlag 2017), 79–88.

7 The current version (2012) is available at www.iucnredlist.org/resources/categories-and-criteria, accessed 22 February 2022.

8 Charles J. Bernard, International Union for the Protection of Nature, established at Fontainebleau 5 October 1948 (IUCN Library: Brussels 1948), 17.

meetings based on scientific data and the presentation of problem solving strategies.[9] It was the first institutionalised attempt at the international level to bring nature conservation into the global focus.[10] The IUPN's initial aim was the preservation of mammals as can easily be taken from its first Red Data Book of 1960 which presented a compilation of more than 130 endangered mammals.[11] In 1956, in the course of 'a public relations exercise',[12] the organisation was renamed in response to tensions between conservationist and preservationist approaches.[13]

The IUCN is neither a traditional international organisation nor a typical non-governmental organisation (NGO). It displays unique features by bringing together governments and non-governmental actors.[14] What emerges from its statutes[15] is that the IUCN enjoys legal personality under Swiss national law. It has four categories of members,[16] including, among others, states as well as NGOs. Organs of the IUCN include the World Conservation Congress; the council; the national and regional committees, and regional fora of members; the commissions; and the secretariat.[17] Among the most important functions assigned to the World Congress are its powers 'to define the general policy of IUCN' and 'to make recommendations to governments and to national and international organisations in any matter related to the objectives of IUCN'.[18] The central role of governments is reflected in the decision-making process of the World Conservation Congress which separates votes by governments from votes by other members.[19]

The IUCN commissions are 'networks of expert volunteers'[20] and they are tasked, among others, to 'analyse issues ... and undertake research ... [and] to provide

9 IUCN, Annual Report of the International Union for Conservation of Nature and Natural Resources for 1973 (Morges, Switzerland 1974), 24.

10 Charlotte Epstein, 'The Making of Global Environmental Norm: Endangered Species Protection', *Global Environmental Politics* 6 (2006), 32–54, at 38.

11 Ibid.

12 Alan Brouder, 'International Union for Conservation of Nature', in Christian Tietje and Alan Brouder (eds.), *Handbook of Transnational Economic Governance Regimes* (Leiden and Boston: Martinus Nijhoff 2009), 953–68, at 954.

13 Epstein, 'The Making of Global Environmental Norm' (n. 10), 38. Modern multilateral environmental agreements which follow a conservationist approach are mainly concerned with 'the "utilization," "rational use," and "management", of natural resources for human benefit. Utilization and rational use clearly reinforce the notion that nature and wild animals are mere resources for human use' (references omitted) (Joan E. Schaffner, 'Value, Wild Animals and Law', in Werner Scholtz (ed.), *Animal Welfare and International Environmental Law: From Conservation to Compassion* (Cheltenham: Edward Elgar 2019), 8–37, at 30, referring to P. van Heijnsbergen, International Legal Protection of Wild Fauna and Flora (Amsterdam: IOS Press 1997).

14 Leif E. Christoffersen, 'IUCN: A Bridge-Builder for Nature Conservation', *Green Globe Yearbook* (1997), 59–70, at 63.

15 See Statutes of World Conservation Congress of 5 October 1948 last amended on 27 September 2016, available at https://bit.ly/3HRmsER, accessed 22 February 2022.

16 Ibid., Part III, para. 4.

17 Ibid., Part IV, para. 15.

18 Ibid., Part V, para. 20.

19 Ibid., Part V, paras. 30–5 and Rules of Procedure of the World Conservation Congress, Part VIII.

20 Ibid., Part VIII, para. 73.

advice on any matter within their fields of competence'.[21] Currently the IUCN benefits from the input of more than 15,000 experts.[22] Among the six commissions operating within the IUCN is the Species Survival Commission with its own mandate and bylaws.[23] Its task 'is to provide information . . . on biodiversity conservation, the inherent value of species, their role in ecosystem health and functioning, the provision of ecosystem services, and their support to human livelihoods. This information is fed into The IUCN Red List of Threatened Species'.[24] Under the bylaws, a group of people called the 'Red List Authority' is charged with implementing Red Listing activities on behalf of the commission and a steering committee is responsible for reviewing, adopting or amending the 'Rules of Procedure for IUCN Red List Assessments'.[25]

The IUCN has provided states with a forum for inclusive law-making, building upon the independent expertise of its networks and participation of civil society. The treaties, facilitated by the IUCN include the CITES,[26] the World Heritage Convention,[27] the Ramsar Convention,[28] the Convention on Migratory Species,[29] the Convention on Biological Diversity,[30] and the Polar Bear Agreement.[31] The IUCN also promoted the law of the sea.[32] The IUCN has emerged 'to a global union', a development which 'mirrors a growing social concern for the health of

21 Ibid., Part VIII, para. 75.

22 https://www.iucn.org/about, accessed 22 February 2022.

23 Further resources on this available at www.iucn.org/species/about/species-survival-commission, accessed 22 February 2022.

24 Ibid. Further details can be taken from the Species Survival Commission's mandate and bylaws.

25 See IUCN 2016, Rules of Procedure for IUCN Red List Assessments 2017–2020, Version 3.0, Approved by the IUCN Species Survival Commission Steering Committee in September 2016.

26 See, among others, Fazeela Ahmed Shaheem, 'Effectiveness of CITES: Analysis in Relation to National Implementing Legislation', in Melissa Lewis, Tuula Honkonen, and Seita Romppanen (eds.), *International Environmental Law-Making and Diplomacy Review* (Helsinki: University of Eastern Finland 2017), 121–31, at 123–5; Peter Sand, 'Whither CITES? The Evolution of a Treaty Regime in the Borderland of Trade and Environment', *EJIL* 8 (1997), 29–58, at 33–4.

27 Christina Cameron and Mechtild Rössler, *Many Voices, One Vision: The Early Years of the World Heritage Convention* (Farnham: Ashgate 2013), 2–11.

28 Convention on Wetlands of International Importance Especially as Waterfowl Habitat of 2 February 1971, 996 UNTS 245. See also Nicholas A. Robinson, 'Biodiversity in International Environmental Law Through the UN Sustainable Development Goals' in Charles R. McManis and Burton Ong (eds.), *Routledge Handbook of Biodiversity and the Law* (London: Routledge 2017), 27–41, at 33.

29 Convention on the Conservation of Migratory Species of Wild Animals of 23 June 1979, 1651 UNTS 333. IUCN, 13th Extraordinary General Assembly, 1977, 81; IUCN, 14th Session of the General Assembly, 1978, 97.

30 1760 UNTS 79. IUCN General Assembly Resolution 15/10 (adopted 1981 in Christchurch at its 15th Session).

31 Agreement on the Conservation of Polar Bears of 15 November 1973, 2898 UNTS 243; IUCN, 11th General Assembly, 1972, 102.

32 A Review of the Impact of IUCN Resolutions on International Conservation Efforts, 7, available at www.iucn.org/downloads/resolutions_eng_web.pdf, accessed 22 February 2022.

humans and nature within the biosphere'.[33] While not treaty-based, a lot of the above suggests that IUCN rather than being an NGO, meanwhile enjoys limited international legal personality.[34]

2.2 *Normative Power of the Concept of Endangered Species*

It does not automatically follow from the above considerations that the Red List possesses legal significance under international law. While many perceive endangered species as a legal concept, in principle, it continues to be an extra-legal notion with only limited legal implications. Nevertheless, and as will be shown in the following, the Red List displays a degree of normative power.

The Red List is a comprehensive inventory of biological species, providing information on their conservation status by using specific criteria to evaluate their extinction risk. It has been described as 'the "mother" of all threatened species lists, the first and most comprehensive attempt at the global listing of all threatened species'.[35] Indeed, the making of the list typically is a natural science exercise, but there are legal and political aspects to it. Over time it 'has evolved from a subjective expert-based system lacking standardized criteria to a uniform and global rule-based system'.[36] The Red List operates on a particular set of criteria, scientifically based. It is applied to all species and regions around the globe. The objective of the list 'is to produce a relative estimate of the likelihood of extinction of a taxon' and the listing process pursues a pragmatic approach based on criteria which determine the level of threat and at the same time it must live with remaining scientific uncertainties.[37] Currently, the Red List classifies taxa into nine categories: Extinct, Extinct in the Wild, Critically Endangered, Endangered,[38] Vulnerable – the last three categories are also characterised as 'Threatened' –, [39] Near Threatened, Least Concern, Data Deficient, and Not Evaluated.[40]

The relevant level of protection for any of such listed species derives from the specific threat to which a multilateral environmental agreement (MEA) refers.

33 Nicholas A. Robinson, 'IUCN as Catalyst for a Law of the Biosphere: Acting Globally and Locally', *Environmental Law* 35 (2005), 249–310, at 307.

34 Ibid., 298–307, referring to Brownlie, Amerasinghe, and others.

35 Irus Braverman, 'The Regulatory Life of Threatened Species Lists', in Irus Braverman (ed.), *Animals, Biopolitics, Law: Lively Legalities* (Abingdon: Routledge 2016), 19–38, at 20.

36 Ibid., 22.

37 Peter-John Meynell, 'Use of IUCN Red Listing Process as a Basis for Assessing Biodiversity Threats and Impacts in Environmental Impact Assessment', *Impact Assessment and Project Appraisal* 23 (2005), 65–72, at 66.

38 According to the IUCN Standards and Petitions Committee (Guidelines for Using the IUCN Red List Categories and Criteria (Version 14, August 2019), 11) a species 'is Endangered when the best available evidence indicates that it meets any of the criteria A to E for Endangered, and it is therefore considered to be facing a very high risk of extinction in the wild'.

39 Ibid., 10.

40 Ibid., 11.

Every species-based MEA follows a different regulatory approach and they vary in terms of their object and purpose.[41] While some of them are rather broad in scope,[42] others focus on particular species,[43] address selected groups of species,[44] their habitats,[45] or practices that are harmful to them.[46] The Red List is instrumental to this end. Thus, Article 7 of the Convention on Biological Diversity requires states parties to identify and monitor 'threatened species' as part of biodiversity components which are important with regard to their conservation. Furthermore, the convention addresses threatened species in several of its work programmes and recognises the red list indices' complementary role in quantifying global trends in the status of biodiversity.[47] The CITES,[48] the Convention on Migratory Species,[49] the Ramsar Convention,[50] and the Protocol concerning Specially Protected Areas

41 See Erika J. Techera, 'Species-Based Conservation', in Elisa Morgera and Jona Razzaque (eds.), *Biodiversity and Nature Protection Law* (Cheltenham: Edward Elgar 2017), 97–109.

42 Convention for the Protection of the Mediterranean Sea against Pollution (Barcelona Convention) of 16 February 1976, 1102 UNTS 27, amended and renamed as the Convention for the Protection of the Marine Environment and the Coastal Region of the Mediterranean of 10 June 1995; UN Convention on the Law of the Sea (UNCLOS) of 10 December 1982, 1833 UNTS 397; Convention for the Protection and Development of the Marine Environment of the Wider Caribbean Region of 24 March 1983 (Cartagena Convention), 1506 UNTS 157; Convention on Biological Diversity of 5 June 1992, 1760 UNTS 79; African Convention on the Conservation of Nature and Natural Resources of 15 September 1968, 1001 UNTS 3, revised on 11 July 2003 and on 7 March 2017.

43 For example African-Eurasian Waterbirds Agreement of 15 August 1996, 2365 UNTS 203; Agreement on the Conservation of Cetaceans in the Black Sea, Mediterranean Sea and Contiguous Atlantic Area of 24 November 1996, 2183 UNTS 303; Agreement on the Conservation of Albatrosses and Petrels of 19 June 2001, 2258 UNTS 257 (all three of them are implementing agreements to the Convention on Migratory Species (n. 29)); Polar Bear Agreement (n. 31); International Convention on the Regulation of Whaling of 2 December 1946, 161 UNTS 72.

44 For instance, the Convention on Migratory Species (n. 29).

45 Such as the Ramsar Convention (n. 28); Protocol concerning Specially Protected Areas and Biological Diversity in the Mediterranean of 10 June 1995, 2102 UNTS 203 (which is a protocol to the Barcelona Convention); Specially Protected Areas and Wildlife Protocol of 18 January 1990, 2180 UNTS 101 (which is a protocol to the Cartagena Convention (n. 42)).

46 For example CITES.

47 UNEP/CBD/AHTEG-2010-Ind/1/INF/9 (7 October 2004), Ad Hoc Technical Expert Group on Indicators for Assessing Progress Towards the 2010 Biodiversity Target, 'Indicators for Assessing Progress Towards the 2010 Target: Change in Status of Threatened Species', 2. See also IUCN World Conservation Congress, 17–25 November 2004, Resolution 3.013: The uses of the IUCN Red List of Threatened Species, referring to the Convention on Biological Diversity (n. 42) documents.

48 See, for example, Decision 16.104 (2013), 27: 'The Animals Committee shall, at its 27th meeting, consider the final IUCN red list assessments for Asian snake species and, if available, incorporate new information and data and make appropriate recommendations, including recommendations to the Standing Committee.'

49 Resolution 11.33 (Rev.COP12) (2017), Annex 1, 3: 'The IUCN Red List Categories and Criteria (Version 3.1, second edition) should be used as suggested below in assessing proposals to list migratory species on Appendices I and II . . . '.

50 Resolution VII.11 (1999), 7: 'To include in the Ramsar List wetlands that include threatened ecological communities or are critical to the survival of endemic species identified as vulnerable, endangered or critically endangered under national endangered species legislation/programs or international designations such as the IUCN Red List . . . '.

and Biological Diversity in the Mediterranean[51] take into consideration IUCN assessments for updating their own scientific assessments with regard to species listing, sometimes, they also deviate from the Red List.[52] It follows from these examples that, notwithstanding its non-binding nature, the Red List serves as a key reference point by providing actors with specific guidelines which 'simplify … complex problems'[53] in the development of policy and/or legal measures and influences their nature conservation measures with regard to species protection to a considerable extent – possibly just due to its alleged apolitical character.[54]

The Red List is part of biopolitical and regulatory technologies (re)producing 'underlying species ontologies by creating, calculating, and governing the boundary between the human and the nonhuman'.[55] Although the Red List may be seen as a 'uniform and global rule-based system',[56] nevertheless, its benefits can also be countered by some limitations. Given the diversity of policy objectives and users, the consequences drawn from such a list may be highly variable and may differ from the original purpose.[57] As regards the utilisation of a threatened species list to limit environmental degradation it would be naïve to rely upon such a list in itself; the list only represents a partial view of environmental components including non-listed species,[58] and it should not be used as a surrogate of biodiversity.[59] Additional criticism against overestimating the list follows from its top down, selective, and narrow approach, the requirement of regularly updating its content, and its unpredictability in the long run. Heterogeneous treatment of the concept within MEAs adds to uncertainties.[60] Beyond the CITES, the Convention on Migratory Species defines it in its Article I(1)(e) as a species '[which] is in danger of extinction throughout all or a significant portion of its range'. In 2014, its Conference of the Parties decided to interpret the term as 'facing a very high risk of extinction in the wild in the near future' and highlighted that coherence with actions 'in other

[51] Decision IG 17/14 (2008), 319: 'The IUCN Red List categories and criteria developed for assessing the conservation status of species are used by most international conventions. It is recommended that they be used for assessing the status of species when examining proposals for amending Annexes II and III of the Protocol' (reference omitted).

[52] Arie Trouwborst et al., 'International Law and Lions (*Panthera Leo*): Understanding and Improving the Contribution of Wildlife Treaties to the Conservation and Sustainable Use of an Iconic Carnivore', *Nature Conservation* 21 (2017), 83–128, at 110.

[53] Hugh P. Possingham et al., 'Limits to the Use of Threatened Species Lists', *Trends in Ecology and Evolution* 17 (2002), 503–7, at 504.

[54] Braverman, 'The Regulatory Life' (n. 35), 22. Concerning the role of such lists in general, see Augustín García-Ureta, 'Nature Conservation' in Emma Lees and Jorge E. Viñuales (eds.), *The Oxford Handbook of Comparative Environmental Law* (Oxford: Oxford University Press 2019), 460–88, at 478.

[55] Braverman, 'The Regulatory Life' (n. 35), 21.

[56] Ibid., 22 with further references.

[57] Possingham, 'Limits to the Use' (n. 53), 503.

[58] Ibid., 504–5.

[59] Ibid., 504.

[60] Heijnsbergen, 'Legal Protection' (n. 13), 95–124.

multilateral fora should be considered'.[61] The Specially Protected Areas and Wildlife Protocol, restricted to the Wider Caribbean region, uses the term 'endangered' as well as 'threatened' (among others Article 1(f)[62] and (g)[63]). The African-Eurasian Waterbirds Agreement applies, *mutatis mutandis*, the Convention on Migratory Species definitions,[64] and the African Convention addresses 'threatened species' meaning 'any species of fauna ... which is considered critically endangered, or vulnerable' (Article V(5)).

Beyond its usage in treaty law, its normative value derives from the assessment 'endangered', which follows from the Red List being part of global administrative law.[65]

2.3 *Endangered Species in Armed Conflict Situations: Conceptual Issues*

As can be taken from the above analysis, the concept oscillates between descriptive and normative elements of categorisation. Science and data-based, it is an important tool to single out a particular segment of the environment, not on the basis of its natural characteristics, but on the basis of an empirical analysis allowing the prognosis that the species concerned are under a threat of extinction. In doing so, it establishes the basis for an ecological imperative:[66] to protect species and prevent their extinction. However, this imperative needs to be translated into precise obligations – a step taken by a broad variety of pertinent MEAs. Hence, in peacetime IEL the concept of endangered species is an intermediate element or a hinge between the problem identified and the measures to be adopted.

Transferring this concept into IHL necessitates a critical reflection about entry points since the concept of endangered species as such is unknown to the law of armed conflict.[67] International humanitarian law does not include any explicit rule addressing the protection of endangered species.

61 UNEP/CMS/Resolution 11.33, para. 1 and Annex, para. 5.

62 '"Endangered species" are species or sub-species of fauna and flora, or their populations, that are in danger of extinction throughout all or part of their range and whose survival is unlikely if the factors jeopardizing them continue to operate.'

63 '"Threatened species" are species or sub-species of fauna and flora, or their populations: i) that are likely to become endangered within the foreseeable future throughout all or part of their range if the factors causing numerical decline or habitat degradation continue to operate; ... '.

64 See Art. I(2), last sentence.

65 See in general Ingo Venzke, 'International Bureaucracies from a Political Science Perspective: Agency, Authority and International Institutional Law', in Armin v. Bogdandy et al. (eds.), *The Exercise of Public Authority by International Institutions: Advancing International Institutional Law* (Heidelberg: Springer 2010), 67–99, at 83.

66 Hans Jonas, *The Imperative of Responsibility* (London: The University of Chicago Press 1984), 185, for instance.

67 This is also the case with the concept of 'biodiversity'. Regarding the latter, see Karen Hulme, 'Armed Conflict and Biodiversity', in Michael Bowman, Peter Davies, and Edward Goodwin (eds.), *Research Handbook on Biodiversity and Law* (Cheltenham: Edward Elgar 2016), 245–69, at 249.

To begin with, in line with doctrine and state practice, MEAs explicitly or implicitly referring to endangered species largely continue to be relevant in times of armed conflict.[68] Furthermore, endangered species are 'common goods', which would be irretrievably lost in the event of their extinction.[69] This means their protection cannot be ignored in times of armed conflict. Indeed, they require adequate protection in times of armed conflict, and it should be recalled that the main purpose of the MEAs mentioned is the protection of common goods.[70]

On the other hand, such relevance does not automatically entail their full applicability as between the parties to a conflict. It must be borne in mind that protection of endangered species in peacetime is not absolute, either. Qualifying clauses in peacetime treaties, such as 'as far as possible and as appropriate' (Article 8 of the Convention on Biological Diversity), play a distinct role when adapting peacetime concepts to situations of armed conflict even if the peacetime treaties remain applicable. The International Court of Justice (ICJ) stated in the advisory opinion on the *Legality of the Threat or Use of Nuclear Weapons*:

> the Court is of the view that the issue is not whether the treaties relating to the protection of the environment are or are not applicable during an armed conflict, but rather whether the obligations stemming from these treaties were intended to be obligations of total restraint during military conflict. . . . States must take environmental considerations into account when assessing what is necessary and proportionate in the pursuit of legitimate military objectives.[71]

68 See ILC, Effects of Armed Conflicts on Treaties. Titles and texts of the draft articles on the effects of armed conflicts on treaties adopted by the drafting Committee on second reading, 11 May 2011, A/CN.4/L.777, Art. 3. As regards theories concerning the applicability of MEAs in armed conflict, see Michael Bothe et al., 'International Law Protecting the Environment During Armed Conflict: Gaps and Opportunities', *International Review of the Red Cross* 92 (2010), 569–92, at 587–8; Silja Vöneky, 'A New Shield for the Environment: Peacetime Treaties as Legal Restraints of Wartime Damage', *Review of European, Comparative & International Environmental Law* 9 (2000), 20–32, at 27; Michael N. Schmitt, 'Green War: An Assessment of the Environmental Law of International Armed Conflict', *Yale Journal of International Law* 22 (1997), 1–110, at 38. The ILC has incorporated these theories in its draft articles to a considerable degree which, due to the lack of a clear consensus among states or in legal discourse on this issue, can only be understood as a 'policy proposal'. See Adrian Loets, 'An Old Debate Revisited: Applicability of Environmental Treaties in Times of International Armed Conflict Pursuant to the International Law Commission's "Draft Articles on the Effects of Armed Conflict on Treaties"', *Review of European, Comparative & International Environmental Law* 21 (2012), 127–36, at 133; Bothe et al., 'International Law Protecting the Environment' (n. 68), 588.

69 Ulrich Beyerlin and Thilo Marauhn, *Abrüstung und Umweltschutz: eine völkerrechtliche Interessenkollision? Disarmament and Environmental Protection: Conflicting Interests in Public International Law?* (Bochum: Dr. N. Brockmeyer 1994), 78–9. With regard to similar terms, see Rüdiger Wolfrum, 'Common Heritage of Mankind', in Anne Peters and Rüdiger Wolfrum (eds.), *Max Planck Encyclopedia of Public International Law* (online edition), 2009, para. 9, available at: www.mpepil.com.

70 See the preamble of CITES: 'wild fauna and flora in their many beautiful and varied forms are an irreplaceable part of the natural systems of the earth which must be protected for this and the generations to come'; Vöneky (n. 68), 28–9.

71 ICJ, *Legality of the Threat or Use of Nuclear Weapons*, advisory opinion of 8 July 1996, ICJ Reports 1996, para. 30.

Hence, peacetime standards protecting endangered species need to be adapted in light of their interaction with IHL norms.[72] By way of example, considerations of military necessity,[73] forming an inherent part of IHL, are thus not precluded but continue to apply, and may have to be read together with the above-mentioned qualifyers of MEAs. In the end, integrating peacetime protection of endangered species into IHL is largely an interpretative effort, which will now be discussed in more detail.

3 ENDANGERED SPECIES AND INTERNATIONAL HUMANITARIAN LAW

The protection of natural resources in times of armed conflict continues to be discussed in a twofold perspective: first, the applicability of peacetime MEAs in times of armed conflict,[74] and, second, the identification of specific IHL rules focusing on the environment.[75] Both perspectives may facilitate answering this chapter's core question whether, how, and to what extent the concept of endangered species can be referred to in situations of armed conflict. Established interpretation, application by analogy, and the determination of customary law may serve as tools to this end. While established interpretation does not necessitate preliminary remarks, reasoning by analogy may be particularly promising in the context of legal uncertainties.[76] Transferability is an issue here, and this requires reassurance of the object and purpose of IHL as such. The aim of IHL is to protect the victims of armed conflict and to this end it seeks to balance military necessity and humanity. Environmental protection, and the protection of animals, are not the ultimate objective of IHL rules. They largely unfold a reflexive protection primarily guided by the intention to prevent indirect harm to humans involved in armed conflicts.[77] Even the International Committee of the Red Cross (ICRC)

72 Michael Bothe, 'The Protection of the Environment in Times of Armed Conflict: Legal Rules, Uncertainty, Deficiencies and Possible Developments', *German Yearbook of International Law* 34 (1991), 54–62, at 54.

73 See Chapter 4: 'The Protection of Animals in Wartime: Rationale and Challenges'. Compare with regard to Art. 236 sentence 2 UNCLOS (n. 42), Wolff Heintschel von Heinegg and Michael Donner, 'New Developments in the Protection of the Natural Environment in Naval Armed Conflicts', *German Yearbook of International Law* 37 (1994), 281–314, at 299. See also Richard Desgagné, 'The Prevention of Environmental Damage in Time of Armed Conflict: Proportionality and Precautionary Measures', *Yearbook of International Humanitarian Law* 3 (2000), 109–29, at 126. See Tara Smith, 'Critical Perspectives on Environmental Protection in Non-international Armed Conflict: Developing the Principles of Distinction, Proportionality and Necessity', *Leiden Journal of International Law* 32 (2019), 759–79, at 774–5.

74 Silja Vöneky, *Die Fortgeltung des Umweltvölkerrechts in internationalen bewaffneten Konflikten* (Berlin: Springer 2001), 133–338.

75 Britta Sjöstedt, *The Role of Multilateral Environmental Agreements: A Reconciliatory Approach to Environmental Protection in Armed Conflict* (Oxford: Hart 2020), 26–135.

76 Fernando Lusa Bordin, *The Analogy between States and International Organizations* (Cambridge: Cambridge University Press 2018), 47.

77 Karsten Nowrot, 'Animals at War: The Status of "Animal Soldiers" under International Humanitarian Law', *Historical Social Research* 40 (2015), 128–50, at 134.

Study on Customary IHL,[78] with the controversies surrounding this study,[79] only displays limited and selective evolutionary potential towards better protection of animals in wartime.

3.1 *Endangered Species as Civilian Objects?*

To begin with, the concept of endangered species could have an impact on the interpretation of Article 52 of Additional Protocol (AP) I. According to Article 48 of AP I 'the Parties to the conflict … shall direct their operations only against military objectives'. Such objectives are defined by Article 52(2) of AP I as 'objects which by their nature, location, purpose or use make an effective contribution to military action and whose total or partial destruction, capture or neutralisation, in the circumstances ruling at the time, offers a definite military advantage'. The two-pronged definition addresses, first, the object's effective contribution to military action focusing on nature, location, purpose, or use, and second, whether the object's destruction offers a definite military advantage in the circumstances ruling at the time. As the definition is contextual and situational, the predominant view that the environment by nature is a civilian object[80] does not automatically mean that components of the environment, such as animals, must be considered civilian objects at all times.[81]

With regard to the first prong, it might be argued that exploiting natural resources does not effectively contribute to military action but only constitutes a 'war sustaining activity'.[82] Irrespective of the difficulty to distinguish between 'effective

78 Jean-Marie Henckaerts and Louise Doswald-Beck (eds.), *Customary International Humanitarian Law. Vol. II: Practice* (Cambridge: Cambridge University Press 2005). The same applies to the ICRC Environmental Guidelines.

79 Yoram Dinstein, 'The ICRC Customary International Humanitarian Law Study', in Anthony M. Helm (ed.), *The Law of War in the 21st Century* (Newport: Naval War College 2007), 99–112; Jeanique Pretorius, 'Enhancing Environmental Protection in Non-International Armed Conflict: The Way Forward', *ZaöRV* 78 (2018), 903–32, at 921–3. As regards the special methodological characteristic of the study, see Heike Spieker, 'The Conduct of Hostilities and the Protection of the Environment', in Andreas Fischer-Lescano et al. (eds.), *Frieden in Freiheit – Peace in Liberty – Paix en Liberté: Festschrift für Michael Bothe zum 70. Geburtstag* (Baden-Baden: Nomos 2008), 741–68, at 759.

80 Stefan Oeter, 'Methods and Means of Combat', in Dieter Fleck (ed.), *The Handbook of International Humanitarian Law* (3rd ed., Oxford: Oxford University Press 2013), 115–230, at 213.

81 With regard to the discussion of the term 'object' in the context of animals, see Marco Roscini, 'Animals and the Law of Armed Conflict', *Israel Yearbook on Human Rights* 47 (2017), 35–67, at 42–8. Compare also ILC, Draft Principles on the Protection of the Environment in Relation to Armed Conflict (2019), reproduced in UN General Assembly, Report of the ILC, Seventy-first session (29 April–7 June and 8 July–9 August 2019), A/74/10, Draft Principle 13(3). 'No part of the natural environment may be attacked, unless it *has become* a military objective' (emphasis added). The ILC's work on the new draft is not yet completed, see Marja Lehto, 'Armed Conflicts and the Environment: The International Law Commission's New Draft Principles', *Review of European, Comparative & International Environmental Law* 29 (2020), 67–75.

82 Cordula Droege and Marie-Louise Tougas, 'The Protection of the Natural Environment in Armed Conflict: Existing Rules and Need for Further Legal Protection', *Nordic Journal of International Law* 82 (2013), 21–52, at 29; de Hemptinne, Chapter 7, 'Animals as Part of the Environment', in this volume.

contribution' and 'war sustaining activities' in general terms, and irrespective of the problem to link the notion of endangered species and their higher level of protection to the terms of the first prong, it remains a matter of situational military assessment.[83] The second prong, however, seems to allow more easily a consideration of endangered species. Given the parallel reading of treaty and customary law so far, Rule 43 (B) of the ICRC Customary Law Database might serve as a door opener. This rule prohibits the destruction of any part of the environment 'unless required by imperative military necessity'.[84] Such necessity may be hard to prove in the case of animals listed as endangered species under peacetime MEAs. Even though the term 'imperative' finds only little support in state practice, this can be considered a plausible interpretation.

An approach that may be better suited for the protection of animals qualifying as endangered species is to consider them as specially protected objects. A contextual approach[85] together with an interpretation in light of object and purpose[86] and adopting a dynamic approach suggests that, if IHL itself recognises specially protected objects such as cultural objects[87]and livestock,[88] it should also be possible to categorise endangered species in a similar way. An argument to this end may be that otherwise it would be easier to consider endangered species as military objectives than livestock – a consequence which would be in contradiction to their character as 'common goods' with an inherent value. However, at the time of negotiating the APs this notion was not borne in mind. On the other hand, it has to be considered that especially Article 54 of AP I serves a very narrow purpose: the protection of objects indispensable for the survival of the civilian population.

3.2 *Endangered Species as Part of the Environment*

This leads to Article 55 of AP I, read together with Article 35(3) of AP I. The question is whether these provisions can be reinterpreted in order to enhance the protection of endangered species. An initial consideration starts from a broad reading of the wider concept of 'natural environment'[89] including endangered

83 Yoram Dinstein, 'Legitimate Military Objectives Under the Current *Jus in Bello*', in Andru E. Wall (ed.), *Legal and Ethical Lessons of NATO's Kosovo Campaign* (Newport: Naval War College 2002), 139–72, at 145–6.

84 William H. Boothby, *Weapons and the Law of Armed Conflict* (2nd ed., Oxford: Oxford University Press 2016), 87.

85 See Art. 31(2) of the Vienna Convention on the Law of Treaties.

86 See Art. 31(1) of the Vienna Convention on the Law of Treaties.

87 Art. 53 of AP I.

88 Art. 54(2) of AP I.

89 See Erik V. Koppe, 'Use of Nuclear Weapons and Protection of the Environment during International Armed Conflict', in Gro Nystuen, Stuart Casey-Maslen, and Annie Golden Bersagel (eds.), *Nuclear Weapons under International Law* (Cambridge: Cambridge University Press 2014), 247–68, at 251.

species as a distinct component[90] thereof, regardless of controversies concerning the precise boundaries of the definition of this term.[91]

In light of debates about their field of application[92] and the cumulative conditions 'widespread, long-term and severe damage',[93] the question arises as to whether increased protection for endangered species in peacetime has an impact on the interpretation of these three terms. In case of extinction of a species, the requirement 'long-term' does not pose a major problem as the damage will last for more than decades.[94] In relation to 'widespread',[95] it may easily be argued that this element is met in the case of migratory species.[96] With regard to other species, a contextual interpretation may help to approve this criterion, based on the habitat of the respective species. Considering that the extinction of a species might have enormous consequences for the entire ecosystem and may, in the long run, also affect ecosystem benefits such as food and biofuels,[97] 'severe'[98] should be read in light of the prevention principle, since the extinction of endangered species always is severe.[99] Otherwise MEAs would not aim at specific regimes for their protection. Such a reading would also conform to the ecosystem approach, which is recognised

90 With regard to the components of the natural environment, see Silja Vöneky and Rüdiger Wolfrum, 'Environment, Protection in Armed Conflict', in Anne Peters and Rüdiger Wolfrum (eds.), *Max Planck Encyclopedia of Public International Law* (online edition), 2016, para. 24, available at: www.mpepil.com.

91 For an in-depth discussion on animals as components of the environment, see de Hemptinne, Chapter 7, 'Animals as Part of the Environment', in this volume.

92 For more details see ibid.; Michael Bothe et al., 'International Law Protecting the Environment During Armed Conflict: Gaps and Opportunities', *International Review of the Red Cross* 92 (2010), 569–92, at 575–6.

93 UNEP, *Protecting the Environment During Armed Conflict: An Inventory and Analysis of International Law* (Nairobi: UNEP 2009), 11; Hulme, 'Armed Conflict and Biodiversity' (n. 67), 249–51.

94 As regards the interpretation of this term, see, among others, Marco Sassòli, *International Humanitarian Law: Rules, Controversies, and Solutions to Problems Arising in Warfare* (Cheltenham: Edward Elgar 2019), 570.

95 See Philippe Antoine, 'International Humanitarian Law and the Protection of the Environment in Time of Armed Conflict', *International Review of the Red Cross* 32 (1992), 517–37, at 526: '"widespread" implies an area of less than several hundred square kilometres'.

96 For instance, for the home range of the Gobi bears, see UNEP/CMS/COP12/Doc.25.1.5 (2017), Proposal for the Inclusion of the Gobi Bear (*Ursus arctos isabellinus*) on Appendix I of the Convention.

97 Claude Gascon et al., 'The Importance and Benefits of Species', *Current Biology* 25 (2015), 431–8, at 434.

98 It has been asserted as regard Article 55 of AP I that it means the collapse of a given ecological framework, with the impossibility of maintaining the previous flora and fauna as an indication, see Stephan Witteler, *Die Regelungen der neuen Verträge des humanitären Völkerrechts und des Rechts der Rüstungsbegrenzung mit direktem Umweltbezug* (Bochum: Dr. N. Brockmeyer 1993), 406. On the other hand, it has also been argued that it involves 'serious or significant disruption or harm to human life, natural economic resources or other assets' (Antoine, 'International Humanitarian Law' (n. 95), 526).

99 For an analysis of these terms, see Peters and de Hemptinne, Chapter 1, 'Wartime', in this volume.

under several biodiversity related conventions.[100] Notwithstanding debates about the customary law status of Articles 35(3)[101] and 55 of AP I[102] the arguments presented here likewise match the challenges of customary IHL.

3.3 *Endangered Species and Excessive Civilian Loss*

Endangered species may become part of what is often labelled as collateral damage. In this context, Article 51(5)(b) of AP I deserves closer consideration. This provision clarifies that attacks which may result in incidental damages to civilian objects 'excessive in relation to the concrete and direct military advantage anticipated' are prohibited.

It may be argued that the extinction of an endangered species as such amounts to excessive civilian loss. However, such a reading falls short of the substance of Article 51(5)(b) of AP I. The balancing required by this provision necessitates the consideration of 'concrete and direct' military advantage, hence runs counter to any abstract weighing. Furthermore, civilian loss must be excessive (not merely extensive)[103] in relation to the concrete military advantage. It can, however, be argued that damage to endangered species has to be attached a special weight in this balancing process, requiring a very special military advantage on the other side, notwithstanding the fact that the application of this principle in the context of environmental protection has posed enormous difficulties in practice.[104] The involvement of endangered species in a situation falling under Article 51(5)(b) of AP I may thus tilt the balance against the permissibility of an attack – but only *in concreto*, not in the abstract.

While Article 51(5)(b) of AP I as such does not apply to ship-to-ship, air-to-air, land-to-air, or land-to-ship hostilities,[105] it is accepted that under corresponding customary international law this rule extends to the mentioned cases.[106]

[100] With regard to the Convention on Biological Diversity (n. 42), see Thilo Marauhn and Ayşe-Martina Böhringer, 'An Ecosystem Approach to the Transboundary Protection of Biodiversity', in Louis J. Kotzé and Thilo Marauhn (eds.), *Transboundary Governance of Biodiversity* (Leiden: Brill Nijhoff 2014), 90–104.

[101] At least parts of Rule 45 of the ICRC Study seem to confirm its customary international law status. See ICRC Customary Law Database.

[102] Vöneky and Wolfrum, 'Environment' (n. 90), para. 35.

[103] Yoram Dinstein, 'The Principle of Distinction and Cyber War in International Armed Conflicts', *Journal of Conflict & Security Law* 17 (2012), 261–77, at 272.

[104] Jean-Marie Henckaerts and Dana Constantin, 'Protection of the Natural Environment', in Andrew Clapham and Paola Gaeta (eds.), *The Oxford Handbook of International Law in Armed Conflict* (Oxford: Oxford University Press 2014), 469–91, at 475, referring to the attack on the Pancevo industrial complex and on a petroleum refinery in Novi Sad by NATO troops during the 1999 Kosovo war as well as to the 2006 Lebanon war.

[105] See Art. 49(3) of AP I. See also Michael Bothe, Karl Josef Partsch, and Waldemar A. Solf (eds.), *New Rules for Victims of Armed Conflicts: Commentary on the Two 1977 Protocols Additional to the Geneva Conventions of 1949* (2nd ed., Leiden and Boston: Martinus Nijhoff 2013), 330.

[106] See Rule 43(C) of the ICRC Customary Law Database; Wolff Heintschel von Heinegg, 'Proportionality and Collateral Damage', in Anne Peters and Rüdiger Wolfrum (eds.), *Max Planck*

3.4 A Dual Perspective on Precaution

When it comes to precaution, we have to distinguish the key concept of precautionary action established in IEL, and the rules on precaution in attack being part of IHL. Turning to IEL first, precautionary action, which is part of customary international law[107] and is expressly laid down in many MEAs,[108] ensures that scientific uncertainty as to causation does not justify inaction or action,[109] however it may be precisely delineated.[110] The integration of such considerations into IHL has recently been discussed more intensely.[111]

First, precautionary action can be applied in favour of the protection of endangered species during armed conflict in particular in cases where new weapons, means, and methods of warfare are employed.[112] Second, precautionary action may be relevant in the context of Article 51 of AP I.[113] The phrase 'expected to cause' may be interpreted as to oblige commanders to consider anticipated indirect damages (even of a third or higher order)[114] that are uncertain, thus adding a further layer to the legality test. In cases involving endangered species covered by the African-Eurasian Waterbirds Agreement, the military commander may thus have to take into account possible collateral damage to endangered species on the basis of reliable information available before authorising an attack under the following conditions. According to the uncertain or vague information available, there are some indications that serious or irreversible harm to endangered species, for example, by destroying their only and last habitat on earth which might lead to their extinction, might occur; sufficient empirical or theoretical scientific basis for the proof of the causal relationship between the activity destroying their last known habitat and the prospective extinction is not needed. As a consequence, the attack might be considered indiscriminate even if there is scientific uncertainty as regards the causal link, provided that the collateral damage is excessive in relation to the anticipated military advantage. This would not be the case where, for example, an

Encyclopedia of Public International Law (online edition), 2015, para. 7, available at: www.mpepil.com.

107 Arie Trouwborst, 'The Precautionary Principle in General International Law: Combating the Babylonian Confusion', *Review of European, Comparative & International Environmental Law* 16 (2007), 185–95, at 188; Kirsten Stefanik, 'The Environment and Armed Conflict: Employing General Principles to Protect the Environment', in Carsten Stahn, Jens Iverson, and Jennifer S. Easterday (eds.), *Environmental Protection and Transitions from Conflict to Peace* (Oxford: Oxford University Press 2017), 93–118, at 113 ('general principle of international law').

108 See Barnabas Dickson, 'The Precautionary Principle in CITES: A Critical Assessment', *Natural Resources Journal* 39 (1999), 211–28.

109 Ulrich Beyerlin and Thilo Marauhn, *International Environmental Law* (Hart: Oxford 2011), 55.

110 Ibid., 52–4.

111 With regard to the terminology, see Stefanik, 'The Environment' (n. 107), 108.

112 Desgagné, 'The Prevention of Environmental Damage' (n. 73), 125.

113 Bothe et al., 'International Law Protecting the Environment' (n. 92), 577–8.

114 In this regard, see Ian Henderson and Kate Reece, 'Proportionality under International Humanitarian Law', *Vanderbilt Journal of Tansnational Law* 51 (2018), 835–55, at 852.

attack is carried out against a munition factory[115] which is located close to a habitat of endangered species.

Turning to precautions in attack as specifically addressed by Articles 57, 58 of AP I, there are crucial differences with regard to precautionary action under IEL.[116] Precaution under IHL is subject to 'feasibility',[117] precautionary action under IEL demands 'serious or irreversible threats'. Article 57(1) of AP I requires the application of precautions and stipulates that in the course of military operations, constant care shall be taken to avoid harming civilians and civilian objects. Whereas this provision does not impose any obligations of result,[118] refraining from an attack[119] may become the preferred, if not the only, option when endangered species are at issue, taking scientific uncertainty as a starting point, in accordance with the concept of precautionary action.[120] It may influence the interpretation of the term 'feasibility' insofar as even if there are only uncertain indications that the existence of endangered species may be threatened, the commander is obliged to refrain from launching an attack.[121] Such a reading finds additional support in Rule 44 of the ICRC Customary Law Database, which introduces the 'due regard' concept and requires that methods and means of warfare must be employed with due regard to the protection and preservation of the natural environment. Interpreted in the light of precautionary action,[122] it enhances the protection of endangered species.

3.5 *Endangered Species in Non-international Armed Conflicts*

In non-international armed conflicts, common Article 3(1)(a) of the four GCs and Articles 4(2)(g), 13, and 14 of AP II are among the main provisions that attract attention. Considering that the extinction of a species might influence the entire ecosystem and may, in the long run, also affect ecosystem benefits such as food, it is possible that 'violence to life and person' in the sense of common Article 3 may occur.[123] Article 4(2)(g) of AP II may provide protection to habitats of endangered

115 Dinstein, 'The Principle of Distinction' (n. 103), 272.

116 See Stefanik, 'The Environment' (n. 107), 113–15.

117 Jean-François Quéguiner, 'Precautions under the Law Governing the Conduct of Hostilities', *International Review of the Red Cross* 88 (2006), 793–821, at 809.

118 International Law Association Study Group on the Conduct of Hostilities in the 21st Century, 'The Conduct of Hostilities and International Humanitarian Law: Challenges of 21st Century Warfare', *International Law Studies* 93 (2017), 322–88, at 332.

119 Art. 57(2)(a)(iii) of AP I.

120 See in this regard, Stefanik, 'The Environment' (n. 107), 114. But see also Karen Hulme, 'Taking Care to Protect the Environment against Damage: A Meaningless Obligation?' *International Review of the Red Cross* 92 (2010), 675–91, at 687–8.

121 See in general, among others, Onita Das, 'Protecting the Environment During Multinational Military Operations', in Robin Geiß and Heike Krieger (eds.), *The 'Legal Pluriverse' Surrounding Multinational Military Operations* (Oxford: Oxford University Press 2020), 322–44, at 333.

122 Michael Bothe, 'Precaution in International Environmental Law and Precautions in the Law of Armed Conflict', *Goettingen Journal of International Law* 10 (2020), 267–81, at 279.

123 See in general Pretorius, 'Enhancing Environmental Protection' (n. 79), 906.

species owned by states.[124] The problem with Article 13 of AP II is that it requires a link to 'civilians'. At best, the same argument as in the context of common Article 3 can be used here. Article 14 of AP II, which leaves no room for military necessity,[125] may only be applicable if habitats of endangered species are at the same time used as areas for the production of foodstuff, for instance. Furthermore, the customary IHL rules discussed above are also relevant in this context. It has been argued that the following minimum standard exists in the form of customary international law of armed conflict: in launching any attack, due regard must be given to the environment and the destruction of or damaging the environment as a civil object is only permitted if it is not excessive in comparison with the anticipated military advantage.[126] Moreover, the MEAs discussed above are applicable.

3.6 *Beyond Interpretation?*

In the light of these findings the question arises whether it is possible to fill any gaps arising from the limited effects of peacetime norms of IEL by analogous application of the concept of endangered species in situations of armed conflict. Here, the Martens Clause can be relied upon, which has been also interpreted in the sense that concepts that remain below the threshold of recognised sources of international law can be invoked under the law of armed conflict.[127]

The following two prerequisites must be fulfilled for the analogous application of the concept: the existence of a regulatory gap and the appropriateness of direct application of the concept in an armed conflict. The latter element refers to the question whether the concept can directly be transferred to this particular situation. To meet this requirement, endangered species must be considered as requiring special protection under the law of armed conflict.

A precondition is therefore first of all that there is no international law provision emanating from the recognised sources according to Article 38(1)(a)–(c) of the ICJ Statute governing the case in question.[128] Primarily, any regulatory gap must be filled by interpreting existing rules according to the applicable rules of interpretation. The principle of the freedom of action of states does not necessarily preclude the possibility of an analogy[129] in international law. Rather, there must be a rule of

[124] Ibid., 908.

[125] Ibid., 910.

[126] Yoram Dinstein, *The Conduct of Hostilities under the Law of International Armed Conflict* (3rd ed., Cambridge: Cambridge University Press 2016), 231. See also ICJ, Nuclear Weapons (n. 71), 242.

[127] Compare, Vöneky and Wolfrum, 'Environment' (n. 90), para. 48.

[128] Silja Vöneky, 'Analogy in International Law', in Anne Peters and Rüdiger Wolfrum (eds.), *Max Planck Encyclopedia of Public International Law* (online edition), 2008, para. 16, available at www.mpepil.com.

[129] As regards the difference between 'deductive justification' and analogy, see Lusa Bordin, *Analogy* (n. 76), 20: '"deductive justification" – applying a well-established rule to facts which that rule undeniably covers – and analogical reasoning – extending a rule to a novel situation by claiming that the situation is 'relevantly similar' to that covered by the rule' (references omitted).

international law that provides for the states' freedom of action in a particular area of international law excluding reasoning by analogy.[130]

The second requirement necessitates that the same legal treatment of a category of endangered species and a category of comparable groups in armed conflict must be appropriate. The concept of protection of groups of persons is not unfamiliar to the law of armed conflict.[131]

Finally, it can basically be said that it cannot be argued against the permissibility of analogous reasoning that the rules of IHL are exhaustive with regard to environmental protection. For instance, the existence of the Martens Clause militates against this assumption. Furthermore, the ICJ's 1996 advisory opinion on the *Legality of the Threat or Use of Nuclear Weapons* supports this idea.[132] With regard to the second requirement, in order to be able to compare two categories of international law, first, it has to be assessed whether it is possible to speak about endangered species as a category of 'protected animals' under international law. Prima facie, this seems to be questionable as a uniform category of protected animals does not exist under general international law at all, which could provide a basis for uniform standards of protection.[133] Rather, it seems to be adequate to regard endangered species as a relative category of protected animals since the protection standard depends on the treaty establishing rights and obligations vis-à-vis its states parties. Beyond that, it appears also questionable whether there is a noteworthy similarity between the category of protected animals and the category of persons entitled to protection under IHL.[134] The category of protected persons under IHL affords protection to people depending on their vulnerability and function,[135] including combatants hors de combat and persons exercising humanitarian functions. However, what makes the comparison difficult are structural differences between the two categories. While endangered species may be considered objects of a 'common concern of humankind' with varying degrees of protection afforded to them, the rationale behind the protection of persons under IHL rules has been the principle of reciprocity, always based on the premise of finding a balance between

130 Albert Bleckmann, 'Analogie im Völkerrecht', *Archiv des Völkerrechts* 17 (1977), 161–80, at 169–72; Ulrich Fastenrath, *Lücken im Völkerrecht: Zu Rechtscharakter, Quellen, Systemzusammenhang, Methodenlehre und Funktionen des Völkerrechts* (Berlin: Duncker & Humblot 1988), 245–6, arguing against a broad understanding of states' freedom of action.

131 On the contrary, one of its main aims has been to provide safeguard rules as regards categories of persons and objects, see Marco Sassòli, Antoine A. Bouvier, and Anne Quintin, *How Does Law Protect in War? Cases, Documents and Teaching Materials on Contemporary Practice in International Humanitarian Law, Volume I* (3rd ed., Geneva: ICRC 2011), for example chapter 7 'Protection of the Wounded, Sick and Shipwrecked' and chapter 8 'The Protection of Civilians'.

132 Vöneky (n. 74), 355; ICJ, Nuclear Weapons (n. 71), 242–3.

133 With regard to international organisations, see Lusa Bordin, *Analogy* (n. 76), 239.

134 With regard to the difference between 'protected persons' and other categories, see Heike Krieger, 'Protected Persons', in Anne Peters and Rüdiger Wolfrum (eds.), *Max Planck Encyclopedia of Public International Law* (online edition), 2011, para. 4, available at www.mpepil.com.

135 Ibid., para. 1.

the principle of humanity and military necessity.[136] A closer look at the IHL rules reveals that animals are only treated as objects.[137] Thus, *de lege lata*, they cannot be equated with protected persons: endangered species do not possess rights and duties under international (humanitarian) law.[138]

4 LEGAL CONSEQUENCES OF A VIOLATION OF THE LEGAL REGIMES PROTECTING ENDANGERED SPECIES

In principle, environmental damage may constitute a war crime under international criminal law if the requirements are fulfilled,[139] activating the individual responsibility of the perpetrator. Given the limited scope of application and high threshold required by Article 8(2)(b)(iv) of the International Criminal Court (ICC) Statute, it is subject to criticism.[140] In the context of endangered species, the explanations given above[141] for the interpretation of the terms 'widespread', 'long-term', and 'severe' can be applied here, as well. However, its proportionality standard and *mens rea* cause significant problems in practice.[142] In the end, the presumption that international criminal law provides protection to animals as species or protects humans from the effects of animal mistreatment is not recognised under international law.[143]

Moreover, the law of state responsibility[144] is relevant in the case of a breach of IHL rules. One of the most important prerequisites is an internationally wrongful act. The problem is that acts of private persons are, in principle, not attributable to states. Furthermore, in practice, the assessment of 'military necessity' is problematic: when it comes to the determination of the legality of an action, the wide margin of appreciation of the actor must always be taken into account.[145] However, such necessity may be hard to prove in the case of endangered species under MEAs.[146]

136 Elizabeth Salmón, 'Chapter 55: Who Is a Protected Civilian?', in Andrew Clapham, Paola Gaeta, and Marco Sassòli (eds.), *The 1949 Geneva Conventions: A Commentary* (Oxford: Oxford University Press 2015), 1135–53, at 1140 and 1153.

137 See Nowrot, 'Animals at War' (n. 77), 136.

138 Ibid. 135.

139 See, for example, Art. 8(2)(b)(iv) of the ICC Statute which is limited to international armed conflicts, or Art. 8(2) (b)(xvi) of the ICC Statute ('pillage'). For an in-depth analysis as regards the scope of application of ICL in the context of animals, see Ventura, Chapter 18: 'Repression of International Crimes'; Ricardo Pereira, 'After the ICC Office of the Prosecutor's 2016 Policy Paper on Case Selection and Prioritisation: Towards an International Crime of Ecocide?', *Criminal Law Forum* 31 (2020), 179–224, at 208–9.

140 Pereira, 'After the ICC Office' (n. 139), 198–200 and 207.

141 See above Section 3.2.

142 For a general discussion, see Jessica C. Lawrence and Kevin Jon Heller, 'The First Ecocentric Environmental War Crime: The Limits of Article 8(2)(b)(iv) of the Rome Statute', *Georgetown International Environmental Law Review* 20 (2007), 61–95, at 71–91.

143 See Ventura, Chapter 18, 'Repression of International Crimes', in this volume.

144 See the 2001 ILC Draft Articles, A/56/10; A/RES/56/83; and A/CN.4/L.602/Rev.1.

145 Richard G. Tarasofsky, 'Legal Protection of the Environment During International Armed Conflict', *Netherlands Yearbook of International Law* 24 (1993) 17–79, at 25.

146 See above Section 3.1.

Furthermore, the necessity test may not only apply between the parties to the conflict, but also between a conflicting party and a neutral party.[147] The no harm concept of IEL may be relevant with regard to the protection of endangered species with the consequence that the belligerent state is responsible for causing damage resulting from its military activities outside the territory of the affected neutral state.[148] Legal challenges arise in relation to non-state actors as they are not covered by that rule, and in areas beyond national jurisdiction.[149]

5 CONCLUDING RECOMMENDATIONS

As has been demonstrated, there are a number of options to enhance the protection of endangered species in times of armed conflict. Mainly, focusing on interpretation, perhaps to some extent on analogy, the rationale of peacetime protection of endangered species may be integrated into IHL. This could, in practice, possibly be best done via an interpretative guidance. We propose the following elements thereof:

Peacetime standards. Endangered species is a normative concept, facilitating detailed peacetime obligations for different dangers and different species. Their common feature is the danger of extinction of a certain species considered to be a 'common good'. Existing IHL rules should be interpreted along the line that factors endangering or likely to endanger the survival of species must be prevented or reduced to the extent feasible and appropriate.

Protection in international armed conflicts. In principle, endangered species are civilian objects. However, they deserve special, non-contextual protection similar to specially protected objects such as cultural objects (Article 53 of AP I) and livestock (Article 54(2) of AP I). By way of interpretation, endangered species should be granted a similar standard of protection. In the absence of a special provision, an interpretative guidance may facilitate agreement to enhance the interpretation of Article 52(1) of AP I from situation to general or abstract. This goes beyond the law as it currently stands, but it would be in line with the peacetime approach to endangered species if they are considered to be specially protected at all times. Customary IHL should be interpreted in the same way.

The term 'expected to cause' in Article 51(5)(b) of AP I should be interpreted in light of the precautionary action concept of IEL to the extent that it obliges commanders to consider anticipated indirect damages (even of a third or higher order) that are uncertain. Hence, an attack might be indiscriminate even if there is scientific uncertainty as regards the causal link, provided that the collateral damage is

147 Bothe et al., 'International Law Protecting the Environment' (n. 92), 585 with further references.

148 Ibid.

149 Silja Vöneky, 'Peacetime Environmental Law as a Basis of State Responsibility for Environmental Damage Caused by War', in Jay E. Austin and Carl E. Bruch (eds.), *The Environmental Consequences of War: Legal, Economic, and Scientific Perspectives* (Cambridge: Cambridge University Press 2000), 190–225, at 191.

excessive in relation to the anticipated military advantage. 'Feasibility' according to Article 57(2)(a)(iii) of AP I should be interpreted in light of this principle, too, insofar as even if there are only uncertain indications for the existence of endangered species, the commander is obliged to refrain from launching an attack.

In case of extinction of a species, the cumulative criteria of Articles 35(3) and 55 of AP I should be read as to be fulfilled in case of listed endangered species.

Protection in non-international armed conflicts. As common Article 3 to the GCs and Article 13 of AP II and customary international law both require a link to 'civilians' or 'persons', these terms should be interpreted in light of the ecosystem approach and the concept of precautionary action. Article 14 of AP II may only be applicable if habitats of endangered species are at the same time used as areas for the production of foodstuff, for instance. Applicable customary international humanitarian law has to be interpreted in the same way as shown in the context of international armed conflicts. Furthermore, MEAs continue to apply.

SELECT BIBLIOGRAPHY

Bothe, Michael et al., 'International Law Protecting the Environment During Armed Conflict: Gaps and Opportunities', *International Review of the Red Cross* 92 (2010), 569–92.

Braverman, Irus, 'The Regulatory Life of Threatened Species Lists', in Irus Braverman (ed.), *Animals, Biopolitics, Law: Lively Legalities* (Abingdon: Routledge 2016), 19–38.

Brouder, Alan, 'International Union for Conservation of Nature', in Christian Tietje and Alan Brouder (eds.), *Handbook of Transnational Economic Governance Regimes* (Leiden: Martinus Nijhoff 2009), 953–68.

Desgagné, Richard, 'The Prevention of Environmental Damage in Time of Armed Conflict: Proportionality and Precautionary Measures', *Yearbook of International Humanitarian Law* 3 (2000), 109–29.

Dinstein, Yoram, 'The Principle of Distinction and Cyber War in International Armed Conflicts', *Journal of Conflict & Security Law* 17 (2012), 261–77.

García-Ureta, Augustín, 'Nature Conservation', in Emma Lees and Jorge E. Viñuales (eds.), *The Oxford Handbook of Comparative Environmental Law* (Oxford: Oxford University Press 2019), 460–88.

Hulme, Karen, 'Armed Conflict and Biodiversity', in Michael Bowman, Peter Davies, and Edward Goodwin (eds.), *Research Handbook on Biodiversity and Law* (Cheltenham: Edward Elgar 2016), 245–69.

Pretorius, Jeanique, 'Enhancing Environmental Protection in Non-international Armed Conflict: The Way Forward', *ZaöRV* 78 (2018), 903–32.

Quéguiner, Jean-François, 'Precautions Under the Law Governing the Conduct of Hostilities', *International Review of the Red Cross* 88 (2006), 793–821.

Robinson, Nicholas A., 'IUCN as Catalyst for a Law of the Biosphere: Acting Globally and Locally', *Environmental Law* 35 (2005), 249–310.

Schmitt, Michael N., 'Green War: An Assessment of the Environmental Law of International Armed Conflict', *Yale Journal of International Law* 22 (1997), 1–110.

Techera, Erika J., 'Species-Based Conservation', in Elisa Morgera and Jona Razzaque (eds.), *Biodiversity and Nature Protection Law* (Cheltenham: Edward Elgar 2017), 97–109.

9

Animals as War Weapons

Chris Jenks

Of all the strange changes happening in war in the 21st century, one of the oddest has to be the return of animals to the battlefield.[1]

1 INTRODUCTION

The UN Convention on Certain Conventional Weapons (CCW) has held meetings of experts on emerging technologies in the area of lethal autonomous weapons systems (LAWS) since 2014.[2] During meetings held in April 2018, a non-governmental organisation (NGO) sponsored a lunchtime side event to discuss an aspect of LAWS. During the question-and-answer period at the end, a reporter probed the nature of the concerns about LAWS by asking whether or not international humanitarian law (IHL) prohibited a state's military from training a pack of wild dogs and then unleashing them to attack opposing belligerents during an armed conflict.

Perhaps it was the incongruous wording of trained wild dogs, but no one in the room seemed to take the question seriously, and it elicited neither substantive response nor discussion. But upon reflection, and notwithstanding the trained/wild issue, the question raises several important points, including that: (i) the IHL applicable as a matter of law to international armed conflicts does not categorically prohibit employing animals as weapons or means and methods of warfare; (ii) humans have used – and continue to use – animals as weapons or means and methods of warfare; and (iii) animals would seem to qualify as LAWS.

This chapter explores those points in considering whether IHL may be leveraged to protect weaponised animals despite the lack of a direct prohibition. It also asserts that the connection between weaponised animals and LAWS may help inform the

[1] Colin Salter, 'Animals and War: Anthropocentrism and Technoscience', *NanoEthics* 9 (2015), 11–21, at 12 (quoting noted Australian moral philosopher Peter Singer in a draft chapter which was not ultimately published. Singer is widely credited for developing the philosophical underpinnings of the animal liberation movement). See Peter Singer, *Animal Liberation: Towards an End to Man's Inhumanity to Animals* (Wellingborough: Thorsons 1975).

[2] See UN Convention on Certain Conventional Weapons, 'Background on Lethal Autonomous Weapons Systems in the CCW', available at https://bit.ly/33tMrTL, accessed 22 February 2022.

discussions on both. It operates along three separate albeit related lines. Each line provides an argument which, if successful, would yield partial protection against weaponising animals in armed conflict. The lines are: first, to rely on international, regional organisation, and domestic law during non-international armed conflict; second, in international armed conflict, to confront states with their obligation to conduct weapons reviews; and third, to call on those states proposing a ban or regulation on LAWS to support comparable action towards weaponised animals. Even collectively the three argument lines would not yield a universal prohibition against weaponising animals. But the admittedly patchwork outcome(s) would offer some measure of protection of animals where little currently exists. Additionally, each line of argument has the potential of gaining additional traction, whether as a matter of law, custom, or policy, thus increasing the protection of animals.

The basis for the first line of argument, leveraging international, regional organisation, and domestic law applicable during non-international armed conflicts, is the recognition that IHL applicable to international armed conflicts as a matter of law 'does not directly deal with the question of [animal] protection'[3] and that there is far more IHL applicable to international armed conflicts than to non-international armed conflicts.[4] How that is considered is a matter of perspective. In the context of animals, the dearth of IHL arguably creates an opportunity for international and domestic law to play a larger, substantive, role in protecting animals in non-international armed conflicts, the far more prevalent type of armed conflict.[5]

The second line of argument, confronting states with their obligation to conduct weapons reviews, is grounded in blunt pragmatism. In terms of international armed conflicts, IHL reflects a 'lack of interest in the welfare of animals' and only indirectly references them, and then as civilian objects or as part of the natural environment.[6] Some have tried arguing otherwise, including that weaponised animals are analogous to child soldiers[7] and/or that animals should receive derivative protection from being considered part of the environment.[8]

3 Jérôme de Hemptinne, 'The Protection of Animals During Warfare', *American Journal of International Law Unbound* 111 (2017) 272–6, at 272.

4 The only portion of the GCs applicable to non-international armed conflict as a matter of law is common Article 3 of the GCs.

5 Estimates are that over the past fifty years, over 90 per cent of the armed conflicts have been non-international armed conflicts. See Uppsala Conflict Data Program, 'Armed Conflicts by Type, 1946–2016 Uppsala Conflict Data Program' (2017), available at https://ucdp.uu.se, accessed 22 February 2022.

6 See Jérôme de Hemptinne, 'Challenges Regarding the Protection of Animals During Warfare', in Anne Peters (ed.), *Studies in Global Animal Law* (2020), 173–83. In fairness to IHL, that law is '[g]eared essentially towards the safeguarding of human beings' (ibid., 174–5).

7 See Karsten Nowrot, 'Animals at War: The Status of "Animal Soldiers" Under International Humanitarian Law', *Historical Social Research* 40 (2015), 128–50, at 141 (analogising the intellectual capacity and criminal responsibility challenges between animals, child soldiers, and persons with severe intellectual disabilities); ILC, Report on the Work of the Seventy-First Session, 10 December 2019, A/74/10, 210 (discussing the protection of the environment in relation to armed conflict).

8 See de Hemptinne, 'Protection of Animals' (n. 3), 273–4 (contending that wildlife is subsumed in the special protection AP I affords the natural environment).

This chapter utilises a different approach for two different reasons. First, those arguments have little chance of delivering meaningful protection in terms of prohibiting weaponising of animals. Even if successful with the quite reasonable contention that animals are part of the natural environment, that would achieve some, but not much, in the way of protection against animals being weaponised.[9] And comparing animals to child soldiers would seemingly require a massive restructuring of IHL's current status-based construct where human beings are either civilians or qualify as prisoners of war.[10] Second, the breadth of these arguments is such that states can respond while avoiding difficult discussions about weaponising animals. This chapter takes the view that in order for the status quo to change regarding weaponising animals, states must be forced to have uncomfortable conversations. The most direct route to that goal requires accepting the unfortunate categorisation within IHL of animals as objects.

Doing so allows the discussion to shift to whether animals may constitute a weapon or a means and method of warfare such that a legal review must be conducted under AP I.[11] To complete the legal review requires, among other things, considering whether the weapon or means and method of warfare can be directed at a specific military objective and whether it is of a nature to cause superfluous injury or unnecessary suffering (to humans).[12] While the weapons review process is macabre when considering the ways by which humans may kill other humans, it may take on a different dimension in considering humans using another sentient entity – animals – to kill other

[9] Considering animals as part of the environment would then invoke Articles 35(3) and 55(1) of AP I (de Hemptinne, 'Protection of Animals' (n. 3), 273). Article 35(3) prohibits the employment of methods or means of warfare which are intended, or may be expected, to cause 'widespread, long-term and severe damage to the natural environment'. Article 55(1) of AP I requires that: '[c]are shall be taken in warfare to protect the natural environment against widespread, long-term and severe damage. This protection includes a prohibition of the use of methods or means of warfare which are intended or may be expected to cause such damage to the natural environment and thereby to prejudice the health or survival of the population.' When animal use constitutes a method or means of warfare, and animals are considered part of the environment, the result then becomes that weaponised animals may not be used to cause widespread, long-term, and severe damage to the natural environment. If the environment includes animals then their weaponised use would be prohibited if the damage to the animals was widespread, long-term and severe.

[10] See de Hemptinne, 'Protection of Animals' (n. 3), 274 (discussing how the definition of civilians from AP I 'only refers to "persons"'); but see Nowrot, 'Animals at War' (n. 7), 137 (arguing for a partial reconceptualisation of IHL and recognition of 'an international legal status of "animal soldiers"'). See also de Hemptinne, Kebebew, and Niyo, Chapter 10, 'Combatants and as Prisoners of War?', in this volume.

[11] Art. 36 of AP I.

[12] Kathleen Lawand, Robin Coupland, and Peter Herby, *A Guide to the Legal Review of New Weapons, Means and Methods of Warfare: Measures to Implement Article 36 of Additional Protocol I of 1977* (Geneva: ICRC 2006) (ICRC Weapons Review).

humans.[13] Sometimes humans react more strongly to the killing of animals than of humans.[14]

There are 174 states parties to AP I that are required to conduct weapons reviews. Admittedly, nowhere near that number actually do so.[15] Indeed, the International Committee of the Red Cross (ICRC) estimates that only fifteen to twenty states 'are known to conduct their own legal reviews; for instance, Australia, Belgium, the Netherlands, Norway, Sweden and the United States'.[16] The weapons review argument line suggests that these states want nothing whatsoever to do with the legal review of animals as a either a weapon or means and method of warfare, despite the fact that certain animal uses appear to qualify as one or the other. At the same time, these states want to be seen as complying with their legal obligations.

Ultimately this argument line leverages that tension and suggests that states could be pressured to either conduct the required legal reviews when they weaponise animals or if they disavow such use of animals then to sign a policy document akin to the Montreux Document, in which states acknowledged their international legal obligations and adopted a series of best practices related to private military security companies.[17]

The third argument line draws from the CCW LAWS discussions referenced at the outset. Currently some thirty states parties to the CCW support regulation – or a ban – on LAWS.[18] As discussed in this chapter, animals may constitute a weapon or means and method of warfare. If autonomy is thought of as the ability to perceive

[13] Humans' inconsistent and even contradictory attitude towards animals is outside the scope of this chapter. As one commentator wrote:

> [w]e should not underestimate the fact, in peacetime, while acts of violence against human beings are, in principle, forbidden, the slaughtering of animals is widely accepted and practiced throughout the world. In this context, it might appear paradoxical that, in situations of armed conflict, where acts of violence against certain individuals, mainly combatants, are admitted and expected, acts of violence against animals might be strictly constrained.

(de Hemptinne, 'Protection of Animals' (n. 3), 273).

[14] The Provisional Irish Republican Army (IRA) reportedly killed more than 1,700 people over twenty-five years. See BBC, 'The Provisional IRA Killed More Than 1,700 People During a 25-year Campaign' (14 August 2019), available at www.bbc.com/news/av/uk-northern-ireland-49337517, accessed 22 February 2022. Yet one of the most widely reported incidents was the 1982 Hyde Park bombing in which the IRA killed eight British Army soldiers but also seven horses (Steven Rattner, 'IRA Bomb Attacks in London Kill 8', *New Yok Times* (21 July 1982)).

[15] ICRC Weapons Review (n. 8), 5 (describing the 'limited number of States known to have put in place mechanisms or procedures to conduct legal reviews of weapons').

[16] ICRC, 'Legal Review of New Weapons: Scope of the Obligation and Best Practices', *Humanitarian Law and Policy* (6 October 2016), available at https://bit.ly/3qj3u40, accessed 22 February 2022 (quoting Dr Gilles Giacca, Legal Advisor at the ICRC).

[17] *The Montreux Document: On Pertinent International Legal Obligations and Good Practices for States Related to Operations of Private Military and Security Companies During Armed Conflict* (Montreux: ICRC 2008).

[18] See Brian Stauffe, 'Stopping Killer Robots: Country Positions on Banning Fully Autonomous Weapons and Retaining Human Control', *Human Rights Watch* (10 August 2020), available at https://bit.ly/3GBCXox, accessed 22 February 2022 (listing the thirty states calling for a treaty banning LAWS).

and react in open or unstructured environments, it seems difficult to argue that animals are not autonomous.[19] For a state's opposition to LAWS to retain consistency and coherence, this argument contends the opposition should extend to weaponised animals.

In terms of the chapter's organisation, Section 2 highlights examples of animals used as weapons, both in antiquity and in present day. That section concludes by explaining that international law would, at most, prohibit only a small number of those uses, essentially those which implicate prohibitions against employing poison or biological weapons. Section 3 begins the first of the three argument lines and attempts to turn the lack of IHL in a non-international armed conflict into a positive. Section 4 explains what is meant by animals as weapons. As referenced above, this section considers animals as objects in order to assess when the use of animals would qualify the animals as either weapons or a means and method of warfare such that a legal review would be required, and what that review entails. Section 5 then transitions to the CCW LAWS discussions and argues that if there are thirty states calling for a ban on LAWS, those states should agree to ban weaponised animals.

2 EXAMPLES OF ANIMALS AS WEAPONS

Humans have used animals as weapons in war for thousands of years. As far back as 4000 BC Egyptian soldiers employed dogs to attack their enemies.[20] Going back 3,000 years, various militaries trained elephants 'to mangle enemies in personal combat'.[21] In response to Carthaginian General Pyrrhus unleashing an elephant army during his 280 BC invasion of Italy,[22] the Romans covered pigs in tar and set fire to them, releasing them in the direction of the elephants.

Pigs are part of a long list of animals to which humans have set fire in an effort to create incendiary weapons. Genghis Khan once offered to end a siege if the city provided him a tribute of 1,000 cats and 1,000 swallows.[23] Khan's troops then tied cloth to the tails of the cats and birds, set fire to the cloth and released the animals, which, burning, raced back to the city, setting it alight.[24] And in the Middle Ages, rats set afire were 'aimed' towards an enemy's camp or

19 See Neil Sharkey, 'Automating Warfare: Lessons Learned from the Drones', *Journal of Law, Information and Science* 21 (2011), 140–54 (describing what is meant by autonomous in the context of machines).

20 John M. Kistler, *Animals in the Military: From Hannibal's Elephants to the Dolphins of the US Navy* (Santa Barbara: ABC-CLIO 2011), 4.

21 Ibid., 55. See also John M. Kistler, *War Elephants* (Westport: Praeger 2005).

22 Jilly Cooper, *Animals in War* (London: Corgi Books 2000), 145. Pyrrhus waited so long in the battle to unleash the war elephants that Carthage, while winning the battle, lost over 4,000 soldiers. This is the origin of the term 'pyrrhic victory', referring to a very costly victory. But the cost was and still is measured in human not animal lives.

23 Kistler, *Animals in the Military* (n. 20), 55. See also Kistler, *War Elephants* (n. 21), 349.

24 Ibid.

city.[25] Humans have not limited themselves to animals, also using insects[26] and reptiles[27] as weapons.

Weaponising animals is by no means limited to antiquity. During World War II, the Japanese developed a plan ('Operation Cherry Blossoms at Night') to use 300,000 rats to produce millions of infected fleas which would then be released over the United States to 'spread plague and cholera'.[28] The rats were provided by locals, while the fleas fed on blood from Japanese prisoners of war.[29] When the Japanese were unable to execute the plan against the United States, they set out to release the fleas on the Soviets but were unable to do so before the end of war.[30] The architect of the plan attempted to mask his involvement by releasing the infected rats into the countryside.[31] This resulted in a plague that 'spread into 22 countries and killed more than 20,000 people'.[32]

For their part during World War II, the United States made considerable but ineffective efforts to make bats an incendiary weapon.[33] The plan entailed surgically attaching small incendiary bombs with string through the bats' chests. The bats would be dropped over Japanese cities following which they were expected to chew or gnaw through the irritating string thus causing the bomb to explode.[34] The United

[25] Alexander J. Knights, 'Unconventional Animals in the History of Warfare', *History Forum within All Empires* (2007).

[26] See Lisa Jean Moore and Mary Kosul, 'Bees, Border and Bombs: A Social Account of Theorizing and Weaponizing Bees', in Ryan Hediger (ed.), *Animals and War: Studies of Europe and North America* (Danvers: Brill 2012), 29–43. According to these authors, '[i]n a battle against Roman Invaders in 198 [CE], the people of Hatra near modern Mosul, Iraq placed scorpions inside a terracotta pot. The terracotta pot was then thrown at the besiegers, unleashing the deadly scorpion bomb'. See also Ana Paulina Morrón, 'Nonhuman Animals as Weapons of War', in Colin Salter, Anthony J. Nocella, and Judy K. C. Bentley (eds.), *Animals and War: Confronting the Military – Animal Industrial Complex* (United States: Lexington Books 2014), 62.

[27] See Knights, *Unconventional Animals* (n. 25) (describing a naval battle during which Carthaginian General Hannibal once hurled thousands of clay jars filled with venomous snakes onto enemy ships. 'As the jars smashed, the snakes crawled out and wreaked absolute havoc.').

[28] Jeffrey A. Lockwood, *Six-Legged Soldiers* (New York: Oxford University Press 2009), 117–27, at 121.

[29] Ibid., 118–22.

[30] Ibid., 119–22.

[31] Ibid.

[32] Ibid., 122–3. The American International Prosecution Section 'determined that the Japanese had conducted human experimentation and disseminated plague-infested fleas on the Chinese people' (*ibid.* 123). But the 'United States Army granted immunity from war crimes prosecution in exchange for Japanese scientific data'. See Nicholas D. Kristof, 'Unmasking Horror: A Special Report', *New York Times* (17 March 1995), A12; Lockwood, *Six-Legged Soldiers* (n. 28), 124. The Soviets, on the other hand, prosecuted the architect and others involved for 'manufacturing biological and chemical weapons following experiments on human guinea pigs'. See Russell Working, 'The Trial of Unit 731', *Japan Times* (5 June 2001), available at https://bit.ly/3r9UCwQ, accessed 22 February 2022; Lockwood, *Six-Legged Soldiers* (n. 28), 124–6. The accused were publicly sentenced 'to labor camps for periods of 2 to 25 years,' but ultimately repatriated to Japan.(ibid.).

[33] Cooper, *Animals in War* (n. 22), 339–42. See also Alexis C. Madrigal, 'Old, Weird Tech: The Bat Bombs of World War II', *The Atlantic* (2011), available at https://bit.ly/3zOQ6bo, accessed 22 February 2022.

[34] Robert E. Lubow, *The War Animals* (New York: Doubleday 1977), 32–3(describing the use of bat bombs).

States spent over 2 USD million and conducted thirty demonstrations before cancelling the project.[35] The project accomplished very little, killing a number of bats in a variety of ways, and accidentally burning down a US military aircraft hangar and a US Army general officer's car.[36]

Not to be outdone, the Soviets spectacularly failed in their World War II attempts to employ explosive laden dogs as anti-tank bombers.[37] Initially the concept was that the dogs would drop an anti-tank mine near a German tank and then return to their handler.[38] After those efforts proved unsuccessful the concept changed to making the dogs essentially 'suicide bombers'.[39] To train the dogs to run under a tank (where the armour is thinnest), the Soviets starved the dogs and served them hot food placed under tanks.[40] This modified approach went even more awry than the initial plan, some of the dogs ran away, frightened by the noise and chaos of the battlefield. Other dogs exploded while still with their Soviet handler and Red Army soldiers had to shoot other dogs who left Soviet lines but were trying to run back to their handlers. The Soviets cancelled the programme, though the reason for the cancellation is very telling about military animal use. The Soviets cancelled the programme because it was bad for Red Army soldiers' morale to see the dogs exploding and even have to shoot the dogs themselves.[41]

Using animals as unwitting suicide bombers has unfortunately continued. In 1989, Israel defended the use of dogs to deliver explosives into bunkers and tunnels in Lebanon, with the Assistant Minister of Defense claiming that 'human life takes precedence over virtually all other considerations'.[42] In 2013, the Taliban reportedly planted explosives on a donkey, turning the animal into an improvised explosive device which killed three US service members and their interpreter.[43] And in 2014, Hamas militants reportedly wired both donkeys and dogs with explosives for use in Gaza against Israeli soldiers.[44]

In 2016, the Netherlands announced that its police forces would employ eagles to counter unmanned aerial vehicles or drones but cancelled the programme a year

35 Madrigal, 'Old, Weird Tech' (n. 33).

36 Ibid.

37 Cooper, *Animals in War* (n. 22), 95. See also Will Stewart, 'Revealed: Stalin's Kamikaze Canines Who Were Trained to Blow Themselves Up as Anti-tank Dogs', *Daily Mail* (3 December 2013), available at https://bit.ly/3ngrD9G, accessed 22 February 2022.

38 Stewart, 'Revealed: Stalin's Kamikaze Canines' (n. 37).

39 Ibid.

40 Ibid.

41 Ibid. (quoting one Red Army conscript, '[t]here are enough people being destroyed. Now they are killing dogs too.').

42 Elizabeth A. Lawrence, 'Animals in War: History and Implications for the Future', *Anthrozoös* 4 (1991), 145–53, at 150.

43 Kevin Sites, 'Donkey Bomber Kills Three US Soldiers and An Interpreter', *VICE News* (25 July 2013), available at https://bit.ly/3zNFwkE, accessed 22 February 2022.

44 Chris Hughes, 'Exploding Donkeys and Dog Bombs Unleashed by Hamas Militants on Israeli Commandos in Gaza', *Mirror* (24 July 2014), available at https://bit.ly/3feLuS3, accessed 22 February 2022.

later because, among other reasons, the eagles 'wouldn't always do what they were trained to do'.[45] The following year the French Army reportedly began an experimental programme to train golden eagles to 'spot drones and perform mid-air takedowns'.[46]

For over sixty years, the US Navy has maintained a 'marine mammal programme' comprised of sea lions and dolphins who perform a variety of tasks, including detecting and finding objects (including mines) at depth or in murky water and detecting – and even facilitating – the detention of enemy divers.[47] In 2019, Norwegian fisherman encountered a beluga whale outfitted with a Russian military harness, leading to reports of the Russian military having restarted its own marine mammal programme.[48]

Finally, not only does the possibility exist that weaponised animals may be employed in contemporary conflicts, animals appear to be models for future combat systems. The US Defense Advance Research Projects Agency has established a Biological Technologies Office (BTO) to 'develop capabilities that embrace the unique properties of biology, replication, complexity and applies those features to revolutionize how the United States defends the homeland and prepares and protects its Soldiers, Sailors, Airmen, and Marines'.[49]

Somewhat surprisingly, IHL has very little to say about weaponised animals. As technological advances have increased mankind's capability to kill and destroy in war, IHL also developed to limit the effects of armed conflict. The origins of IHL can

[45] Thuy Ong, 'Dutch Police Will Stop Using Drone-Hunting Eagles since They Weren't Doing What They're Told', *The Verge* (12 December 2017), available at https://bit.ly/3ffzPCm, accessed 22 February 2022.

[46] Jeff John Roberts, 'France Is Training Eagles to Kill Drones', *Fortune* (23 February 2017), available at https://fortune.com/2017/02/22/drones-eagles-france/, accessed 22 February 2022. The French programme purportedly 'involves soldiers raising the eagles from chicks, and training them to associate the drones with food' (ibid.).

[47] Naval Information Warfare Systems Command, 'U.S. Navy Marine Mammal Program' (no date), available at https://bit.ly/3njjoJZ, accessed 22 February 2022. As will be discussed in this chapter, at least one function the marine mammals perform, sea lions attaching clamps to the legs of enemy divers, likely qualifies the sea lions as weapons or a means and method of warfare under IHL. Jane G. Lee, 'Military Whales and Dolphins: What Do They Do and Who Uses Them?', *National Geographic* (3 May 2019), available at https://on.natgeo.com/3GhwIpw, accessed 22 February 2022. See also Daniel Brown, 'Here's How Military Dolphins are Used to Protect US Nukes and Spot Enemy Mines', *Business Insider* (3 May 2017), available at https://bit.ly/3r4DZ5K, accessed 22 February 2022.

[48] Hannah Ellis-Peterson, 'Whale with Harness Could Be Russian Weapon, Say Norwegian Experts', *Guardian* (29 April 2019), available at https://bit.ly/3eWcE01, accessed 22 February 2022.

[49] Defense Advanced Research Projects Agency, 'Biological Technologies Office' (no date), available at www.darpa.mil/about-us/offices/bto, accessed 22 February 2022. One program within the BTO is the 'Technologies for Host Resilience' which 'aims to develop new methods to maintain and optimize force health in the face of new and emerging infectious diseases. The goal is to discover the molecular mechanisms for tolerance of infection in animals, and develop therapeutic strategies that modulate the resilience of humans against infection' (Linda Chrisey, 'Program Information Technologies for Host Resilience (THoR)' (no date), available at www.darpa.mil/program/technologies-for-host-resilience, accessed 22 February 2022).

be found at the same time as the earliest uses of animals as weapons.[50] References to IHL are also found in the texts of the world's leading religions.[51] But early IHL is either silent on or accepting of weaponised animals. For example, similar to Genghis Khan's burning of cats and birds discussed above, the Bible's Book of Judges discusses Samson capturing 300 foxes, 'igniting their tails, and setting them loose to run through the Philistine's fields, vineyards and groves'.[52]

Despite the prominent role animals have played in armed conflict and that IHL is designed to limit the effects of armed conflict, animals have no legal status and receive no specific protections.[53] Even as IHL became more formalised with the nineteenth-century Geneva and Hague Conventions and their twentieth-century additions, along with AP I and AP II, IHL makes surprisingly little reference to animals, and even then the references are in relation to humans. For example, the 1996 Protocol II to the 1980 Convention on Prohibitions or Restrictions of the Use of Certain Conventional Weapons Which May be Deemed to be Excessively Injurious or to Have Indiscriminate Effects prohibits the use of booby traps and other devices which are 'in any way attached to or associated with . . . animals or their carcasses'.[54] According to one commentator this is the only direct reference to animals in any IHL treaty.[55] The other references to animals in IHL instruments reflect that animals are 'mere objects'.[56] This includes the 1907 Hague Convention IV dictating that prisoners of war 'have the right to keep all their personal belongings, "except arms, horses, and military papers"' and AP I prohibiting the destruction and removal of livestock because livestock constitutes an 'object' indispensable to the survival of the civilian population.[57] Another, albeit indirect, way by which IHL references animals is as part of the 'environment'. More than one IHL treaty prohibits means and methods of warfare which are intended, or may be expected to cause widespread, severe, damage to the environment.[58]

50 Elchin Mameday, 'What Are the Origins of International Humanitarian Law?', *ICRC Blog* (7 August 2017), available at https://bit.ly/33ulTC8, accessed 22 February 2022 (referring to Hammurabi, then King of Babylon, as proclaiming the first laws of war in in 1754 BC).

51 Amanda Alexander, 'A Short History of International Humanitarian Law', *European Journal of International Law* 26 (2015), 109–38, at 109. See also Ahmed Al-Dawoody, 'IHL and Islam: An Overview' (14 March 2017), *Humanitarian Law and Policy*, available at https://bit.ly/3zOPAd4, accessed 22 February 2022.

52 Morrón, 'Nonhuman Animals' (n. 26), 55.

53 See Nowrot, 'Animals at War' (n. 7), 134.

54 Art. 6(1)(x) of Protocol II on Prohibitions or Restrictions on the Use of Mines, Booby-Traps and Other Devices (Protocol II) of 10 October 1980 (as amended on 3 May 1996) annexed to the Convention on Prohibitions or Restrictions on the Use of Certain Conventional Weapons Which May Be Deemed Excessively Injurious or to Have Indiscriminate Effects of 10 October 1980, 1342 UNTS 137 (Convention on Certain Convention Weapons).

55 Nowrot, 'Animals at War' (n. 7), 136.

56 Ibid., 136.

57 Ibid.

58 ICRC Customary Law Database, Rule 45.

The perverse state of IHL as applied to animals is perhaps best illustrated by the fact that IHL does not prohibit using animals as suicide bombers but draws a line at placing booby traps on animals or their carcasses.[59] Why? Because of the concern of humans being tricked into thinking it was safe to do what humans always do, use animals, only for the human to be injured or killed by the booby trap. Indeed, when the examples of weaponised animals discussed in Section 1 are considered against the corpus of IHL, only launching diseased animals against an enemy is clearly prohibited.[60] By way of further illustration as to the challenge of looking to IHL for definitive prohibitions regarding weaponised animals, it is by no means clearly settled in 2022 that launching a basket of poisonous snakes against one's enemy in armed conflict would violate IHL.[61] As a result, the opportunity cost for first considering non-international armed conflict, where there is even less IHL applicable as a matter of law, is not high. Arguably the lack of IHL is a positive as the gap allows for the possibility of international, regional organisation, and domestic law to moderate at least some weaponised animal usage.

3 NON-INTERNATIONAL ARMED CONFLICT

The first line of argument in the effort to limit the weaponising of animals in armed conflict is to consider non-international armed conflict. While there are a number of approaches to the interplay between other bodies of law and IHL during armed conflict, the argument for applying that other law seems strongest when there is minimal IHL in general and none which specifically applies to animals.[62] That situation is found during non-international armed conflict. The three potential sources of law which may still bind – or limit – a state during a non-international armed conflict are international law (Section 3.1), regional organisation law (Section 3.2), and domestic law (Section 3.3). As discussed in the next section, international law proves of little assistance and regional organisation's contribution may be to prompt the development of domestic law recognising animals as living entities and not objects.

59 See Art. 6(1)(x) of Protocol II annexed to the Convention on Certain Convention Weapons (n. 54). Under the protocol, a '"Booby-trap" means any device or material which is designed, constructed or adapted to kill or injure, and which functions unexpectedly when a person disturbs or approaches an apparently harmless object or performs an apparently safe act' (ibid., Art. 2(2)).

60 Two twentieth-century biological warfare treaties would likely prohibit launching diseased animals against an enemy. See Protocol for the Prohibition of the Use in War of Asphyxiating, Poisonous or Other Gases and of Bacteriological Methods of Warfare of 17 June 1925, 94 LNTS 95; Convention on the Prohibition of the Development, Production and Stockpiling of Bacteriological (Biological) and Toxin Weapons and or Their Destruction of 10 April 1972, 1015 UNTS 163.

61 While Article 23(a) of the Hague Regulations states that 'it is especially forbidden . . . to employ poison or poisoned weapons', there is no universal definition for what constitutes poison or poisoned weapon.

62 See Daragh Murray, *Practitioners' Guide to Human Rights in Armed Conflict* (New York: Oxford University Press 2016); Cordula Droege, 'Elective Affinities? Human Rights and Humanitarian Law', *International Law Review of the Red Cross* 90 (2008), 501–48.

3.1 *International Law*

As one commentator has noted, 'although various international law instruments address the protection of endangered species, habitat protect, and biological diversity, very little attention is given to the welfare of animals, let alone animal rights'.[63] In 1978, a Universal Declaration of Animal Rights was presented to UNESCO.[64] Over a decade later, the declaration was modified and submitted to UNESCO.[65] It 'went well beyond the scope of existing international regulation, and went nowhere'.[66]

There are at least two texts of a proposed 'Universal Declaration for the Welfare of Animals' as the result of conferences in the Philippines in 2002 and in Costa Rica in 2005, but neither have been adopted.[67] And in 2018, a pre-draft of a proposed UN Convention on Animal Health and Protection was released but has not made substantive progress toward adoption.[68]

While general international law has proven no more useful than IHL, regional instruments, in particular one from Europe, may provide some assistance albeit not directly.

3.2 *Regional Organisation Law*

In 1987, the European Convention for the Protection of Pet Animals was opened for signatures.[69] In 1992, following the fourth ratification the convention entered force.[70] As of February 2020 some twenty-three members of the Council of Europe have ratified the convention.[71]

As the convention's title makes clear, the subject is pet animals, a subset of animals. The convention defines pet animal as 'any animal kept or intended to be

63 Anne Peters, 'Global Animal Law: What It Is and Why We Need It', *Transnational Environmental Law* 5 (2016), 9–23, at 13. See also Michael J Bowman, 'The Protection of Animals under International Law', *Connecticut Journal of International Law* 4 (1989), 487–99 (explaining the need for a truly global animal law instrument with effective enforcement procedures).

64 'Compromise & the Universal Declaration of Animal Welfare', *Animal People* (July–August 2005), 3, available at https://bit.ly/3qmFNYs, accessed 22 February 2022. See also Jean-Marc Neumann, 'The Universal Declaration of Animal Rights or the Creation of a New Equilibrium Between Species', *Animal Law* 19 (2012), 91–109.

65 'Animal People' (n. 64), 3.

66 Ibid.

67 World Society for the Protection of Animals, 'Universal Declaration of Animal Welfare' (2007), available at www.wspa-usa.org/wspaswork/udaw/Default.html, accessed 22 February 2022. See also Miah Gibson, 'The Universal Declaration of Animal Welfare', *Deakin Law Review* 16 (2011), 539–67.

68 Global Animal Law Association, UN Convention on Animal Health and Protection of 23 August 2018, available at www.globalanimallaw.org/database/universal.html, accessed 22 February 2022.

69 Council of Europe: European Convention for the Protection of Pet Animals of 13 November 1987, available at https://bit.ly/3HWbEFw, accessed 22 February 2022.

70 Ibid.

71 Council of Europe, 'Chart of Signatures and Ratifications of Treaty 125', available at https://bit.ly/31QT6Hr, accessed 22 February 2022.

kept by man in particular in his household for private enjoyment and companionship'.[72] As a result, in and of itself the convention does not prohibit weaponising animals. Even where the weaponised animal is of a type which would qualify as a pet, for example a dog, if a state intended to have a dog serve as an unwitting suicide bomber à la the Soviets in World War II, that dog was not 'intended to be kept by man in particular in his household for private enjoyment and companionship'.[73] Accordingly, an explosive laded canine is an animal but not a pet animal under the convention.

Ultimately it is not what the convention does directly that factors into protecting animals, but indirectly, through the development of domestic law recognising animals.

3.3 *Domestic Law*

An important first step is to dereify animals' status as things. In 1988, Austria was the first to modify its civil code to reflect that animals were not things, followed by Germany in 1990, Switzerland in 2003, Catalonia in Spain in 2006, the Netherlands in 2011, and the Czech Republic in 2012.[74] However, as the Global Animal Network noted, 'while innovative, [those code] statement[s] say what the animals are not, but not much what the animals legally are. We simply know that they are distinct from common things. In the civil law of these countries, the status of animals is therefore a "non-thing" status.'[75] As unclear as that seems, it is actually worse. The civil code of the countries listed above still specify that 'provisions applying to things also apply to animals. This implies a type of "non-thing thing" status for animals.'[76]

But change and progress continue. In 2015, France, New Zealand and Quebec 'amended their laws to recognize animals as sentient beings'.[77] In September, 2018, Slovakia revised the definition of animals in its civil code to 'reflect that they are living beings, not things' and, according to one Slovakian media outlet, 'animals will enjoy special status and value as living creatures that are to perceive the world with their own senses'.[78] In November, the Brussels Parliament introduced legislation which would recognise animals as a special category of 'a living being endowed with

[72] Art. 1(1) of the European Convention for the Protection of Pet Animals (69).

[73] Ibid.

[74] Sabine Brels, 'The Evolution of the Legal Status of Animals: From Things to Sentient Beings', *The Conscious Lawyer* (January 2016), available at https://bit.ly/3GgrpXr, accessed 22 February 2022.

[75] Ibid.

[76] Ibid. For example, while it declares that 'animals are not objects; they are protected by special laws', the civil code of Austria acknowledges that if no contrary regulation exists then '[t]he provisions in force for the things apply to animals' (Civil Code (Allgemeines Bürgerliches Gesetzbuch) (ABGB), Art. 285(a)).

[77] Nicole Pallotta, 'Brussels Recognizes Animals as Sentient Beings Distinct from Objects, Animal Legal Defense Fund' *Animal Legal Defense Fund* (8 December 2018), available at https://bit.ly/3qmoHdC, accessed 22 February 2022.

[78] Ibid.

sensitivity, interests of its own and dignity, that benefits from special protection'.[79] The Brussels Secretary of State is quoted as saying that the ultimate aim is 'for animals to benefit finally from the legal status that corresponds to their biological nature'.[80] Of note, as referenced in the introduction and discussed at the end of this chapter, the ability to perceive the world is a significant component of the definition of autonomous as applied to autonomous weapons.

The admittedly patchwork and varied result is that, particularly in Europe, at least some domestic law in some countries provides increased protections to animals. That domestic law is obviously operative in peacetime. In the case of civil unrest, that domestic law, unless derogated, would still be operative. And as civil unrest crossed the armed conflict threshold that domestic law would potentially still apply.[81] Each state of course has its own mechanisms for when lawsuits may be filed. Without delving into the legal mechanisms of each and every state which has revised how animals are considered, the point is that there is the potential, particularly in some European countries, to make the argument that weaponising animals violates domestic law which may still be operative during non-international armed conflict. This may implicate only a few states. A handful of additional states might be added as the result of the next line of argument, leveraging the weapons review process in international armed conflict.

4 INTERNATIONAL ARMED CONFLICT

This section considers whether states are meeting their international law obligations if animal objects qualify as weapons under IHL and thus should be subject to legal review.

Animals used as weapons means quite literally that; an animal as the weapon as opposed to animals which transport a weapon, say a cavalry trooper on horseback, or tow or pull a weapon, say mules pulling artillery, or animals delivering messages (pigeons) or serving as sentries/providing early warning (dogs).[82]

Where certain animals and/or their usage qualifies as weapons or means and methods of warfare, states would be required to conduct a legal review. At least certain animals and/or their usage would seem to qualify as weapons, a point not a single state has formally acknowledged. And despite animals being used as weapons, no state has publicly acknowledged conducting the legal review international law

79 Ibid.

80 Ibid.

81 ICTY, *Prosecutor* v. *Duško Tadić*, decision of 2 October 1995, IT-94-1-AR72, para. 49 (detailing factors to consider in determining the existence of an armed conflict).

82 See, for example, Cooper, *Animals in War* (n. 22) (discussing a wide range of war animals); John C. Burham, *A Soldier's Best Friend* (New York: Union Square Press 2008) (discussing military working dogs); John E. O'Donnell, *None Came Home: The War Dogs of Vietnam* (1st Book Library 2001) (discussing military working dogs); Michael G. Lemish, *War Dogs: Canines in Combat* (Lincoln: Potomac Books 1996) (discussing military working dogs).

requires. If IHL insists on treating animals as objects then states should be held to account for when those 'objects' constitute weapons. Ideally increased public scrutiny of animals as weapons could lead to states disavowing their use and even signing a declaration to that effect. But at a minimum, states using animals as weapons should have to own their actions and perform the required legal review.

4.1 *Weapons under International Humanitarian Law*

Under the 1907 Hague Convention IV, 'the right of belligerents to adopt means of injuring the enemy is not unlimited'.[83] Means of injuring the enemy includes weapons but also means and methods of warfare.

The ICRC considers weapons 'weapons of all types – be they anti-personnel or anti-material, "lethal" or non-lethal weapons systems'.[84] The US Department of Defense Law of War Working Group utilises a more expansive definition under which what constitutes weapons includes:

> all arms, munitions, materiel, instruments, mechanisms, or devices that have an intended effect of injuring, damaging, destroying or disabling personnel or property, and the term "weapon system" refers to the weapon itself and those components required for its operation, including new, advanced or emerging technologies which may lead to development of weapons or weapon systems and which have significant legal and policy implications. Weapons systems are limited to those components or technologies having direct injury or damaging effect on people or property (including all munitions and technologies such as projectiles, small arms, mines, explosives, and all other devices and technologies that are physically destructive or injury producing).[85]

Means of warfare is more difficult to determine. According to one commentator, 'the concept refers to military equipment that is not a weapon per se but "nonetheless has an impact on the offensive capability of the force to which it belongs"'.[86] Means of warfare is a broader than a weapon and encompasses 'acts of violence against the adversary, whether in offence or in defence'.[87] More precisely, as noted by Heather A. Harrison Dinniss and Jann K. Kleffner, 'Methods of warfare refers to activities designed to adversely affect the enemy's military operations or military capacity and extends to the various general categories of operations (bombing, ground, close-air support, etc.), as well as the specific tactics used for attack. A common shorthand for methods of

83 Art. 22 of the Hague Convention IV.
84 ICRC Weapons Review (n. 12), 1.1.
85 W. Hays Parks, Office of The Judge Advocate General of the Army, 'Weapons Review Programme of the United States', presented at the Expert Meeting on Legal Reviews of Weapons and the SIrUS Project, Jongny sur Vevey, Switzerland, 29–31 January 2001.
86 Vincent Boulanin and Maaike Verbruggen, 'Article 36 Reviews: Dealing with the Challenges Posed by Emerging Technologies' (Stockholm: SIPRI 2017), 3, available at www.sipri.org/sites/default/files/2017-12/article_36_report_1712.pdf, accessed 22 February 2022.
87 Art. 49(1) of AP I.

warfare is "the way in which [weapons] are used" in hostilities.'[88] In considering whether military equipment constitutes a means of war, it is necessary 'to understand how it works and how it may be used on the battlefield ... [thus] [t]he terms "means" and "method of warfare" must therefore be read together'.[89] For the ICRC,

> the words 'methods and means' include weapons in the widest sense, as well as the way in which they are used. The use that is made of a weapon can be unlawful in itself, or it can be unlawful only under certain conditions. For example, poison is unlawful in itself, as would be any weapon which would, by its very nature, be so imprecise that it would inevitably cause indiscriminate damage. ... However, a weapon that can be used with precision can also be abusively used against the civilian population. In this case, it is not the weapon which is prohibited, but the method or the way in which it is used.[90]

The question then becomes do – or may – animals qualify as a weapon and/or means and method of warfare?

4.2 *Animals as Weapons*

The analysis of whether animals constitute weapons or means and method of warfare is relatively straightforward because, as discussed, IHL considers animals as objects. Most of the contemporary uses of animals appear to involve animals as delivery mechanisms for the application of both lethal (dogs and donkeys laden with explosives) and non-lethal (sea lions attaching clamps to the legs of enemy divers) force. Here the animals would not be considered weapons but would constitute a means and method of warfare. By contrast, the Dutch and French example of eagles used against drones is one where the animal itself is the offensive capability and thus the eagles would be considered as a weapon. Here we see the second or third order effect of IHL not affording animals a status. Despite being alive and sentient, under IHL animals are essentially indistinguishable from a helicopter outfitted with missiles (functional equivalent of dogs/donkeys carrying explosives) or the missile itself (eagle attacking drones).

Without question there are ways in which animals could be – and already have been – utilised that would constitute either a weapon or a means and method of warfare. Given that, such use is subject to a legal review, at least for states parties to AP I.

4.3 *Legal Review*

The international community could – but has thus far not – decided to regulate, or ban, the use of animals as weapons. Indeed, some weapons are per se illegal as the

88 Heather A. Harrison Dinniss and Jann K. Kleffner, 'Soldier 2.0: Military Human Enhancement and International Law', *International Law Studies* 92 (2016), 432–82, at 437.

89 Boulanin and Verbruggen, 'Article 36 Reviews' (n. 86), 3.

90 AP I Commentary, para. 1402.

result of a treaty restricting or banning their use. This includes: explosive projectiles weighing less than 400 grammes,[91] bullets that expand or flatten in the human body,[92] poison and poisoned weapons,[93] chemical weapons,[94] biological weapons,[95] weapons that injure by fragments which, in the human body, escape detection by X-rays,[96] incendiary weapons,[97] blinding laser weapons,[98] mines, booby traps and other devices,[99] anti-personnel mines,[100] explosive remnants of war,[101] and cluster munitions.[102] Most weapons are not illegal per se, meaning that 'use may be lawful in some circumstances, although unlawful in others'.[103] This category of not illegal per se weapons includes animals and are subject to a required review.

Under Article 36 of AP I: 'In the study, development, acquisition or adoption of a new weapon, means or method of warfare, a High Contracting Party is under an obligation to determine whether its employment would, in some or all circumstances, be prohibited by this Protocol or by any other rule of international law applicable to the High Contracting Party.'[104] AP I is of course binding on its 174 states parties. The ICRC contends that '[t]he requirement that all new weapons, means and methods of warfare be systematically assessed is arguably one that applies to all States'.[105] The United States, which is not a party to AP I, claims to not be bound by the obligation of Article 36.[106] However, as a matter of long-standing policy predating AP I, the United States conducts legal reviews of the intended

[91] Declaration of Saint Petersburg Renouncing the Use, in Time of War, of Explosive, Projectiles Under 400 Grammes Weight of 29 November and 11 December 1868.

[92] Hague Declaration concerning Expanding Bullets, 29 July 1899.

[93] Art. 23(a) of the Hague Regulations.

[94] Convention on the Prohibition of the Development, Production, Stockpiling and Use of Chemical Weapons and on Their Destruction of 13 January 1993, 1974 UNTS 317.

[95] Protocol for the Prohibition of the Use in War of Asphyxiating, Poisonous or Other Gases and of Bacteriological Methods of Warfare (n. 60); Convention on the Prohibition of the Development, Production and Stockpiling of Bacteriological (Biological) and Toxin Weapons and on Their Destruction (n. 60).

[96] Protocol I on Non-Detectable Fragments annexed to the Convention on Certain Convention Weapons (n. 54).

[97] Protocol III on Prohibitions or Restrictions on the Use of Incendiary Weapons of 10 October 1980 annexed to the Convention on Certain Conventional Weapons (n. 54).

[98] Protocol IV on Blinding Laser Weapons of 13 October 1995 annexed to the Convention on Certain Convention Weapons (n. 54).

[99] Protocol II annexed to the Convention on Certain Convention Weapons (n. 54).

[100] Convention on the Prohibition of the Use, Stockpiling, Production and Transfer of Anti-Personnel Mines and on their Destruction of 18 September 1997, 2056 UNTS 211.

[101] Protocol V on Explosive Remnants of War of 28 November 2003 annexed to the Convention on Certain Convention Weapons (n. 54).

[102] Convention on Cluster Munitions of 30 May 2008.

[103] US Department of Defense, *Law of War Manual* (Washington, DC: Office of General Counsel, US Department of Defense 2016), para. 6.1.1 (distinguishing the legality of the weapon itself (per se) from the legality of the use of the weapon).

[104] Art. 36 of AP I.

[105] ICRC Weapons Review (n. 12), 4.

[106] Boulanin and Verbruggen, 'Article 36 Reviews' (n. 86), 18.

procurement, acquisition, and use of weapons and weapons systems, but not means and methods of warfare.

Neither Article 36 nor its associated commentary provide information or detail on the process by which states are to review weapons and means and methods of warfare. As a general proposition, the review must include assessing:

whether the weapon's intended use is calculated to cause superfluous injury;
whether the weapon is inherently indiscriminate; and
whether the weapon falls within a class of weapons that has been specifically prohibited.

Even where a weapon is not prohibited, there may be specific legal restrictions on the weapon's use. These specific legal restrictions largely have nothing to do with animals and include cluster munitions, incendiary weapons, laser weapons (except blinding lasers which are per se illegal), riot control agents, herbicides, nuclear weapons, and explosive ordnance. The one specific legal restriction which implicates animals is the already discussed prohibited on booby-trapping animals or animal carcasses.

It is important to recognise the difference between a weapons system which is per se unlawful because it cannot be aimed versus an inaccurate weapon system which, depending on how it is used, may or may not be unlawful. As Mike Schmitt and Jeff Thurnher explain,

> The classic case is that of the SCUD missiles launched by Iraq during the 1990–1991 Gulf War. While it is true that the missiles were inaccurate, they were not unlawful per se because situations existed in which they could be employed discriminately. In particular, the missiles were capable of employment against troops in open areas such as the desert, and they actually struck very large military installations without seriously endanger the civilian population. However when launched in the direction of cities, as repeatedly occurred during the conflict, their use was undeniably unlawful.[107]

A similar argument has been made concerning animals as weapons. If a military were to field a weaponised rhino in an urban battlefield that contains innocent civilians, we would be reasonably worried that the war-rhino does not comply with Article 36, if rhinos cannot reliably discriminate friends from foe, for example, a rhino may target and charge a non-combatant child in violation of the principle of distinction.[108] That a war-rhino cannot reliably distinguish between a non-combatant child and an enemy belligerent is of course problematic. But unless the point is that war-rhinos are of a nature to strike combatants, military objectives, civilians, and

[107] Michael N. Schmitt and Jeffrey S. Thurnher, '"Out of the Loop": Autonomous Weapon Systems and the Law of Armed Conflict', *Harvard National Security Journal* 4 (2013), 231–81, at 246.

[108] Patrick Lin, Maxwell J. Mehlman, and Keith Abney, *Enhanced Warfighters: Risk, Ethics, and Policy* (San Luis Obispo: California Polytechnic State University 2013), 29.

civilian objects without distinction then the war-rhino is not per se illegal. Similar to the SCUD missile, the lawful use of the war-rhino would simply be limited and not include urban battlefields.

The idea that the manner by which humans are using animals in the military and during armed conflict might require legal review has not been the subject of much, really any, discussion. But at least one group of commentators and a prominent practitioner have directly or indirectly lent support. In their 2013 book, Patrick Lin, Maxwell Mehlman, and Keith Abney wrote of the challenges stemming from enhancing human warfighters.[109] In arguing that enhanced humans might require legal review they noted that '[t]hroughout history, humans have employed animals in the service of war, such as dogs, elephants, pigeons, sea lions, dolphins, and possibly rhinoceroses . . . [and that] other organisms are plausibly weapons subject to an Article 36 review'.[110]

In 2016, the International Institute for Humanitarian Law focused its annual 'roundtable' meeting on Weapons and the International Rule of Law.[111] Marie Van Hoofstat, then the Legal Advisor for the Belgian Ministry of Defense, provided the Belgian perspective on the legal review of weapons. In explaining how the Belgian Commission charged with reviewing weapons had thus far only reviewed weapons or weapons systems, Ms. Hoofstat added that '[t]he Belgian Commission has not (yet) conducted a review of military working dogs, but one could wonder whether they qualify as a means of warfare. Or are they to be considered as a weapon and should their use be evaluated as a method of warfare?'[112]

The point of this section is not that animals as weapons or means and methods of warfare would or would not pass a legal review but that there are number of states that would appear to be required to conduct such a review yet there is no indication of their being completed. This issue is much broader than as applied to animals, all states – or all states with an armed forces – are required to conduct these reviews but they are not required to release them. As discussed in the introduction, fewer than twenty states conduct any reviews. But those states who do conduct legal reviews could – and arguably should – be put on the spot to either disavow weaponising animals or to acknowledge they have weaponised animals and conducted the requisite review. Particularly if and when a state reviews an animal as weapon, how the state answers the question of whether the weapon's intended use is calculated to cause superfluous injury and whether the weapon is inherently indiscriminate would be interesting on its own, and also potentially assist the LAWS discussion.

109 Ibid.

110 Ibid.

111 Baldwin De Vidts and Gian Luca Beruto (eds.), *Weapons and the International Rule of Law: 39th Round Table on Current Issues of International Humanitarian Law* (San Remo: International Institute of Humanitarian Law 2017).

112 Marie Van Hoofstat, 'Legal Reviews of New Weapons: Process and Procedures', in Baldwin De Vidts and Gian Luca Beruto (eds.), *Weapons and the International Rule of Law* (n. 111), 51–7, at 52.

5 ANIMALS AND LAWS

Arguably, in order for IHL to maintain logical coherence, society cannot move forward on autonomous weapons without confronting what has been wilfully overlooked: how IHL applies to animals used as weapons. Perhaps it is fitting that it may have taken developments in the emerging technologies autonomous weapons to facilitate a long-overdue examination of animals as weapons. And as referenced above, there are aspects of weaponising animals which may help inform the LAWS discussion.[113]

In terms of the weapons review question of whether the weapon's intended use is calculated to cause superfluous injury, that is normally thought of in the context of whether the weapon, once it has rendered a target hors de combat, is designed to continue to injure. The classic examples include use of glass as shrapnel, which will be difficult for X-rays to detect, or coating a sharpened stake with excrement with the goal of the resulting puncture wound being made worse through infection.[114]

In terms of LAWS, some may question whether there is additional moral injury caused by using a robotic machine and not a human.[115] In terms of weaponised animals, what injury is actually calculated in using the animal is unclear but there may be a similar question as to whether an animal as the modality of injury is somehow the source of injury and whether that injury is considered superfluous.[116]

In terms of the legal review question of whether the weapon is inherently indiscriminate, the comparison between weaponised animals and LAWS seems even more apt. In determining how discriminating a LAWS would have to be to pass legal muster, is that more, less, or the same as a weaponised animal? Dogs did not seem to be particularly discriminating about who or what to blow up when employed by the Soviets in World War II. Is that the low bar autonomous weapons must equal or surpass? Perhaps the answer to the various World War II examples is that they did not violate IHL at the time, but would today. But is that actually the

[113] But see Rebecca Crootof, 'Autonomous Weapon Systems and the Limits of Analogy', *Harvard National Security Journal* 9 (2018), 51–83(discussing the problems with analogizing between LAWS and both animals and child soldiers). Crootof acknowledges that '[i]n many ways, animals are the best analogy for autonomous weapon systems' and that the animal analogy is 'conceptually useful'. But Crootof contends the utility is limited as 'there is no international "law of animal combatants"' (to this author's thinking that only increases, not lessens, the value of the analogy) (ibid., 78).

[114] ICRC Customary Law Database, Rule 70.

[115] Christof Heyns, Autonomous Weapons Systems and Human Rights Law, Presentation made at the informal expert meeting organised in Geneva on 13–16 May 2014 by the state parties to the Convention on Certain Conventional Weapons (n. 54).

[116] The first time planes or tanks were introduced on the battlefield, in addition to confusion no doubt enemy soldiers were terrified of this new, unknown, weapon. Some of that fear may well have been desired and even intended, as in the sirens on a German Stuka dive bomber. But that does not mean that caused superfluous injury. See Rebecca Grant, 'The Stuka Terror', *Air Force Magazine* (1 October 2008), available at www.airforcemag.com/article/1008stuka/, accessed 22 February 2022. Neil Prior, 'WW1: Tanks Inspired War Effort as British "Iron Landships"', *BBC News* (30 August 2014), available at www.bbc.com/news/uk-wales-28605164, accessed 22 February 2022.

case? Would suicide dog bombers be per se prohibited by IHL? Israel did not seem to think so as recently as the 1980s. And there are European countries experimenting with using birds as counter drone weapons and the US and Russian marine mammal programmes, at a minimum, to consider.

Given how circular the LAWS discussion has been thus far, perhaps CCW states parties might benefit from discussing weaponised animals, whether they constitute LAWS, and whether/under which circumstances would weaponised animals violate IHL.

Humans have a status under IHL and with that status come obligations and protections. But LAWS, like animals, do not possess agency, cannot assume legal obligations, and are considered objects under IHL. Do we have the same concerns about LAWS as objects as with animals? Could the accountability question as applied to weaponised animals help inform that same discussion in the LAWS context? While some observers believe accountability when using autonomous weapons will pose a challenge to IHL, at least one commentator has analogised employing autonomous weapons to employing 'animal soldiers' – that 'any violations of the laws of war committed by or least with assistance of animal soldiers will, in the same way as it is already currently the case, continue to be attributed to those human combatants who have deployed the animals and are thus responsible for supervising them appropriately'.[117]

Finally, and returning to using the LAWS discussion as backhanded way of prohibiting weaponised animals, some thirty states are calling for LAWS to be banned. Those states are Algeria, Argentina, Austria, Bolivia, Brazil, Chile, China, Colombia, Costa Rica, Cuba, Djibouti, Ecuador, Egypt, El Salvador, Ghana, Guatemala, Holy See, Iraq, Jordan, Mexico, Morocco, Namibia, Nicaragua, Pakistan, Panama, Peru, State of Palestine, Uganda, Venezuela, and Zimbabwe.[118] According to Human Rights Watch, the Non-Aligned Movement, comprised of 125 states, has also called for prohibition or regulation of LAWS.[119]

Presenting those states with the question of the IHL legality of weaponised animals may facilitate the LAWS discussions. It seems hard to argue that animals are not autonomous or that in certain circumstances could be weapons or means and methods of warfare. That would seemingly yield an autonomous weapon. So rather than speculate about future, as yet undeveloped, autonomous weapons, why not discuss the extant animal autonomous weapons?

6 CONCLUDING RECOMMENDATIONS

The overall goal of this chapter was to provide legal arguments for achieving a measure of protection of animals from being weaponised during armed conflict.

[117] Nowrot, 'Animals at War' (n. 7), 142.
[118] Stauffe, 'Stopping Killer Robots' (n. 18).
[119] Ibid.

This chapter assumed a utilitarian, ends-focused, approach. Varied and patchwork protected, while by no means ideal, seems better than the status quo of virtually no protection.

Each line of argument: the recognition that the lack of non-international armed conflict IHL may allow increased incorporation of domestic law; the leveraging of states weapons review obligations in international armed conflict; and the shifting of the CCW LAWS discussion to consider animals has the potential to yield some protection. The protection would come in different, piecemeal, ways: law, custom, and policy. Taken together, the three lines of argument may yield both synergy and momentum towards an IHL prohibition against using animals as weapons or means and method of warfare in armed conflict.

SELECT BIBLIOGRAPHY

Boulanin, Vincent and Maaike Verbruggen, 'Article 36 Reviews: Dealing With the Challenges Posed by Emerging Technologies' (Stockholm: SIPRI 2017), 3, available at https://bit.ly/33ra8MP, accessed 22 February 2022.

Cooper, Jilly, *Animals in War* (London: Corgi Books 2000).

Hediger, Ryan (ed.), *Animals and War: Studies of Europe and North America* (Danvers: Brill 2012).

Kistler, John M., *Animals in the Military: From Hannibal's Elephants to the Dolphins of the US Navy* (Santa Barbara: ABC-CLIO 2011).

Lawand, Kathleen, Robin Coupland, and Peter Herby, *A Guide to the Legal Review of New Weapons, Means and Methods of Warfare: Measures to Implement Article 36 of Additional Protocol I of 1977* (Geneva: ICRC 2006).

Nowrot, Karsten, 'Animals at War: The Status of "Animal Soldiers" under International Humanitarian Law', *Historical Social Research* 40 (2015), 128–50.

10

Animals as Combatants and as Prisoners of War?

Jérôme de Hemptinne, Tadesse Kebebew and Joshua Joseph Niyo[*]

1 INTRODUCTION

Many animals serve in the military around the world in various capacities.[1] For instance, horses, donkeys, mules, elephants, and camels are employed to carry heavy loads – such as food, water, ammunition, or medical supplies – to soldiers located in war zones. Pigeons are instructed to deliver strategic messages, and eagles to combat drones. Elephants, dogs, and rats are trained to detect anything from explosives and booby traps to humans buried in rubble.[2] Dogs patrol and protect military bases. Dolphins and sea lions are used to find or lay underwater mines, to locate enemy combatants, or to seek and destroy submarines using kamikaze methods.[3] Dogs, cats, and other animals, such as monkeys, are kept as mascots to raise troops' morale and provide them with company and peace of mind.

But, when they are deployed in the theatre of hostilities to participate in military operations, should animals be treated as combatants? In that case, can they be targeted at all times? Given the sacrifices that they make during warfare and the many lives they save by performing dangerous tasks that are usually devoted to human beings, are these animal soldiers protected when captured by the enemy? Should they be entitled to a status similar to that of prisoner of war with the associated safeguards? Alternatively, if they do not fulfil all the requirements for such status, should they be entitled to equivalent treatment under international

* The authors are indebted to Giulio Bartolini for his helpful comments on an earlier draft.

1 For a description of the various military usages of animals, see Jenks, Chapter 9: 'War Weapons', in this volume.

2 Michael Ray, 'Fightin' Fauna: 6 Animals of War', *Encyclopedia Britannica*, no date, available at: www.britannica.com/list/fightin-fauna-6-animals-of-war. On the use of military dogs in the United States, see S. D. Cruse, 'Military Working Dogs: Classification and Treatment in the US Armed Forces', *Animal Law* 21 (2014–15), 250–83, available at: https://bit.ly/3Hg3ZRw. See generally '12 Ways Animals Have Helped the War Effort', *Imperial War Museums* (no date), available at: https://bit.ly/3sdlNZx.

3 Terrill Ceiridwen, 'Romancing the Bomb: Marine Animals in Naval Strategic Defense', *Organization & Environment* 14 (2001), 105–13. See also John M. Kistler, *Animals in the Military: From Hannibal's Elephants to the Dolphins of the US Navy* (Santa Barbara: ABC-CLIO 2011), 311–26.

humanitarian law (IHL)? Should this treatment be adapted to the specific needs of non-human creatures?

When addressing these questions, we must keep in mind that, under IHL, animals are usually treated as objects and not as persons.[4] As noted in previous chapters, this body of law exclusively reserves the latter category for human beings. However, we felt it important to examine whether applying to animals the status of combatant and prisoner of war, or the equivalent treatment thereof, could improve their fate when they are actively involved in hostilities and when they fall into the power of the enemy. Indeed, IHL can no longer ignore the evolution of animals' protection in many jurisdictions around the world. In the same way that the strengthening of human rights, and the increased awareness of environmental challenges after World War II, have impacted the development of IHL, the increasing concern for animal welfare during the last decades should also progressively guarantee that animals are protected, not as mere objects of war, but as true subjects of war.[5] Of course, this course of action could appear to many scholars, non-governmental organisations (NGOs), or military persons as inappropriate, particularly in a context where human beings themselves are often confronted with extreme violence and are left largely unprotected. Nevertheless, as emphasised in the introduction to this book,[6] safeguarding animals and protecting human beings are two separate issues that can usually run in parallel, without necessarily having a negative impact on each other. Indeed, the protection of animals' interests does not automatically interfere with – or run contrary to – the guaranteeing of human needs.[7] Moreover, based on the proportionality principle, IHL guarantees that fundamental human values prevail over animal interests when, in extreme circumstances, it is necessary to choose between the two.[8] On the other hand, we should bear in mind that, by referring to human categories in order to reinforce the protection of animals involved in war, we run the risk of reaching anthropomorphist conclusions, which would attribute human characteristics to animals.[9] This is precisely why we must continuously assess to what extent the concrete protections offered to combatants and prisoners of war, and their underlying rationale, are adapted to the specific needs of animals.

It is in light of this quest for animal personhood in wartimes that we will examine the aforementioned questions with a view to assessing whether Geneva Convention (GC) III and Additional Protocol (AP) I could provide satisfying and realistic protections for animal soldiers. Following the pattern of analysis developed in other chapters of this book, we will first delineate the scope of application for the provisions governing the status of combatant and prisoner of war (Section 2). We will

[4] See Roscini, Chapter 5, 'Property and Objects', in this volume.

[5] Jérôme de Hemptinne, 'The Protection of Animals During Warfare', *American Journal of International Law Unbound* 111 (2017), 272–6, at 273.

[6] See Peters and de Hemptinne, Chapter 1, 'Wartime', in this volume.

[7] de Hemptinne, 'Animals' (n. 5), 273.

[8] Ibid.

[9] See Krieger and Martínez Soria, Chapter 4, 'Rationale and Challenges', in this volume.

then critically consider the content and limits of this regime (Section 3). We will finally analyse the legal consequences that flow from violating fundamental norms of IHL (Section 4). All of this is geared towards proposing recommendations to ameliorate the fate of animals during warfare (Section 5).

2 SCOPE OF APPLICATION OF THE LAWS APPLICABLE TO COMBATANTS AND PRISONERS OF WAR

Despite the long history of animals used in warfare, IHL does not formally address the question of their protection when they participate in hostilities or fall into the power of the enemy. Various solutions could be envisaged. The first one – which appears to be the most consistent with IHL's current texts, spirit, and practice – would be to treat animals as mere objects, properties, or equipment used by soldiers for military purposes.[10] In that case, animals would constitute military objectives when they take part in the hostilities and when the requirements of Article 52(2) of AP I are met. Once captured and neutralised by the enemy, they should not be 'destroyed' since they could no longer contribute to military action. However, as they would be assimilated to inanimate objects, animals would not benefit from any legal entitlements aiming at 'humanising' their protection and treatment. A second approach, envisaged by Chris Jenks, would be to consider that animals constitute, in certain circumstances, means and methods of warfare and weapons. Their use would not be per se illegal, but potentially subject to legal review.[11] That said, this conception also reduces animals to pure things and does not create any obligation to treat them with respect and dignity.

This leads us to consider a third solution – a dual-faceted approach: assimilating animals to human beings, and, on the one hand, allowing them to benefit from the status of combatant and of prisoner of war once the requirements for the obtention of these status contained in GC III and AP I are met, or on the other, considering animal soldiers as benefiting from equivalent treatment even if they do not formally qualify for the status. The logic of this dual-faceted approach is grounded in the structure of protection of persons under GC III and AP I, where the loss of status does not necessarily lead to the loss of protection under these instruments.[12] This section will now proceed to explore whether animal soldiers could meet the requirements of combatant and prisoner of war. Three considerations are relevant in this regard.

First consideration – 'functional conception'. The term 'combatant' designates members of regular and irregular armed forces who directly participate in hostilities and who have a right to so. It excludes all civilians – including civilian prisoners who are not entitled to combatant status, immunity, or privilege. The status of 'prisoners of war' is granted to different categories of persons because they contribute to the war

10 See Roscini, Chapter 5, 'Property and Objects', in this volume.
11 See Jenks, Chapter 9, 'War Weapons', in this volume.
12 Art. 44(4) of AP I.

effort. This status is primarily offered to regular[13] and irregular[14] armed forces. It also extends to two categories of civilians who are so close to regular or irregular armed forces that they often run the risk of being interned with them: those who accompany these forces, without actually being members thereof, and members of the merchant marine and the crews of civil aircraft.[15] Thus, the status of prisoner of war is essentially contingent upon the exercise by individuals of activities that are closely connected to military operations: proper combat functions, or indirect contributions to the war effort, by providing support to the armed forces.

Assimilating animals to such categories of combatants or prisoners of war is not an easy task since they seem reserved by IHL for human persons. Indeed, when determining the groups of individuals that can benefit from this status, neither GC III nor AP I refer to animals. Moreover, many of the safeguards that these treaties offer seem exclusively adapted to the needs of human soldiers. We will come back to this point below when analysing the content and limits of the legal regimes attached to these persons. The AP I Commentary on Article 43 is explicit in this regard when it states that '[t]he expression "armed forces" means "members of the armed forces", *i.e.*, *persons*, as explicitly stated in paragraph 2'[16], and that '[i]n itself it ... does not allow, for example, the use of *animals* trained to attack, who are incapable of distinguishing between an able-bodied enemy and an enemy who is "hors de combat"'.[17]

However, in contrast to this interpretation, an argument could theoretically be made that the notion of armed forces contained in Article 4(A)(1) to (3) of GC III, and in Article 43 of AP I, is mainly '*purpose/use oriented*': armed forces – and persons accompanying them – are protected, not owing to their intrinsic nature, but owing to their contribution to the war effort. In other words, it is because they are specifically entrusted by states to fight on their behalf, that these forces – and persons accompanying them – deserve to be treated as combatants and as prisoners of war. Accordingly, GC III and AP I could, in theory, encompass animals based on the exclusive military membership and functions that they perform during warfare and, in particular, on the basis of the support that they provide to states' armies. Moreover, contrary to the above statement of the AP I Commentary according to which animal soldiers have no capacity of discernment, such animals are generally trained to discharge their military duties with a certain degree of autonomy. These activities can be executed with some independence by the animal soldiers while acting under the instructions of armed forces, and at the same time, being controlled by them. For instance, animal soldiers are often able, by themselves, to identify military targets,

[13] Art. 4(A)(1) of GC III. This also includes categories provided under Article 4(A)(3).
[14] Art. 4(A)(2) of GC III.
[15] Art. 4(A)(3) and (4) of GC III.
[16] AP I Commentary, para. 1672.
[17] Ibid. (emphasis added).

mines, or soldiers in need of rescue, as well as to carry loads, or to watch military bases.

That said, in response to the assertions related to animal independence, it could still be sustained in objection that their capacity to understand and autonomously assess the military situation on the ground is relatively limited compared to humans. Indeed, when conducting military operations, animals remain under the strict authority of soldiers, who train and deploy them and, accordingly, take full responsibility for their actions. Consequently, this would seem to render the 'functional conception' of the notion of armed forces as inapplicable to animal soldiers, on account of the fairly limited aptitude of non-human creatures to take decisions in armed conflict. However, what the 'functional conception' focuses on, is the purpose and duty of engagement in combat functions – that is, the *purpose/use oriented'* approach – which does not include any assessment of the subjective/mental element of those involved in military operation. Hence, it is theoretically possible for animal soldiers to fulfil the 'functional conception' assessment.

Second consideration – requirement of distinction. Under customary international law, combatants belonging to armed forces who, at the time of falling into the power of the enemy, fail to individually distinguish themselves from the civilian population – by not wearing a uniform or a distinctive sign – lose combatant status and, thus, forfeit prisoner of war status.[18] In addition, according to GC III, irregular armed forces must meet other collective conditions of organisation, distinction, and respect of IHL in order for their members to benefit from the status of prisoner of war.[19] This entails that members of irregular armed forces who, for instance, individually comply with these conditions while belonging to a group that does not collectively respect them, are deprived of the protection of GC III.[20]

Therefore, the question is, should we impose the same requirement of distinction on animal soldiers and demand that they carry a distinctive sign, which is recognisable at a certain distance? This criterion could indeed, to a certain extent, make sense for animals, so that the adversary may be able to distinguish those animals that participate in hostilities, from those that do not. Thereby, armed forces would be in a position to know which animals can be targeted or placed in custody. However, in theory, animal soldiers should not lose their protection just because they do not satisfy a requirement over which they have no control, being unable to guarantee its compliance. It would seem logical that animal soldiers, at the very least, benefit from

18 ICRC Customary Law Database, Rule 106. See also Laura Olson, 'Status and Treatment of Those Who Do Not Fulfil the Conditions for Status as Prisoners of War' in Andrew Clapham, Paola Gaeta, and Marco Sassòli (eds.), *The 1949 Geneva Conventions* (Oxford: Oxford University Press 2015), 911–37, at 915.

19 Art. 4(A)(2) of GC III. According to this provision, members of irregular armed forces must respect the following conditions: '(a) that of being commanded by a person responsible for his subordinates; (b) that of having a fixed distinctive sign recognizable at a distance; (c) that of carrying armed openly; (d) that of conducting their operations in accordance with the laws and customs of war.'

20 Olson, 'Status and Treatment' (n. 18), 913–14.

the protections guaranteed in this legal regime, even if they may not qualify for the status on account of their failure and general inability to distinguish themselves.[21] In effect, only soldiers who use animals in combat operations without providing them with a distinctive sign should, themselves, be held accountable for this act. Indeed, this could be considered a form of perfidy, which is prohibited if it results in killing, injuring, or capturing an adversary.[22] For the same reason – as will be discussed later – only soldiers should bear full responsibility for serious violations of IHL that are committed by animal soldiers, which are deliberately used in combat operations.

Third consideration – affiliation to state armed forces. It should be emphasised that, in order to benefit from the combatant and prisoner of war status, an individual must be part of a group of regular or irregular armed forces which must itself belong to a party to an international armed conflict.[23] Individual membership in regular armed forces is generally regulated by domestic law and expressed through formal integration into permanent units distinguishable by uniforms, insignia, and equipment. Such membership ceases, and civilian protection is restored, when a member disengages from active duty and re-integrates into civilian life. Membership in irregular armed forces is usually not regulated by domestic law and can only be reliably determined based on functional criteria.[24] Thus, in theory, animal soldiers involved in hostilities should also be linked to state regular or irregular armed forces, to be granted the same status as these forces. This condition could be regulated by national laws or assessed in light of the concrete functions that animal soldiers exercise during hostilities alongside armed forces. Some states have taken steps to try and officially include 'canine members' in the state armed forces through legislation.[25] Moreover, de facto affiliation, showing that animals provide direct or indirect contributions to state armed forces, should be sufficient to establish the existence of such a linkage.

That said, it could be contended that recruiting animal soldiers in armed forces remains problematic since, unlike human beings, they supposedly do not act willingly and are unaware of the dangerous conditions under which they will be forced to operate.[26] Moreover, these animals cannot willingly disengage from active duty like human-members of armed forces: they remain entirely dependent on the goodwill of the soldiers who exercise authority over them. According to this argument, it is difficult to ascribe membership to animal soldiers in view of their assumed limited capacities, presumed absence of willingness to participate in hostilities, and a claimed particular vulnerability in these circumstances.

21 Art. 44(4) of AP I.
22 Art. 37 of AP I.
23 Sean Watts, 'Who Is a Prisoner of War?', in Clapham, Gaeta, Sassòli, *The 1949 Geneva Conventions* (n. 18), 889–910, at 891–7.
24 Sean Watts, 'Who Is a Prisoner of War?' (n. 23), 896–8.
25 US: S.2134 Canine Members of the Armed Forces Act (2011–12).
26 Anne Peters, 'Animals in International Law', *Collected Courses of The Hague Academy of International Law: Recueil des Cours* Vol. 410 (Leiden: Brill 2020), 377.

However, we should not place an undue emphasis on the subjective elements rather than the factual (objective) conditions for the determination of status under IHL. Legally, the two conditions for obtaining status are membership of the armed forces and a belonging to a party to an international armed conflict. Accordingly, the individual mental state, that is, cognition and volition to be a member or participate in the armed conflict, is immaterial. The same could be said regarding human soldiers involuntarily or legally conscripted into state armed forces against their will. In theory, these subjective considerations should not exclude them – animals or humans – from protection under GC III and AP I.

It is interesting to note in this regard, that a general rise in public sensibility of the necessity to improve animal conditions in those circumstances is progressively emerging. There are encouraging signs of a shift in attitudes, especially for certain animals like dogs or horses, which have entertained close emotional bonds with soldiers for centuries. As noted by Marco Roscini,

> A legislative proposal submitted to the US Congress, the US Canine Members of the Armed Forces Act, provided, for instance, that military working dogs should not be considered as 'equipment' but should be reclassified as canine members of the armed forces. In some cases, at least unofficially, dogs have been given a military rank and wear a sign distinctive of their rank on their body armour.[27]

The symbolic practices of decorating animals that have distinguished themselves on the battlefield, and of establishing war memorials commemorating animals that have served in the army, also illustrate the intention of some armies to treat certain combatant animals differently from mere commodities.[28] In the wars conducted by the United States in Afghanistan and in Iraq, '[s]ignificant progress was made in the direction of inclusiveness, and canine soldiers are currently treated much like human soldiers in many ways'.[29] That said, as noted earlier, we should not forget that these attitudes are profoundly anthropomorphic, in that, they celebrate only animals that have fought heroically alongside armed forces.

In brief, based on the foregoing assessment, animal soldiers could potentially meet the first and third requirements regarding the centrality of membership of a party to the armed conflict, as well as engagement in military operations. Nevertheless, our second observation was that animal soldiers will not be able to guarantee that the requirement of distinction be respected. Consequently, this makes it unlikely for animal soldiers to obtain the status of prisoner of war as such. However, we are of the view that they should still benefit from some sort of

27 Marco Roscini, 'Animals and the Law of Armed Conflict', *Israel Yearbook of Human Rights* 47 (2017), 35–67, at 44.

28 Karsten Nowrot, 'Animals at War: The Status of "Animal Soldiers" under International Humanitarian Law', *Historical Social Research* 40 (2015), 128–50, at 140.

29 Janet M. Alger and Steven F. Alger, 'Canine Soldiers, Mascots, and Stray Dogs in US Wars: Ethical Considerations', in R. Hediger (ed.), *Animals and War: Studies of Europe and North America* (Leiden: Brill 2013), 66–104.

equivalent treatment under GC III and AP I. As we will argue below, this treatment should also be adapted to their specific needs.

In non-international armed conflicts, the status of combatant and prisoner of war are legally non-existent. Non-state actors, which do not formally belong to a party to the conflict, are usually treated as de facto armed forces without any right of participation in hostilities. Therefore, they are only protected by minimal norms.[30] Logically, animal soldiers used by armed groups should be similarly treated and should benefit from the same minimal safeguards that are offered to these groups. One might question whether the protection of animal soldiers should be contingent upon the categories of belligerents established by IHL – state or non-state entities – which are grounded on the fact that only states' armies have the monopoly to use legitimate force.[31]

3 CONTENTS AND LIMITS OF THE LAWS APPLICABLE TO COMBATANTS AND PRISONERS OF WAR

Naturally, if treated as combatants, animal soldiers may lawfully engage in military activities. Concomitantly, they may be lawfully targeted at all times when belonging to armed forces. But while human beings willingly and deliberately join armed forces, perfectly cognisant that this situation could lead to lethal consequences, animals have no freedom of choice in this regard. They are not aware of the exact role that they play in the conduct of hostilities[32] and are unable to react autonomously to any military action undertaken by adverse military forces against them. Moreover, they do not benefit from any immunity of prosecution that is available to those human beings who have the legal right to participate in hostilities, because they are not subjected to criminal prosecution anyway. In this context, one must recognise that qualifying animals as proper combatants would not be very satisfying. [33]

30 See common Art. 3 of the GCs and AP II.

31 Marco Sassòli, *International Humanitarian Law: Rules, Controversies, and Solutions to Problems Arising in Warfare* (Cheltenham: Edward Elgar 2019), 249.

32 Peters, 'Animals' (n. 26), 376–7.

33 It is tempting to treat animals like civilians who remain protected at all times against the conducted of hostilities. However, considering that the interests of human beings – be they combatants or civilians – should prevail over those of animals in extreme circumstances, such qualification as a civilian would come with a caveat. When animals are used to perform concrete acts of hostilities – for instance, when they are employed as delivery systems for explosives – that could potentially inflict death or serious injury on persons protected against direct attack, the general presumptive protection that should be offered to all animals against military attacks could be temporarily removed for the duration of their concrete involvement in hostilities. This would aim at protecting those individuals who may be harmed by their actions. Accordingly, applying to animals a similar status as the one of 'civilians directly participating in hostilities', instead of a status akin to 'combatants', even if these animals are enrolled into armed forces and intimately linked to them would seem to better ensure their protection and needs, at the same time respecting general military considerations. That said, Anne Peters has also shown that the authoritative definition of the notion of 'direct participation in hostilities' articulated

However, when animal soldiers fall into the hands of the enemy, offering them equivalent protections to those contained in GC III and AP I could be more meaningful if these safeguards were adapted to their specific needs. Indeed, some existing rules that are applicable to prisoners of war are not directly relevant to animals, for instance, the rules on discipline, clothing, ranks, religious and intellectual activities, interrogation, financial resources and remuneration, representation, retention of civil capacities, escape, or sanctions. In any event, the application of the full regime of protection for animal soldiers envisaged in GC III and AP I would be unrealistic and unnecessary. Besides, in situations where armed forces are already unable to protect the well-being of human detainees, safeguarding the interests of animal soldiers would certainly not constitute a priority for these forces.

It should also be observed that the overarching rationale of the internment regime of prisoners of war, as well as the related matter of release and repatriation, do not fit for animals. Indeed, the internment of prisoners of war is mainly justified by the necessity to prevent combatants from future involvement in hostilities.[34] However, animals cannot necessarily represent a real threat of future involvement once they are not under the patronage of their handlers. Indeed, it is less likely that they could re-join their armed forces by themselves in order to participate again in combat efforts. The main reason that may justify, in exceptional circumstances, their 'internment', is mostly to guarantee their own survival, by providing them with the necessary medical care and means of subsistence, and by preserving them from the danger of hostilities. In this context, decisions to 'liberate' animals should, therefore, be based on an evaluation of their capacities to subsist by themselves in the difficult circumstances of war, or on the possibility of returning to their countries of origin without creating danger.

It remains critical to guarantee that all animal soldiers, which have been involved in hostilities by performing concrete combat activities alongside soldiers, be treated with the required dignity and respect as soon as they fall into the power of the enemy. Consequently, we propose a broad framework that should guide the use and treatment of animals, from the point of their possible 'recruitment' to the point at which, on detention, they may be released to return to the armed forces to which they belong. This regime is grounded on four principles, which are, to a certain extent, inspired by certain essential provisions contained in GC III and AP I and which should be implemented whenever it is actually feasible. Indeed, belligerents may often be incapable of respecting these principles in the difficult circumstances of war.

by the ICRC based on three cumulative criteria – threshold of harm, direct causation, and belligerent nexus – is not easily transposable to animals. (See in that regard Peters, 'Animals' (n. 26), 376–7; ICRC, *Interpretive Guidance on the Notion of Direct Participation in Hostilities Under International Humanitarian Law* (Geneva: ICRC 2009).)

34 Marco Sassòli, 'Release, Accommodation in Neutral Countries, and Repatriation of Prisoners of War', in Clapham, Gaeta, Sassòli, *The 1949 Geneva Conventions* (n. 18), 1039–66, at 1040–4.

First principle – no military involvement. First of all, it should be made clear that animals should not, in principle, be used to carry out military functions, except when absolutely necessary for essential tasks that cannot be accomplished by human beings; such tasks as searching for or rescuing wounded soldiers. Thus, the usage of animals as weapons of war should, in theory, be banned. This would not only preserve animals from the cruelty of wars, but it would also considerably reduce the number of those that could be detained because of their past involvement in military activities.

Second principle – subsidiarity. Banning, once and for all, the usage of animals for military purposes remains, at this stage, rather utopian. Indeed, while technological advancements have reduced the need for several species to be employed by militaries around the world, many animals, such as dogs, horses, mules, or camels are still seen as vital to their work. That said, one could argue that, if they have at their disposal inanimate objects – such as weapons or trucks – which allow them to conduct military operations in the same manner as living creatures, belligerents should, in principle, have recourse to these objects as a priority. Of course, they cannot be required to acquire such non-living objects. Parties to the conflict should only be obliged to do what is feasible, depending on the means available at the time.[35]

Third principle – humane treatment and animal dignity. In the case of detention, belligerents should ensure, to the greatest practicable extent, that the dignity of animal soldiers be respected by providing them with satisfactory conditions of detention. These conditions could be inspired by those of nutrition, safety, and health applicable to prisoners of war.[36] The physical and mental integrity of animal soldiers should always be preserved. All forms of cruel treatment, torture, mutilation, or medical experiments should be strictly prohibited.[37] Animal soldiers should be accommodated in an area 'affording every guarantee of hygiene and healthfulness.'[38] Thus, they should not be located in the vicinity of dangerous areas or installations, nor should they be placed in regions where essential resources, like water, are not available or cannot be provided. They should not be interned close to warzones, where they run the risk of being killed or injured. Concerning labour, an argument could be made that animal soldiers could be used for work within the camp, but not for military purposes (as foreseen in Articles 49 to 57 of GC III). Thus animal soldiers should be granted basic 'humane' treatment based on GC III and AP I, but tailored to their own specific needs. Lastly, it could be envisaged that, when effectively possible, the respect of these conditions be monitored by a third party, such as a 'non-

35 Michael Schmitt, 'War, Technology and the Law of Armed Conflict' in Anthony Helm (ed.), *The Law of War in the 21st Century: Weaponry and the Use of Force* (Newport: Naval War College International Studies 2006), 137–82, at 137.

36 Art. 15, 26, 29–31 and 38 of GC III. See also Silvia Sanna, 'Treatment of Prisoners of War?' in Clapham, Gaeta, Sassòli, *The 1949 Geneva Conventions* (n. 18), 985–6, 997–9, 998–9.

37 Art. 13 and 130 of GC III; Art. 11 of AP I. See also Sanna, 'Treatment of Prisoners of War?' (n. 36), 983.

38 Art. 22 of GC III. See also Sanna, 'Treatment of Prisoners of War?' (n. 36), 996.

governmental animal welfare organisation', which would be allowed to report its findings and suggestions for improvement directly to the detaining authority.[39]

Fourth principle – liberation or return to their homeland. Belligerents have no obligation to intern the armed forces of the enemy who are *hors de combat* when they encounter them in the contact zone.[40] This principle is particularly relevant for animal soldiers. Since captured animal soldiers may not always represent a military threat to the security of the adversary (in comparison to human combatants), they should, as far as possible, be freed if they can survive by themselves, or be returned to their homeland. This course of action would allow armed forces to set up detention facilities only for animal soldiers, which are endangered because of warfare and which cannot be sent back to their country of origin.

4 LEGAL CONSEQUENCES OF A VIOLATION OF THE LAWS APPLICABLE TO COMBATANTS AND PRISONERS OF WAR

The GCs, the APs, and the International Criminal Court (ICC) Statute being deeply anthropocentric, contain explicit provisions on grave breaches and war crimes against prisoners of war, which protect only confined human persons. Yet, some of the acts constituting grave breaches or war crimes, such as wilful killing, inhumane treatment, and causing great suffering or serious injury to body or health of human victims[41] could be adapted to the specific needs of other sentient beings, or in our case, animal soldiers. Indeed, the criminalisation of atrocities committed against animal victims would reflect the fact that animals are capable of suffering in physical and psychological terms from the impact of criminal conduct. As early as the 1960s, the Council of Europe had declared that 'the *humane treatment* of animals is one of the hallmarks of Western civilisation'.[42] Along this line, there is merit in applying the provisions on grave breaches and war crimes to acts committed against animal soldiers. Arguably, the war crime of compelling a prisoner of war to serve in the forces of a hostile power[43] could also apply to animals.

Concerning the conduct of animal soldiers, or acts committed with their assistance, which might constitute grave breaches or war crimes, animal soldiers do not stand trial under the current state of the law.[44] As aptly noted by Anne Peters, 'It seems impossible that dogs could distinguish a combatant from a civilian, for example. And even if a dog could be successfully trained to make the distinction,

[39] See the regime of ICRC visits contained in Art. 126 of GC III. See also Sassòli, *International Humanitarian Law* (n. 31), 268.

[40] Sassòli, *International Humanitarian Law* (n. 31), 264.

[41] Art. 129 and 130 of GC III.

[42] Parliamentary Assembly of the Council of Europe, *International Transit of Animals*, Recommendation 287 (1961), 22 September 1961 (emphasis added).

[43] Art. 8(2)(a)(v) of ICC Statute.

[44] For some historical account of criminal trial and punishment of animals, see Edward P. Evans, *The Criminal Prosecution and Capital Punishment of Animals* (London: William Heinemann 1906).

it does not have the mental set-up to recognise the *criminal* character of a possible violation. The dog cannot incur guilt, it cannot have a *mens rea*.'[45] Under the general principle of criminal law, when animals are used for the commission of criminal acts, the person who employs them is directly responsible for the conduct. International criminal law is not also alien to the approach of attributing the responsibility for the conduct of subordinate soldiers, in accordance with the principle of 'command responsibility', as stipulated in the Articles 86(2) and 87 of AP I. In the same way, it could be argued that the conduct of animal soldiers should be attributed to the human combatants who deploy and supervise them, for purposes of criminal responsibility.[46] As discussed above, animal soldiers should, in principle, be distinguishable when engaged in hostilities; failure of which, could amount to an act of perfidy that is prohibited under IHL, where it results in the killing, injuring, or capture of an adversary.[47] In such perfidious circumstances, and also in general, those who deploy or instruct the animal soldiers bear full responsibility in case the latter performs acts that are contrary to IHL.

5 CONCLUDING RECOMMENDATIONS

Animal soldiers are *de lege lata* not subjects of IHL as such. The proposal that animal soldiers should benefit from protection similar to combatants or prisoners of war under GC III and AP I, is likely to be regarded by most – possibly excluding ardent proponents of animal rights – as somewhat utopian. Nevertheless, the normative recognition of the idea that those sentient animals which are 'subjects-of-a-life' (Tom Regan) must be legally protected and even might bear rights, has been gaining some recognition, at least at the domestic level. In the same manner that IHL has progressively offered a series of protection to human beings in armed conflicts, the broader recognition of animal rights could influence the way certain existing IHL principles are interpreted and applied to animals. Better still, it might even influence the law's progressive development. The 'humane' treatment of the dog captured in Afghanistan by the Taliban, epitomises the practical need for the protection of captive animal soldiers.[48] Against this backdrop, this chapter calls for a treatment of animal soldiers adapted to their specific needs, which respects the following nine basic principles.

First, animal soldiers should not, in principle, be used to carry out military functions, except when absolutely necessary for essential tasks that cannot be accomplished by human beings. Second, if they have at their disposal inanimate objects which allow them to conduct military operations in the same manner as living creatures, belligerents should, in principle, have recourse to these objects as

45 Peters, 'Animals' (n. 26), 377.
46 Nowrot, 'Animals' (n. 28), 142.
47 Art. 37 of AP I.
48 Nowrot, 'Animals' (n. 28), 128–9.

a priority. Third, animal soldiers as members of the armed forces can be legally targeted only when they directly participate in hostilities and for such time of their participation. Fourth, since captured animal soldiers may not always represent a military threat to the security of the adversary (in comparison to human combatants), they should, as far as possible, be freed if they can survive by themselves, or be returned to their homeland. Fifth, in case of detention, belligerents should ensure, to the greatest practicable extent, that the dignity of animal soldiers be respected by providing them with satisfactory conditions of detention. Sixth, these conditions could be inspired by those of nutrition, safety, and health, which are applicable to prisoners of war. Seventh, the physical and mental integrity of animal soldiers should always be preserved. Eighth, when effectively possible, the respect of these conditions should be monitored by a third party, such as a non-governmental animal welfare organisation. Finally, the conduct of animal soldiers should be attributed to the human combatants who deploy and supervise them, for purposes of criminal responsibility.

SELECT BIBLIOGRAPHY

Evans, Edward P., *The Criminal Prosecution and Capital Punishment of Animals* (London: William Heinemann 1906).

Levie, Howard S., *Prisoners of War in International Armed Conflict* (Newport: Naval War College 1978).

Sassòli, Marco *International Humanitarian Law, Rules, Controversies, and Solutions to Problems Arising in Warfare* (Cheltenham: Edward Elgar 2019).

Nowrot, Karsten, 'Animals at War: The Status of "Animal Soldiers" under International Humanitarian Law', *Historical Social Research* 40 (2015), 128–50.

Olson, Laura, 'Status and Treatment of Those Who Do Not Fulfil the Conditions for Status as Prisoners of War' in Andrew Clapham, Paola Gaeta, and Marco Sassòli (eds.), *The 1949 Geneva Conventions* (Oxford: Oxford University Press 2015), 911–37.

Peters, Anne, 'Animals in International Law', *Collected Courses of The Hague Academy of International Law: Recueil des Cours* Vol. 410 (Leiden: Brill 2020).

Sandoz, Yves, Christophe Swinarski, and Bruno Zimmermann (eds.), *Commentary on the Additional Protocols of 8 June 1977 to the Geneva Conventions of 12 August 1949* (Geneva: ICRC 1987).

Schmitt, Michael, 'War, Technology and the Law of Armed Conflict' in Anthony Helm (ed.), *The Law of War in the 21st Century: Weaponry and the Use of Force* (Newport: Naval War College International Studies 2006), 137–82.

Watts, Sean, 'Who Is a Prisoner of War?' in Andrew Clapham, Paola Gaeta, and Marco Sassòli (eds.), *The 1949 Geneva Conventions* (Oxford: Oxford University Press 2015), 889–910.

11

Animals as Means of Medical Transportation, Search and Rescue

*Jérôme de Hemptinne**

1 INTRODUCTION

Many animals that possess highly developed sense of smell, such as dogs, are employed to search on the battlefield for missing combatants or civilians in need of medical assistance.[1] Often these animals receive sophisticated training to find such persons and to bring them medical equipment, food and water, especially when they are out of the reach of ambulances or medical personnel. 'Cadaver dogs' are used to locate the remains of deceased victims and 'mercy dogs' to accompany severely wounded soldiers as they perish. Other animals – such as horses, mules, donkeys or camels – exercise similar search and rescue activities in inaccessible areas. In many cases, these animals are simply employed to transport the wounded and sick, medical personnel or facilities. But, like dogs, they can also be trained to search for wounded persons, using their keen senses of sight, scent and hearing.[2]

Accordingly, during World Wars I and II, thousands of animals were used for medical purposes, with varying degrees of success, by American, Austrian, British, French, German and Italian troops.[3] During these conflicts, the British Red Cross employed specially trained dogs to provide help to stricken soldiers on the battlefield.[4] However, while performing medical activities, they were widely killed and, when wounded, they rarely received treatment. This situation was prompted by the fact that animals were left unprotected by the early 1864, 1906 and 1929 Geneva Conventions (GCs). Moreover, after World War II, the GCs and their Additional Protocols (APs) did not include provisions to improve their fate.

That said, some general principles enshrined in GCs I and IV as well as in AP I regarding the protection of medical transports, equipment and personnel could potentially provide minimum safeguards to animals when used as means of medical

* I would like to thank Marco Roscini for his valuable comments.

[1] Eric Baratay, *Bêtes de tranchées: Des vécus oubliés* (Paris: CNRS éditions 2013), 111–13.

[2] Ibid.

[3] Ibid.

[4] Mark Cox, 'Dogs of War: The First Aiders on Four Legs', *British Red Cross Blog* (no date), available at https://bit.ly/3Gr3uET, accessed 22 February 2022.

transportation (Section 2) or as means of search and rescue (Section 3). However, the current international humanitarian law (IHL) regime remains inappropriate to the protection of animals in many respects. The application of *sui generis* principles, tailored to the specific needs of sentient beings, should thus be conceived in light of developments which have recently occurred in the welfare and rights of animals in peacetime (Section 4).

2 ANIMALS AS MEANS OF MEDICAL TRANSPORTATION

Animals are frequently used to transport wounded and sick soldiers and civilians located in remote areas. They are often trained to bring them the necessary personnel and facilities so that they receive adequate treatment. Means of medical transportation by land are duly protected by the detailed legal regime contained in GC I and GC IV as well as in AP I. After describing the scope of application of this regime (Section 2.1), I will analyse its content and limits (Section 2.2) as well as the legal consequences that flow from violating the fundamental rules governing it (Section 2.3). In each section, I will distinguish between the theoretical provisions as they currently exist in IHL and their concrete application to animals.

2.1 *Scope of Application of the Laws on Medical Transportation*

2.1.1 General Rules

International humanitarian law grants detailed legal protections to means of medical transportation operating in international armed conflicts. Indeed, as noted by Geoffrey S. Corn, '[o]ne of the key principles of humanitarian protection of the wounded and sick is that they and the required medical personnel and equipment be transported as quickly as possible to a place where they can receive care'.[5] While GC I protects medical means of transportation assisting wounded and sick members of armed forces,[6] GC IV accords protection to medical transports devoted to the care of civilian persons.[7] The notion of transports is not, as such, defined in the GCs. However, Article 8(h) of AP I – which is today considered to have acquired a customary international law status[8] – provides the following 'purpose/use oriented definition' of this concept: 'any means of transportation, whether military or civilian, permanent or temporary, assigned exclusively to medical transportation' by a competent authority of a party to the conflict. This entails that, once it is assigned to medical transportation, a given vehicle needs to be exclusively engaged in such functions in order to be protected by IHL. Conversely, the moment it ceases to be

5 ICRC Commentary on GC I (2016), para. 2363.
6 Art. 35 of GC I.
7 Art. 21 of GC IV.
8 ICRC Customary Law Database, Rule 29.

used to perform medical duties, it loses its protected status.[9] Such assignment needs not be permanent, that is, made exclusively for medical purposes for an indefinite period of time. It can be temporary when the vehicle is employed in a medical transport capacity at least for a defined, albeit possibly short, period of time.[10] The AP I Commentary adds that the expression of transport is understood 'in a wide sense, as it covers all means of transportation by land'[11] as long as they are linked, directly or indirectly, to wounded and sick persons. The link is direct when the persons being transported are the wounded and sick themselves. It is indirect when these are medical personnel, or medical equipment and supplies.[12]

I will show below that medical transports are protected when they are used not only in international armed conflicts but also in non-international armed conflicts. According to the International Committee of the Red Cross (ICRC), in the absence of a definition of medical transports in common Article 3 of the GCs and in AP II, these terms must be understood as applying in non-international armed conflicts in the same sense as in international armed conflicts.[13] Accordingly, the definition contained in Article 8(h) of AP I applies in both contexts.

2.1.2 Applicability to Animals

Could animals be treated as medical transports for the purpose of IHL? It could be contended that the notion of transports is limited to inanimate objects, as exemplified by the list of means of transportation cited in the ICRC Commentary on GC I (2016), which mentions, among other things, automobiles, trucks, trains, motorcycles, small all-terrain vehicles and inland boats.[14] At first sight, animals seem thus to be excluded from this regime. It is true that, aside from a few multilateral treaties protecting endangered species, the welfare of animals has always been poorly regulated at the international level.[15] As we know, this is especially valid for IHL, which is, by definition, eminently anthropocentric.[16] Nevertheless, the multiple functions that dogs, horses, donkeys, mules or camels played during World Wars I

[9] ICRC Commentary on GC I (2016), para. 2374. Military medical transports must be differentiated from mobile medical units (Art. 19 of GC I): 'the transport function in principle prevails in the case of "transports", while the possibility of administering care prevails in the case of "mobile medical units"' (ICRC Commentary on GC I (2016), para. 1782). When animals are used for medical purposes, the transport function prevails over the possibility of administering care. Hence, in this section, animals are only treated as means of medical transportation.

[10] ICRC Commentary on GC I (2016), para. 2380.

[11] AP I Commentary, para. 387.

[12] Ibid.

[13] ICRC Customary Law Database, Rules 28 and 29.

[14] ICRC Commentary on GC I (2016), para. 2372.

[15] Anne Peters, 'Global Animal Law: What It Is and Why We Need It', *Transnational Environmental Law* 5 (2016), 13–16.

[16] Michael Schmitt, 'Green War: An Assessment of the Environmental Law of Armed Conflict', *Yale Law Journal* 22 (1997), 1–110, at 6.

and II – and continue to play today in many conflicts – in transporting wounded and sick, medical personnel and equipment can no longer be ignored. This has to be seen in light of a general rise in public awareness of the necessity to improve the welfare and the protection of animals whose lives are threatened by modern hostilities, especially when they are used to save the lives of combatants or civilians. The object and purpose of GC I and GC IV should also be duly taken into account, that is, to guarantee that appropriate means be deployed by all belligerents with a view to dispensing necessary care to the wounded and sick on a non-discriminatory basis. In addition, I will argue in Section 3.1 below that assimilating animals into the category of medical personnel is not an easy task, since this category is clearly reserved by IHL to human beings. Thus, to avoid any gap in protection and to further the goals of the GCs, animals cannot but fall within the category of medical transports when employed to extract persons requiring medical assistance or to provide such assistance.

Furthermore, this approach is consistent with the definition of Article 8(h) of AP I studied above for two main reasons. First, such definition is open-ended: despite the limited examples of means of transportation given by the AP I Commentary, Article 8 (h) does not, as such, restrict its scope of application to inanimate objects. On the contrary, it refers to 'any means of transportation'. This commentary also acknowledges that no means of transportation 'is excluded, from the oxdrawn cart to the supersonic jet, or any future means of transportation; the absence of an exhaustive list leaves the field open for the latter'.[17] Second, being 'purpose/use-oriented', the definition of Article 8(h) entails that, like any other means of transportation, animals must benefit protection, not because of their intrinsic characteristics, but because of their assignment to medical purposes. In other words, animals should be safeguarded by GCs I and IV on account of the medical functions they perform. As long as they are assigned to exercise such functions, there is no reason to exclude them from the protection of IHL. Indeed, as just emphasised, their protection can only contribute to the achievement of its humanitarian goals. That said, their assignment to medical goals need be neither permanent nor direct. Indeed, it can last only for a short period of time and be exercised, not only in favour of wounded and sick persons themselves, but also in favour of medical personnel, equipment or supplies.

2.2 *Contents and Limits of the Laws on Medical Transportation*

2.2.1 General Rules

According to Article 35 of GC I, medical transports 'shall be respected and protected in the same way as mobile medical units'.[18] Article 21 of GC IV directly governs the

[17] AP I Commentary, para. 384.
[18] Art. 21 of AP I; ICRC Customary Law Database, Rule 29.

protection of transports used to convey wounded and sick civilians.[19] In a nutshell, such a protection entails that 'Parties to the conflict may not unduly hold up, obstruct the passage of, or otherwise prevent military medical transports from fulfilling their task. They must also actively ensure and enforce respect by any third parties that may seek to unjustifiably interfere with medical transports'.[20] Moreover, such transports, whether civilian or military, shall never be intentionally destroyed or attacked.[21] Not only direct and indiscriminate attacks, but also attacks which may be expected to cause excessive harm, are prohibited against them on account of their medical, non-combatant functions.[22] Furthermore, belligerents must take all feasible precautions to spare medical transports from attack and from the effects of attacks.[23] In this regard, they must do everything feasible to verify that objectives to be attacked are not entitled to special medical protection.[24] They must abort or suspend attacks when it becomes apparent that the target is subject to such protection.[25] Belligerents must also take all feasible precautions in the choice of means and methods of attack with a view to avoiding, or in any event minimising, incidental civilian harm to medical transports.[26]

However, such protection can be temporarily removed when medical transports, civilian or military, are used outside their humanitarian functions, to commit acts harmful to the enemy.[27] This means that, in these circumstances, such transports may become legitimate military targets and may thus be directly attacked and even destroyed by the adversary.[28] While neither GCs I or IV nor AP I provide a definition of the notion of 'acts harmful to the

19 For an analysis of the protection of buildings, material and transports under IHL, see Katja Schöberl, 'Buildings, Material, and Transports' in Andrew Clapham, Paola Gaeta and Marco Sassòli (eds.), *The 1949 Geneva Conventions: A Commentary* (Oxford: Oxford University Press 2015), 825–38. One could make the argument that means of transportation should also be respected and protected when used to transport (and rescue) wounded and sick animals (instead of wounded and sick persons as envisaged by IHL).

20 ICRC Commentary on GC I (2016), para. 2387.

21 Art. 19(1) of GC I; Art. 12(1) of AP I. See also ICRC Customary Law Database, Rule 28.

22 AP I Commentary, para. 540. See also Alexander Breitegger, 'The Legal Framework Applicable to Insecurity and Violence Affecting the Delivery of Health Care in Armed Conflicts and other Emergencies', *International Review of the Red Cross* 95 (2013) 83–127, at 108.

23 Breitegger, 'The Legal Framework' (n. 22), 108.

24 Ibid.

25 Ibid.

26 Ibid.

27 Art. 21 and 22 of GC I; Art. 13 of AP I. See also ICRC Customary Law Database, Rule 28.

28 Tom Haeck, 'Loss of Protection' in Clapham, Gaeta and Sassòli, *The 1949 Geneva Conventions* (n. 19), 839–54, at 847. It should be noted that, when an attack is taking place, the basic principles of proportionality and precaution should be fully respected. The impact on the wounded and sick treated by the transport unit targeted should also be duly evaluated. Moreover, after an attack and the military disadvantage removed from the unit, the transport unit should, in principle, regain its full protection and be allowed to be used for its medical purposes. When used to 'commit acts harmful to the enemy', a medical unit will lose its protection, but may not necessarily be destroyed. For it to be legal, the destruction must offer a sufficiently concrete military advantage at the time. See generally Rain Liivoja, 'Status of Medical Personnel: Clear as Mud?', *ICRC Blog Humanitarian Law and Policy* (25 February 2019), available at https://bit.ly/3rlAc4i, accessed 22 February 2022.

enemy',[29] it is usually understood as meaning any 'acts the purpose or effect of which is to harm the adverse party, by facilitating or impeding military operations'[30] including transporting weapons, ammunition or able-bodied soldiers. The loss of specific protection of medical transports is subject to further conditions under IHL before it becomes effective – namely, non-compliance with a due warning that is accompanied, in all appropriate cases, by a reasonable time limit.[31] Furthermore, as far as possible, medical transports shall not be located in the vicinity of military objectives[32] and, under no circumstances, be used in an attempt to shield military objectives from an attack.[33] In order to reinforce the protection of all medical equipment employed by medical services, which include any mean of transport, and to render them visible during hostilities, a distinctive emblem can be displayed on them.[34] That said, the emblem does not confer protection as such[35]: '[l] egally speaking, a medical unit that does not display the emblem remains protected; however, the risk of inadvertent attack as a result is significantly higher'.[36] Lastly, it should be observed that the military importance in modern warfare of medical transports used by the armed forces medical services has been duly recognised by Article 35(2) of GC I.[37] Indeed, when falling into the hands of the detaining power, they remain subject to the laws of war on condition that this power ensures the care of the wounded and sick who are in these means of transport.[38] They thus become booty of war and may be destroyed or converted to military use if the distinctive emblem is removed.[39]

Common Article 3 of the GCs does not provide any specific protection to means of medical transportation in non-international armed conflicts. Nonetheless, such a protection is traditionally inferred from the fact that this provision requires that the wounded and sick be searched for, collected and protected against pillage and ill-treatment, as well as that they receive adequate care.[40] Indeed, to fully guarantee respect for these obligations, means of medical transportation must, in turn, be

[29] However, Articles 22 of GC I and 13(2) of AP I indicate several types of acts which do not constitute 'acts harmful to the enemy', for example when a medical unit is guarded.

[30] Breitegger, 'The Legal Framework' (n. 22), 110. See also Schöberl, 'Buildings, Material, and Transports' (n. 22), 842.

[31] Art. 21 of GC I.

[32] Art. 19(2) of GC I. See also ICRC Customary Law Database, Rule 28.

[33] Art. 12(4) of AP I. See also ICRC Customary Law Database, Rule 28.

[34] Art. 39 of GC I. See also Corn, 'Protection' (n. 9), para. 2403.

[35] ICRC Customary Law Database, Rule 28.

[36] Antoine Bouvier, 'The Use of the Emblem' in Clapham, Gaeta and Sassòli, *The 1949 Geneva Conventions* (n. 19), 855–85, at 863.

[37] ICRC Commentary GC I (2016), para. 2413.

[38] Schöberl, 'Buildings, Material, and Transports' (n. 19), 829.

[39] Ibid.

[40] Ibid. See Art. 7 and 8 of AP II.

respected and protected at all times, and must not be attacked.[41] This rule is explicitly set forth in AP II.[42]

2.2.2 Applicability to Animals

Obviously, the provisions on medical transports outlined above provide significant safeguards to animals when medically involved in international or non-international armed conflicts. In both instances, animals cannot be attacked, nor harmed in any way, nor their medical functioning be impeded, even if they do not momentarily bear any wounded and sick or medical equipment.[43] They fully benefit from the rule governing precautions in attacks and from the effects of attacks. They cannot be located in the vicinity of military objectives or used to commit acts harmful to the enemy. It is only if, and when, they are employed for military purposes – for instance, to transport able soldiers or munitions, to serve as 'living bombs' or to detect explosives – that they may lose such a protection. Moreover, providing assistance to military and civilian wounded in the field, animals could theoretically be identified as a protective device, using the emblem of the GCs.[44]

Nevertheless, assimilating animals as purely 'inanimate vehicles of transportation' is reductive in many respects. Generally speaking, it is important to recall that, in several jurisdictions around the world, animals are increasingly recognised as a separate category besides the Roman law category of 'things' (*res*), and in some codes even as 'sentient beings' and not simply as inanimate objects.[45] Of course, there would be no incentive among states to create a new category of living beings that could benefit from specific safeguards when they are used to provide care during warfare. That said, in the same manner that human rights law has progressively offered many protections to human beings in armed conflicts,[46] animal rights could progressively influence the conditions under which medical transports should take place when undertaken by living

41 Bouvier, 'The Use of the Emblem' (n. 36), 863.

42 Art. 11(1) of AP II.

43 It could be argued that the protection offered to animals in this context should apply when they transport (and rescue), not only wounded and sick humans, but also wounded and sick animals, especially when these animals are involved in war. It would, however, be unrealistic that belligerents be obliged 'to respect and protect' all wounded and sick animals even when they are used for military purposes.

44 Bouvier, 'The Use of the Emblem' (n. 41), 855–85.

45 Austria: General Civil Code (Allgemeines Bürgerliches Gesetzbuch) (ABGB), para. 285(a); Germany: Civil Code (Bürgerliches Gesetzbuch) (BGB), Section 90 a); Switzerland: Civil Code, Art. 641 a); The Netherlands: Civil Code (Burgerlijk wetboek), Book 3, Title 1, Section 1, Art. 2a); Czech Republic: Civil Code, section 494; France: Civil Code, Art. 515-14; Canada: Quebec Civil Code, Art. 898.1; Colombia: Civil Code, Art. 655; New Zealand: Section 4 of the Animal Welfare Amendment Act (No 2) 2015.

46 See generally Louise Doswald-Beck, *Human Rights in Times of Conflict and Terrorism* (Oxford: Oxford University Press 2012).

creatures.[47] Four basic principles – which should influence the way IHL principles on medical transport are interpreted and apply concretely – illustrate this proposition.

First principle – animal dignity. When using animals for medical purposes, belligerents should ensure, to the greatest practicable extent, that their dignity be respected by providing them with satisfactory conditions of nutrition, safety and health, especially when these animals are wounded on the battlefield. This is all the more important since treating living means of transportation decently is in the interest of the wounded and sick themselves, whose evacuation and treatment often require prompt medical intervention and thus animals which are fit to carry out these tasks. Ultimately, this first principle aims at reinforcing the humanitarian goals of IHL.

Second principle – subsidiarity. If they have at their disposal inanimate vehicles of transportation which allow them to provide treatment to wounded and sick of the same level and quality as living means of transportation, belligerents should, in principle, use the former means of transportation as a priority. Of course, they cannot be required to acquire such non-living vehicles. Parties to the conflict should only be obliged to do what is feasible depending on the means of transport available at the time, together with the concrete needs of wounded or sick on the theatre of hostilities.[48]

Third principle – no military involvement. Animals should not be employed outside their medical functions to perform military tasks such as carrying able-bodied soldiers or weapons. Indeed, if this happens, they could lose their protection and be targeted. As we know, when attacks are launched on combatants, IHL prohibits the use of means and methods of warfare that cause superfluous injury or unnecessary suffering.[49] By nature, this prohibition does not apply to inanimate objects. In order to reinforce their protection by avoiding that they be negatively affected by the use of such means and methods of warfare, animals should be regarded as living beings experiencing emotions, including pain and distress when injured.

Fourth principle – return to homeland. When falling into enemy hands, it is unjustified that, like medical vehicles, animals be disposed of by the enemy for military purposes as if they were military vehicles. An alternative regime – based on the one applicable to equipment contained in mobile medical units falling into the hands of adverse military forces – should be envisaged: animals should be either

47 Jérôme de Hemptinne, 'The Protection of Animals During Warfare', *American Journal of International Law Unbound* 111 (2017), 272-276, at 273.

48 Michael Schmitt, 'War, Technology and the Law of Armed Conflict' in Anthony Helm (ed.), *The Law of War in the 21st Century: Weaponry and the Use of Force* (Newport: Naval War College International Studies 2006), 137–82, at 137.

49 Art. 35(2) of AP I. For an extensive analysis of the application of such a prohibition to animals, see Marco Roscini, 'Animals and the Law of Armed Conflict', *Israel Yearbook on Human Rights* 47 (2017), 35–67, at 51–6.

returned to their homeland or, when impossible, retained to perform medical duties only. I will get back to this issue in Section 3.2 below.

2.3 *Consequences of Violations of the Laws on Medical Transportation*

2.3.1 General Rules

In international armed conflicts, the extensive destruction and appropriation of protected property, not justified by military necessity and carried out unlawfully and wantonly, constitutes a grave breach of the GCs[50] and is a war crime under the International Criminal Court (ICC) Statute.[51] The concept of protected property, unlike protected person, is not defined by the GCs. However, medical transports are usually considered protected under these conventions.[52] The requirement of extensiveness is generally interpreted to exclude isolated acts of destruction and appropriation.[53] It should be added that, under the ICC Statute, intentionally directing attacks against 'medical units and transports ... using the distinctive emblems of the Geneva Conventions in conformity with international law' constitutes a war crime in both international[54] and non-international armed conflicts.[55] Moreover, acts committed against medical transports in non-international armed conflicts could be prosecuted under the charge of pillage[56] and destruction or seizure of property not imperatively demanded by the necessities of the conflict.[57]

2.3.2 Applicability to Animals

The provisions on grave breaches and on war crimes cited above could potentially apply to animals which perform medical functions. Indeed, medical transports are protected property and, according to the above interpretation, they include animals which exclusively perform medical functions. This approach poses however several difficulties. By definition, the vocabulary of destruction, appropriation, seizure or pillage contained in the GCs and in the ICC Statute is suited only for inanimate objects. They do not capture the essence of living creatures which, like human beings, may experience pain, distress and suffering as a result of criminal activities conducted against them. The grave breaches or crimes of wilful killing,[58] inhumane

50 Art. 50 of GC I; Art. 50 of GC II; Art. 147 of GC IV.
51 Art. 8(2)(a)(iv) of ICC Statute.
52 Schöberl, 'Buildings, Material, and Transports' (n. 19), 836.
53 Ibid.
54 Art. 8(2)(b)(xxiv) of ICC Statute.
55 Art. 8(2)(e)(ii) of ICC Statute.
56 Art. 8(2)(e)(v) of ICC Statute.
57 Art. 8(2)(e)(xii) of ICC Statute.
58 Art. 50 of GC I; Art. 51 of GC II; Art. 147 of GC IV; Art. 8(2)(a)(i) and (c)(i) of ICC Statute.

treatment[59] and causing great suffering or serious injury to body or health[60] that apply to individuals, including those exercising medical tasks, would be better adapted to the specific needs of other sentient beings such as animals. Indeed, these incriminations would reflect the fact that animals are capable of physically and psychologically suffering from criminal activities.[61] However, if animals are treated as means of transport for IHL purposes, they must also be treated in the same manner for international criminal law purposes. I will return to this delicate question in Section 3.3.2 below.

That said, it is very unlikely that today criminal activities committed on medical animals alone would meet the ICC gravity threshold.[62] In other words, it is currently unconceivable that such activities be considered as constituting the most serious crimes that require action at the international level. In fact, there are very few cases that have been brought before international courts and tribunals which concern the protection of property. Nonetheless, if an attack is launched on medical personnel and, at the same time, on medical animals accompanying them – especially if this attack would also put in danger wounded and sick persons themselves – one could envisage that the ICC considers that persons be prosecuted and tried for this kind of attack directed at simultaneously medical personnel, wounded and sick as well as animals.

3 ANIMALS AS MEANS OF MEDICAL SEARCH AND RESCUE

Animals are also used to perform search and rescue activities. They are often highly trained to do so. These activities are indirectly protected by the regime contained in GC I and GC IV as well as in AP I. In the interest of clarity, I will proceed as I did previously for animals that are employed as means of transportation. After describing the scope of application of this regime (Section 3.1), I will analyse its content (Section 3.2) and the legal consequences that flow from violating the fundamental rules governing it (Section 3.3).

3.1 *Scope of Application of the Laws on Medical Search and Rescue*

3.1.1 General Rules

Belligerents must take all feasible measures to search for and rescue the wounded and sick in order to protect them against dangers arising from the battlefield.[63]

59 Art. 50 of GC I; Art. 51 of GC II; Art. 147 of GC IV; Art. 8(2)(a)(ii), (iii) and (c)(i), (ii) of ICC Statute.
60 Ibid.
61 This approach would also be consistent with the legislations of several states which protect the life, physical integrity and well-being of animals as fellow creatures against acts of killing or cruelty, such as brutally inflicting severe pain or suffering.
62 See Art. 17(1)(d) of ICC Statute.
63 Art. 18(1) of GC II; Art. 16(2) of GC IV; Art. 10 of AP I; Art. 8 of AP II.

Under customary international law, these obligations apply in both international and non-international armed conflicts.[64] The search obligation extends to missing combatants and civilians, including those who are dead.[65] Such tasks are usually carried out by medical personnel or members of humanitarian organisations, such as the ICRC. In both categories of conflicts, these subjects benefit from the detailed regime of protection offered by the GCs and the APs. It should finally be noted that medical units and their material used for search and rescue operations are also duly protected.

Article 8(c) of AP I provides the following definition – which is widely accepted[66] – of medical personnel: those persons assigned, by a party to the conflict, exclusively to the search for, collection, transportation, diagnosis or treatment, including first-aid treatment, of the wounded, sick and shipwrecked, and the prevention of disease, to the administration of medical units or to the operation or administration of medical transports. The ICRC notes in this regard that:

> The essence of the definition is that medical personnel have to be exclusively assigned to medical duties in order to enjoy the specific protection to which they are entitled. If the medical assignment is permanent, respect and protection are due at all times. If the medical assignment is only temporary, respect and protection are due only during the time of assignment.[67]

Pursuant to Article 8(e) of AP I, the term 'medical units' refers to 'establishments and other units, whether military or civilian, organized for medical purposes, be they fixed or mobile, permanent or temporary'. Furthermore, according to the ICRC Commentary on GC I (2016), mobile medical units are 'establishments which can move from place to place as circumstances require and according to the movements of the troops'.[68] Fixed medical establishments are permanent buildings used as hospitals and stores. It is usually accepted that these definitions apply in the contexts of both international and non-international armed conflicts.[69]

3.1.2 Applicability to Animals

With an acute sense of smell, much stronger than any human's, dogs have proved to be particularly useful to detect human scents. In many armies around the world, they are trained and employed to locate survivors of hostilities and to identify the remains of deceased victims. But, when engage in these activities, how are these animals protected by IHL, if at all? It might be tempting to argue that they should

64 ICRC Customary Law Database, Rule 109.
65 Art. 15(1) of GC I; Art. 18(1) of GC II; Art. 16(2) of GC IV; Art. 17 (2) of AP I; Art. 8 of AP II. See also ICRC Customary Law Database, Rule 112.
66 ICRC Customary Law Database, Rule 25.
67 Ibid.
68 ICRC Commentary GC I (2016), para. 2326.
69 ICRC Customary Law Database, Rule 28.

enjoy the same status as medical personnel in order to avoid any gap in protection. Indeed, by comparison, when involved in medical transportation, animals benefit from the legal protection specifically designed for means of medical transport. But no such regime exists for means that are deployed in search and rescue activities. One could also contend that the definition of medical personnel contained in Article 8(c) of AP I is mainly 'purpose/use oriented': just like means of medical transportation, medical personnel are protected, not because of their intrinsic nature, but because of their assignment to medical duties.[70] Animals could thus theoretically fall within the scope of this provision on the basis of the exclusive medical functions they perform during warfare. Lastly, it should be emphasised that, while usually accompanying medical personnel, animals often retain some degree of autonomy when discharging their search and rescue duties.

That said, this progressist interpretation is difficult to reconcile with the terms of Article 8(c) of AP I. Indeed, this provision expressly refers only to 'persons'. It therefore seems to exclude other living beings. Moreover, if they were considered as such, animals would rarely be in position to exercise the duties associated with the status of medical personnel[71] (even if this would not theoretically prevent them from benefiting from their rights). The independence of animals in exercising medical tasks referred to above is limited. They are unable to understand and obey autonomously the various legal obligations incumbent upon medical personnel under the GCs and APs which understanding is required to guarantee the well-being of the wounded and sick, be they soldiers or civilians.[72] In reality, animals must be trained by individuals to exercise, with a certain degree of independence, minimum search and rescue tasks. In such a context, under the current IHL regime, medical working dogs appear to be more 'medical equipment'[73] which could potentially benefit from the specific protection afforded to mobile or fixed medical units to which they belong.[74] In other words, if they are used by medical personnel for search or rescue activities, animals could constitute means of search or rescue, but not medical

70 For an analysis of the notion of 'assignment to medical duties', see generally Rain Liivoja, 'Status of Medical Personnel: Clear as Mud?' (n. 28); M. Sassòli, 'Medical Care in Armed Conflict, Part I', *ICRC Blog Humanitarian Law and Policy* (24 January 2019), available at https://bit.ly/3GwoJFq, accessed 22 February 2022.

71 Roscini, 'Animals' (n. 49), 44–5.

72 Karsten Nowrot, 'Animals at War: The Status of "Animal Soldiers" under International Humanitarian Law', *Historical Social Research* 40 (2015), 128–50, at 140.

73 This interpretation could be disputed. Indeed, the ICRC Commentary on Article 35 of GC I (2016) states that 'medical includes drugs, bandages, medical instruments, stretchers and other supplies needed for the care of the wounded and sick.' At first sight, animals seem to be excluded from this regime. That said, such definition is open-ended: despite the limited examples it provides, the ICRC Commentary on GC I (2016) does not, as such, restrict its scope of application to inanimate objects. Moreover, one could argue that the ICRC approach is 'purpose/use-oriented'. This would entail that, like any other equipment, animals must benefit protection, not because of their intrinsic characteristics, but because of their assignment to medical purposes.

74 See the similar conclusions reached by Marco Roscini regarding animals involved in hostilities ('Animals and the Law of Armed Conflict' (n. 49), 45).

personnel as such. In all circumstances, animals benefit from the general protection offered to objects under IHL.

3.2 *Contents and Limits of the Laws on Medical Search and Rescue*

3.2.1 General Rules

Medical units, including their equipment, are protected by the same legal regime as the one applicable to medical transport.[75] One distinctive characteristic deserves particular attention. The material of medical units having fallen into enemy hands is treated differently depending on whether it is part of a mobile medical or a fixed medical establishment (or means of transport).[76] When belonging to a mobile unit, this material must be reserved for the care of the wounded and sick. It is interesting to recall in this regard that Article 33 of GC I no longer requires their restitution to their home land because of the 'practical obstacles to the restoring of equipment under war conditions'.[77] When belonging to fixed medical establishments (or to transport units), material remains subject to the laws of war and the rules on seizure of property, including war booty and confiscation of movable property.[78] Thus, as with means of medical transportation, they can be used for military purposes provided that previous arrangements are made for the welfare of the wounded and sick which benefit from their care.[79] In non-international armed conflicts, no such rules allowing or prohibiting the taking of war booty have been identified.[80] Therefore, domestic law is the applicable legal regime in this context.[81]

3.2.2 Applicability to Animals

Applying the regime of equipment of mobile medical units to animals when they fall into enemy hands, even if they belong to fixed medical units, seems appropriate for two main reasons. First, the military importance of animals in modern warfare is much less significant than any equipment or vehicle which can easily be converted for military purposes. Second, and more importantly, the suffering of animals resulting from their involvement in hostilities should be prevented as much as possible. It could even be argued that animals should always be returned to their country of origin (with all the necessary care).[82] However, practical obstacles linked

75 Art. 33(1) of GC I.
76 Schöberl, 'Buildings, Material, and Transports' (n. 19), 828.
77 Pictet Commentary on GC I, para. 273.
78 Schöberl, 'Buildings, Material, and Transports' (n. 19), 828.
79 Art. 33(2) of GC I.
80 Schöberl, 'Buildings, Material, and Transports' (n. 19), 835–6.
81 Ibid.
82 This entails that, during transfer, the detaining authorities should provide medical animals with sufficient water and food, adequate shelter and the necessary medical attention.

to the conduct of hostilities will often bar such returns. Accordingly, animals could be retained by the detaining power and, when necessary and possible, used for the care of wounded and sick. In those circumstances, at a minimum, medical animals should be treated with dignity and respect.

3.3 *Consequences of Violations of the Laws on Medical Search and Rescue*

3.3.1 General Rules

Pursuant to Articles 49 and 50 of GC I, wilful killing, torture, inhumane treatment, or wilfully causing great suffering or serious injury to the body or health of medical personnel constitutes a grave breach of GC I. However, attacking medical personnel may be legal if such personnel are engaged in acts harmful to the enemy. Moreover, the ICC Statute makes it a war crime in both international[83] and non-international armed conflicts[84] intentionally to direct attacks against medical personnel that are 'using the distinctive emblems of the Geneva Conventions in conformity with international law'. As I have already explained, the extensive destruction and appropriation of protected property, not justified by military necessity and carried out unlawfully and wantonly, constitutes a grave breach of the GCs[85] and a war crime under the ICC Statute.[86] Medical units are usually considered as being protected under these conventions.[87] Moreover, acts committed against medical units in non-international armed conflicts could also be prosecuted under the charge of pillage[88] and destruction or seizure of property not imperatively demanded by the necessities of the conflict.[89]

3.3.2 Applicability to Animals

On the one hand, according animals the same status as medical personnel for the sake of sanctioning serious violations of IHL committed against them would be contrary to the explicit texts of the GCs and the APs. On the other hand, when such violations are committed against animals, treating them in this way would be all the more justified. Indeed, as noted in Section 2.3.2 above, these violations appropriately reflect the nature of the violence inflicted upon living beings and its serious consequences on their mental or physical health. It would, however, be illogical to submit animals simultaneously to two different legal regimes: the regime governing medical equipment when applying IHL and the regime governing medical personnel when

83 Art. 8(2)(b)(xxiv) of ICC Statute.
84 Art. 8(2)(e)(ii) of ICC Statute.
85 Art. 50 of GC I; Art. 50 of GC II; Art. 147 of GC IV.
86 Art. 8(2)(a)(iv) of ICC Statute.
87 Schöberl, 'Buildings, Material, and Transports' (n. 19), 836.
88 Art. 8(2)(e)(v) of ICC Statute.
89 Art. 8(2)(e)(xii) of ICC Statute.

applying international criminal law. A consistent approach between IHL and international criminal law is required when identifying norms of IHL the violation of which is prosecuted and tried under international criminal law. That said, if the prosecution and the trial of such a violation is envisaged at the international level – which, as we know, is currently rare – one may wonder whether the suffering of animals could be taken into consideration at sentencing level, when assessing the seriousness of crimes committed against them. Indeed, as foreseen by Article 78 of the ICC Statute, the court shall take into account such factors as the gravity of the crime when determining the appropriate sentence. Thus, at that stage, it could be acknowledged that the destruction or the appropriation of medical equipment are particularly heinous crimes and must therefore be aggravated because the equipment is made up of living beings experiencing pain and suffering.

4 CONCLUDING RECOMMENDATIONS

Two final observations should be made. On a factual level, the number of animals performing medical functions in a given armed conflict is often relatively modest. Moreover, exercising these functions is not necessarily running against military interests, especially when the lives of combatants are at stake. In this context, it would make sense to impose upon belligerents the respect of a sophisticated regime of protection. That said, on a legal level, IHL is ill-equipped for duly protecting non-human living creatures: only the regime applicable to inanimate objects can easily be transposed to these creatures. Hence, to guarantee the full protection of animals and to facilitate the performance of their medical duties, this regime must be reinforced and tailored to the specific needs of sentient beings.

In light of these considerations and the above analysis, the following seven general guidelines should influence the way basic IHL principles governing means of medical transportation, search and rescue are interpreted and applied concretely. First, when used for medical purposes in both international and non-international armed conflicts, animals should benefit from the regime of protection offered by the GCs, the APs and customary IHL to means of medical transportation or mobile medical units. Second, in these circumstances, belligerents should ensure, to the greatest practicable extent, that their dignity be respected by providing them with satisfactory conditions of nutrition, safety and health. Third, if they have at their disposals inanimate medical means which allow them to provide treatment to wounded and sick of the same level and quality as living medical means, belligerents should use the former means as a priority. Fourth, animals should not be employed outside their medical functions to perform military tasks. If that happens, animals could lose their protection and be targeted. But, in that case, they should never be submitted to means and methods of warfare that cause superfluous injury or unnecessary suffering. Fifth, when falling into enemy hands, animals should be either returned to their home country or, when impossible, retained to perform medical duties. Sixth, the provisions on grave breaches and on war crimes that protect medical objects should apply to animals performing medical duties. Seventh, the suffering of these animals should be duly taken into consideration at sentencing level, when assessing the seriousness of crimes committed against them.

SELECT BIBLIOGRAPHY

Baratay, Eric, *Bêtes de tranchées: Des vécus oubliés* (Paris: CNRS éditions 2013).

Bouvier, Antoine, 'The Use of the Emblem' in Andrew Clapham, Paola Gaeta and Marco Sassòli (eds.), *The 1949 Geneva Conventions* (Oxford: Oxford University Press 2015), 855–85.

Breitegger, Alexander, 'The Legal Framework Applicable to Insecurity and Violence Affecting the Delivery of Health Care in Armed Conflicts and Other Emergencies', *International Review of the Red Cross* 95 (2013), 83–127.

Haeck, Tom, 'Loss of Protection' in Andrew Clapham, Paola Gaeta and Marco Sassòli (eds.), *The 1949 Geneva Conventions* (Oxford: Oxford University Press 2015), 839–54.

Liivoja, Rain, 'Status of Medical Personnel: Clear as Mud?', *ICRC Blog Humanitarian Law and Policy* (25 February 2019).

Nowrot, Karsten, 'Animals at War: The Status of "Animal Soldiers" under International Humanitarian Law', *Historical Social Research* 40 (2015), 128–50.

Peters, Anne, 'Global Animal Law: What It Is and Why We Need It', *Transnational Environmental Law* 5 (2016), 13–16.

Roscini, Marco, 'Animals and the Law of Armed Conflict', *Israel Yearbook on Human Rights* 47 (2017), 35–67.

Schmitt, Michael, 'War, Technology and the Law of Armed Conflict' in Anthony Helm (ed.), *The Law of War in the 21st Century: Weaponry and the Use of Force* (Newport: Naval War College International Studies 2006).

Schöberl, Katia, 'Buildings, Material, and Transports' in Andrew Clapham, Paola Gaeta and Marco Sassòli (eds.), *The 1949 Geneva Conventions* (Oxford: Oxford University Press 2015), 825–38.

Sassòli, Marco, 'Medical Care in Armed Conflict, Part I', *ICRC Blog Humanitarian Law and Policy* (24 January 2019).

12

Veterinary Personnel

Katharine Fortin

1 INTRODUCTION

To properly analyse the protection of veterinary personnel under international humanitarian law (IHL), it is first important understand the different roles that animals have played, and continue to play, in armed conflict. Before and up to World War II, horses, oxen and mules were the primary means by which supplies and combatants were brought to areas of combat. Horses and mules were used to accompany infantry divisions, pull artillery batteries and travel together with artillery crews. Cavalry units, consisting of mounted fighting troops, were an essential part of any army, as their mobility, speed and shock value offered significant advantages over infantry divisions. Horse-drawn ambulances were also widely used for the collection and transportation of the sick and wounded. It was said in 1864 that the Union Army had 220,000 horses and mules for 426,000 men – one animal for every two men.[1] In the 1899–1902 Boer War, the high number of human casualties suffered by the British (e.g. 22,000 men) was dwarfed by the vast number of animal casualties (e.g. 326,073 horses, 51,399 mules and 195,000 oxen).[2] In those days when animals played such a vital role in the waging of war, there were tens of thousands of sick and wounded animals that needed care and medical attention.[3] The high death rates of the animals referred to above are testament to the fact that animals often did not receive this care. Indeed, most literature assessing the provision of veterinary services in armed conflict in the late nineteenth and early twentieth century demonstrates that veterinary care was deeply inadequate and that the wastage of animals was appalling and unnecessary. The very few military veterinary hospitals that existed

[1] Gene Armistead, *Horses and Mules in the Civil War: A Complete History with a Roster of More Than 700 War Horses* (Jefferson: McFarland 2013), 10.

[2] Sandra Swart, 'Horses in the South African War, c. 1899–1902', *Society and Animals* 18 (2010), 348–66, at 348 and 349; Frederick Smith, *A Veterinary History of the War in South Africa 1899–1902* (London: H. & W. Brown 1914).

[3] Steven J. Corvi, 'Men of Mercy: The Evolution of the Royal Army Veterinary Corps and the Soldier-Horse Bond During the Great War', *Journal of the Society for Army Historical Research* 76 (1998), 272–84

were poorly organised and had to be supplemented by those run by charitable institutions, such as the UK Blue Cross and the UK Royal Society for the Prevention of Cruelty to Animals (RSPCA).[4] Due to the immense suffering of animals during the Boer War, there were calls from some quarters for the provisions of IHL to be extended to animals employed in warfare and veterinary surgeons.[5] While these legal changes were not made, veterinary care in the British Army at least was radically overhauled to offer more effective treatment of sick and wounded animals in World War I.

Although a number of horses, mules and oxen carried on being employed in much smaller numbers during World War II, they were gradually replaced with motor vehicles as the first half of the twentieth century progressed.[6] As the ratio of animals per human in state militaries radically reduced, the role of veterinary surgeons drastically changed, moving away from the care of horses and mules toward the care of other animals. Today, army veterinary personnel are assigned to varied duties that include providing medical attention to the explosive ordinance detection dogs that are used to inter alia sniff out improvised explosive devices (IEDs) placed by armed groups, such as the Taliban and Islamic State.[7] A military dog's keen sense of smell enables it to work with its handler to detect explosives, track militants and find the wounded among the rubble.[8] Veterinary personnel also take care of other animals that are used in the army's operations. Some countries use dolphins and sea lions in anti-mining operations and other sea mammals, such as beluga whales and seals, to guard entrances to naval bases, identifying intruders in restricted areas and finding lost equipment.[9] State militaries employ a range of personnel responsible for

4 Blue Cross, *The Blue Cross at War, 1914–'18 and 1939–45* (Oxford: Blue Cross 1990). See also Smith, *Veterinary History* (n. 2) for an account of the difficulties and chaos that reigned due to the deficient organisation of the veterinary service, leading to the death of animals. While some accounts of the battle of Solferino indicate that more veterinary surgeons than doctors were involved on the battlefield, this should not be taken as a sign that the care of animals was good. Martin Gumpert estimates that there were roughly four veterinarians for every 1,000 horses, as opposed to two doctors for every 6,000 wounded (Martin Gumpert, *Dunant: The Story of the Red Cross* (New York: Oxford University Press 1938), 46).

5 Henry Salt, *Horses in Warfare* (National Peace Council 1912), available at www.henrysalt.co.uk/library/article/horses-in-warfare/, accessed 22 February 2022.

6 Eric Darre and Emmanuel Dumas, 'Vétérinaires et droit international humanitaire: Réflexions sur une controverse' *Military Law and Law of War Review* (2004) 43, 111–36, at 117.

7 For an overview of the duties of veterinary personnel in the Swiss, Dutch and French armies, see Joris Wijnker and Judith Gooijer, 'The Military Veterinarian: Its Position and Function in the Royal Netherlands Army', *Nederlands Geneeskundig Tijdschrift* (January 2014).

8 Robert Chesshyre, 'Dogs of War: Sniffer Dogs Lead the Way in Afghanistan', *Telegraph* (20 January 2011), available at https://bit.ly/3nmPrsp accessed 22 February 2022. Alex Horton, 'The Dog Who Helped Kill Baghdadi Visited the White House. But Conan is Just the Latest War Hero', *The Seattle Times* (26 November 2019), available at https://bit.ly/3tfIA63, accessed 28 February 2022

9 Marco Roscini, 'Animals and the Law of Armed Conflict' *Israel Yearbook on Human Rights* 35 (2017), 35–67, at 35. See also Jane Lee, 'Military Whales and Dolphins: What Do They Do and Who Uses Them?', *National Geographic* (3 May 2019), available at https://on.natgeo.com/3GhwIpw, accessed 22 February 2022

the training and care of these animals, including veterinary personnel. Veterinary personnel in state armies around the world also take an active role in the protection of the health of military personnel, taking responsibility for hygiene, epidemiology and disease control, as well as the safety and quality of food and water.[10]

Although it is hard to find specific information on veterinary personnel and armed groups, it has been rightly commented that whenever animals are used in combat, humans are assigned to their care.[11] Certainly, evidence exists that armed groups sometimes use animals in military operations. These groups very often adopt the same tactics or behaviours as states, especially when they are sophisticated or when their existence is attributed to a military coup. As evidence of the latter points, it is notable that Franco's army had a very effective cavalry division, which originated in the Spanish army. His forces also made extensive use of mules, which were essential for supplying troops to Franco's forces in difficult terrain.[12] Their handlers (*acemileros*) were said to be the rural heroes of Nationalist zones. They delivered food, munitions, medicine, weapons and transported the sick, injured and dead. The Tuaregs in Mali used camels for transportation in the first Tuareg rebellion in the 1960s.[13] Today, many armed groups, like states, have swapped animals for motorised vehicles. But, as states, several armed groups continue to use animals for the transportation of persons and goods across difficult terrain.[14] They also employ animals in combat. Some reports mention that contemporary armed groups, such as the Revolutionary Armed Forces of Colombia (FARC), Hamas and the Taliban, have used animals, like dogs, mules and donkeys as 'suicide bombers' – a practice already developed by the Soviet Union in World War II.[15] Several armed groups in

10 See Wijnker and Gooijer, 'The Military Veterinarian' (n. 7).

11 Darre and Dumas, 'Vétérinaires et DIH' (n. 6), 113.

12 Michael Seidman, *The Victorious Counterrevolution: The Nationalist Effort in the Spanish Civil War* (Wisconsin: University of Wisconsin Press 2011).

13 Kalifa Keita, 'Conflict and Conflict Resolution in the Sahel: The Tuareg Insurgency in Mali' (Carlisle: Strategic Studies Institute, US Army War College 1998), 10 available at www.files.ethz.ch/isn/47576/Conflict_Conflict_Resolution.pdf, accessed 22 February 2022

14 Naharet Newsdesk, 'From Camels to 4x4s: A History of the Tuareg Rebels', *Naharet* (24 March 2012), available at www.naharnet.com/stories/en/34453, accessed 22 February 2022. There are many accounts of the FARC using mules. See US Senates, Hearing Before the Permanent Subcommittee on Investigations of the Committee on Governmental Affairs, One Hundred Second Congress, First Session, 'Arms Trafficking, Mercenaries and Drug Cartels' (27 and 28 February 1991), 22; Marjolein van der Water, 'The FARC Guerilleros' Final Journey', *de Volkskrant* (30 November 2016).

15 For accounts of the Soviet Union using suicide dogs, see Boris Egorov, 'Why Did the Soviets Use 'Suicide' Dogs to Blow Up Nazi Tanks?', *Russia Beyond* (22 August 2018), available at www.rbth.com/history/329005-soviets-used-suicide-dogs, accessed 22 February 2022. For accounts of the FARC using mules, dogs and horses to detonate bombs, see Report Submitted to the Committee on Foreign Affairs, US House of Representatives and Committee on Foreign Relations, US Senate by the Department of State in Accordance with Sections 116(d) and 502B(b) of the Foreign Assistance Act of 1961, as Amended, Volume 2, 2479. For accounts of the Taliban using donkeys to carry and detonate explosive devices, see Michael Evans, 'Donkey "Suicide" Bombing is Latest Tactic against Patrols', *Times* (30 April 2009), available at https://bit.ly/3rim5wi, accessed 22 February 2022. Associated Press, 'Bomb Attached to Donkey Kills Policeman in Eastern Afghanistan', *FoxNews* (5 April 2013), available at https://fxn.ws/3HZSOxg, accessed 22 February 2022.

the Sahel region of Africa are known for carrying out mounted attacks on horseback or camelback.[16] Hamas is reported to have a canine unit, as part of its *Nohba* tunnel unit belonging to the organisation.[17] In instances where armed groups are using animals in their military operations, it can be assumed that they have individuals who are responsible for these animals' care and health. Some groups almost certainly also engage individuals for the tasks mentioned above relating to food hygiene and disease control.

2 SCOPE OF APPLICATION OF THE LAWS POTENTIALLY APPLICABLE TO VETERINARY PERSONNEL

When analysing manner in which IHL applies to veterinary personnel, it is helpful to make a distinction between international armed conflicts (Section 2.1) and non-international armed conflicts (Section 2.2).

2.1 *General Rules in International Armed Conflicts*

Although during the drafting of Articles 8 and 9 of the 1929 Geneva Convention (GC) on the protection of the sick and wounded in the field it was proposed that veterinary personnel should benefit from the same protections as medical and health personnel; these suggestions were rejected and have never since been implemented.[18] As a result, under the modern framework of IHL that applies to international armed conflicts, veterinary personnel *generally* do not have a special status akin to medical personnel and veterinary hospitals or clinics are not protected in the same way as medical establishments and units. However, it will be shown below that veterinary personnel may fall within the scope of Article 24 of GC I, which provides special respect and protection to medical personnel, medical administrators and chaplains due to their functions.

The International Committee of the Red Cross (ICRC) Commentary on GC I (2016) confirms that a veterinarian who, as a member of the armed forces, takes care of animals that are deployed to assist combat activities will be deemed a combatant.[19] This reflects the traditional position that veterinary personnel engaged with the care of animals used in combat are treated like ordinary members of the armed forces

[16] The best-known group carrying out such attacks is the Janjaweed in Darfur. Janjaweed translates as 'devils on horseback'. For the use of camels by Boko Haram, see Reuters, 'Suspected Boko Haram Militants Riding Camels Kill Five in Niger', *YahooNews* (4 September 2016), available at https://yhoo.it/3nn92bO, accessed 22 February 2022.

[17] Mordechai Sones, 'Hamas Canine Unit Revealed, Israeli Expert Sceptical', *Arutz Sheva 7* (9 February 2017), available at www.israelnationalnews.com/News/News.aspx/224713, accessed 22 February 2022.

[18] Procès-Verbaux, Des Séances de la première Commission Révision de laConvention de Genève, Séances I à XXI, Séance III, 123. See Section 3 for a review of these proceedings.

[19] ICRC Commentary GC I (2016), Art. 24.

engaged in hostilities. This means that they are not immune from being targeted and are eligible for prisoner of war status upon capture. Some countries recognise that there can be members of the armed forces who do not have a combat mission, for instance military lawyers, cooks and labourers.[20] According to the IHL definition, these individuals are still held to have combatant status if they are members of the armed forces.[21] Veterinary personnel who are not members of the armed forces, but simply accompany these forces as civilians, are eligible for prisoner of war status if they receive authorisation from the armed forces which they accompany, as attested by an identity card which is granted to them. Any civilian veterinary personnel accompanying the armed forces which do not fulfil these conditions will benefit from the protections of GC IV upon capture.[22]

If veterinary personnel are exclusively assigned to duties that match those of medical personnel, it may be possible for them to fall within the scope of Article 24 of GC I which provides special respect and protection to medical personnel, medical administrators and chaplains. This provision specifies that '[m]edical personnel exclusively involved in the search for, or the collection, transport or treatment of the wounded or sick, or in the prevention of disease, staff exclusively engaged in the administration of medical units and establishments, as well as chaplains attached to the armed forces, shall be respected and protected in all circumstances'. The term 'prevention of disease' was added to the text of Article 24 in 1949, to take account of the fact that hygiene and prophylactic measures for the prevention of disease often forms an important part of the work of medical staff.[23] The term 'exclusively' is understood to indicate that an individual's assignment to such duties must be 'permanent', meaning that individuals who have different duties or a temporary assignment to the tasks enumerated in Article 24 will not fall within this provision.[24] The idea that temporary medical personnel engaged with the prevention of disease are also protected while they are exclusively assigned to medical tasks was introduced later by Article 8 of AP I.[25]

The insertion of the phrase 'prevention of disease' into Article 24 of GC I and its later enumeration in Article 8 of AP I is relevant to understanding when and how some veterinary personnel may be protected as 'medical personnel'. Historically and today, veterinary personnel have been responsible for protecting members of the armed forces from disease. They are very often responsible for carrying out food inspections and water checks, prevention of zoonoses (i.e. diseases that pass from

20 See also Art. 3 of the 1907 Hague Convention (IV).

21 Knut Ipsen 'Combatants and Non-combatants', in Dieter Fleck (ed.), *The Handbook of International Humanitarian Law* (3rd ed., Oxford: Oxford University Press 2013), 80–115, at 85–7 and 96–7.

22 An example of volunteer civilian veterinary personnel accompanying the armed forces is the Blue Cross.

23 Pictet Commentary GC I (2016), 219; ICRC Commentary GC I (2016), para. 1958.

24 Pictet Commentary GC I (2016), 219.

25 Art. 8 of AP I.

animals to humans), and even public health initiatives.[26] The ICRC Commentary on GC I (2016) states that, when veterinary personnel are 'exclusively' assigned to activities related to the prevention of disease vis-à-vis human beings, they will fall within the scope of Article 24.[27] The ICRC Commentary on GC I (2016) notes that these days there are 'more and more' veterinarians engaged exclusively in this protected activity.[28] However, it also observes that these activities remain exceptional and the more traditional activities of veterinarians – like the care of animal health care – 'fall in principle' outside the scope of Article 24, even if veterinary personnel are formally held to be members of the armed forces' medical service.[29] It notes that '[a] veterinarian who, as a member of the armed forces, takes care of animals that deployed to assist combat activities would, for example, be deemed a combatant'.[30] The ICRC Commentary on GC I (2016) does not say anything about veterinarians who are exclusively assigned to duties relating to taking care of animals that *are not deployed* to assist combat activities, such as a veterinary surgeon that is solely responsible for the treatment of dogs used to sniff out the wounded or dead in the rubble of buildings. There seems room to argue that these personnel could also fall under Article 24, on the basis that they are medical personnel exclusively involved in the search for, or the collection, transport or treatment of the wounded or sick.

Veterinary hospitals and units that are devoted to the care of animals used in combat are also not given special protection under IHL, akin to the protection that is given to medical units. However, recognising that there is often some mixing between the work and duties of medical and veterinary personnel, Article 22(4) of GC I specifies that, when the personnel and equipment of the veterinary service are found in the unit of medical unit without forming an integral part thereof, that unit will not be deprived of its protection under IHL.

2.2 *General Rules in Non-international Armed Conflicts*

It can be presumed that, just as in international armed conflicts, veterinary personnel in non-international armed conflicts will benefit from the protection given to medical personnel where they are exclusively assigned to the prevention of human diseases within their ranks. It is noteworthy that the content of Article 24 of GC I has been held to have customary international law status and apply in both international and non-international armed conflicts.[31]

26 See Wijnker and Gooijer, 'The Military Veterinarian' (n. 7). See also Vicky Fogelman et al., 'The Role of Veterinary Public Health and Preventive Medicine during Mobilization and Deployment' in Patrick Kelley (ed.), *Military Preventive Medicine: Mobilization and Deployment, Vol. I* (1st ed., Office of the Surgeon General, US Army 2003), 669–81

27 ICRC Commentary GC I (2016), para. 1959.

28 Ibid.

29 Ibid. See also Darre and Dumas, 'Vétérinaires et DIH' (n. 6) for examples.

30 ICRC Commentary GC I (2016), para. 1959.

31 ICRC Customary Law Database, Rule 25.

The status of individuals who are not exclusively assigned to these duties raises additional difficulties as it requires a consideration of whether the duties of a vet relating to animal care are such to cause these individuals to lose their protection under IHL. According to the ICRC, individuals associated with an armed group may lose their protection in one of two ways.[32] In instances where they are integrated into an armed group and hold a continuous functional role within the organisation that involves the preparation, execution or command of acts or operations amounting to direct participation in hostilities, they will lose their protection so long as they hold that function within the group.[33] Persons who are not integrated within such a group can lose their protection temporarily as a result of carrying out certain activities that are associated with the armed group's combat activities.[34] In these instances, these individuals will only lose their civilian protection for the duration of those activities. Although the exact content of such legal tests is contested, they both require an evaluation of the extent to which activities contribute to a group's military action.

3 CONTENTS AND LIMITS OF THE LAWS POTENTIALLY APPLICABLE TO VETERINARY PERSONNEL

It follows from the above analysis that in both international and non-international armed conflicts, veterinary personnel will be protected under IHL when they are exclusively assigned to the prevention of disease within their ranks. Veterinary personnel falling within the scope of Article 24 of GC I and its customary equivalent in non-international armed conflict are entitled to be *respected* by parties to an armed conflict and must not be the subject of attack or ill-treatment.[35] They are also allowed to be *protected* by parties to an armed conflict, meaning that these parties must take steps to ensure that they can carry out their work without interference.[36] If veterinary personnel exclusively responsible for medical duties fall into enemy hands, they will not become prisoners of war and may not be detained as such. They shall only be retained insofar as the state of health and number of the prisoners of war require. If they are retained, they will receive the benefits and protections of the GC III and be given the facilities they need to provide for the medical care of the prisoners of war.[37]

The protection conferred to veterinary personnel falling under Article 24 of GC I is generally thought to be limited and will cease if they commit an act harmful to the enemy, but only if due warning has been given and remained

32 ICRC, *Interpretive Guidance on the Notion of Direct Participation in Hostilities Under International Humanitarian Law* (Geneva: ICRC 2009).
33 Ibid., 34 and 72.
34 Ibid., 34–5 and 65–8.
35 See ICRC Commentary GC I (2016), paras. 1987–90.
36 Ibid., paras. 1991–2.
37 See Art. 28, 30 and 31 of GC I; Art. 4(c) and 33 of GC III.

unheeded.[38] In general, taking a part in hostilities, in violation of the principle of strict neutrality and outside the humanitarian function of medical personnel, is considered an act harmful to the enemy.[39] This would include taking part directly in the hostilities and it *may* also encompass activities that do not amount to direct involvement in hostilities.[40] Veterinary personnel falling within the scope of Article 24 are required to wear a water resistant armlet affixed to their left arm bearing the distinctive emblem of the Red Cross, issued and stamped by the military authority to which they belong.[41] They are also obliged to possess a special identity card bearing the distinctive emblem of the Red Cross.[42]

In order to determine when and whether veterinary personnel not engaged in medical duties will enjoy protection in non-international armed conflict, it is necessary to analyse whether their functions (i.e. the care and treatment of military animals) amount to direct participation in hostilities. In order to make this determination, the ICRC has indicated that attention must be given to a cumulative three-part test. Although this test is not universally accepted, it provides a useful initial framework through which this issue can be studied.[43] Attention needs to be given to whether (i) the act is likely to inflict harm of a certain threshold on the adversary, (ii) the causal link between the act and this harm, and (iii) the nexus between the act and the military operation that the act supposedly supports.[44] In instances where veterinary personnel care for animals that are exclusively used for humanitarian purposes, their action will clearly not inflict any harm on the adversary. In circumstances where veterinary personnel provide medical treatment or care to animals that are used in active combat, the provision of veterinary services may contribute to a party's ability to inflict harm on the enemy by rendering it capable of disarming IEDs to enable a particular military operation or identifying militants.[45] However, the contribution is likely to be too far removed to constitute 'direct participation in hostilities' such as to remove a person's civilian protection. The word 'direct' in Article 51(3) of AP I – on which the ICRC's test is based – was

38 ICRC Commentary GC I (2016), paras. 1995–2010 and para. 1881.

39 ICRC Customary Law Database, Rule 25.

40 For a definition of direct participation in hostilities, see below. For a discussion of the phrase 'act harmful to the enemy outside their humanitarian duties', see ICRC Commentary GC I (2016), paras. 1998–2010. This makes clear that medical personnel are not prohibited from carrying a light weapon for the defence of themselves or for the defence of the sick or wounded.

41 See Art. 40 of GC I. See also ICRC Commentary GC I (2016), para. 2590 (indicating that an exception may be made when medical personnel are deemed to be better protected when they do not use the emblem).

42 Ibid.

43 ICRC, *Direct Participation* (n. 32).

44 Ibid., 46–64.

45 For the notion that demining can constitute direct participation in hostilities depending on the circumstances, see Lindsey Cameron and Vincent Chetail, *Private Military and Security Companies under Public International Law* (Cambridge: Cambridge University Press 2013), 442.

included to make clear that the provision refers only to 'acts of war which by their nature or purpose are likely to cause actual harm to the personnel and equipment of the enemy armed forces'.[46] The ICRC explains that the requirement that harm be 'direct' excludes war sustaining activities (e.g. design, production or shipment of weapons, construction or repair of roads) or the general war effort (e.g. production of agricultural or non-military goods or political propaganda).[47] While taking care of animals used in active combat has a closer link to hostilities than some of these examples the ICRC provides, it does not fulfil the requirement that the harm in question is brought about in one causal step.[48] A civilian veterinary surgeon providing treatment to sick animals used in combat can be compared to a civilian mechanic maintaining vehicles or equipment back at base, which although essential, does not directly impact on military actions.[49] As a result, the provision of veterinary services to combat animals will likely be excluded from the definition of 'direct participation in hostilities'. This means that, under the ICRC guidance, veterinary personnel providing exclusive medical care to animals used by an armed group in military operations will not lose their protection under IHL in non-international armed conflict, either by virtue of being a member of this group or by virtue of directly participating in hostilities. If individuals associated with an armed group play a mixed role, for example by not only providing care to animals but also accompanying animals on military operations as 'handlers', they are likely to lose their protection under IHL at least for the duration of the military activity. Physically guiding or providing direct instructions to animals to find explosives or militants in the context of a specific military operation is likely to amount to direct participation in hostilities.

When reflecting on the contents and limits of the rules protecting veterinary personnel in IHL, one is struck by the conceptual awkwardness in the notion that veterinary personnel generally have combatant status in international armed conflict. It is not self-evident why veterinary personnel do not enjoy the same protected status as medical personnel in all circumstances and not just when they are involved in the prevention of diseases that threaten humans. Indeed, the fact that the duties of veterinary personnel are closely associated with the duties of medical personnel is recognised in Article 22(4) of GC I, which anticipates that there may be significant mixing between veterinary and medical personnel and mixing of materials. It is not clear why the legal framework forces us to compare veterinary personnel to the mechanic, rather than the surgeon. It is testament to the anthropocentric nature of IHL that it protects individuals involved in the care and medical treatment of

[46] Art. 51(3) of AP I; AP I Commentary, para. 1944.

[47] ICRC, *Direct Participation* (n. 32), 51

[48] Ibid., 53

[49] Michael, N. Schmitt, 'Humanitarian Law and Direct Participation in Hostilities by Private Contractors and Civilian Employees', *Chicago Journal of International Law* 5(2) (2005), 511–46, at 544–5.

humans even if those humans are combatants, but does not provide safeguards to individuals involved in the care and medical treatment of animals when used in combat.[50]

This difference of treatment between veterinary personnel and medical personnel is certainly rooted in history. Indeed, before World War I, veterinary personnel sometimes took part in combat alongside the cavalry regiments.[51] It is also known that there was a staggeringly great loss of animal lives in armed conflicts pre-dating the twentieth century and in its early years during the Boer War. The appallingly large number of animal deaths indicate a widespread (but not universal) attitude that animals were disposable, like other military equipment. Indeed, if animals are treated as inanimate 'objects', it makes more sense that the people that take care for them are accorded less protection than those who care for humans. When considering this puzzle, it is interesting to look more closely at the drafting papers documenting the discussion whether veterinary personnel should benefit from the same protections as medical and health personnel contained in Articles 8 and 9 of the 1929 Geneva Convention on the protection of the sick and wounded in the field. The Secretary General of the Conference, Paul De Gouttes, indicated that he thought it more appropriate that veterinary personnel be given their own protection under Article 9, so that they would be given the same protection as those helping the sick and wounded and administrating health establishments.[52] The Romanian delegation put forward a similar proposal. These suggestions were not received favourably by other states.[53] The reasoning of these states was based on three points. First, it was asserted that the humanitarian role of the veterinary service on the battlefield had not been demonstrated.[54] Second, it was argued that, if special protection was granted to new categories of individuals, it would have to be entrusted to other people as well.[55] Third, it was maintained that it would be hard to give members of the veterinary service the white armband with the red cross.[56]

Later in the conference, the Romanian delegate took the opportunity to explain how he felt the humanitarianism of the veterinary service had indeed been demonstrated. He argued that everyone had heard of the important role played by famous French veterinary surgeons, such as Nocard, Chaveau and Vallée.[57] He then

[50] For the anthropocentric nature of IHL, see Michael Schmitt, 'Green War: An Assessment of the Environmental Law of Armed Conflict', *Yale Law Journal* 22 (1997), 1–110, at 6.

[51] Darre and Dumas, 'Vétérinaires et DIH' (n. 11), 115–16.

[52] Procès-Verbaux (n. 18), 123.

[53] Ibid. The states expressing verbal opposition to this proposal (which was rejected by a majority vote) were France, the UK, and the United States.

[54] Ibid., 124. (View expressed by France.)

[55] Ibid.

[56] Ibid. (View expressed by the United States.)

[57] Procès-Verbaux, Des Séances de la première Commission Révision de la Convention de Genève, Séances I à XXI, Séance IV, 125-6. Edmond Nocard (1850–1903) was a French veterinarian and microbiologist who served briefly in the military. Auguste Chaveau (1827–1917) was a French professor and veterinarian who worked in microbiology, virology, biochemistry, muscle thermodynamics and

emphasised the important role that the veterinary service played in the care of the sick, the development of vaccines, as well as the preparation and production of food from fatally injured horses. Pointing this out, he indicated that he did not see how veterinary personnel should be protected less well than health personnel.[58] While at first glance it might seem that the Romanian delegate was going out on a limb to propose something quite radical, in fact these examples belie any notion that he was asserting a less anthropocentric approach to IHL. It is striking that to demonstrate the 'humanitarian' nature of veterinarians, the Romanian delegate pointed out how these professionals have assisted humans – and he did not mention the assistance that they have rendered to animals. A similar philosophy is demonstrated by the provisions of GC I which assert that, when veterinarians who are exclusively working to better *human* health (e.g. in hygiene, water or food supplies), they can be protected as medical personnel, but when they are working to improve animal health, they are not protected.[59]

These observations lead to a reflection on the desirability of IHL paying more attention to the care of animals. It might be said that it is inappropriate or unrealistic to critique IHL's anthropocentric character on the basis that one of its key purposes is to protect humanity. But equally, it might be argued that there is a short-sightedness to such a position. Perhaps now there is an imperative to argue that it is wise and appropriate to find space for (non-human) animals within the concept of humanity? The development of such a conceptual framework could draw inspiration from efforts to treat the seabed, ocean-floor and environment as the 'common heritage of mankind' – finding respect for animal life as an endeavour to be supported by all humanity.[60] Notably such a rethinking would not require a radical reconfiguration of the anthropocentric nature of IHL, as it is increasingly understood that the survival of humankind is dependent on the survival of other species. This is true, not only on a grand scale, in the sense of warnings of an impending 'mass extinction' if we do not take better care of our planet, but also on a local scale, where the care of animals is often fundamentally important for the survival of local communities. It is for this reason that military veterinarians and humanitarian charities often provide veterinary advice and assistance to local communities alongside more traditional assistance such as food and medical support. They recognise that a community's ability to survive is often dependent on – or connected to – the survival and health of their livestock or animals for food or the transportation of supplies or firewood.[61]

cardiology. Despite attempts, the author has not been able to ascertain the identity of the veterinarian 'Vallée' who was also referred to.

58 Ibid., 126.

59 Art. 24 of GC I.

60 See Art. 136 of the UNCLOS.

61 'Dealing With the Aftermath: The Role of the Vet Following Conflict or Disaster', *The Veterinary Record* (14 May 2005), available at https://doi.org/10.1136/vr.156.20.625, accessed 22 February 2022. It

Yet by proceeding to address this puzzle by evaluating whether the term 'humanity' is broad enough to encompass the animal kingdom with references to 'humankind', one is arguably missing the other meaning attached to the word which refers to the 'quality of being humane, kind, benevolent'. This alternate meaning also holds potential to see the protection of animals as integrated within the principle of humanity. One is reminded of the poem written at the beginning of the twentieth century that is cited in a Blue Cross publication on animals in World War I:

> I'm only a cavalry charger,
> And I'm dying as fast as I can
> (For my body is riddled with bullets –
> They've potted both me and my man);
> And, though I've no words to express it,
> I'm trying this message to tell
> To kind folks who work for the Red Cross
> – Oh, please help the Blue One as well![62]

Indeed, it is notable that much writing on animals in warfare emphasises the close bond between animals and combatants.[63] Writers criticising the poor care of horses during the Boer War lamented this behaviour as 'wanting' in 'humanity'.[64] Henry Salt, writing in 1912, argued that: '[n]o branch of the humanitarian movement can be carried to a successful conclusion with [sic] does not have regard to the suffering of all sentient beings – human and sub-human alike'.[65] If 'humanity' were interpreted more broadly, it opens up a more solid basis to argue that, by protecting animals that are *hors de combat*, veterinary personnel are engaged in humane work that falls into the spirit of IHL and thus deserve protection. Conferring protection to such animals is arguably justified since animal activities are much less harmful than those of human beings, and animals usually entirely depend on human beings to conduct warfare.

This alternate interpretation of the term 'humanity' highlights a related point that there is conceptual space for the protection of military animals to be given greater attention within IHL under the principle of 'honour' which is often referred to as another important bedrock of the legal framework.[66] It is interesting to note in this

notes that, in a refugee camp in Darfur, the provision of food for donkeys only belatedly became a priority after 10,000 donkeys died due to the priority that had been put on helping people. Not enough attention had been given to the fact that people relied on the donkeys for transportation and gathering firewood.

62 Blue Cross, *The Blue Cross at War* (n. 4), 14.

63 For a reflection on these sources, see Swart, 'Horses in the South African War' (n. 2), 359–60. This is not always the case of course. Frederick Smith also laments the ill-treatment of horses by their riders (*Veterinary History* (n. 2), 236–7).

64 Smith, 'Veterinary History' (n. 2), viii.

65 Salt, *Horses in Warfare* (n. 5).

66 For a discussion of the relevance of honour to modern-day compliance with IHL, see ICRC, *Roots of Restraint in War* (Geneva: ICRC 2020), 32–3 and 65.

respect that at the time when horses were used on the battlefield, their treatment was seen as a 'hallmark of civility'.[67] Still today, we see instances in which the care and welfare of animals has been secured through unexpected collaborations between fighting parties. An example is the rescue of the vulture in Syria; an operation that required collaboration between the Islamic State, the Free Syrian Army, Al-Nusra and Israel.[68]

4 LEGAL CONSEQUENCES OF VIOLATIONS OF THE LAWS POTENTIALLY APPLICABLE TO VETERINARY PERSONNEL

According to analysis above, the protection that is due to veterinary personnel will depend on (i) the nature of their functions and (ii) the classification of an armed conflict.

Notably, directing attacks against personnel using the distinctive emblem, in accordance with IHL, is a war crime in both international and non-international armed conflicts.[69] This means that attacking veterinary personnel is a war crime in these contexts, when these personnel are exclusively engaged in activities related to the prevention of human disease and possibly also the care of animals used in humanitarian operations. Due to their status as 'protected persons', any acts listed in Article 50 of GC I committed against such medical personnel in the context of an international armed conflict will constitute a grave breach.

In non-international armed conflicts, it will be necessary to look carefully at an individual's function at the time of the attack in order to determine whether the attack constitutes a war crime under Article 8(2)(c) or Article 8(2)(e)(i) of the ICC Statute. If the individuals were engaged in providing medical treatment to sick animals (no matter what their use) or the prevention of disease of humans, they will be protected. This will not be the case if these individuals were actively involved in guiding or providing direct instructions to combat animals, in the context of specific military operations.

5 CONCLUDING RECOMMENDATIONS

This chapter has highlighted the conceptual awkwardness in the idea that veterinary personnel in international armed conflicts have combatant status. It has argued that there are good reasons of law and logic to contend that veterinary personnel should have the same status as medical personnel even when they are taking care of animals that are used in combat. On the basis that there has been very little discussion of the protection of veterinary personnel under IHL in academic literature before,

67 Swart, 'Horses in the South African War' (n. 2), 361.

68 Olaf Koens, *Paarden vliegen businessclass: Verhalen over mens en dier in het Midden-Oosten* (Amsterdam: Nijgh & Van Ditmar 2019), 38.

69 Art. 8(2)(b)(xxiv) and 8(2)(e)(ii) of ICC Statute.

a sensible next step might be for the issue to be discussed in more detail at a conference convened by military veterinary personnel, for military veterinary personnel. Here attention could be given to veterinary personnel's own views about whether such a protected status is necessary and whether the current legal framework is satisfactory.[70] Attention could be given inter alia to the three points raised to deny their protected status during the drafting of the 1929 Geneva Convention, namely: (i) the humanitarian role of the veterinary service on the battlefield; (ii) the argument that if special protections are granted to new categories of individuals they will have to be granted to other people as well; and (iii) the argument that it is undesirable to give members of the veterinary service the white armband with the red cross.

The chapter has also shed light on a more general propensity of the IHL framework to define 'humanity' narrowly to refer almost solely to human beings. It has argued that this anthropocentric approach is a potentially missed opportunity that does not sufficiently take into account the fact that the fate of the human race is intricately bound up with the fate of the other animal and plant species with which it shares the planet. Taking this fact seriously, the principle of 'humanity' is broad enough to be interpreted in a manner to pay attention to other animal species. There is also room for more consideration to be given to animal welfare by interpreting the principle of humanity to include notions of kind and humane treatment. Connectedly, concern for animal welfare can potentially be brought to bear on the framework of IHL through the principle of honour, which calls upon the values of individual combatants.

SELECT BIBLIOGRAPHY

Corvi, Steven, 'Men of Mercy: The Evolution of the Royal Army Veterinary Corps and the Soldier-Horse Bond During the Great War', *Journal of the Society for Army Historical Research* 76 (1998), 272–84.

Darre, Eric and Emmanuel Dumas, 'Vétérinaires et droit international humanitaire: Réflexions sur une controverse', *Military Law and Law of War Review* (2004) 43, 111–36.

Fogelman, Vicky et al., 'The Role of Veterinary Public Health and Preventive Medicine during Mobilization and Deployment' in Patrick Kelley (ed.), *Military Preventive Medicine: Mobilization and Deployment*, Vol. I (Office of the Surgeon General, US Army 2003), 669–81.

Swart, Sandra, 'Horses in the South African War, c. 1899–1902', *Society and Animals* 18(2010), 348–66.

Wijnker, Joris and Judith Gooijer, 'The Military Veterinarian: Its Position and Function in the Royal Netherlands Army', *Nederlands Geneeskundig Tijdschrift* (January 2014).

70 Noting the 1929 rejection of the proposal to put veterinary personnel on the same footing as the medical service, Jean Pictet stated that this 'question appears to have lost some of its importance owing to the fact that modern armies are mechanized' (Pictet Commentary on GC I, 205). This chapter has shown that it remains a matter of relevance.

PART III

The Protection of Animals in Specific Situations

Part III concentrates on specific situations in which animals may find themselves during warfare and to which special legal regimes are attached: occupied territory (Chapter 13), protected zones (Chapter 14), sea warfare (Chapter 15), and disasters situations (Chapter 16). It also deals with animals that are used as means of medical experimentation (Chapter 17).

13

Animals in Occupied Territory

Marco Longobardo[*]

It is not a straightforward question of man versus beast.[1]

1 INTRODUCTION

Situations of occupation are as likely to affect the life and well-being of both wild and domestic animals. For example, during World War I, the German forces that occupied Poland cut down the local forests and hunted the wisent to the extent that the animal was declared extinct in its natural habitat.[2] Similarly, during World War II, the Nazi occupying troops in Norway destroyed the local ecosystem so that the reindeers' population dropped to 50 per cent of what it had been.[3] During the 1991 Iraqi occupation of Kuwait, around 8,000 camels were killed,[4] and the deliberate oil spills in the Gulf led to the death of a huge number of birds, fish, and other marine species.[5] The Iraqi occupation also led to the termination of the project to save the endangered species of Arabian oryx,[6] and, generally, Kuwait was unable to resume its wildlife protection programmes for seven years due to Iraqi trenches, foxholes, and minefields.[7] Moreover, Azerbaijan claimed responsibility for damage to fauna and killing of animals in areas allegedly occupied by Armenian forces.[8] The violence connected to hostilities in occupied territory has affected animals

* I thank Eyal Benvenisti, Katharine Fortin, Charles Garraway, and Saba Pipia for some exchanges on this topic.

1 Glen Plant, 'Remarks', *International Law Studies* 69 (1996), 76–7, at 77.
2 Nada Al-Duaij, *Environmental Law of Armed Conflict* (New York: Transnational Publishers 2004), 26.
3 Ibid., 27.
4 Ibid.
5 Ibid., 28; Samira A.S. Omar et al., 'The Gulf War Impact on the Terrestrial Environment of Kuwait: An Overview', in Jay E. Austin and Carl E. Bruch (eds.), *The Environmental Consequences of War* (Cambridge: Cambridge University Press 2000), 316–37, at 326–9.
6 Al-Duaij, *Environmental Law* (n. 2), 27–8.
7 Omar et al., 'The Gulf War' (n. 5), 328–9.
8 See A/71/607-S/2016/944, 10 November 2016, 2; A/74/676-S/2020/90, 7 February 2020, para. 235.

in several zoos, such as that in Kuwait City in 1990,[9] the private zoo of Saddam Hussein in Baghdad in 2003,[10] and the Gaza zoo in 2008/2009.[11]

Notwithstanding these instances, writing a chapter on the legal protection of animals in occupied territory may appear, prima facie, a pointless exercise since the law of occupation never mentions explicitly animals. Unsurprisingly, to the best knowledge of this author, no study on this topic has been published so far. However, as in relation to other areas of international humanitarian law (IHL),[12] some rules embodied in the law of occupation and concerned with the protection of private and public property apply to animals. The law of occupation also allows, under certain conditions, the application of other branches of international law that may be relevant for the protection of animals.

This chapter explores this intricate legal regime, offering an overview of the ways in which international law can offer protection to animals in occupied territory. The indirect nature of this protection, coupled with the scant state practice, will be crucial in order to assess the effectiveness of animal protection in these circumstances.

In line with the well-established distinction between rules on invasion and rules on occupation,[13] this chapter does not address issues pertaining to the protection of animals during the invasion of a territory, even if an occupation follows the invasion. Similarly, this chapter does not deal with the rules applicable to animals involved in hostilities that occur in the occupied territory during occupation.[14] The findings of other chapters of this book related to the protection of animals in the conduct of hostilities will apply.[15]

2 SCOPE OF APPLICATION OF THE LAWS ON OCCUPATION

2.1 *Relevant Principles and Rules of the Law of Occupation*

The law of occupation[16] only embodies obligations incumbent upon occupying powers, whereas no duty is imposed upon the population of the occupied

[9] Frank R. Finch, 'This Land Is Our Land: The Environmental Threat of Army Operations', *International Law Studies* 69 (1996), 99–115, at 111; Al-Duaij, *Environmental Law* (n. 2), 28.

[10] Sally Williams, 'The Man Who Risks His Life to Rescue Zoo Animals from War Zones', *Telegraph* (8 December 2017).

[11] George Bisharat et al., 'Israel's Invasion of Gaza in International Law', *Denver Journal of International Law and Policy* 38 (2009), 42–114, at 72.

[12] See Roscini, Chapter 5, 'Property and Objects', in this volume.

[13] See US Military Tribunal, Nuremberg, *Wilhelm List et al.* (19 February 1948), 9 Law Reports of Trials of War Criminals 34, 55–6; US Department of Defense, *Law of War Manual* (Washington, DC: Office of General Counsel, US Department of Defense 2016), section 11.1.3.1.

[14] For example, the UN mission dispatched by the Human Rights Council found that Israel has targeted animals during the 2008/2009 military operation in the Gaza Strip in violation of Article 54 of AP I (A/HRC/12/48, 25 September 2009, para. 1929).

[15] See Jenks, Chapter 9, 'War Weapons'; de Hemptinne, Kebebew, and Niyo Chapter 10, 'Combatants and as Prisoners of War?', in this volume.

[16] Among recent works, see, for example, Robert Kolb and Sylvain Vité, *Le droit de l'occupation militaire: perspectives historiques et enjeux juridiques actuels* (Brussels: Bruylant 2009); Eyal Benvenisti, *The International Law of Occupation* (2nd ed., Oxford: Oxford University Press 2012);

territory or the ousted sovereign.[17] The law of occupation was first codified by the 1989 and 1907 Regulations annexed to the relevant Hague Conventions, which still today form the basis of the applicable legal regime. Under Article 42 of the Hague Regulations, '[t]erritory is considered occupied when it is actually placed under the authority of the hostile army. The occupation extends only to the territory where such authority has been established and can be exercised.' Under Article 43 of the Hague Regulations, the occupying power 'shall take all the measures in his power to restore, and ensure, as far as possible, public order and civil life, while respecting, unless absolutely prevented, the laws in force in the country.'[18] This provision places upon the occupying power also a duty of vigilance that private actors in occupied territory do not violate IHL and international human rights law (IHRL).[19] Under this rule, the occupying power might be responsible for private activities such as poaching, as long as they are prohibited under the rules of IHL and IHRL.

Geneva Convention (GC) IV complements the Hague Regulations[20] by providing a number of rules on the protection of the local population, demanding that the hostile administration of the occupying power has as its main goal the welfare of the local population. Some of the rules embodied in Additional Protocol (AP) I also apply in times of occupation, complementing the protection offered by the previous instruments.

International humanitarian law does not exhaust the rules that are applicable in occupied territory, but rather, other rules may apply. This principle has been affirmed by the International Court of Justice (ICJ) in relation to rules such as the principle of self-determination of peoples[21] and IHRL.[22] Indeed, in principle, the law of occupation can be seen as an open system in which other international law

Yoram Dinstein, *The International Law of Belligerent Occupation* (2nd ed., Cambridge: Cambridge University Press 2019).

17 Marco Longobardo, *The Use of Armed Force in Occupied Territory* (Cambridge: Cambridge University Press 2018), 148.

18 Reference to 'civil life' is mandated by the French-only authoritative text, which employs '*vie publique*'. See Benvenisti, *The International Law* (n. 16), 68.

19 See Eritrea-Ethiopia Claims Commission (EECC), Partial Award: Central Front – Eritrea's Claims 2, 4, 6, 7, 8 and 22 of 28 April 2004, para. 67; ICJ, Armed Activities on the Territory of the Congo (*DRC* v. *Uganda*), judgment of 19 December 2005, ICJ Reports 2005, paras. 178 and 250; *Armed Activities on the Territory of the Congo (DRC v. Uganda)*, judgment of 9 February 2022, paras. 78 and 359. See, also, Marco Longobardo, 'State Responsibility for International Humanitarian Law Violations by Private Actors in Occupied Territories and the Exploitation of Natural Resources', *Netherlands International Law Review* 63 (2016), 251–74.

20 Art. 154 of GC IV.

21 ICJ, *Legal Consequences of the Construction of a Wall in the Occupied Palestinian Territory*, advisory opinion of 9 July 2004, ICJ Reports 2004, para. 118.

22 Ibid., para. 106; ICJ, *DRC* v. *Uganda* 2005 (n. 19), para. 216. See also Yutaka Arai-Takahashi, *The Law of Occupation* (Leiden: Brill 2009); Noam Lubell, 'Human Rights Obligations in Military Occupation', *International Review of the Red Cross* 94 (2012), 317–337; Longobardo, *The Use* (n. 17), 62–82.

rules are presumed to apply[23] if their application is not barred as result of the armed conflict.[24]

2.2 *Animals as Public and/or Private Property in Occupied Territory*

Some rules on the protection of public and private property[25] may be relevant to the protection of animals in occupied territory. For instance, Article 46 of the Hague Regulations, which demands respect for private property and prohibits its confiscation, is applicable to animals that are private property (thus, excluding wildlife). Since under Article 56 of the Hague Regulations '[t]he property of municipalities, that of institutions dedicated to religion, charity and education, the arts and sciences … shall be treated as private property', this protection extends also to animals that are property of some public institutions. It is reinforced by the IHRL rules on private property,[26] which should be interpreted in light of IHL.[27]

Under Article 53 of GC IV, animals that are private or public property in occupied territory cannot be destroyed unless this is rendered absolutely necessary by military operations. According to the ICJ, this provision is the only IHL rule governing the destruction of property in occupied territory[28] since it is more specific than Article 23(g) of the Hague Regulations.[29]

Similarly, the ban on pillage pursuant to Article 47 of the Hague Regulations and Article 33(3) of GC IV is applicable to animals that belong to individuals or the state, since pillage encompasses the appropriation of both private and public property.[30] The applicability of pillage to animals is confirmed by the findings of the ICJ, which has applied the ban on pillage to natural resources in occupied territory.[31]

Although private property cannot be confiscated and both private and public property cannot be destroyed, the law of occupation embodies some rules on the ways in which an occupied power can use property located in the occupied territory. These rules apply to animals as well.[32] For instance, Article 52 of the Hague

23 Longobardo, *The Use* (n. 17), 43–7.

24 See ILC, Effects of Armed Conflicts on Treaties: Titles and texts of the draft articles on the effects of armed conflicts on treaties adopted by the drafting Committee on second reading, 11 May 2011, A/CN.4/L.777.

25 On public property, see Anicée van Engeland, 'Protection of Public Property', in Andrew Clapham, Paola Gaeta and Marco Sassòli (eds.), *The 1949 Geneva Conventions: A Commentary* (Oxford: Oxford University Press 2015), 1535–50(with an overview on the different criteria envisaged to distinguish the two categories). On private property, see Yutaka Arai-Takahashi, 'Protection of Private Property', ibid., 1515–34.

26 See generally Ursula Kriebaum and August Reinisch, 'Property, Right to, International Protection' in *Max Planck Encyclopedias of International Law, Online* (2019).

27 Art. 31(3)(c) of the Vienna Convention on the Law of Treaties.

28 ICJ, Wall (n. 21), paras. 132 and 135.

29 Longobardo, *The Use* (n. 17), 260–1.

30 See, for example, ICTY, *Prosecutor* v. *Zejnil Delalić et al.*, trial judgment of 16 November 1998, IT-96-21-T, para. 590; ICC, *Prosecutor* v. *Katanga*, trial judgment of 7 March 2014, ICC-01/04-01/07, para. 115.

31 ICJ, *DRC* v. *Uganda* 2005 (n. 19), para. 245; *DRC* v. *Uganda* 2022 (n. 19), para. 359.

32 Gerhard von Glahn, *The Occupation of Enemy Territory* (Minneapolis: University of Minnesota Press 1957), 167.

Regulations allows requisitions in kind of movable public and private property if four cumulative conditions are met: first, needs of the army of occupation; second, proportionate relationship to the resources of the territory; third, order by a commander; and fourth, payment for the requisitions.[33] There is well-established case law on the applicability of this rule to animals in occupied territory. For example, a Polish court in 1921 held that Article 52 of the Hague Regulations prohibits requisition of horses for reasons different from the needs of the occupying army.[34] This view was confirmed by a French court in 1945,[35] is reflected in the preparatory works of the 1989 and 1907 Hague Conventions,[36] and is supported by the Danish Military Manual that includes 'cattle' in the scope of Article 52 of the Hague Regulations.[37]

Moreover, under Article 53(1) of the Hague Regulations, the occupying power 'can only take possession of cash, funds, and realizable securities which are strictly the property of the State, depots of arms, means of transport, stores and supplies, and, generally, all movable property belonging to the state which may be used for military operations'. This rule is applicable to animals that are property of the state and which may be used during military operations (e.g., horses).[38] It prohibits the occupying power from taking possession of any other animal, as confirmed by the Democratic Republic of the Congo (DRC)'s argument regarding wildlife as protected property.[39]

Article 53(2) of the Hague Regulations governs the legal regime of animals that can be used as means of transportation.[40] Under this provision, '[a]ll appliances . . . adapted for . . . the transport of persons or things . . . may be seized, even if they belong to private individuals, but must be restored and compensation fixed when peace is made'. Accordingly, the occupying power must compensate the seizure of animals used as means of transportation.[41] This reading is confirmed by the preparatory works of the Hague Regulations. In 1899, the Russian delegation suggested to insert in this provision the words 'as well as teams, saddle animals, draft and pack animals',[42] but the proposal was dropped because of the Swiss resistance to include a specific enumeration.[43] Interestingly, the Belgian government argued that the taking of a horse by the

33 Arai-Takahashi, *The Law* (n. 22), 226–8.

34 *Siuta* v. *Guzkowski* (15 February 1921), 1 International Law Reports 480, 481–2.

35 *Secret* v. *Loizel* (18 January 1945), 12 International Law Reports 457, 458.

36 William M. Franklin, 'Municipal Property under Belligerent Occupation', *American Journal of International Law* 38 (1944), 383–96, at 393.

37 Danish Ministry of Defence/Defence Command Denmark, *Military Manual on International Law Relevant to Danish Armed Forces in International Operations* (Copenhagen 2016), 448.

38 Jérôme de Hemptinne, 'The Protection of Animals During Warfare', *American Journal of International Law Unbound* 111 (2017), 272–6, at 276.

39 ICJ, *DRC* v. *Uganda* (n. 19), DRC, Public sitting held on 13 April 2005, C2005/5, para. 15.

40 See, in a broader context, Marco Roscini, 'Animals and the Law of Armed Conflict', *Israel Yearbook on Human Rights* 47 (2017), 35–67, at 56–7.

41 See Civil Affairs Department of The Judge Advocate General's School, *Law of Belligerent Occupation* (JAGS TEXT No. 12, 1945), 168 and 206.

42 Doris Appel Graber, *The Development of the Law of Belligerent Occupation 1863–1914* (New York: Columbia University Press 1949), 184.

43 Ibid.

German occupying forces without any form of payment was governed by Article 53(2) of the Hague Regulations on means of transportations rather than by Article 52 of the Hague Regulations on lawful seizure of movable property.[44]

Article 55 of the Hague Regulations provides that the occupying power acts as 'administrator and usufructuary of public buildings, real estate, forests, and agricultural estates belonging to' the occupied state and that it 'must safeguard the capital of these properties, and administer them in accordance with the rules of usufruct'. The protection of forest was considered paramount due to the heavy exploitation of timber during most occupations over the nineteenth century.[45] Article 55 of the Hague Regulations protects animals from two different perspectives. First, since the rule applies to forest and agricultural estates, it encompasses the animals living in those areas. Second, the list in Article 55 is just illustrative and the relevant regime applies to natural resources belonging to the occupied state at large,[46] which include wildlife.[47] Significantly, the DRC clarified before the ICJ that wildlife is a component of public property under Article 55 of the Hague Regulations,[48] while the court included findings on hunting of endangered species in the plundering of natural resources.[49] Accordingly, the occupying power, following the rules on usufructus,[50] can use the public animals located in a forest or another area under its actual authority as long as it does not deplete irremediably their stock.[51] This rule is, therefore, very important since it demands the occupying power to preserve the endangered fauna in lieu of the ousted sovereign.

2.3 *Other Relevant Rules of the Law of Occupation*

Other sources of indirect protection of animals can be found in rules on the fundamental rights of the local population of the occupied territory. For example, under Article 56(1) of GC IV, the occupying power has the duty of ensuring the 'adoption and application of the prophylactic and preventive measures necessary to combat the spread of contagious diseases and epidemics. Medical personnel of all categories shall be allowed to carry out their duties.' This duty covers measures to

44 *Laurent* v. *Le Jeune* (3 March 1921), 1 International Law Reports 481, 482.

45 On the debate about the legal regime of forests in occupied territories, see Graber, *The Development* (n. 42), 170–2.

46 Iain Scobbie, 'Natural Resources and Belligerent Occupation: Perspectives from International Humanitarian and Human Rights Law', in Susan M. Akram et al. (eds.), *International Law and the Israeli-Palestinian Conflict* (London: Routledge 2010), 229–52, at 233–4.

47 Arie Trouwborst, 'Wildlife and Landscapes', in Elisa Morgera and Kati Kulovesi (eds.), *Research Handbook on International Law and Natural Resources* (Cheltenham: Edward Elgar 2016), 198–217, at 198–9.

48 ICJ, *DRC* v. *Uganda*, DRC, Public sitting (n. 39), para. 15.

49 ICJ, *DRC* v. *Uganda* 2005 (n. 19), para. 223.

50 *Iustiniani Institutiones Digestum Vetus* D.7.1.1, available at http://amshistorica.unibo.it/176, accessed 22 February 2022. See generally Simon McKenzie, *Disputed Territories and International Criminal Law* (London: Routledge 2020), 163–9, noting that, under Roman law, usufructus is applicable to animals (ibid., 163).

51 Scobbie, 'Natural Resources' (n. 46), 233; McKenzie, *Disputed Territories* (n. 50), 165–6.

avoid the spreading of diseases among animals and between animals and humans, which are usually undertaken by veterinarians.[52] Clearly, the human right to health on the prevention, treatment, and control of diseases,[53] which is binding upon occupying powers,[54] supports this view.

Moreover, Article 58(2) of GC IV may be relevant for some animals as well. Under this provision, the occupying power shall also accept consignments of 'articles required for religious needs and shall facilitate their distribution'. If animals are *employed* during religious rites, they could receive protection under this provision, whereas they do not enjoy such a protection if they are considered to be sacred but are not actually *required* for religious rites.[55] However, both sacred animals and animals employed in religious rites are indirectly protected by freedom of religion,[56] which is applicable in occupied territory.[57]

Also Article 54(2) of AP I is relevant for the protection of animals in occupied territory. According to this provision, '[i]t is prohibited to attack, destroy, remove or render useless objects indispensable to the survival of the civilian population, such as . . . livestock . . . for the specific purpose of denying them for their sustenance value to the civilian population or to the adverse Party, whatever the motive'. Livestock and other animals that are objects indispensable to the survival of the civilian population in occupied territory fall into the scope of this rule, as demonstrated by the findings of the UN mission dispatched by the Human Rights Council to investigate the 2008/2009 military operation in the Gaza Strip.[58]

Finally, it might be argued that the protection offered by the first sentence of Article 55 of AP I applies to occupied territory as well, so that wildlife would be protected by this rule as a component of the environment. Indeed, the provision reads that '[c]are shall be taken in *warfare* to protect the natural environment against widespread, long-term and severe damage'. There is room to argue that the concept of 'warfare' is as broad as to comprehend not only the conduct of hostilities, but also situations of occupation. Such an obligation would be in line with the conservative

52 On the application of this rule to the 2020 Covid19 pandemic, which originated from wildlife, see Marco Longobardo, 'The Duties of Occupying Powers in Relation to the Fight against Covid-19', *EJIL:Talk!* (8 April 2020), available at https://bit.ly/3fAWuJD, accessed 22 February 2022; Marco Longobardo, 'The Duties of Occupying Powers in Relation to the Prevention and Control of Contagious Diseases Through the Interplay between International Humanitarian Law and the Right to Health', *Vanderbilt Journal of Transnational Law*, 55 (2022), available at: https://papers.ssrn.com/sol3/papers.cfm?abstract_id=3929320, accessed 22 February 2022. On the protection of veterinaries, see Fortin, Chapter 12, 'Veterinary Personnel', in this volume.

53 See Art. 12(2)(c) of the International Covenant on Economic, Social and Cultural Rights of 16 December 1966, 993 UNTS 3.

54 E/C.12/ISR/CO/4, 12 November 2019, paras. 58–9.

55 See Roscini, 'Animals' (n. 40), 57, on sacred animals under the rules protecting sacred places during hostilities.

56 See Art. 18 of the International Covenant on Civil and Political Rights (ICCPR) of 16 December 1966, 999 UNTS 171.

57 ICJ, Wall (n. 21), para. 111 (on the ICCPR in general).

58 A/HRC/12/48, 25 September 2009, para. 1929.

principle embodied in Articles 43 and 55 of the Hague Regulations. From this perspective, however, only this generic obligation of care would be applicable to occupied territories, whereas other obligations under the same provisions would be applicable only if hostilities occur in occupied territory.

2.4 *Protection of Animals through Customary Environmental Rules*

Animals are components of the environment and thus they are protected under environmental rules applicable to occupied territory. In particular, animals are portions of the wildlife, and as such, they are parts of the environment.[59] This idea is in line with the well-established trend of considering damage to wildlife as a portion of environmental damage.[60] Contrary to other branches of IHL, the law of occupation does not embody any specific rule on the protection of the environment. However, albeit in the context of the conduct of hostilities, the ICJ affirmed that states must take environmental considerations into account in armed conflict, mentioning Principle 24 of the 1992 Rio Declaration in support of this position;[61] this statement is relevant for occupied territories as well since occupation is a kind of armed conflict.[62] Noteworthy, the International Law Court (ILC) is in the process of codifying rules on the protection of the environment in occupied territory, which may be relevant for animals located therein.

Moving from the perspective that IHL and IHRL complement each other in relation to the protection of the environment in occupied territory,[63] the ILC has drafted two provisions pertaining to the protection of the environment in occupied territory.[64] Neither of these provisions refers to animals, fauna, or wildlife as a such. Draft Principle 20 – 'general obligations of an Occupying Power' – comprises three different obligations. First, the principle affirms that the occupying power 'shall respect and protect the environment of the occupied territory' in the administration of the occupied territory, taking into account 'environmental considerations'. This provision should be read in the context of the powers conferred to the occupant by Article 43 of the Hague Regulations. The Draft Principle goes on to affirm that an occupying power 'shall take appropriate measures to prevent significant harm to the

59 Trouwborst, 'Wildlife' (n. 47), 198.

60 Philippe Sands and Richard B. Stewart, 'Valuation of Environmental Damage: US and International Law Approaches', *Review of European, Comparative & International Environmental Law* 5 (1996), 290–6, at 291.

61 ICJ, *Legality of the Use or Threat of Nuclear Weapons*, advisory opinion of 8 July 1996, ICJ Reports 1996, para. 30.

62 Art. 2(2) of GC IV.

63 ILC, First Report on Protection of the Environment in Relation to Armed Conflicts by Marja Lehto, Special Rapporteur, 30 April 2018, A/CN.4/720, paras. 51–62.

64 Draft Principle 22 is not analysed because it bans environmental harm outside the occupied territory, in line with the general duty not to use the occupied territory to harm other states. (Marco Longobardo, 'The Relevance of the Concept of Due Diligence for International Humanitarian Law', *Wisconsin International Law Journal* 32 (2019), 44–87, at 75.)

environment of the occupied territory that is likely to prejudice the health and well-being of the population'.[65] These two provisions convey the idea that, since the occupying power must act in the interests of the local population,[66] these interests must comprise the respect for the environment, which includes fauna as one of its components.

Draft Principle 21 governs the use of natural resources, providing that the occupying power must administer and use the natural resources under the law of occupation 'in a way that ensures their sustainable use and minimises environmental harm'. This rule draws significantly from the spirit and common interpretation of Article 55 of the Hague Regulations and, as such, it applies to animals *qua* natural resources.

2.5 *Protection of Animals through Environmental Treaty Rules*

Finally, it has been suggested that environmental law treaties – which are normally applied in peacetime – are applicable also during armed conflict and occupation.[67] If this assertion proves correct, some environmental treaties may provide protection to animals in occupied territory.

Although sometimes environmental treaties embody provision regarding their applicability in armed conflict and occupation, most environmental treaties pertaining to the protection of animals – such as the CITES and the 1979 Convention on the Conservation of Migratory Species of Wild Animals (CMS) – are silent on this point. According to one view, similarly to what happens in relation to IHRL conventions, environmental treaties that are silent on their application in times of armed conflict should be considered in principle to be applicable.[68] The ILC confirmed this idea in the framework of the codification of the effects of armed conflicts upon treaties. It stated that international environmental treaties in principle apply in situations of armed conflict.[69] The UN has confirmed that the obligations embodied in the CITES are binding upon peacekeepers, even though the sending states, rather than the UN, are responsible for lack of implementation.[70] However, one has to ascertain whether a specific environmental treaty might apply

65 See, generally, Karen Hulme, 'Enhancing Environmental Protection during Occupation through Human Rights', *Goettingen Journal of International Law* 10 (2020), 203–41.

66 Michael Bothe, 'The Administration of Occupied Territory', in Clapham, Gaeta and Sassòli, *The 1949 Geneva Conventions* (n. 25), 1455–84, at 1466–7.

67 See, for example, Silja Vöneky, 'A New Shield for the Environment: Peacetime Treaties as Legal Restraints of Wartime Damage', *Review of European, Comparative & International Environmental Law* 9 (2003), 20–32; Patricia Birnie, Alan Boyle and Catherine Redgwell, *International Law and the Environment* (3rd ed., Oxford: Oxford University Press 2009), 207; Britta Sjostedt, *The Role of Multilateral Environmental Agreements* (Oxford: Hart 2020).

68 Vöneky, 'A New Shield' (n. 67), 32; Sjostedt, *The Role* (n. 67), 150–8.

69 See the Annex to Art. 7 of the ILC Draft Articles on the Effects of Armed Conflicts on Treaties (endorsed by Philippe Sands et al., *Principles of International Environmental Law* (4th ed., Cambridge: Cambridge University Press 2018), 832).

70 *UN Juridical Yearbook* (1994), 450.

during an occupation in light of the rules of that treaty regarding its scope of application. For instance, although the CITES does not embody any specific provision, Articles I, II, XIV, and XVI mention actions to be taken within the jurisdiction of the contracting states, which is a concept that encompasses also occupied territories.

It follows that animals would receive protections from two different perspectives: they would be protected both by environmental treaties as part of the environment, and by specific conventions for the protection of animals that should be considered as environmental treaties. Accordingly, the CMS and the CITES are mentioned among those environmental treaties that would be applicable in armed conflict and occupied territory.[71]

However, in the past, other authors have opposed this view[72] and most scholars, even today, adopt a cautious approach to the applicability of these conventions in times of occupation.[73] The issue was left unresolved by the ICJ in the advisory opinion on the *Legality of the Threat or Use of Nuclear Weapons* where the court, after having affirmed that customary international environmental law should be taken into account by the belligerents, concluded that 'the issue is not whether the treaties relating to the protection of the environment are or are not applicable during an armed conflict'.[74]

3 CONTENT AND LIMITS OF THE LAWS ON OCCUPATION

The protection offered to animals in occupied territory is subject to a number of limitations that affect its effectiveness. Some of these limitations are linked to the fact that the law of occupation is not concerned with the protection of animals as such, whereas others depend on the rules of the law of occupation.

As with any portion of IHL, the law of occupation has a marked anthropocentric approach to the environment and the protection of animals.[75] The main objectives of the law of occupation are the protection of the sovereignty of the occupied state, the basic protection of the local population, and the

71 Vöneky, 'A New Shield' (n. 67), 28.

72 Michael Bothe, 'The Protection of the Environment in Times of Armed Conflict', *German Yearbook of International Law* 34 (1991), 54–62, at 54–5; Marina Castellaneta, 'La responsabilità internazionale degli stati per danni all'ambiente causati nel corso di conflitti armati', *Rivista di diritto internazionale* 71 (1998), 632–72.

73 See, for example, these two conventions are listed as 'silent' on their applicability in armed conflict by Jean-Marie Henckaerts and Dana Constantin, 'Protection of the Natural Environment', in Andrew Clapham and Paola Gaeta (eds.), *The Oxford Handbook of International Law in Armed Conflict* (Oxford: Oxford University Press 2014), 469–91, at 484. See also Michael Bothe et al., 'International Law Protecting the Environment during Armed Conflict: Gaps and Opportunities', *International Review of the Red Cross* 92 (2010), 569–92.

74 ICJ, *Nuclear Weapons* (n. 61), para. 30.

75 Michaela Halpern, 'Protecting Vulnerable Environments in Armed Conflict: Deficiencies in International Humanitarian Law', *Stanford Journal of International Law* 51 (2015), 119–46, at 140–1.

preservation of the military interests of the occupying power.[76] States during the negotiations of the Hague Regulations or the GC IV overlooked animal interests in favour of the protection of other human interests that were considered more urgent.[77] As a result, the rules embodied in the law of occupation that are applicable to animals only consider them as a portion of the occupied state's resources or a property of the local population.[78] Similarly, most environmental conventions do not focus on animals as such, but rather, address animal protection mainly as a component of the maintenance of a healthy environment, which is in itself an anthropocentric approach to environmental protection as a human rights issue.[79]

Accordingly, any protection offered to animals in occupied territory is indirect, since animals are only protected as property, natural resources, or portions of the environment. This reality is in stark conflict with the emerging debate on animal rights and interests in national and international law, which aims at changing the anthropocentric approach to animals as human property, and at emancipating animal rights from environmental protection and the management of natural resources.[80] From the analysis of the rules of occupation, and irrespective of possible developments that are emerging in other fields of international law,[81] it must be concluded that animals do not enjoy any right as such in occupied territory under international law.[82]

Other limits to the protection of animals in occupied territory are the consequence of the way in which the law of occupation developed and is applied. For example, the administration of the occupying power in relation to the protection of animals is subject to strict limitations. Indeed, it is questionable that the occupying power can alter the legal regime in force in the occupied territory to offer a better protection to the animals living therein. Scholars often mention, as an example of state practice, the British decision after World War I to introduce new legislation against cruelty to animals in occupied Palestine, in conflict with the Ottoman law in

76 See Longobardo, *The Use* (n. 17), 82–7.

77 Boyd van Dijk, 'Human Rights in War: On the Entangled Foundations of the 1949 Geneva Conventions', *American Journal of International Law* 112 (2018), 553–82, at 581–2.

78 See ILC, First Report by Lehto (n. 63), para. 50.

79 See the Final Report of the Independent Expert on the Issue of Human Rights Obligations Relating to the Enjoyment of a Safe, Clean, Healthy and Sustainable Environment, John H. Knox, A/HRC/37/59, 24 January 2018; ILC, First Report by Lehto (n. 63), paras. 63–76.

80 See, for example, Gary Francione, *Animals as Persons: Essays on Abolition of Animal Exploitation* (New York: Columbia University Press 2008); Alexander Gillespie, *International Environmental Law, Policy, and Ethics* (2nd ed., Oxford: Oxford University Press 2014), 111–29; Anne Peters, 'Global Animal Law: What It Is and Why We Need It', *Transnational Environmental Law* 5 (2016), 9–23.

81 See, for example, and compare Malgosia Fitzmaurice, *Whaling and International Law* (Cambridge: Cambridge University Press 2015), 153–65, with Anne Peters, 'Rights of Human and Nonhuman Animals: Complementing the Universal Declaration of Human Rights', *American Journal of International Law Unbound* 111 (2018), 355–60.

82 See, with reference to IHL in general, Niccolò Pons, 'Animals', in Dražan Djukić and Niccolò Pons (eds.), *The Companion to International Humanitarian Law* (Leiden: Brill 2018), 170–2.

force at the time.[83] However, caution is necessary to prevent the occupying power from using arguments based on animal protections to violate its duty not to alter the law in force in the occupied territory under Article 43 of the Hague Regulations. For instance, it has been reported that Israel has declared a number of areas in the West Bank to be national park in order to seize Palestinian territory unlawfully in breach of pre-existing law.[84] Such a conduct is clearly illegal under the law of occupation.

Different is the case of an occupying power that implements environmental obligations binding upon the ousted sovereign. In this case, those environmental obligations, whether international or domestic in nature, are parts of the law in force in the occupied territory and, as a result, should not be altered by the occupying power, but rather, must be implemented as the ousted sovereign would have done.[85] Accordingly, if the occupied state has ratified one convention on the protection of animals, then the occupying power must not alter the way in which that convention is implemented in the occupied territory on pain of violating Article 43 of the Hague Regulations.[86] Interestingly, the ILC's Special Rapporteur has acknowledged that an occupying power can implement those international environmental treaties that had been ratified by the ousted sovereign and transplanted in the legal system of the occupied territory.[87] As a result, the domestic law protection in force in the occupied territory must be respected and implemented by the occupying power.

From this perspective, the Israeli programme to reintroduce the endangered Mountain Gazelle in the occupied Golan Heights should be assessed.[88] At the end of the 1967 Six-Day War field surveys found no gazelles in the area, despite contrary expectations, so the Israeli Nature Reserves Authority transferred 350 specimens to the southern Golan and by the early 1980s the local population of gazelles reached 6,000 units.[89] Since then, the populations of gazelles fluctuated in relation to the different policies adopted by the Israeli administration, sometimes in order to reduce the gazelle numbers as requested by farmers, sometimes to support the growth of their population.[90] Given that the Golan Heights are sovereign Syrian territory under Israeli occupation,[91] the programme of reintroduction of the gazelle

83 Norman Bentwich, 'The Legal Administration of Palestine under the British Military Occupation', *British Yearbook of International Law* 1 (1920–1), 139–48, at 145; Dinstein, *The International Law* (n. 16), 128.

84 Bothe, 'The Administration' (n. 66), 1477.

85 See, *mutatis mutandis*, the reasoning offered in Longobardo, *The Use* (n. 17), 186–90.

86 Adam Roberts, 'Transformative Military Occupation: Applying the Laws of War and Human Rights', *American Journal of International Law* 100 (2006), 580–622, at 589; Benvenisti, *The International Law* (n. 16), 83; Bothe, 'The Administration' (n. 66), 1478.

87 ILC, First Report by Lehto (n. 63), para. 49.

88 See Rachelle Adam, 'Finding Safe Passage through a Wave of Extinctions: Israel's Endangered Mountain Gazelle', *Journal of International Wildlife Law & Policy* 19 (2016), 136–58.

89 Ibid., 141.

90 Ibid., 142.

91 See Ray Murphy and Declan Gannon, 'Changing the Landscape: Israel's Gross Violations of International Law in the Occupied Syrian Golan', *Yearbook of International Humanitarian Law* 11 (2008), 139–74.

would be legitimate only if conducted in compliance with the law in force in the area prior to the occupation and to restore a pre-existing community of gazelles that was displaced due to the Six-Day War. This assumption is confirmed by the ILC's Draft Principles, which clarify that the protection of the environment does not widen the powers attributed to the occupying power by IHL.

However, reliance on pre-occupation law is only a viable solution when such a legislation exists and is implemented effectively. In areas under occupation, especially when life conditions are difficult, laws protecting animals are often not implemented. For example, a study on the wildlife in the Gaza Strip demonstrated a lack of implementation of the environmental legislation for wildlife protection and nature conservation adopted throughout the successive periods of British mandate, Egyptian administration, and Israeli occupation.[92] Natural reserves created by the Palestinian administration are severely threatened by the activities of the local authorities and by the Israeli military operations.[93]

Other specific rules of the law of occupation offer only limited protection to animals. For instance, Article 52 of the Hague Regulations protects animals from requisition only in relation to the resources of the state, since one of the conditions for lawful requisition is a proportionate relationship between the requisition and the resources of the territory. Although, prima facie, this rule could allow the occupying power to starve an individual by requisitioning all of their cattle as long as this does not deplete significantly the resources of the country,[94] this risk is reduced today since the GC IV demands the occupying power to provide for the basic needs of the population of the occupied territory, including foodstuff.[95] Anyway, for the purposes of the present chapter, it should be noted that private and public property are protected under Article 52 of the Hague Regulations only from the standpoint of the protection of the resources of the occupied country – which is the main interest of the rules embodied in that instrument.

Moreover, the principles codified by the ILC are worded as due diligence obligations of conduct rather than as obligations of result.[96] Draft Principle 20(3) clarifies that environmental concerns do not widen the powers of the occupying administration, but rather, the occupying power 'shall respect the law and institutions of the occupied territory concerning the protection of the environment and may only introduce changes within the limits provided by the law of armed conflict'. This means that environmental concern does not alter the occupying power's duty to

[92] Magad M. Yassim et al., 'Preliminary Survey of Terrestrial Vertebrate Fauna and People's Awareness Towards Wildlife in the Northern Governorate of the Gaza Strip', *Al-Azhar Bulletin of Science* 17 (2006), 17–40, at 27.

[93] See Abdel Fattah N. Abd Rabou et al., 'The Avifauna of Wadi Gaza Nature Reserve, Gaza Strip – Palestine', *The Islamic University Journal (Series of Natural Studies and Engineering)* 15 (2007), 39–85.

[94] Ernst H. Feilchenfeld, *The International Economic Law of Belligerent Occupation* (Washington, DC: Carnegie Endowment for International Peace 1942), 37.

[95] Art. 55 of GC IV. See also Kolb and Vité, *Le droit* (n. 16), 439.

[96] Longobardo, 'The Relevance' (n. 64), 75.

administer the occupied territory 'while respecting, unless absolutely prevented, the laws in force in the country',[97] which is still today one of the basic tenets of the law of occupation.[98]

4 LEGAL CONSEQUENCES OF VIOLATIONS OF THE LAWS ON OCCUPATION

This subsection briefly addresses the legal consequences of violations of the aforementioned rules of international law that are applicable to animals in occupied territory. Both state responsibility and individual responsibility are taken into account.

4.1 *State Responsibility*

As a matter of state responsibility, any violation of the law of occupation entails the responsibility of the state with the entire array of consequences codified by the ILC in the Articles on State Responsibility.[99] This is in line with Article 3 of the 1907 Hague Convention IV that commands states to pay reparations for violations of the law of armed conflict.[100] Moreover, since the law of occupation embodies obligations *erga omnes partes*,[101] every state that is a party to the relevant treaties has the possibility to invoke responsibility for violations before international courts with jurisdiction.[102]

However, it should be noted that judicial ascertainment of responsibility for violations of rules applicable to animals is scarce. The ICJ, in the *Wall* opinion, has affirmed Israeli responsibility for violations of the law of occupation, prescribing both restitution and reparation.[103] Similarly, in the *DRC* v. *Uganda* case, the same court has ascertained the violations of some rules of the law of occupation pertaining to public and private property, also assessing the responsibility of the occupying power for failing to prevent private looting of property and natural resources.[104] However, neither of these decisions addressed directly compensation for loss of animals,[105] even though the destruction of olive orchards mentioned by the *Wall*

97 Art. 43 of the Hague Regulations. See also Art. 64(2) of GC IV, which slightly widens the grounds for changing the local law.

98 Benvenisti, *The International Law* (n. 16), 89–104. More generally, see Andrea Carcano, *The Transformation of Occupied Territory in International Law* (Leiden: Brill 2015).

99 A/56/49 (Vol. I)/Corr. 4, 12 December 2001.

100 On the differences between this provision and the ILC's Articles, see Marco Longobardo, 'Rapporti fra strumenti di codificazione: il progetto di articoli sulla responsabilità degli Stati e le convenzioni di diritto internazionale umanitario', *Rivista di diritto internazionale* 101 (2018), 1136–63, at 1145–7.

101 ICJ, *Wall* (n. 21), paras. 155, 157.

102 ICJ, *Questions Relating to the Obligation to Prosecute or Extradite (Belgium* v. *Senegal)*, judgment of 20 July 2012, ICJ Reports 2012, paras. 68–70; ICJ, *Application of the Convention on the Prevention and Punishment of the Crime of Genocide (The Gambia* v. *Myanmar)*, order of 23 January 2020, para. 41.

103 ICJ, *Wall* (n. 21), paras. 152–3.

104 ICJ, *DRC* v. *Uganda* 2005 (n. 19), paras. 246, 248–50.

105 ICJ, *Wall* (n. 21), para. 153 (referring to 'any form of material damage'); ICJ, *DRC* v. *Uganda* (n. 19), paras. 259–61 (mentioning natural resources).

opinion had an impact on the protection of autochthonous birds.[106] Only in 2022, in the reparation phase of the *DRC v. Uganda* case, has the ICJ finally examined state responsibility, and related compensation, for damage caused to fauna.[107]

On other occasions, international courts patently failed to identify the law of occupation as the relevant legal framework. For example, the rule codified by Article 55 of the Hague Regulations should have been taken into account by the European Court of Justice (ECJ) in dealing with stocks of fish in the waters of Western Sahara, which is a territory under Moroccan occupation. Regrettably, the ECJ did not apply the law of occupation,[108] thus failing to consider stocks of fish as protected by the rule of Article 55 of the Hague Regulations on natural resources.[109]

Conversely, some non-adjudicative bodies have mentioned damage to animals when assessing occupying powers' responsibility. For instance, the Commission for Reception, Truth and Reconciliation in East-Timor mentioned 'stealing of … herds of animals to West Timor' by the Indonesian occupying forces and affiliated armed groups in the context of 'looting and stealing from civilians suspected of opposing the occupation'.[110] Likewise, in relation to the damage to fauna and other components of the environment caused by fires in the occupied portions of Azerbaijan, upon pressure of the UN General Assembly[111] Azerbaijan and Armenia agreed to allow a mission led by the Organization for Security and Cooperation in Europe access to the area. The mission acknowledged damage to fauna in occupied territory, without ascertaining any state responsibility.[112] Accordingly, such references are usually very generic and are not linked to the assessment of state responsibility for the violation of specific rules.

Moreover, as aforementioned, domestic courts have dealt with the application to the law of occupation in relation to protection of property rights at the end of some occupations.[113] However, this practice is limited to some specific animals – such as horses and cattle – and is linked to a purely anthropocentric approach to animals as property.

106 Simon Awad and Omar Attum, 'The Biodiversity Value of Olive Groves in Palestine', *Jordan Journal of Natural History* 4(4) (2017), 29–36, at 33.

107 See *DRC v. Uganda* 2022 (n. 19), paras 551–363.

108 See ECJ, *Front Polisario* v. *Council*, 10 December 2015, T-512/12; ECJ, *Council v. Front Polisario*, 21 December 2016, C-104/16 P; ECJ, *Western Sahara Campaign UK* v. *Commissioners*, 27 February 2018, C-266/16.

109 Marco Longobardo, 'The Occupation of Maritime Territory under International Humanitarian Law', *International Law Studies* 95 (2019), 322–61, at 352–3.

110 Commission for Reception, Truth and Reconciliation in East-Timor, Final Report, January 2006, Chapter 7.5, para. 232.

111 UN General Assembly Resolution of 15 September 2006, A/RES/60/285.

112 A/61/696, 12 January 2007, section 3.5.3.

113 See above Section 2.2.

4.2 *Individual Criminal Responsibility*

Under certain circumstances, individual criminal responsibility may follow the violations of some rules applicable to the protection of animals in occupied territory. Again, these rules protect animals as portions of property in occupied territory.

Article 147 of GC IV lists 'extensive destruction and appropriation of property, not justified by military necessity and carried out unlawfully and wantonly' as a grave breach of the convention. Since this rule refers also to destruction prohibited under Article 53 of GC IV,[114] the penal regime of the grave breaches also applies to animals protected as property by this latter provision,[115] as confirmed by the ICTY.[116] The grave breach regime does not apply to animals protected by rules of the Hague Regulations concerning property,[117] and is relevant only for extensive destruction and appropriation, whereas isolated incidents would not be enough.[118]

Moreover, the International Criminal Court (ICC) Statute embodies some criminal provisions that may be relevant in relation to the punishment of individuals involved in acts against animals in armed conflict. In particular, Article 8(2)(a)(iv) of the ICC Statute considers to be a war crime the '[e]xtensive destruction and appropriation of property, not justified by military necessity and carried out unlawfully and wantonly'. This provision refers also to property located in occupied territory and protected by Article 53 of GC IV, animals included.[119]

Additionally, pursuant to Article 8(2)(b)(xiii) of the ICC Statute, '[d]estroying or seizing the enemy's property unless such destruction or seizure be imperatively demanded by the necessities of war' is a war crime. This crime refers also to property in occupied territory and is applicable to destruction or seizure of animals in violation of Articles 46, 52, 53, 55, and 56 of the Hague Regulations.[120] One chamber of the ICC considered this rule also relevant in relation to destruction in violation of Article 53 of GC IV.[121]

114 Pictet Commentary on GC IV, 601.

115 Carlson M. LeGrand, 'Framing the Issues', *International Law Studies* 69 (1996), 23–31, at 27; Adam Roberts, 'The Law of War and Environmental Damage', in Austin and Bruch, *The Environmental Consequences* (n. 5), 47–86, at 56–7; Michael N. Schmitt, 'War and the Environment: Fault Lines in the Prescriptive Landscape', ibid., 87–136, at 96–7.

116 See, for example, ICTY, *Prosecutor* v. *Brđanin*, judgment of 1 September 2004, IT-99-36-T, para. 630.

117 Relevant case law does not support the contrary view suggested by Knut Dörmann, *Elements of War Crimes* (Cambridge: Cambridge University Press 2002), 87–8, at 90–1.

118 Pictet Commentary on GC IV, 601.

119 Knut Dörmann, 'Article 8, Paragraph 2(a)(iv): Extensive Destruction and Appropriation of Property', in Kai Ambos (ed.), *The Rome Statute of the International Criminal Court: A Commentary* (4th ed., Berlin: C. H. Beck/Hart/Nomos 2022), 380–4, at 380.

120 Dörmann, *Elements* (n. 119), 257–9; Robin Geiß and Andreas Zimmermann, 'Article 8, Paragraph 2 (b)(xiii): Prohibited Destruction', in Ambos (ed.), *The Rome Statute* (n. 119), 492–500, at 493.

121 ICC, *Prosecutor* v. *Katanga and Ngudjolo Chui*, decision on the confirmation of charges of 26 September 2008, 01/04-01/07, para. 314.

Finally, Article 8(2)(b)(xvi) of the ICC Statute, which criminalises 'pillaging a town or place, even when taken by assault', may be relevant in relation to animals in occupied territory. Indeed, as already discussed,[122] animals fall into the protective scope of the ban on pillage.

5 CONCLUDING RECOMMENDATIONS

The protection of animals in occupied territory is scant and does not take into account the complex needs of animals. Although the applicable rules are not limited only to IHL, but rather, other sources of international law may be relevant, the legal protection offered to animals in occupied territory needs to be strengthened in three main areas. First, occupying powers should pay more attention to the local legislation protecting animals, and to their duty to implement it in light of their obligation to restore and ensure public order and civil life. Second, an approach based on animals' needs as such, rather than on animals as property or parts of the environment, would be useful to enhance the protection of animals in occupied territory. Third, special agreements between the occupying power and the representatives of the local population of the occupied territory, concluded under Article 47 of GC IV, might be good tools to enhance animal protection.

SELECT BIBLIOGRAPHY

Al-Duaij, Nada, *Environmental Law of Armed Conflict* (New York: Transnational Publisher 2004).

Finch, Frank R., 'This Land is our Land: The Environmental Threat of Army Operations', *International Law Studies* 69 (1996), 99–115.

Hulme, Karen, 'Enhancing Environmental Protection During Occupation through Human Rights', *Goettingen Journal of International Law* 10 (2020), 203–41.

[122] See above Section 2.2.

14

Animals in Protected Zones

Matthew Gillett

1 INTRODUCTION

Although human values are axiomatic to international humanitarian law (IHL),[1] this field of law can also protect non-humans.[2] Examining the capacity of IHL to shield animals from the ravages of war is critical. As anthropocentric harm to the environment escalates in this globalized age, we stand on the precipice of a mass loss of animal species.[3] This would be the first anthropogenic extinction.[4] At the same time, wars continue to flare up around the world. Armed conflicts heavily impact animals,[5] despite the fact that they do not choose to participate in hostilities but only 'struggle for survival' therein.[6]

Within the framework of IHL, protected zones present a unique and under-explored means of sheltering animals. As spatial concepts, they afford protection to humans and non-humans alike, as long as situated within their physical parameters.[7]

1 See Karsten Nowrot, 'Animals at War: The Status of "Animal Soldiers" under International Humanitarian Law', *Historical Social Research* 140 (2015), 128–50, at 135 ('the scope of application of the *ius in bello* – as strongly indicated by its more recent labelling as international "humanitarian" law – has always been and continues to be exclusively human-oriented'). See further Sandesh Sivakumaran, 'International Humanitarian Law', in Daniel Moeckli et al. (eds.), *International Human Rights Law* (3rd ed.) (Oxford: Oxford University Press 2017), 507; Anne Peters, *Animals in International Law* (Leiden: Brill/Nijhoff 2021), 334.

2 Marco Roscini, 'Animals and the Law of Armed Conflict', *Israeli Yearbook of Human Rights* 47 (2017), 35–67, at 58–66.

3 Gerardo Ceballosa, Paul R. Ehrlich and Rodolfo Dirzo, 'Biological Annihilation Via the Ongoing Sixth Mass Extinction Signalled by Vertebrate Population Losses and Declines', *Proceedings of the National Academy of Sciences of the United States of America* 114 (2017), 1. This mass extinction is also referred to as the Holocene or Anthropocene extinction, due to its link with human activity.

4 Anthony D. Barnosky et al., 'Has the Earth's Sixth Mass Extinction Already Arrived?' (2011) *Nature* 471.

5 Roscini, 'Animals and the Law of Armed Conflict' (n. 2), 35–6; ICRC, 'Natural Environment: Neglected Victim of Armed Conflict' (5 June 2019), available at https://bit.ly/3qZirbN, accessed 22 February 2022.

6 'They had no choice', as noted on the Inscription on the Animals in War memorial outside Hyde Park, London (2004) cited in Peters, *Animals in International Law* (n. 1), 333–4.

7 See Section 3.7.2 below, referring to Niccolò Pons, 'Animals', in Dražan Djukić and Niccolò Pons (eds.), *The Companion to International Humanitarian Law: International Humanitarian Law Series, Volume* 55 (Leiden: Brill 2018), 171–2.

This geographic quality de-links such zones from the 'personal' status of animals or the anthropomorphism of their suffering. In this way, protected zones open up a pathway to animal protection that is not contingent on equating them with human beings.[8]

Contrastingly, other IHL protections touted for animal protection are based on personal status (as civilian or combatant) or unnecessary[9] harm (in terms of prohibited means and methods of war). The applicability of these constructs will pivot on whether ecocentric interpretations can be applied to the underlying 'cardinal' IHL principles of distinction and unnecessary suffering.[10] Given that distinction and unnecessary suffering have historically been conceived of as anthropocentric, their direct applicability to animals remains contested and largely contingent on further developments in IHL.[11]

The International Law Commission's (ILC) recent Draft Principles on the Protection of the Environment in Relation to Armed Conflicts highlight the normative adaptability of protected zones to ecocentric purposes.[12] Principle 4 (previously I-(x), 5), on 'Designation of protected zones', and Principle 17 (previously II-5, 13), on 'Protected zones' explicitly seek to protect 'areas of major "environmental importance"'.[13] By enshrining these area-based constructs into the Draft Principles, the ILC has signaled that they constitute a significant means to potentially prevent or mitigate environmental harm.[14]

Nonetheless, despite the ecological promise of protected zones, the ILC Commentary does not address their applicability to animals.[15] Similarly, scholarly works on the protection of animals in war, which remain few in number,[16] lack any analysis of protected zones in this respect.[17] Accordingly, this study is both apposite

8 Such a designated area 'may lose its protection if a party to an armed conflict has military objectives within the area, or uses the area to carry out any military activities during an armed conflict', but the area's status will still be determined on a spatial rather than personal basis; ILC, Draft Principles on the Protection of the Environment in Relation to Armed Conflict (2019) ('ILC Draft Principles'), reproduced in UN General Assembly, Report of the ILC, Seventy-First Session (29 April–7 June and 8 July–9 August 2019), A/74/10, Annex I, at 260.

9 The ICJ has defined 'unnecessary' as 'a harm greater than that unavoidable to achieve legitimate military objectives'; ICJ: *Legality of the Threat or Use of Nuclear Weapons*, Advisory Opinion [1996] ICJ Reports 226, para. 78.

10 ICJ: *Nuclear Weapons* (n. 9), para. 78; Sivakumaran, 'International Humanitarian Law' (n. 1), 504.

11 Roscini, 'Animals and the Law of Armed Conflict' (n. 2), 45 ('Even admitting, for argument's sake, that certain animals could have combatant status, it would be difficult to qualify the animals not enlisted in the armed forces as civilians.'); 51–6 ('It can be *argued*, then, that the principle of unnecessary suffering now applies not only to humans, but also to animals') (emphasis added).

12 ILC Draft Principles (n. 8), 212–13.

13 ILC Draft Principles (n. 8), 223 (noting that the term 'cultural' is used alongside 'environmental' In Draft Principle 4 to 'indicate the existence of a close linkage to the environment.').

14 ILC Draft Principles (n. 8), 213.

15 Whereas the ILC Commentary to the Draft Principles refers to the notions of environmental protection and biodiversity in generalized terms, they do not specifically analyse how protected zones would address harm to animals (see 221, 224 in particular).

16 Roscini, 'Animals and the Law of Armed Conflict' (n. 2) 36.

17 See, for example, Natalino Ronzitti, 'Protected Areas', in Andrew Clapham, Paola Gaeta and Marco Sassòli (eds.), *The 1949 Geneva Conventions: A Commentary* (Oxford: Oxford University

and timely. It fills a gap in the literature regarding protected zones and animals, which is ever more pressing given the threat facing non-humans during times of war.

While the study of protected zones and animals set out below is novel and original,[18] it must remain anchored to the axiomatic precepts of the law of armed conflict. Normatively, this requires assessing protected zones in light of the anthropocentric ontology and orientation of IHL.[19] Of course, preserving the environment serves human ends. As observed by the International Court of Justice (ICJ) '[t]he environment is not an abstraction but represents the living space, the quality of life and the very health of human beings, including generations unborn'.[20] But that human-centred utility risks subordinating ecocentric concerns to anthropocentric concerns at the conceptual and normative level. Equally, it raises practical issues, such as the deleterious impact on animals of being brought into close proximity with human populations. Accordingly, the normative coherence and operational implications of using protected zones for animals are addressed herein. This analysis is necessary, as the graveyard of international law reform is littered with superficially attractive initiatives that failed to take account of conceptual coherence with applicable legal frameworks,[21] the historical and contemporary realities of state proclivities,[22] and unintended consequences on the ground.[23]

Press 2015), 369–87 (making no reference to animals). Roscini (n. 2), looks to some provisions of IHL that could be applied to animals in his article entitled 'Animals and the Law of Armed Conflict' (which he claims is the 'first ever in-depth study of how the law of armed conflict applies to animals and fills a serious gap in the literature'), but makes no mention of protected zones. Nowrot in 'Animals at War' (n. 1) reviews IHL personal protections regarding animals, by equating them with human combatants or civilians, but does not refer to protected zones. Yoram Dinstein, in *The Conduct of Hostilities under the Law of International Armed Conflict* (3rd ed., Cambridge: Cambridge University Press 2016), at 106, only touches on animals when discussing 'military objectives'. The ICRC's *Guidelines on the Protection of the Natural Environment in Armed Conflict: Rules and Recommendations Relating to the Protection of the Natural Environment under International Humanitarian Law* (ICRC 2020), ('ICRC Environmental Guidelines'), 82–3 refers to protected zones as means to shield the environment but make no explicit mention of animals in this respect. Similarly, Cordula Droege and Marie-Louise Tougas in 'The Protection of the Natural Environment in Armed Conflict: Existing Rules and Need for Further Legal Protection', *Nordic Journal of International Law* 82(1) (2013), 21–52 make no reference to animals in relation to protected zones.

18 See references in footnote 17, reflecting that there are no other major scholarly work examining the applicability of protected zones to animals.

19 Nowrot, 'Animals at War' (n. 1), 135.

20 ICJ: *Nuclear Weapons* (n. 9), para. 29.

21 Andreas Zimmermann, 'Crimes Within the Jurisdiction of the Court', in Otto Triffterer and Kai Ambos (eds.), *The Rome Statute of the International Criminal Court: A Commentary* (3rd ed., C. H. Beck, Hart, Nomos, 2016), 113 (listing the conceptual and practical incongruities of including transnational crimes such as terrorism or drug-trafficking in the Rome Statute of the International Criminal Court) and 125 ('the crimes of terrorism and drug-trafficking were not even seriously considered during the Kampala review process [of the ICC]').

22 Philippe Sands, *Principles of International Environmental Law* (4th ed., Cambridge: Cambridge University Press, 2018), 72 ('In July 1993, the ICJ established a seven-member Chamber for Environmental Matters, but this was disbanded [due to a complete lack of use] in 2006.').

23 See Nina H. B. Jørgensen, 'Children Associated with Terrorist Groups in the Context of the Legal Framework for Child Soldiers', *Questions of International Law* 60 (2019), 19, observing that the

To fill this lacuna, the following analysis explores the potential utility of protected zones for animal populations. Because of the dearth of systematic discussions of protected zones, it first provides a detailed taxonomy of the various types of protected zones and their legal bases. It then surveys examples of protected zones established during armed conflicts, both international and non-international, since the birth of modern IHL. Based on these legal and factual foundations, it engages in doctrinal, normative, and operational analyses of the potential use of protected zones in relation to animals threatened by armed conflict, including the risks engendered by bringing internally displaced persons into zones traditionally habitat to animal species.

The assessment looks at the intra-IHL coherence of using protected zones for animals, and also addresses the impact of international environmental law, cultural heritage law, and international criminal law. In doing so, it seeks to de-fragmentalise the applicability of international law. The study draws on a variety of interdisciplinary sources, including evolutionary biology,[24] ecology, history and conservation management,[25] and the political theory of animal rights.[26] A rich tapestry is woven by these materials, providing a platform to assess the novel issue of protected zones and animals in armed conflict.

2 SCOPE OF APPLICATION OF THE LAWS ON PROTECTED ZONES

Protected zones are locations and geographic spaces that are accorded area-based protected status under IHL.[27] To retain this status, these areas must be free from military objectives and not defended militarily. On a terminological note, whereas 'locality' is taken to mean a specific place of limited area, generally containing buildings, 'zone' is used in the context of protected areas to describe a larger area of land than a locality and may include multiple localities.[28]

divergence between the threshold age of *fifteen* regarding child soldiers under the Rome Statute and the threshold age of *eighteen* for the participation of children in hostilities provided inter alia in the Optional Protocol to the Convention on the Rights of the Child (2000), creates a 'grey area'. The grey area exacerbates the risk of opportunists using children aged fifteen to eighteen in hostilities, knowing that this will not constitute a crime on their part and nor will the children be prosecutable before the ICC, as they fall below the eighteen-year jurisdictional age limit set out in Article 26 of the Rome Statute. Note also that the use of United Nations 'safe zones' in Bosnia in the 1990s had the unintended effect of corralling Bosnian Muslims into the Srebrenica and Zepa enclaves, which then fell under Bosnian Serb control and were the scenes of large-scale and genocidal executions in July 1995, as discussed in Section 2.

24 See, for example, Joshua H.Daskin and Robert M. Pringle, 'Warfare and Wildlife Declines in Africa's Protected Areas', *Nature* 553 (2018), below, Section 3.7.2.

25 See, for example, Kwi-Gon Kim, *The Demilitarized Zone (DMZ) of Korea: Protection, Conservation and Restoration of a Unique Ecosystem* (Heidelberg: Springer 2013), below, Section 3.6.1.

26 See, for example, Nowrot, 'Animals at War' (n. 1), 130, referring to the political theory of animal rights.

27 Vito Todeschini, 'Specially Protected Zones', in Djukić and Pons, *Companion to International Humanitarian Law* (n. 7), 655.

28 ICRC Commentary GC I (2016), paras. 1913 and 1916–26; ICRC Customary Law Database, Rule 35.

Protected zones are explicitly provided for in the law applicable to international armed conflicts, in Article 23 of Geneva Convention (GC) I, Articles 14 and 15 of GC IV, and Articles 59 and 60 of Additional Protocol (AP) I. However, similar arrangements may also be made in non-international armed conflicts, despite the silence of the relevant instruments in this respect.[29] Consistent with the tenor of IHL, there is no explicit mention of animals in the provisions undergirding protected zones.[30]

Protected zones under IHL differ from protected areas established by the UN Security Council.[31] Whereas 'IHL protected zones' are typically subject to agreement by the parties to the conflict,[32] UN Security Council protected areas are established unilaterally by a supra-national entity. United Nations' areas may be demilitarised, and/or no-fly zones, and may be subject to UN peacekeeping protection. They are not subject to any limitations on size (unlike protected zones under IHL) and will not lapse simply due to the violation of the conditions of the protected area by one or more parties to the conflict.[33] Examples include the UN Security Council protected areas established in Srebrenica and Zepa during the conflict in the former Yugoslavia in the 1990s, which were eventually overrun by Bosnian Serb forces, leading to the murder of thousands of Bosnian Muslim men and boys and the expulsion of the females sheltering therein.[34]

Other analogous types of arrangements include 'open relief centres'. The UN High Commissioner for Refugees (UNHCR) established such a centre during the armed conflict in Sri Lanka, with the consent of the government of Sri Lanka and, reportedly, the Liberation of Tigers of Tamil Eelam (LTTE).[35] Similar arrangements are set up as 'zone or space for peace'. The 'Ginapaladtaka Declaration' in the Philippines provided that certain villages were to be respected as peace zones and not used for fighting, even while fighters continued living in those locations.[36]

The purpose of protected zones is to exclude these areas from the theatre of hostilities. In turn, this 'provid[es] shelter and care to the wounded and sick,

29 Sandesh Sivakumaran, *The Law of Non-international Armed Conflict* (Oxford: Oxford University Press 2012), 383–5; Ronzitti, 'Protected Areas' (n. 17), 370.

30 See, for example, Art. 23 of GC I; Art. 14 and 15 of GC IV; Art. 59 and 60 of AP I. See also Pons, 'Animals' (n. 7), 170. Article 54 of AP I prohibits inter alia the destruction and removal of 'livestock', but only as part of the 'protection of objects indispensable to the survival of the civilian population'; Nowrot, 'Animals' (n. 1), 136.

31 Sivakumaran, *The Law of Non-international Armed Conflict* (n. 29), 385.

32 See below Section 3.1.

33 Ronzitti, 'Protected Areas' (n. 17), 370.

34 UN Security Council Resolution 819 of 16 April1993, S/RES/819; UN Security Council Resolution 824 of 6 May 1993, S/RES/824; Sivakumaran, *The Law of Non-international Armed Conflict* (n. 29), 385.

35 Sivakumaran, *The Law of Non-international Armed Conflict* (n. 32), 386; Memorandum of Understanding among the Government of the Socialist Republic of Sri Lanka and the Office of the UN High Commissioner for Refugees (UNHCR) relating to the Repatriation of Sri Lankan Refugees and Displaced Persons, 1 February 1993.

36 Sivakumaran, *The Law of Non-international Armed Conflict* (n. 29), 386.

pregnant women, and/or to civilians generally'.[37] In this sense, the underlying goal of protected zones is to shelter or protect more effectively persons who do not or no longer take direct part in hostilities.[38]

Protected zones establish area-based protections for the spaces per se, rather than specifically protecting the people sheltered within them. However, people sheltering therein continue to be protected by the other generally applicable provisions of IHL (such as GC I for the wounded and sick and GC IV for civilians).[39]

There is a fundamental tension between the ontological precept of protected zones, which is the protection of human beings, and the goal of protecting animals. Bringing humans and animals together will typically act to the detriment of the latter.[40] Anthropogenic factors are by far the greatest threat to animal well-being and survival.[41] During armed conflict food is scarce and non-livestock animals may be exploited to make up the shortfall.[42] Even when humans do not intend to harm animals, their attacks on other human populations could collaterally decimate animal populations. Thus, the optimal protection for animals is distance from not only the fighting, but also from any sizeable human populations.

While protected zones were conceived with anthropocentric interests in mind, significant developments have occurred recently which may broaden this scope of protected interests. As noted above, the ILC Draft Principles include Principle 4 (I-(x), 5), on 'Designation of protected zones', whereby 'States should designate, by agreement or otherwise, areas of major environmental and cultural importance as protected zones', and Principle 17 (II-5, 13) on 'Protected zones', whereby '[a]n area of major environmental and cultural importance designated by agreement as a protected zone shall be protected against any attack, as long as it does not contain a military objective'.[43] Whilst it has been said that the ILC Draft Principles are based on anthropocentric considerations,[44] they are broad enough to protect animals per se, as part of the environment.[45] The opening up of IHL to encompass and legitimize eco-zones, or biodiversity zones, would enable this field of law to serve the interests of humans and non-humans alike.[46]

37 Ronzitti, 'Protected Areas' (n. 17), 370.

38 See UN General Assembly Resolution 2675 of 9 December 1970, A/RES/2675, providing that '[p]laces or areas designated for the sole protection of civilians, such as hospital zones or similar refuges, should not be the object of military operations'. This principle reflects customary international law; Sivakumaran, *The Law of Non-international Armed Conflict* (n. 29), 383.

39 Sivakumaran, *The Law of Non-International international Armed Conflict* (n. 5), 385.

40 See, for example, ICRC, 'Natural Environment' (n. 5).

41 Sean L. Maxwell et al., ' Biodiversity: The Ravages of Guns, Nets and Bulldozers', *Nature* (2016), available at https://go.nature.com/3uevEQj, accessed 22 February 2022.

42 See Longobardo, Chapter 13, 'Occupied Territory', in this volume.

43 ILC Draft Principles (n. 8).

44 See Krieger and Martínez Soria, Chapter 4, 'Rationale and Challenges', in this volume.

45 ILC Draft Principles (n. 8), 211.

46 See also ICRC Environmental Guidelines (n. 17), 83–4, calling for the designation of areas of environmental importance but not addressing the separation of animals and humans.

3 CONTENTS AND LIMITS OF THE LAWS ON PROTECTED ZONES

As discussed at the outset, protected zones are various locations and areas that are accorded protected status, subject to meeting the requirements of the relevant provision or rule of IHL. Due to the gap in the scholarship regarding the implications of protected zones for animals, it is important to systematically provide a taxonomy of the relevant IHL provisions and principles, in order to provide a robust legal foundation from which to assess this novel yet significant potentiality.

3.1 *The Legal Parameters of Protected Zones*

Among the myriad IHL area-based constructions, Article 23 of GC I provides for hospital zones and localities. Together with safety zones and neutralised zones regulated in Articles 14 and 15 of GC IV, this forms a wider system of protected zones. The system is further developed in AP I, which provides special protection to non-defended localities and thirteen demilitarised zones.

Several features are common to all protected zones. First, their special protections under IHL are contingent on the formal requirements prescribed by treaty law being met. Second, they must typically be recognised by adverse parties to the conflict.[47] Third, they must not be employed for military activities, including the movement of troops and materiel, and must not be militarily defended.[48] Fourth, they must be clearly marked and their boundaries must be sufficiently demarcated. If any of these core conditions are violated, the opposing party may, after a reasonable time has lapsed without rectification, declare the agreement terminated.[49]

3.2 *Hospital Zones and Localities and Safety Zones*

Hospital and safety zones are referred to in several IHL provisions concerning international armed conflicts. Under Article 23(1) of GC I, parties may, optionally,[50] organise 'hospital zones and localities so … as to protect the wounded and sick from the effects of war, as well as the personnel entrusted with the organization and administration of these zones and localities and with the care of the persons therein assembled'.[51] They may establish these zones 'in their own territory and, if the need arises, in occupied areas'.[52] The parties concerned 'may conclude agreements on mutual recognition of the hospital zones and localities they have created'. A draft agreement of this nature is annexed to GC I (Draft Agreement

47 See, for example, Art. 23(1) of GC I. But see the ambiguity in relation to non-defended localities; Ronzitti, 'Protected Areas' (n. 17), 371, 386.
48 See, for example, ICRC Commentary GC I (2016), paras. 1914–15.
49 Ronzitti, 'Protected Areas' (n. 17), 373.
50 See ICRC Commentary GC I (2016), para. 1889.
51 Art. 23(1) of GC I.
52 Ibid.

annexed to GC I).[53] Attacks against hospital zones are prohibited, as reflected in Article 11 of the Draft Agreement annexed to GC I, which states: '[i]n no circumstances may hospital zones be the object of attack. They shall be protected and respected at all times by the Parties to the conflict.'[54]

Hospital zones and localities under Article 23 of GC I may be established in peacetime and during armed conflict.[55] The protecting powers and the International Committee of the Red Cross (ICRC) are encouraged to support the institution and recognition of these hospital zones and localities by lending their good offices to the parties in this respect.[56] Premised on agreement, protected zones require recognition by the adverse party(ies).[57] Pending such agreement, persons *hors de combat* and otherwise subject to protections under IHL will continue to be protected by the generally applicable rules of IHL.[58]

Article 14 of GC IV, which concerns the protection of civilians, largely repeats the wording of Article 23(1) of GC I. However, Article 14 uses the term 'hospital and safety zones and localities', thereby extending beyond Article 23(1)'s scope to the additional category of safety zones,[59] which encompasses more sizeable areas than hospitals and their surroundings.[60]

The ICRC Commentary provides for the establishment of 'hospital zones and localities *outside areas where fighting is taking place*'.[61] This is in order to shelter vulnerable persons from long-range artillery attacks, missiles and aerial bombardments.[62] Similarly, the Draft Agreement annexed to GC I[63] states that such zones 'shall be far removed and free from all military objectives, or large industrial or administrative establishments'.[64] According to the ICRC, '[r]emoteness from military objectives [is] – the essential condition – the very essence of the whole scheme – is that there should be no military objective either within the zones or in their vicinity'.[65]

53 Draft Agreement Relating to Hospital Zones and Localities, Annex 1 to GC I (Draft Agreement annexed to GC I).
54 See ICRC Commentary GC I (2016), para. 1906.
55 Art. 23(1) of GC I; Art. 14 of GC IV.
56 Art. 23 (1) GC I.
57 ICRC Commentary GC I (2016), para. 1928; Ronzitti, 'Protected Areas' (n. 17), 371.
58 ICRC Commentary GC I (2016), para. 1900.
59 Ronzitti, 'Protected Areas' (n. 17), 373.
60 In terms of the scope of GC IV, Article 13 indicates that part II (which contains the provisions on protected zones) covers 'the whole of the populations of the countries in conflict, without any adverse distinction based, in particular, on race, nationality, religion or political opinion, and are intended to alleviate the sufferings caused by war'. Article 4 states that persons falling under the protection of GC I, GC II, GC III shall not qualify as protected persons under GC IV. However, GC IV forms a residual safety net whereby anybody in enemy hands who is not covered by one of the other GCs is granted protection; Pictet Commentary on GC VI, 52.
61 ICRC Commentary GC I (2016), para. 1884 (emphasis added).
62 Ibid., para. 1904.
63 Ronzitti, 'Protected Areas' (n. 17), 370.
64 Draft Agreement annexed to GC I.
65 Pictet Commentary on GC I, Annex I, Art. 4; Art. 4 of Draft Agreement Relating to Hospital and Safety Zones, Annex 1 to GC IV (Draft Agreement annexed to GC IV).

While no specific conventional provision provides for hospital and safety zones in non-international armed conflicts,[66] common Article 3(3) of the GCs, which applies to international and non-international conflicts, states that the '[t]he Parties to the conflict should further endeavour to bring into force, by means of special agreements, all or part of the other provisions of the present Convention.'[67] The ICRC has stated that prohibition on directing attacks against protected zones forms part of customary IHL.[68] In line with these sources, the ILC's Draft Principles suggest that non-state actors should be able to conclude agreements to designate areas of ecological importance as demilitarised zones.[69]

Examples of hospital zones in non-international armed conflicts include the ICRC's establishment, in November 1990, of rules to protect the Jaffna Teaching Hospital, which had been damaged by fighting between the Sri Lankan security forces and the LTTE. The parties agreed to the rules and established a hospital zone. The rules required the clear marking of the hospital and surrounds with red crosses, the prohibition of armed personnel and military vehicles from the compound or surrounding area, and the prohibition of firing on the area.[70]

Although invocations of Article 23(1) of GC I are rare, parties 'have made use of the general concept of protected zones provided for in the Conventions both in international and non-international conflicts'.[71] Examples include the 'agreement declaring the hospital of Osijek and its surroundings a protected zone',[72] and the analogous example of Argentina and the UK during the 1982 Falklands/Malvinas conflict, which designated an area to allow hospital ships to hold position and to exchange wounded, both of which are discussed below in Section 3.6.3.

The ICRC considers that 'the purpose of the hospital zones and localities provided for in Article 23 is to "protect" certain categories of *persons*'.[73] Conventional understandings of IHL consider the term persons to refer to human beings, and not animals.[74] However, incidental protection for animals may arise. For example, the local civilian population who normally live within the protected zone and any domestic animals or livestock owned by them will normally be protected by agreements under Article 23(1).[75]

An essential requirement is that the zone or locality must contain no military objectives and must not be defended militarily.[76] However, '[t]he adverse Party is not prohibited from taking over the zone or locality but remains bound to respect all its

66 Ronzitti, 'Protected Areas' (n. 17), 370.
67 See also ICRC Commentary GC I (2016), para. 1885.
68 ICRC Customary Law Database, Rule 35.
69 ILC Draft Principles (n. 8), 222.
70 Ibid. See also Sivakumaran, *The Law of Non-international Armed Conflict* (n. 32), 383.
71 ICRC Commentary GC I (2016), para. 1886.
72 Ibid., para. 1886.
73 Ibid., para. 1903 (emphasis added).
74 See Lostal, Chapter 19, 'Reparation and Rehabilitation', in this volume.
75 ICRC Commentary GC I (2016), paras. 1924–6.
76 ICRC Commentary GC I (2016), paras. 1914–15.

obligations towards the protected zone or locality and the persons and objects sheltered therein'.[77]

Temporally, establishing a protected zone during peacetime would send a hostile message to potential adversaries. However, the ICRC has noted the prophylactic benefit of designating hospitals and protected zones in advance of hostilities.[78] Given that 'aspects of setting up and managing a hospital zone or locality risk being neglected during the early days of an armed conflict',[79] and that indirectly protected entities such as animals are the most at risk of being ignored, this *ex ante* aspect of protected zones is particularly important to mitigate harm to animals. Moreover, establishing ecological protected zones for animals may be seen as less provocative by potential adversaries than human-centred protective zones, particularly if grounded in precepts of international environmental law.

The model Draft Agreements annexed to GC I and GC IV provide an indication of the intended use and parameters of such protected zones.[80] Regarding geographic scope, the Draft Agreements provide that hospital zones and localities shall 'comprise only a small part of the territory governed by the Power which has established them'.[81] According to the Pictet Commentary, '[i]t would obviously be inadmissible for a State to establish a hospital zone covering half the country' because '[t]he very idea of zones of refuge implies a relatively limited area, and in any case the adverse Party would be unlikely to accord recognition to very large zones which might seriously impede military operations.'[82] Conversely, protected zones established by the UN Security Council have no such restriction. During the conflict in Rwanda in 1994, the UN Security Council established secure areas and humanitarian zones that covered much of the country's territory,[83] leading to significant negative impacts for the animal populations therein.[84]

In theory, the larger the protected zone the greater the protection for animals. However, warring parties are unlikely to agree that vast swathes of territory could be designated as hospital, safety, neutralised or demilitarised, or other types of protected zones, particularly as they would have to ensure there were no military objectives throughout these areas. Moreover, areas of relatively limited size will usually be sufficient to shelter large numbers of civilians or combatants *hors de combat*, as demonstrated by the examples of hospitals and their surrounds. However, prior to

77 Ibid.

78 ICRC Commentary GC I (2016), para. 1896. See also Ronzitti, 'Protected Areas' (n. 17), 371. According to Ronzitti, '[t]he creation of a zone in peacetime is quite unrealistic, since it foresees a possible conflict with a neighbouring state that a country will usually not wish to emphasize'. See also ICRC Environmental Guidelines (n. 17), 14.

79 ICRC Commentary GC I (2016), para. 1896.

80 Pictet Commentary on GC IV, 129.

81 Art. 4 of Draft Agreement annexed to GC I; Art. 4 of Draft Agreement annexed to GC IV.

82 Pictet Commentary on GC IV, 129; Art. 4 of Draft Agreement annexed to GC IV.

83 Ibid., 384.

84 See Section 3.7.6 below.

armed conflict erupting states may be more receptive to designating larger areas for ecological protection, as urged by the ILC's Draft Principle 4.

An efficient use of protected zones to benefit animals would focus on existing delimited animal habitats (presuming that humans would not be introduced in large numbers to these areas). Such zones would be unlikely to constitute any more than a small proportion of a state's territory. For example, Tanzania, with its high proportion of natural reserves (approximately 114,000 km^2), still only designates well below 50 per cent of its land area (approximately 945,000 km^2) to this end.[85] Despite the lack of any specific quantitative threshold, the references to limited size reinforces their focus on protecting members of the human species, and supports the arguments for developing new forms of animal protection zones in armed conflict, particularly in advance of hostilities flaring up.

3.3 *Neutralised Zones*

Under Article 15 of GC IV,

> [a]ny Party to the conflict may, either direct[ly] or through a neutral state or some humanitarian organization, propose to the adverse Party to establish, in the regions where fighting is taking place, neutralised zones intended to shelter from the effects of war the following persons, without distinction: (a) Wounded and sick combatants or non-combatants; (b) civilian persons who take no part in hostilities, and who, while they reside in the zones, perform no work of a military character.

These zones are based on the same idea as the hospital and safety zones covered by Article 14 and are explicitly anthropocentrically oriented.[86]

The major distinction between these and the former categories is that neutralized zones are 'established in the actual regions where fighting is taking place and are intended to give shelter to both civilian and military wounded and sick, as well as all civilian persons who take no part in hostilities'.[87] Moreover, neutralised zones would usually be 'set up on a temporary basis to meet the tactical situation at a particular moment, whereas hospital and safety zones tend to be more permanent in character'.[88]

There is no specific conventional provision explicitly providing for the organisation of neutralised zones in non-international armed conflicts. However, their establishment aligns with common Article 3(3) of the GCs and customary IHL, particularly the prohibition on directing attacks against zones established to shelter the wounded and sick and the prohibition of attacks directed against civilians.

85 See, for example, The United Republic of Tanzania: National Environment Statistics Report (2017), xxiv, available at https://bit.ly/3qZhL6f, accessed 22 February 2022.
86 Pictet Commentary on GC IV, 129.
87 Ibid.
88 Ibid.

Historically, neutralised zones in non-international armed conflicts include in a district in Madrid during the Spanish Civil War (prompted by the ICRC);[89] three zones in Jerusalem during the conflict in Palestine in 1948 (directed and administered by the ICRC); and a neutralised zone in Shanghai in 1937, during the Sino-Japanese war, named the Jacquinot Zone in honour of the man who organized it.[90]

Irrespective of the nature of the conflict, the agreement of the parties to the conflict is required for a neutralised zone to be operationalised. During the conflict between the Sri Lankan Security Forces and the LTTE the Sri Lankan forces unilaterally declared a 35-km^2 'safe zone' for civilians. However, in the absence of a formal agreement with the LTTE, the presence of the LTTE in the zone and the shelling of the zone by government forces did not amount to violations of the IHL provisions concerning protected zones (even if they may have constituted attacks on civilians).[91]

3.4 *Demilitarised Zones*

Many of the considerations concerning the preceding protected zones apply to demilitarised zones. Under Article 60 of AP I, parties may agree to establish demilitarised zones, subject to the following:

(a) all combatants, as well as mobile weapons and mobile military equipment, must have been evacuated;
(b) no hostile use shall be made of fixed military installations or establishments;
(c) no acts of hostility shall be committed by the authorities or by the population; and
(d) any activity linked to the military effort must have ceased.[92]

In principle, these demilitarised zones 'are primarily concerned with protecting the population residing there and do not constitute places of refuge'.[93]

Though there are historic examples of areas that have been demilitarised, they would not constitute demilitarised zones under Article 60.[94] Outside the specific ambit of IHL, some peace treaties have required the defeated party to maintain the demilitarisation of areas. These include areas around the Rhine under Articles 42 to 44 of the Treaty of Versailles of 1919 and islands such as Pantelleria and the Dodecanese Islands demilitarised under the 1947 Peace Treaty between the Allied Powers and Italy, and ceded by Italy to Greece. There have been demilitarised areas

89 See Ronzitti, 'Protected Areas' (n. 17), 376.
90 Pictet Commentary on GC IV, 129.
91 Human Rights Watch, 'War on the Displaced, Sri Lankan Army and LTTE Abuses against Civilians in the Vanni' (February 2009), paras. 12–16. See also ICRC Online Platform, *How Does the Law Protect in War?*, available at https://bit.ly/3AuZK31, accessed 22 February 2022.
92 Art. 60(3) of AP I. See also Sivakumaran, *The Law of Non-international Armed Conflict* (n. 32), 384; Principle 4 of the ILC Draft Principles (n. 8).
93 AP I Commentary, para. 2312.
94 Ibid., para. 2302.

established following armistices, which are often referred to as 'buffer zones', such as the demilitarised zones in Korea and in the Middle East between Israel and its neighbours.[95]

Regarding animals, Article 60 of AP I is not specific but 'allows that an agreement on a demilitarized zone be tailored to each specific situation'.[96] The protection of areas of significant species diversity could be enhanced, even when situated close to hostilities, if belligerents were to agree to formally classifying them as 'demilitarized zones'. In this respect, a draft Convention on the Prohibition of Hostile Activities in Protected Areas has been developed in order to grant territorial protection to areas of great environmental importance.[97] In a similar vein, the World Heritage Convention recognises states' duties to identify and safeguard certain places that constitute part of the common heritage of humankind, including the habitat of threatened species of animals 'of outstanding universal value from the point of view of science or conservation'.[98]

Given the broad ratification of the World Heritage Convention, and the customary international law status of its obligation to safeguard sites of outstanding universal value, an argument can be made that states are obliged to establish demilitarised zones, or an equivalent arrangement, for such habitats of threatened species.[99] This novel argument is bolstered by Article 8 of the Convention on Biological Diversity,[100] which requires that '[e]ach Contracting Party shall, as far as possible and as appropriate: (a) [e]stablish a system of protected areas or areas where special measures need to be taken to conserve biological diversity'.

However, detractors from this argument may assert that these instruments from other areas of international law cannot affect the express criteria under IHL, and that the establishment of demilitarised and other protected zones must remain completely voluntary unless IHL itself is altered. The argument demonstrates the stultifying impact of IHL's insistence on consent in relation to protected zones. At the same time, it highlights the normative potentialities of developing IHL in light of the principles and provisions of international environmental law and cultural heritage law.[101]

3.5 *Open Towns, Non-defended Localities*

The considerations concerning other protected zones largely govern open towns and non-defended localities. Under Article 59 of AP I,

95 Ibid., para. 2301.
96 Art. 60(3) of AP I; ICRC Customary Law Database, Rule 36.
97 Jérôme de Hemptinne, 'The Protection of Animals During Warfare', *American Journal for International Law Unbound* 111 (2017), 272–6, at 276 citing UNEP, *Protecting the Environment during Armed Conflict: An Inventory and Analysis of International Law* (Nairobi: UNEP 2009).
98 Arts. 2–4 of the World Heritage Convention.
99 See UNEP, Protecting the Environment (n. 115), 38.
100 Convention on Biological Diversity of 5 June 1992, 1760 UNTS 79.
101 See ILC Draft Principles (n. 8), 222–3, which also seek to draw together these areas of international law.

> [t]he appropriate authorities of a Party to the conflict may declare as a non-defended locality any inhabited place near or in a zone where armed forces are in contact which is open for occupation by an adverse Party. Such a locality shall fulfil the following conditions: (a) All combatants, as well as mobile weapons and mobile military equipment must have been evacuated; (b) no hostile use shall be made of fixed military installations or establishments; (c) no acts of hostility shall be committed by the authorities or by the population; and (d) no activities in support of military operations shall be undertaken.

No special agreement is required between the parties to establish non-defended localities: they 'may be established by a unilateral declaration or by agreement'.[102] As with attacks on demilitarised zones, attacks on non-defended localities would entail potential consequences under international criminal law, as such a violation is considered a grave breach under Article 85(3)(d) of AP I.

3.6 *Examples of Protected Zones and Their Impact on Animals*

The following exegesis sets out examples of protected zones established during armed conflict. This is not a comprehensive survey of all such protected zones, but rather seeks to point out potentialities for the impact of such zones on the well-being of animals.

3.6.1 Democratic People's Republic of Korea and the Republic of Korea

A notable example demonstrating the potential benefits of protected zones for wildlife is provided by the demilitarised zone between the Democratic People's Republic of Korea and the Republic of Korea (Korean DMZ).[103] Established in 1953 under an armistice and comprising a strip of land 250 kilometres long and 4 kilometres wide,[104] both sides were prohibited from conducting any hostile act within, from, or against the demilitarised zone. Each side was allowed up to 1,000 military personnel inside the zone at any point in time.[105] Accordingly, very little human activity has occurred in the demilitarised zone since its creation.

In this pristine environment, fauna and flora have flourished.[106] For example, red-crowned cranes and white-naped cranes are now among its 'most famous and visible denizens'.[107] Moreover, 'nearly 100 species of fish, perhaps 45 types of amphibians

102 AP I Commentary, para. 3487. But see Ronzitti, 'Protected Areas' (n. 17), 376, noting that '[i]t is not specified whether mere acquiescence by the enemy is enough, or whether a formal acknowledgement is required'.

103 Pons, 'Animals' (n. 7), 1712.

104 Kim, *The Demilitarized Zone (DMZ) of Korea* (n. 25), 172.

105 ICRC Customary Law Database, Rule 36 (see practice mentioned).

106 Kim, The Demilitarized Zone (DMZ) of Korea (n. 25), 172.

107 Lisa Brady, 'Korea's Green Ribbon of Hope: History, Ecology, and Activism in the DMZ', 3 *Solutions* 1 (2012), 94–8, at 95.

and reptiles and over 1,000 different insect species are also supposed to exist in the protected zone'.[108] Bordering the demilitarised zone, there is also a civilian control zone, which is primarily used for agriculture by way of fields and rice paddies.[109] The aims of this demilitarised zone were not directed towards the well-being of animals. Nonetheless, its positive impact on wild species evidences the potential use of demilitarised zones and other similar protective regimes to assist animals.

The South Korean government has advocated for the entire demilitarised zone to be named a biosphere reserve through UNESCO. In 2012, the South Korean government requested this designation, but was not successful, due, in part, to the lack of rules regulating development by landowners in the surrounding areas.[110] The South Korean Ministry of Environment has reportedly claimed that over 5,000 species of plants and animals have been identified in the area, including more than 100 that are protected, such as the Siberian musk deer, white-naped crane, red-crowned crane, Asiatic black bear, cinereous vulture, and long-tailed goral (a species of wild goat).[111]

3.6.2 Croatia

In December 1991, an agreement declaring the hospital of Osijek and its surroundings 'a protected zone according to the principles of Article 23 of the First Geneva Convention and of Articles 14 and 15 of the Fourth Geneva Convention' was concluded under the auspices of the ICRC.[112] Pursuant to the agreement, the protected zone was not to be made the object of attack under any circumstances.[113] The protected zone was to be clearly delimited and marked by means of large red crosses, visible at night.[114] Access was to be limited to civilians, soldiers who were *hors de combat*, medical personnel, and ICRC delegates, as well as persons who normally lived within the protected zone and were not taking any part in hostilities.[115]

108 Ibid.

109 National Public Radio, 'In Korean DMZ, Wildlife Thrives: Some Conservationists Worry Peace Could Disrupt It' (20 April 2019) (NPR on Korean DMZ), available at https://n.pr/3nXVjIS, accessed 22 February 2022.

110 Ibid.

111 Ibid.

112 ICRC Commentary GC I (2016), para. 1886. The ICRC referred to the Memorandum of Understanding on the Application of IHL between Croatia and the Socialist Federal Republic of Yugoslavia and the Agreement between Croatia and the Socialist Federal Republic of Yugoslavia on a Protected Zone around the Hospital of Osijek of 27 December 1991 (Art. 1, 2(1) and 4(1)) (Agreement), available at www.peaceagreements.org/masterdocument/1880, accessed 22 February 2022. See also Sivakumaran, *The Law of Non-international Armed Conflict* (n. 32), 385.

113 Agreement (n. 112), para. 11.

114 Ibid., para. 3.

115 Ibid.

Reportedly, hospitals in the region of Eastern Croatia were intentionally shelled despite being clearly marked as hospitals.[116] The Vukovar hospital was hit by multiple shells. Osijek was regularly targeted as it was a strategic location in Eastern Slavonia. The Osijek hospital itself had been shelled by Federal forces prior to the concluding of the agreement, for example on 16 September 1991.[117] After the agreement was signed, there were some violations and the ICRC issued a communication to the press objecting to these attacks.[118]

Also during the Balkans war, a 1991 Memorandum of Understanding on the Application of IHL was agreed between Croatia and the Socialist Federal Republic of Yugoslavia (SFRY). Pursuant to this instrument, neutralised zones were established at the Franciscan Monastery and the New Hospital in Dubrovnik, under ICRC supervision.[119]

While there are documented accounts of the establishment of these protected zones, there is very little information as to their impact on animal populations . Witnesses before the International Criminal Tribunal for the former Yugoslavia (ICTY) referred to large numbers of animals killed in and around Vukovar.[120] However, they did not elaborate on the details of those killings, as animal deaths were not usually the focus of ICTY proceedings. There are reports that the conflict resulted in significant releases of metal contaminants in the soil in Croatia[121] and a significant loss of livestock.[122] Nonetheless, there is a lack of specific information concerning the fate of animal populations in these protected zones.

3.6.3 Falklands/Malvinas War in the South Atlantic

Although IHL concerning conflict at sea does not specifically provide for protected zones, a quasi-neutralised one was established at sea in the South Atlantic (the so-called

[116] US Department of State Dispatch Supplement, September 1992, Vol. 3, No 6, 28–9.

[117] See Netherlands Institute for War Documentation, 'Srebrenica: A "Safe" Area – Appendix XIII – Chronology of the Bosnian Conflict 1990–1995'. This document refers to the 16 September 1991 shelling of Osijek Hospital.

[118] ICRC, Communication to the Press No 92/1, 'Conflict in Yugoslavia: Review of ICRC activities' (2 January 1992); ICRC, Communication to the Press No 92/7, 'Yugoslavia: Dialogue Continues as Plenipotentiaries Meet in Geneva' (27 March 1992); ICRC, Press Release No 1710, 'Yugoslavia: New Attack on Osijek hospital' (24 April 1992), both referenced at https://bit.ly/36DowDc, accessed 22 February 2022.

[119] ICRC Customary Law Database, Rule 35 (see practice mentioned); ICRC, 'Communication No 92/1' (n. 118).

[120] See, for example, ICTY, *Prosecutor* v. *Mile Mrksic et al.*, testimony of Zoran Basic, IT-95-13/1, 8 September 2006, T.11651 (referring to 15,000 animal carcasses in the Vukovar area).

[121] Domagoj Vidosalvjevic et al., 'Soil Contamination as a Possible Long-Term Consequence of War in Croatia', *Acta Agriculturae Scandinavica, Section B – Soil & Plant Science* 63(4) (March 2013).

[122] See, for example, ARCOTRASS – Consortium, *Study on the State of Agriculture in Five Applicant Countries: Croatia* (2006), 21. According to this study, '[b]efore the war in the first half of the 90s the livestock sector was of considerable economic importance in Croatia. The consequences were severe. Herd size and production were significantly reduced for all livestock.'

Red Cross Box), during the 1982 conflict between Argentina and the United Kingdom. An area with a diameter of approximately twenty nautical miles was designated on the high seas to allow hospital ships to hold position and to exchange wounded.[123]

Little information is available as to its impact of this zone on animals. There are indications that the 1982 conflict led to a significant downturn in the growth of the king penguin population which had colonised the Falklands, as the concentrated fighting fell within the king penguin's foraging zone.[124] However, there is no established connection between the maritime zone established by the parties and the well-being of this animal population. Effects of the conflict, such as landmines planted by Argentinean forces seeking to slow the British counter-attack, appear to have potentially benefited local animal populations by excluding humans.[125] In fact, the prospect of oil or gas in the waters around the Falklands/Malvinas may present an even greater threat to animal species, including marine species, than the conflict in 1982 itself.[126]

3.6.4 Uganda

The city of Kampala was designated as a demilitarised and neutralised zone pursuant to the Nairobi Peace Agreement of 1985 between the Government of Uganda and the National Resistance Movement (NRM).[127] The fighting in Uganda had negatively impacted animal populations. For example, '[b]etween 1983 and 1995, while the Lord's Resistance Army terrorised Uganda, topi and roan, two species of antelope, were wiped out completely in the country's Pian Upe reserve'.[128] Environmental problems, including loss of biodiversity, continued as the fighting continued over the years. A 2010 report by Uganda's National Environment Management Agency (NEMA) found that the country was experiencing 'soil erosion and declining soil fertility, deforestation, pollution of land, water and air resources, loss of biodiversity and over-harvesting of forests, fisheries and water resources'.[129] By contrast, in Kampala, there are indications that species such as marabou storks

123 ICRC Commentary GC I (2016), para. 1887. See also International Institute of Humanitarian Law (IIHL), San Remo Manual on International Law Applicable to Armed Conflicts at Sea (San Remo: IIHL 1994), rule 160, providing that '[t]he parties to the conflict may agree, for humanitarian purposes, to create a zone in a defined area of the sea in which only activities consistent with those humanitarian purposes are permitted'.

124 Sophie Panel and Antoine Pietri, *God Did Not Save the Kings: Environmental Consequences of the 1982 Falklands War*, Center for Environmental Economics – Montpelier, Working Paper 2020-17, at 3–4, 8.

125 Matthew Teller, 'The Falklands Penguins That Would Not Explode', *BBC News* (7 May 2017), available at www.bbc.com/news/magazine-39821956, accessed 22 February 2022.

126 Panel and Pietri, *Environmental Consequences of the 1982 Falklands War* (n. 124) 9.

127 Sivakumaran, *The Law of Non-international Armed Conflict* (n. 29), 384.

128 'Conflicts other Casualties: How War Affects Wildlife', *The Economist* (11 January 2018).

129 Advisory Consortium on Conflict Sensitivity (ACCS), *Northern Uganda Conflict Analysis* (September 2013), 50 citing National Environment Management Agency (NEMA), *State of the Environment Report for Uganda* (2010).

flourished in the 1990s.[130] However, it is difficult to establish the specific impact of the protected zone covering Kampala on wildlife and domestic animals living there.

3.6.5 Ukraine

Large parts of Eastern Ukraine have been affected by the fighting in recent years and will no doubt be further impacted following the Russian invasion of 24 February 2022. The fighting inevitably impacts humans, infrastructure providing essential services, including health-care facilities, electricity stations, and water treatment and distribution facilities and transport networks. Since 2017, the ICRC has been facilitating negotiations between 'the Ukrainian authorities, the Organization for Security and Co-operation in Europe, and representatives of non-government-controlled areas in Donetsk and Lugansk' with a view to create safety zones along the confrontation line. This would allow for the continued operation of an important water filtration system.[131]

Although there has been no organised monitoring of animal populations in areas affected by the recent fighting in Ukraine, residents and ecologists have observed a significant regeneration of the wildlife in the region. Wolves have reappeared in significant numbers, and there appear to have been large increases in the numbers of wild boar, rare marbled polecats and endangered steppe marmots.[132] At the same time, the conflict has reportedly led to the destruction of large areas of land and many ecosystems, including eighteen wildlife reserves, which is of negative impact on the present animal populations.[133]

3.7 *Protection of Animals in Protected Zones*

The impetus to establish zones to protect animals and their habitats from the ravages of war is growing. Protected zones feature in multiple provisions of the ILC's Draft Principles.[134] Similarly, the ICRC has suggested that protected zones could be established in national parks, natural reserves, and endangered species' habitats,[135] and has drafted a model pledge based on the ideal of removing fighting from areas of major ecological importance or fragility.[136] Demilitarised zones could be set up in uninhabited ecological zones; whereas non-defended localities would be suitable for inhabited places.[137]

130 See Derek Pomeroy and Michael Kibuule, 'Increasingly Urban Marabou Storks Start Breeding Four Months Early in Kampala, Uganda', *Ostrich* 88(3) (2017), 261–6.

131 See Emanuela-Chiara Gillard, '"Safe Areas": The International Legal Framework', *International Review of the Red Cross* 99 (2017), 1075–101, at 1086.

132 Lily Hyde, 'All Wild on Ukraine's Eastern Front', *Politico* (17 July 2018).

133 UNEP, 'Ukraine's Donbas Bears the Brunt of Toxic Armed Conflict' (25 July 2018).

134 See ILC Draft Principles (n. 8), Principles 4 and 17.

135 ICRC Environmental Guidelines (n. 17), 14.

136 Ibid., 61.

137 Ibid., 82. See also Art. 59(2) of AP I.

The ICRC has suggested that the following specific types of locations could be established as protected zones: 'groundwater aquifers, key biodiversity areas (which could be national parks or endangered species habitats), ecological connectivity zones, or areas important for coastal protection, carbon sequestration or disaster prevention'.[138] To foster the coherence of international law and avoid its fragmentation, areas could be designated based on regimes such as the 'World Heritage List, the National Biodiversity Strategies and Action Plans of Parties to the Convention on Biological Diversity, or listed in IUCN's conservation databases, such as the Red List of Ecosystems, the World Database of Key Biodiversity Areas and the World Database on Protected Areas', as well as domestic legislation.[139]

3.7.1 Direct Protection of Animals in Protected Zones

Because protected zones are spatial in nature, they do not provide animals with any direct legal protection. As with humans, protected zones benefit animals indirectly through their area-based prohibitions of attacks.

Innovative arguments have been made to the effect that animals could fit into the definition of members of the armed forces.[140] However, the framework of IHL makes it clear that the classification of 'combatant' was intended to apply to persons rather than animals.[141] The division of combatants and civilians is less structured under the law governing non-international armed conflicts, but revolves around the concept of direct participation in hostilities[142] which is also largely anthropocentric. To fit animals under its rubric would require adjusting the oft-repeated maxim 'farmer by day, soldier by night' and would clash with the anthropocentric presuppositions underlying IHL.

It has been argued that animals may qualify as civilian objects.[143] In the context of protected zones, the attribution of civilian object status would provide a double layer of protection. For example, if military activity were undertaken in a protected zone, thereby potentially depriving it of its status, the animals qualifying as civilian objects would still be legally protected from being the direct targets of attacks. However, classifying animals as objects or equipment would be incongruous with animal rights political theory and efforts to have animals recognised as worthy of protection in their own right.[144]

[138] ICRC Environmental Guidelines (n. 17), 82.

[139] Ibid.

[140] See de Hemptinne, Kebebew, and Niyo, Chapter 10, 'Combatants and as Prisoners of War?'; Krieger and Martínez Soria, Chapter 4, 'Property and Objects', in this volume.

[141] See AP I Commentary, para. 1672. According to AP I Commentary to Article 43, '[t]he expression "armed forces" means "members of the armed forces"'.

[142] See ICRC, *Interpretive Guidance on the Notion of Direct Participation in Hostilities under International Humanitarian Law* (Geneva: ICRC 2009).

[143] See Krieger and Martínez Soria, Chapter 4, 'Property and Objects', in this volume.

[144] See, for example, Art. 60 of AP I. This provision requires that, for demilitarised zones, 'all combatants, as well as mobile weapons and mobile military equipment, must have been evacuated'.

Addressing the merits of animals qualifying as civilian objects, Roscini argues that '"objects" are not limited to inanimate things, but also include living beings that are susceptible of appropriation and ownership'.[145] He notes that animals have been characterised as property by inter alia the ICTY[146] and the Eritrea-Ethiopia Claims Commission (EECC).[147] Jérôme de Hemptinne notes that 'in most legal systems, animals have traditionally been considered as being "moveable objects"'.[148] On this basis, animals could be targeted during armed conflict when used for military purposes and when targeting them would offer a definite military advantage.[149] Conversely, to the extent animals qualify as civilian objects,[150] then any attack directed against them would violate Article 52(2) of AP I, which reflects customary international law and potentially constitute a war crime.[151]

Animals could also be protected as objects necessary for the survival of the human population. Under Article 54 of AP I, depriving the civilian population of objects indispensable for its survival is prohibited. On this basis, collateral damage to animals that are necessary for the survival of the civilian population would potentially constitute a violation of IHL.[152] However, these protections would be contingent on re-characterising key IHL terms in a manner that is ecocentrically motivated but renders animals akin to anthropocentric property. The alternative approach of applying area-based protected zones obviates the need for such interpretive gymnastics.

3.7.2 Indirect Protection of Animals in Protected Zones

Animals could indirectly benefit from protected zones in two primary ways. First, because the prohibition of attacking protected zones applies in a spatial manner. Animals located in these zones will generally benefit from incidental protection due to the reduced likelihood of harm through collateral damage.[153] This is not insignificant; collateral damage has been shown to result in multiple animal deaths in modern conflicts such as the Balkans war.[154] Given that the occurrence of conflict

145 Roscini, 'Animals and the Law of Armed Conflict' (n. 2) 13–14.

146 ICTY, *Prosecutor* v. *Ante Gotovina, Ivan Čermak and Mladen Markač*, judgment of 15 April 2011, IT-06-90-T, para. 1783. See also Krieger and Martínez Soria, Chapter 4, 'Property and Objects', in this volume.

147 EECC, *Partial Award, Western Front, Aerial Bombardment and Related Claims – Eritrea's Claims* 1, 3, 5, 9–13, 14, 21, 25 and 26, 19 December 2005, paras. 29–30. See also Krieger and Martínez Soria, Chapter 4, 'Property and Objects', in this volume.

148 de Hemptinne 'The Protection' (n. 97), 275.

149 Ibid.

150 In this respect, see Krieger and Martínez Soria, Chapter 4, 'Property and Objects', in this volume.

151 See, for example, Art. 8(2)(b)(ii) of ICC Statute. ('Intentionally directing attacks against civilian objects, that is, objects which are not military objectives'.)

152 Art. 54 of AP I. See also de Hemptinne 'The Protection' (n. 97), 275; Federica D'Alessandra and Matthew Gillett, 'The War Crime of Starvation in Non-International Armed Conflict', *Journal of International Criminal Justice* 17 (2019), 815–847, at 836.

153 Pons, 'Animals' (n. 7), 171–2.

154 ICTY, *Prosecutor* v. *Kupreškić et al.*, judgment of 14 January 2000, IT-95-16-T, para. 762. The ICTY Trial Chamber in the *Kupreškić* case acknowledged the fact that the destruction of livestock may be

inside animal habitats predicts the severity of population declines of animal species in those areas, establishing zones that exclude hostilities is likely to benefit animal populations.[155] Animals will also flourish due to the rehabilitation of the environment in zones that are not subject to military attacks.

However, if animals are crowded together with humans in protected zones, the lack of attacks may be a two-edged sword. Human populations left to engage in industrious and economic activity unmolested by attacks are likely to have an increased impact on the natural environment.[156] Even the mere presence of large numbers of humans in the same areas as wild animals is likely to disrupt their normal feeding and foraging behaviour and negatively impact their well-being. Conversely, if humans are largely excluded from the protected zones, as is the case in the Korean DMZ, animal populations will flourish.

Second, the welfare of all animals, including wild animals, will be a factor to be duly considered when undertaking a proportionality assessment before conducting an attack that may cause collateral damage.[157] This factor would be relevant if attacks were launched against military targets adjacent to protected zones established for animals. Already, potential harm to non-combatant humans (including those in protected zones) is a key component in any proportionality assessment. Incorporating harm to animals in the proportionality equation would mark a significant ecocentric advance. Such assessments would be difficult and vulnerable to claims of subjectivity, as it 'depends on the value attributed to animals' and 'animal considerations must be weighed against human considerations (as opposed to military advantage)'.[158] However, it is 'increasingly accepted that animals should also acquire value in their own right and, as a consequence, that their interests should no longer be automatically subordinated to those of human ones.'[159] Moreover, the ILC has stated: 'If the rules relating to proportionality are applied in relation to the protection of the natural environment, it means that attacks against legitimate military objectives must be refrained from if such an attack would have incidental environmental effects that exceed the value of the military objective in question.'[160] Nonetheless, when engaging in proportionality assessments, a common view holds that 'when human interests conflict with animal interests, human life or suffering should prevail over those of animals'.[161] The spatial nature of protected zones obviates the need to weigh human interests against those of animals, at least in

lawful damage incidental to an attack on a military objective, but the tribunal found that the damage was not 'collateral', but rather 'it was the primary purpose of the attack'.

155 See Daskin and Pringle, 'Warfare and Wildlife' (n. 24), 328.

156 See Longobardo, Chapter 13, 'Occupied Territory', in this volume.

157 Pons, 'Animals' (n. 7), 171.

158 Michael Schmitt, 'Green War: An Assessment of the Environmental Law of Armed Conflict', *Yale Law Journal* 22 (1997) 1–110, at 58–61; de Hemptinne 'The Protection' (n. 115), 275.

159 de Hemptinne 'The Protection' (n. 97), 275.

160 Report of the ILC, Seventy-First Session (n. 43), 256.

161 de Hemptinne 'The Protection' (n. 97), 275.

the legal proportionality context; all living entities inside such zones will benefit from their protection from attack. In fact, the presence of civilian humans together with animals in such zones will weigh against the proportionality of any attacks against them.

However, two countervailing risks for animals will arise from the use of protected zones. First, the anthropogenic threats of habitat destruction, resource depletion and hunting for bushmeat will escalate when humans are co-located with animals.[162] Second, and more invidiously, protected zones under IHL are subject to the agreement of the parties to hostilities. However, according to the *pacta tertiis* principle of international law, such agreements would not bind third parties.[163] In the complex, multi-party armed conflicts that currently plague the world, it will be difficult to obtain consent from all parties.[164] But without consent of all parties, any protection existent between a sub-set of the warring factions will be illusory, as the other parties will not be bound to respect the sanctity of the designated area. Counter-intuitively, risks may in fact be heightened due to a false sense of security on the part of those inside purportedly protected zones, as well as the increased potential for large-scale abuses against persons crowded into geographically delineated areas, as was notoriously demonstrated by the events in Srebrenica in July 1995.[165] Such attacks would likely breach other provisions of IHL, irrespective of protected zones, and may amount to criminal conduct. However, history has shown the potential for elevated risks notwithstanding legal protections, and the risk of crowding together in exposed zones, would fall on humans and animals alike.

3.7.3 Protection Through the Application of International Environmental Law

In addition to or notwithstanding any protections under IHL instruments, animals may benefit from the continued application of protecting conventions during armed conflict (to the extent these are not incompatible with IHL). In this respect, obligations under international environmental treaties are not automatically suspended when armed conflict occurs. The ILC Draft Articles on the Effects of Armed Conflicts on Treaties indicate a presumption in favour of the continued applicability of environmental obligations.[166]

162 Panel and Pietri *Environmental Consequences of the 1982 Falklands War* (n. 124) 4–6.

163 ILC Draft Principles (n. 8), 222, 260. See also PCIJ: *Factory at Chorzów*, P.C.I.J., Series A, No. 17, p. 45; and article 34 of the Vienna Convention on the Law of Treaties (Vienna, 23 May 1969), United Nations, Treaty Series, vol. 1155, No. 18232, p. 331.

164 The parties may include non-state actors according to the ILC; ILC Draft Principles (n. 8), 222.

165 See discussion of the crimes committed against those gathered in the Srebrenica and Zepa enclaves, above Section 2.

166 ILC, Effects of Armed Conflicts on Treaties: Titles and texts of the draft articles on the effects of armed conflicts on treaties adopted by the drafting Committee on second reading, 11 May 2011, A/CN.4/L.777, Annex – Indicative list of treaties referred to in Article 7.

However, the extent and operational impact of international environmental law during armed conflict remains prospective and uncertain. Although there are some multilateral treaties protecting endangered species, the welfare of animals has not yet been adequately regulated at the international level,[167] resulting in very few enforceable and binding international treaties concerning the welfare of animals. Nonetheless, instruments such as the Convention on International Trade in Endangered Species (CITES), seek to protect vulnerable animals. Along with other international instruments, including the World Heritage Convention and the Convention on Biological Diversity, these may provide the conceptual basis for an obligation to establish environmentally focused protected zones in the context of armed conflict.

Basing protected zones on these sources has the advantage of conceptual coherence and reduces doctrinal fragmentation between domains of international law. However, states have been reluctant to implement environmental law provisions during armed conflicts, and have conditioned IHL provisions seeking to protect the environment on exacting requirements, as reflected, for example, in Article 35(3) of Additional Protocol I and the corresponding war crime in Article 8(2)(b)(iv) (which is even more exacting).[168] The likelihood of states developing their practice, and in turn the law, and forming an environmental obligation to establish protected zones remains an aspirational goal rather than an established part of the doctrine.

3.7.4 Specially Affected Animal Groups

Throughout history, all manner of animals have been used in armed conflicts, including horses, elephants, dogs, bats, camels, seals, pigeons, dolphins, donkeys, belugas, oxen or cormorants.[169] However, it is not only these animals that are directly used for military purposes, but also several other types of animals that will typically suffer as a result of armed hostilities. The following section surveys the major types of animal populations which will potentially be present in war zones and which may benefit from the establishment of protected zones.

3.7.5 Domestic and Farm Animals

Local populations living in areas falling within the theatre of armed conflict will likely have domestic animals and stock.[170] These animals are susceptible

167 de Hemptinne 'The Protection' (n. 97), 272, citing Anne Peters, 'Global Animal Law: What It Is and Why We Need It', 5 *Transnational Environmental Law* (2016), 9–23.

168 See Matthew Gillett, 'Chapter 10. Eco-Struggles: Using International Criminal Law to Protect the Environment During and After Non- International Armed Conflict' in Carsten Stahn et al. (eds.), *Environmental Protection and Transitions from Conflict to Peace: Clarifying Norms, Principles and Practices* (Oxford: Oxford University Press 2017).

169 Nowrot, 'Animals at War' (n. 1), 130.

170 See, for example, ARCOTRASS – Consortium, *Study on the State of Agriculture* (n. 122), 21.

to harm during hostilities. Lord Paddy Ashdown recounted during his testimony in the *Milošević* case how '[i]n his journey through western Kosovo, [he] saw villages and towns razed to the ground, uninhabited, all the properties roofless, having been set on fire, evidence of gunfire, with shell holes and putrefying dead cows strewn in the fields'.[171] Other witnesses in ICTY proceedings frequently detailed the killing of livestock and pets by armed forces and paramilitary groups.[172]

Soldiers engaged in armed conflict often obtain dogs, cats and other animals to serve as pets and military mascots to raise morale and comfort soldiers.[173] These domestic animals and stock may suffer as indirect victims of forced displacement of civilian populations. As human populations flee, these animals are typically abandoned and left to wander the fields or streets without proper food or water being left for them. Given that war is at times accompanied by famine,[174] domestic animals face the risk of consumption by remaining humans looking for food. In this respect, an Imam in Syria issued a fatwa in 2013 allowing the starving local population to eat cats, dogs and donkeys,[175] which is usually impermissible under Islamic dietary laws. If protected zones were established, the populations would be less likely to flee and therefore less likely to abandon their animals.

In terms of legal protection, domestic animals and stock located in protected zones will typically be considered civilian objects, as the property of the civilian inhabitants to whom they belong.[176] However, if those civilians take part in hostilities they would lose their civilian protection.[177] In turn, their pets would no longer be civilian property, as least during their owner's active participation. Nonetheless, the indirect shelter provided by the protected zone would continue to apply as long as the owner's military activities were not significant enough to vitiate the area-based protection.

171 ICTY, *Prosecutor* v. *Slobodan Milosevic*, summary of testimony of Paddy Ashdown of 14 and 15 March 2002, IT-02-54.

172 See for example, ICTY, *Prosecutor* v. *Vlastimir Djordjevic*, judgment of 23 February 2011, IT-05-87/1-T, paras. 331, 1102; ICTY, *Prosecutor* v. *Goran Hadzic*, testimony of Adnan Abd El Razek, IT-04-75-T, 1 July 2013, T.6465-6466.

173 Roscini, 'Animals and the Law of Armed Conflict' (n. 2), 1. These pets may also serve as operational dogs as discussed below.

174 See D'Alessandra and Gillett, 'The War Crime of Starvation' (n. 152), 815–47, at 816.

175 Saad Abedine, Hala Gorani, and Laura Smith-Spark, 'Syria: Reported Fatwa Allows the Hungry to Eat Cats and Dogs', *CNN* (18 October 2013), available at https://cnn.it/3qXb4BN, accessed 22 February 2022.

176 See Krieger and Martínez Soria, Chapter 4, 'Rationale and Challenges', in this volume. Heike Krieger and José Martínez Soria noted that most legal orders equate animals with tangible objects of which private property or public ownership is possible, and that therefore animals are covered by the rules on military or civilian objects, prohibitions against pillage and plunder and other property-related rules.

177 See Article 15 of GC IV.

3.7.6 Wild Animals

Wild animals may arguably be considered property of the state, or, if they live on private property, of the owner of the private property. If so, they may benefit from direct protection as civilian objects, in addition to the indirect protection arising from living in a zone protected from attacks. However, classing wild animals as property is contentious. For example, David Favre argues that wildlife is not property per se, even if governments can control access to it.[178] If not considered property, then wild animals would receive incidental protection based on their presence in an area that happened to be legally protected from attack. However, wild species may range over vast areas that will not necessarily coincide with the limits of protected zones. On leaving those confines, they will be legally bereft of any particular protections under IHL other than their potential characterization as civilians and the prohibitions against disproportionate harm to the environment.[179]

The direct and indirect impact of warfare on wild animals can be devastating. The ICRC has noted that 'from 1946 to 2010, conflict was the single most important predictor of declines in certain wildlife populations'.[180] These declines often reached existential levels. For example, '[d]uring the 15-year civil war in Mozambique, the Gorongosa National Park lost more than 90% of its animals'.[181]

Whilst they offer unique protection due to their area-based nature, protected zones themselves may exacerbate animal suffering in unintended ways. For instance, in 1994 Rwandan refugees ended up occupying areas previously largely unused by humans, depriving wild animals of their natural habitat essential to their thriving and survival. Many Rwandan refugees were relocated to the vicinity of the Virunga National Park in the Democratic Republic of Congo (DRC)[182] despite the fact that UNESCO conveyed to the UNHCR that utmost care had to 'be taken to avoid establishment of refugee camps in or near national parks.'[183] As a result 'every day an estimated 30,000 adults and children forage in the park with their machetes, emerging with loads averaging 40 pounds'.[184] Because of the threat to animals and their habitats posed by fighting and by the humans displaced by fighting, Virunga National Park was inscribed on the list of World Heritage in

178 David Favre, 'Living Property: A New Status for Animals within the Legal System', 93 *Marquette Law Review* 1021 (2009–2010), 1021–70, at 1044.

179 See, for example, Article 35(3) of AP I.

180 ICRC, 'Natural Environment' (n. 5), p. 1.

181 Ibid., 4.

182 The Virunga National Park was declared a world heritage site in 1979 because of its outstanding universal value due in part to its exceptional biodiversity ('the top African National Park for biological diversity'). See UNESCO, Virunga National Park Description (no date), available at https://whc.unesco.org/en/list/63/, accessed 22 February 2022.

183 UNESCO, World Heritage Committee report of its 18th session of 12–17 December 1994, WHC-94/CONF.003/16, 21.

184 Raymond Bonner, 'Flood of Rwanda Refugees is Destroying Ecological Treasure', *New York Times* (15 November 1994).

danger in 1994.[185] It has remained listed ever since, with repeated conflicts in the DRC extending hostilities to this renowned natural site.[186]

In the case of the Gorongosa National Park in Mozambique, animals were harmed not only by clashes between the right-wing RENAMO, or Resistência Nacional Moçambicana, rebel forces which took refuge there, and government forces, but also poaching by professional hunters and encroachment into the park by the 100,000 or so people living on its edges who mostly survived on subsistence farming.[187] The results were devastating; 'the African buffalo went down from 14,000 to 100 individuals, and the hippo population from 3,500 to 100 ... the elephant population declined from 2,000 to 200'.[188] Though the Gorongosa National Park did not fulfil the criteria for a protected zone per se, its fate demonstrates the ecocentric risks of bringing large numbers of humans into animal habitats.

4 LEGAL CONSEQUENCES OF VIOLATIONS OF PROTECTED ZONES

The Geneva Conventions do not list attacks against protected zones as grave breaches.[189] However, attacking protected zones, such as hospital zones and localities, could amount to several international crimes, including the war crime of '[i]ntentionally directing attacks against ... places where the sick and wounded are collected';[190] the war crime of '[a]ttacking or bombarding, by whatever means, towns, villages, dwellings or buildings which are undefended and which are not military objectives';[191] and attacks on the civilian population or objects or on buildings using the distinctive emblems of the GCs.[192] Additional Protocol I supports this criminalisation, as it includes 'making non-defended localities and demilitarized zones the object of attack' as grave breaches, 'when committed wilfully, in violation of the relevant provisions of this Protocol, and causing death or serious injury to body or health'.[193]

In the context of non-international armed conflicts, the ICRC's Customary International Humanitarian Law Study indicated that '[d]irecting an attack against a demilitarised zone agreed upon between the parties to the conflict is prohibited'

185 See World Heritage Committee, Decision CONF 003 IX (1–19), Monitoring of the State of Conservation of the World Heritage Cultural and Natural Properties, 18th session of the World Heritage Committee (CONF 003), 1994.

186 UNEP, *The Democratic Republic of the Congo: Post-Conflict Environmental Assessment: Synthesis for Policy Makers* (Nairobi: UNEP 2011), 26.

187 David Quammen, 'National Geographic: How one of Africa's Great Parks is Rebounding from War', *National Geographic* (May 2019).

188 ICRC, 'Natural Environment' (n. 5), 4.

189 Art. 50 of GC I; Art. 147 of GC IV. See also Ronzitti, 'Protected Areas' (n. 17), 385.

190 ICRC Commentary GC I (2016), para. 1908 (citing Art. 8(2)(b)(ix) and (e)(iv) of ICC Statute).

191 Ibid. (citing Art. 8(2)(b)(v) of ICC Statute). See also Art. 3(c) of ICTY Statute.

192 Ibid. (citing Art. 8(2)(b)(i), (e)(i), (b)(ii), and (b)(xxiv) and (e)(ii) of ICC Statute.

193 Art. 85(3)(d) of AP I.

and is a norm of customary international law, which would thereby be applicable in non-international armed conflicts and may form a basis for criminal prosecution.[194]

Aside from, and in addition to, criminal responsibility, violations of the IHL provisions and corresponding agreements concerning protected zones could provide a basis to seek reparations for the violation of IHL from the perpetrating state. Reparations may be sought, for example, pursuant to Article 3 of the 1907 Hague Convention IV and pursuant to Article 91 of AP I.[195] However, claims by individuals against states for acts harming the environment or animals will often be frustrated by considerations of sovereign immunity in foreign courts.[196]

5 CONCLUDING OBSERVATIONS AND RECOMMENDATIONS

As area-based constructs, protected zones bear a unique potential to shelter animals from hostilities. The ICJ has recognised the spatial dimension of the environment, noting that it 'is not an abstraction but represents the living space' of human beings, including future generations.[197] By attaching to an area, rather than any specific person therein, protected zones can obviate the need for contentious legal approaches, such as equating animals with human civilians. Yet the historical record indicates that even these area-based protections are no panacea for the threat posed to animals during armed conflict. Whereas the Korean DMZ demonstrates the ecological promise of protected zones,[198] other examples, such as in Rwanda, highlight the risk of causing severe ecological harm by drawing human populations to wildlife habitats.[199] This highlights a fundamental operational tension – the intended beneficiaries of protected zones (human beings) are the single greatest threat to animal survival.[200] Establishing protected zones in order to protect both humans and animals may be self-defeating, at least insofar as wild animals are concerned.[201] At the normative level, the use of protected zones to shelter non-humans is incongruous, as it clashes with the anthropogenic origins and orientation of IHL, which prioritise human interests over those of the environment.

Nonetheless, examples such as the Korean DMZ, indicate that the normative and operational tensions can be reconciled under specific conditions. They suggest that animals will prosper to a greater degree from separately established ecological zones,

194 ICRC Customary Law Database, Rule 36; Sivakumaran, *The Law of Non-international Armed Conflict* (n. 29), 384–5.

195 Ronzitti, 'Protected Areas' (n. 17), 386.

196 Ibid.

197 ICJ: *Nuclear Weapons* (n. 9), para. 29.

198 Kim, The Demilitarized Zone (DMZ) of Korea (n. 25), 172; Panel and Pietri *Environmental Consequences of the 1982 Falklands War* (n. 124) 4.

199 See above, Section 3.7.6.

200 Sean L. Maxwell et al., 'Biodiversity: The Ravages of Guns, Nets and Bulldozers', *Nature* 536 (2016), 143–5.

201 In relation to domestic animals at least, anthropocentric protected zones may be beneficial during times of war.

rather than through their co-mingling with human populations. Moreover, the analysis shows that establishing protected ecological zones prior to the outbreak of hostilities has legal basis under IHL that corresponds to the precepts of international environmental law and will enhance the impact of such zones during war.[202]

Operational measures that would increase the protections of these zones include identifying, in advance, the likely location of such zones and, to the extent humans and animals are to be co-located, ensuring they have the infrastructure to adequately protect the sheltered persons. Preparatory measures may also be taken to accommodate the needs of pets and other animals located in the protected zone. Any particularly vulnerable animal species or groups should be taken into consideration – for instance by delineating nature-only areas within the protected zone or by ensuring the presence of sufficient food and handlers for zoo animals. Agreements to respect protected zones should be obtained from all parties to the conflict, as gathering large numbers of animals in small areas could increase their exposure to harmful acts, in the same way that human populations sheltered in so-called safe zones have been rendered vulnerable to attack, as occurred in Srebrenica and Zepa in 1995.[203]

If the natural habitat of wild animals falls within a designated protected zone, measures should ensure that the sheltered persons, who will often increase significantly in number, do not encroach excessively onto those animals' habitats. This could be done through signage, information campaigns and monitoring. However, the natural habitats of wild animals will often fall outside any anthropocentric protected zone.[204] These animals should be permitted to remain in their natural habitats in all but the most extenuating circumstances. Again, given the advisability of allowing wild animals to remain in situ, it would be preferable to create designated ecocentric protected zones to shelter vulnerable animal populations during armed conflict, as opposed to using anthropocentric protected zones for this purpose.[205] The creation of a network of such zones could be achieved in a systematic manner through reliance on other pre-existing multilateral conventions and treaties such as the Convention on Biological Diversity and the World Heritage Convention.[206]

Based on the foregoing, one promising approach would be to establish animal protected zones for particularly valuable protected areas or threatened environmental hotspots, particularly those of outstanding universal value or areas of 'major

202 ICRC Environmental Guidelines (n. 17), 82–3.

203 Ronzitti, 'Protected Areas' (n. 17), 386.

204 Animals with extremely large natural habitats and migratory species will present additional complications in this respect.

205 But see Krieger and Martínez Soria, Chapter 4, 'Rationale and Challenges'. The authors argued that the anthropocentric versus ecocentric debate has lost relevance because 'any informed anthropocentric approach will be aware of and protect the interdependencies and complexities of ecological systems' and therefore protect those interests.

206 ICRC Environmental Guidelines (n. 17), 82.

environmental importance'.[207] The International Union for the Conservation of Nature has advocated for the adoption of a Draft Convention on the Prohibition of Hostile Military Activities in Protected Areas, according to which the UN Security Council would designate protected areas to be marked 'non-target' or demilitarised areas during conflicts, and a listing process would establish criteria to demarcate an 'international protected area'. However, to date, the Draft Convention has not been supported by the UN Security Council and has not been adopted.[208]

In a similar vein, the United Nations Environment Programme (UNEP) recommends the creation and adoption of a new legal regime 'for place-based protection of critical natural resources and areas of ecological importance during armed conflicts', incorporating precautionary measures prior to the commencement of active hostilities. As explained by UNEP, 'this could include protection for watersheds, groundwater aquifers, agricultural and grazing lands, parks, national forests, and the habitat of endangered species'.[209]

A broader approach would see 'a registry of protected areas . . . [based on] UN List of National Parks and Equivalent Reserves, the Ramsar Wetlands of International Importance, the UNESCO Biosphere Reserves, and the Council of Europe's Biogenic Reserves . . . adopted immediately'. For other areas not in these lists, studies would be required to determine their vulnerability to military activities.[210] This approach would bring together different registries drawn up under different standards by different institutions, thus contributing to the systemic harmonisation of international law and practice regarding the protection of the environment. In this respect, it has been noted that the ILC's Draft Principles could have drawn stronger links to 'environmental treaties such as the World Heritage Convention, the Ramsar Convention on International Wetlands and the Biological Diversity Convention'.[211]

Ultimately, the establishment of animal protection zones will become more pressing over the coming years for countries at war or facing the prospect of war. Whereas humans suffer during armed conflict, many animal species are disappearing from the face of the earth at a historically alarming rate. Assessing novel questions, such as the use of spatial concepts like protected zones to shelter animals, is critical in the search for legal protections that can mitigate the harmful impact of war on nature.

[207] See ILC Draft Principles (n. 8), Draft Principle 4. Several states expressed 'general support' for the inclusion of a draft principle on the designation of areas of major environmental and/or cultural importance as protected zones – including Denmark, Finland, Germany, Greece, Iceland, Iran, Italy, Morocco, Norway, Sweden, Peru and Portugal – whereas a small number of other states – including the Russian Federation and Turkey – expressed caution in this respect. See also ICRC Environmental Guidelines (n. 17), 83 (and references therein).

[208] UNEP, Protecting the Environment (n. 97), 20.

[209] Ibid.

[210] Schmitt, 'Green War' (n. 158), 25.

[211] Anne Dienelt and Britta Sjöstedt, 'Is the ILC's Work Enhancing Protection for the Environment in Relation to Warfare? A Reply to Stavros-Evdokimos Pantazopoulos and Karen Hulme', *Questions of International Law* (8 July 2017).

Such doctrinal assessments must remain cognisant of, and congruent with, the guiding principles of IHL, as emphasised in the preceding systematic analysis of the applicable provisions and principles of this domain. On this basis, they provide an opportunity to seek the normative harmonisation of international law, particularly between IHL and international environmental law, cultural heritage law and international criminal law, and thereby to reduce its fragmentation and consequent loss of coherence, respect and ultimately effectiveness.

The foregoing analysis demonstrates that protected zones have the potential to constitute a significant legal tool, capable of providing relief to animals from the harms of war. If crafted appropriately, with sufficient safeguards for humans and non-humans alike, they entail a unique form of protection for animals in war, which accords with the principles underlying IHL, as well as the related areas of international law aimed at the protection of nature and all its entities.

SELECT BIBLIOGRAPHY

Daskin, Joshua H, and Robert M. Pringle, 'Warfare and Wildlife Declines in Africa's Protected Areas', *Nature* 553 (2018), 328–32.

Kim, Kwi-Gon, *The Demilitarized Zone (DMZ) of Korea: Protection, Conservation and Restoration of a Unique Ecosystem* (Heidelberg: Springer 2013).

Maxwell, Sean L. et al., 'Biodiversity: The Ravages of Guns, Nets and Bulldozers', *Nature* 536 (2016), 143–5.

Pons, Niccolò, 'Animals', in Dražan Djukić and Niccolò Pons (eds.), *The Companion to International Humanitarian Law* (Leiden: Brill 2018).

Ronzitti, Natalino, 'Protected Areas', in Andrew Clapham, Paola Gaeta and Marco Sassòli (eds.), *The 1949 Geneva Conventions: A Commentary* (Oxford: Oxford University Press 2015), 369–87.

Roscini, Marco, 'Animals and the Law of Armed Conflict', 47 *Israeli Yearbook of Human Rights* 61 (2017), 35–67.

Schmitt, Michael N., 'Green War: An Assessment of the Environmental Law of Armed Conflict', *Yale Law Journal* 22 (1997), 1–110.

Sivakumaran, Sandesh, *The Law of Non-international Armed Conflict* (Oxford: Oxford University Press 2012).

Todeschini, Vito, 'Specially Protected Zones' in Dražan Djukić and Niccolò Pons (eds.), *The Companion to International Humanitarian Law* (Leiden: Brill 2018), 655–6.

15

Animals in Sea Warfare

Etienne Henry

It is an important and popular fact that things are not always what they seem. For instance, on the planet Earth, man had always assumed that he was more intelligent than dolphins because he had achieved so much – the wheel, New York, wars and so on – while all that dolphins had ever done was muck about in the water having a good time. But conversely, the dolphins had always believed that they were far more intelligent than man – for precisely the same reasons.

Douglas Adams, *The Hitchhiker's Guide to the Galaxy*[1]

1 INTRODUCTION

Even though a few international humanitarian law (IHL) norms do apply to animals, in particular those norms dealing with the protection of the environment, the law applicable to naval warfare – and the law of armed conflict in general[2] – only rarely regulates in explicit terms the treatment accorded to animal life. The fate of animals in sea warfare raises three interrelated sets of issues. The first two concern the fact that animals in warfare are vulnerable to both injury and death, either (1) when they take part in hostilities or (2) when they suffer the incidental consequences of attacks on military objectives.[3] Additionally, in the context of prize law, (3) some animals have historically been contraband goods, and thus susceptible to being seized when on board neutral vessels heading toward enemy ports.

This chapter provides a cursory analysis of the treatment of these issues under extant international law. In doing so it takes note of recent trends indicating a growing recognition that enhanced protection of animals is needed.[4] Without

[1] As quoted in Thomas I. White, *In Defense of Dolphins* (Oxford: Blackwell Publishing 2007), 117.

[2] See Jérôme de Hemptinne, 'The Protection of Animals During Warfare', *American Journal of International Law Unbound* 111 (2017), 272–6, at 272.

[3] See Karsten Nowrot, 'Animals at War: The Status of "Animal Soldiers" under International Humanitarian Law', *Historical Social Research* 40 (2015), 128–50, at 130; Marco Roscini, 'Animals and the Law of Armed Conflict', *Israel Yearbook on Human Rights* 47 (2017), 35–67, at 35–6.

[4] See, for example, Anne Peters, 'Global Animal Law: What It Is and Why We Need It', *Transnational Environmental Law* 5 (2016), 9–23.

adopting a definite position in the debate between the 'animal welfare' and 'animal rights' approaches, the chapter's concluding recommendations critically assess *lex lata* on the basis of pragmatic considerations. These recommendations call for an increased recognition of the inherent dignity of animals as sentient beings and for the creation of a *sui generis* status, separate from the classic dichotomy between movable things and persons under the law applicable to sea warfare.[5] An area where the law particularly needs reinterpretation and/or revision concerns the military use of marine mammals, which are usually considered to count among the most sentient beings on this planet, dolphins included. The normative basis for enhancing their protection is therefore not likely to raise major controversies.[6]

2 SCOPE OF APPLICATION OF THE LAW ON NAVAL WARFARE

Because of the influence of domestic legal orders, 'animals cannot but fall within the category of objects'[7] rather than persons – whether civilian or combatant. As will be seen below, this distinction is confirmed by the three sets of issues identified in this chapter: The military use of marine mammals (Section 2.1), animals as victims of naval conflicts (Section 2.2), and prize law (Section 2.3).

2.1 *The Use of Marine Mammals as a Means of Warfare?*

The use of animals in naval warfare for hostile purposes primarily concerns marine mammals.[8] Sea mammals have notoriously been used to accomplish military tasks,[9] such as mine-clearing operations,[10] recovering lost equipment,[11] intelligence gathering,[12]

[5] See, in this regard, Nowrot, 'Animals' (n. 3), 129; Gary L. Francione, 'Reflections on Animals, Property, and the Law and Rain without Thunder', *Law and Contemporary Problems* 70 (2007), 9–58.

[6] See, in this sense, Roscini, 'Animals' (n. 3), 67. See also White, *In Defense* (n. 1), x; de Hemptinne, Chapter 7 'Part of the Environment', in this volume.

[7] de Hemptinne, 'The Protection' (n. 2), 274.

[8] It was reported in early 2020 that France has launched a programme involving albatrosses for the purpose of detecting illegal fishing in its waters in the Indian Ocean. There is no indication that these birds could also serve military purposes. See Caroline Stevan, 'Des albatros recrutés pour détecter les pêcheurs illégaux', *Radio-Télévision suisse* (1 February 2020), available at https://bit.ly/3HiGbxh, accessed 22 February 2022.

[9] See, for various historical examples of World War I, including photographs of sea lions trained as 'U-Boat hunters', Lucinda Moore, *Animals in the Great War: Rare Photographs from Wartime Archives* (Barnsley: Pen & Sword Military 2017), 16–40.

[10] William Gasperini, 'Uncle Sam's Dolphins', *Smithsonian Magazine* (September 2003), available at https://bit.ly/3AIhV5m, accessed 22 February 2022 (referring to operations in Umm Qasr's harbour, Iraq).

[11] Jane J. Lee, 'Military Dolphins and Sea Lions: What Do They Do and Who Uses Them?', *National Geographic News* (29 March 2014), available at https://on.natgeo.com/307RWPJ, accessed 22 February 2022.

[12] See Rick Noack, 'Alleged Russian Spy Whale Is Refusing to Leave and Seeking Norwegians' Devotion, Authorities Say', *Washington Post* (5 February 2019), available at https://wapo.st/345KFZR, accessed 22 February 2022.

or in the defence of military locations like harbours.[13] Publicly available information on respective state practice is limited to the US, Russia, and perhaps Iran.[14] Despite their considerable length, neither the US government's 2016 *Law of War Manual*[15] nor the *Commander's Handbook on the Law of Naval Operations*[16] address legal issues raised by the military use of animals.

Other authors have rightly come to the conclusion that animals qualify as objects rather than persons.[17] If animals are used as agents of violence, the inescapable conclusion is that they qualify as a 'means of warfare' under Article 35(1) of Additional Protocol (AP) I.[18] The concept of 'means' of warfare is not explicitly defined in treaty law. Its origin, however, dates back at least to Article 12 of the Brussels Project of an International Declaration of 27 August 1874 concerning the Laws and Customs of War – the wording of which later served as the basis for Article 22 of the Hague Regulations. According to said provision, '[t]he right of belligerents to adopt *means of injuring the enemy* is not unlimited'.[19] The term has therefore been understood to refer to weapons, for the obvious reason that these are primarily used for the purpose of injuring the enemy. However, nothing in Article 35(1) of AP I prevents the inclusion of animals among means of warfare whenever they are used for hostile purposes.

2.2 *Animals as 'Victims' of Sea Warfare*

The very existence of navies – even during peace time – represents a threat to the environment, especially given the frequent exemption clauses for warships in treaties for the protection of the marine environment.[20] Naval combats can of course affect marine species directly, but indirect effects are also significant, for example through the destruction of the living ecosystems – such as coral

[13] See Josh Frey, 'Anti-Swimmer Dolphins Ready to Defend Gulf', *America's Navy* (12 August 2003), available at www.navy.mil/submit/display.asp?story_id=8978, accessed 8 May 2019.

[14] See the official page of the US Navy program, US Navy, 'US Navy Marine Mammal Program', *America's Navy*, available at https://bit.ly/3s7rEOv, accessed 10 May 2019. Concerning the use of marine mammals by the Russian Navy, see 'Crimean Military Dolphins to Serve in Russian Navy', *Sputnik News* (26 March 2014), available at https://bit.ly/3N94ykp, accessed 22 February 2022. See also White, *In Defense* (n. 1), 216. Thomas White writes that the USSR sold dolphins trained for military purposes to Iran. The annexation of Crimea is said to have put an end to the Ukrainian programme.

[15] US Department of Defense, *Law of War Manual* (Washington, DC: Office of General Counsel, US Department of Defense 2016).

[16] US Department of the Navy, *The Commander's Handbook on the Law of Naval Operations* (Arlington County, US Department of the Navy 2007).

[17] Roscini, 'Animals' (n. 3), 44–8. See also Nowrot, 'Animals' (n. 3), 137–8; Roscini, Chapter 5, 'Property and Objects'.

[18] See Jenks, Chapter 9, 'War Weapons'.

[19] Emphasis added.

[20] See, for example, Art. VII(4) of the London Convention on the Prevention of Marine Pollution by Dumping of Wastes and Other Matter of 29 December 1972, 1046 UNTS 138; Art. 236 of the UNCLOS; Art. 3(2) of the International Convention on the Control of Harmful Anti-fouling Systems on Ships of 18 October 2001, British Treaty Series No. 13 (2012).

reefs – that sustain them.[21] However, the pollution caused by the conduct of hostilities, whether it originates on land or sea, can also have devastating ecological consequences. Widely reported precedents in this regard include the massive spilling of crude oil as a result of the destruction of oil facilities, as occurred during the so-called tanker war between Iraq and Iran in the 1980s, in Kuwait in 1991, or more recently during the 2006 Lebanon War. But the sinking of warships is also reported as a potential cause of pollution. In 2018 for instance, the Norwegian government announced a project for capping the shipwreck of a World War II submarine in order to avoid mercury pollution.[22] More so, one is forced to contemplate with foreboding the disastrous consequences of targeting nuclear-powered warships, which potentially carry nuclear weapons as well. In this regard it is worth mentioning the Treaty of Moscow and Washington on the Prohibition of the Emplacement of Nuclear Weapons and Other Weapons of Mass Destruction on the Sea-Bed and the Ocean Floor and in the Subsoil Thereof,[23] applicable in all maritime spaces beyond twelve nautical miles from the coast.

The issue of war-related pollution raises the complex question of the extent to which environmental provisions remain applicable in times of armed conflict.[24] An answer to this question requires a case by case analysis, in particular taking into account the terms of each specific treaty, the position of the parties with respect of the armed conflict, including *jus contra bellum*, and the various maritime zones where different states exercise distinct degrees of jurisdiction.[25] A detailed examination of the matter would go beyond the scope of the present chapter.[26] There is,

[21] See, for example, reported cases of whales mistaken for submarines and killed by contact mines, Moore, *Animals* (n. 9), 36–7.

[22] See 'Environmental Solution for the Shipwreck of the WW II Submarine U-864', *Ministry of Transport and Communications* (15 October 2018), available at https://bit.ly/3IQQaud, accessed 22 February 2022.

[23] Treaty on the Prohibition of the Emplacement of Nuclear Weapons and Other Weapons of Mass Destruction on the Sea-Bed and the Ocean Floor and in the Subsoil Thereof of 11 February 1971, 955 UNTS 115.

[24] See, for further discussion, Julian Wyatt, 'Law-Making at the Intersection of International Environmental, Humanitarian and Criminal Law: The Issue of Damage to the Environment in International Armed Conflict', *International Review of the Red Cross* 92 (2010), 593–646. See also de Hemptinne, Chapter 7, 'Part of the Environment', in this volume.

[25] See ILC, Draft Articles on the Effects of Armed Conflicts on Treaties, in Report of the ILC on the work of its sixty-third session (26 April–3 June and 4 July–12 August 2011), A/66/10, *Yearbook of ILC, II, Part Two* (2011), 106–30.

[26] See, for a generally sceptical view, Natalino Ronzitti, 'Le droit humanitaire applicable aux conflits armés en mer', *Recueil des cours de l'Académie de droit international de La Haye* 242 (1993-V), 9–196, at 106–9; Wolff Heintschel von Heinegg and Michael Donner, 'New Developments in the Protection of the Natural Environment in Naval Armed Conflicts', *German Yearbook of International Law* 37 (1994), 281–314, at 298–300. See also, though not discarding altogether the relevance of UNCLOS, Thomas A. Mensah, 'Environmental Damages under the Law of the Sea Convention', in Jay E. Austin and Carl E Bruch (eds.), *The Environmental Consequences of War* (Cambridge: Cambridge University Press 2000), 226–49, at 248–9; Jinxing Ma and Shiyan Sun, 'Restrictions on

however, at least a rebuttable presumption that 'treaties relating to the international protection of the environment' and 'multilateral law-making treaties' are generally meant to remain applicable during armed conflict.[27] The general principle of Article 192 of the United Nations Convention on the Law of the Sea (UNCLOS) thus remains applicable: 'States have the obligation to protect and preserve the marine environment.'

Moreover, the existence of an armed conflict is not a sufficient ground to justify substantial transboundary pollution in areas under the jurisdiction of neutral states.[28] If hostilities take place in the Exclusive Economic Zones of neutral states, belligerents shall 'have due regard for the rights and duties of the coastal State, inter alia, for … the protection and preservation of the marine environment'.[29] Even though it is not mentioned in Article 87 of the UNCLOS – and despite the principle affirmed in Article 88 of the UNCLOS that '[t]he high seas shall be reserved for peaceful purposes' – it is usually understood that the conduct of hostilities counts among the 'freedoms' of the high seas, whereby belligerents have only a duty to respect the rights of exploration and exploitation of natural resources by neutral states in areas beyond national jurisdiction.[30]

When they are not used to perform military tasks, animals arguably qualify as civilian objects, either as an 'enemy's property'[31] or as part of the natural environment.[32] Their protection under *lex lata* therefore results primarily from the application of the general principles applicable to the law of targeting, such as military necessity, distinction, precautions in attack, proportionality, and the more specific rules derived therefrom.[33] Furthermore, animals are also conferred protection by rules applicable more specifically to the protection of the environment. In this regard, two instruments deserve mention: the Environmental Modification (ENMOD) Convention and Articles 35(3) and 55(1) of AP I. The relevance of the latter provision is, however, curtailed by Article 49(3) of AP I, which specifies that it

the Use of Force at Sea: An Environmental Protection Perspective', *International Review of the Red Cross* 98 (2016), 515–41, at 527–9.

27 ILC, Draft Articles on the Effects of Armed Conflicts on Treaties (n. 25), 107–8, Art. 7 and Annex.

28 See ICJ, *Legality of the Threat or Use of Nuclear Weapons*, advisory opinion of 8 July 1996, ICJ Reports 1996, paras. 93–4.

29 San Remo Manual on International Law Applicable to Armed Conflicts at Sea, prepared by international lawyers and naval experts convened by the International Institute of Humanitarian Law, adopted in Livorno in June 1994 (San Remo Manual), para. 34. See also, concerning the laying of mines, ibid., para. 35.

30 Ibid., para. 36.

31 Article 23(g) of the Hague Regulations.

32 See de Hemptinne, Chapter 7, 'Part of the Environment', in this volume.

33 See UN Secretary-General, UN Decade of International Law: Report of the Secretary-General, 19 August 1994, A/49/323, Annex: Guidelines for Military Manuals and Instructions on the Protection of the Environment in Times of Armed Conflict, 49, para. 4. See also ICRC Customary Law Database, Rule 43; ILC, Draft Principles on the Protection of the Environment in Relation to Armed Conflict (2019), reproduced in Report of the UN General Assembly, ILC, Seventy-first session (29 April–7 June and 8 July–9 August 2019), A/74/10, Chap. VI.

applies only to the effects that sea operations have on the land or to attacks directed from the sea against objectives located on land.

Finally, the use of animals to perform military tasks raises the issue of their treatment upon capture and subsequent detention. As discussed in Section 3.1, there is no obvious ground to confer to animals the treatment afforded to prisoners of war under a strict interpretation of extant law, as animals are not persons under *lex lata*.

2.3 *Animals and Prize Law*

Animals that qualify as contraband are liable to capture when found on neutral merchant vessels headed for enemy ports. Historically, horses were considered contraband.[34] According to Article 22(7) of the London Declaration of 26 February 1909 concerning the Laws of Naval War, '[s]addle, draught, and pack animals suitable for use in war' found on neutral merchant vessels may be 'treated as contraband of war, under the name of absolute contraband'.[35] More recently, foodstuffs were sometimes included in the category of conditional contraband – a category, though now abandoned in practice, encompassing things that could but did not necessarily serve a belligerent purpose – including livestock.[36]

According to the most recent restatement of the law, '[c]ontraband is defined as goods which are ultimately destined for territory under the control of the enemy and which may be susceptible for use in armed conflict'.[37] Animals trained or purported to be used for the accomplishment of military tasks, such as sea mammals, navy or war dogs, or homing pigeons are therefore liable to be captured as contraband, provided that they have been mentioned in lists published by the captor state.[38] Conversely, animals purported to serve as foodstuff for the civilian population or pet animals (including mascots) are deemed 'free goods' and are therefore not liable to capture.[39] Given the dubious relevance of prize law as it currently stands for

34 See, with references to major international treaties from the seventeenth and eighteenth centuries, including the treaty of Utrecht, Ludwig Gessner, *Le droit des neutres sur mer* (2nd ed., Paris: Librairie Guillaumin et Cie; Paul Ollendorff 1876), 86–7. See also Elihu Lauterpacht, 'The Hague Regulations and the Seizure of *Munitions de Guerre*', *British Yearbook of International Law* 32 (1955–6), 218–43, at 227; Douglas Howland, 'Contraband and Private Property in the Age of Imperialism', *Journal of the History of International Law* 13 (2011), 117–53, at 118.

35 During the 1909 London Naval Conference, the UK and Japan expressed the view that horses should have been considered as conditional contraband. See James Brown Scott (ed.), *The Declaration of London, February 26, 1909: A Collection of Official Papers and Documents Relating to the International Naval Conference Held in London, December, 1908–February, 1909* (Oxford: Oxford University Press 1919), 199, 216 and 239.

36 See, with reference to the '*viandes sur pied ou abattues*', Henri Fromageot, 'Les vivres considérés comme contrebande de guerre', *Journal du droit international privé et de la jurisprudence comparée* 27 (1900), 29–48, at 32.

37 Para. 148 of the San Remo Manual (n. 29).

38 Ibid., para. 149.

39 Ibid., para. 150.

contemporary armed conflicts,[40] as well as the limited practice of maritime transportation of live animals, the matter will not be further discussed in this chapter.

3. CONTENTS AND LIMITS OF THE LAW ON NAVAL WARFARE

3.1 *Marine Mammals Directly Participating in Hostilities?*

The classification of animals used for hostile purposes as means of warfare implies, in particular, that they can be deployed only if they are able to distinguish between military objectives and civilian objects or persons.[41] A further implication is that when they are used to perform tasks of a military nature animals qualify as 'military objectives', under the customary definition reflected in Article 52(2) of AP I, and can therefore be attacked[42] whenever they 'make an effective contribution to military action' and when their 'total or partial destruction, capture or neutralization, in the circumstances ruling at the time, offers a definite military advantage'.[43] In the context of naval warfare, activities such as mine-sweeping[44], intelligence gathering,[45] and the carrying of military material[46] are typically construed as 'mak[ing] an effective contribution to military action'.

Regarding the means used in fighting animals, belligerents who suspect that the enemy is deploying cetaceans trained for military purposes might, for instance, be tempted to use sonar as a weapon to disable them. There is indeed increasing evidence that some types of military sonar dangerously affect cetaceans and have already been the likely cause of mass stranding events.[47] According to a 2010 report by the International Whaling Commission, sonar could be responsible for up to

[40] See, in this sense, Steven Haines, 'War at Sea: Nineteenth-Century Laws for Twenty-First Century Wars?', *International Review of the Red Cross* 98 (2016), 419–47, at 431–2 and 438–40.

[41] See, for further discussion, Chapter 10: 'Animals as Combatants and as Prisoners of War?'. Some authors have expressed doubts in this respect. See Nowrot, 'Animals' (n. 3), 139; de Hemptinne, 'The Protection' (n. 2), 274.

[42] See Yoram Dinstein, *The Conduct of Hostilities under the Law of International Armed Conflict* (3rd ed., Cambridge: Cambridge University Press 2016), 106; Ian Henderson, *The Contemporary Law of Targeting* (Leiden: Martinus Nijhoff 2009), 43.

[43] See San Remo Manual (n. 29), para. 40. See also Art. 52(2) of AP I (as a reflection on customary international law on the matter).

[44] Para. 60(a) of the San Remo Manual (n. 29).

[45] Ibid., paras. 60(c) and 70(d).

[46] Ibid., paras. 60(g) and 70(e).

[47] See Antonio Fernández et al., '"Gas and Fat Embolic Syndrome" Involving a Mass Stranding of Beaked Whales (Family Ziphiidae) Exposed to Anthropogenic Sonar Signals', *Veterinary Pathology* 42 (2005), 446–57; Ronald Filadelfo et al., 'Correlating Military Sonar Use with Beaked Whale Mass Strandings: What Do the Historical Data Show?', *Aquatic Mammals* 35 (2009), 435–44; Antonio Fernández, Manuel Arbelo and Martín Vidal, 'No Mass Strandings since Sonar Ban: Whales', *Nature* 497 (2013), 317; Whitney Campbell, 'Loud and Clear: Marine Mammals and Military Sonar', *Green Screen: Emerging Research Impacting Earth's Environment* (30 May 2013), available at https://go.nature.com/3KWKpNg, accessed 22 February 2022.

22 per cent of stranding events from 1982 to 2007.[48] If belligerents cannot ensure that no other cetaceans are swimming in the relevant area, the use of sonar as a weapon would be characterised by its indiscriminate effects and therefore forbidden.[49] Furthermore, such use of sonar would likely 'render death inevitable' in the sense of the Preamble of the Saint Petersburg Declaration of 29 November/11 December 1868 Renouncing the Use, in Time of War, of Explosive Projectiles Under 400 Grammes Weight and would therefore run against the prohibition of 'means and methods of warfare which are of a nature to cause superfluous injury or unnecessary suffering'.[50] As a matter of strict law, however, the principle of unnecessary suffering is not applicable to the targeting of animals, as opposed to enemy combatants.

A reference to the terms of the 'Martens clause' would nonetheless support the application of the principle to sentient animals. According to the clause, as it appears in Article 1(2) of AP I: 'In cases not covered by this Protocol or by other international agreements, civilians and combatants remain under the protection and authority of the principles of international law derived from established custom, from the principles of humanity and from the dictates of public conscience.'[51] Indeed, and despite the essentially humanistic, and therefore putatively anthropocentric, intellectual origins of the clause, reference to the latter in the context of environmental protection seems warranted.[52] In particular, it seems that there are increasing

48 See Michael Stachowitsch, Naomi A. Rose and E. C. M. Parsons (eds.), *State of the Cetacean Environment Report (SOCER) 2010* (International Whaling Commission 2010), SC/62/E1, 13.

49 See para. 42(b) of the San Remo Manual (n. 29).

50 ICRC Customary Law Database, Rule 70.

51 See Giovanni Distefano and Etienne Henry, 'Final Provisions, Including the Martens Clause', in Andrew Clapham, Paola Gaeta and Marco Sassòli (eds.), *The 1949 Geneva Conventions: A Commentary* (Oxford: Oxford University Press 2015), 155–88, at 183–5.

52 See UN Secretary General, UN Decade of International Law (n. 33), 50, para. 7. See also Richard A. Falk, 'Environmental Welfare and Ecocide Facts, Appraisal and Proposals', *Revue belge de droit international* 9 (1973), 1–27, at 5; Michael Bothe, 'The Protection of the Environment in Times of Armed Conflict', *German Yearbook of International Law* 34 (1991), 54–62, at 56; Betsy Baker, 'Legal Protections for the Environment in Times of Armed Conflict', *Virginia Journal of International Law* 33 (1992), 351–84, at 352; Wil D. Verwey, 'Protection of the Environment in Times of Armed Conflict: In Search of a New Legal Perspective', *Leiden Journal of International Law* 8 (1995), 7–40, at 21–4; Dinah Shelton and Alexandre Kiss, 'Martens Clause for Environmental Protection', *Environmental Policy and Law* 30 (2000), 285–6, at 285; Elizabeth Mrema, Carl Bruch and Jordan Diamond, *Protecting the Environment during Armed Conflict: An Inventory and Analysis of International Law* (Nairobi: UNEP 2009), 12; Michael Bothe et al., 'International Law Protecting the Environment during Armed Conflict: Gaps and Opportunities', *International Review of the Red Cross* 92 (2010), 569–92, at 588–9; Art. 36(2) of the Draft International Covenant on Environment and Development of the International Union for Conservation of Nature (IUCN), in IUCN, The World Conservation Union et al., *Draft International Covenant on Environment and Development* (4th ed., Gland and Bonn: IUCN Environmental Law Programme; International Council of Environmental Law 2010), 14; Cordula Droege and Marie-Louise Tougas, 'The Protection of the Natural Environment in Armed Conflict: Existing Rules and Need for Further Legal Protection', *Nordic Journal of International Law* 82 (2013), 21–52, at 40; Ma and Su, 'Restrictions' (n. 26), 541; ILC, Protection of the Environment in Relation to Armed Conflicts (n. 33), Draft Principle 12. See, for a more sceptical view, Harry

elements of state practice and public opinion pointing towards the need for increased respect for elementary considerations of animal welfare as a manifestation of the 'dictates of public conscience'.[53]

Upon capture, animals are neither conferred protection comparable to the treatment of prisoners of war[54] nor do they have the right to receive veterinary treatment in case they have been injured or are sick. As far as they qualify as booty of war, and can therefore be appropriated by the captor state, the latter would even be entitled to slaughter them on the spot.[55] This could happen in cases where the captors do not have the ability to keep marine mammals in captivity and want to prevent them from returning to their masters if released. This resonates with the long-standing debates on the alleged right to kill prisoners of war in analogous situations of 'necessity' before the adoption of the Hague Regulations.[56]

3.2 *Animals as Victims of Sea Warfare*

The ENMOD Convention was largely inspired by the use of chemical agents in counterinsurgency operations – especially during the Vietnam War. The convention purports to prohibit the deliberate use of 'military or any other hostile use of environmental modification techniques having widespread, long-lasting or severe effects'.[57] In this context, the term 'widespread' is defined as 'encompassing an area on the scale of several hundred square kilometres'; 'long-lasting' means 'lasting for a period of months, or approximately a season'; and 'severe' means 'involving serious or significant disruption or harm to human life, natural and economic resources or other assets'.[58] Tsunamis are expressly considered phenomena that could be caused

H. Almond, 'Weapons, War and the Environment', *Georgetown International Environmental Law Review* 3 (1990), 117–82, at 163.

53 See, in this sense, Roscini, 'Animals' (n. 3), 52–6. See, arguing that the protection of animal welfare has become a general principle of law, Katie Sykes, 'Nations Like unto Yourselves: An Inquiry into the Status of a General Principle of International Law on Animal Welfare', *Canadian Yearbook of International Law* 49 (2011), 3–50. See also Leslie C. Green, 'The Environment and the Law of Conventional Warfare', *Canadian Yearbook of International Law* 29 (1991), 222–37, at 225. The wording of the Martens clause does not, however, require establishing the existence of a general principle of law, as it explicitly calls for an assessment of public opinion. See Michael Byers, *War Law: International Law and Armed Conflict* (London: Atlantic Books 2005), 122.

54 For a discussion on the applicability of the status of combatant and prisoner of war to animals, see also de Hemptinne, Kebebew and Niyo, Chapter 10, 'Combatants and as Prisoners of War?', in this volume.

55 ICRC Customary Law Database, Rule 49. See also Jean-Marie Henckaerts and Louise Doswald-Beck (eds.), *Customary International Humanitarian Law, Volume I: Rules* (Cambridge: CUP 2005), 174: 'Practice . . . indicates that booty may be used without restriction and does not have to be returned to the adversary.'

56 See Etienne Henry, *Le principe de nécessité militaire: Histoire et actualité d'une norme fondamentale du droit international humanitaire* (Paris: Pedone 2017), 157, 222 and 326–7.

57 Art. 1(1) of the ENMOD Convention.

58 UN General Assembly, Report of the Conference of the Committee on Disarmament, Vol. I, Official Records, Thirty-First Session, Supplement No. 27, 1976, A/31/27, 91.

by the use of environmental modification techniques,[59] even though it was admitted at the time that no state had the capacity to deliberately cause a tsunami.[60]

Under Article 35(3) of AP I, '[i]t is prohibited to employ methods or means of warfare which are intended, or may be expected, to cause widespread, long-term and severe damage to the natural environment'. The qualifiers in this sentence have been understood as having a different meaning to those in the ENMOD Convention, thus setting a much higher threshold of application for Article 35(3) of AP I. For instance, '"long-term" was interpreted as a matter of decades'.[61] They are also meant to apply cumulatively rather than alternatively.[62] In contrast to the ENMOD Convention, Article 35(1) of AP I can apply to damage not caused deliberately if there was previous knowledge of the likelihood of the damage, as indicated by the phrase 'or may be expected, to cause'. As a result, incidental collateral damages are prohibited even if they are not 'excessive in relation to the concrete and direct military advantage anticipated', so long as they are 'widespread, long-term and severe'.[63] In this context, the concrete assessment of what might be expected should be informed by relevant developments in scientific knowledge, with the consequence that an action that is considered as in compliance with the requirement of Article 35(1) of AP I at some point in time might well turn out not be at a later point, if scientific research renders evident the widespread, long-term and severe nature of a kind of damage previously thought not to be so.[64]

Given the limited reach of provisions especially dealing with the environment, a cursory look at the general regime applicable to targeting is warranted. As already briefly mentioned, the principle of distinction requires that military objectives and civilian objects are distinguished, including, of course, animals.[65] In particular, animals must not be made the object of direct attacks, unless they have become military objectives as a result of their involvement in hostilities.[66] Thus, the 'preventive' targeting of wild or domesticated marine mammals kept for entertainment or research purposes would never be allowed. Moreover, belligerent parties must take all feasible precautions to avoid causing incidental 'damage' to animals.[67] This

59 Ibid., 92.

60 Ibid., 74, para. 337 (Federal Republic of Germany). See also, for the view that the ENMOD Convention does 'not even reflect existing capabilities', Yoram Dinstein, 'Protection of the Environment in International Armed Conflict', *Max Planck Yearbook of United Nations Law* 5 (2001), 523–50, at 530.

61 AP I Commentary, para. 1452.

62 Ibid., para. 1457.

63 See Dinstein, 'Protection' (n. 60), 536.

64 Ibid., 533.

65 San Remo Manual (n. 29), para. 39.

66 Ibid., para. 41. See also ILC, Protection of the Environment in Relation to Armed Conflicts (n. 33), Draft Principle 13(3).

67 San Remo Manual (n. 29), para. 46. See also ibid., para. 44. In this sense, see IUCN, The World Conservation Union et al., *Draft International Covenant* (n. 52), 13, Art. 36(1)(b); Ma and Su, 'Restrictions' (n. 26), 539.

is especially true with regards to protected species.[68] A useful tool for the implementation of this obligation of 'due regard' is to agree on the creation of protected zones where no combat will take place, especially 'in marine areas containing: (a) Rare or fragile ecosystems; or (b) the habitat of depleted, threatened or endangered species or other forms of marine life'.[69]

Under the principle of military necessity and as a minimum threshold, the 'destruction of the environment, not justified by military necessity and carried out wantonly, is clearly contrary to existing international law'.[70] Arguably this principle prohibits the causation of militarily unnecessary harm in a much broader and all-encompassing fashion and, where several courses of actions are conducive to a similar military advantage, imposes the least harmful among them to be chosen.[71] Thus whenever feasible in concrete situations, belligerents should consider capturing rather than killing marine mammals used as 'weapons' by the enemy. The incidental maiming or killing of animals is regulated by the principle of proportionality in attack. According to Article 51(5)(b) of AP I, an attack is to be considered indiscriminate – and therefore unlawful – if it 'may be expected to cause incidental loss of civilian life, injury to civilians, damage to civilian objects, or a combination thereof, which would be excessive in relation to the concrete and direct military advantage anticipated.'

Furthermore, it is well-established that: 'States must take environmental considerations into account when assessing what is necessary and proportionate in the pursuit of legitimate military objectives. Respect for the environment is one of the elements that go to assessing whether an action is in conformity with the principles of necessity and proportionality.'[72] From a macro perspective, all animal species considered an essential component of the natural environment are granted protection against eradication under the principle of proportionality. The operationalisation of the proportionality test is, however, beset with difficulties, resulting, inter alia, from the scientific expertise required to assess the risks to the marine environment.[73] Here again it should be stressed that, as far as possible, state-of-the-art scientific knowledge and the risk of long-term damage should be taken into account. The fact that some animal species are specifically protected in international instruments indicates that risks to their well-being should carry a special weight in the context of the proportionality assessment.[74] Indeed, according to paragraph 13(c) of the San

68 See, in this sense, de Hemptinne, 'The Protection' (n. 2), 275.

69 San Remo Manual (n. 29), para. 11. See also ILC, Protection of the Environment in Relation to Armed Conflicts (n. 33), Draft Principle 17.

70 UN General Assembly Resolution 47/37 of 9 February 1993, Protection of the Environment in Times of Armed Conflict, A/47/37. See also San Remo Manual (n. 29), para. 44.

71 See Henry, *Le principe* (n. 56), 529–680.

72 ICJ, Nuclear Weapons (n. 28), para. 30. See also ILC, Protection of the Environment in Relation to Armed Conflicts (n. 33), Draft Principle 15.

73 See Henry, *Le principe* (n. 56), 609–16 and references. See also de Hemptinne, 'The Protection' (n. 2), 274.

74 See de Hemptinne, 'The Protection' (n. 2), 275.

Remo Manual, '"collateral" casualties or collateral damage means the loss of life of, or injury to, civilians or other protected persons, and damage to or the destruction of the *natural environment* or objects that are not in themselves military objectives.'[75] However, as has been forcefully argued in another context,[76] the constraints of necessity and proportionality are likely to be of limited relevance in practice, given that animals as 'objects' are susceptible to be attributed a relatively minor weight in the equation.

From a micro perspective, that is beyond the species' survival, should the welfare of individual sentient animals be considered in the proportionality assessment? This issue overlaps in part with the question of the applicability of the prohibition of unnecessary suffering. Again, while in strict law animal welfare is not covered, an extensive application is warranted by recourse to the 'dictates of public conscience'.[77]

4 LEGAL CONSEQUENCES OF A VIOLATION OF THE LAW ON NAVAL WARFARE

The criminal repression of grave breaches of IHL and war crimes does not appear to present problems that are specific to sea warfare.[78] Regarding the responsibility of states and international organisations for internationally wrongful acts, difficulties might arise when identifying injured states in cases where the causation of unlawful damages to wildlife occurs in spaces beyond national jurisdiction, namely on the high seas or in the Area.[79] As far as the latter is concerned, the International Tribunal on the Law of the Sea (ITLOS) noted the *erga omnes* character of the obligations flowing from the regime applicable to the Area as a 'common heritage of mankind' under Part XI of the UNCLOS.[80] It held that '[s]ubjects entitled to claim compensation may include the Authority, entities engaged in deep seabed mining, other users of the sea, and coastal States'.[81]

5 CONCLUDING RECOMMENDATIONS

As reflected above, *lex lata* provides optimal protection neither for animals considered as a constitutive part of the marine environment[82] nor for animals in

75 Louise Doswald-Beck (ed.), *San Remo Manual on International Law Applicable to Armed Conflicts at Sea* (Cambridge: Cambridge University Press 1995), 85 (emphasis added).

76 See Francione, 'Reflections' (n. 5), 9–10 and 35–6.

77 See, in this sense, de Hemptinne, 'The Protection' (n. 2), 275.

78 See Ventura, Chapter 18, 'International Crimes', in this volume.

79 Art. 1(1) of UNCLOS (n. 20) defines the Area as 'the seabed and ocean floor and subsoil thereof, beyond the limits of national jurisdiction'.

80 International Tribunal for the Law of the Sea, *Responsibilities and Obligations of States with Respect to Activities in the Area*, advisory opinion of 1 February 2011, ITLOS Reports 2011, 59, para. 180.

81 Ibid., para. 179.

82 See also Ma and Su, 'Restrictions' (n. 26), 516.

themselves considered as sentient beings. This state of the law does not reflect the growing recognition that enhanced protection is necessary. Although some of the deficiencies could be remedied through a progressive interpretation of relevant norms, there is no certainty that military commanders will effectively do so. Moreover, it appears that difficulties arise mainly as a result of the qualification of animals as objects. As far as animals are used for the performance of military tasks, this qualification seems somewhat counterintuitive. Indeed, commentators tend to use terms designed for persons when referring to the use of animal 'combatants'.[83]

The extension of the status of combatant to animals 'taking a direct part in hostilities' would provide the important benefit of ensuring them protection against superfluous injury and unnecessary suffering.[84] It would also entail, so the argument goes, an obligation to treat sentient animals 'humanely' upon capture, including through the provision of food and veterinary care. However, it would bring with it the disadvantage – at least from a military standpoint – of obligating 'animal combatants' to wear distinctive signs and markers in order to comply with the requirement of Article 44(3) of AP I.[85] In this regard, the use of marine animals is comparable to the case of amphibious operations.[86]

The analogy with human combatants is nevertheless inappropriate in several respects. First, it is highly questionable whether animals should enjoy some form of citizenship status, resulting in bonds of allegiance with a specific state.[87] If that were the case, one could argue that animals should not be forced to switch sides as a result of capture under Article 23(h) of the Hague Regulations and Article 51 of GC IV. But I fail to see what criteria should be used to determine the nationality of marine animals, given that their ecosystems are largely situated in areas beyond state jurisdiction. Indeed, marine mammals are sometimes bought on the international market.[88] It would be ethically questionable to consider that the simple transfer of propriety rights could entail the creation of a bond of allegiance towards the buyer, unless one accepts the analogy with the nationality of slaves. Moreover, given that navies largely contribute to the killing of marine mammals even in peacetime, one can seriously doubt whether marine mammals would knowingly adhere to the purposes of the selfsame institutions that threaten their very existence. Their first 'political right' in this regard, if there is any, would arguably be the freedom not to take part and not to be negatively affected by human warfare.

From a normative standpoint, the concept of 'agency' arguably plays an important underlying role in the context of the law on targeting: if someone decides to become

83 Nowrot, 'Animals' (n. 3), 135.
84 See de Hemptinne, 'The Protection' (n. 2), 275–6.
85 It appears that the 'innocent' appearance of animals indeed constitutes a military advantage, especially when marine mammals are used for intelligence collection.
86 See Ronzitti, 'Le droit humanitaire' (n. 26), 41–3.
87 But see Nowrot, 'Animals' (n. 3), 132–3.
88 See Karin Brulliard, 'Russia's Military is Recruiting Dolphins, and their Mission is a Mystery', *Washington Post* (3 November 2016), available at https://wapo.st/3gbrQH7, accessed 22 February 2022.

a combatant or to take an active part in hostilities, then this person will be liable to attack by enemy armed forces. My point here is not to deny that some animals have advanced forms of intelligence and have some degree of agency, but rather to question whether any animal has the capacity to knowingly decide on such far-reaching issues as enrolment in a state's armed forces. It is true that, as a result of domestic legislations on conscription, soldiers do not always freely choose to become a member of the armed forces.[89] But they are at least aware that their condition as combatants exposes them to attack. Like children, marine mammals are likely not even able to appreciate the risks they are taking until placed in – and suffering the consequences of – a real combat situation.[90] The inescapable conclusion, in terms of progressive development of international law, would therefore be a prohibition on the military use of marine mammals.[91] Such an objective does not appear totally unrealistic given the limited numbers of states involved in such practices and the alternative options increasingly offered by the deployment of unmanned maritime systems.[92]

In addition, I have formulated the following recommendations aimed at the enhancement of animal welfare in the context of sea warfare. First, the creation of a *sui generis* status for sentient animals with the object and purpose of extending to them the protection conferred by the principle of superfluous injury and unnecessary suffering and the right to be treated 'humanely' upon capture. Second, given the harm that they cause to cetaceans, there is also a need for a regulation or, if need be, a prohibition on the use of some kinds of military sonar, even in peacetime.[93] Third, as already mentioned in Section 3.2,[94] belligerents are strongly encouraged to agree, on an ad hoc basis, on the creation of protected zones where no combat activities are to take place.

SELECT BIBLIOGRAPHY

Doswald-Beck, Louise (ed.), *San Remo Manual on International Law Applicable to Armed Conflicts at Sea* (Cambridge: Cambridge University Press 1995).

Ma, Jinxing and Shiyan Sun, 'Restrictions on the Use of Force at Sea: An Environmental Protection Perspective', *International Review of the Red Cross* 98 (2016), 515–41.

Roscini, Marco, 'Animals and the Law of Armed Conflict', *Israel Yearbook on Human Rights* 47 (2017), 35–67.

White, Thomas I., *In Defense of Dolphins* (Oxford: Blackwell Publishing 2007).

89 See Nowrot, 'Animals' (n. 3), 133.

90 See also de Hemptinne, Kebebew and Niyo, Chapter 10, 'Combatants and as Prisoners of War?', in this volume.

91 See, in this sense, Philip Hoare, 'Let Slip the Dolphins of War', *New York Times* (20 December 2017), available at https://nyti.ms/3rcy2Fc, accessed 22 February 2022. See also White, *In Defense* (n. 1), 216–17.

92 See Michael N. Schmitt and David S. Goddard, 'International Law and the Military Use of Unmanned Maritime Systems', *International Review of the Red Cross* 98 (2016), 567–92.

93 See Tom Batchelor, 'Scientists Demand Military Sonar Ban to End Mass Whale Strandings', *Independent* (30 January 2019), available at https://bit.ly/30dndRg, accessed 22 February 2022.

94 See above n. 69 and accompanying text.

16

Animals in Disaster Situations

Giulio Bartolini[*]

1 INTRODUCTION

As maintained in the introduction to this volume, '[t]he impact of armed conflict on wildlife is often acknowledged, but its scale is largely underestimated ... Livestock and companion animals, which are highly dependent on human care, are also direct victims of hostilities'.[1] A similar statement could be replicated for disasters.[2]

When viewed from an anthropocentric perspective, the impact that disasters have on animals implies particularly negative consequences for affected communities, especially in terms of food security in the Global South.[3] However, in line with the research agenda of this volume, which explores the 'preservation of the interests of animals'[4] based on an 'emerging recognition in international law that animals have some significance in themselves and as individual beings',[5] it is imperative we recognise that disasters represent a challenge for

* This research is part of the activities of the Jean Monnet Project 'Disseminating Disaster Law for Europe'.

1 See Peters and de Hemptinne, Chapter 1, 'Wartime', in this volume.

2 According to Article 3(a) of the Draft Articles on the Protection of Persons in the Event of Disasters, a disaster means 'a calamitous event or series of events resulting in widespread loss of life, great human suffering and distress, mass displacement, or large-scale material or environmental damage, thereby seriously disrupting the functioning of society'. The commentary on this definition excludes armed conflicts from this definition. See UN General Assembly, Report of the ILC, Sixty-eight session, 2 May–10 June and 4 July–12 August 2016, A/71/10, 22, para. 2. Similarly, the UN excluded armed conflicts from the notion of a hazard capable of generating a disaster. See UN General Assembly, Report of the Open-Ended Intergovernmental Expert Working Group on Indicators and Terminology Relating to Disaster Risk Reduction, 1 December 2016, A/71/644, 22. See also Giulio Bartolini, 'A Taxonomy of Disasters in International Law', in Flavia Zorzi Giustiniani et al. (ed.), *Routledge Research Handbook of Human Rights and Disasters* (London: Routledge 2018), 10–26.

3 For more information, see Roderick Campbell and Tristan Knowles, 'The Economic Impacts of Losing Livestock in a Disaster: Final Report Prepared for the World Society for the Protection of Animals', *Economists at Large* (2011), available at https://bit.ly/35DcWHH, accessed 22 February 2022; UN Food and Agriculture Organization, '2017: The Impact of Disasters and Crises on Agriculture and Food Security' (2018), available at www.fao.org/3/I8656EN/i8656en.pdf, accessed 22 February 2022.

4 See Peters and de Hemptinne, Chapter 1, 'Wartime', in this volume.

5 Katie Sykes, 'Nations Like unto Yourselves: An Inquiry into the Status of a General Principle of International Law on Animal Welfare', *Canadian Yearbook of International Law* 49 (2011), 3–50, at 10.

animals as well.[6] Estimates related to animal deaths emphasise heavy consequences both for wild animals, which the approximately 500 million deaths attributed to Australia's 2019–20 wildfires sadly attests to,[7] and domesticated livestock, exemplified by the 2010 Pakistan floods in which 1.2 million ruminants and 6 million poultry died.[8] Additionally slow onset disasters such as droughts have severe impacts on animals. Furthermore, animal losses are not factored into disaster management activities. During Hurricane Katrina in the United States in 2005, for example, around 70,000 animals lost their lives because evacuations occurred without safeguarding the lives or well-being of people's pets.[9] Disaster settings, therefore, represent an additional test case for analyses grounded on the recognition of animals as sentient beings[10] and consequently allow us to explore measures guaranteeing the well-being of animals and thus adding an additional layer to current research in global animal law studies.[11] Trained animals, particularly dogs, also play a unique role during disasters through their involvement in search and rescue operations, including cross-border operations. The legal framework related to the use of rescue dogs during disasters might therefore represent a complementary scenario for issues around armed conflict analysed in this volume.[12]

Against this background, Section 2 of this chapter will examine how issues explored elsewhere in this volume related to armed conflicts[13] have been analysed in disaster settings, paying particular attention to instruments and initiatives related to international disaster law (IDL).[14] This analysis will thus supplement some of the intertwining goals of this volume: 'to create an inventory of the international legal framework available for the protection of animals in armed

6 See James Sawyer and Gerardo Huertas, *Animal Management and Welfare in Natural Disasters* (London: Routledge 2018); Dick Green, *Animals in Disasters* (Cambridge, MA: Butterworth-Heinemann 2019).

7 Mihir Zaveri and Emily S. Rueb, 'How Many Animals Have Died in Australia's Wildfires?', *New York Times* (11 January 2020), available at https://nyti.ms/3s8l2PU, accessed 22 February 2022.

8 UN World Food Programme, 'Pakistan Flood Impact Assessment' (September 2010), available at https://bit.ly/3Gl7BkJ, accessed 22 February 2022.

9 Karin Brulliard, 'How the Chaos of Hurricane Katrina Helped Save Pets from Flooding in Texas', *Washington Post* (31 August 2017), available at https://wapo.st/3rZvLwa, accessed 22 February 2022.

10 Donald Broom, *Sentience and Animal Welfare* (Wallingford: CABI 2014).

11 Anne Peters, 'Global Animal Law: What It Is and Why We Need It', *Transnational Environmental Law* 5 (2016), 9–23. See further Anne Peters (ed.), *Studies in Global Animal Law* (Heidelberg: Springer 2020); Sabrine Brels, *Le droit du bien-être animal dans le monde: Évolution et universalisation* (Paris: L'Harmattan 2017).

12 See de Hemptinne, Chapter 11, 'Medical Transport, Search and Rescue', in this volume.

13 See chapters in Part II, 'The Protection of Animals in International and Non-international Armed Conflicts'.

14 For an overview, see Andrea de Guttry, Marco Gestri and Gabriella Venturini (eds.), *International Disaster Response Law* (Heidelberg: Springer 2012); Susan C. Breau and Katja Samuel (eds.), *Research Handbook on Disasters and International Law* (Cheltenham: Edward Elgar 2016). See also Giulio Bartolini, 'Charting an Emerging Subject: The Role of the Yearbook of International Disaster Law', *Yearbook of International Disaster Law* 1 (2018), 1–4.

conflicts';[15] the identification of which animals are protected by IDL instruments and their underlying rationale; and an assessment of the structural capacity of IDL to move away from an overwhelmingly anthropocentric body of law towards a system able to factor animal concerns into its legal and operational documents. This chapter might conversely also permit to assess how inputs pertaining to IDL are able to influence initiatives and instruments addressing animals, thus providing an additional model for similar efforts related to international humanitarian law (IHL).

This survey will also explore ways of enhancing the protection of animals during armed conflicts through instruments beyond IHL. Even if IDL instruments analysed in this chapter have been designed to be applied in peacetime, such instruments might also be invoked during armed conflicts. This point, for instance, has recently been addressed by the International Law Court (ILC) in its Draft Articles on the Protection of Persons in the Event of Disasters. Article 18 maintains that for disasters occurring during an armed conflict, the doctrine of *lex specialis* would ensure that IHL provisions take precedence, as still maintaining the possibility for the Draft Articles to be applied to the extent that legal issues raised by this instrument are not covered by IHL rules.[16] If this approach could be maintained in general terms for IDL instruments, it would therefore be possible to introduce further legal elements for the protection of animals in armed conflicts or, at least, such instruments might provide further inputs for the interpretation of existing IHL norms.

2 ANIMALS AND DISASTERS: BETWEEN IDL AND GLOBAL ANIMAL LAW

In order to identify relevant provisions and initiatives, this section provides an overview of the main issues addressed in international law with regard to animals and disasters. In particular, two main areas of interest are identified: the protection of animals during disasters (Section 2.1), and the involvement of animals in international relief operations (Section 2.2).

2.1 *Protection of Animals During Disasters*

James Sawyer and Gerardo Huertas have observed that regardless of the negative effects that disasters have imposed on animals, '[i]n the past, the most common reaction when disaster management for animals was mentioned were looks of puzzlement, often followed by comments about rescuing cats from trees'.[17] As a result, recent focus on this scenario deserves some of our attention also.

Within the area of IDL the current universal point of reference to the issue of protecting animals during disasters is provided by the Sendai Framework for Action

[15] See Peters and de Hemptinne, Chapter 1, 'Warfare' in this volume.
[16] UN General Assembly, Report of the ILC (n. 2), 73, para. 9.
[17] Sawyer and Huertas, *Animal* (n. 2), ix.

(2015–30), which was elaborated by the Third World Disaster Conference in 2015 and endorsed by the UN General Assembly[18] as part of current efforts to make disaster risk reduction a guiding element of international and domestic agendas.[19] Its aim is to guide states and other relevant stakeholders towards its final outcome, namely '[t]he substantial reduction of disaster risk and losses in lives, livelihoods and health and in the economic, physical, social, cultural and environmental assets of persons, businesses, communities and countries', as spelled out through seven global targets and four priorities of action. In comparison with previous frameworks (Yokohama and Hyogo), the Sendai Framework has introduced some elements related to animal protection due to their link to livelihoods as well as economic and environmental assets. Within Priority 3 in particular – namely '[i]nvesting in disaster risk reduction for resilience' – a series of measures to be adopted at national and local levels have been identified, including requests '[t]o strengthen the protection of livelihoods and productive assets, including livestock [and] working animals', as well as 'to strengthen and promote collaboration and capacity-building for the protection of [these] productive assets' at global and regional levels.[20]

Its rationale is thus grounded on utilitarian premises as livestock and working animals are an international concern largely due to their economic link with humans. Nevertheless, these references might facilitate measures to be adopted by states for the protection of animals in case of disasters. Indeed, the Sendai Framework, regardless of its soft law character, has been complemented by thirty-eight indicators.[21] The aim of these indicators, which are based on voluntary national reports, is to assess states' performance with regard to the framework's seven global targets.[22] Animal issues have been included in indicators related to Target C, which encourages states to '[r]educe direct disaster economic loss in relation to global gross domestic product (GDP) by 2030'. In particular, indicator C-2 focuses on '[d]irect agricultural loss attributed to disasters', namely damages to 'crops, livestock, fisheries, apiculture, aquaculture and forest sectors as well as associated facilities and infrastructure'.[23] Through references included in Priority 3 and indicator C-2, states are being encouraged to regard the adoption of tailored actions to protect animals in these contexts as a prerequisite for reaching the aforementioned global target.

18 UN General Assembly, Sendai Framework for Disaster Risk Reduction 2015–30, 23 June 2015, A/RES/69/283.

19 On its impact, see Katja L. H. Samuel, Marie Aronsson-Storrier and Kirsten Nakjavani Bookmiller (eds.), *The Cambridge Handbook of Disaster Risk Reduction and International Law* (Cambridge: Cambridge University Press 2019).

20 UN General Assembly, Sendai (n. 20), paras. 30 (p) and 31 (f).

21 UN General Assembly, Report of the Open-Ended Intergovernmental Expert Working Group (n. 2).

22 This monitoring system is available at https://sendaimonitor.unisdr.org, accessed 22 February 2022.

23 UN General Assembly, Report of the Open-Ended Intergovernmental Expert Working Group (n. 2), 6.

Novelties introduced in the Sendai Framework, regardless of having a sectoral target in relation to animals, represent a recognition of animal concerns in disaster management and might have top-down effects on further initiatives at various levels. Indeed, the consolidation of disasters as a driving topic in international/national agendas, as well as the emerging relevance of animal concerns within the same disaster management community have generated a parallel activism by institutional stakeholders involved in animal protection who favour a focus on disasters in their agendas. A prominent example thereof is provided by the activities carried out by the World Organisation for Animal Health (OIE),[24] which is currently composed of 182 states. Indeed, regardless of its original limited mandate – sharing information on epizootic diseases to prevent their spread[25] – the OIE has progressively become an active player on animal welfare issues. Since 2004 the OIE World Assembly of Delegates started to introduce in its Terrestrial and Aquatic Animal Health Codes a series of international standards addressing animal welfare that could play a guiding role at the international level[26] regardless of their recommendatory character.[27]

The OIE's animal welfare agenda has recently been extended to disaster settings. In 2011, Resolution 22 of the World Assembly of Delegates created an 'ad hoc group on animal health and welfare and public health concerns during natural disasters'[28] that was charged to discuss proposals on standard-setting activities in this area. As highlighted in several OIE discussion papers,[29] different options were assessed, ranging from providing inputs to existing private initiatives, as in the Livestock Emergency Guidelines and Standards Handbook (analysed below), to the possibility of including a specific section in the Terrestrial Animal Health Code or adopting guidelines on technical requirements. This latter option was eventually endorsed through the Guidelines on Disaster Management and Risk Reduction in Relation to Animal Health, Animal Welfare and Veterinary Public Health released by OIE in 2016.[30] Furthermore, this document was endorsed in 2016 by the World Assembly of Delegates in Resolution 28 on animal welfare, which recommends that:

> Veterinary Services of each Member Country take steps to engage with governmental and non-governmental organisations to apply the guidelines on disaster

[24] As it was founded in 1924 as the Office International des Epizooties, OIE remains the organisation's official acronym.

[25] See Art. 4 of the Organic Statutes of the Office International des Epizooties of 25 June 1924.

[26] For a positive appraisal of its mandate, see Michael Bowman, Peter Davies and Catherine Redgwell, *Lyster's International Wildlife Law* (Cambridge: Cambridge University Press 2010), 698–9.

[27] David Favre, 'An International Treaty for Animal Welfare', *Animal Law Review* 18 (2012), 237–79, at 252.

[28] See OIE, 79th General Session of the World Assembly of Delegates: Final Report, 22–27 May 2011, 42 and 52; Resolution 22, ibid., 162–3.

[29] See, for example, Sarah Khan, 'Discussion Paper on the Future Role of the OIE with Respect to Animals and Disasters' (June 2013), available at https://bit.ly/3rbpWwu, accessed 22 February 2022.

[30] OIE, Guidelines on Disaster Management and Risk Reduction in Relation to Animal Health, Animal Welfare and Veterinary Public Health, May 2016, available at https://bit.ly/3Ga33xP, accessed 22 February 2022.

> management and risk reduction in relation to animal health and welfare and veterinary public health including, as appropriate, the possible need to strengthen the relevant regulatory frameworks, and improve their capacity to respond to any kind of disaster.[31]

Interestingly, one of the driving factors behind its elaboration was the parallel interest within international agendas on disaster issues, as emphasised when the chairman of the Animal Welfare Working Group stated that '[t]he work is in line with the United Nations Sendai Framework for Disaster Risk Reduction'.[32] This element thus confirms the capacity of disaster issues to influence the agendas of international actors, as complemented by the extensive use in the Guidelines of Terminologies adopted by UN Office for Disaster Risk Reduction (UNISDR) and the International Federation of Red Cross and Red Crescent (IFRC) to define key terms related to disaster management. Furthermore, the OIE's Guidelines adopt an impressively wide scope of application. Contrary to the Sendai Framework, which focuses on livestock and the instrumental uses of animals, the OIE's guidelines avoid taking a position on which animals are deserving of protection, using this latter term without qualification. As a result, pleas made in the OIE's guidelines for the need for states to adopt proactive measures to protect animals during disasters and fully integrate animal health, welfare concerns, and veterinary services into the domestic disaster-management framework can be broadly interpreted. However, regardless of its timely character and interesting features, the guidelines have a number of shortcomings.

First, the decision not to add a specific section devoted to disaster issues in the Terrestrial Animal Health Code lowered the impact of initiatives on this issue. Indeed, even if this code is a non-binding instrument, approved on a consensus basis by the World Assembly of Delegates, due to its technical and specialised character the Terrestrial Animal Health Code represents the guiding document in the OIE system, both for mandatory activities and reporting obligations, as well as other areas where it plays a more informal guiding role, for instance concerning the identification of standards aimed at structurally assessing the quality of veterinary services.[33] Furthermore the potential inclusion of a specific section on animals and disasters in the Terrestrial and Aquatic Health Codes would have prospectively permitted to benefit from the planned follow-up mechanism, namely the Observatory on Implementation of OIE Standards,[34] and for this potential new

[31] See OIE, 84th General Session of the World Assembly of Delegates, Final Report, 22–6 May 2016, 55; Resolution 28, ibid., 160–1.

[32] Ibid., 55.

[33] See the Performance of Veterinary Services Pathway, available at www.oie.int/solidarity/pvs-pathway, accessed 22 February 2022. On-site visits and assessments, based on the codes, are made in involved countries whose results could be made public with the consensus of concerned states.

[34] On this planned mechanism, see OIE, 86th General Session of the World Assembly of Delegates, Final Report, 20–5 May 2018, Resolution 36, Implementation of OIE Standards by OIE Member Countries: State of Play and Specific Capacity Building Needs, 184.

standard's inclusion among technical issues to be assessed under OIE's review programmes on the performance of veterinary services.

Second, not translating the OIE's guidelines into a technical standard resulted in an even 'lighter' document than this latter category, thus hardly qualifiable as exhaustive or capable of driving concrete actions expected by states in this area. Although the guidelines mainly aim to highlight the relevance of this problem in contemporary scenarios 'with the objective of protecting animal health, animal welfare and veterinary public health during disaster events', they nevertheless fail to provide concrete guidance as '[t]he document does not prescribe how Veterinary Services should act, but leaves it to each OIE Member Country to adapt to local needs'.[35] This approach, which represents the guidelines' main shortcoming, might testify to the challenges faced by the OIE once it gets involved in activities unrelated to its core issues. In particular, addressing animal welfare in disaster settings would have probably required expanding this latter notion further in terms of positive measures to be adopted and adding an additional component to domestic disaster management frameworks, which are usually anthropocentric and characterised by shortages in resources.

Paradoxically, the best suited operational guidelines to provide inputs on states in this area are those provided by private initiatives. This is the case for the Livestock Emergency Guidelines and Standards (LEGS) Handbook.[36] Originally published in 2009 and then updated in 2014 by this NGO, the LEGS Handbook was born out of a wide consultation process of relevant stakeholders, as reflected in its steering committee – composed by staff of international organisations such as the Food and Agricultural Organization (FAO) and the African Union, the International Committee of the Red Cross (ICRC), and non-state actors like academics and veterinary experts. Its aim was to provide international guidelines and standards for designing, implementing, and evaluating livestock interventions in humanitarian crises, including disasters. Clearly this approach mirrored previous non-state driven standard-setting initiatives in the humanitarian sector, such as the Sphere Project's handbook,[37] which aimed both to integrate a rights-based approach with a needs-based one and to determine specific minimum technical standards to guarantee the quality of international assistance. This link was formally reinforced in 2011, once the Sphere Project officially recognised LEGS as its formal companion, thus increasing its sectoral priority.[38]

35 OIE, Guidelines (n. 31), 2.

36 LEGS, *Livestock Emergency Guidelines and Standards* (2nd ed., Warwickshire: Practical Action Publishing 2014), available at https://bit.ly/346FUzh, accessed 22 February 2022.

37 Tommaso Natoli, 'Non-State Humanitarian Actors and Human Rights in Disaster Scenarios: Normative Role, Standard Setting and Accountability', in Zorzi Giustiniani (ed.), *Routledge Handbook* (n. 2), 149–64.

38 See 'The Sphere Project and the Livestock Emergency Guidelines and Standards Sign Companionship Agreement' (18 October 2011), LEGS, available at https://bit.ly/3Gl7Vjr, accessed 22 February 2022.

Indeed LEGS, apart from its main purpose to provide guidelines for decision-making activities and their assessment, also claims to be underpinned by a rights-based approach focused on the right to food and an adequate standard of living, and complementing this traditional human-based perspective with a particular focus on animal welfare. The OIE's guidelines recognise that, even if 'LEGS is not based on animal welfare, many LEGS interventions lead to improve[d] animal welfare, thus contributing to the "five freedoms" commonly used as a framework for assessing animal welfare'.[39] This fact is exemplified, for instance, in the section devoted to '[t]echnical standards for the provision of water', whose comprehensive chapter is based on the assumption that '[t]he provision of water contributes to the first of the animal welfare "five freedoms" ... namely "freedom from hunger and thirst" – by ready access to fresh water and a diet to maintain full health and vigour'.[40] This reference confirms support for the basic premises of animal welfare theories, as the well-known five freedoms originally identified them in the 1965 Brambell Report[41] and subsequently encapsulated in the OIE Terrestrial Animal Health Code[42] and additional standard-setting initiatives.[43] At the same time LEGS does not aim to address all manner of animals: companion animals are outside its main focus. Consequently, LEGS represents another example of self-standard-setting instruments elaborated by non-state humanitarian actors and based on wide consultation processes normally involving traditional subjects of international law. Still, regardless of their formal value, which is softer even than soft law,[44] such documents have acquired a certain standing in light of their capacity to capture elements pertaining to this area of law and provide oriented solutions for involved actors. On some occasions such instruments have obtained a formal endorsement in binding international acts as guiding documents to inform activities of states and international organisations. Moreover, their acceptance has from a pragmatic perspective been imposed by states and international organisations as a precondition for humanitarian organisations to apply for their funding opportunities.[45]

With regards to LEGS, a first indicator of its potential relevance has been provided by the FAO. In 2016, the FAO published *Livestock-Related Interventions during Emergencies: The How-To-Do Manual*, which makes an extensive use of LEGS, claiming that '[t]his manual complements LEGS and provides specific and

39 LEGS, *Livestock Emergency Guidelines and Standards* (n. 36), xii.

40 Ibid., 179.

41 Francis William Rogers Brambell, *Report of the Technical Committee of Enquire into the Welfare of Animals Kept under Intensive Livestock Husbandry Systems* (London: HMSO 1965).

42 OIE, *Terrestrial Animal Health Code* (28th ed., 2019), Art. 7.1.2, available at https://bit.ly/34mqMO7, accessed 22 February 2022.

43 Miah Gibson, 'The Universal Declaration of Animal Welfare', *Deakin Law Review* 16 (2011), 539–67.

44 Walter Kälin, 'How Hard is Soft Law? The Guiding Principles on Internal Displacement and the Need for a Normative Framework', *Brookings Institution* (19 December 2001), 6, available at https://brook.gs/3rhoHfo, accessed 22 February 2022.

45 Dug Cubie, 'An Analysis of Soft Law Applicable to Humanitarian Assistance: Relative Normativity in Action?', *International Humanitarian Legal Studies* 2 (2011), 177–215.

technical "How-to-do-it" information for the most common livestock interventions … and readers should already be acquainted with the LEGS guidelines'.[46] In essence, the approach proposed by the FAO is to use LEGS as the planning and decision-making tool for emergency interventions related to livestock, while its own technical manual could provide guidance for the effective implementation of relevant measures, thus confirming the blurring and complementary dynamics involving different stakeholders in the humanitarian arena.

Furthermore, as both IDL and global animal law rely extensively on multilevel and transnational perspectives to provide content to international inputs, domestic and subnational levels should also be taken into account. Some states have indeed already started to pay attention to animal concerns in their domestic disaster management regulations and policies. However, the current framework is characterised by different formal legal values and perspectives, ranging from the inclusion of animal protection among the global goals of disaster management authorities to sectoral documents detailing procedures for relevant domestic stakeholders or categories of animals, as livestock or pets.

For instance, the protection of animals has been included in the competencies of disaster management authorities and in documents providing a general national framework. For example, Article 1 of the 2018 Italian Civil Protection Code includes – for the first time – the protection of animals among the functions to be performed by the civil protection service, as complemented by Article 2.6, which refers to 'interventions aimed at ensuring the relief and assistance to populations and animals affected by calamitous events'.[47] This framework has been reinforced by a memorandum of cooperation, involving the Italian Civil Protection Department and a network of NGOs focused on animal welfare, aimed at implementing the abovementioned provisions devoted to the protection of animals included in the Italian Civil Protection Code. Interestingly, this instrument was complemented by references to a number of international instruments 'recognising animals as sentient being', ranging from the EU Lisbon Treaty to the 1978 Universal Declaration on Animal Rights. On such grounds this memorandum of cooperation engages parties to identify operational procedures for the management of animals in disaster settings, including the possibility of mobilising volunteers and staff members belonging to such NGOs' animal welfare associations in governmental relief operations.[48]

References to the protection of animals have also been included in documents defining the roles and functions for domestic authorities, such as the 2010 Standing

46 Philippe Ankers, Suzan Bishop, Simon Mack and Klaas Dietze (eds.), *Livestock-Related Interventions during Emergencies: The How-To-Do Manual* (Rome: FAO 2016), 1–2.

47 Italy: Decreto Legislativo No. 1 of 2 January 2018, Codice della protezione civile: Art. 1, 'to protect life, physical integrity, property, settlements, animals and the environment' against disasters, available at https://bit.ly/3vuhKd9, accessed 22 February 2022.

48 Italy: Protocollo d'Intesa of 21 September 2018, available at https://bit.ly/3470GSp, accessed 22 February 2022.

Orders on Disasters by Bangladesh;[49] the 2015 New Zealand National Civil Defence Emergency Management Plan Order, which devotes a full section to envisaging how animal welfare might be supported by specialised NGOs;[50] the 2015 Disaster Risk Management Act of Jamaica;[51] the 2016 National Disaster Management Plan of India;[52] and the 2015 Costa Rica National Risk Management Policy.[53] Similarly such references could be present in documents enacted by subnational entities in charge of civil protection functions, as in the Emergency Animal Welfare Plan of the Australian State of Victoria.[54]

Additionally, domestic instruments having a sectoral approach can be mentioned. This applies to documents related to veterinary services and their role in disaster settings. For instance, Costa Rica has developed specific guidelines and contingency plans relevant for such authorities,[55] while a 2018 survey managed by the EU Commission on veterinary services during disasters emphasised that only five member states have developed disaster management plans in this area.[56] Similarly a sectoral approach might imply a specific focus on certain categories of animals, as is the case for the disaster management plan developed by the Indian Ministry of Agriculture in 2016 and tailored specifically to the protection of livestock,[57] or conversely the 2006 US Pets Evacuation Transportation Standards Act that addresses the preparedness of operational plans during disasters.[58]

Finally, specialised transnational NGOs have been able to support states to develop their domestic normative frameworks or to advocate at both international and domestic fora. The primary example in this regard is the World Animal Protection, formerly the World Society for Animal Protection, as it is one of the

49 Bangladesh: Standing Order on Disaster of April 2010, available at https://bit.ly/3ufs5ZN, accessed 22 February 2022.

50 New Zealand: National Civil Defence Emergency Management, Order of 2 June 2015, available at https://bit.ly/3s23mWs, accessed 22 February 2022.

51 Jamaica: National Disaster Risk Management Act of 19 February 2015, available at http://extwprlegs1.fao.org/docs/pdf/jam145358.pdf, accessed 25 February 2022.

52 India: National Disaster Risk Management Plan of May 2016, available at http://pibphoto.nic.in/documents/rlink/2016/jun/p20166201.pdf, accessed 25 February 2022.

53 Costa Rica: Comisión Nacional de Prevención de Riesgos y Atención de Emergencias, Política Nacional de Gestión del Riesgo 2016–2030 of 2015 available at https://bit.ly/3hzeqFr, accessed 22 February 2022.

54 Australia: Victorian Emergency Animal Welfare Plan (revision 2) of October 2019, available at https://bit.ly/3ufqi7d, accessed 22 February 2022.

55 Costa Rica: Reglamento al Título IV, Dispositivo de Emergencias, de la Ley General del Servicio Nacional de Salud Animal, No. 8495 y procesos de contratación en situaciones de emergencia of 7 August 2013, available at www.imprentanacional.go.cr/pub/2013/08/07/comp_07_08_2013.pdf, accessed 22 February 2022.

56 European Commission, Directorate-General for Health and Food Safety, Overview Report on Emergency Preparedness among Veterinary Services for Dealing with Natural Disasters, DG(SANTE) 2018–6518, available at https://bit.ly/3KYdqZ6, accessed 22 February 2022.

57 India: Ministry of Agriculture and Farmers Welfare, Disaster Management Plan of 26 February 2016, available at https://bit.ly/3uccDOj, accessed 22 February 2022.

58 US: Pets Evacuation and Transportation Standards Act of 6 October 2006, Public Law 109–308, available at www.congress.gov/109/plaws/publ308/PLAW-109publ308.pdf, accessed 22 February 2022.

few NGOs with a specialised focus on animals and disasters with regard not only to tailored relief activities but through its involvement in the elaboration of domestic normative and guiding standards – as occurred for the Costa Rican and Indian instruments[59] – and its advocacy activities in global and regional institutional fora devoted to disaster risk reduction.[60]

2.2 *Animals in Search and Rescue Operations*

As analysed elsewhere this volume,[61] trained dogs have been used in armed conflicts for detecting the presence of humans. Similarly, once a disaster occurs, the need to involve search and rescue teams (USAR) in relief efforts could be present, a phenomenon that led in 1991 to the creation of the UN International Search and Rescue Advisory Group (INSARAG), a global professional network of governmental and non-governmental USAR teams. This network, whose secretariat is provided by the UN Office for the Coordination of Humanitarian Affairs, aims to establish minimum international standards, certifications, and methodologies for international coordination and deployment in international relief missions. Its mandate was endorsed by UN General Assembly Resolution 57/150 (2002),[62] the final result of several previous attempts to elaborate a universal treaty concerning USAR teams.[63] Such scenarios have raised a series of legal challenges.

In relation to armed conflicts, the legal status of trained dogs has been identified as pertaining to mobile or fixed medical units.[64] This regime could also be invoked for rescue operations carried out during complex emergencies, namely disasters occurring in territories affected by armed conflicts, as was confirmed by Article 18 of the ILC Draft Articles and its commentary, which maintain the *lex specialis* character of IHL rules in this scenario.[65] However, rescue operations normally occurring during peacetime might benefit from solutions provided by IDL: based on practice,[66]

59 For India, see the acknowledgments in the Disaster Management Plan quoted above (n. 58); for Costa Rica see World Animal Protection, 'Country Profiles: Cost Rica', available at https://animalsindisasters.org/country-profile/costa-rica, accessed 22 February 2022.

60 For instance, this NGO has managed side-events and advocacy activities at world disaster conferences and global and regional disaster risk reduction platforms.

61 See de Hemptinne, Chapter 11, 'Medical Transport, Search and Rescue', in this volume.

62 UN General Assembly, Strengthening the Effectiveness and Coordination of International Urban Search and Rescue Assistance, 16 December 2002, A/RES/57/150.

63 Kirsten Nakjavani Bookmiller, 'The International Law of 96 Hours: Urban Search and Rescue Teams and the Current State of International Disaster Response Law', in David Caron, Michael Kelley and Anastasia Telesetsky (eds.), *The International Law of Disaster Relief* (Cambridge: Cambridge University Press 2004), 111–35.

64 See de Hemptinne, Chapter 11, 'Medical Transport, Search and Rescue', in this volume.

65 UN General Assembly, Report of the ILC (n. 2), 73, para. 9.

66 See, for instance, Art. 2 of the Agreement between the Republic of Austria and the Republic of Albania on Mutual Assistance in the Case of Disasters or Serious Accidents of 27 January 2010. This provision identifies 'Equipment' as 'material, in particular technical devices, the vehicles and the rescue dogs for the deployment, as well as items for personal use'.

rescue dogs are normally qualified as 'equipment', as confirmed by Article 3 (g) of the ILC Draft Articles ('Use of Terms'). Article 3 (g) includes within its definition of 'equipment and goods' the reference to 'specially trained animals', which are therefore considered – as specified in the commentary – 'technical "equipment" required by the disaster relief personnel to perform their functions'.[67]

Consequently, some IDL instruments have addressed issues relevant for rescue dogs. The INSARAG Guidelines, for example, include references to animal welfare concerns in relation to the deployment of rescue dogs, for instance requiring rest periods, nutrition, stress control, and appropriate means of transportation.[68] Elements provided by the INSARAG Guidelines, therefore, might act as a source of inspiration for IHL taking into account how in this latter context animal welfare concerns are not mentioned at all once addressing dogs involved in medical search and rescue activities.

Additionally, IDL treaties address the most recurring regulatory problem related to rescue dogs, namely that their deployment into areas affected by a disaster is either delayed or entirely prevented due to legal barriers related to sanitary measures like quarantine periods, as was experienced in the aftermath of the 2011 Japanese earthquake.[69] IDL treaties might provide facilitations, as exemplified by Article 8 of the Swiss-Venezuelan Cooperation Agreement, which maintains that parties shall: 'ensure the rapid transport to the disaster area and simplify and exempt from formalities the Emergency Teams, their dogs, the equipment and emergency aid . . . Individuals shall be accredited with a valid form of identification and the dogs with a valid vaccination certificate. All the veterinary formalities for entry, including quarantine requirements, shall be waived.'[70] Such facilities could not, however, be taken for granted as other treaties reiterate how the 'border crossing procedure and stay within the territory of the requesting Party for the search-dogs teams shall be defined according to the state quarantine regulations of the requesting Party'.[71]

The scenario is no better for universal treaties, such as the instruments elaborated by the World Customs Organisation (WCO), due to their limited participation and

67 UN General Assembly, Report of the ILC (n. 2), 28, para. 31.

68 UN Office for the Coordination of Humanitarian Affairs, 'Guidelines, Vol. III: Operational Field Guide', INSARAG, 15–18, available at https://bit.ly/3C8hgL1, accessed 22 February 2022.

69 See the report commissioned by the IFRC, 'The Impact of Regulatory Problems and Gains from Legal Preparedness in Recent Response Operations' (10 March 2015), 11 (on file with the author).

70 Art. 8 of the Agreement of Cooperation in Case of Disaster between Switzerland and Venezuela of 30 September 1998, 2409 UNTS 151. See also Agreement between the Swiss Federal Council and the Government of the Republic of the Philippines on Cooperation in the Event of Natural Disaster or Major Emergencies of 6 December 2001, available at https://bit.ly/3IUpicW, accessed 22 February 2022.

71 See Art. 9 of the Agreement between the Government of the Russian Federation and the Government of Greece on Cooperation in the Sphere of Prevention and Mitigation of Emergency Situations of 21 February 2000, available at https://bit.ly/3KWrC4S, accessed 22 February 2022. See also Art. 9.8 of the Agreement between the Government of the Republic of Lithuania and the Government of the Republic of Belarus on Cooperation in the Field of Prevention and Elimination of Consequences of Catastrophes, Natural Disasters and Serious Accidents of 16 December 2003, 2339 UNTS 203.

inability to attribute clear exemptions. In this context reference should be made to the 1990 Istanbul Convention on Temporary Admission and its Annexes. Ratified by around seventy states,[72] Annex D maintains that specific categories of animals, including detector dogs, shall be granted temporary admission in accordance with Article 2 of this convention. Under this latter provision a temporary admission guarantees a 'total conditional relief from import duties and taxes and without application of import restrictions or prohibitions of economic character'. Therefore, this provision does not address safety regulations eventually applied by the affected state, as in quarantine requirements. Additionally, Annex J of the WCO Kyoto Convention, originally adopted in 1973 as the International Convention on the Simplification and Harmonization of Customs Procedures, revised in 1999, and currently in force in around 120 states[73] regulates 'relief consignments', including 'specially trained animals'. In this case a series of measures are imposed on states through 'standards' in order to give priority to the clearance of relief consignments for temporary admission and import (Article 2), while as a 'recommended practice' Article 5 maintains that '[i]n the case of relief consignments any economic export prohibitions or restrictions and any export duties or taxes otherwise payable should be waived'. Moreover, sanitary requirements are also not addressed and this has a non-binding character.

At the regional level a specific regulation is provided by the EU system through its Regulation (EU) No. 576/2013 related to the non-commercial movement of pets, which also addresses rescue dogs. This instrument largely facilitates their free movement within member states based on a series of predefined requirements, including marking, anti-rabies vaccinations, and other sanitary requirements.[74] A similar regime covers movements from non-EU countries, with the additional requirement that they enter the EU through designated entry points identified by member states. However, in order to facilitate search and rescue activities, Article 10.3 of the Regulation provides, by way of derogation, that 'Member States may authorise registered military or search-and-rescue dogs to move through a point of entry other than a travellers' point of entry' on the condition that the accompanying person has been granted a permit in advance by the relevant member state and compliance with the abovementioned sanitary requirements is subsequently carried out at a place designated by the member state.

In other circumstances, some solutions could be inferred from regional disaster law treaties in relation to facilitations provided for the entry and departure of 'equipment' functional to international relief teams as search dogs are routinely

72 Convention on Temporary Admission of 26 June 1990, available at https://bit.ly/3AK3QnQ, accessed 22 February 2022.

73 International Convention on the Simplification and Harmonization of Custom Procedures (as Amended) of 26 June 1999, available at https://bit.ly/3AJFQkO, accessed 22 February 2022.

74 See EU: Regulation No. 576/2013 of the European Parliament and of the European Council of 12 June 2013 on the non-commercial movement of pet animals, repealing Regulation (EC) No. 998/2003, Official Journal of the EU L 178/1, 28 June 2013.

qualified as 'equipment' as analysed above. Examples of this are the Agreement on Disaster Management and Emergency Response developed by the Association of Southeast Asian Nations, which provides that a state party '[i]n accordance with its national laws and regulations … shall: b. facilitate the entry into, stay in and departure from its territory of personnel and of equipment, facilities and materials involved or used in the assistance',[75] and the 1991 Inter-American Convention, which makes reference to 'best efforts'.[76] Clearly such provisions can hardly be qualified as self-executing or capable of solving potential sanitary barriers.

Consequently, another possibility would be to rely on domestic legislations, as maintained by the abovementioned UN General Assembly Resolution 57/150 (2002), urging:

> all States, consistent with their applicable measures relating to public safety and national security, to simplify or reduce, as appropriate, the customs and administrative procedures related to the entry, transit, stay and exit of international urban search and rescue teams and their equipment and materials, taking into account the Guidelines of the International Search and Rescue Advisory Group, particularly concerning visas for the rescuers and the quarantining of their animals.[77]

Similarly, guidance on solutions to be adopted at the domestic level could be provided by IDL documents elaborated by the IFRC. For instance, its Model Act for the Facilitation and Regulation of International Disaster Relief and Initial Recovery Assistance suggests states to temporarily admit trained dogs without the need for quarantine.[78] However, the inherent limits of these approaches is to make the operativity of search and rescue teams unpredictable and dependent on uncertain and variegated domestic solutions.

3 CONCLUDING RECOMMENDATIONS

This chapter has attempted to provide a snapshot of current legal issues involving animals during disasters. Regardless of their fragmented approach, some trends have been identified and it would therefore be helpful to introduce some recommendations in this area as well as some points of reference for issues relevant for IHL, as disaster scenarios provide further examples of ways to introduce animal welfare perspectives into areas of international law.

75 Art. 14 of the Agreement on Disaster Management and Emergency Response of 26 July 2005, available at https://bit.ly/3G9pQd2, accessed 22 February 2022.

76 Art. 5 of the Inter-American Convention to Facilitate Disaster Assistance of 7 June 1991, available at www.oas.org/juridico/english/treaties/a-54.html, accessed 22 February 2022.

77 UN General Assembly, Strengthening (n. 64), para. 3.

78 IFRC, Model Act for the Facilitation and Regulation of International Disaster Relief and Initial Recovery Assistance (March 2013), available at www.ifrc.org/PageFiles/125656/MODEL%20ACT%20INGLES.pdf, accessed 22 February 2022. See in particular Art. 41 and its commentary on 'Search Dogs'.

Firstly, animal concerns are increasingly being factored into legal and operational approaches related to the management of disasters commonly via soft law documents. This trend has also resulted in mutual cross-fertilisations involving different perspectives, namely disaster management and animal welfare issues, as well as diverse stakeholders like international organisation, states, and NGOs. This interesting novelty, however, still lacks coherence. The potential relevance of international inputs analysed in this chapter could be examined further. This should seek to intensify a dialogue among experts belonging to different backgrounds, be they veterinary services or disaster management communities. So far, some initiatives have been driven by utilitarian and anthropocentric premises that address specific categories of animals, while other initiatives have adopted a more encompassing welfare perspective.

Animal concerns should be integrated in disaster management activities. For example, this issue could be included in the UN cluster system established to facilitate international coordination in major disasters.[79] Particularly the OIE and its technical experts could be the leading actor in the early recovery cluster led by the United Nations Development Programme, so as to magnify the impact of relief activities tailored for the protection of animals carried out by international actors in the aftermath of disasters. Additionally, the potential role of normative domestic frameworks to provide protection to animals during disasters should not be ignored, as they are capable of operationalising international inputs. Their recognition in several domestic systems might pave the way for further initiatives at the international level.

In any case, it is now clear that the protection of animals during disasters might suffer from challenges related to weak normative frameworks, as it is the case for the protection of animals during armed conflicts. Protective measures might be stifled by competing and anthropocentric interests and a lack of resources by domestic authorities. Nonetheless they ought to be proactively adopted and supported. Taking into account the novelty of these issues in international and national disaster management agendas, it is hard to assess whether such concerns can play an effective role in the future or whether they will be relegated to mere aspirational standards, even if some embryonic interests can now be recognised.

Finally, IDL instruments address the role of animals as an active component of international relief operations. Interestingly, specialised transnational actors have started to regard welfare issues for deployed rescue dogs as a key component to recommended practices in this area. This introduces an operational element that might work as a reference parameter for IHL scenarios too. Regarding rescue dogs, furthermore, a critical problem is the lack of a uniform international legal framework aimed to facilitate the deployment of rescue dogs in relief operations. As

[79] See, on the cluster system, Giovanni de Siervo, 'Actors, Activities and Coordination in Emergencies', in De Guttry, Gestri and Venturini, *International Disaster Response Law* (n. 16), 485–516.

explored, indeed, domestic sanitary regulations might potentially hinder the performance of rescue activities in cross-border relief operations. In this regard, attempts have been made to introduce some derogations to domestic regulations in order to facilitate such rescue activities. The legal framework provided by IDL instruments, however, is still characterised by fragmentation, thus making the use of rescue dogs subject to potential domestic legal hurdles. Independently from possible international regulations, it is suggested here to introduce domestic provisions aimed at derogating from standard procedures, for instance waiving sanitary and other restrictions especially for those teams acting under INSARAG Guidelines, which maintains specific standards in terms of vaccinations and immunisations.

The survey over the multifaceted character of issues addressed in this chapter has confirmed that the 'animal turn'[80] has, similarly as in IHL, started to play a role with regard to disasters and the related legal issues.

SELECT BIBLIOGRAPHY

Bartolini, Giulio, 'Charting an Emerging Subject: The Role of the Yearbook of International Disaster Law', *Yearbook of International Disaster Law* 1 (2018), 1–4.

Brels, Sabrine, *Le droit du bien-être animal dans le monde: Évolution et universalisation* (Paris: L'Harmattan 2017).

de Guttry, Andrea, Marco Gestri and Gabriella Venturini (eds.), *International Disaster Response Law* (Heidelberg: Springer 2012).

Green, Dick, *Animals in Disasters* (Cambridge, MA: Butterworth-Heinemann 2019).

Peters, Anne (ed.), *Studies in Global Animal Law* (Heidelberg: Springer 2020).

Sawyer, James and Gerardo Huertas, *Animal Management and Welfare in Natural Disasters* (London: Routledge 2018).

80 Harriet Ritvo, 'On the Animal Turn', *Daedalus* 136 (2007), 118–22.

17

Animals as Means of Military Experimentation

Veronika Bílková[*]

1 INTRODUCTION

'My pig?' he said. 'They shot him twice in the face with a 9-millimeter pistol, and then six times with an AK-47 and then twice with a 12-gauge shotgun. And then he was set on fire.' 'I kept him alive for 15 hours,' he said. 'That was my pig.'[1]

Animals have accompanied humans to war since time immemorial. They have also helped them get ready for war. One way of doing so is through military experiments. Millions of animals are subject to enormous suffering and ultimately find death in experiments similar to the one just described. They sacrifice their life and well-being (or, rather, have those sacrificed) to make humans better able to kill each other. Experiments on animals are certainly not specific for military research. Animals are 'used' in biology lessons, medical testing, chemical, drug, food and cosmetics testing, or simply curiosity-driven experiments. When compared to hundreds of millions of animals killed or maimed in these experiments, military research might appear modest and innocuous. That is probably why it has so far escaped scholarly attention. Another reason may be the relative dearth of data, as states tend to keep information about their military research classified. Finally, the legal regulation is scarce and dispersed in diverse sources, which makes the field less accessible.

This chapter shows that the lack of scholarly and legislative attention is not warranted. Military experiments on animals, as is described in Section 2, are an important phenomenon, not only because of the number of animals affected by them but also because of harm and suffering inflicted on these animals. Section 3 gives an overview of two main sets of legal rules that are of relevance in this field: national legal acts and international treaties or other rules of international law. Whereas these rules are primarily designed for civil research, they either apply or

[*] I would like to thank the participants of the online workshop of 1 June 2020 for their valuable comments.

[1] C. J. Chivers, 'Tending a Fallen Marine, With Skill, Prayer and Fury', *New York Times* (2 November 2006), available at www.nytimes.com/2006/11/02/world/middleeast/02medic.html, accessed 22 February 2022.

could apply to military experiments as well. Based on the analysis of these two sets of rules, Section 4 describes the main parameters of the gradually emerging legal regulation of military experiments on animals (scope of application, content, and legal consequences of violations).

2 MILITARY EXPERIMENTS ON ANIMALS IN PRACTICE

Animals are regularly used in experiments. This applies both to civil and military research. They are subject to various cruel practices and millions of them die every year. So much we know for sure. It is more difficult to find specific data about the countries which engage in such research, the number of animals used for this purpose, the concrete treatment these animals are exposed to, and the assessment of the usefulness of such testing. Some data are nonetheless available. They are used in this section, first, to discuss the scale of military testing of animals (Section 2.1), and second, to give an overview of the main types of such testing (Section 2.2).

2.1 *Scale of Military Experiments*

In 2012, the US-based animal rights organisation People for the Ethical Treatment of Animals (PETA) carried out a survey to examine the prevalence of animal use for military medical training exercises among the twenty-seven member states of NATO.[2] In the survey, six states (Canada, Denmark, Norway, Poland, the UK, and the United States) indicated they were using animals in those exercises, whereas the remaining twenty-one states answered in the negative. From the perspective of this chapter, this survey suffers from three limitations. Of all the forms of animal testing, its focuses solely on military medical training experiments. It is, moreover, limited to NATO countries and, since it was carried out in 2012, some of the data it contains might already be outdated.[3]

Despite these limitations, the data produced by the survey are still the most complete dataset on military testing of animals available. In addition, this chapter relies on the information provided by the authorities of several NATO countries, and the information collected from the media and the websites of animal rights/welfare non-governmental organisations (NGOs). There is uncertainty as to the correctness and completeness of this information. We know that animals are used in military testing. We also know some countries which engage in this type of testing and certain practices that animals are subject to. Yet, many things remain unclear. Which other

[2] Shalin G. Gala, Justin R. Goodman, Michael P. Murphy, Marion J. Balsam, 'Use of Animals by NATO Countries in Military Medical Training Exercises: An International Survey', *Military Medicine* 177 (2012), 907–810.

[3] 'Poland banned the use of animals for military trauma training in 2013', available at https://bit.ly/3geDu42, accessed 22 February 2022.

states run programmes involving military testing of animals?[4] How many animals are subject to testing? Which species are used? These questions are important, not only to understand the factual situation, but also to be able to address moral and legal concerns that arise in this context.

2.2 *Types of Military Experiments*

Military researchers use animals for a variety of purposes. Some of them correspond to uses in civil research (testing of new vaccines), others are specific for military purpose (testing of new weapons). Three types of experiments may be distinguished: experiments to test weapons, experiments to test military surgical techniques, and experiments carried out for other purposes.[5]

Animals are used in experiments to test weapons. The aim of these experiments is to find out how new weapons harm human beings. Pigs and other animals that are supposedly similar to human beings are usually used for these purposes. They are exposed to compounds or procedures which are known, or even specifically designed, to cause severe suffering, harm, and possibly death to humans. Tested weapons include both conventional weapons and weapons of mass destruction (biological, chemical, and nuclear weapons). Weapons are tested not only when states intend to deploy them, but also when they look for ways to counter the effects of their use by other states.

One of the best-known and most deadly experiments happened in 1946. In the course of the so-called Operation Crossroads, some 4,000 animals were intentionally exposed to the nuclear testing on ships.[6] Other weapons of mass destruction have also been tested on animals. The Porton Down laboratory in the UK is one of the places notorious for chemical testing. It was reported that in 2017 alone, 4,000 animals were experimented on at this location (73 monkeys, 26 pigs, 126 guinea pigs, 240 rats, and 3,400 mice). Some of them were poisoned with a deadly nerve agent VX which 'left them writhing, gasping and shaking'.[7] The same laboratory also uses animals to test biological weapons. The experiments involve poisoning monkeys with deadly biological agents, such as Q fever, and infecting them with Ebola.[8]

4 The top nine animal testing countries are supposedly the US, Japan, China, Australia, France, Canada, the UK, Germany, and Brazil. Although the data are based on civil research, it is likely that countries using animals for civil research may be inclined to use them in military research as well. 'Facts and Figures on Animal Testing', available at https://bit.ly/3Hmwlug, accessed 22 February 2022; 'Military Research on Animals', available at https://bit.ly/30aqW23, accessed 22 February 2022.

5 'Military Research on Animals' (n. 4).

6 See William A. Shurcliff, *Operation Crossroads: The Official Pictorial Record* (New York: William H. Wise 1946).

7 Jane Dalton, 'Deadly Porton Down Nerve Agent Tests Left Animals Gasping, Writhing and Shaking before Dying', *Independent* (20 February 2019), available at https://bit.ly/3gfVz1G, accessed 22 February 2022.

8 Rob Waugh, 'Ministry of Defence "Tested Biological Weapons on Monkeys" at Military Lab', *Metro* (26 September 2017), available at https://bit.ly/3LojQqM, accessed 22 February 2022.

Similar experiments have been reported in other countries.[9] Conventional weapons, such as various explosives, are tested upon animals as well.[10]

Testing military surgical techniques is probably the most common form of animal experiments. Animals are killed or harmed to allow doctors and medical staff to train to be ready to heal humans in the battlefield. The situation has been monitored by PETA for years. In 2014, for instance, PETA published information about the Danish trauma-causing exercises, taking place at the Jægerspris Kaserne, and involving also military from other countries such as the UK.[11] The use of animals in trauma-causing exercises has also been recorded in Canada, Germany, Norway, Poland, and the United States.[12] The trend has been to replace animals with modern human-patient simulators which seem to provide equally, if not more relevant results. Despite that, PETA estimates that still, 'more than 10,000 live animals are shot, stabbed, mutilated, and killed in cruel military training exercises'[13] each year.

Other purposes for which animal testing is used involve creating vaccines and testing resistance to physical assaults or to adverse conditions. Experimentations on animals for creating vaccines (for humans or animals) has a long tradition in both civil and military research. Within the EU only, some five million animals, including mice, rats, fish, chickens, rabbits, dogs, and primates, are used each year in the discovery and development of new medicines, vaccines, and medical devices.[14] Experiments to test resistance to physical assaults focus on the capacity to withstand certain kinds of physical damage. Rats, rabbits, monkeys, and other animals have been employed in this type of tests. They may be immersed in boiling water, set on fire, or shocked with electricity.[15] Experiments to test resistance to adverse conditions consists of hurting animals in various ways to see how much they can resist certain extreme situations such as high pressure. For instance, in 2000–7, the UK military tested the effects of decompression on live goats.[16]

3 APPLICABLE LEGAL RULES ON MILITARY EXPERIMENTS

There is no legal instrument dealing specifically with military testing on animals at the international or national level. Two sets of legal rules are nonetheless of

9 Bela Toth, 'A Critical Review of Experiments in Chemical Carcinogenesis Using Newborn Animals', *Cancer Research* 28 (1968), 727–38.

10 Tom Rawstorne, 'Is it Really Right to Blow Up Pigs Even If It Saves Our Soldiers' Lives?', *Mail Online* (28 May 2010), available at https://bit.ly/34mqc2H, accessed 22 February 2022.

11 PETA, 'Photos: Inside the Secretive Military Training Facility Where Animals Are Mutilated and Killed', available at https://bit.ly/30fZNc2, accessed 22 February 2022.

12 PETA, 'The Military's War on Animals', available at https://bit.ly/3Lojnoo, accessed 22 February 2022.

13 PETA, '5 Horrific Animal Experiments Happening Now', available at www.peta.org/features/current-animal-experiments, accessed 22 February 2022.

14 Dinesh K. Badyal, Chetna Desai, 'Animal Use in Pharmacology Education and Research: The Changing Scenario', *Indian Journal of Pharmacology* 46 (2014), 257–65.

15 T. Dai et al., 'Animal Models of External Traumatic Wound Infections', *Virulence* 2 (2011), 296–315.

16 'UK Navy to End Goat Experiments', *BBC News* (6 February 2008).

relevance for this area. One consists of national legal acts related to animal testing (Section 3.1). The other encompasses certain rules of international law that apply, directly or indirectly, to this testing (Section 3.2). Since the legal regulation is rudimentary and dispersed, other normative systems, especially ethical standards, serve as a source of inspiration.[17] They influence the debate about what the desirable legal rules should be (*de lege ferenda*). Some ethical standards, especially the 3Rs principle,[18] have already become part of legal regulation in some countries and, partly, at the international level (*de lege lata*).

3.1 *Domestic Legal Regulations*

States began enacting legal acts applicable to experiments on animals in the late nineteenth century.[19] The first piece of this type was, purportedly, the Cruelty to Animals Act,[20] adopted in the UK in 1876. Other states have quickly followed. The relevant acts usually apply to both civil and military experiments or, at least, the latter are not explicitly excluded. This section focuses on the regulation adopted in three NATO states which, in the 2012 PETA survey, indicated the use of animals in military experiments (the UK, the United States, and Poland). One non-NATO state which might, with some probability, engage in animal testing as well (Russia) is also included.

In the UK, animal experiments are regulated by the Animals (Scientific Procedures) Act (ASPA).[21] Enacted in 1986 and revised in 2013, ASPA applies to ‘regulated procedures’, defined as ‘any procedure applied to a protected animal for a qualifying purpose which may have the effect of causing the animal a level of pain, suffering, distress or lasting harm equivalent to, or higher than, that caused by the introduction of a needle in accordance with good veterinary practice’ (Article 2(1)). Protected animals encompass all living vertebrates other than humans, under the responsibility of humans. Some animals (primates, cats, dogs, and horses) enjoy enhanced protection. The act introduces a licensing system. Animal testing may only be carried out by licensed persons, in designated establishments, based on a Home Office-approved programme of work. Violations of ASPA entail penalties.

In the United States, the first federal act regulating research on animals was the Animal Welfare Act (AWA) adopted in 1966.[22] This act has been repeatedly

[17] Jane A. Smith, Kenneth M. Boyd (eds.), *Lives in The Balance: The Ethics of Using Animals in Biomedical Research* (Oxford: Oxford University Press 1994); Vera Baumans, ‘Use of Animals in Experimental Research: An Ethical Dilemma?’, *Gene Therapy* 11 (2004), 64–6; Donna Yarri, *The Ethics of Animal Experimentation* (Oxford: Oxford University Press 2005); Andrew Knight, *Costs and Benefits of Animal Experiments* (London: Palgrave Macmillan 2011).

[18] William M. S. Russell, Rex L. Burch, *The Principle of Humane Experimental Technique* (London: Methuen 1959).

[19] See ‘EU and National Regulations for Animal Experimentation’, available at https://bit.ly/3uhDXKP, accessed 22 February 2022.

[20] UK: An Act to amend the Law relating to Cruelty to Animals of 15 August 1876.

[21] UK: Animals (Scientific Procedures) Act 1986.

[22] US: Animal Welfare Act 1966, P.L. 89-544.

amended and its scope extended to regulate not only the use of animals in laboratory, but also the treatment of animals in research, exhibition, transport and by dealers. The Animal Welfare Act sets standards for humane treatment of animals used in research. All individuals and businesses engaging in animal research must be licensed or registered. Animals must be provided with basic standards of veterinary care. In research, methods to avoid or minimise discomfort, distress, and pain must be used, unless withholding them is scientifically justified. Tests are overseen by special committees established within research facilities and by a national inspection service. Violations of AWA entail sanctions.

Poland has a long tradition of regulating animal experiments.[23] The first legal act in this field was the Act on Animal Protection adopted in 1928.[24] The current regulation dates to the 1990s–2000s. It includes the Act on Animal Protection (AAP) adopted in 1997[25] and the Act on Experiments on Animals (AEA) adopted in 2005.[26] Under these acts, experiments on animals can be carried out, if truly necessary, for scientific, educational, or health-protecting purposes. They should be planned and conducted in a manner that does not expose animals to unnecessary pain, suffering and distress, or lasting harm. Proper use of anaesthetics and humanitarian killing of animals is required. The principle of humanitarian treatment of animals is repeatedly stressed. Testing should be conducted by competent persons, though no specific qualification is required. Supervision is ensured by ethical committees and the 'Veterinary Inspectorate'. Violations of the acts entail sanctions.

Unlike Poland and the UK, the Russian Federation does not have a special law on animal experiments.[27] The area is regulated by the Decree of the Ministry of Health on measures of further improvement of the organisational forms of the work with the use of experimental animals,[28] adopted under the Soviet Union, in 1977. The decree contains, and confirms, the Rules on the Execution of Work with the Use of Experimental Animals, which regulate the use of animals in experiments conducted in scientific and educational institutions. It also includes four annexes to the Rules, applicable to the equipment of experimental laboratories, treatment of animals in

23 See Mariusz Zbigniew Felsmann et al., 'Protection of Animals Used in Experiments in Polish Law History, Present Day and Perspective: A Review', 59 *Veterinarni Medicina* (2014), 117–23.

24 Poland: Rozporządzenie Prezydenta Rzeczypospolitej z dnia 22 marca 1928 r. o ochronie zwierząt (Regulation of the President of the Republic of 22 March 1928 on the protection of animals).

25 Poland: Ustawa z dnia 21 sierpnia 1997 r. o ochronie zwierząt (Act of 21 August 1997 on the protection of animals).

26 Poland: Ustawa z dnia 21 stycznia 2005 r. o doświadczeniach na zwierzętach (Act of 21 January 2005 on animal experiments).

27 In 2018, the Federal Law on Responsible Treatment of Animals (Федеральный закон от 27.12.2018 N 498-ФЗ Об ответственном обращении с животными) was adopted. This law does not apply to relations in the area of retention and use of laboratory animals (Art. 1(2)).

28 USSR: Приказ Минздрава СССР от 12.08.1977 N 755 О мерах по дальнейшему совершенствованию организационных форм работы с использованием экспериментальных животных (Order of the Ministry of Health of the USSR dated 12.08.1977 N 755 On measures to further improve the organizational forms of work using experimental animals).

vivarium, the course of experiments, and euthanasia of animals. The main principle of the regulation is humane treatment of animals. Experiments must be carried out by persons with specialised qualifications, equipped with a special permit. Violations of the rules may entail responsibility, though no details are provided.

3.2 *International Legal Regulations*

No international legal instrument regulates military experiments on animals specifically. There are however certain, mostly regional, instruments that apply to experiments on animals as such. The application of more general rules of international law, especially international humanitarian law (IHL) and international environmental law (IEL), should also be considered.

Within the Council of Europe, the European Convention for the Protection of Vertebrate Animals Used for Experimental and other Scientific Purposes (European Convention) was adopted in 1986.[29] The European Convention entered into force in 1991 but it has secured only twenty-two ratifications, including that by the EU. It 'applies to any animal used or intended for use in any experimental or other scientific procedure where that procedure may cause pain, suffering, distress or lasting harm' (Article 1(1)). The European Convention establishes the requirement of general care and accommodation and sets the basic rules for the 'procedures', that is, 'any experimental or other scientific use of an animal which may cause it pain, suffering, distress or lasting harm' (Article 2(c)). Experiments may only take place in registered establishments and must be conducted by competent persons duly authorised to do so. States should collect statistical data on the use of animals and share them to the extent possible. Military research is neither excluded nor explicitly included into the scope of application of the European Convention.

While the European Convention establishes the basic standard, the regulation adopted within the EU is more detailed and comprehensive. The first EU legal act in this area is the European Council Directive 86/609/EEC of 24 November 1986 on the approximation of laws, regulations, and administrative provisions of the member states regarding the protection of animals used for experimental and other scientific purposes. The current legal framework dates from 2009–20. It encompasses the Directive 2010/63/EU on the protection of animals used for scientific purposes (2010 Directive),[30] the Regulation 2019/1010 on the alignment of reporting obligations in the field of legislation related to the environment (2019 Regulation),[31] and the Implementing Decision 2020/569 establishing a common format and

29 EU: European Convention for the Protection of Vertebrate Animals Used for Experimental and other Scientific Purposes of 18 March 1986, ETS No. 123.

30 EU: Directive 2010/63/EU of the European Parliament and of the European Council of 22 September 2010 on the protection of animals used for scientific purposes.

31 EU: Regulation (EU) 2019/1010 of the European Parliament and of the European Council of 5 June 2019 on the alignment of reporting obligations in the field of legislation related to the environment.

information content for the submission of the information to be reported by member states (2020 Decision).[32]

The 2010 Directive, replacing its 1986 predecessor, introduced comprehensive and detailed rules 'for the protection of animals used for scientific or educational purposes' (Article 1). It is, as the first international instrument, explicitly based on the 3Rs principle which is expressed in its Article 4. It applies to live non-human vertebrate animals and live cephalopods, with higher protection being granted to some animals (non-human primates and endangered species). Experiments, labelled as procedures, may only be conducted by competent persons, with a special authorisation. Research institutions have to keep records on animals and to establish an animal-welfare body. They should be inspected by the designated national bodies. States should also establish national committees that would have advisory powers with respect to national authorities. Military research is not one of the areas explicitly excluded from the scope of the 2010 Directive under its Article 1(5) and it should therefore fall under it.

The other two acts, the 2019 Regulation and the 2020 Decision, elaborate upon the 2010 Directive. The 2019 Regulation seeks to improve transparency and reporting obligations under the 2010 Directive by establishing a central, open access EU database for the publication of annual statistics and certain other data. The 2020 Decision introduces a common format for submitting information on the use of animals for scientific purposes. The format should make it easier to assess the implementation of the 2010 Directive and help ensure consistency in its application. Apart from this specific legislation, it is important to recall that the Treaty on the Functioning of the EU in its Article 13 recognises that 'animals are sentient beings', whose welfare requirements shall be paid full regard in various areas of the EU policies, including research.[33]

The regulation within Europe is quite unique and does not have counterparts in other regions or at the universal level. One exception are non-binding standards issued by the World Organization for Animal Health (OIE), a reference organisation of the WTO.[34] The Terrestrial Animal Health Code, adopted by the OIE in 1968 and regularly updated since then, describes the 3Rs principle as one of the guiding principles of animal welfare, which 'provide(s) valuable guidance for the use of animals in science' (par. 7.1.2(3)). This is confirmed in section 7.8 related to the use of live animals in research and education. Research is defined broadly as 'basic and applied research, testing and the production of biological materials' (Preamble), with no exclusion for military research. The OIE recognises the legitimacy of the use

[32] EU: Commission Implementing Decision 2020/569 of 16 April 2020 establishing a common format and information content for the submission of the information to be reported by member states.

[33] EU: Treaty on the Functioning of the EU of 26 October 2012.

[34] Some instruments issued by the Organisation for Economic Co-operation and Development (OECD) are also of relevance, especially the 1979 *Principles of Good Laboratory Practice* and the 1981 *Guidelines for the Testing of Chemicals.*

of animals in research but stresses that such use may only take place if necessary, ethically justified, and if no alternatives exist. Animals should be treated humanely and in accordance with the principle of animal welfare.

More general international rules may be of relevance, albeit mostly indirectly, as well, especially those of IHL and IEL. IHL contains no rules on military experiments as such. This can be explained by the general disinterest that IHL shows to animals and by the fact that military research, though linked to armed conflicts, does not take place only during these conflicts when IHL applies. The Geneva Conventions (GCs) prohibit 'physical mutilation or medical or scientific experiments of any kind which are not justified by the medical, dental or hospital treatment … and carried out in/the patient's/interest'.[35] Yet, the prohibition only concerns protected persons, that is humans, and is applicable only in an armed conflict.

Another rule of limited import is Article 36 of AP I, on new weapons, which stipulates that 'in the study, development, acquisition or adoption of a new weapon, means or method of warfare', states need to determine whether its employment would be prohibited by IHL. Although the provision is in force in times of peace and war alike and although it should apply to experiments on animals, to the extent that they make part of the study or development of new weapons, the obligation to determine compatibility with rules of international law introduced by it only concerns the employment of the new weapons, not the study and development as such. More general principles of IHL, such as the Martens clause,[36] do not regulate animal testing, due to the war-centred and human-centred approach they adopt.

International environmental law encompasses many legal instruments that protect either certain animal species or animals in a certain geographic area/situation. With the exception of the European acts discussed above, there are no legal instruments on experiments on animals, let alone military experiments.

A provision on animals used in scientific research was included in the Draft International Convention for the Protection of Animals (ICPA), put forward by animal welfare activists in 1988.[37] The provision, draft Article 9, would read as follows: '[t]he Contracting Parties shall take all appropriate steps to minimize the use of animals in scientific research, testing, and education, and to prevent cruelty and reduce suffering to the minimum in those animals which are used'.

35 Art. 13 of GC III; Art. 12 of GC I; Art. 12 of GC II; Art. 32 of AP I. See also Art. 50 of GC I; Art. 51 of GC II; Art. 130 of GC III; Art. 147 of GC IV, which rank 'biological experiments, wilfully causing great suffering or serious injury to body or health' among grave breaches of the GCs, yet again when committed against protected persons.

36 The Martens clause stipulates that '[u]ntil a more complete code of the laws of war has been issued …, the inhabitants and the belligerents remain under the protection and the rule of the law of nations, as they result from the usages established among civilized peoples, from the laws of humanity and the dictates of public conscience.' (Preamble to the 1907 Hague Convention (IV).)

37 Draft International Convention for the Protection of Animals of 4 April 1988, available at https://bit.ly/3gfSL4w, accessed 22 February 2022.

The convention has not so far been adopted. As an alternative to it, experts have been advocating for the adoption of a Universal Declaration of Animal Welfare (UDAW).[38] The declaration would recognise that animals are living, sentient beings who deserve due consideration and respect. It would promote the idea of animal welfare and declare the 3Rs principle as the leading guidance for the use of animals in experiments. The UDAW has not been, however, formally adopted either.

From more general rules of IEL, the principles of no harm and of precaution might potentially apply. Those principles indicate that states may not use or permit the use of their territory in a manner to cause serious, foreseeable, and preventable harm to other states and that when an activity raises threats of harm to humans or the environment, precautionary measures should be taken even in the situation of scientific uncertainty. Whether harm caused to animals in animal testing would fall under the no harm principle and to what extent the principle of precaution would apply to an activity carried out to dispel scientific uncertainty, remains however unclear. The 'animal turn' in IEL might bring about a broader use of these principles with respect to animal testing. Such broader use has not however yet materialised.

4 EMERGING LEGAL REGULATIONS ON EXPERIMENTS

The previous section has shown that the absence of any international or domestic legal instrument that would deal specifically with military experiments on animals does not necessarily entail the absence of legal rules in this area. In fact, the important commonalities which exist between various legal acts applicable to animal testing suggest that a new legal regulation has been gradually emerging, based on certain shared rules and principles. This section first discusses the scope of application of the emerging legal regulation (Section 4.1), then identifies the main principles and rules making up this regulation (Section 4.2), and finally considers what legal consequences would follow from the violation of these principles and rules (Section 4.3).

4.1 *Scope of Application of the Laws on Medical Experiments*

The emerging legal regulation should regulate military experiments on animals. Two terms – military experiments and animals – thus have to be defined to determine the scope of application of the regulation *ratione materiae*. From the temporal and territorial point of view (application *ratione temporis* and *ratione loci*), the legal acts currently in force apply equally in times of peace and in times of armed conflict. And they apply to animal testing carried out in the territory of the states bound by

38 World Society for The Protection of Animals, 'Animal Welfare Matters. The Case for a Universal Declaration on Animal Welfare' (2007), available at www.udaw.org, accessed 22 February 2022.

these acts, though experiments carried out outside this territory, if performed and/or controlled by state agents, as is almost always the case for military experiments, would most likely be within their scope of application as well.

No existing legal act contains a definition of military experiments. They do, conversely, define experiments as such, using either this term (AEA) or some alternative expressions ('procedure' in the European Convention and in the 2010 Directive). The definitions have two main elements. One relates to the nature of the activity – the use of animals for scientific purposes; the other to its effects on animals – the use may cause them pain, suffering, distress, and lasting harm.[39] The European Convention stresses that '[a] procedure starts when an animal is first prepared for use and ends when no further observations are made for that procedure' (Article 1(2)(c)). Military experiments, as a subcategory of experiments/procedures, could then be defined in two ways: by the actor, as experiments carried out by the armed forces; or by the goal, as experiments primarily carried out to increase the offensive or defensive capacities of the armed forces. Provided that military and civil research might to some extent overlap and that they have been and most probably will continue to be subject to largely identical legal rules, having an autonomous definition of military experiments might turn out not to be absolutely necessary.

The term animal is, conversely, explicitly defined in virtually all the legal acts dealing with animal testing. Most acts adopt a general descriptive definition. As an exception, the AWA suggests an enumeration of concrete species considered as 'animals' in the act. In either of the approaches, the term animal does not refer to all living organisms. In the first approach, it denotes (non-human) vertebrate animals, including free-living and/or reproducing larva forms and excluding foetal forms.[40] The latter approach is usually even more restrictive. The AWA applies only to 'live or dead dog, cat, monkey (nonhuman primate mammal), guinea pig, hamster, rabbit, or such other warm-blooded animal, as the Secretary may determine' (para. 2132(g)). In this way, the animals most widely used in experiments (birds, mice, and rats) are left out of the scope of AWA. The general definition, which is present in all recently adopted legal acts, on the contrary includes all these species.

4.2 *Content of the Laws on Military Experiments*

The emerging legal regulation encompasses a set of principles and rules that can be found in the various international and national legal acts applicable to experiments on animals. The principles set general requirements that such experiments must respect. The rules bring in more concrete guidelines as to the manner in which these requirements should be fulfilled. The principles and rules apply to civil and military

[39] Art. 1(2)I of European Convention (n. 29); Art. 3(1) of 2010 Directive (n. 30); Art. 2(1) of UK ASPA (n. 21); Art. 2(6) of the AEA (n. 26).

[40] Art. 1(2)(a) of European Convention (n. 29); Art. 1(3) of 2010 Directive (n. 30); Art. 2(1) of AEA (n. 26).

experiments alike, though the nature of the experiment might affect their implementation and the assessment as to whether they have been respected.

The first principles applicable to animals testing are the principle of humanitarian (humane) treatment and the prohibition of excessive cruelty and of unnecessary suffering. The former is enshrined in national legal acts, the European Convention, the 2010 Directive and the draft ICPA. It can also be found in IHL, although here, it has traditionally applied to human beings only.[41] It is notorious that the 'humanitarian (humane) treatment' is not easy to define, as 'the details of such treatment may ... vary according to circumstances ... and to what is feasible'.[42] This is even more so when the principle is used with respect to non-humans. The prohibition of excessive cruelty and of unnecessary suffering provides one clear example of a behaviour which is considered incompatible with the principle of humanitarian (humane) treatment. Repeated references to the prohibition appear, in one form or another, in virtually all legal acts scrutinised in Section 3. For instance, the European Convention indicates that '"humane method of killing" means the killing of an animal with a minimum of physical and mental suffering appropriate to the species' (Article 1(2)(j)).

In recent years, the principle of humanitarian (humane) treatment has been more and more often complemented by the 3Rs principle, known from moral philosophy. The first international instrument to explicitly invoke the principle is the 2010 Directive (Article 4). The principle is also enshrined in the draft UDAW. The 3 Rs stand for 'Replacement, Reduction and Refinement. Replacement means that whenever suitable alternatives to testing on animals exist, they should be given precedence. States should use these alternatives when available and actively work to find them, when not (yet) available. Reduction consists of limiting the number of animals used in testing to what is really necessary. Increasingly, the type of animals (species) is concerned as well. For instance, the 2010 Directive stipulates that in the choice between various procedures, those using the minimum number of animals (Article 13(2)(a)) and also 'involving animals with the lowest capacity to experience pain, suffering, distress or lasting harm' (Article 13(2)(b)) should be favoured. Refinement suggests that methods that cause the least pain, distress, and harm to animals should be used. This can be seen as a new and somewhat revised formulation of the prohibition of excessive cruelty and of unnecessary suffering. Generally, the 3Rs principle introduces the requirements of last resort (replacement), minimal use (reduction), and minimal harm (refinement).

The last principle is that of effectiveness, which relates to the capacity of animal testing to provide scientifically and/or practically relevant and significant outcomes.

41 The Pictet Commentary on GC I defines humane treatment as a treatment reserved to humans, as opposed to animals, noting that '[i]t would therefore be pointless and even dangerous to try to enumerate things with which a human being must be provided for his normal maintenance as distinct from that of an animal.' (Pictet Commentary on GC I, 53.)

42 Ibid.

So far, this principle has found its main expression in the provisions restricting the purposes for which experiments may be performed. The European Convention indicates six such purposes in Article 2, namely: 'a) avoidance or prevention of disease … and diagnosis or treatment of disease …; b) detection, assessment, regulation or modification of physiological conditions in man, vertebrate and invertebrate animals or plants; c) protection of the environment; d) scientific research; e) education and training; f) forensic inquiries.' The 2010 Directive contains a similar list in Article 5. Military research is not explicitly mentioned in either instrument. Most of its forms could however be subsumed under one of the (vaguely formulated) enlisted purposes. Moral philosophers question the legitimacy of imposing pain and suffering on animals to develop instruments that are used to kill (other humans or animals).[43] Yet, this debate has not so far affected legal regulation. In a broader sense, the principle of effectiveness also includes the 'usefulness' of the data produced by animal testing. It has been asserted that 90 per cent of drugs tested on animals fail on humans.[44] Although the results might vary for different types of experiments, the lack of reliability of the data produced in animal testing might also cast doubt on its necessity and legitimacy.

The principles applicable to experiments on animals translate into more concrete rules. The divergences between the various sources adopted at the national and international level show that these rules are still in the process of formation. It is nonetheless already possible to identify some of these emerging rules.

One set of such rules applies to the actors competent to conduct (military) experiments on animals. Virtually all legal acts scrutinised in Section 3 limit this circle, at the institutional level, to research or educational institutions, and at the personal level, to individuals with relevant education and a special permission or authorisation.[45] What the relevant education is and under what conditions, and by whom, the permission or authorisation is granted, differs from one source to another and is often left relatively vague.[46] All the sources nonetheless stem from the postulate that experiments on animals may only be carried out by institutions and persons that are, in principle, able and willing to respect the legal regulation. Military installations and researchers should be well placed to meet these conditions, though the recent trend of outsourcing some parts of research involving animal testing to private institutions might give rise to concerns.[47]

43 Geneviève Florence et al., 'Ethics and Animal Experimentation in Military Research Centers', *Sciences et Techniques de l'Animal de Laboratoire* 26 (2001), 95–103.

44 PETA, 'Animal Testing Is Bad Science: Point/Counterpoint', available at https//bit.ly/3GhQiBj, accessed 22 February 2022.

45 Art. 13 of European Convention (n. 29); Art. 20 of 2010 Directive (n. 30).

46 See Felsmann et al., 'Protection of Animals' (n. 23).

47 In 2012, the Defence Research and Development Canada subcontracted testing of a new taser projectile (involving firing projectiles on pigs) to a US university. See David Pugliese, 'Defence Department Still Wounding Anesthetized Animals in "Live Tissue Training"', *National Post* (8 January 2019).

Another set of rules pertains to the conditions under which experiments on animals take place. Although these rules show high variability, some seem to be well settled and largely shared. This is so, for instance, with the rules requiring proper use of anaesthetics for animals subject to testing[48] and the rules on the care for, and the well-being of, experimental animals. The latter entail that animals must be provided with accommodation, have access to food and water, have some freedom of movement, be transported in appropriate conditions and have their health state regularly checked.[49] They may not be used repeatedly in various experiments and should be put to death in a humane manner if, after the experiment, they could either not be restored to normal health or would remain in lasting pain and distress.[50] All these rules are, however, usually subject to various qualifications (as far as possible, if reasonably and practically available, for exceptional and scientifically justifiable reasons, etc.), which make them relatively easy to bypass, especially in an area where important interests might be said to be at stake, such as military research.

The third set of rules relates to the supervision of experiments. There is a consensus that experiments on animals may not be left uncontrolled. Bodies exercising oversight should be established within research institutions as well as on a higher (local, regional, or national) level. The competencies of such bodies may again differ, but the principle is that there should be 'an effective system of control and supervision' (Article 3 of the European Convention). Supervision, as was clearly foreseen already in the 1928 Polish AAP, has to be ensured also for military research, though here the line might be separate from that for civil research (special military supervisory bodies, etc.).

4.3 *Legal Consequences of Violations of the Laws on Military Experiments*

All legal acts applicable to military experiments on animals foresee, explicitly or implicitly, that their violations will entail certain consequences. International legal acts usually expect, or require, that such consequences be specified at the national level. Thus, for instance, Article 60 of the 2010 Directive stipulates that: 'Member States shall lay down the rules on penalties applicable to infringements of the national provisions adopted pursuant to this Directive and shall take all measures necessary to ensure that they are implemented. The penalties provided for must be effective, proportionate and dissuasive.' National legal acts, partly in the implementation of the 2010 Directive, contain more detailed regulation. The AEA introduces criminal liability for ten new offences, for example for exposing experimental animals to unnecessary pain, fear, or permanent damage to the

48 Art. 8 of European Convention (n. 29); Art. 14 of 2010 Directive (n. 30); Art. 30(1) of AEA (n. 26).

49 Art. 5 of European Convention (n. 29); Art. 33 of 2010 Directive (n. 30); Art. 29(3) of AEA (n. 26).

50 Art. 11 of European Convention (n. 29); Art. 6 of 2010 Directive (n. 30); Art. 10 of AEA (n. 26).

organism (Article 38) or for conducting experiments without adequate anaesthesia (Article 39). Similar offences are enshrined in the ASPA (Section 22). The failure to implement the international acts on experiments on animals, such as the European Convention, could amount to an internationally wrongful act, triggering state responsibility under the 2001 Draft Articles on Responsibility of States.[51]

5 CONCLUDING RECOMMENDATIONS

Military experiments on animals are a fact of life. Each year, thousands of animals are subject to extreme pain and suffering to help humans improve their military capacities. So far, this topic has attracted only limited scholarly attention. This should change. We need, first, to learn more about the reality of military experiments on animals. Although some data are available, we still do not know exactly which states use animals in military research, what they do with them, and what the outcomes of such research are. Secrecy surrounding military research makes it difficult to analyse this phenomenon and to comprehend its full scope and nature. Yet such understanding is crucial to address the various moral and legal concerns that arise in this context.

Legal regulation applicable to military experiments on animals also deserves closer scrutiny. While no legal instruments deal specifically with these experiments, the matter is not left unregulated. Both national legal acts and certain instruments and rules of international law are of relevance in this domain. The important commonalities which exist between these different sources suggest that a new legal regulation has been gradually emerging. It should apply to all experiments, including military ones, that are carried out on animals, defined as non-human vertebrate animals, in times of peace or of armed conflict. The regulation is based on the principle of humanitarian (humane) treatment, the prohibition of excessive cruelty and of unnecessary suffering the 3Rs principle, and the principle of effectiveness. The principles are complemented by concrete rules which relate to the actors competent to conduct animal testing, the conditions under which this testing may take place, and its supervision. Violations of these rules entail criminal sanctions and may trigger state responsibility.

The regulation of military experiments on animals is not radically different from the regulation of civil experiments of this type, though some adjustments might be in place to reflect the specific nature of the former. At this moment, we should not focus too much on the need for specific rules in some instances, but rather highlight that military research is generally subject to the same legal rules as its civil counterpart.

[51] ILC, Draft Articles on Responsibility of States for Internationally Wrongful Acts, Report of the ILC on the Work of its Fifty-third session, November 2001, A/56/10, 43–59.

SELECT BIBLIOGRAPHY

Baumans, Vera, 'Use of Animals in Experimental Research: An Ethical Dilemma?', *Gene Therapy* 11 (2004), 64–6.

Felsmann, Mariusz Zbigniew et al., 'Protection of Animals Used in Experiments in Polish Law – History, Present Day and Perspective: A Review', *Veterinarni Medicina* 59 (2014), 117–23.

Florence, Geneviève et al., 'Ethics and Animal Experimentation in Military Research Centers', *Sciences et Techniques de l'Animal de Laboratoire* 26 (2001), 95–103.

Gala, Shalin G. et al., 'Use of Animals by NATO Countries in Military Medical Training Exercises: An International Survey', *Military Medicine* 177 (2012), 907–10.

Knight, Andrew, *Costs and Benefits of Animal Experiments* (London: Palgrave Macmillan 2011).

Russell, William M. S. and Rex L. Burch, *The Principle of Humane Experimental Technique* (London: Methuen 1959).

Shurcliff, William A., *Operation Crossroads: The Official Pictorial Record* (New York: William H. Wise 1946).

Smith, Jane A. and Kenneth M. Boyd (eds.), *Lives in the Balance: The Ethics of Using Animals in Biomedical Research* (Oxford: Oxford University Press 1994).

Yarri, Donna, *The Ethics of Animal Experimentation* (Oxford: Oxford University Press 2005).

PART IV

Enforcement Regimes for the Protection of Animals in Wartime

Part IV deals with the various enforcement regimes that can be put in place in order to guarantee effective protection of animals during warfare: Repression of international crimes (Chapter 18), reparation and rehabilitation measures (Chapter 19), the special regime of wildlife trafficking (Chapter 20), and the roles played by the UN Security Council in this regard (Chapter 21).

18

Repression of International Crimes

Manuel J. Ventura[*]

1 INTRODUCTION

International humanitarian law (IHL) has one broad overarching aim: the betterment of the human condition in situations of armed conflict. Further, through the criminalisation of serious IHL violations, international criminal law (ICL) seeks, inter alia, to condemn, deter and repress conduct that humanity has deemed unacceptable in armed conflict and to punish persons that commit war crimes and/or are complicit in them. This is for good reason: such conduct is detrimental not to any one state but to humanity as a whole. Because IHL is generally anthropocentric in character, one can reasonably expect criminal cases that arise from IHL violations to reflect this. So does this mean that ICL has played no role in the repression of crimes that have affected animals in war? Instinctively, one might say 'it is likely', 'perhaps' or 'not sure'. If sufficiently familiar with the case law, one could perhaps point to anecdotal examples. But in the absence of any detailed study that has focused on animals it is difficult to be sure. A baseline by which to begin a discussion of such matters is conspicuously absent.

This chapter seeks to fill this gap. First, it explores ICL's scope of application by considering how its underlying crimes (with less emphasis on contextual or *dolus specialis*/specific intent requirements) could apply to conduct negatively affecting animals during armed conflict.[1] Second, it considers the content of ICL in this area by presenting a review (up to July 2020) of all judgments from the International Criminal Tribunal for the Former Yugoslavia (ICTY) and International Criminal Tribunal for Rwanda (ICTR), the Extraordinary Chambers in the Courts of Cambodia (ECCC) and the Special Court for Sierra Leone (SCSL) where war crimes allegations were adjudged and animals were featured.[2] Decisions of the ICC

[*] The views expressed herein are those of the author alone and do not necessarily reflect the views of the Organisation for the Prohibition of Chemical Weapons in general.

[1] This chapter excludes reparations in international criminal law (ICL) for such conduct. On this topic, see Lostal, Chapter 19, 'Reparations and Rehabilitation', in this volume.

[2] This chapter excludes the IRMCT, the Kosovo Specialist Chambers (KSC) (no IRMCT or KSC judgments presently exist in which animals are featured within the context of war crimes), the Special

issuing arrest warrants or confirming charges, as well as judgements concerning war crimes allegations, were also reviewed. What emerges is the first detailed account of how ICL has been used to address and repress crimes affecting animals during armed conflict which will then facilitate an exploration of ICL's limits and gaps in this area.

2 SCOPE OF APPLICATION OF THE REGIME OF ICL

International criminal law is commonly agreed to comprise of four core crimes: war crimes, crimes against humanity, genocide and aggression. From this, we can readily exclude aggression as it concerns the unlawful use of force in international affairs and has little bearing on the topic at hand.

2.1 *War Crimes*

The most obvious candidate for the repression of crimes affecting animals in armed conflicts are war crimes – the criminalisation of conduct that constitutes grave IHL violations (assuming, of course, a nexus between the underlying conduct and the armed conflict and an accused's knowledge of the armed conflict[3]). Indeed, it is known that war has contributed to the decline in animal populations more than any other factor.[4] However, IHL treaties (almost)[5] contain no provisions that expressly and directly prohibit specific conduct vis-à-vis animals.[6] The International Committee of the Red Cross (ICRC)'s customary IHL study also did not identify any such rules. In their absence, war crimes that directly address conduct against animals cannot exist. This is why Article 8 of the ICC Statute lists no such war

Tribunal for Lebanon (as it has no jurisdiction *ratione materiae* over war crimes) and ICTR cases that did not include war crimes charges.

3 ICTY, *Prosecutor* v. *Kunarac et al.*, appeal judgment of 12 June 2002, IT-96–23 & IT- 96–23/1-A, para. 58; ICTY, *Prosecutor* v. *Kordić and Čerkez*, appeal judgment of 17 December 2004, IT-95–14/2-A, para. 311; ICTY, *Prosecutor* v. *Naletilić and Martinović*, appeal judgment of 3 May 2006, IT-98–34-A, para. 119.

4 Joshua H. Daskin and Robert M. Pringle, 'Warfare and Wildlife Declines in Africa's Protected Areas', *Nature* 553 (2018), 328–32. Further, research suggests that civil wars generally impact wildlife indirectly – through institutional and socio-economic changes – as opposed to direct impact via military tactics. See Franciany Braga-Pereira et al., 'Warfare-Induced Mammal Population Declines in Southwestern Africa are Mediated by Species Life History, Habitat Type and Hunter Preferences', *Scientific Reports* 10 (2020), 15428.

5 One exception is the prohibition on the placement of booby-traps and other explosive devices on animals or their carcasses. See Art. 7(1)(j) of the Protocol on Prohibitions or Restrictions on the Use of Mines, Booby-Traps and Other Devices as amended (Protocol II) annexed to the Convention on Prohibitions or Restrictions on the Use of Certain Conventional Weapons which may be deemed to be Excessively Injurious or to have Indiscriminate Effects of 3 May 1996, 2048 UNTS 93.

6 This is to be distinguished from international environmental treaties that do address animals directly but are not considered to form part of IHL even if they may apply during armed conflict. This includes, for example, the CITES and the Convention on the Conservation of Migratory Species of Wild Animals of 23 June 1979, 1651 UNTS 333.

crimes (and neither did the statutes of the ad hoc and hybrid international tribunals with jurisdiction over war crimes).

But this still leaves open the application of IHL rules *indirectly* to animals. The most obvious are those rules concerning the environment. In this respect, Articles 35(1) and 55(1) of AP I[7] – which prohibit conduct that causes or could be expected to cause, and mandates that care shall be taken to avoid, 'widespread, long-term and severe damage to the natural environment' – are most relevant; its violation is specifically criminalised at the ICC, KSC and the (yet to be established) African Court of Justice and Human Rights under the Malabo Protocol (2014) (ACJHR) (albeit only in IACs).[8] Such an offence has a dual benefit vis-à-vis animals: it protects the natural environment in which they reside but also protects them as part of the natural environment. Indeed, the ILC, the ICRC and academics have all opined that the 'natural environment' should be understood to encompass fauna.[9] Accordingly, the prosecution of environmental crimes during armed conflict could conceivably encompass the illegal poaching/trafficking of wildlife, particularly as this phenomenon fuels and funds armed conflict.[10] Additionally, war crimes that arise from other IHL violations that indirectly protect the environment (and animals as part of said environment) could also be engaged, including employing poison or poisoned weapons;[11] employing asphyxiating, poisonous or other gases,

7 Art. 35(3) and 55(1) of AP I. Although these provisions only apply in international armed conflicts (IACs), the ICRC has concluded such environmental protection is part of customary IHL that 'arguably' applies in non-international armed conflicts (NIACs) as well. See ICRC Customary Law Database, Rules 43 to 46; ICRC Environmental Guidelines, para. 47.

8 Art. 8(2)(b)(iv) of ICC Statute; Art. 14(1)(b)(iv) of the Law No. 05/L-053 on the Kosovo Specialist Chambers and Specialist Prosecutor's Office of 3 August 2015 (KSC Law); Art. 28D(b)(iv) of the Protocol on Amendments to the Protocol on the Statute of the African Court of Justice and Human Rights of 27 June 2014 (Malabo Protocol). These provisions criminalise '[i]ntentionally launching an attack in the knowledge that such attack will cause . . . widespread, long-term and severe damage to the natural environment which would be clearly excessive in relation to the concrete and direct overall military advantage anticipated'.

9 ILC, Report of the ILC on the Work of its Forty-Third Session (29 April–19 July 1991, A/46/10, Commentary to Art. 26 (Wilful and severe damage to the environment) of the Draft Code of Crimes Against the Peace and Security of Mankind, in *Yearbook of the ILC 1991, Vol. II, Part Two* (New York/Geneva: UN 1994), A/CN.4/SER.A/1991/Add.1 (Part 2), 94–107, at 107, para. (4). See also AP I Commentary, para. 2126; ICRC Environmental Guidelines, para. 16 (both expressing the view that, in addition to fauna, the 'natural environment' also includes animals that are, or may be, the product of human intervention such as livestock). Michael N. Schmitt, 'Green War: An Assessment of the Environmental Law of International Armed Conflict', *Yale Journal of International Law* 22 (1997), 1–109, at 5; Ines Peterson, 'The Natural Environment in Times of Armed Conflict: A Concern for International War Crimes Law?', *Leiden Journal of International Law* 22(2) (2009), 325–43, at 328. See also de Hemptinne, Chapter 7, 'Animals as Part of the Environment', in this volume.

10 Christian Nellemann et al. (eds.), *The Environmental Crime Crisis: Threats to Sustainable Development from Illegal Exploitation and Trade in Wildlife and Forest Resources* (Nairobi/Arendal: UNEP/GRID-Arendal 2014), 48; David H. Barron, 'How the Illegal Wildlife Trade is Fueling Armed Conflict', *Georgetown Journal of International Affairs* 16(2) (2015), 217–27.

11 In IACs, see Art. 8(2)(b)(xvii) of ICC Statute; Art. 14(1)(b)(xvii) of KSC Law (n. 8); Art. 28D(b)(xviii) of Malabo Protocol (n. 8). In NIACs, see Art. 8(2)(e)(xiii) of ICC Statute; Art. 14(1)(d)(xiii) of KSC Law (n. 8); Art. 28D(e)(xiii) of Malabo Protocol (n. 8).

and all analogous liquids, materials or devices);[12] employing weapons which use microbial or other biological agents or toxins;[13] and the use of weapons, projectiles and material and methods of warfare which are inherently indiscriminate.[14]

Rules of IHL that apply in all armed conflicts that specifically protect civilian objects[15] and public/private property,[16] and whose violation form the basis of other war crimes, can also repress crimes affecting animals during armed conflict. This includes animals, such as cattle, that are subject to ownership but can also encompass wildlife as part of the natural environment as a civilian object.[17] Here, we can identify a number of war crimes that can, depending on context, apply. This includes the extensive destruction and appropriation of property not justified by military necessity and carried out unlawfully and wantonly,[18] intentionally directing attacks against civilian objects,[19] intentionally launching attacks knowing that they

12 In IACs, see Art. 8(2)(b)(xviii) of ICC Statute; Art. 14(1)(b)(xviii) of KSC Law (n. 8); Art. 28D(b)(xix) of Malabo Protocol (n. 8). In NIACs, see Art. 8(2)(e)(xiv) of ICC Statute; Art. 14(1)(d)(xiv) of KSC Law (n. 8); Art. 28D(e)(xiv) of Malabo Protocol (n. 8).

13 In IACs, see Art. 8(2)(b)(xxvii) of ICC Statute. In NIACs, see Art. 8(2)(e)(xvi) of ICC Statute. Note, however, that as of 11 February 2022, only 11 States have accepted/ratified these provisions as amendments to the ICC Statute.

14 In IACs, see Art. 8(2)(b)(xx) of ICC Statute (requiring a list of such weapons, projectiles and material and methods of warfare as an annex to the ICC Statute, which has not been agreed to); Art. 14(1)(b)(xx) of KSC Law (n. 8); Art. 28D(b)(xxi) of Malabo Protocol (n. 8).

15 'Civilian objects are all objects which are not military objectives', that is, 'objects which by their nature, location, purpose or use make an effective contribution to military action and whose total or partial destruction, capture or neutralization, in the circumstances ruling at the time, offers a definite military advantage'. Where in 'doubt whether an object which is normally dedicated to civilian purposes . . . is being used to make an effective contribution to military action, it shall be presumed not to be so used'. See Art. 52(1)–(3) of AP I.

16 While domestic jurisdictions increasingly view animals as more than mere 'objects' (thus subjecting them to human ownership) and have in some cases, through strategic litigation, accorded them legal personality and rights (see generally 'Gradually, Nervously, Courts are Granting Rights to Animals: Chimpanzees and Elephants First', *The Economist* (22 December 2018), available at https://econ.st/3umQvRv, accessed 22 February 2022 (recounting cases in the US, Argentina, India, Brazil and Colombia)), IHL provisions that apply to (human) 'persons' are particularly inapposite to animals, as they can entail specific obligations (such as abiding by proportionality, military necessity and distinction principles) or the application of specific legal concepts (such as nationality or 'allegiance theory' in IACs) that animals are simply not a position to fulfil or satisfy. See Jérôme de Hemptinne, 'The Protection of Animals During Warfare', *American Journal of International Law Unbound* 111 (2017) 272–6, at 274–5.

17 On the environment, and the wildlife therein, constituting a 'civilian object', see Marco Sassòli, *International Humanitarian Law, Rules, Controversies, and Solutions to Problems Arising in Warfare* (Cheltenham: Edward Elgar 2019), 569–70, para. 10.187 and ICRC Environmental Guidelines, paras. 18–19, 21 (both noting that some controversy surrounds this view). See Roscini, Chapter 5, 'Animals as Property and Objects', in this volume.

18 As a grave breach of the GCs (and for which a state of occupation is necessary: ICTY, *Prosecutor v. Prlić et al.*, appeal judgment of 29 November 2017, IT-04-74A, para. 303), see Art. 8(2)(a)(iv) of ICC Statute, Art. 2(d) of ICTY Statute; Art. 14(1)(a)(iv) of KSC Law (n. 8); Art. 28D(a)(iv) of Malabo Protocol (n. 8), Art. 6 of the ECCC Law) (note that this latter provision does not require the destruction to be 'extensive' nor does it expressly include the 'appropriation' of property).

19 In IACs, see Art. 8(2)(b)(ii) of ICC Statute; Art. 14(1)(b)(ii) of KSC Law (n. 8); Art. 28D(b)(ii) of Malabo Protocol (n. 8).

would cause damage to civilian objects which would be clearly excessive in relation to the concrete and direct overall military advantage anticipated,[20] destroying or seizing the property of the enemy/adversary unless such destruction or seizure was imperatively demanded by the necessities of war,[21] pillaging,[22] plunder[23] and devastation not justified by military necessity.[24]

A final category of war crimes can also incidentally protect animals: those that shield civilians from the knock-on effects of conduct that affect animals. One example is where the animals in question are a source of sustenance (e.g. cattle and other farm animals as sources of food) and whose looting and killing, as a military tactic, leads to acute food shortages or deprivation. Here, the most apt war crime is that of intentionally using starvation of civilians as a method of warfare by depriving them of objects indispensable to their survival[25] and, where death results, it is possible to envisage wilful killing or murder as well.[26] Tactics that result in such consequences could also be considered as intentionally directing attacks[27] against the civilian population[28] or, alternatively, depending on context, as intentionally launching attacks knowing that they would cause incidental loss of life or

20 In IACs, see Art. 8(2)(b)(iv) of ICC Statute; Art. 14(1)(b)(iv) of KSC Law (n. 8); Art. 28D(b)(iv) of Malabo Protocol (n. 8). In NIACs, see Art. 28D(e)(xviii) of Malabo Protocol (n. 8) (note that this latter provision does not expressly require the damage to be excessive in relation to the concrete and direct overall military advantage anticipated).

21 In IACs, see Art. 8(2)(b)(xiii) of ICC Statute; Art. 14(1)(b)(xiii) of KSC Law (n. 8); Art. 28D(b)(xiv) of Malabo Protocol (n. 8). In NIACs, see Art. 8(2)(e)(xix) of ICC Statute; Art. 14(1)(d)(xii) of KSC Law (n. 8); Art. 28D(e)(xii) of Malabo Protocol (n. 8).

22 In IACs, see Art. 8(2)(b)(xvi) of ICC Statute; Art. 14(1)(b)(xvi) of KSC Law (n. 8); Art. 28D(b)(xvii) of Malabo Protocol (n. 8). In NIACs, see Art. 8(2)(e)(v) of ICC Statute; Art. 14(1)(d)(v) of KSC Law (n. 8); Art. 4(f) of ICTR Statute; Art. 3(f) of the SCSL Statute; Art. 28D(e)(v) of Malabo Protocol (n. 8).

23 As a violation of the laws or customs of war, see Art. 3(e) of ICTY Statute.

24 As a violation of the laws or customs of war, see Art. 3(b) of ICTY Statute.

25 In IACs, see Art. 8(2)(b)(xxv) of ICC Statute; Art. 14(1)(b)(xxv) of KSC Law (n. 8); Art. 28D(b)(xxvi) of Malabo Protocol (n. 8). In NIACs, see Art. 8(2)(e)(xix) of ICC Statute (note, however, that as of 11 February 2022, on 7 States have accepted/ratified this provision as an amendment to the ICC Statute; Art. 28D(e)(xvi) of Malabo Protocol (n. 8). For further discussion of this war crime, see Dapo Akande and Emanuela-Chiara Gillard, 'Conflict-Induced Food Insecurity and the War Crime of Starvation of Civilians as a Method of Warfare: The Underlying Rules of International Humanitarian Law', *Journal of International Criminal Justice* 17(4) (2019), 753–79.

26 In IACs, see Art. 8(2)(a)(i) of ICC Statute; Art. 14(1)(a)(i) of KSC Law (n. 8); Art. 28D(a)(i) of Malabo Protocol (n. 8); Art. 2(a) of ICTY Statute; Art. 6 of ECCC Law (n. 18). In NIACs, see Art. 8(2)(c)(i) of ICC Statute; Art. 14(1)(c)(i) of KSC Law (n. 8); Art. 28D(c)(i) of Malabo Protocol (n. 8); Art. 4(a) of ICTR Statute; Art. 3(a) of SCSL Statute.

27 'Attack' under IHL is defined in Article 49(1) of AP I as 'acts of violence against the adversary, whether in offence or defence'. This has been interpreted, in the present context, to encompass acts that have a direct or, as is the case here, indirect consequences on civilians. See Knut Dörmann, 'Article 8(2)(b)(i)', in Otto Triffterer and Kai Ambos (eds.), *The Rome Statute of the International Criminal Court: A Commentary* (3rd ed., Munich/Oxford/Baden-Baden: Verlag C. H. Beck/Hart Publishing/Nomos 2016), 355–62, at 355–6, margin No. 85.

28 In IACs, see Art. 8(2)(b)(i) of ICC Statute; Art. 14(1)(b)(i) of KSC Law (n. 8); Art. 28D(b)(i) of Malabo Protocol (n. 8). In NIACs, see Art. 8(2)(e)(i) of ICC Statute; Art. 14(1)(c)(i) of KSC Law (n. 8); Art. 28D (e)(i) of Malabo Protocol (n. 8). In IACs/NIACs, see Art. 4(a) of SCSL Statute.

injury to civilians which would be clearly excessive in relation to the concrete and direct overall military advantage anticipated.[29] Further, because of the severe consequences on health and well-being that the onset of starvation brings with it, a number of other war crimes can be envisaged. These include torture or inhumane treatment,[30] wilfully causing great suffering or serious injury to body or health,[31] and committing outrages upon personal dignity.[32] Finally, where coercive acts – such as, inter alia, the looting and/or killing of civilian property like cattle – leads to an exodus of the civilian population from their homes in which they are lawfully present and in the absence of a genuine choice to do so, the war crime of unlawful deportation or transfer[33] is also possible.

2.2 *Crimes against Humanity*

While crimes against humanity do not require the existence of an armed conflict, it is often the case that they go hand-in-hand with war crimes during armed conflict. Notwithstanding, crimes against humanity have their own independent requirements that must be satisfied. Thus, its underlying crimes must be committed within particular a context, namely, a widespread or systematic attack[34] against a civilian population;[35] the underlying crimes must form part of said attack; an accused must have knowledge of the attack; and

29 In IACs, see Art. 8(2)(b)(iv) of ICC Statute; Art. 14(1)(b)(iv) of KSC Law (n. 8); Art. 28D(b)(iv) of Malabo Protocol (n. 8). In NIACs, see Art. 28D(e)(xviii) of Malabo Protocol (n. 8) (note that this provision does not expressly require the damage to be excessive in relation to the concrete and direct overall military advantage anticipated).

30 As a grave breach of the GCs, see Art. 8(2)(a)(ii) of ICC Statute; Art. 14(1)(a)(ii) of KSC Law (n. 8); Art. 28D(a)(ii) of Malabo Protocol (n. 8); Art. 6 of ECCC Law (n. 18); Art. 2(b) of ICTY Statute.

31 As a grave breach of the GCs, see Art. 8(2)(b)(iii) of ICC Statute; Art. 14(1)(a)(iii) of KSC Law (n. 8); Art. 28D(a)(iii) of Malabo Protocol (n. 8); Art. 6 of ECCC Law (n. 18); Art. 2(c) of ICTY Statute.

32 In IACs, see Art. 8(2)(b)(xxi) of ICC Statute; Art. 14(1)(b)(xxi) of KSC Law (n. 8); Art. 28D(b)(xxii) of Malabo Protocol (n. 8). In NIACs, see Art. 14(1)(c)(ii) of KSC Law (n. 8); Art. 28D(c)(ii) of Malabo Protocol (n. 8); Art. 4(e) of ICTR Statute; Art. 3(e) of SCSL Statute.

33 In IACs, see Art. 8(2)(a)(vii) and Art. 8(2)(b)(viii) (requiring a state of occupation) of ICC Statute; Art. 14(1)(a)(vii) and Art. 14(1)(b)(viii) (requiring a state of occupation) of KSC Law (n. 8); Art. 28D(a)(vii) and Art. 28D(b)(ix) (requiring a state of occupation) of Malabo Protocol (n. 8); Art. 6 of ECCC Law (n. 18); Art. 2(g) of ICTY Statute. Note that deportation requires civilians to cross a *de jure* state border or a *de facto* border. See ICTY, *Prosecutor* v. *Stakić*, appeal judgment of 22 March 2006, IT-97-24-A, paras. 289 and 300.

34 An 'attack' in this context refers to a series of violent as well as, in some cases, non-violent acts. See ICTR, *Nahimana et al.* v. *Prosecutor*, appeal judgment of 28 November 2007, ICTR-99-52-A, para. 918; ICTR, *Prosecutor* v. *Akayesu*, trial judgment of 2 September 1998, ICTR-96-4-T, para. 581. 'Widespread' refers to the large-scale nature of the attack and the number of victims, while 'systematic' refers to the organized nature of the attack. See ICTY, *Kunarac et al.* appeal judgment (n. 3), para. 94; ICTY, *Prosecutor* v. *Blaškić*, appeal judgment of 29 July 2004, IT-95-14-A, para. 101.

35 While the target of the attack must be civilians, a person *hors de combat* may be a victim if the act in question was part of a widespread or systematic attack against any civilian population. See ICTY, *Prosecutor* v. *Martić*, appeal judgment of 8 October 2008, IT-95-11-A, para. 313; ICTY, *Prosecutor* v. *Mrkšić and Šljivančanin*, appeal judgment of 5 May 2009, IT-95-13/1-A, paras. 29–32.

that his/her acts were part of said attack.[36] On the assumption that conduct affecting animals during an armed conflict occurs within such a context, a number of the same underlying crimes considered above as war crimes can also constitute underlying crimes as crimes against humanity. However, no underlying crimes exist which directly protect the environment, civilian objects and/or property as such (as one finds in war crimes). For conduct affecting animals to fall within the crimes against humanity prism it should, ultimately, affect human beings.

Accordingly, the category of crimes described above that have knock-on effects on human beings as war crimes could, depending on context, also constitute crimes against humanity. Where animals are a source of food and their killing (either directly or because of conduct that affects the environment) or their theft leads to starvation among civilians and deaths ensue, murder and – where large scale deaths occur – extermination[37] charges are possible, together with torture[38] and inhuman or degrading treatment as an other inhumane act[39] (in light of the effects of starvation on the human body).[40] Additionally, in cases where civilians are forcibly displaced from an area in which they are lawfully present due to coercive acts such as, inter alia, the destruction and theft of property – including cattle and other animals – or damage against the natural environment (and animals as part of said environment), then deportation and forcible transfers can also be envisaged.[41] Where any or all of these underlying crimes[42] are carried out with the specific intent to discriminate against any identifiable social group on

36 Art. 7(1) of ICC Statute; Art. 13(1) of KSC Law (n. 8); Art. 28C(1) of Malabo Protocol (n. 8); Art. 2 of SCSL Statute. Note that at the ICC, but not under customary international law, said attack must be pursuant to, or in furtherance of, a state or organisational policy. See Art. 7(2)(a) of ICC Statute. Knowledge of the precise details of the attack is not necessary, nor must an accused necessarily share the purpose or goal of the attack. See ICTY, *Kunarac et al.* appeal judgment (n. 3), paras. 102, 104 and 124; ICTY, *Blaškić* appeal judgment (n. 34), para. 124.

37 Art. 7(2)(b) of ICC Statute. This provision provides that extermination 'includes the intentional infliction of conditions of life, *inter alia* the deprivation of access to food . . ., calculated to bring about the destruction of part of a population'.

38 Note that, at the ICC, torture requires 'the intentional infliction of severe pain or suffering . . . upon a person in the custody or under the control of the accused'. See Art. 7(2)(e) of ICC Statute.

39 ICTY, *Prosecutor* v. *Kupreškić et al.*, trial judgment of 14 January 2000, IT-95-16-T, para. 566.

40 Art. 7(1)(a)–(b), (f) of ICC Statute; Art. 13(1)(a)–(b), (f) of KSC Law (n. 8); Art. 28C(1)(a)–(b), (f) (also including 'cruel, inhuman and degrading treatment or punishment') of Malabo Protocol (n. 8); Art. 5(a)–(b), (f) of ICTY Statute; Art. 3(a)–(b), (f) of ICTR Statute; Art. 2(a)–(b), (f) of SCSL Statute; Art. 5 of ECCC Law (n. 18). On prosecuting starvation as murder, extermination and torture as a crime against humanity, see Manuel J. Ventura, 'Prosecuting Starvation Under International Criminal Law: Exploring the Law Possibilities', *Journal of International Criminal Justice* 17(4) (2019), 781–814, at 793–8.

41 Art. 7(1)(d) of ICC Statute; Art. 13(1)(d) of KSC Law (n. 8); Art. 28C(1)(d) of Malabo Protocol (n. 8); Art. 5(d) of ICTY Statute; Art. 3(d) of ICTR Statute; Art. 2(d) of SCSL Statute; Art. 5 of ECCC Law (n. 18).

42 ICTY, *Prosecutor* v. *Brđanin*, appeal judgment of 3 April 2007, IT-99-36-A, para. 296; ICC, *Prosecutor* v. *Ntaganda*, trial judgment of 8 July 2019, ICC-01/04-02/06-2359, para. 994.

specific grounds (i.e. *dolus specialis*)[43] and discriminate in fact,[44] then they can also constitute acts of persecution.[45]

A further residual underlying crime is available as a crime against humanity: other inhumane acts.[46] This includes conduct of a similar character and gravity as the existing enumerated/underlying crimes against humanity which cause serious suffering or serious injury to body or to mental or physical health.[47] Here one could potentially include conduct during armed conflict that affect human beings and, incidentally, animals but which is not already captured by existing underlying crimes. This could include environmental damage (and damage to animals as part of said environment) or the use of poison, gases, microbial agents and/or toxins in war. Ultimately, this would involve a value judgement as to how similar in character the relevant conduct is in relation to existing underlying crimes.[48] Given the somewhat flexible nature of other inhumane acts, the right facts – and incidental effects on animals – could render this an attractive option.

2.3 *Genocide*

Genocide is distinguished by its underlying acts being committed with a *dolus specialis* requirement 'to destroy, in whole or in part,[49] a national, ethnical, racial

[43] Art. 7(1)(g) of ICC Statute (stipulating that persecution means 'the intentional and severe deprivation of fundamental rights contrary to international law by reason of the identity of the group or collectivity').

[44] ICTY, *Stakić* appeal judgment (n. 33), para. 327; ICTR, *Nahimana et al.* appeal judgment (n. 34), para. 985.

[45] Art. 7(1)(h) of ICC Statute; Art. 13(1)(h) of KSC Law (n. 8); Art. 28C(1)(h) of Malabo Protocol (n. 8); Art. 5(h) of ICTY Statute; Art. 3(h) of ICTR Statute, Art. 2(h) of SCSL Statute; ECCC Law (n. 18), Art. 5.

[46] Art. 7(1)(k) of ICC Statute; Art. 13(1)(j) of KSC Law (n. 8); Art. 28C(1)(k) of Malabo Protocol (n. 8); Art. 5(i) of ICTY Statute; Art. 3(i) of ICTR Statute; Art. 2(i) of SCSL Statute; Art. 5 of ECCC Law (n. 18).

[47] Art. 7(1)(k) of ICC Statute; Art. 28C(1)(k) of Malabo Protocol (n. 8); ICTR, *Kayishema and Ruzindana*, trial judgment of 21 May 1999, ICTR-95-1-T, paras. 151 and 154; ICTY, *Prosecutor* v. *Krnojelac*, trial judgment of 15 March 2002, IT-97-25-T, para. 130; ICTY, *Prosecutor* v. *Karadžić*, trial judgment of 24 March 2016, IT-95-5/18-T, para. 494; ICTY, *Kordić and Čerkez* appeal judgment (n. 3), para. 117. This severity requirement 'must be assessed on a case-by-case basis with due regard for the individual circumstances'. See ICTY, *Kordić and Čerkez* appeal judgment (n. 3), para. 117; ICC, *Prosecutor* v. *Katanga and Ngudjolo*, decision on the confirmation of charges of 30 September 2008, ICC-01/04-01/07-717, para. 454.

[48] Christopher Keith Hall and Carsten Stahn, 'Article 7: Crimes against humanity – Section B(I)(2)(k) (other inhumane acts)', in Triffterer and Ambos, *Rome Statute: A Commentary* (n. 27), 239, margin No. 99 ('guidance may be derived from norms prohibiting inhumane treatment under human rights law and international humanitarian law', but '[u]ltimately, the similarity assessment ... involves a value judgment').

[49] 'In part' denotes a substantial part of the relevant protected group so that it has an impact on the group as a whole; a specific numerical threshold is not required. See ICTY, *Prosecutor* v. *Krstić*, appeal

or religious group, as such'.[50] This denotes the physical or biological (but not cultural) destruction of any of the four aforementioned human groups; the victims must be targeted for who they are (rather than who they are not).[51] It is evident that in order to qualify as genocide, conduct affecting animals during armed conflict must have a concurrent effect on one or more particular groups of human beings. Like crimes against humanity, genocide is anthropocentric in character. This means that there is little to no scope for the protection of animals directly; at best, the protection of animals would be concomitant to the protection afforded to human beings by the concept of genocide.

Assuming that the accused acts with specific intent, three underlying acts of genocide are most relevant: killing members of the group; causing serious bodily or mental harm to members of the group; and deliberately inflicting conditions of life calculated to bring about physical destruction of the group in whole or in part.[52] Where animals are a source of food for the population, and their theft and/or killing leads to starvation among members of a targeted group, each of the three acts of genocide could be appropriate.[53] Where deaths results from said starvation, charges of killing would be viable, as would serious bodily and mental harm due to the effects of starvation on the human body, particularly in light of the aforementioned potential for its characterisation as torture and/or inhuman or degrading treatment as well.[54] The theft and/or killing of animals, as a means of depriving targeted human groups of food or as a means to expel them from their homes, could also be characterised as deliberately inflicting conditions of life[55] calculated to destroy the targeted group. Finally, the devastation of the natural environment – and animals as part of said environment – can potentially lead to the same charge, as could the use of poison, gases, microbial agents and/or toxins.

judgment of 18 April 2004, IT-98-33-A, paras. 8 and 12; ICTR, *Gacumbitsi* v. *The Prosecutor*, appeal judgment of 7 July 2006, ICTR-01-64-A, para. 44.

50 Art. II of the Convention on the Prevention and Punishment of the Crime of Genocide of 9 December 1948, 78 UNTS 277.

51 ICTY, *Krstić* appeal judgment (n. 49), para. 25; ICTY, *Prosecutor* v. *Tolimir*, appeal judgment of 8 April 2015, IT-05-88/2-A, para. 230; ICTY, *Stakić* appeal judgment (n. 33), paras. 20–8.

52 Art. 6(a)–(c) of ICC Statute; Art. 28B(a)–(c) of Malabo Protocol (n. 8); Art. 4(2)(a)–(c) of ICTY Statute; Art. 2(2)(a)–(c) of ICTR Statute; Art. 4 of ECCC Law (n. 18); Art. II(a)–(c) of Genocide Convention (n. 50).

53 On prosecuting starvation pursuant to these three acts of genocide, see Ventura, 'Prosecuting Starvation Under ICL' (n. 40), 808–10.

54 Art. 6(b), fn. 3 of ICC Elements of Crimes (The Hague: ICC 2011) (noting that '[t]his conduct may include, but is not necessarily restricted to, acts of torture … or inhuman or degrading treatment').

55 Art. 6(c), fn. 4 of ICC Elements of Crimes (n. 54) (noting that this term 'may include, but is not necessarily restricted to, deliberate deprivation of resources indispensable for survival, such as food … or systematic expulsion from homes').

3 CONTENT AND LIMITS OF THE REGIME OF INTERNATIONAL CRIMINAL LAW

3.1 *Crimes and Conduct Affecting Animals Incidental to Charged Crimes*

It is often the case that crimes affecting animals were evidenced and/or established in ICL cases not because the prosecution had actually charged such acts as crimes per se, but rather because they were incidental to findings concerning other charged crimes. For example, the forcible handover of cows by civilians to non-state armed groups was found in *Lubanga* when it addressed entirely different offences, namely, the conscription, enlistment and use of child soldiers.[56] Similarly, in *Taylor*, the theft of livestock by armed children were held to constitute the use of child soldiers to participate in hostilities,[57] while the looting of cows or cattle in *Stanišić and Župljanin*[58] and *Halilović*[59] was the result of the adjudication of murder charges as war crimes and/or crimes against humanity. In *Đorđević*, the killing of pets and farm animals was noted while adjudicating charges of persecution via the destruction of religious property,[60] while *Tadić* found that livestock was burned alive while adjudicating on charges of murder/wilful killing and cruel treatment/other inhumane acts as war crimes and crimes against humanity.[61] At the ECCC and the ICTY, ox and horse-drawn carts were often used by authorities as a means to transport people to detention facilities or by the civilian population to leave their homes and escape violence or a coercive environment.[62] In one instance in *Nuon and Khieu* (Case 002/01), people and animals were transported together in train carts to their assigned locations.[63] In such cases, the international crimes concerned were usually deportation and/or forcible transfers (other inhumane acts) as crimes against humanity.

The looting and killing of animals have also been utilised as background information. Thus, in *Stakić*, a soldier's killing of a dog for barking was recounted as part of the ordeal of a witness as a representative sample of the persecution inflicted on

56 ICC, *Prosecutor* v. *Lubanga*, decision on the confirmation of charges of 29 January 2007, ICC-01/04-01/06-803-tEN, para. 392, fn. 329.

57 SCSL, *Prosecutor* v. *Taylor*, trial judgment of 18 May 2012, SCSL-03-01-T, paras. 1544 and 1546.

58 ICTY, *Prosecutor* v. *Stanišić and Župljanin*, trial judgment of 27 March 2013, Vol. I, IT-08-91-T, para. 557.

59 ICTY, *Prosecutor* v. *Halilović*, trial judgment of 16 November 2005, IT-01-48-T, paras. 460–1.

60 ICTY, *Prosecutor* v. *Đorđević*, trial judgment of 23 February 2011, IT-05-87/1-T, paras. 1102 and 1842–4.

61 ICTY, *Prosecutor* v. *Tadić*, trial judgment of 7 May 1997, IT-94-1-T, paras. 342 and 345.

62 ECCC, *Co-Prosecutors* v. *Nuon and Khieu*, trial judgment (Case 002/01) of 7 August 2014, 002/19-09-2007/ECCC/TC-E313, paras. 591, 593–4, 600–, 622, fns. 1797, 1803, 1858, 1862–3 and 1865; ICTY, *Đorđević* trial judgment (n. 60), paras. 437, 965, 1173, 1179 and 1677; ICTY, *Prosecutor* v. *Haradinaj et al.*, retrial judgment of 29 November 2012, IT-04-84*bis*-T, paras. 436–7 and 442–3, fn. 1569; ICTY, *Prosecutor. Gotovina et al.*, trial judgment of 15 April 2011, IT-06-90-T, paras. 423, 510, 1446 and 1604; ICTY, *Karadžić* trial judgment (n. 47), para. 1457.

63 ECCC, *Nuon and Khieu* trial judgment (Case 002/01) (n. 62), paras. 596–7, fn. 1832 (resulting in deaths from exhaustion and starvation).

the Bosnian Muslim population of Prijedor Municipality.[64] Similarly, in *Gotovina et al.*, the evidence of one witness that had travelled through relevant areas was reviewed as illustrative, noting that, inter alia, dead animals were seen rotting alongside the road, soldiers looted livestock and loaded them onto trucks, animals were hung from trees, pigs were dragged behind trucks and a pig was shot and run over.[65] In relation to events during the Srebrenica genocide, one particularly notorious incident can be highlighted: in a meeting between Bosnian Muslim and UN representatives and Bosnian Serb forces, the latter deliberately orchestrated the killing of a pig within audible distance, with the animal's death squeals/screams being used as a means of frightening those in attendance as an intimidation tactic.[66]

At the ICTR, many cases considered evidence of, and made findings about, such acts in the adjudication of various massacres in Rwanda charged as genocide and murder/extermination as crimes against humanity, as in *Akayesu*,[67] *Musema*,[68] *Bagilishema*,[69] *Kamuhanda*,[70] *Ntagerura et al.*,[71] *Setako*,[72] *Ndindiliyimana et al.*,[73] *Nyiramasuhuko et al.*[74] *Karemera and Ngirumpatse*[75] and *Nizeyimana*.[76] Additionally, findings concerning crimes affecting animals were also found within the context of adjudicating upon rape as in *Nyiramasuhuko et al.*[77] and persecution as a crime against humanity, as in *Kayishema and Ruzindana*.[78] This was facilitated by the fact

64 ICTY, *Prosecutor* v. *Stakić*, trial judgment of 31 July 2003, IT-97-24-T, para. 849.

65 ICTY, *Gotovina et al.* trial judgment (n. 62), paras. 534–7, 540–1, 543 and 546 (but noting that it would consider this evidence when discussing particular incidents).

66 ICTY, *Prosecutor* v. *Krstić*, trial judgment of 2 August 2001, IT-98-33-T, paras. 128 and 341; ICTY, *Prosecutor* v. *Blagojević and Jokić*, trial judgment of 17 January 2005, IT-02-60-T, para. 155, fn. 531; ICTY, *Popović et al.* trial judgment (n. 144), paras. 949 and 951; ICTY, *Prosecutor* v. *Tolimir*, trial judgment of 12 December 2012, IT-05-88/2-T, para. 251; ICTY, *Karadžić* trial judgment (n. 47), para. 5045; ICTY, *Prosecutor* v. *Mladić*, trial judgment of 22 November 2017, IT-09-92-T, paras. 2466 and 2477. Video/sound of this incident is available on YouTube: 'Second and Third Meetings in the Hotel Fontana', *IRMCT YouTube Channel*, at 1:12–1:31, available at https://youtu.be/pia1iQZIpbQ, accessed 22 February 2022.

67 ICTR, *Akayesu* trial judgment (n. 34), paras. 353 and 354.

68 ICTR, *Prosecutor* v. *Musema*, trial judgment of 27 January 2000, ICTR-96-13-T, paras. 384, 423, 663–6 and 696–7 (ultimately finding the evidence unreliable).

69 ICTR, *Prosecutor* v. *Bagilishema*, trial judgment of 7 June 2001, ICTR-95-1A-T, paras. 586 and 601–3.

70 ICTR, *Prosecutor* v. *Kamuhanda*, trial judgment of 23 January 2003, ICTR-99-54A-T, paras. 320–2, 398, 430, 513 and 518.

71 ICTR, *Prosecutor* v. *Ntagerura et al.*, trial judgment of 25 February 2004, ICTR-99-46-T, paras. 501 and 530-538.

72 ICTR, *Prosecutor* v. *Setako*, trial judgment of 25 February 2010, ICTR-04-81-T, paras. 188–90 and 192.

73 ICTR, *Prosecutor* v. *Ndindiliyimana et al.*, trial judgment of 17 May 2011, ICTR-00-56-T, paras. 1253–4, 1257–8, 1261, 1266 and 1270.

74 ICTR, *Prosecutor* v. *Nyiramasuhuko et al.*, trial judgment of 24 June 2011, ICTR-98-42-T, paras. 830, 1319, 1323, 1328, 1410, 1412, 1414, fn. 3378, 1521, 1557, 1571, 1590, 1756, 2034, 2045, 2069, 2080, 2229, 2781, 4332 and 4645.

75 ICTR, *Prosecutor* v. *Karemera and Ngirumpatse*, trial judgment of 2 February 2012, ICTR-98-44-T, para. 1148.

76 ICTR, *Prosecutor* v. *Nizeyimana*, trial judgment of 19 June 2012, ICTR-00-55C-T, paras. 224, 231, 243, 266 and 311, fn. 510.

77 ICTR, *Nyiramasuhuko et al.* trial judgment (n. 74), paras. 2229 and 2781.

78 ICTR, *Kayishema and Ruzindana* trial judgment (n. 47), paras. 293, 306 and 315.

that many fleeing Tutsi took their most valuable possessions with them, particularly cattle. When they sought refuge in various churches or stadiums only to be killed en masse, their animals were either stolen or killed.

3.2 *Crimes and Conduct Affecting Animals in Detention Facilities/ Concentration Camps and as Forced Work*

Animals also featured in detention facilities/concentration camps, with evidence being adduced that detainees were forced to tend to cattle, pigs, chickens, cows and buffalo while in detention, as in *Nuon and Khieu* (Case 002/02),[79] *Krnojelac*,[80] *Naletilić and Martinović*[81] and *Stanišić and Simatović*;[82] or that townspeople and/or detainees were forced to fish and catch frogs, as in *Sesay et al.*,[83] *Taylor*[84] and *Nuon and Khieu* (Case 002/02).[85] These were, in many cases, prosecuted as forced labour/ enslavement or as attacks against human dignity (other inhumane acts) as crimes against humanity or war crimes. In other cases, passing reference to work concerning animals was made, but not prosecuted as such, as in *Krajišnik*[86] and *Stanišić and Župljanin*.[87] The raising or tending of pigs and its location (such as in a mosque), was also used as a means to offend the religious sensitives of persons of particular faiths.[88] Detention conditions resulting in, inter alia, the slaughtering and eating of poorly cooked meat were also legally characterised as other inhumane acts as a crime against humanity in *Bagilishema*.[89] In *Tadić*, a detainee was forced to eat a live pigeon.[90]

79 ECCC, *Co-Prosecutors* v. *Nuon and Khieu*, trial judgment (Case 002/02) of 16 November 2008, 002/ 19-09-2007/ECCC/TC-E465, paras. 1034, 1038, 1044, fn. 3351, 2655, 2672–3, 2678, 2746, fns. 9007, 9026, 9279 and 9312.

80 ICTY, *Krnojelac* trial judgment (n. 47), paras. 393–5 (but finding that it had not been established that the detainees were forced to carry out such work).

81 ICTY, *Prosecutor* v. *Naletilić and Martinović*, trial judgment of 31 March 2003, IT-98-34-T, paras. 329–32 (burying of dead cattle; finding that it had not been proven that detainees were compelled to perform labour).

82 ICTY, *Prosecutor* v. *Stanišić and Simatović*, trial judgment of 30 May 2013, IT-03-69-T, paras. 197–8 and 752 (detainees being forced to 'gather', 'catch' and 'drive' livestock).

83 SCSL, *Prosecutor* v. *Sesay et al.*, trial judgment of 2 March 2009, SCSL-04-15-T, paras. 1230, 1428, 1478–82 and 2036–7.

84 SCSL, *Taylor* trial judgment (n. 57), paras. 520, 523, 1799, 1803, 1810, 1812, 1843, 1844 and 5750. See also SCSL, *Prosecutor* v. *Taylor*, Appeal Judgement of 26 September 2013, SCSL-03-01-A, paras. 261, 263 and 296, fn. 611.

85 ECCC, *Nuon and Khieu* trial judgment (Case 002/02) (n. 79), para. 2672, fn. 9007 (catching frogs).

86 ICTY, *Prosecutor* v. *Krajišnik*, trial judgment of 27 September 2006, IT-00-39-T, para. 343.

87 ICTY, *Stanišić and Župljanin* trial judgment (n. 58), Vol. I, para. 408.

88 ECCC, *Nuon and Khieu* trial judgment (Case 002/02) (n. 79), para. 3253, fn. 10896 (as pigs are offensive to persons of the Muslim faith), para. 1105, fn. 13306 (raising and housing pigs in Buddhist religious buildings).

89 ICTR, *Bagilishema* trial judgment (n. 69), paras. 466, 471, 474, 477, 481, 487 and 489–94.

90 ICTY, *Tadić* trial judgment (n. 61), paras. 194 and 222.

3.3 Use of Animals in the Commission of International Crimes

Another category concerns the indirect use of animals in the commission of underlying crimes. This can be seen in circumstances where people were transported by horse or ox cart for execution[91] or, in this way, enforced disappearances were carried out.[92] In other cases, dogs were used to guard, search, separate persons or prevent escape so as to facilitate killings or mistreatment (as in *Nizeyimana*,[93] *Krstić*,[94] *Blagojević and Jokić*,[95] *Popović et al.*[96], *Tolimir*,[97] *Stanišić and Simatović*,[98] *Karadžić*[99] and *Mladić*[100]); accompanied forces that attacked civilians (as in *Blagojević and Jokić*,[101] *Karadžić*[102] and *Mladić*[103]); or were used to search for civilians or the enemy in order to subsequently subject them to criminal acts (as in *Blagojević and Jokić*,[104] *Popović et al.*,[105] *Gotovina et al.*[106] and *Tolimir*).[107] Among the charges for such conduct were persecution and forcible transfers (other inhumane acts) as a crime against humanity.[108]

A further subset can be identified. These are cases where animals were directly used to physically *perpetrate* crimes. Thus, persons were chained and pulled by ox or cows and dragged to their death[109] and camels and horses were ridden by militias in carrying out attacks against civilians in Darfur, Sudan, as in the *Harun and Kushayb*[110] and *Al Bashir*[111] cases. Indeed, the use of horses and camels by militias to carry out crimes in Darfur was so notorious that the act of

91 ECCC, *Nuon and Khieu* trial judgment (Case 002/02) (n. 79), paras. 965, 1070, 1077, 3296–7, 3346 and 3483, fn. 11162.
92 ECCC, *Nuon and Khieu* trial judgment (Case 002/02) (n. 79), para. 1709.
93 ICTR, *Nizeyimana* trial judgment (n. 76), paras. 1120, 1128, 1131, 1133 and 1135.
94 ICTY, *Krstić* trial judgment (n. 66), paras. 150–1 and 158, fn. 334.
95 ICTY, *Blagojević and Jokić* trial judgment (n. 66), paras. 128 and 171, fn. 418.
96 ICTY, *Popović et al.* trial judgment (n. 144), paras. 328, 342, 394 and 426.
97 ICTY, *Tolimir* trial judgment (n. 66), paras. 265, 287 and 337.
98 ICTY, *Stanišić and Simatović* trial judgment (n. 82), para. 500.
99 ICTY, *Karadžić* trial judgment (n. 47), paras. 5093, 5098, 5113, 5120, 5158 and 5186.
100 ICTY, *Mladić* trial judgment (n. 66), paras. 382, 2256, 2453, 2504, 2516, 2937 and 2981.
101 ICTY, *Blagojević and Jokić* trial judgment (n. 66), para. 163.
102 ICTY, *Karadžić* trial judgment (n. 47), para. 5035.
103 ICTY, *Mladić* trial judgment (n. 66), paras. 1557, 2413, 2448 and 2968.
104 ICTY, *Blagojević and Jokić* trial judgment (n. 66), para. 235.
105 ICTY, *Popović et al.* trial judgment (n. 144), para. 305, fn. 2054.
106 ICTY, *Gotovina et al.* trial judgment (n. 62), paras. 496 and 1645.
107 ICTY, *Tolimir* trial judgment (n. 66), para. 518.
108 ICTY, *Popović et al.* trial judgment (n. 144), paras. 918 and 925; ICTY, *Karadžić* trial judgment (n. 47), paras. 5626 and 5647.
109 ECCC, *Nuon and Khieu* trial judgment (Case 002/02) (n. 79), paras. 4444 and 3100, fn. 10484.
110 ICC, *Prosecutor* v. *Harun and Kushayb*, decision on the Prosecution application under Article 58(7) of the Statute of 27 April 2007, ICC-02/05-01/07-1-Corr, paras. 55–7 and 63.
111 ICC, *Prosecutor* v. *Al Bashir*, decision on the Prosecution's application for a warrant of arrest against Omar Hassan Ahmad Al Bashir of 4 March 2009, ICC-02/05-01/09-3, paras. 85, 91, fns. 74, 94, 97 and 112.

providing such animals to the militia concerned is specifically alleged in the *Hussein* case.[112] Other animals, in particular dogs (German Shepherds) were used to attack and maul detainees in *Naletilić and Martinović*,[113] *Brđanin*,[114] *Krajišnik*,[115] *Stanišić and Župljanin*,[116] *Karadžić*[117] and *Mladić*.[118] These resulted in cruel treatment/wilfully causing great suffering as war crimes,[119] torture as a war crime and as a crime against humanity[120] and persecution (inhumane treatment) as a crime against humanity.[121]

3.4 *International Crimes and Conduct Affecting Animals Prosecuted as Such*

It has been killings and/or theft that have affected animals the most in war. How such conduct has been legally characterised differs. It has been prosecuted as pillage/plunder/extensive expropriation of property, wanton destruction of property, and attacks against civilians and civilian objects as war crimes, as in *Mbarushimana*,[122] *Ngudjolo*,[123] *Katanga*,[124] *Bemba*,[125] *Ongwen*,[126] *Ntaganda*,[127] *Blaškić*,[128] *Kordić and*

112 ICC, *Prosecutor* v. *Hussein*, public redacted version of 'Decision on the Prosecutor's Application under Article 58 relating to Abdel Raheem Muhammad Hussein' of 1 March 2012, ICC-02/05-01/12-1-Red, para. 25.
113 ICTY, *Naletilić and Martinović* trial judgment (n. 81), paras. 434 and 680, fn. 1145.
114 ICTY, *Prosecutor* v. *Brđanin*, trial judgment of 1 September 2004, IT-99-36-T, paras. 501–2 and 535.
115 ICTY, *Krajišnik*, trial judgment (n. 86), paras. 459, 568 and 802.
116 ICTY, *Stanišić and Župljanin* trial judgment (n. 58), Vol. I, para. 441.
117 ICTY, *Karadžić* trial judgment (n. 47), paras. 2198 and 2494.
118 ICTY, *Mladić* trial judgment (n. 66), paras. 440 and 963.
119 ICTY, *Naletilić and Martinović* trial judgment (n. 81), para. 436.
120 ICTY, *Brđanin*, trial judgment (n. 114), paras. 480, 524.
121 ICTY, *Krajišnik*, trial judgment (n. 86), para. 802.
122 ICC, *Prosecutor* v. *Mbarushimana*, decision on the confirmation of charges of 16 December 2011, ICC-01/04-01/10-465-Red, paras. 177 and 178 (theft of, inter alia, goats).
123 ICC, *Prosecutor* v. *Ngudjolo*, judgment pursuant to Article 74 of the Statute of 18 December 2012, ICC-01/04-02/12-3-tENG, paras. 334 and 338 (theft of, inter alia, livestock, cows, heifers, calves, goats and hens).
124 ICC, *Prosecutor* v. *Katanga*, judgment pursuant to Article 74 of the Statute of 7 March 2014, ICC-01/04-01/07-3436-tENG, paras. 928, 932, 938, 950, 953, 956–7, 1660, 1662 and 1665 (theft of, inter alia, livestock, cattle, cows, calves, heifers, goats, chickens, fowl; these animals were described as being integral and essential to the daily life of the civilian population and thus were of great value to them).
125 ICC, *Prosecutor* v. *Bemba*, decision pursuant to Article 61(7)(a) and (b) of the Rome Statute on the charges of the prosecutor against Jean-Pierre Bemba Gombo of 15 June 2009, ICC-01/05-01/08-424, paras. 322, 324 and 330–2 (theft of, inter alia, livestock); ICC, *Prosecutor* v. *Bemba*, judgment pursuant to Article 74 of the Statute of 21 March 2016, ICC-01/05-01/08-3343, paras. 509, 549, 554, 566, 643, 646 and 648 (killing and looting of sheep/livestock; noting that these acts had grave consequences for the victims).
126 ICC, *Prosecutor* v. *Ongwen*, decision on the confirmation of charges against Dominic Ongwen of 23 March 2016, ICC-02/04-01/15-422-Red, para. 50.
127 ICC, *Ntaganda* trial judgment (n. 42), paras. 526, 578, 1032, fn. 1564, 1032–3, 1036, 1040 and 1042–3.
128 ICTY, *Prosecutor* v. *Blaškić*, trial judgment of 3 March 2000, IT-95-14-T, paras. 424–5, 568, 572, 579, 604, 630, 495, 531, 590, 592, 640, 659, 661, 749–54 and Disposition (setting stables on fire, burning cattle alive and slaughtering livestock).

Čerkez,[129] *Brđanin*,[130] *Hadžihasanović and Kubura*,[131] *Martić*,[132] *Gotovina et al.*,[133] *Prlić et al.*,[134] *Fofana and Kondewa*[135] and *Taylor*.[136] Notwithstanding, *Hadžihasanović and Kubura* noted that in the face of a looming famine, livestock could be appropriated/plundered on the basis of a state of necessity.[137] In *Prlić et al.*, in combination with other attacks on villages, it was found to have constituted inhuman/cruel treatment as a war crimes,[138] while in *Orić* the destruction of property housing animals was specifically cited instead of, or in addition to, the destruction of animals.[139]

Furthermore, the killing and theft of animals have assisted in establishing a causal link to specific crimes. Thus, in *Milutinović et al.*,[140] *Đorđević*,[141] *Stanišić and Simatović*[142] and *Karadžić*[143] such conduct, inter alia, was found to have forced the

129 ICTY, *Prosecutor* v. *Kordić and Čerkez*, trial judgment of 26 February 2001, IT-95-14/2-T, paras. 805–6 and 808 (but finding that some of the property was not specifically protected under the GCs or located in occupied territory).

130 ICTY, *Brđanin* trial judgment (n. 114), fn. 1567, paras. 622, 630, 637–8 and 660 (but finding that a state of occupation could not be established and that the property (animals and cattle) in question was not accorded general protection under the GCs).

131 ICTY, *Prosecutor* v. *Hadžihasanović and Kubura*, trial judgment of 15 March 2006, IT-01-47-T, paras. 1860–1, 1894–5 and 1912–14 (theft of, inter alia, livestock) and paras. 1854, 1887, 1906 and 1927.

132 ICTY, *Prosecutor* v. *Martić*, trial judgment of 12 June 2007, IT-95-11-T, paras. 180, 227, 357 and 382 (looting of cattle and sheep). See also ICTY, *Martić* appeal judgment (n. 35), paras. 184 and 203.

133 ICTY, *Gotovina et al.* trial judgment (n. 62), paras. 224, 305, 355, 357, 361–6, 389–90, 405, 492, 497, 499, 559, 565, 567, 576, 578, 582, 587, 619, 626, 644, 650–1, 653, 656, 659, 667–8, 684, 692, 707–8, 710, 713, 723 (witness claimed the sheep were abandoned livestock), 726, 737, 744, 748, 757–8, 760 (dog shot for barking), 761–2, 764, 771, 774–5, 777, 782, 793, 817, 838, 840, 842, 892, 936, 938–9, 946, 949, 953, 962, 969, 974, 976–7, 979–80, 984, 988–9, 996, 999, 1004–5, 1018, 1021, 1023–4, 1028–9, 1034, 1037–8, 1041, 1067, 1079–81, 1089, 1094, 1097–99, 1102–5, 1109, 1122–3, 1292, 1559, 1666, 1713 (livestock/cattle, cows, calves, horses, sheep, donkeys, goats, lambs, oxen, poultry, pigs, puppies and dogs were looted and/or killed (some specifically shot or burned alive)), 1767, 1772–5, 1780, 1783, 1785 and 1789.

134 ICTY, *Prosecutor* v. *Prlić et al.*, trial judgment of 29 May 2013, Vol. III, IT-04-74-T, paras. 1629–31, 1650–3, 1661–3, 1674–6 and 1681–3. But see paras. 1530 (finding that some of the slaughtered livestock were not in occupied territory) and 1646 (finding that the theft of livestock was insufficiently extensive).

135 SCSL, *Prosecutor* v. *Fofana and Kondewa*, trial judgment of 2 August 2007, SCSL-04-14-T, paras. 644, 650 and 697 (looting of livestock).

136 SCSL, *Taylor* trial judgment (n. 57), paras. 1935, 1937 (theft and killing of sheep and chickens). See also SCSL, *Taylor* appeal judgment (n. 84), fn. 785.

137 ICTY, *Hadžihasanović and Kubura* trial judgment (n. 131), para. 53.

138 ICTY, *Prlić et al.* trial judgment (n. 134), Vol. III, paras. 1212, 1302 and 1404 (killing and looting of livestock).

139 ICTY, *Prosecutor* v. *Orić*, trial judgment of 30 June 2006, IT-03-68-T, paras. 600, 613 and 667 (destruction of barns and outbuildings, driving away cattle, torching stables and burning livestock).

140 ICTY, *Prosecutor* v. *Milutinović et al.*, trial judgment of 26 February 2009, Vol. II, IT-05-87-T, paras. 312, 1026, 1067, 1207–8 and 1253–5.

141 ICTY, *Đorđević* trial judgment (n. 60), paras. 528, 715, 723, 1640 and 1641. See also ICTY, *Prosecutor* v. *Đorđević*, appeal judgment of 27 January 2014, IT-05-87/1-A, para. 706, fn. 1727.

142 ICTY, *Stanišić and Simatović* trial judgment (n. 82), paras. 255 (collection of dead animals), 394 (poisoning of livestock), 566 (burying dead animals and persons in a mass grave), 997, 1003, 1049 and 1054 (but not specifically alluding to the looting and killing of cattle when making legal findings on deportation/forcible transfers as a crime against humanity).

143 ICTY, *Karadžić* trial judgment (n. 47), paras. 2465, 2468–9, 2475 and 2520 (but not specifically alluding to the looting and killing of cattle when making legal findings on deportation/forcible transfers as a crime against humanity).

civilian population to leave their homes for the purposes of forcible transfers/ deportation as crimes against humanity. In *Popović et al.*, when finding that forcible transfers as a crime against humanity had been established, such conduct was used as evidence to demonstrate that there had been no intention for the displaced to be allowed to return.[144] When carried out with discriminatory intent, such conduct has also been categorised as acts of persecution as a crime against humanity, as in *Yekatom and Ngaïssona*,[145] *Kupreškić*,[146] *Blaškić*,[147] *Kordić and Čerkez*,[148] *Todorović*,[149] *Simić et al.*,[150] *Gotovina et al.*,[151] *Karadžić*[152] and *Mladić*.[153] Indeed, the legal finding that the destruction and plundering of property, including livestock in particular, can constitute persecution is firmly established in the jurisprudence.[154]

3.5 *Limits and Gaps in the Repression of International Crimes Affecting Animals*

The above review has demonstrated the various ways crimes affecting animals in war have been addressed by ICL and the specific crimes that have been prosecuted therein. Predominantly, it was the theft and killing of animals that resulted in criminal charges. Indirectly, such conduct was used to establish forcible transfers or deportation as crimes against humanity, or where discriminatory intent existed, persecution as well. Additionally, it directly established pillaging, plunder or extensive expropriation of property, wanton destruction of property and attacks against civilians and civilian objects as war crimes, or in combination with other acts, constituted inhuman or cruel treatment as war crimes. Further, the use of animals

144 ICTY, *Prosecutor* v. *Popović et al.*, trial judgment of 10 June 2010, IT-05-88-T, paras. 723, fns 2657, 949 and 951.

145 ICC, *Prosecutor* v. *Yekatom and Ngaïssona*, decision on the confirmation of charges against Alfred Yekatom and Patrice-Edouard Ngaïssona of 11 December 2019, ICC-01/14-01/18-403-Red, paras. 135 and 138, fn. 315.

146 ICTY, *Kupreškić et al.* trial judgment (n. 39), paras. 338, 749, 751, 762 and 763.

147 ICTY, *Blaškić* trial judgment (n. 128), paras. 495, 531, 590, 592, 640, 659, 661 and 749–54.

148 ICTY, *Kordić and Čerkez* trial judgment (n. 129), para. 827 (citing to its previous findings on plunder).

149 ICTY, *Prosecutor* v. *Todorović*, sentencing judgment of 31 July 2001, IT-95-9/1-S, para. 47.

150 ICTY, *Prosecutor* v. *Simić et al.*, trial judgment of 17 October 2003, IT-95-9-T, paras. 98–102 and 866, fn. 2053 (noting the creation of an inventory of collected 'abandoned' property and the spoils of war – mainly cattle and perishable goods – and that livestock were transported to agricultural enterprises and farms); paras. 871, 876 and 1029 (noting action taken to limit looting); para. 1027 (finding that the accused had knowledge of the looting but did not intentionally participate therein).

151 ICTY, *Gotovina et al.* trial judgment (n. 62), paras. 1873, 1881–2 and 1890.

152 ICTY, *Karadžić* trial judgment (n. 47), paras. 2540, 2544, 2547, fns. 8554 and 8556 (citing to prior findings concerning, inter alia, the looting of cattle).

153 ICTY, *Mladić* trial judgment (n. 66), paras. 1385, 1388, 1396, 1400 (looting of, inter alia, cattle), 3388(e), 3398, 3400–1 and 3405.

154 ICTY, *Kordić and Čerkez* trial judgment (n. 129), para. 205; ICTY, *Stakić* trial judgment (n. 64), para. 763; ICTY, *Prosecutor* v. *Deronjić*, sentencing judgment of 30 March 2004, IT-02-61-S, para. 123; ICTY, *Simić et al.* trial judgment (n. 150), paras. 102–3; ICTY, *Milutinović et al.* trial judgment (n. 140), Vol. I, fn. 373.

(dogs) also established persecution, torture and forcible transfers (as crimes against humanity) and cruel treatment, torture and wilfully causing great suffering (as war crimes), while the tending and catching of animals (usually in concentration camp cases) constituted forced labour/enslavement as crimes against humanity and war crimes. This, of course, does not include all the identified conduct outline above or the entire gambit of potential crimes identified in Sections 2.1–2.3 above. But one should appreciate that the pursuit of crimes committed against animals in war per se is not a high priority for international criminal tribunals and courts. There are many variables at play in international criminal prosecutions and so the choices made may have been entirely justified. Looking from the outside in, it is difficult to make definitive assessments.

Notwithstanding, certain limits and gaps can be pointed out. Indeed, an overarching theme can be identified from the prosecuted conduct: it generally reflects or recognises that animals are viewed as (civilian) objects and/or as the property of, or that attacks against animals can affect, human beings. Absent is the notion that the unjustified killing or infliction of suffering on animals have effects on the animals *themselves* or that animals are more than simply objects that require protection from looting or destruction for the benefit of humanity. This is likely a reflection of the generally anthropocentric nature of ICL and IHL. But this is not to say that ICL has no means at its disposal. As aforementioned, IHL affords protection to animals as part of the natural environment.[155] However, there has never been a case in ICL that has prosecuted environmental crimes in armed conflict as such. Even cases that have featured elements of environmental crimes are few and far between.[156]

This can be explained, at least in part, by jurisdictional limitations. For example, the ICTR and the SCSL had jurisdiction over violations of Common Article 3 of the Geneva Conventions (GCs) and AP II, while the ECCC only had jurisdiction over grave breaches of the GCs (1949).[157] However, provisions directly addressing the environment are found in AP I – which is why at the ICC, KSC and the (yet to be established) ACJHR, environmental crimes are only penalised in IACs[158] – when the majority of today's armed conflicts are actually NIACs.[159] Regardless, the ICTY, in addition to jurisdiction over grave breaches of the GCs, also had jurisdiction over violations of the laws or customs of war, that is, customary IHL,[160] which could have

155 See above n. 9.

156 Matthew Gillett, 'Environmental Damage and International Criminal Law', in Sébastein Jodoin and Marie-Claire Cordonier Segger (eds.), *Sustainable Development, International Criminal Justice, and Treaty Implementation* (Cambridge: Cambridge University Press 2013), 73–99, at 92–5.

157 Art. 4 of ICTR Statute; Art. 3 of SCSL Statute (the SCSL also had jurisdiction over 'other serious violations of international humanitarian law', but the list in its statute did not include environmental crimes: Art. 4(a)–(c)) of SCSL Statute); Art. 6 of ECCC Law (n. 18).

158 See above n. 8.

159 In 2018, only eighteen of at least sixty-nine armed conflicts were IACs. See Annyssa Bellal, *The War Report: Armed Conflicts in 2018* (Geneva: Academy of International Humanitarian Law and Human Rights 2019), 19.

160 Art. 2 and 3 of ICTY Statute.

encompassed the relevant environmental provisions of AP I. But no such cases were ever brought at the ICTY. When one adds the substance of the war crime itself and the difficulties which entail from the requirement of widespread, long-term *and* severe damage to the natural environment[161] – a very high cumulative standard – one may begin to understand why a lack of cases for this crime persists.

Regardless, in 2016 the ICC office of the prosecutor (OTP) released a policy paper which included an environmental outlook in considering the gravity of crimes. It stated that the manner of the commission of crimes and their impact could be assessed in light of, inter alia, actions that result in 'the destruction of the environment' and the 'environmental damage inflicted on the affected communities'.[162] The paper went on to assert that the ICC OTP would 'give particular consideration to prosecuting Rome Statute crimes that are committed by means of, or that result in, *inter alia*, the destruction of the environment [and] the illegal exploitation of natural resources'.[163] While this has been heralded as a potential landmark for the prosecution of crimes against the environment – and, incidentally, indirectly protecting animals that reside therein – it remains to be seen how this shift in focus is actioned in practice. Nevertheless, even in this context animals would come into play only *as part* of the natural environment rather than as independent entities.

Here, one should contrast the status of animals at international law versus that in domestic jurisdictions. Due in large part to the contemporary animal rights movement, domestic law is far ahead of international law – so much so that litigation claiming rights for animals has been initiated in various jurisdictions around the world.[164] Although such litigation has achieved mixed results, it builds upon established notions on the treatment of animals in peacetime, namely, that animals should be generally protected from mistreatment, neglect or indeed death per se. This has been achieved in many states via the passage of animal cruelty laws which have been applied domestically in peacetime. Thus, if an animal is made to suffer or is killed inhumanely or unjustifiably, then criminal prosecution for such actions is a distinct possibility. But because ICL and IHL have no equivalent, the idea that international criminal protection should accorded to animals does not exist. Should international law drift, or evolve, into this direction?

On its face, it makes little objective sense for criminal law to ban animal cruelty in peacetime, simply to deny the same or comparable protection in war time under international law. After all, the pain and suffering inflicted on animals is no different. Arguably, it is worse in war in light of its inherently violent nature. Since many states have deemed it fit to protect animals from such conduct in peacetime, attempting to incrementally shift the law in this direction in wartime under

161 See above n. 8.
162 ICC Office of the Prosecutor, *Policy Paper on Case Selection and Prioritisation* (The Hague: ICC 2019), paras. 40–1.
163 Ibid., para. 41.
164 See above n. 16.

international law would not represent a radical legal departure. After all, this study has revealed the commission of specific acts of cruelty against animals in armed conflict. Thus, in *Tadić* a live bird was forcibly eaten by a detainee;[165] a pig was deliberately slaughtered – in *Krstić, Blagojević and Jokić, Popović et al., Tolimir, Karadžić* and *Mladić* – simply to ensure that its squeals and death cries were audible so as to frighten and intimidate;[166] a dog was killed merely because it was barking in *Stakić*,[167] and in *Gotovina et al.*, pigs were dragged behind trucks, shot and run over.[168] Cruelty against animals in armed conflict is not a mere hypothetical.

Be that as it may, one must concede that it is difficult to envisage resorting to a breach of existing IHL as a basis for animal cruelty as a war crime. There is no specific protection under IHL that encompasses such conduct. While one may point to the Martens clause, it is doubtful that, in modern times, it alone may form the legal basis for an IHL rule[169] for the purposes of war crimes, particularly in light of the principle of legality. Put simply, the indirect protection afforded to animals by existing IHL is detached from the reality of how animals are increasingly viewed in domestic jurisdictions. This is not necessarily IHL's fault. After all, IHL was predominantly carved out at a time predating the modern animal rights movement and the identified shift in domestic jurisdictions. It is similarly difficult to envisage genocide playing any role. Due to its express focus on the protection of particular human groups, it is an inherently anthropocentric crime.

And yet, ICL does have one underlying crime that was purposefully tailored to be open-ended, amenable to adaptation and which may assist in breaking free from the paradigm that sees animals as mere inanimate objects: other inhumane acts as a crime against humanity. Could one construct an argument that animal cruelty satisfies its requirements?[170] The problem is that crimes against humanity is also anthropocentric in character – all of its existing enumerated underlying crimes (rape, murder, etc.) seek to protect *human beings*, not animals. On one view, this makes it difficult to argue that animal cruelty is similar in character as existing underlying crimes. But one could argue that animal cruelty as an other inhumane act seeks to protect human beings from the result of violence inflicted upon animals and, in particular, the shock and horror of witnessing such cruelty or to witness its aftermath. This would work best if there is a particularly strong and meaningful connection between the relevant animal and a (or many) human being(s).[171] In this

165 See above n. 90.
166 See above n. 66.
167 See above n. 64.
168 See above n. 65.
169 Antonio Cassese, 'The Martens Clause: Half a Loaf or Simply Pie in the Sky?', *European Journal of International Law* 11(1) (2000), 187–216, at 211; Mary Ellen O'Connell, 'Historical Development and Legal Basis', in Dieter Fleck (ed.), *The Handbook of International Humanitarian Law* (3rd ed., Oxford: Oxford University Press 2013), 1–42, at 34, margin No. 131(2).
170 On the requirements of other inhumane acts as a crime against humanity, see above Section 2.2.
171 An example can be seen in *Tadić*, where a witness testified that, after fleeing his home in the wake of paramilitary attacks, he returned to feed his birds and then fled again – seemingly ignoring the grave

way, we can overcome the similar character problem by bringing the focus back on protecting human beings. At the same time, this is regressive: it reinforces the 'animal as property' paradigm, since it is usually the case that strong bonds form between humans and animals when the latter is the property of the former. One class of animals that would not be of this category are those that are sacred/holy to persons of particular faiths, since such animals are not seen as 'property' due to religious conviction. Nonetheless, this would only apply to a very narrow set of animals.

To encompass cruelty against all animals generally, the argument would have to be made that animal cruelty is indeed similar in character to other underlying crimes against humanity. One could turn to domestic law and note that many countries have criminalised animal cruelty, but ultimately a value judgement will have to be made: should the protection of animals from cruelty stand alongside the protection of human beings from cruelty? Here, one may rely on the fact that domestic jurisdictions are increasingly according (some) legal personality to animals. So, while it is true that all existing enumerated crimes against humanity protect those that the law deems to be its subjects (i.e. human beings), the fact that the law is increasingly viewing animals as its subjects as well (through the recognition of legal personality) means that they may have *more* in common with human beings than we instinctively think – at least in a legal sense. After all, animal cruelty need not be of the same character as the existing underlying crimes, but it must be *similar* in character. The recognition of legal personality for animals can be the hook for the purposes of the similarity assessment. Should this be overcome, we are then faced with the requirement that animal cruelty must cause serious suffering or serious injury to body or to mental or physical health. Again, this has traditionally always been inflicted on human beings. But when viewed through the lens of animals with legal personality, it is conceivable that the suffering or serious injury in question could be inflicted on said animals per se. And so, rather than showing that a human being was affected by animal cruelty, one would instead have to demonstrate such effects on the animal in question.

As is apparent, what will greatly assist the aforementioned proposition is the recognition of legal personality for animals by the law. While we are not quite there yet, if in the future according animals (at least some) legal personality eventually becomes generally accepted, then the argument that animal cruelty could constitute an other inhumane act becomes much stronger. We have cause to be optimistic: through judicial rulings and changes in legislation, domestic law is

danger to which he was exposing himself. On appeal, the defence challenged the witness's concern about the welfare of his pet pigeons in light of the presence of paramilitaries and that, accordingly, the account of what he saw was implausible. The ICTY appeals chamber dismissed the challenge, remarking that '[i]t [wa]s conceivable that a person may do such a thing, even though one might think such action to be an irrational risk'. See ICTY, *Tadić* trial judgment (n. 61), para. 331; ICTY, *Prosecutor* v. *Tadić*, appeal judgment of 15 July 1999, IT-94-1-A, paras. 58 and 66.

increasingly, albeit incrementally, moving in this direction. And the more it does, the more enticing the argument presented herein becomes.

4 CONCLUDING RECOMMENDATIONS

This chapter has provided the first glimpse into how ICL has sought to repress crimes that affect animals in war. After outlining potential crimes under which such conduct could be prosecuted, this chapter has identified that animals have in many cases been the 'victims' of crimes (mainly through killing and theft), while in others they have been used to perpetrate crimes. The jurisprudential review has also shown that adjudicated crimes overwhelmingly protect human beings from their effects and ignores the welfare of animals per se: they are seen as mere objects or property. It has been argued that this is increasingly out of step with domestic developments and the contemporary animal rights movement. While the infliction of environmental damage as a war crime offers some protection to animals, it suffers from jurisdictional and substantive limitations. Accordingly, the recognition of animal cruelty as an 'other inhumane' act as a crime against humanity has been suggested. While this proposition has limitations, the increasing domestic trend to accord legal personality to some animals may make it more palatable as time goes on. At the very least, we must begin to question and critically analyse why animal cruelty is outlawed in peacetime by many and varied states but is seemingly unregulated by international law when carried out in armed conflict.

SELECT BIBLIOGRAPHY

Akande, Dapo and Emanuela-Chiara Gillard, 'Conflict-Induced Food Insecurity and the War Crime of Starvation of Civilians as a Method of Warfare: The Underlying Rules of International Humanitarian Law', *Journal of International Criminal Justice* 17(4) (2019), 753–79.

de Hemptinne, Jérôme, 'The Protection of Animals During Warfare', *American Journal of International Law Unbound* 111 (2017), 272–6.

Gillett, Matthew, 'Environmental Damage and International Criminal Law', in Sébastien Jodoin and Marie-Claire Cordonier Segger (eds.), *Sustainable Development, International Criminal Justice, and Treaty Implementation* (Cambridge: Cambridge University Press 2013), 73–99.

Nellemann, Christian et al. (eds.), *The Environmental Crime Crisis: Threats to Sustainable Development from Illegal Exploitation and Trade in Wildlife and Forest Resources* (Nairobi/Arendal: UNEP/GRID-Arendal 2014).

Peterson, Ines, 'The Natural Environment in Times of Armed Conflict: A Concern for International War Crimes Law?', *Leiden Journal of International Law* 22 (2009), 325–43.

Schmitt, Michael N., 'Green War: An Assessment of the Environmental Law of International Armed Conflict', *Yale Journal of International Law* 22 (1997), 1–109.

Ventura, Manuel J., 'Prosecuting Starvation Under International Criminal Law: Exploring the Law Possibilities', *Journal of International Criminal Justice* 17 (2019), 781–814.

19

Reparation and Rehabilitation

Marina Lostal[*]

1 INTRODUCTION

As famously stated in the *Factory at Chorzów* case, 'reparation must, as far as possible, wipe out all the consequences of the illegal act'.[1] The aim of reparations,[2] therefore, is to re-establish the conditions in existence prior to the commission of a breach of international law. The obligation to make reparations, though hitherto only an aspect of inter-state disputes, has now been extended to human rights claims and, more recently, to international criminal law (ICL).[3] Reparations can be individual and/or collective[4] and might adopt different remedies

* The views expressed in this chapter are written in my personal capacity and reflect my own views. I am indebted to Anne Peters, Jérôme de Hemptinne, Britta Sjöstedt, and Matthew Gillett for their comments on an earlier draft; the participants of the online workshop in June 2020, particularly Marco Longobardo, Marco Roscini, and Giulio Bartolini for their helpful comments; and to my former ICC colleagues Adeline Bedoucha, Cheihk Fall, Fin-Jasper Langmack, Erin Rosenberg, Ana Ugalde, and Tars van Litsenborgh for their thoughts and interest on animals and reparation. The usual disclaimers apply.

1 Permanent Court of International Justice, *The Factory at Chorzow (Germany* v. *Poland)*, judgment of 13 September 1928, 1928 PCIJ (ser. A), n. 17, para. 125.

2 Reparations, in its plural form, is a term generally used in the context of war reparations and ICL, whereas reparation, in its singular form, refers to the right to receive it. See Christian Marxsen, 'Unpacking the International Law on Reparation for Victims of Armed Conflict', in Christian Marxsen and Anne Peters (eds.), *Reparations for Victims of Armed Conflict: Impulses from the Max Planck Trialogues* (Heidelberg: Max Planck Institute Research Paper Series 2018–19), 3–22, at 4.

3 Art. 28(h) of the Protocol on the Statute of the African Court of Justice and Human Rights of 1 July 2008; Art. 63(1) of the American Convention on Human Rights of 22 November 1969; Art. 41 of the European Convention for the Protection of Human Rights and Fundamental Freedoms (as amended by Protocols No. 11 and 14) of 4 November 1950, ETS 5; UN General Assembly Resolution of 21 March 2006, Basic Principles and Guidelines on the Right to a Remedy and Reparation for Victims of Gross Violations of International Human Rights Law and Serious Violations of International Humanitarian Law, A/RES/60/147; Art. 75(1) of ICC Statute. For an overview of reparations at different international criminal tribunals, see Philipp Ambach, 'The International Criminal Court Reparations Scheme: A Yardstick for Hybrid Tribunals?', in Gerhard Werle and Andreas Zimmermann (eds.), *The International Criminal Court in Turbulent Times* (The Hague: T. M. C. Asser Press 2019), 131–44.

4 Rule 98(1) and (2) of the Rules of Procedure and Evidence of the ICC.

or modalities,[5] such as restitution, compensation, rehabilitation, and symbolic measures.[6] Restitution means returning property to the victims, compensation entails monetary awards, and rehabilitation 'is aimed at restoring the victims to their former condition [and] may include economic development ... social, medical or legal services'.[7] Symbolic measures are geared towards acknowledging the harm caused through, for example, public functions or memorials.[8]

An issue that has been under-researched is that animals have figured to a greater or lesser extent in all three areas of reparations. With regard to inter-state disputes, for example, the International Court of Justice (ICJ) in the *Armed Activities on the Territory of the Congo* case found Uganda responsible, inter alia, for looting, plundering, and exploiting Congolese natural resources – including the hunting of protected species – and was consequently ordered to provide appropriate reparations.[9] Similarly, the Eritrea–Ethiopia Claims Commission (EECC) found Eritrea liable to pay USD 12 million for looting livestock required by rural families for subsistence;[10] and the UN Compensation Commission (UNCC) concluded that Iraq was to pay compensation to remedy the 'significant and widespread environmental damages, including loss of habitats and disturbance to ecological equilibria' they had caused during their invasion of Kuwait.[11] Furthermore, in *Peasant Community of Santa Barbara* v. *Peru*,[12] which concerned a massacre that also involved the disappearance of several domestic animals at the hands of soldiers, the Inter-American Court of Human Rights ordered Peru to either return those animals to their former human owners or pay them fair compensation for their loss.[13] The *Indigenous Communities of the Lhaka Honhat Association*

5 James Crawford, *State Responsibility: The General Part* (New York: Cambridge University Press 2013) 506; ICC, *Prosecutor* v. *Thomas Lubanga Dyilo*, amended order for reparations annexed to the judgment on the appeals against the 'Decision establishing the principles and procedures to be applied to reparations' of 7 August 2012 with amended order for reparations of 3 March 2015, ICC-01/04–01/06–3129-AnxA (Lubanga Reparations Principles), para. 33.

6 ILC, Art. 34 of the Draft Articles on Responsibility of States for Internationally Wrongful Acts, November 2001, Supplement No. 10, A/56/10; Art. 75(1) of ICC Statute.

7 ICC, *Prosecutor* v. *Ahmad Al Faqi Al Mahdi*, reparations order of 17 August 2017, ICC-01/12–01/15–236, para. 48 (Al Mahdi reparations order).

8 See Luke Moffett, *Justice for Victims before the International Criminal Court* (London: Routledge 2014), 37.

9 ICJ, *Armed Activities on the Territory of the Congo (Democratic Republic of the Congo* v. *Uganda)*, judgment of 19 December 2005, ICJ Reports 2005, paras. 223, 259, 261 and 345(4). The settlement of reparations is currently before the ICJ. See ICJ, 'Overview of the Case', available at www.icj-cij.org/en/case/116, at 1:12–1:31, accessed 22 February 2022.

10 EECC, *Final Award, Ethiopia's Damages Claims*, decision of 17 August 2009, para. 126. The award also notes that men and boys caring for livestock appear to have been particularly common victims of killings. They were shot and their animals stolen. Ethiopia initially included a claim of USD 8 million for the loss of wild birds (see ibid. paras. 95 and 274).

11 UNCC, 'State of Kuwait', available at https://uncc.ch/state-kuwait, accessed 22 February 2022. See also UN Security Council Resolution 687 of 8 April 1991, S/RES/687(1991), para. 16.

12 Inter-American Court of Human Rights, *Peasant Community of Santa Barbara* v. *Peru*, preliminary objections, merits, reparations and costs, judgment of 1 September 2015, IACtHR (ser. C) No. 299.

13 Ibid., paras. 197, 201 and 304.

v. *Argentina*[14] concerned a creole population whose sudden presence in ancestral lands had diminished the autochthonous fauna and flora of an indigenous community's by fencing off and introducing livestock into the area. The Inter-American Court of Human Rights ordered the displacement of the creole population because their actions had breached the community's rights to communal property, a healthy environment, adequate food and water, and a secure cultural identity, all of which were dependent on their ability to hunt, forage, and fish.[15]

This chapter is concerned with the reparative framework of the International Criminal Court (ICC) context, for three reasons. First, given its jurisdiction over war crimes, the ICC often deals with cases that have occurred during armed conflicts, which is the overarching topic of this book. Second, animals have appeared in all reparations proceedings before the court and are likely to continue doing so. This is because for reparations to have an actual restorative effect the specific measures chosen need to be meaningful to the lived experiences of victims, and many situations before the ICC are located in areas like the Sahel and west Africa where animals are a key part of cultural and economic life. As expressed by the legal representative of victims in the *Katanga* case: 'Cattle play an important role in the family and societal relations of the victims . . . animals allow the family to provide . . . a dowry at a wedding, and to guarantee an inheritance for one's children. [Owning animals] represents an important form of social status.'[16] This fact naturally leads victims to communicate preferences for remedies involving animals. And third, the reparative framework at the ICC is amenable to adaptation because, having been introduced late into the negotiations of the ICC Statute, its content was largely left to judicial development, particularly through principles laid down in case law.[17]

Section 2 of this chapter notes that the protection of animals in the regulatory framework of the ICC is non-existent. Then, it argues that, under the current legal framework, animals could only receive a favourable treatment during reparations proceedings in two scenarios: if institutions dedicated to the conservation and protection of animals were admitted as victims and requested reparations in favour of animals, or if animals were considered protected objects in cases concerning war crimes against the environment. Section 3 shows how animals have been used as objects in all reparations proceedings. Section 4 argues that the ICC should now take stock of the fact that the treatment of animals as mere objects is no longer an unquestionable practice.[18]

14 Inter-American Court of Human Rights, *Indigenous Communities of the Lhaka Honhat Association* v. *Argentina*, merits, reparations and costs, judgement of 6 February 2020 (ser. C) No. 400.

15 Ibid., paras. 168, 202–43 and 330.

16 ICC, *Prosecutor* v. *Germain Katanga*, 'propositions des victimes sur des modalités de réparation dans la présente affaire (article 75 du Statut et norme 38-1-f du Règlement de la Cour)' of 8 December 2016, ICC-01/04-01/07-3720, para. 19.

17 Conor McCarthy, *Reparations and Victim Support in the International Criminal Court* (Cambridge: Cambridge University Press 2012), 36.

18 I have expanded on this argument in Marina Lostal, 'De-objectifying Animals: Could they Qualify as Victims before the International Criminal Court?', *Journal of International Criminal Justice* 19/3 (2021), 583–610.

2 ANIMALS AS RECIPIENTS OF REPARATIONS

Animals are nowhere mentioned, let alone receive any sort of protection, within the legal instruments governing the ICC. However, there are two avenues that could indirectly enable them to receive reparations: through the legal representation of institutions which mandate includes the conservation or protection of animals (Section 2.1) and as protected objects in cases concerning war crimes against the environment (Section 2.2). In both instances the likelihood of awarding reparations in favour of animals is remote.

2.1 *Legal Representation of Institutions Dedicated to the Protection of Animals*

Reparations in favour of victims are foreseen in Article 75 of the ICC Statute. The concept of 'victims' is defined in Rule 85 of the ICC Rules of Procedure and Evidence (RPE), according to which:

(a) Victims means natural persons who have suffered harm as a result of the commission of any crime within the jurisdiction of the Court;
(b) Victims may include organizations or institutions that have sustained direct harm to any of their property which is dedicated to religion, education, art or science or charitable purposes, and to their historic monuments, hospitals and other places and objects for humanitarian purposes.

Natural persons, so the ICC says, is a concept restricted to human beings.[19] Animals cannot a priori fit into Rule 85(b) of the RPE because legal persons must have suffered direct harm to their property to be deemed victims, and animals cannot own things in any legal sense. Organisations and institutions in the sense of Rule 85(b) of the RPE could encompass any legal person[20] with functions concerning the conservation or protection of animals, from large environmental agencies and anti-poaching foundations to zoos and local animal shelters.

Legal persons must have suffered harm to their property to qualify as victims. Many organisations dedicated to the conservation of nature may feel uneasy about labelling animals as property in the sense of Rule 85(b) of the RPE. Nevertheless, the term 'property' need not be narrowly construed. This is because in *Prosecutor* v. *Ahmad Al Faqi Al Mahdi*, which concerned the destruction of world heritage sites in Mali, the trial chamber initially admitted several organisations to participate in the proceedings[21] despite the inappropriateness of speaking about cultural heritage sites, which in part belong to humanity as a whole, in terms of property rights. As

[19] ICC, *Situation in the Democratic Republic of the Congo*, decision on the application for participation in the proceedings VPRS 1, VPRS 2, VPRS 3, VPRS 4, VPRS 5 and VPRS 6 of 17 January 2006, ICC-01/04-101-tEN-Corr, para. 80.

[20] ICC, Lubanga Reparations Principles (n. 5), para. 8.

[21] ICC, *Prosecutor* v. *Ahmad Al Faqi Al Mahdi*, public redacted version of 'Second Decision on Victim Participation at Trial' of 12 August 2016, ICC-01/12-01/15-156-Red, para. 7.

such, institutions dedicated to the conservation of animals and the environment could be admitted as victims, even though they cannot strictly claim ownership over the environment or its animal life.

To earn an entitlement to reparations, the ICC first needs to have entered a conviction against an individual. The victim-organisations at hand would then need to prove that their 'property' – that is any animals and/or their habitat belonging to them – had suffered harm as a result of the commission of such crimes. It is important to note, however, that said property need not have been the target of the crime, it just needs to have been harmed as a result of the crime's commission. This could play out as follows.

In war crimes involving the deportation or forced displacement of civilian populations,[22] two different kinds of institutions dedicated to animals could claim harm to their property: zoos located in the now abandoned city or organisations managing any natural reserves that a displaced population comes to occupy. This is because the forcible displacement of a population could lead to (1) a corollary disappearance of staff members running and managing the zoo, leaving the animals to face a slow death caused by starvation or disease; and (2) the displaced group may settle in an area previously populated by animals, and thereby affect the habitat to an extent that the ecosystem's equilibrium becomes compromised and thus also endangering the area's animal life. This latter scenario happened in 1994 when Rwandan refugees were relocated to the Virunga National Park, a natural world heritage site located in the Democratic Republic of the Congo (DRC). It was reported that there were refugee settlements located at a walking distance from the park, and that 'every day an estimated 30,000 adults and children forage[d] in the park with their machetes, emerging with loads averaging 40 pounds'.[23] Precisely because of the threats posed by refugees, the Virunga National Park was in the same year included on UNESCO's List of World Heritage in Danger,[24] where it has remained ever since.

The causal link that the ICC requires for harm to be considered a result of the commission of a crime in the sense of Rule 85(b) of the RPE consists in pairing the 'but/for' test with the 'proximate cause' standard, where the logic of the former means that *but for* the crime, the harm would not have occurred, whereas the logic of the latter means that it 'was reasonably foreseeable that the acts and conduct underlying the conviction would cause the resulting harm'.[25] Both the zoo and the deportation examples above could reasonably meet these tests, as abandoning zoo animals to their fate is a common occurrence during armed

[22] See Art. 8(2)(a)(vii)-1, 8(2)(b)(viii) and 8(2)(e)(viii) of ICC Statute.

[23] Raymond Bonner, 'Flood of Rwandan Refugees is Destroying Ecological Treasure', *New York Times* (15 November 1994), available at https://nyti.ms/3Hmxt13, accessed 22 February 2022.

[24] UNESCO, World Heritage Committee, 'Inscription on the List of World Heritage in Danger: Virunga National Park (Zaire)' of 12–17 December 1994, CONF 003 IX.

[25] ICC, Al Mahdi reparations order (n. 7), para. 44; ICC, Lubanga Reparations Principles (n. 5), para. 59.

conflicts[26] and there had already been warnings concerning the establishment of refugee camps in or near national parks and the dangers this would involve for the habitat.[27]

Therefore, in the above example, both the local zoo and the agency managing the conservation of the natural park could be entitled to reparations. The decision of what specific remedies they would receive belongs ultimately to the judges overseeing the case. Judges, however, do not make this determination in a vacuum and are largely informed by several considerations, including the views of the victims' legal representatives, which in turn are supposed to reflect the preferences of victims. Thus, there are two circumstances that must concur for animals to benefit from reparations: that the legal persons entitled to reparations use the opportunity to request remedies for the benefit of their animals, and that the judges concur with such a request. While possible, this only constitutes a potential scenario and has not taken place in practice.

2.2 *Animals as Protected Objects in Cases Concerning the Environment*

The *Al Mahdi* case generated a precedent where the ICC ordered a remedy to repair the objects that had been the target of the attacks of the case. The accused, Ahmad Al Faqi Al Mahdi, was convicted for destroying ten cultural and religious sites in the Malian world heritage city of Timbuktu; the conviction was entered for the war crimes concerning attacks against cultural property.[28] The protected buildings of Timbuktu, albeit outside the confines of Rule 85 of the RPE qua non-humans and non-organisations, were given a victim-like treatment when the trial chamber stated that: 'The attacks on the Protected Buildings lie at the heart of this case and form the basis for Mr Al Mahdi's conviction. The Chamber is satisfied that Mr Al Mahdi's crime is the actual and proximate cause of the damage to the Protected Buildings.'[29] In other words, the trial chamber extended tests that were hitherto reserved for victims –the 'but/for' test and the 'proximate cause' standard – to the protected objects of the war crime, and ordered measures intended for their rehabilitation and maintenance.[30]

Since animals are a part of the protected object in the war crime against the environment,[31] reparations based on convictions for this crime could lead to

26 This is a common occurrence in armed conflict. See, for example, Sharon Guynup, 'How Syrian Zoo Animals Escaped a War-Ravaged City', *National Geographic* (5 October 2017), available at https://on.natgeo.com/3Hn6YZi, accessed 22 February 2022; Anonymous, 'Lions Starve to Death in Yemen's National Zoo', *Middle East Monitor* (29 January 2020), available at https://bit.ly/3KZ8hA2, accessed 22 February 2022.

27 UNESCO, World Heritage Committee, report of its 18th session of 31 January 1995, WHC-94/CONF.003/16, 21.

28 Art. 8(2)(e)(iv) of ICC Statute.

29 ICC, Al Mahdi reparations order (n. 7), para. 64.

30 Ibid., para. 104(i).

31 ILC, Draft Code of Crimes Against the Peace and Security of Mankind, *Yearbook of the ILC* 43/2 (1991), 107. For a discussion regarding the definition of the notion of environment in IHL, see de Hemptinne, Chapter 7, 'Part of the Environment', in this volume.

awarding reparations in the benefit of animals. The ICC Statute says: 'Intentionally launching an attack in the knowledge that such attack will cause incidental loss of life or injury to civilians or damage to civilian objects or widespread, long-term and severe damage to the natural environment which would be clearly excessive in relation to the concrete and direct overall military advantage anticipated.'[32] However, a conviction based on this crime is unlikely due to the high harm threshold required and because it only applies to international armed conflicts.[33] This latter restriction constitutes a major blind spot. For example, the widespread poaching activities carried out by the Lord's Resistance Army (LRA)[34] in central Africa can be argued to meet the crime's harm threshold, especially when having the effect of bringing some species to the brink of extinction.[35] The ICC even has an arrest warrant against Joseph Kony, the alleged leader of the LRA.[36] However, Kony and the LRA are involved in the armed conflict taking place in Uganda, which the ICC so far has characterised as non-international in nature.[37] In sum, the possibility of animals receiving reparations when classified as targets in war crimes against the environment is not only remote but undesirable because it presupposes widespread, long-term, and severe harm.

3 ANIMALS IN THE PRACTICE OF THE ICC

Despite the legal instruments of the ICC making no mention of animals and/or their treatment, animals are constantly being voluntarily brought into the reparations programmes designed for the (human) victims of crimes. Animals have been used in two types of remedies: as a means to provide economic rehabilitation to the individuals victimised and as symbolic reparations that commemorate that which was lost.[38]

32 Art. 8(2)(b)(iv) of ICC Statute.

33 This is so despite the Office of the Prosecutor's intent on awarding priority to crimes against the environment. See ICC, 'Policy Paper on Case Selection and Prioritisation' of 15 September 2016, para. 41, available at https://bit.ly/35vCJRW, accessed 22 February 2022. For a discussion regarding the protection of the environment in non-international armed conflicts, see de Hemptinne, Chapter 7, 'Part of the Environment', in this volume.

34 Cathy Haenlein, Thomas Maguire, and Keith Somerville, 'Poaching, Wildlife Trafficking and Terrorism', *Whitehall Papers* 86/1 (2016), 58–76, at 71–4.

35 For more on how poaching continues to steer elephants dangerously nearer to extinction, see World Wildlife Fund, 'The Status of African Elephants: *Loxodonta Africana*', available at https://wwf.to/3HnqrJE, accessed 22 February 2022.

36 ICC, *Situation in Uganda,* decision on warrant of arrest for Joseph Kony issued on 8 July 2005 as amended on 27 September 2005, ICC-02/04-01/05-53.

37 ICC, *Prosecutor* v. *Dominic Ongwen,* decision on the confirmation of charges against Dominic Ongwen of 23 March 2016, ICC-02/04-01/15-422-Red, para. 71.

38 In the context of the ongoing Colombian peace process, animals have also made an appearance as candidates for symbolic reparations. One of the victims, Jenner Alfonso Mora Moncaleano, used to rescue stray animals from the street, taking care of them while finding them a new home. For this reason, his parents specifically requested that reparations should include a project where animals would be rescued

3.1 *Animals in the* Lubanga *Case*

The *Lubanga* case concerned events connected to an armed conflict in the north of the DRC where the accused was found guilty of enlisting and conscripting children under the age of fifteen into the Force patriotique pour la libération du Congo between 2002 and 2003. Mr Lubanga was sentenced to twelve years imprisonment and for reparations purposes his liability set at USD 10 million.[39] Even though the charge that Mr Lubanga faced had nothing to do with animals, they were nonetheless considered during the reparations phase as a means to redress the harm suffered by his victims. For example, one proposed measure included the husbandry of 'goats, chickens or pigs'.[40] With respect to female child soldiers, the legal representative of victims requested that rehabilitation measures had to take into account 'the property that the girls' parents could have received as a bride price when the girls were married. In their culture and customs, when a young girl gets married, her bride price includes animals that are intended to be bred in order to establish a supply of livestock from which the family can draw to marry their sons.'[41] While the exact measures being implemented remain confidential, one could reasonably expect some of these suggestions to have been taken into account since they were based on the wishes of the victims.

3.2 *Animals in the* Katanga *Case*

Animals have featured more prominently in *Prosecutor* v. *Germain Katanga*. The *Katanga* case centred on an attack against the village of Bogoro (DRC). Carried out on 24 February 2003, the specific target of the attack was the Hema ethnic group living in the village. The fact that they were 'herders by tradition'[42] was, in the words of Mr Katanga, a motivating factor behind the attack: 'the Hema … are graziers.

and put up for adoption as a tribute to the life and dreams of their son. In this regard, see 'Audiencia de regimen de condicionalidad, Mondoñedo II' [video], *YouTube* (28 November 2018), at 01:02h, available at youtube.com/watch?v=h_tddODdjso&t=5278s, accessed 22 February 2022. See also JEP, 'Comunicado 98: Sala de Definición de Situaciones Jurídicas de la JEP realizó audiencia de régimen de condicionalidad por la Masacre de Mondoñedo' (28 November 2018), available at https://bit.ly/3L6vJuw, accessed 22 February 2022.

39 ICC, *Prosecutor* v. *Thomas Lubanga Dyilo*, corrected version of the 'Decision Setting the Size of the Reparations Award for which Thomas Lubanga Dyilo is Liable' of 21 December 2017, ICC-01/04-01/06-3379-Red-Corr-tENG, para. 281.

40 ICC, *Prosecutor* v. *Thomas Lubanga Dyilo*, draft implementation plan for collective reparations to victims submitted to the amended reparations order of 3 March 2015 in the case against Thomas Lubanga Dyilo (ICC-01/04-01/06) of 3 November 2015, ICC-01/04-01/06-3177-AnxA, para. 161. See also ICC, *Prosecutor* v. *Thomas Lubanga Dyilo*, filing on reparations and draft implementation plan of 3 November 2015, ICC-01/04-01/06-3177-Red, para. 302.

41 ICC, *Prosecutor* v. *Thomas Lubanga Dyilo*, observations of team V02 on the draft implementation plan for reparations submitted by the Trust Fund for Victims to Trial Chamber II on 3 November 2015 of 1 February 2016, ICC-01/04-01/06-3195-tENG, para. 23(b).

42 ICC, *Prosecutor* v. *Germain Katanga*, decision on sentence pursuant to article 76 of the Statute of 23 May 2014, ICC-01/04-01/07-3484-tENG-Corr, para. 724.

They are herders. So, as regards them . . . it was said that we would be driven from our land for it to become pasture for the animals. So, that was it.'[43] An important element of the attack against Bogoro, therefore, involved the taking of animals belonging to the Hema population. For these actions, Mr Katanga was convicted of pillaging,[44] sentenced to twelve years imprisonment,[45] and his liability set at USD 1 million.[46] In arriving at this sum, the trial chamber took into account the market value of the livestock lost, namely 'USD 400 for a cow, USD 50 for a goat, and USD 8 for a hen'.[47] While it estimated that the harm resulting from the pillaging of livestock amounted to USD 524,[48] the human victims that the trial chamber identified ended up receiving a symbolic amount of USD 250 on account of the harm they had suffered above and beyond what was pillaged.[49] The trial chamber also ordered a myriad of collective reparations 'in the form of support for housing, support for an income-generating activity, support for education and psychological support'.[50] It was proposed that such income-generating activities should include vocational animal husbandry training and the provision of small livestock and veterinary kits.[51] The use of animals did not end there. Since cows are a totemic figure in the Hema culture, the legal representative of victims proposed that those individuals who had suffered the loss of a close relative receive 'one cow with 4 teeth and a corresponding veterinary kit'.[52]

3.3 *Animals in the* Al Mahdi *Case*

As outline in Section 2.2, Mr Al Mahdi pleaded guilty to participating in the destruction of nine mausolea and the door of a mosque in the Malian world heritage city of Timbuktu between June and July of 2012. While several victims alleged having had their domestic animals and livestock pillaged,[53] the trial and conviction focused solely on the charges concerning cultural property. Mr Al Mahdi was sentenced to nine years imprisonment and made liable to pay USD 2.7 million in the reparations phase of the proceedings.[54]

43 ICC, *Prosecutor* v. *Germain Katanga*, judgement pursuant to Art. 74 of the Statute of 7 March 2014, ICC-01/04-01/07-3436-tENG, para. 712.

44 Art. 8(2)(e)(v) of ICC Statute.

45 ICC, *Katanga* (n. 43), paras. 950 and 957.

46 ICC, *Prosecutor* v. *Germain Katanga*, order for reparations pursuant to Art. 75 of the Statute of 24 March 2017, ICC-01/04-01/07-3728-tENG, 118.

47 Ibid., para. 218.

48 Ibid.

49 Ibid., para. 300.

50 Ibid., para. 306.

51 ICC, *Prosecutor* v. *Germain Katanga*, draft implementation plan relevant to 'Trial Chamber II's order for reparations of 24 March 2017 ICC-01/04-01/07-3728' of 25 July 2017, ICC-01/04-01/07-3751-Red, para. 128.

52 Ibid., para. 96. The teeth of cattle are used to determine its age.

53 ICC, Al Mahdi reparations order (n. 7), para. 101.

54 ICC, *Prosecutor* v. *Ahmad Al Faqi Al Mahdi*, judgment and sentence of 27 September 2016, ICC-01/12-01/15-171, 49; ICC, Al Mahdi reparations order (n. 7), para. 134.

An early draft implementation plan of reparations proposed a ceremonial sacrifice of ten bulls in order to restore the sacred nature to the destroyed buildings and to then distribute the sacrificial meat among the poor.[55] This initiative was later abandoned in an updated plan for reparations that is currently being implemented. The trial chamber ordered economic rehabilitation measures for the population of Timbuktu because the destruction of the protected buildings had caused a decline in tourists and pilgrims visiting the city.[56] The updated plan for reparations foresees the setting up of an economic resilience facility – with a funding package of USD 1 million – which includes small livestock trading as well as cattle and fish farming.[57] Here, as in *Lubanga*, animals are a part of the reparations programme even though the charges and ensuing conviction against Mr Al Mahdi had nothing directly to do with animals.

3.4 *Animals in the* Ntaganda *Case*

Prosecutor v. *Bosco Ntaganda* is the last case at the ICC to have entered a conviction[58] and reparations phase. The *Ntaganda* case is so far the one with the most extensive list of crimes and scope of victims. Mr Ntaganda was the former deputy of the Forces Patriotiques pour la Libération du Congo, the same group as Mr Lubanga's, and was found guilty of eighteen counts of war crimes and crimes against humanity involving, inter alia, murder, rape, sexual slavery, persecution, forcible transfer, conscripting children under the age of fifteen, and pillaging. This last crime included livestock and was conducted in the context of the *ratissage* against Mongbwalu – a small town in the DRC province of Ituri.[59] Mr Ntaganda was convicted of a total of thirty years imprisonment.[60] His liability was set at USD 30

55 ICC (Trust Fund for Victims), *Prosecutor* v. *Ahmad Al Faqi Al Mahdi*, 'Corrected version of Draft Implementation Plan for Reparations, With public redacted Annex I, 20 April 2018, ICC-01/12-01/15-265-Conf', 30 April 2018 ICC-01/12-01/15-265-Conf-Corr+Corr-Anx, ICC-01/12-01/15-265-Corr-Red, 18 May 2018, para. 267. This initiative was later abandoned in an updated version of the plan.

56 ICC, Al Mahdi reparations order (n. 7), para. 83.

57 ICC (Trust Fund for Victims), *Prosecutor* v. *Ahmad Al Faqi Al Mahdi*, Lesser public redacted version of 'Updated Implementation Plan' submitted on 2 November 2018 ICC-01/12-01/15-291-Conf-Exp, ICC-01/12-01/15-291-Red3, 14 October 2019, para. 127 approved in ICC, *Prosecutor* v. *Ahmad Al Faqi Al Mahdi*, decision on the updated implementation plan from the Trust Fund for Victims of 4 March 2019, ICC-01/12-01/15-324-Red, para. 84.

58 The *Ntaganda* case is currently on appeal. See ICC, *Prosecutor* v. *Bosco Ntaganda*, prosecution appeal brief of 7 October 2019, ICC-01/04-02/06-2432; ICC, *Prosecutor* v. *Bosco Ntaganda*, defence appeal brief – Part I of 11 November 2019, ICC-01/04-02/06-2443.

59 ICC, *Prosecutor* v. *Germain Ntaganda*, judgment of 8 July 2019, ICC-01/04-02/06-2359, para. 1032. Interestingly, when enquired about the scope of the meaning of the term '*ratissage*' in military operations, a prosecution witness stated that '"[r]atissage" means clean up everything you find across your path, clean everything, insects, birds, animals, men, hit everything, spare nothing, nothing at all'. See ICC, *Prosecutor* v. *Ntaganda*, transcript from the trial hearing No. 89 of 25 April 2016, ICC-01/04-02/06-T-89-Red2-ENG, p. 74.

60 ICC, *Prosecutor* v. *Germain Ntaganda*, sentencing judgement of 7 November 2019, ICC-01/04-02/06-2442, 117.

million, and the proposed reparations implementation plan is not public yet. However, since he victimised members of the Lendu and Hema populations, which are by tradition farmers and herders respectively,[61] it is likely that animals will once again figure in the chosen remedies.[62]

3.5 *Beyond the ICC: Other Uses of Animals in Rehabilitation Measures*

The use of animals for reparations purposes at the ICC has focused on economic rehabilitation and symbolic measures. Outside the ICC, however, animals have been used in physical and psychological rehabilitation measures for humans. Animal-assisted therapy is a common technique for individuals undergoing motor rehabilitation practices and those suffering from mental health issues,[63] including, for example, military personnel experiencing post-traumatic stress disorder (PTSD) or victims of sexual assault.[64]

Dealing with animals can have a calming effect on people, which has been shown to generate positive psychological results[65] even in scenarios involving armed conflict. For example, during the 2003 Iraq War, it was common for US soldiers to take care of cats and dogs roaming the streets of Baghdad. These animals were often flea-bitten and starving, but the contact the soldiers had with them and the care that they provided in turn gave the soldiers 'a temporary exit pass from reality'[66] and thus acted as a much-needed psychological buttress against the stresses of combat.

As far as sexual assault victims are concerned, several organisations in the DRC, including the Jane Goodall Institute, work with local rape survivors from the war in taking care of endangered apes, such as gorillas, bonobos, and chimpanzees. This initiative engages 'young rape victims in tree planting to provide food sources to wild

[61] Legal Representative of Victims, *Prosecutor* v. *Germain Katanga*, 'Propositions des victimes sur des modalités de réparation dans la présente affaire (Art. 75 du Statut et norme 38-1-f du Règlement de la Cour)' of 8 December 2016, ICC-01/04-01/07-3720, para. 19.

[62] For example, the legal representative of victims of the attacks, which in great part were Lendu, noted in relation to reparations that 'most of them were themselves engaged in subsistence farming or small scale business and suffered significant losses due to the pillage of tools, the pillage of livestock, devastation of farming land, or physical injury preventing them to continue their farming activities'. See ICC, *Prosecutor* v. *Bosco Ntaganda*, submissions by the common legal representative of the victims of the attacks on reparations of 28 February 2020, ICC-01/04-02/06-2477-Red, para. 65.

[63] See Giovanni Ballarini, 'Pet Therapy: Animals in Human Therapy', *Acta Bio Medica* 74 (2003), 97–100, at 97–98.

[64] For example, a number of institutions dealing with veterans in the US use therapeutic practices with horses and dogs to alleviate the symptoms of PTSD. See, in general, Andrea Beetz et al., 'Positive Effects of a Short-Term Dog-Assisted Intervention for Soldiers with Post-Traumatic Stress Disorder: A Pilot Study', *Frontiers in Veterinary Science* (2019), 1–14, at 2.

[65] Ballarini, 'Pet Therapy' (n. 63), 98.

[66] Dana Marie Pannella, 'Animals Are Property: The Violation of Soldiers' Rights to Strays in Iraq', *Case Western Reserve Journal of International Law* 43/1 (2010), 513–35, at 514. See also Rebecca Frankel, *War Dogs: Tales of Canine Heroism, History, and Love* (New York: St Martin's Press 2014), 77.

chimpanzees',[67] while others are employed as surrogate mothers for orphaned gorillas. In these settings, '[a]nimals can act as transitional objects, which allows people to first establish a bond with them and then extend this bond to people'.[68] The manifold ways in which animals can be used to repair human harm indicates that their appearance in reparations proceedings is, if anything, likely to increase.

4 CONCLUDING RECOMMENDATIONS

This chapter has shown that, if in the future animals are to benefit from reparations measures, it will happen either indirectly through the backdoor, namely when institutions dedicated to their protection and conservation are permitted to stand as victims under Rule 85(b) of the RPE, or in reparations connected to convictions for a war crime against the environment. In either instance, however, this eventuality remains unlikely.

The recurring consideration of animals in the reparations practice of the ICC coupled with the absolute lack of regulation on their treatment is problematic. There is now an increasing mass of international and domestic rules that no longer consider animals as objects and instead afford them some degree of special consideration. At the international level, a World Trade Organisation (WTO) panel affirmed in 2014 that 'animal welfare is a globally recognized issue'[69] when it upheld a trade ban on seal-derived products because it was believed that clubbing seals and their offspring to death was against public morals. According to a recognition in the Treaty on the Functioning of the European Union that animals are in fact sentient, EU members – all of which are parties to the ICC – are required to take this sentience into account when formulating and implementing the Union's agriculture, fisheries, transport, internal market, research and technological development, and space policies.[70] Similarly, the World Organisation for Animal Health (OIE) has issued several international standards on animal welfare that address, for example, the transportation and slaughter of animals.[71] At the domestic level, courts in Argentina, India, and Pakistan have conferred legal rights to animals, signalling a definitive departure from the 'legal tradition of categorizing animals as rightless things'.[72] For example, a number of states

[67] Tina Deines, '"Gorilla Moms": The Women Rescuing Congo's Endangered Primates', *Guardian* (14 June 2017), available at https://bit.ly/3Jo4aSB, accessed 22 February 2022.

[68] Dilek Tunçay Elmaci and Sibel Cevizci, 'Dog-Assisted Therapies and Activities in Rehabilitation of Children with Cerebral Palsy and Physical and Mental Disabilities', *International Journal of Environmental Research and Public Health* 12/5 (2015), 5046–60, at 5047.

[69] WTO, *European Communities: Measures Prohibiting the Importation and Marketing of Seal Products*, Panel Report, WTO Docs WT/DS400/R and WT/DS401/R, 25 November 2013 (*EC – Seal Products*), para. 7420.

[70] EU: Art. 13 of the Treaty on the Functioning of the EU of 26 October 2012.

[71] See World Organisation for Animal Health, *Terrestrial Animal Health Code* (28th ed. 2019), section 7, chapters 1–14, available at https://bit.ly/3un1XMZ, accessed 22 February 2022.

[72] Saskia Stucki, 'Toward Hominid and Other Humanoid Rights: Are We Witnessing a Legal Revolution?', *Verfassungsblog* (30 December 2016), available at https://bit.ly/3ux6yfF, accessed 22 February 2022. See, for example, Poder Judicial de Mendoza and Tercer Juzgado de Garantías,

now proclaim in their civil codes that animals are not things[73] and thus afford them 'legal requirements and rules of common law, reasonable restrictions, obligations and principles of law, as well as public order and morality'.[74] In 2018, strategic litigation against the arbitrary confinement of animals in the US led to a judicial opinion that labelled the binary division between persons and things 'a deep dilemma of ethics and policy that demands our attention'.[75]

While these changes have not yet reached a level that would allow us to speak of a new international custom or general principle of international law, they are also not anecdotal. These changes point to a trend in international and domestic law that has embodied the animal turn by questioning the classical understanding and treatment of animals as things.[76] In light of the principle *iura novit curia* – meaning 'the court knows the law' – the systemic silence within the ICC is starting to tail behind international and domestic legal developments.

At this stage there should be at least a *prise de conscience* that the treatment of animals by humans as mere things to be used and abused no longer constitutes a ubiquitous legal status quo.[77] Eventually, this should lead to a discussion about what place and treatment animals should be afforded. Embedding animal issues into the reparative framework of the ICC is feasible because, unlike the statute and other instruments, it does not require an amendment by the state parties. The reparative framework is largely developed through case law and thus does not necessitate qualified majorities and lengthy inter-state negotiations. Provided that there is an awareness and willingness to deal with the animal question, there are a number of ways in which judges could seek advice and opinions on whether to introduce, for example, welfare standards vis-à-vis animals. They could, for example, hire thematic advisers through the usual recruitment channels, request *amici curiae* in connection to a reparations case, and/or appoint experts in the reparations phase pursuant to Rule 97(2) of the RPE. The profile of these individuals could range from ethologists and animal welfare specialists to experts in applied ethics. The benefits of

'Presentación efectuada por A.F.A.D.A. respecto del chimpancé "Cecilia": Sujeto no humano' (3 November 2016), Expediente n° P-72.254/15; Turkey: Islamabad High Court, *Islamabad Wildlife Management Board through its Chairman versus Metropolitan Corporation Islamabad through its Mayor & 4 others*, 25 April 2020 W.P. No. 1155/2019.

73 Austria: Civil Code (Allgemeines Bürgerliches Gesetzbuch) (ABGB), Art. 285(a); Germany: Civil Code (Bürgerliches Gesetzbuch) (BGB), Art. 90 ; Switzerland: Civil Code, Art. 641a; France: Civil Code, Art. 515-14; The Netherlands: Civil Code (Burgerlijk Wetboek), Book 3, Title 1, Section 1, Art. 2a); Czech Republic: Civil Code, Section 494; Spain: Catalunya Civil Code, Art. 511-1(3); Canada: Quebec Civil Code, Art. 898.1; Colombia: Civil Code, Art. 655; New Zealand: Section 4 of the Animal Welfare Amendment Act (No. 2) 2015.

74 The Netherlands: Civil Code (*Burgerlijk Wetboek*), Book 3, Title 1, Section 1, Art. 2a).

75 State of New York Court of Appeals: Motion No. 2018-268 in the Matter of Nonhuman Rights Project, Inc., on Behalf of Tommy, *Appellant*, v. *Patrick C. Lavery, & c., et al.*, Respondents, 8 May 2018, 5.

76 Harriet Ritvo, 'On the Animal Turn', *Daedalus* 136/4 (2007), 118–22, at 121.

77 Sabine Brels, *Le Droit de Bien-Être Animal Dans Le Monde: Évolution et Universalisation* (Paris: L'Harmattan 2017), 13.

bringing in animal-related expertise to the ICC would go beyond the immediate concern of their use in reparations proceedings.

Lastly, there is another area at the ICC where, one day, advice regarding animals could be urgently needed: the seizure and freezing of assets of a person under investigation.[78] The court has so far dealt with, though not very efficiently, liquid assets and inanimate objects such as villas and planes.[79] What would happen if the person under investigation possessed live animals?[80] Or what if they were in possession of animal derivatives such as elephant tusks or rhinoceros horns acquired through poaching? This scenario could very well be the case for someone like Joseph Kony or even Saif al-Islam Gaddafi – the third son of the former Libyan leader Muammar Gaddafi – who was known for having a private zoo containing lions, ostriches, and camels and for whom there is an ICC arrest warrant.[81] This all goes to show that regulation in the ICC reparative framework regarding the treatment of animals is a pending and inexorable question that needs to be addressed sooner rather than later.

SELECT BIBLIOGRAPHY

Brels, Sabine, *Le droit de bien-être animal dans le monde: Évolution et universalisation* (Paris: L'Harmattan 2017).

Crawford, James, *State Responsibility: The General Part* (New York: Cambridge University Press 2013).

Haenlein, Cathy, Thomas Maguire and Keith Somerville, 'Poaching, Wildlife Trafficking and Terrorism', Whitehall Papers 86 (2016).

Lostal, Marina, 'De-objectifying Animals: Could they Qualify as Victims before the International Criminal Court?', *Journal of International Criminal Justice* 19/3 (2021), 583–610.

McCarthy, Conor, *Reparations and Victim Support in the International Criminal Court* (Cambridge: Cambridge University Press 2012).

Moffett, Luke, *Justice for Victims before the International Criminal Court* (Abingdon: Routledge 2014).

Pannella, Dana Marie, 'Animals Are Property: The Violation of Soldiers' Rights to Strays in Iraq', *Case Western Reserve Journal of International Law* 43 (2010), 513–35.

Stucki, Saskia, 'Toward Hominid and Other Humanoid Rights: Are We Witnessing a Legal Revolution?', *Verfassungsblog* (30 December 2016), available at https://bit.ly/3ux6yfF.

78 Art. 93(1)(k) of ICC Statute. Such measures are, in particular, for the ultimate benefit of victims in the reparations phase, according to Art. 57(3)(e) of ICC Statute. For a commentary on this function, see Daley J. Birkett, 'Pre-Trial "Protective Measures for the Purpose of Forfeiture" at the International Criminal Court: Safeguarding and Balancing Competing Rights and Interests', *Leiden Journal of International Law* 32 (2019), 585–602.

79 See Daley J. Birkett, 'Managing Frozen Assets at the International Criminal Court: The Fallout of the Bemba Acquittal', *Journal of International Criminal Justice* 18/3 (2020), 1–26.

80 The author thanks Erin Rosenberg for signalling this issue.

81 ICC, *Situation in the Libyan Arab Jamahiriya*, warrant of arrest for Saif Al-Islam Gaddafi of 27 June 2011, ICC-01/11-1. See also Luke Harding, 'Gaddafi's Son Abandons his Lions in Fight for Tripoli', *Guardian* (30 August 2011), available at https://bit.ly/342QzLt, accessed 22 February 2022.

20

The Special Regime for Wildlife Trafficking

Karsten Nowrot

1 INTRODUCTION

Disputes over the use and distribution of natural resources are rarely the primary reason for the outbreak of civil war and the accompanying formation of armed rebel groups. However, it is by now generally recognised that resource-rich countries, in particular those that rely heavily on the export of primary commodities, at times suffer from the multifaceted so-called natural resource curse.[1] More so, these same countries are also at times confronted with what the World Trade Organisation (WTO) describes as the 'most severe manifestation' of this phenomenon:[2] an overall higher risk of prolonged and increasingly intensified international – and especially non-international – armed conflicts precisely because the production of, and international trade in, raw materials such as diamonds and other gemstones, gold, timber, rare minerals, oil, and illegal narcotics often accounts for one of the primary sources of funding for insurgents and other organised armed groups. In order to illustrate and substantiate the proposition that natural recourses have a significant potential to 'fuel' ongoing civil wars, one only needs to refer to the respective conditions prevailing in conflict-affected countries like Angola, Colombia, Myanmar, Sierra Leone, Peru, Somalia, Cambodia, Iraq, Libya, the Central African Republic, and – last but unfortunately surely not least – in the Democratic Republic of the Congo (DRC). Moreover, it should be noted here that the DRC in particular also 'possesses an outstanding megabiodiversity reservoir that ranks fifth in importance at the global level and is unequalled in Africa'.[3]

And indeed, as more recently increasingly recognised, these same findings regarding raw materials apply also to the international and non-international trade in wildlife, including the trafficking of specimens of endangered and legally protected species.

[1] On the phenomenon of the so-called natural resource curse, see, for example, WTO, *World Trade Report 2010: Trade in Natural Resources* (Geneva: 2010), 91–96.

[2] *Ibid.*, 94.

[3] UNEP, *The Democratic Republic of the Congo: Post-Conflict Environmental Assessment, Synthesis for Policy Makers* (Nairobi: UNEP 2011), 22.

Although the exact importance of these activities as factors contributing to the prolongation of armed conflicts remains contested, and notwithstanding their variation from conflict to conflict,[4] it is in principle widely acknowledged that poaching and the trafficking of wildlife constitutes one of the more notable sources of funding for certain governmental actors, but first and foremost also for organised non-state armed groups, in particular in some regions of Africa, enabling these actors to sustain themselves materially and (crucially) militarily, which can and often does contribute to the prolongation of armed conflicts.[5] Thereby, in particular also endangered species and their products are much 'wanted', considering their financial value as 'commodities' in both legal and illegal international trade relations.[6]

This phenomenon certainly adds another regrettable dimension to the already well-developed – and thus rather profitable – peacetime illegal trade in wildlife commodities by further threatening the survival of many of the world's already and soon-to-be endangered species. Whereas the continuing destruction of natural habitats has for quite some time been regarded as the most serious threat to endangered and other vulnerable animals around the world, the local as well as in particular transboundary trade in these species and their products arguably also constitutes one of the truly crucial factors contributing to their decline and further endangerment. Wildlife trafficking is already for quite some time said to be the third most valuable illicit commerce in the world after drugs and weapons, and appears to be on the rise. Whereas in the 1990s the global illegal wildlife trade was estimated to generate USD 5–10 billion annually,[7] more recent estimates already put this number above USD 20 billion.[8] These figures serve as a clear indication that in particular also the participation of organised criminal groups in the illegal wildlife trade, attracted by the prospect of considerable profits resulting from what is often viewed as a comparatively low-risk criminal activity, constitutes already in peacetime a severe threat to wildlife populations around the world.

4 For a rather sceptical account, see for example Stéphane Crayne and Cathy Haenlein, 'Poaching, Wildlife Trafficking and Conflict', in Cathy Haenlein and M. L. R. Smith (eds.), *Poaching, Wildlife Trafficking and Security in Africa: Myths and Realities* (London: Routledge 2016), 38–57.

5 Generally thereto for example Christian Nellemann et al., *The Rise of Environmental Crime: A Growing Threat to Natural Resources, Peace, Development and Security, An UNEP–INTERPOL Rapid Response Assessment* (Nairobi: UNEP 2016), 16, 67–71, at 86; Jérôme de Hemptinne, 'The Protection of Animals During Warfare', *American Journal of International Law Unbound* 111 (2017), 272–6, at 272; Joshua H. Daskin and Robert M. Pringle, 'Warfare and Wildlife Declines in Africa's Protected Areas', *Nature* 553 (2018), 328–32. See Daskin and Pringle, Chapter 3, 'Ecological Effects of Warfare on Wildlife', in this volume.

6 See, for example, UNEP, CITES, IUCN and TRAFFIC, *Elephants in the Dust: The African Elephant Crisis* (Nairobi: UNEP 2013), 40–1; David H. Barron, 'How Illegal Wildlife Trade is Fuelling Armed Conflict', *Georgetown Journal of International Affairs* 16 (2015), 217–27, at 219–21.

7 Elisabeth M. McOmber, 'Problems in Enforcement of the Convention on International Trade in Endangered Species', *Brooklyn Journal of International Law* 27 (2002), 673–701, at 674.

8 EU: European Parliament, Resolution of 24 November 2016 on the EU action plan against wildlife trafficking (2016/2076(INI)), para. A.

However, the situation is made substantially worse by armed conflicts, considering that also these 'civilian' poachers and their smuggling networks can – and commonly do – take advantage of the frequently chaotic wartime circumstances, including the significantly weakened capacity of the countries concerned to control their territory and to effectively enforce their international obligations and domestic laws aimed at preventing and combatting the illegal wildlife trade. Accordingly, even in those cases where wildlife trafficking does not seem to constitute a significant source of funding for belligerents, the protection of animals is often substantially complicated by the existence of armed conflicts, therefore illustrating the complex and growing negative consequences of wartime conditions for endangered species particularly and wildlife in general.

Nevertheless, in particular as far as the activities of insurgents and other organised armed groups are concerned, the increasing recognition of the linkages between conflict prevention and containment – and thus also the issue of international peace and security – on the one hand as well as the need for effective protection of wild animals on the other hand[9] could also, more optimistically, be perceived as a new opportunity to improve the existing normative frameworks on the prevention and combatting of wildlife trafficking and its enforcement mechanisms. These possible improvements would be for the benefit of conflict-affected humans and animals alike and – when again considered optimistically – have the potential to also more effectively combat the illegal trade in wildlife and its products during peacetime.

Against this background and in order to illustrate this more hopeful proposition, this chapter intends to approach the normative governance regimes dealing with wildlife trafficking in the present context of the protection of animals in wartime from an enforcement perspective in two main steps. Section 2 attempts to identify and address the practical challenges arising in connection with the effective implementation of these legal compliance instruments, with particular emphasis on the respective problems resulting from ongoing armed conflict. In light of the findings arrived at in Section 2, Section 3 elaborates on how to adequately address these challenges and thus to adapt the regime for combatting wildlife trafficking to the specific circumstances of wartime with the aim of making the overall normative framework more effective for the animals concerned.

[9] See in this connection also for example the respective statements in UN General Assembly Resolution 73/343 of 20 September 2019, A/RES/73/343 (2019); UN Security Council Resolution 1236 of 30 January 2014, S/RES/2136 (2014); UN Security Council Resolution 1234 of 28 January 2014, S/RES/2134 (2014); UN Security Council Resolution 2217 of 28 April 2015, S/RES/2217 (2015). See also Anne Peters, 'Elephant Poaching and Ivory Trafficking as a Threat to the Peace', *American Journal of International Law Unbound* 108 (2014), 162–5. See also Sjöstedt, Chapter 21, 'Enforcement Powers of the United Nations Security Council', in this volume.

2 CHALLENGES TO EFFECTIVELY ENFORCING THE INTERNATIONAL REGIME FOR WILDLIFE TRAFFICKING IN WARTIME

In light of the in principle incontrovertible fact that wildlife trafficking constitutes one of the most serious threats to endangered and non-endangered animals around the world in times of peace and war, it is hardly surprising and fortunate that a considerable number of international agreements for the protection of animals address, inter alia, also the issue of suppressing illegal trade in wildlife. When categorising the respective regulatory approaches from an enforcement perspective, and in order to reduce the existing factual and normative complexities by way of systemisation, it seems reasonable to broadly distinguish in this regard between three main types of stipulations, namely implementation provisions, compliance control and enforcement instruments as well as compliance facilitation and enabling mechanisms.[10]

International wildlife treaties are thus in general characterised by a variety of often quite sophisticated implementation and compliance mechanisms aimed at preventing and combatting wildlife trafficking. While it is sadly well known that, in spite of these regimes, the phenomenon of wildlife trafficking persists and to some extent even flourishes, which indicates that the respective normative frameworks are for a variety of reasons suffering from certain structural and/or enforcement deficiencies already in the rather 'ordinary' scenario of peacetime. That said, the at least equally pressing issue that this section of the chapter will focus on concerns the specific, additional practical challenges that arise in connection with the effective application of the respective implementation and compliance approaches under the 'extraordinary' circumstances of armed conflict.

When considering this topic from the formal perspective of public international law, the first and overarching question obviously arising in this regard concerns the effects of armed conflict on international wildlife treaties.[11] Whereas some agreements, like Article XV(1) of the 2003 African Convention on the Conservation of Nature and Natural Resources,[12] explicitly address specific obligations of the contracting parties in wartime and thus indirectly provide for their continued application during hostilities, most respective treaties, prominently including the long-time multilateral 'flagship wildlife agreement',[13] the Convention on International Trade in Endangered Species of Wild Fauna and Flora (CITES), remain silent on this issue. However, even if one – rightly – assumes that also the protection provided by

[10] For a respective assessment see, for example, more recently Karsten Nowrot, *Illegal Trade in Wild Animals and Derived Products During Armed Conflicts: What Role for International Wildlife Agreements?* (Hamburg: Hamburg University 2020), 8–17, with numerous additional references.

[11] For further discussions on this topic, see also de Hemptinne, Chapter 7, 'Part of the Environment', in this volume.

[12] African Convention on the Conservation of Nature and Natural Resources of 11 July 2003.

[13] Rosalind Reeve, 'Enhancing the International Regime for Protecting Endangered Species: The Example of CITES', *Zeitschrift für ausländisches öffentliches Recht und Völkerrecht* 63 (2003), 333–54, at 333.

those international wildlife treaties that contain no reference to their applicability or non-applicability during armed conflict can at least be presumed to continue to apply in wartime to the extent that the respective obligations do not conflict with relevant IHL,[14] the underlying fundamental issue remains whether and to what extent a contracting party involved in an armed conflict can and should be expected to comply with its respective treaty obligations in basically the same way as if the conflict did not exist.[15] Although recognising, or even explicitly providing for, the continued application of international wildlife treaties can be considered 'laudable', it might not be too far-fetched to assume that 'those actively involved in conflicts may well in practice be unlikely to regard protection of wildlife and of the wider environment as immediate and pressing concerns in times of war'.[16]

However, the issue in the present context is not merely one of subjective motivation and thus, depending on the perspective adopted, an understandable or regrettable unwillingness on the side of conflict-affected countries to effectively combat poaching and trafficking of wildlife during hostilities. Rather, one of the, if not even the, central challenge relates to the respective contracting parties' objective capacity to successfully implement and enforce the treaty regimes, a capacity that is often significantly weakened as a result of ongoing armed conflict.[17] Prominent among the respective issues is the limited control the affected treaty parties have over parts of their territory and the related activities undertaken therein. It is this aspect in particular that ultimately has also the potential to cause severe consequences as far as the workability and remedial functions of treaty compliance mechanisms are concerned.

We would do well to look at two examples. First, a valid and convincing argument can be made that any acts related to wildlife trafficking committed by insurgents or other organised armed groups during an armed conflict that contravene protection standards enshrined in wildlife agreements are not attributable to the affected contracting party. Consequently, such situations of non-compliance are for example not appropriately addressed by recourse to the in principle quite effective CITES Compliance Procedure, in particular the option, granted to the Standing Committee of the Conference of the Parties (COP), to recommend on the basis of Article XIII(3) CITES the adoption of trade sanctions against the party concerned.[18]

14 On this approach, see also more recently, for example, ILC, Second Report on Protection of the Environment in Relation to Armed Conflicts by Marja Lehto, Special Rapporteur, 27 March 2019, A/CN.4/728, para. 28; UN General Assembly, ILC, First Report on Protection of the Environment in Relation to Armed Conflicts by Marja Lehto, Special Rapporteur, 30 April 2018, A/CN.4/720, paras. 77–80, with further references.

15 See thereto also already Michael Bothe et al., 'International Law Protecting the Environment During Armed Conflict: Gaps and Opportunities', *International Review of the Red Cross* 92 (2010), 569–92, at 581.

16 Michael Bowman, Peter Davies and Catherine Redgwell, *Lyster's International Wildlife Law* (2nd ed., Cambridge: Cambridge University Press 2010), 290.

17 See also ILC, Second Report (n. 14), para. 28.

18 CITES Resolution Conf. 14.3 (CITES Compliance Procedures) as last amended at COP 18 in August 2019, Annex. For further details on this compliance enforcement mechanism, see, for example, Nowrot, *Illegal Trade* (n. 10), 12–14, with additional references.

This finding is not solely based on the international legal regime on state responsibility, especially the rules concerning the (non-)attribution of conduct of insurrectional and secessionist movements to the state at issue as for example enshrined – at least implicitly – in Article 10 of the Articles on State Responsibility developed by the International law Commission (ILC) and also reflecting customary international law.[19] Rather, this approach also finds its manifestation in the regulatory structure and stipulations of the 2007 Guide to CITES Compliance Procedure itself, requiring the Standing Committee of the COP, when deciding about the recommendation of trade suspensions, to take into account, among others, 'the capacity of the Party concerned' as well as 'such factors as the cause, … of the compliance matter', and 'the appropriateness of the measures'.[20]

Second, in addition to the general inappropriateness of trade sanctions regimes like the one created under CITES, it seems necessary to briefly recall that first and foremost also many of the compliance facilitation and enabling approaches explicitly foreseen in international wildlife agreements or developed in subsequent treaty practice[21] – for example the provision of financial and technical assistance, capacity-building, the exchange of information and good practices, as well as other means of capacity-building – are for a variety of obvious reasons frequently unable to achieve their intended positive effects on the compliance level of affected contracting parties during ongoing armed conflicts.

In sum, when assessing the respective scenarios from an enforcement perspective, it becomes quite obvious that wildlife treaty compliance mechanisms are in general unsuited to promote the legal protection of animals in wartime with their remedial potential and overall workability being frequently and significantly weakened by armed conflict, at least as far as conflict-affected countries – and the activities taking place in their territories – are concerned.

3 SOME THOUGHTS ON POSSIBLE ENFORCEMENT PATHS LESS TAKEN IN TREATY PRACTICE

In light of the findings arrived at in Section 2, I will presently discuss some ideas on how to adapt the regime for preventing and combatting wildlife trafficking to the specific circumstances of wartime and thus adequately address the aforementioned challenges. The aim of this adaptation is to make the overall normative framework more effective at defending the interests of animals. In this regard, it is submitted that it seems potentially promising – and with that the chapter turns towards its end

[19] See UN, Draft Articles on Responsibility of States for International Wrongful Acts, with Commentaries, in *Yearbook of the ILC* 2001, Vol. II, Part Two, 50–2, with additional references.

[20] See CITES Resolution Conf. 14.3 (CITES Compliance Procedures) as last amended at COP 18 in August 2019, Annex, para. 32 (a), (b) and (c) respectively.

[21] See, generally, Nowrot, *Illegal Trade* (n. 10), 14–17, with further references.

to perceptions already introduced in its very beginning[22] – to start by taking a closer look at those domestic, supranational, and international governance mechanisms that have been devised – especially in the last two decades – with the aim to suppress or at least limit the funding of parties to armed conflicts by means of transboundary trade in other (non-living) natural resources.

Among these hard and soft law approaches, probably the most well-known example is the Kimberley Process Certification Scheme: a joint initiative formally launched in 2003 between governments, civil society groups, and representatives of the diamond industry. This regime portrays itself as an attempt to curb the transboundary trade in so-called conflict or blood diamonds, which are used by armed insurgent groups to finance the continuation of civil wars, particularly in Africa.[23] In addition to the Kimberley Process Certification Scheme, reference should be made in the present context to the Organisation for Economic Co-operation and Development (OECD) Due Diligence Guidance for Responsible Supply Chains of Minerals from Conflict-Affected and High-Risk Areas, adopted by the OECD Council at Ministerial level on 25 May 2011 and subsequently amended on 17 July 2012 as well as on 25 September 2015. The central purpose of this soft law governance instrument is 'to help companies respect human rights and avoid contributing to conflict through their mineral sourcing practices' by clarifying how economic actors can identify and better manage risks throughout the entire mineral supply chain.[24] Other examples from the realms of domestic and supranational legislations are section 1502 of the Dodd-Frank Wall Street Reform and Consumer Protection Act (Dodd-Frank Act) that became effective on 21 July 2010 following its approval by the US Congress,[25] and the EU Regulation 2017/821 laying down supply chain due diligence obligations for Union importers of tin, tantalum and tungsten, their ores, and gold originating from conflict-affected and high-risk areas of 17 May 2017 (EU Conflict Minerals Regulation).[26]

Let me be clear, I am most certainly not suggesting here that the regulatory structures and various governance approaches foreseen in these hard as well as soft law instruments be transferred and applied 'lock, stock, and barrel' to address and cope with the problems of wildlife trafficking in wartime. Aside from the general fact that animals are rightly increasingly recognised as sentient beings, or at least not

[22] See Section 1, above.

[23] Further information on this regime and its governance approaches are available at https://www.kimberleyprocess.com, accessed 22 February 2022.

[24] OECD, *Due Diligence Guidance for Responsible Supply Chains of Minerals from Conflict-Affected and High-Risk Areas: Third Edition* (Paris: OECD Publishing 2016), 3, available at https://bit.ly/3IRFs6L, accessed 22 February 2022.

[25] US: Dodd-Frank Wall Street Reform and Consumer Protection Act, Public Law 111-203 – 21 July 2010, 124 Stat. 1375 (2010), available at https://bit.ly/30fhWZy, accessed 22 February 2022

[26] EU: Regulation 2017/821 of the European Parliament and of the European Council of 17 May 2017 laying down supply chain due diligence obligations for Union importers of tin, tantalum and tungsten, their ores, and gold originating from conflict-affected and high-risk areas (OJ EU L 130/1 of 19 May 2017).

merely as legal objects,[27] and thus cannot easily be compared to minerals and other raw materials, the respective call for caution is in particular also supported by the frequently divergent regulatory goals pursued by conflict minerals governance schemes on the one hand and international wildlife regimes on the other hand. Whereas the former are exclusively aimed at promoting responsible commercial transactions in raw materials and obviously lack any protective, trade-discouraging dimension with regard to the often also quite rare commodities concerned, the latter are generally first and foremost intended to provide care for endangered species and, in this regard, frequently either stipulate a more or less comprehensive prohibition on commercial transactions in specimens or protect them against over-exploitation through trade.

Moreover, it should be recalled that the more recently devised governance instruments dealing with the issue of conflict minerals were created, and some of them have established respective certification and disclosure mechanisms, in what used to be more or less a kind of normative 'no man's land'. To the contrary, in the realm of international wildlife regimes, such reporting obligations and, as far as permitted trade in wild animals is concerned, also quite elaborate mandatory permit and certificate schemes by national authorities (especially under CITES) have been in place already for a number of decades. Consequently, it is surely not a general lack of governance instruments per se that prevents the treaty frameworks for combatting wildlife trafficking from becoming more effective in wartime and that could be remedied by relying on and copying from models and templates provided by conflict minerals regimes.

That said, it is nevertheless submitted that we can, especially also in the present context of protecting animals during hostilities, learn some useful lessons and gain some valuable inspiration from the existence, context, and regulatory approaches of these conflict minerals regulations; in particular if we view and assess them from a more overarching perspective. In an attempt to illustrate and substantiate this perception, I would like to make two main observations.

3.1 *Recognising the Potential Benefits of the Securitisation of Wildlife Trafficking in Wartime*

To begin with, the emergence of these conflict minerals governance regimes serves as a quite clear indication for the potential influence exercised by – as well as the normative consequences resulting from – the phenomenon and approach of what is frequently referred to as 'securitisation'. Primarily discussed and theorised in the field of political science, the concept of securitisation is in particular grounded by a recognition that security issues are not always based on objective findings of threats existing in reality but are often also – or even exclusively – based on socially and discursively constructed threats.[28]

27 See also Peters and de Hemptinne, Chapter 1, 'Wartime', in this volume.

28 See thereto for example Ole Wæver, 'Securitization and Desecuritization', in Ronnie D. Lipschutz (ed.), *On Security* (New York: Columbia University Press 1995), 46–86, at 54; Barry Buzan,

Against this background, securitisation is understood as a 'more extreme version of politicization'[29] and refers to a process by which securitising actors, commonly among them 'political leaders, bureaucracies, governments, lobbyists, and pressure groups',[30] present a certain issue or development as a fundamental threat to a reference subject or object and thus portray it as a matter of security; a strategy in the sense of a 'securitizing move' that will result in a successful securitisation 'if and when the audience accepts it as such'.[31] The primary motivation for, and 'reward' to be expected from, a successful securitisation move concerns the substantial increase in political attention and superior financial resources associated with issues related to national and international security challenges.[32]

Viewed from a normative perspective, these assets have also the potential to translate into new governance instruments, as demonstrated by the more recently created conflict minerals regimes. It is probably no exaggeration to assume that adding a securitisation context to the sourcing of, and transboundary trade in, minerals from conflict areas has strongly, if not even decisively, contributed to the establishment of quite effective soft law instruments like the Kimberley Process Certification Scheme and their incorporation into hard law[33] as well as also to the adoption of legally binding regulations such as the Dodd-Frank Act and the EU Conflict Minerals Regulation; governance regimes that ultimately also serve other public interests aside from addressing security concerns.[34]

In light of these findings, it seems reasonable to predict that the increasingly visible recognition, not the least also in the practice of the UN Security Council,[35] of

Ole Wæver and Jaap de Wilde, *Security: A New Framework for Analysis* (Boulder: Lynne Rienner 1998), 23–40.

29 Buzan, Wæver and de Wilde, *Security* (n. 28), 23.

30 Ibid., 40.

31 Ibid., 25.

32 See also, for example, Yuen Foong Khong, 'Human Security: A Shotgun Approach to Alleviating Human Misery?', *Global Governance* 7 (2001), 231–6, at 232; Andrew Mack, 'The Concept of Human Security', in Michael Brzoska and Peter J. Croll (eds.), *Promoting Security: But How and for Whom?* (Bonn: Bonn International Center for Conversion (BICC) Brief 30 2004), 47–50, at 49.

33 See, for example, EU: Council Regulation (EC) No. 2368/2002 of 20 December 2002 implementing the Kimberley Process Certification Scheme for the international trade in rough diamonds (OJ EC L 358/28 of 31 December 2002).

34 See in this connection, for example, respective excerpts from the preamble of the EU Conflict Minerals Regulation

> (3) Human rights abuses are common in resource-rich conflict-affected and high-risk areas and may include child labour, sexual violence, the disappearance of people, forced resettlement and the destruction of ritually or culturally significant sites. . . . (26) Preventing the profits from the trade in minerals and metals being used to fund armed conflict through due diligence and transparency will promote good governance and sustainable economic development.'

See EU: Regulation 2017/821 of the European Parliament and of the European Council of 17 May 2017 laying down supply chain due diligence obligations for Union importers of tin, tantalum and tungsten, their ores, and gold originating from conflict-affected and high-risk areas (OJ EU L 130/1 of 19 May 2017).

35 See thereto already Section 1.

linkages between conflict prevention and containment on the one hand and the need for effectively combatting wildlife trafficking on the other hand – and therefore the ongoing securitisation of global illegal wildlife trade – has in principle a quite notable potential to result in an, perhaps in particular also legal, enhancement of the protection provided to wild animals during armed conflicts; a potential that – despite possible challenges that might also arise in this connection[36] – arguably will and ought to be developed further and exploited more fully in the foreseeable future.

3.2 *Broadening the Compliance Focus and Diversifying the Implementation Mechanisms of International Wildlife Treaties in Wartime*

Nevertheless, it is not merely, and perhaps not even primarily, the potential benefits of a continued securitisation that should attract our attention when taking a closer look at the more recently emerging conflict minerals regimes in the present context. Rather, we might also learn some useful lessons from the regulatory approaches foreseen in these instruments. Most of these governance structures do not predominantly focus on the conflict-affected countries where extraction activities take place directly but first and foremost address the subsequent supply chains by formulating normative expectations or even creating legally binding obligations for consumer countries as well as in particular for importers, manufacturers as well as other 'downstream' businesses.

Bearing in mind the considerable challenges to effectively enforcing the transnational regime for wildlife trafficking in wartime as far as the conflict-affected countries themselves are concerned, it is submitted that a comparable broadening and shifting of the compliance focus of international wildlife regimes to the whole chains of supply and demand of the legal as well as in particular also the illegal wildlife trade, combined with a diversification of the respective implementation mechanisms, can be regarded as a promising enforcement strategy for making the international normative frameworks for preventing and combatting wildlife trafficking more responsive to the specific circumstances of armed conflicts and thus also more supportive of the welfare of animals concerned. Such a broader and more diversified regulatory approach, which does not primarily concentrate its compliance facilitation and enforcement efforts on the conflict-affected source countries but instead takes into account the supply and demand chains in their entirety, allows the governance structures (and their creators) to identify and normatively address all of the – voluntary and involuntary – actors involved in, or concerned with, the legal and illegal wildlife trade.[37]

36 For a more sceptical perception, see, for example, Lorraine Elliott, 'The Securitization of Transnational Environmental Crime and the Militarization of Conservation', in Lorraine Elliott and William H. Schaedla (eds.), *Handbook of Transnational Environmental Crime* (Cheltenham: Edward Elgar 2016), 68–87, at 81–3.

37 See also already Annecoos Wiersema, 'CITES and the Whole Chain Approach to Combatting Illegal Wildlife Trade', *Journal of International Wildlife Law & Policy* 20 (2017), 207–25, at 215.

And indeed, it seems appropriate to emphasise that the respective approaches are most certainly not entirely unknown to the current international regime for wildlife trafficking. Recent years have borne witness to a number of related efforts, both within and outside the framework of individual international wildlife agreements. All of them have in common the aim of more holistically and thus also more effectively preventing and combatting the illegal trade in wildlife and, in this regard, focusing on other segments of, and public as well as private actors in, the supply chain aside from the source countries.

One quite prominent and important class of approaches targets the relevant transit routes and concentrates in this connection specifically also on the companies involved in the transportation sector.[38] In this regard, attention should be directed towards initiatives like the Reducing Opportunities for Unlawful Transport of Endangered Species (ROUTES) Partnership. Financed by the US Agency for International Development (USAID) and closely cooperating with the CITES Secretariat, ROUTES brings together transport and logistics companies, government agencies, and civil society groups with the aim to combat wildlife trafficking by reducing the use of legal transportation supply chains.[39] In addition, the International Air Transport Association (IATA) has concluded a memorandum of understanding with the CITES Secretariat in June 2015 intended to foster cooperation in, among others, the fields of 'the transport of CITES specimens for legal international trade and the combatting of illegal trade in CITES specimens'.[40]

Moreover, the 2016 IATA Annual General Meeting adopted a resolution on illegal wildlife trade that, inter alia:

> 'calls on member airlines to increase passenger, customer, client, and staff awareness about the nature, scale, and consequences of the illegal wildlife trade', 'calls on airlines, airports, freight forwarders and all other stakeholders within the air transport sector to work proactively with enforcement agencies and conservation organizations to address the problem', 'calls on member airlines to consider the adoption of appropriate policies and procedures that discourage this illegal trade, taking into account the importance of awareness programs, information sharing and incident reporting systems' and 'encourages member airlines to sign the United for Wildlife Transport Taskforce Buckingham Palace Declaration'.[41]

The last mentioned encouragement refers to a declaration agreed upon in March 2016 by a diverse group of actors, among them CITES, the International Maritime Organization (IMO), the UN Development Programme (UNDP), the

[38] Ibid., 218–19.

[39] Additional information on ROUTES is available at https://routespartnership.org, accessed 22 February 2022.

[40] Memorandum of Understanding between the CITES Secretariat and IATA of 8 June 2015, para. 2.5, available at https://bit.ly/3HfiMge, accessed 22 February 2022.

[41] IATA, 72nd IATA Annual General Meeting 2016, Resolution on the Illegal Trade in Wildlife, paras. 2, 4, 5 and 6, available at www.iata.org/en/policy/environment/wildlife-trafficking, accessed 22 February 2022.

World Customs Organisation (WCO),[42] IATA, the WWF UK as well as numerous transport industry associations and companies, that stipulates eleven commitments aimed at combatting the illegal trade in wildlife by focusing on transit routes and in particular the role played by the transportation sector.[43]

Another type of governance approach that attempts to address the issue of wildlife trafficking by taking into account other parts of the supply chain focuses on aspects related to consumer countries. Two regulatory strategies seem particularly worth highlighting in this regard. One of them concerns and targets the role as well as potential consequences of legal domestic markets for endangered species. While traditionally considered to be outside CITES's scope of application, the contracting parties to this wildlife treaty have more recently quite firmly taken up this issue; at least as far as the admittedly in many ways rather special case of (domestic) ivory markets is concerned. In the course of COP 17 in September and October 2016, they decided – despite concerns expressed by the CITES Secretariat – to amend CITES Resolution Conf. 10.10 (Trade in Elephant Specimens).[44] The resolution in its current applicable version as last amended at COP 18 in August 2019 recalls the by now almost undisputed finding that 'legal domestic markets for ivory may increase the risk to elephant populations and local communities, due to the opportunity it creates for the laundering of illegal ivory under the guise of legality'.[45] Against this background, the resolution, inter alia, recommends 'that all Parties and non-Parties in whose jurisdiction there is a legal domestic market for ivory that is contributing to poaching or illegal trade, take all necessary legislative, regulatory and enforcement measures to close their domestic markets for commercial trade in raw and worked ivory as a matter of urgency'.[46]

The second – and somehow related – regulatory strategy that focuses on the role of consumer countries attempts to tackle perhaps the central factor contributing to the phenomenon and profitability of wildlife trafficking, namely demand in the legal as well as in particular also the illegal consuming markets. The issue of demand and its potential to negatively influence treaty compliance has for some time most certainly

42 More generally on the role and activities of the WCO in combatting illegal wildlife trade, see, for example, Kunio Mikuriya, 'Illicit Wildlife Trade and the Role of Customs', *University of Pennsylvania Asian Law Review* 12 (2016), 55–64.

43 Additional information on the United for Wildlife Transport Taskforce Buckingham Palace Declaration and its signatories are available at www.unitedforwildlife.org/the-buckingham-palace-declaration, accessed 22 February 2022.

44 Wiersema, 'CITES and the Whole Supply Chain' (n. 37), 221.

45 Preamble of CITES Resolution Conf. 10.10 (Trade in Elephant Specimens) as last amended at COP 18 in August 2019. On this concern, see also, for example, Anneeoos Wiersema, 'Incomplete Bans and Uncertain Markets in Wildlife Trade', *University of Pennsylvania Asian Law Review* 12 (2016), 65–87, at 81–3.

46 CITES Resolution Conf. 10.10 (Trade in Elephant Specimens) as last amended at COP 18 in August 2019, para. 3. See, however, also for respective challenges in this regard for example Peter H. Sand, 'Japan's Ivory Trade in the Face of the Endangered Species Convention', *Journal of International Wildlife Law & Policy* 21 (2018), 221–38.

been identified and recognised as a very important driver for illegal wildlife trading.[47] Moreover, the overall importance of, among others, public awareness campaigns has been emphasised in a number of more recently concluded international wildlife agreements. Respective examples in this regard are provided by Article 4(7) of the 1994 Lusaka Agreement on Co-operative Enforcement Operations Directed at Illegal Trade in Wild Fauna and Flora,[48] and Article 7(7)(a) of the 1999 Southern African Development Community (SADC) Protocol on Wildlife Conservation and Law Enforcement.[49] However, for a variety of reasons respective efforts specifically aimed at reducing the demand in consumer countries have traditionally not been undertaken within the framework of CITES – and only rather cautiously undertaken by other relevant actors like civil society groups.[50]

Nevertheless, of late there have been clear indications that the situation is beginning to change. Campaigns initiated by NGOs in various important consumer countries have gained momentum, in particular since the middle of the 2010s.[51] In addition, the UN General Assembly has more recently supported this approach.[52] And last, but surely not least, also the contracting parties of CITES have taken the quite remarkable step of adopting at COP 17 in September/October 2016 the CITES Resolution Conf. 17.4 (demand reduction strategies to combat illegal trade in CITES listed species), thereby explicitly and rather comprehensively addressing the issue of demand reduction as a notable and promising strategy to prevent and combat the illegal wildlife trade.[53]

It is quite notable that these regulatory and other activities aimed at addressing the problem of the illegal trade in wildlife from a more holistic perspective by focusing on the whole supply chain, and thus in particular also on transit and consumer countries as well as the various public and private actors involved, have primarily been initiated or at least considerably intensified in the previous decade only. Already this finding serves as an indication that the emerging securitisation of wildlife trafficking during armed conflicts has, most certainly together with other

47 See, for example, Peter H. Sand, 'Whither CITES? The Evolution of a Treaty Regime in the Borderland of Trade and Environment', *European Journal of International Law* 8 (1997), 29–58, at 52.

48 Lusaka Agreement on Co-Operative Enforcement Operations Directed at Illegal Trade in Wild Fauna and Flora of 8 September 1994, 1950 UNTS 35.

49 SADC Protocol on Wildlife Conservation and Law Enforcement of 18 August 1999, available at https://bit.ly/3IRiXPe, accessed 22 February 2022.

50 See thereto for example Kirsten Conrad, 'Trade Bans: A Perfect Storm for Poaching?', *Tropical Conservation Science* 5 (2012), 245–254, at 249–250.

51 For respective examples see, for example, Sabrina Persaud, 'Losing Our "CITES" on the "Traffic": How Taxing Ivory Trafficking Can Save the African Elephant from its Bloody Extinction', *Journal of International Wildlife Law & Policy* 20 (2017), 295–320, at 319–20.

52 UN General Assembly Resolution 73/343 of 20 September 2019, A/RES/73/343 (2019), para. 13. See also already for example UN General Assembly Resolution 69/314 of 19 August 2015, A/RES/69/314 (2015), para. 7.

53 CITES Resolution Conf. 17.4 (Demand reduction strategies to combat illegal trade in CITES listed species) of September/October 2016. See, in this connection, also for example CITES Resolution Conf. 10.10 (Trade in Elephant Specimens) as last amended at COP 18 in August 2019, para. 7 lit. d.

factors and motives, exercised a considerable influence on the progressive development of compliance efforts in this field. Moreover, it seems not too far-fetched to predict that the continued influence of this phenomenon has a considerable potential to lead to quantitatively and qualitatively even more intensified action in the foreseeable future.

Finally, and more specifically addressing the prospective role of CITES in this context, another conceivable enforcement approach vis-à-vis transit and consumer countries concerns the possibility of applying the CITES Compliance Procedure, in particular including the option, granted to the Standing Committee of the COP, to recommend on the basis of Article XIII(3) of the CITES the adoption of trade sanctions, more frequently and rigorously against respective contracting parties that do not sufficiently fulfil, among others, their obligations under Article VIII(1) of the CITES; an enforcement approach that seems in principle quite promising, in particular also as far as combatting wildlife trafficking in the present context of wartime is concerned, but has until now not been utilised in the CITES treaty practice in anything even close to a comprehensive and determined way. Indeed, it seems quite astonishing – and, taking into account the important role played by considerations of fairness and thus, among others, equal treatment of the contracting parties for the continued acceptability and viability of a treaty regime, most certainly also potentially worrisome – that until now more than 90 per cent of the CITES parties targeted by respective trade embargoes were 'source countries' from the 'third world'.[54] This initially rather surprising empirical finding[55] has already been criticised as potentially revealing a kind of 'inherent hidden bias in the system as currently practised' and thus pointing at a major structural and legitimacy challenge for the CITES as a whole.[56]

Such a negative perception of the current sanctions practice is in principle obviously not without merit. Nevertheless, a more optimistic view might again, and thus also in this connection, draw attention to the potential benefits of a continued securitisation of wildlife trafficking during armed conflicts in the sense of providing a stronger incentive, for developing and developed contracting parties alike, to address this structural enforcement challenge and provide for a more balanced, and therefore also more legitimate and effective, application of the CITES Compliance Procedure to the benefit of conflict-affected animals.

54 See thereto as well as for a rightly critical assessment of this finding, Peter H. Sand, 'Enforcing CITES: The Rise and Fall of Trade Sanctions', *Review of European Community & International Environmental Law* 22 (2013), 251–63, at 261.

55 For a certainly not entirely implausible explanation, see, for example, Peter H. Sand, 'International Protection of Endangered Species in the Face of Wildlife Trade: Whither Conservation Diplomacy?', *Asia Pacific Journal of Environmental Law* 20 (2017), 5–27, at 26 ('For diplomatic reasons, other Member States will inevitably think twice before antagonizing such a heavy-weight member country by allegations of non-compliance (. . .).').

56 Sand, 'Enforcing CITES' (n. 54), 261.

4 CONCLUDING RECOMMENDATIONS

Armed conflicts undoubtedly add another regrettable dimension to the already well-developed trade in wildlife and its products. This chapter has tried to illustrate that the often quite sophisticated implementation and compliance mechanisms for preventing as well as combatting wildlife trafficking, as foreseen in international treaty regimes or developed in practice, are in general not well suited to promote and ensure the protection of animals in wartime. In order to adequately address and remedy these enforcement challenges, some useful lessons can be learned from the more recently emerging instruments dealing with conflict minerals that focus on the whole supply chain. This approach can lead to notable improvements of the regime for wildlife trafficking in general. It thus might even have the potential to result in more effectively preventing and combatting the illegal trade in wildlife during peacetime as well. After all, what works for diamonds and gold might very well work for our precious 'living jewels'.

SELECT BIBLIOGRAPHY

Asch, Edward van, 'The International Consortium on Combatting Wildlife Crime (ICCWC)', in Lorraine Elliott and William H. Schaedla (eds.), *Handbook of Transnational Environmental Crime* (Cheltenham: Edward Elgar 2016), 469–77.

Ayling, Julie, 'What Sustains Wildlife Crime? Rhino Horn Trading and the Resilience of Criminal Networks', *Journal of International Wildlife Law & Policy* 16 (2013), 57–80.

Baker, Joni E., 'A Substantive Theory of the Relative Efficiency of Environmental Treaty Compliance Strategies: The Case of CITES', *Journal of International Wildlife Law & Policy* 2 (1999), 1–45.

Elliott, Lorraine, 'The Securitization of Transnational Environmental Crime and the Militarization of Conservation', in Lorraine Elliott and William H. Schaedla (eds.), *Handbook of Transnational Environmental Crime* (Cheltenham: Edward Elgar 2016), 68–87.

Kasimbazi, Emmanuel B., 'The Lusaka Agreement Task Force as a Mechanism for Enforcement Against Wildlife Crime', in Michael Faure, Peter De Smedt and An Stas (eds.), *Environmental Enforcement Networks: Concepts, Implementation and Effectiveness* (Cheltenham: Edward Elgar 2015), 239–62.

McOmber, Elisabeth M., 'Problems in Enforcement of the Convention on International Trade in Endangered Species', *Brooklyn Journal of International Law* 27 (2002), 673–701.

Nowrot, Karsten, *Illegal Trade in Wild Animals and Derived Products during Armed Conflicts: What Role for International Wildlife Agreements?* (Hamburg: Hamburg University 2020).

Reeve, Rosalind, *Policing International Trade in Endangered Species: The CITES Treaty and Compliance* (London: Routledge 2002).

Sand, Peter H., 'Enforcing CITES: The Rise and Fall of Trade Sanctions', *Review of European Community & International Environmental Law* 22 (2013), 251–63.

Wiersema, Annecoos, 'CITES and the Whole Chain Approach to Combatting Illegal Wildlife Trade', *Journal of International Wildlife Law & Policy* 20 (2017), 207–25.

Zimmerman, Mara E., 'The Black Market for Wildlife: Combatting Transnational Organized Crime in the Illegal Wildlife Trade', *Vanderbilt Journal of Transnational Law* 36 (2003), 1657–90.

21

Enforcement Powers of the United Nations Security Council

Britta Sjöstedt[*]

1 INTRODUCTION

The United Nations (UN) Security Council is the leading organ on international peace and security in the UN system. It has an exclusive mandate to identify and address threats and breaches to international peace in accordance with Chapter VII of the UN Charter. It can adopt binding decisions and even authorise military means to maintain and restore international peace and security.[1] The UN Security Council is not typically associated with animal protection. However, wildlife issues have become a security concern.[2] Wildlife poaching and trafficking of wildlife products finance transnational criminal networks and armed groups, which the UN Security Council has acknowledged in recent years. Elephant tusks and rhino horns, in particular, represent high-value wildlife commodities, which drive these species to extinction.[3] The UN Security Council has adopted several resolutions addressing wildlife poaching and trafficking as commodities with implications on international security. For instance, it has contributed to protect wildlife in Central Africa. Furthermore, the security implications of poaching and trafficking of wildlife have led to integrated responses combining biodiversity conservation with professional militarised anti-poaching enforcement – on a few occasions in cooperation with UN peacekeeping forces. The militarised responses have had some direct effects to halt species loss but they also risk to further escalate the violence affecting local communities in states engaged in fighting wildlife poaching. The chapter argues that the UN Security Council needs to address wildlife poaching and

[*] The author wishes to thank the editors as well as the participants at the online workshop of June 2020 providing valuable feedback on an earlier draft. The author also wishes to thank Daniëlla Dam de-Jong for her insightful comments. Finally, the author would like to thank Stiftelsen för rättsvetenskaplig forskning for funding her postdoctoral research.

[1] See Art. 41 and 42 of the UN Charter.

[2] Cathy Haenlein and M. L. R. Smith, 'Conclusions', in Cathy Haenlein and M. L. R. Smith (eds.), *Poaching, Wildlife Trafficking and Security in Africa: Myths and Realities* (London: Royal United Services Institute, Whitehall Papers Series 2016), 102–18, at 102.

[3] Ibid., 103–4.

trafficking broadly using its exclusive mandate to adopt binding decisions on UN member states and only as a last and temporary resort, authorise military means.

The chapter begins with giving an overview of the authority of the UN Security Council. It raises questions about the scope of its enforcement powers and its expanding mandate to address new types of security threats, including those related to the environment. Thereafter, the third section provides a general background on how wildlife links with international security. The fourth section studies how the issue of wildlife ended up on the agenda of the UN Security Council through the work of the other UN organs. This chapter mainly focuses on the UN Security Council's work on commodity sanctions relating to wildlife, as it directly connects the Security Council's enforcement powers to animal protection. The chapter also analyses the intensified military responses to poaching and investigates the appropriateness of such militarised conservation practices, particularly when involving the UN peacekeepers. Finally, the chapter offers some conclusions and suggests further recommendations.

2 THE AUTHORITY OF THE UN SECURITY COUNCIL

The UN Charter, adopted in 1945 at the end of World War II, aimed at creating a system of global collective security to prevent a new world war. According to the UN Charter, the UN Security Council has the principal responsibility to ensure international peace and security. It consists of five permanent members, namely the winning states of World War II: China, France, the Soviet Union (today Russia), the United Kingdom and the United States (US). These members are referred to as the 'P5' and they can block a decision by using their veto power. The UN Security Council also has ten elected members, rotating for a period of two years.[4]

Article 39 of the UN Charter constitutes the starting point of the legal basis for the UN Security Council to act, namely to 'determine the existence of any threat to the peace, breach of the peace, or act of aggression' and in such cases the council 'shall make recommendations, or decide what measures shall be taken in accordance with Articles 41 and 42, to maintain or restore international peace and security'. In the *Tadić* case, the International Criminal Tribunal for the former Yugoslavia (ICTY) stated: '[w]hile the "act of aggression" is more amenable to a legal determination, the "threat to the peace" is more of a political concept. But the determination that there exists such a threat is not a totally unfettered discretion, as it has to remain, at the very least, within the limits of the Purposes and Principles of the Charter.'[5] While a breach of peace or an act of aggression are formulated in restricted and legally

[4] Sebastian von Einsiedel and David M. Malone, 'Security Council', in Thomas G. Weiss and Sam Daws (eds.), *The Oxford Handbook on the United Nations* (2nd ed., Oxford: Oxford University Press 2018), 141–63, at 143.

[5] ICTY, *Prosecutor* v. *Duško Tadić*, decision on the defence motion for interlocutory appeal on jurisdiction of 2 October 1995, IT-94-1-A, para. 29.

connoted terms,[6] the determination of the existence of a threat seems to be a grey area 'open for normatively justifiable interpretation'.[7]

Traditionally, the notion of threat to international peace refers to military threats between states, but over the years the UN Security Council has become increasingly concerned with non-traditional non-military and intra-state threats. For instance, it has addressed acts of terrorism performed by non-state actors, responsibility to protect civilians, humanitarian crisis, exploitation of natural resources and migration as threats to international peace and security. Thematic debates on women, peace and security, poverty, environmental degradation and climate change have been categorised as threats to peace by the UN Security Council. The notion of threat has been described as the 'broadest and most indistinct concept in Article 39' covering 'the widest range of behaviour by a State'.[8] Hence, the notion of 'any threat to peace' constitutes the lowest threshold when the UN Security Council can act.[9] Since the UN Security Council alone decides what falls under the scope of Article 39, it has a far-reaching mandate.

Once identifying a threat, breach of peace, or an act of aggression, the UN Security Council is empowered to impose collective security provisional measures under Article 40, economic and political measures under Article 41 and, as a final resort, coercive action under Article 42.[10] The decisions of the council are binding for all the UN member states.[11] Article 41 enables the UN Security Council to impose sanctions, including adopting weapon embargos, establishing panels of experts, freezing assets of certain individuals and even establishing new institutions including criminal courts dealing with criminal accountability. There is no mechanism in place to question the legality of the UN Security Council's actions or decisions. Debates whether the UN Security Council has acted *ultra vires* have been raised on several occasions, for instance in regard to establishing new institutions such as the ICTY, or addressing threats of terrorism or climate change, but in reality as long as none of the P5 vetoes a decision, there is nothing for the rest of the international community to do to prevent the council to act.

3 LINKING WILDLIFE TO INTERNATIONAL SECURITY

Wildlife and wildlife products are valuable commodities used for food, pets, skins, medicine, trophies and ornaments. With an increased demand for these products,

[6] Although reference to the use of aggression has rarely been employed by the UN Security Council. See Karel Wellens, 'The UN Security Council and New Threats to the Peace: Back to the Future', *Journal of Conflict and Security Law* 8 (2003), 15–70, at 31.

[7] Ibid., 28.

[8] Ibid., 18.

[9] Ibid., 31.

[10] Trina Ng, 'Safeguarding Peace and Security in our Warming World: A Role for the Security Council', *Journal of Conflict and Security Law* 15 (2010), 275–300, at 288–9.

[11] Art. 25 of the UN Charter.

poaching has augmented and intensified. Today, it takes place in areas previously not used for hunting.[12] In general, there is a lack of reliable verifiable data in regard to poaching and species loss. But the two highest-value and most desirable wildlife resources, namely ivory and rhino horn, are well documented. Trade with these commodities have been documented for centuries.[13]

Rhino horns have been used in China for medical purposes between since 200 BC. The demand for rhino horn has expanded in modern days for medical practices, despite the lack of evidence for being effective, and for symbols of status. The number of rhinos has dramatically dropped from hundreds of thousands in early 1900s to around 75,000 in the early 1970s. The increase in trafficking of fauna and flora in the 1970s led to the adoption in 1973 of the Convention on International Trade in Endangered Species of Wild Fauna and Flora (CITES). An international trade ban on rhino horns was adopted under CITES in 1977, but the ban has not been effective as domestic sales continued to be legal in countries such as China, Taiwan, South Korea and Yemen.[14] Although a drop was noted during the 1990s, since mid-2000s poaching of rhinos has increased again.[15] According to the World Wildlife Fund (WWF), around 27,000 rhinos remain in the world. Most of these live inside national parks and nature reserves, as they struggle to survive outside protected areas due to poaching and habitat loss.[16] Africa is reaching alarming rates of rhino loss. In 2013, 1,215 rhinos were killed in South Africa alone.[17] Of the five species of rhino, three are critically endangered, namely black, Javan and Sumatran rhino, while the Greater one-horned rhino is considered vulnerable and the white rhino near threatened.[18] The sub-species Africa's Western black rhino is permanently extinct[19] and the Northern white rhino is at the brink of extinction with only two individuals left, both female.[20]

In the 1970s, a rising demand for ivory in China and Japan among other states led to a huge drop in the elephant population, which persisted during the 1980s. The population dropped from 1.3 million in 1979 to 600,000 in 1989. All commercial trade of ivory has been prohibited under CITES since 1989. A decrease in poaching of elephants could be noted as a consequence of the ban, which allowed some

12 Cathy Haenlein and M. L. R. Smith, 'Introduction', in Cathy Haenlein and M. L. R. Smith (eds.), *Poaching, Wildlife Trafficking and Security in Africa: Myths and Realities* (London: Royal United Services Institute, Whitehall Papers Series 2016), 1–2.

13 Ibid.

14 Haenlein and Smith, 'Introduction' (n. 12), 14.

15 Ibid.

16 World Wildlife Fund website, available at www.worldwildlife.org/species/rhino, accessed 22 February 2022.

17 Andre Viollaz, 'UN Security Council Cracking Down on Ivory Poaching and Illegal Wildlife Trading', *Business Insider* (3 February 2014), available at https://bit.ly/3HlfTKY, accessed 22 February 2022.

18 World Wildlife Fund website (n. 16).

19 Haenlein and Smith, 'Introduction' (n. 12), 9–10.

20 World Wildlife Fund website (n. 16).

elephant populations to recover. However, the complete ban on ivory was lifted and a few exceptions in regard to trade of older ivory were permitted. Allowing some ivory to be sold lawfully has boosted illegal poaching, leading to a decrease in the number of elephants once again. In Africa, the elephant population has shrunk to among the lowest levels recorded. In its latest report published in 2016, the Species Survival Commission's African Elephant Specialist Group of the International Union for Conservation of Nature (IUCN) estimated the number of elephants to be around 415,000, which is a decline of more than 100,000 elephants since 2007.[21] An estimated 30,000 elephants are poached each year in Africa. The other species of elephant, namely the Asian elephant, is considered endangered with fewer than 50,000 individuals according to the WWF.[22] In addition to elephants and rhinos, other species are also subject to wildlife poaching and trafficking, such as pangolins, live reptiles and big cats. Birds, turtles and tropical fish seem to have fallen in numbers as well, albeit these are difficult to monitor.[23]

The expansion of trafficking of poached wildlife profits armed groups and criminal gangs. Transnational criminal networks have grown and generate enormous revenues.[24] The illegal trade of ivory and other wildlife products is the fourth most profitable income source for criminal gangs in Africa, only challenged by drug trafficking, counterfeiting and human trafficking.[25] In 2015, the value of rhino horn was estimated at USD 65,000 per kilo on the black market, which is more than gold, while ivory could be sold for USD 2,000 per kilo on the black market. The most common destination for most of the wildlife commodities is Asia.[26]

Similar to exploitation of natural resources, poaching does not only threaten biodiversity, but also leads to corruption and erosion of the rule of law.[27] The economic value of wildlife commodities, mainly high-value commodities such as rhino horn and ivory, have had destabilising consequences, particularly in Africa. In the last ten years, wildlife commodities are often referred to as drivers of conflict or funders of terrorism. In several armed conflicts, wildlife poaching and trafficking constitute sources of income for armed groups.[28] For instance, the ivory trade has

[21] African Elephant Status Report 2016, Paper No. 60, International Union for Conservation of Nature and Natural Resources, available at https://bit.ly/3HlZeHd, accessed 22 February 2022. See also Haenlein and Smith, 'Introduction' (n. 13), 9.

[22] World Wildlife Fund website (n. 16).

[23] Haenlein and Smith, 'Introduction' (n. 12), 10–11.

[24] Ibid., 1–2.

[25] UN General Assembly, Annex to the letter dated 9 December 2015 from the Permanent Representatives of Angola and Lithuania to the UN addressed to the Secretary-General, Summary of the informal Arria-formula meeting of the Security Council on the impact of the illicit transfer of small arms and light weapons on poaching in Africa, A/70/614-S/2015/953.

[26] Viollaz, 'UN Security Council Cracking Down on Ivory Poaching and Illegal Wildlife Trading' (n. 17).

[27] UN General Assembly, Summary of the informal Arria-formula meeting (n. 25), 3.

[28] Peter Aldinger, Carl Bruch and Sofia Yazykova, 'Revisiting Securitization: An Empirical Analysis of Environment and Natural Resource Provisions in United Nations Security Council Resolutions

funded the Janjaweed in Sudan, the Lord's Resistance Army in Uganda, and other armed groups in the Democratic Republic of the Congo (DRC) and Central African Republic (CAR).[29]

In 2012, the US Secretary of State Hillary Clinton stated that illegal wildlife poaching and trafficking had become a security concern, which was confirmed by the US Senate's Committee on Foreign Relations in the same year. In 2013, the issue of wildlife poaching and trafficking was addressed by the UN Secretary-General Ban Ki-Moon as a threat to sustainable peace and security and later the issue was addressed by the UN Security Council.[30] Thus, the concern for wildlife poaching and trafficking goes beyond conservation and animal welfare.[31] However, concerned voices have expressed that the description of wildlife poaching and trafficking as a conflict driver or financer of terrorism is exaggerated and rarely grounded in substantial evidence, being merely speculations or generalisations.[32] Nevertheless, there is an established connection between poaching and trafficking of wildlife and instability. The increased number of conflicts correlates with escalating illegal wildlife killing and biodiversity loss.[33] For instance, the armed conflicts in the Sahara-Sahel region have increased since 2011, which has led to large-scale killings of wildlife.[34] In most war zones, wildlife population decreases are due to increased proliferation of arms and lack of control. In those places, uncontrolled poaching is carried out not only by members of armed groups but also by members of state armies, criminal networks, as well as displaced persons and civilians.[35] In addition, poachers are difficult to tackle as they are becoming more heavily armed with access to more advanced weapons and methods.[36]

4 RESPONSES TO WILDLIFE POACHING AND TRAFFICKING WITHIN THE UN: MAKING ITS WAY TO THE SECURITY COUNCIL

The need for a robust protection of wildlife has been acknowledged in various forums, in and outside the UN, and numerous agencies work for wildlife protection from different perspectives. With the adoption of CITES, bans on international trade of certain endangered wildlife items have entered into force, which has been influential to prevent trade of certain species. The UN Convention against

1946–2016', in Ashok Swain and Joakim Öjendal (eds.), *Handbook of Environmental Conflict and Peacebuilding* (Abingdon: Routledge 2018), 143–72, at 152.

29 Ibid.

30 Haenlein and Smith, 'Introduction' (n. 12), 2.

31 Ibid.

32 Ibid., 16.

33 José Carlos Brito et al., 'Armed Conflicts and Wildlife Decline: Challenges and Recommendations for Effective Conservation Policy in Sahara-Sahel', *Conservation Letters* 11 (2018), 1–13, at 2.

34 Ibid., 3–6.

35 Emmanuel de Merode et al., 'The Impact of Armed Conflict on Protected Area Efficacy in Central Africa', *Biology Letters* 3 (2007), 299–301, at 299.

36 Viollaz, 'UN Security Council Cracking Down on Ivory Poaching and Illegal Wildlife Trading' (n. 19).

Transnational Organized Crime (UNCTOC)[37] and the UN Convention against Corruption (UNCAC)[38] have been important instruments for state parties to use in order to tackle wildlife trafficking.[39]

In 2010, the CITES Secretariat established the International Consortium on Combating Wildlife Crime (ICCWC) between CITES Secretariat, INTERPOL, the UN Office on Drugs and Crime, the World Bank and the World Customs Organisation. The purpose of ICCWC is to provide support to agencies working on issues related to wildlife trafficking on different levels with ivory as a major area of focus. In practice, the ICCWC is implementing the three conventions: CITES, UNCTOC and UNCAC.[40]

In the 2010s with a peak in 2013–14, wildlife poaching and trafficking, particularly of ivory and rhino horns in Central Africa, were intensively discussed as a security item within the UN. In 2013, the UN Secretary-General issued a report in which he described wildlife poaching, mainly focused on elephants, as a transnational criminal activity and a growing security concern in Central Africa, including in the CAR, Gabon, Cameroon and Chad.[41] The UN Secretary-General highlighted the growing threat of ivory poaching in Central Africa and its importance to fund armed groups, including the infamous Lord's Resistance Army.[42] According to the report of the UN Secretary-General, poachers are using advanced and powerful weapons, which presumably are coming illegally from Libya.[43] The report concluded that poaching and its links to other criminal activities is a grave threat to peace and security in Central Africa.[44] It was later discussed by the UN Security Council and its president made a statement encouraging the UN, the African Union (AU) and the Economic Community of Central African States (ECCAS) to work together including through joint field assessments and investigate alleged elephant poaching.[45] Ten members of the council expressed concern for the poaching activities, including two of the permanent members (France and Russia).[46]

37 UN Convention Against Transnational Organized Crime of 15 November 2000 (UNTOC), 2225 UNTS 209.

38 UN Convention Against Corruption of 31 October 2003 (UNCAC), 2349 UNTS 41.

39 Radha Ivory, 'Corruption Gone Wild: Transnational Criminal Law and the International Trade in Endangered Species', *American Journal of International Law Unbound* 111 (2017), 413–18, at 415. See also Nowrot, Chapter 20, 'Wildlife Trafficking', in this volume.

40 See Nowrot, Chapter 20, 'Wildlife Trafficking', in this volume for further information and analysis on the work of CITES.

41 UN Security Council, Report of the Secretary-General on the activities of the United Nations Regional Office for Central Africa and on the Lord's Resistance Army-affected areas, 20 May 2013, S/2013/297, para. 7.

42 Ibid. See also Daniëlla Dam-de Jong, 'UN Natural Resources Sanction Regimes: Incorporating Market-Based Responses to Address Market-Driven Problems', in Larissa van den Herik (ed.) *Research Handbook on UN Sanctions and International Law* (Cheltenham: Edward Elgar 2017), 147–74, at 166.

43 UN Security Council, Report of the Secretary-General (n. 41), para. 9.

44 Ibid.

45 UN Security Council, 6971st meeting record of the UN Security Council, 29 May 2013, S/PV.6971.

46 Ibid.

In the same year, the UN General Assembly announced 3 March, the day of the adoption of CITES, as World Wildlife Day in order to celebrate and raise awareness of the world's wild fauna and flora.[47] Maintaining this international momentum, the UN Environmental Assembly (UNEA) adopted in June 2014 a resolution addressing illegal wildlife trade, including timber. The resolution highlighted the increasing illegal poaching and trade in wildlife and its negative impacts from an economic, social, environmental and security perspective. It strongly encouraged states to commit to adopt targeted actions to eliminate supply, transit and demand for illegal wildlife products. The resolution focused on the need to implement existing commitments, ensure synergies, cooperation and coordination of efforts to address illegal wildlife trade. It also favoured a policy to develop sustainable alternative livelihoods for communities adversely affected by the illegal trade.[48] It also called upon the UN General Assembly to consider the issue of wildlife trafficking and poaching.[49] In 2015 at its sixty-ninth session, the UN General Assembly adopted Resolution 69/314 that specifically addressed illicit wildlife trafficking and how to tackle it building on the resolution previously adopted by the UNEA. The resolution urged member states at the national level to take steps to prevent, combat and eradicate illegal trade in wildlife and also to investigate and prosecute the illegal trade. It also urged states to strengthen enforcement and criminal justice responses in accordance with national and international law and it acknowledges that ICCWC can provide valuable technical assistance.[50] In the resolution, the UN General Assembly strongly encouraged states to support the development of sustainable and alternative livelihoods for communities affected by illicit trafficking in wildlife. It underscored the importance to fully engage the communities living in or close to wildlife habitats as active partners in conservation and enhance the rights and capacity within the communities to manage and benefit from wildlife.[51] The resolution has been regarded as 'a landmark event' that indicates an international and unified commitment to address wildlife crimes. The commitments were reaffirmed in UN General Assembly Resolutions 70/301 in 2016[52] and 71/326 in 2017.[53]

47 UN General Assembly, Resolution adopted by the General Assembly on 20 December 2013, 68/205 World Wildlife Day, 20 December 2013, A/RES/68/205.

48 UN Environmental Programme, 'First UN Resolution on Wildlife Trafficking Historic Step Forward, Chief of UN Environment Programme Says' (31 July 2015), available at https://bit.ly/3ulVoLU, accessed 22 February 2022.

49 Achim Steiner, 'Putting a Stop to Global Environmental Crime Has Become an Imperative', *UN Chronicle* (no date), available at https://bit.ly/346oCSR, accessed 22 February 2022.

50 UN General Assembly, Resolution adopted by the General Assembly on 30 July 2015, 69/314, Tackling illicit trafficking in wildlife, A/RES/314, para. 3.

51 Ibid., para. 8.

52 UN General Assembly, Resolution adopted by the General Assembly on 9 September 2016, 70/301, Tackling illicit trafficking in wildlife, A/RES/70/301.

53 UN General Assembly, Resolution adopted by the General Assembly on 11 September 2017, 71/326, Tackling illicit trafficking in wildlife, A/RES/71/326.

In 2019, the UN General Assembly adopted the most recent Resolution 73/343 on the theme 'Tackling illicit trafficking in wildlife',[54] which urged the member states to take decisive steps nationally, regionally and internationally to prevent, combat and eradicate the illegal trade in wildlife on the supply, transit and demand sides, as encouraged in the earlier resolutions. Such efforts include the strengthening of the requisite legislation and regulations necessary for the prevention, investigation, prosecution and appropriate punishment of such illegal trade, as well as the enhancement of enforcement and criminal justice responses. The representative for China stressed the importance of tackling the root causes of the illegal trade by addressing poverty reduction and economic development, meeting the needs of developing countries and improving people's livelihoods.[55]

Resolution 73/343 expressed its serious concern about the rate of species extinctions, as indicated in the alarming findings of the Intergovernmental Science-Policy Platform on Biodiversity and Ecosystem Services Global Assessment Report, released earlier the same year, and stressed the urgent need to address the unprecedented global decline in biodiversity. The resolution highlighted the continued increasing scale of poaching and illegal trade in wildlife products and its adverse economic, social and environmental impacts. It expressed serious concern over the detrimental levels of poaching of rhinos and elephants in Africa and the significant increase in illicit pangolin trafficking, as well as the illegal trade in other protected wildlife species. Furthermore, Resolution 73/343 recognised 'the essential engagement role of indigenous peoples and local communities to ensure a sustainable solution to addressing the illegal wildlife trade'.[56]

5 TARGETED WILDLIFE SANCTIONS BY THE UN SECURITY COUNCIL

The UN Security Council can be associated with animal protection in three streams of its work. Firstly, in its work on conflict prevention and root causes of conflict, the UN Security Council addresses illegal and unsustainable exploitation of natural resources funding criminal organisations and armed groups.[57] To this end, the UN Security Council has adopted commodity sanctions in accordance with Article 41 of the UN Charter. The commodity sanctions concern mainly non-living natural resources, such as hydrocarbons, mineral resources and timber, but more recently also wildlife and wildlife products.[58] In addition, environmental security more

[54] UN General Assembly, Resolution adopted by the General Assembly on 16 September 2019, 73/343, Tackling illicit trafficking in wildlife, A/RES/73/343.

[55] UN, Meetings Coverages and Press Release, 'General Assembly Advocates Labour Rights, Ending Illicit Wildlife Trade' (16 September 2019), available at www.un.org/press/en/2019/ga12175.doc.htm, accessed 22 February 2022.

[56] UN General Assembly, Resolution 73/343 (n. 54), preamble para. 12.

[57] Amanda Kron, 'Environmental Peacebuilding and the UN Security Council', in Nico J. Schrijver and Niels M. Blokker (eds.), *Elected Members of the Security Council: Lame Ducks or Key Players?* (Leiden/Boston: Brill 2019), 248–66, at 251.

[58] Ibid., 252.

broadly has entered the agenda of the UN Security Council's work in conflict prevention. A number of meetings have been held on topics including protection of the environment during armed conflict, scarcity of freshwater, climate change, loss of biodiversity as well as exploitation of natural resources.[59] Addressing climate change and destruction of ecological integrity as a threat to international security has been both praised and criticised. Environmental degradation, climate change and biodiversity loss are factors together with poaching and trafficking of wildlife leading to the very high levels of species loss.[60] Thus, any of the work of the council that may contribute to improve general environmental protection, will have positive implications on protection of animals as such.

Secondly, the UN Security Council has the potential to protect animals when establishing organs aimed at providing remedies to breaches of international peace and violations of international law. For instance, the council installed the Fund and the UN Compensation Commission as a response to Iraq's 1990 invasion of Kuwait and the following occupation that constituted a breach of Article 2(4) UN Charter.[61] The UN Compensation Commission provided humanitarian compensations for the victims of the war and occupation. It also granted compensations for claims related to the environmental degradation caused by Iraq intentionally setting fire to oil wells and spilling crude oil into the Gulf as well as indirect environmental harm caused by displaced persons.[62] It contributed to restoration of the environment, including habitats of animals and thus also contributed to protect animals in the region affected by the war.

Thirdly, potentially the UN Security Council's work stream on global health issues could be related to animal protection, even though this is not yet the case. Major health crises have been considered to endanger the maintenance of international peace by the council, including the spread of HIV/AIDS,[63] the Ebola outburst in Western Africa in 2014[64] and in the DRC in 2018[65], and the latest in line the global COVID-19 pandemic.[66] These diseases are linked to humans' interference with wildlife. Human contact with wildlife through capturing,

59 See, for example, UN Security Council, Protection of the Environment during Armed Conflict, Arria Formula meeting (6 November 2018), available at https://bit.ly/35ujI2f, accessed 22 February 2022. Formal meetings were organised under the umbrella of 'Maintenance of international peace and security'. See UN Security Council, Water, peace and security, S/PV.7818 (2016); UN Security Council, Understanding and addressing climate-related security risks, S/PV.8307 (2018); and UN Security Council, Root causes of conflict – role of natural resources, S/PV.8372.

60 Haenlein and Smith, 'Introduction' (n. 12), 1.

61 UN Security Council Resolution of 20 May 1991, S/RES/692, para. 3.

62 For further reading on the UN Compensation Commission, see Cymie Payne and Peter Sand (eds.), *Gulf Wars Reparations and the UN Compensation Commission* (Oxford: Oxford University Press 2011).

63 UN Security Council Resolution 1983 of 7 June 2011, S/RES/1983.

64 UN Security Council Resolution 2177 of 18 September 2014, S/RES/2177.

65 UN Security Council Resolution 2439 of 30 October 2018, S/RES/2439.

66 UN Security Council Resolution 2532 of 1 July 2020, S/RES/2532.

slaughtering, selling, trafficking, trading and consuming can transfer pathogens from animals to humans. The illegal trade in wildlife is not subject to appropriate sanitary controls and can therefore potentially lead to the spread of zoonotic diseases, like SARS-CoV-2 that caused the COVID-19 pandemic.[67] COVID-19 is likely linked to a pathogen found in wild bats that may have been passed to humans, possibly via an intermediary. To prevent future pandemics and health crises, protecting biodiversity will be a key measure, including addressing wildlife trafficking.[68] The UN Security Council could take the lead in this work together with other key actors, such as the World Health Organization (WHO) and the secretariat for the Convention on Biological Diversity.[69]

This chapter focuses on the first work stream, mainly on commodity sanctions, as it directly links the enforcement powers of the UN Security Council with animal protection. The other work streams of the UN Security Council are only indirectly addressing animal protection although they might evolve towards having more prominent connections with protecting animals in the future.

The adoption of commodity sanctions is aimed at breaking the link between exploitation of natural resources and hostilities. In 1998, the UN Security Council confirmed for the first time a direct link between natural resources and armed conflict by recognising the role diamonds have in financing and fuelling the conflict taking place in Angola.[70] Many UN Security Council resolutions followed this path connecting 'conflict minerals' such as diamonds, gold, oil and coltan with the threats to international peace in regard to the DRC, Cambodia, Liberia, Sierra Leone and Côte d'Ivoire, to mention a few examples.[71] As discussed above, wildlife poaching and trafficking are increasingly noted for their serious implications for international security. Already in 2001, a panel of experts appointed by the UN Security Council referred to wildlife trafficking as a source, among other natural resources, to finance military operations in the DRC.[72] This panel mentioned in particular the well-organised elephant poaching and the seizures of ivory.[73] It repeated in this in its interim report of 2002.[74] However, the UN Security Council

67 UN Office on Drugs and Crime (UNODC), *World Wildlife Crime Report 2020: Trafficking in Protected Species* (Vienna: UNODC 2020), 34.

68 Ibid., 19.

69 Convention on Biological Diversity of 5 June 1992, 1760 UNTS 79.

70 UN Security Council Resolution of 12 June 1998, S/RES/1173. See also Aldinger, Bruch and Yazykova, 'Revisiting Securitization' (n. 28), 144.

71 See a general discussion in UNEP, *From Conflict to Peacebuilding: The Role of Natural Resources and the Environment* (Nairobi: UNEP 2009).

72 UN Security Council, Letter dated 8 April 2001 from Secretary General to the President of the Security Council, 12 April 2001, S/2001/357, paras. 61–2. See the discussion by Daniëlla Dam-de Jong, 'UN Natural Resources Sanctions Regimes: Incorporating Market-Based Responses to Address Market-Driven Problems', in Larissa van den Herik (ed.), *Research Handbook on UN Sanctions and International Law* (Cheltenham: Edward Elgar: 2017), 147–76, at 166.

73 Ibid., para. 9.

74 UN Security Council, Letter dated 22 May 2002 from the Secretary-General addressed to the President of the Security Council, 22 May 2002, S/2002/565, para. 52.

did not take any further action in regard to wildlife poaching but focused instead on the traditional non-living conflict minerals in the subsequent resolutions in regard to the situation of the DRC.

It was only in 2013 that the UN Security Council decided to address wildlife poaching and trafficking in its resolutions. Spurred by the report issued by the UN Secretary-General highlighting the growing threat of ivory and elephant poaching in Central Africa, the UN Security Council adopted Resolutions 2121 and 2127 that condemned the destruction of the natural heritage and affirmed poaching and trafficking of wildlife as a factor fuelling the armed conflict in the CAR.[75] This was the first time a resolution referred to living resources as natural resources that could be illegally exploited and constitute a threat to international peace and security.[76] Later in the same year, in Resolution 2134, the UN Security Council expressed concern for illegal exploitation of natural resources including wildlife poaching as a destabilizing force in the CAR. It also decided that member states shall adopt sanctions against individuals and entities 'providing support for armed groups or criminal networks through illicit exploitation of natural resources, including diamonds and wildlife and wildlife products, in regard to the CAR'.[77] The sanctions included preventing entry or transit through the territory as well as freezing assets and economic resources. Only a few weeks later, the council adopted similar measures against persons and entities involved in trafficking of wildlife products, in particular ivory in the DRC.[78]

In later resolutions adopted in 2015 regarding CAR and the DRC, the UN Security Council has encouraged national authorities, neighbouring states and members of the Great Lakes Conference to cooperate to investigate and prosecute crimes related to wildlife poaching and wildlife trafficking, but without specifying further what kind of measures that should be undertaken.[79]

In November 2015, the Permanent Missions of Lithuania and Angola to the UN co-hosted an Arria-formula meeting of the UN Security Council to discuss the impacts of the illegal transfer of small arms and light weapons on poaching in Africa. An Arria-formula meeting is an informal intermittent meeting enabling the council to meet with civil society to receive briefings outside the council chamber.[80] The objective of the Arria-formula meeting was to invite representatives of all member states, in particular those affected by poaching, international organizations

75 UN Security Council Resolution 2121 of 10 October 2013, S/RES/2121, preamble; and UN Security Council Resolution 2127 of 5 December 2013, S/RES/2127, preamble.

76 Anne Peters, 'Novel Practice of the Security Council: Wildlife Poaching and Trafficking as a Threat to the Peace', *EJIL Talk!* (12 February 2014), available at https://bit.ly/3ARD8Kk, accessed 22 February 2022.

77 UN Security Council 2134 of 28 January 2014, S/RES/2134, para. 37 (d).

78 UN Security Council 2136 of 30 January 2014, S/RES/2136, para. 4(g).

79 UN Security Council Resolution 2198 of 29 January 2015, S/RES/2198, para. 26; and UN Security Council Resolution of 28 April 2015, S/RES/2198, para. 38.

80 von Einsiedel and Malone, 'Security Council' (n. 4), 151.

and civil society to attend and make statements to explain why poaching should be considered a threat to international peace and propose measures on how the UN Security Council could tackle such a threat.[81]

At the Arria-formula meeting, members of the UN Security Council discussed the implications of poaching being a major source of revenues for armed groups that increases corruption and distrust in state officials, which weakens the state's authority.[82] This leads to destabilisation of states affected by poaching and trafficking of wildlife. Therefore, poaching needs to be seen from a wider security and rule of law perspective. Such a perspective would involve a need to strengthen the affected states' environmental laws and ensure strategies and plans at a local level to deal with poaching, which was highlighted at the Arria-formula meeting and supported by states affected by poaching.[83] Furthermore, the UN Security Council members emphasised that the problem needs to be addressed from a demand perspective, but also include the illegal trade of arms. The member states also discussed the major differences among the affected states which means that the solutions must be adjusted to the different situations. At the meeting it was recommended that the UN Security Council should make better use of available instruments in particular to include poaching-related activities in the designation criteria for sanctions measures.[84] The members of the UN Security Council recommended that all actors in the UN system including UN peacekeeping operations should do more and coordinate efforts in fighting poaching and illegal trafficking in arms.[85] Moreover, the UN Security Council was recommended to work with local communities to minimise the threats to civilians that are facing increased militarisation of poaching as well as anti-poaching activities and to adopt long-term solutions that involve tackle corruption, improve implementation of existing environmental laws and ensure accountability for wildlife crimes.[86]

Other suggestions pointed out during the Arria-formula meeting were: criminalising poaching and related offences as serious crimes consistent with UNCTOC and its Protocol on firearms; increasing regional and sub-regional cooperation, including joint operations, information sharing, communication protocols or even cross-border relocation of animals to ensure their safety; improving capability to collect information about weapons and ammunitions found at poaching sites to better identify its origins and establish pattern of diversion and detect where wildlife and weapons intersect; and strengthening preventive arms control measures, such as marking and record keeping, import and export of control systems, stockpile and ammunition management, marking and tracing weapons, and sharing technologies.

81 UN General Assembly, Summary of the informal Arria-formula meeting (n. 25).
82 Ibid., 4.
83 Ibid.
84 Ibid., 5.
85 Ibid., 4.
86 Ibid., 5.

It was also suggested that the Arms Trade Treaty[87] regulating international trade in conventional arms with the aim to hinder illicit trade of conventional arms could be a crucial tool.[88] However, several of the affected states, such as the DRC, South Sudan and Uganda, have not ratified this treaty.[89]

6 MILITARY MEANS TO PROTECT WILDLIFE, ALSO WITH A UN SECURITY COUNCIL MANDATE?

The increased sophistication in arms and technology among poachers was one of the concerns raised at the Arria-formula meeting of the UN Security Council in 2015. Poachers use advanced weaponry and technologies such as AK-47s, sophisticated hunting rifles, drones, GPS, night-vision goggles and even helicopters.[90] The weapons frequently come from the black market and illegal trade, which makes them very cheap to buy but difficult to trace.[91] In several states, for example the CAR, the DRC and South Sudan, armed groups engaged in poaching are operating on a scale that cannot be handled with traditional law enforcement. This puts more pressure on park rangers protecting the animals and other staff engaged in conservation when performing an increasingly more dangerous job.[92] Poachers are 'prepared to shoot to kill both animals and rangers that get in their way. Rangers can often encounter heavily armed poachers during patrols, and shots are regularly exchanged.'[93] The conservation staff are frequently under attack and park stations are repeatedly looted. Park rangers are in many times underequipped and insufficiently trained to handle 'combat poachers' using advanced military-style techniques. Poaching has become a 'high profit/low risk activity'.[94]

Armed groups use national parks, nature reserves and other protected areas as hiding places because of their inaccessible and isolated locations as well as their richness in natural resources and wildlife to sustain their military operations and to enrich themselves. Protected areas, which provide sanctuary to wildlife in many parts of the world, are therefore often under threat in times of armed conflict.[95] If

87 Arms Trade Treaty of 2 April 2013, 3013 UNTS 1.

88 UN General Assembly, Summary of the informal Arria-formula meeting (n. 25), 5.

89 See ratifying parities at the Arms Trade Treaty website, available at https://thearmstradetreaty.org, accessed 22 February 2022.

90 Rosaleen Duffy and Jasper Humphreys, 'Poaching, Wildlife Trafficking and Human Security', in Cathy Haenlein and M. L. R. Smith (eds.), *Poaching, Wildlife Trafficking and Security in Africa: Myths and Realities* (London: Royal United Services Institute, Whitehall Papers Series 2016), 22–37, at 33. See also UN General Assembly, Summary of the informal Arria-formula meeting (n. 25), 3–4.

91 UN General Assembly, Summary of the informal Arria-formula meeting (n. 25), 3.

92 Viollaz, 'UN Security Council Cracking Down on Ivory Poaching and Illegal Wildlife Trading' (n. 17).

93 Duffy and Humphreys, 'Poaching, Wildlife Trafficking and Human Security' (n. 90), 33.

94 UN General Assembly, Summary of the informal Arria-formula meeting (n. 25), 4. See also Viollaz, 'UN Security Council Cracking Down on Ivory Poaching and Illegal Wildlife Trading' (n. 17).

95 de Merode et al., 'The Impact of Armed Conflict on Protected Area Efficacy in Central Africa' (n. 35), 299. See also International Law and Policy Institute (ILPI), 'Protection of the Natural Environment in Armed Conflict: An Empirical Study', Report 12/2014.

anti-poaching operations can remain operational in protected areas in instable times it would contribute to protect wildlife.[96] However, park authorities often struggle to keep the protected areas and the wildlife sanctuaries safe from poachers in unstable and war-torn places.[97] For instance, in the DRC, several armed groups are active and using automatic weapons for wildlife poaching for ivory, rhino horns and bush-meat, among other commodities inside the national parks declared as natural World Heritage sites.[98] A large number of rangers have been killed while patrolling protected areas. According to the Thin Green Line foundation approximately 1,000 rangers have been killed worldwide in the last ten years while at duty.[99] In the DRC, almost 200 park rangers were killed while on duty between 1996 and 2007 alone in the World Heritage site Virunga National Park.[100]

Conservation agencies have called for responding with 'military-style conservation' using military force to deal with poachers.[101] Many countries are increasingly militarising their responses to poaching, for instance, by providing military training and arms to park rangers, employing the national army to fight poachers, hiring conservation organisations or private firms.[102] As stated by Duffy and Humphreys: '[a]s the militarised activities of poachers are matched by corresponding militarised responses, the result has increasingly been framed as an existential "war for wildlife"'.[103] In the DRC, Cameroon and Colombia, the army protects national parks and wildlife.[104] In the DRC, a special brigade of the Congolese army had a specific mandate to protect the World Heritage site Garamba National Park.[105] In 2013, fifteen governments[106] in West and Central Africa concluded an agreement for creating a regional security network to protect their wildlife. The agreement included obligations to suppress and prevent of cross-border criminal

96 de Merode et al., 'The Impact of Armed Conflict on Protected Area Efficacy in Central Africa' (n. 35), 299.

97 UN General Assembly, Summary of the informal Arria-formula meeting (n. 25), 2.

98 Britta Sjöstedt, 'The Role of Multilateral Environmental Agreements in Armed Conflict: 'Green-Keeping' in Virunga Park: Applying the UNESCO World Heritage Convention in the Armed Conflict of the Democratic Republic of the Congo', *Nordic Journal of International Law* 82 (2013), 129–53, at 132.

99 The Thin Green Line Foundations, 'Our Story' (no date), available at https://thingreenline.org.au/story, accessed 22 February 2022.

100 Sjöstedt, 'The Role of Multilateral Environmental Agreements in Armed Conflict' (n. 98), 134.

101 Duffy and Humphreys, 'Poaching, Wildlife Trafficking and Human Security' (n. 90), 33.

102 Viollaz, 'UN Security Council Cracking Down on Ivory Poaching and Illegal Wildlife Trading' (n. 17).

103 Duffy and Humphreys, 'Poaching, Wildlife Trafficking and Human Security' (n. 90), 33.

104 UN Security Council, Report of the Secretary General on the Activities of the United Nations Regional Office for Central Africa and on the Lord's Resistance Army-affected areas, 20 May 2013, S/2013/297, para. 9.

105 Sjöstedt, 'The Role of Multilateral Environmental Agreements in Armed Conflict' (n. 98), 144–5.

106 The countries involved are Cameroon, Ivory Coast, Benin, Burkina Faso, Democratic Republic of Congo, Republic of Congo, Chad, Gabon, Guinea Bissau, Equatorial Guinea, Niger, Nigeria, Sao Tomé-et-Principe, Togo and Gambia.

activities, including illegal forest exploitation and poaching of endangered animal species.[107]

Conservation sectors and conservation initiatives are increasingly becoming more integrated with security. Retired General Jooste, head of anti-poaching in South Africa's national parks, declared that his country was 'under the attack from armed foreign nationals' describing it as an ongoing war that needed to be won.[108]

A noteworthy incident illustrating how the conservation sector was triggered to become securitised occurred in May 2013, when twenty-six elephants were slaughtered, most likely for their ivory, at a famous watering hole for elephants known as the 'village of elephants', in Dzanga Bai – a natural World Heritage site in the CAR.[109] The armed group Séléka and Sudanese poachers armed with automatic rifles have adversely impacted the CAR's wildlife and protected areas.[110] At the same time, it is difficult for park rangers in this country to get access to weapons.[111] As a response to the killings of the elephants, in August 2013 the WWF hired the environmental security firm Maisha Consulting to establish a presence in the CAR to protect national parks and also to make contact with the Séléka forces through Maisha Consulting's Wildlife Security Operation. A former Israeli paratrooper in charge of the Wildlife Security Operations explained the operation 'as a holistic union of war and wildlife protection'.[112] The firm managed to enter an agreement with the Séléka to spare wildlife and permit park rangers to patrol the World Heritage site.[113]

The need to strengthen the park rangers has also been requested by the World Heritage Committee on some occasions. In regard to the DRC, the World Heritage Committee requested weapons, ammunition and military training for the park rangers. As a result, the park rangers have been trained by Special Forces of France and Belgium and have formed an advanced force with a paramilitary structure able to respond to armed groups engaged in poaching as well as to other regular poachers.[114]

The World Heritage Committee, the executive organ of the World Heritage Convention, has requested the UN Security Council to include a mandate for UN peacekeepers to protect World Heritage sites and support the park rangers to

107 Elias Ntungwe Ngalame, 'West, Central Africa Agree Security Force to Protect Forests, Seas', *Thomson Reuters Foundation News* (19 July 2013), available at https://tmsnrt.rs/3ulUQ7g, accessed 22 February 2022.

108 Duffy and Humphreys, 'Poaching, Wildlife Trafficking and Human Security' (n. 90), 36.

109 Ibid., 47–8.

110 Stephane Crayne and Cathy Haenlein, 'Poaching, Wildlife Trafficking and Conflict', in Cathy Haenlein and M. L. R. Smith (eds.), *Poaching, Wildlife Trafficking and Security in Africa: Myths and Realities* (London: Royal United Services Institute, Whitehall Papers Series, 2016), 38–57, at 45.

111 UNGA, Summary of the informal Arria-formula meeting (n. 25), 4.

112 Duffy and Humphreys, 'Poaching, Wildlife Trafficking and Human Security' (n. 90), 34.

113 Crayne and Haelein, 'Poaching, Wildlife Trafficking and Conflict' (n. 110) 50–1.

114 Sjöstedt, 'The Role of Multilateral Environmental Agreements in Armed Conflict' (n. 98) 147.

disarm and evacuate armed groups from the World Heritage sites in its resolutions regarding the DRC. The suggestion did not end up in any of the resolutions adopted by the council.[115] Yet, since 2003, UN peacekeeping troops have provided informal support to the park rangers to protect the World Heritage sites in the DRC. For instance, disarmament operations of armed groups have been performed by park rangers in collaboration with UN peacekeepers without being officially authorized by the Security Council.[116] This support has contributed to prevent exploitation of natural resources and poaching of wildlife.[117]

Wildlife poaching and trafficking has been declared to constitute a threat to international peace in accordance with Article 39 of the UN Charter, as discussed above. Thus, it is possible for the UN Security Council to act to protect wildlife within its mandate. This could even include authorising military means if non-coercive action is insufficient in accordance with Article 42 of the UN Charter.

In regard to CAR, an exception to weapons embargo was issued by the UN Security Council in accordance with Article 41 of the UN Charter in order to allow park rangers to have access to weapons to ensure the protection of the Sangha River Tri-national Protected Area. Supply of small arms and other related equipment for *international* patrols to defend against poaching, smuggling of ivory and arms was decided.[118] A similar exception for anti-poaching patrols was not granted in any of the DRC resolutions. Still, in the DRC military training as well as weapons have been provided to the park rangers contrary to the weapons embargo.[119] Despite the absence of the weapon embargo exception in the DRC, such a practice appears to have been tolerated on the ground in order to protect wildlife.

The militarised responses have been successful in decreasing the number of animals killed overall. However, there are other examples where poaching has increased even when members of the national army have been involved in poaching activities.[120] Furthermore, using militarised responses sanctioned by the UN Security Council to ensure wildlife protection raises other concerns. The employment of weaponised conservation risks to lead to an escalation of violence and instability. It also moves wildlife conservation to an international level that may undermine a community-based approach.[121] Communities living close to wildlife are considered as key partners to tackle wildlife poaching and other wildlife crimes. As stated in the 2020 World Wildlife Crime Report, 'community-led patrols and community-based crime prevention initiatives can be vital extensions of national

115 Britta Sjöstedt, *The Role of Multilateral Environmental Agreements: A Reconciliatory Approach to Environmental Protection in Armed Conflict* (Oxford: Hart 2020), 241.

116 Sjöstedt, 'The Role of Multilateral Environmental Agreements in Armed Conflict' (n. 98).

117 Ibid.

118 UN Security Resolution 2127 of 5 December 2013, S/RES/2127, para. 54 (d).

119 Sjöstedt, 'The Role of Multilateral Environmental Agreements in Armed Conflict' (n. 98), 150–1.

120 Ibid.

121 Duffy and Humphreys, 'Poaching, Wildlife Trafficking and Human Security' (n. 90), 34–5.

law enforcement networks'. They can play a fundamental role to protect wildlife and form 'the so-called first line of defense'.[122]

To sum up, although there is currently no extensive practice to address wildlife poaching and trafficking by using military means authorised by the UN Security Council, there is nothing blocking such a development in the future. The question is though if such development is desirable. Also, all poaching taking place may not reach the level of constituting a threat to international peace and thus operate outside the mandate of the UN Security Council. This is a limitation of the ability for the UN Security Council to enforce wildlife protection. In addition, other units outside and within the UN, such as the international collaboration of ICCWC or regional ECCAS may be in a better position to handle these types of operations. As pointed about by Dam-de Jong, several anti-poaching initiatives have been undertaken within the framework of ECCAS, but the council has not provided the international support needed for these initiatives.

7 CONCLUDING RECOMMENDATIONS

The UN Security Council has the powers to adopt binding decisions for all UN member states on matters regarding international peace and security. On several occasions, it has identified wildlife poaching and trafficking as a threat to international peace in accordance with Article 39 of the UN Charter. Therefore, it could use its powers to address gaps in the existing international legal framework for protecting wildlife against poaching and trafficking. The UN Security Council should continue to develop the commitments adopted in the UN General Assembly resolutions on tackling illicit trafficking in wildlife. For instance, in accordance with Articles 39 and 41 of the UN Charter, the UN Security Council could call for improved legislation and enforcement of national environmental and criminal laws, facilitate cooperation and inter-agency work and further intelligence to investigate and prosecute high-level wildlife crime. The UN Security Council could also strengthen financial investigation tools to deal with corruption. In addition, as suggested by the WWF, in states affected by poaching, it could contribute to provide ranger training programmes to gather forensic evidence from poaching sites; establish regulatory and monitoring frameworks for the management and disposal of confiscated weapons and ammunition. The UN Security Council could also establish formal mechanisms for collation and exchange of information between ranger forces and international mechanisms, such as INTERPOL's firearms tracing system, and CITES' Monitoring of Illegal Killing of Elephants system. Also, as proposed by the WWF, the UN Security Council should appoint a Special Envoy for wildlife crime.[123]

122 UN Office on Drugs and Crime, World Wildlife Crime Report 2020 (n. 67), 25.

123 World Wildlife Fund, 'UN Security Council Can Boost Fight against Poaching by Linking It to Trafficking in Small Arms' (30 November 2015), available at https://wwf.to/3uxyujx, accessed 22 February 2022.

The UN Security Council has addressed wildlife protection in different ways. For instance, the adoption of Resolution 2217 in regard to the CAR calls upon neighbouring states to cooperate on a regional level. Yet, as highlighted by Dam-de Jong, the UN Security Council could have specifically called UN member states to work with the existing ICCWC and to endorse the recommendations issued under CITES, which could strengthen the efforts on ivory.[124] Such an approach would have been in line with the recommendations included in the UN General Assembly resolutions to prevent, combat and eradicate the illegal trade in wildlife, on the supply, transit and demand sides, including by strengthening the requisite legislation and regulations for prevention, prosecution and enforcement, as well as to increase efforts to raise awareness about the problem.

The UN Security Council has implicitly acknowledged the need for militarised anti-poaching responses by adopting an exception for park rangers and conservation from the weapons embargo in the CAR. This may raise questions, in particular if the anti-poaching operations are conducted by foreign private military firms such as Maisha Consulting. Furthermore, the UN Security Council has the mandate to authorise military means to maintain and restore international peace. So far the council has not authorised military means specifically in regard to wildlife protection but informal collaborations have taken place in the DRC between UN peacekeepers and park rangers. If anti-poaching operations can be conducted in protected areas even against heavily armed poachers, it contributes to safeguard wildlife. However, the militarised responses come with certain backlashes including increasing militarisation and escalation in violence. Therefore, these responses should not be regarded as a long-term solution for animal protection – with or without the blessing of the UN Security Council, but rather as temporary emergency measures. Instead the main focus of the council should be to build strong institutions that hopefully also can contribute to support local communities and ensure alternative livelihoods.

SELECT BIBLIOGRAPHY

Aldinger, Peter, Carl Bruch and Sofia Yazykova, 'Revisiting Securitization: An Empirical Analysis of Environment and Natural Resource Provisions in United Nations Security Council Resolutions 1946–2016', in Ashok Swain and Joakim Öjendal (eds.), *Handbook of Environmental Conflict and Peacebuilding* (Abingdon: Routledge 2018).

Dam-de Jong, Daniëlla, *International Law and Governance of Natural Resources in Conflict and Post-Conflict Situations* (Cambridge: Cambridge University Press 2015).

Haenlein, Cathy and M. L. R. Smith (eds.), *Poaching, Wildlife Trafficking and Security in Africa: Myths and Realities* (London: Royal United Services Institute, Whitehall Papers Series 2016).

Sjöstedt, Britta, 'The Role of Multilateral Environmental Agreements in Armed Conflict: "Green-Keeping" in Virunga Park: Applying the UNESCO World Heritage Convention in

124 Dam-de Jong, 'UN Natural Resources Sanctions Regimes' (n. 72) 170–1.

the Armed Conflict of the Democratic Republic of the Congo', *Nordic Journal of International Law* 82 (2013), 129–53.

van den Herik, Larissa (ed.), *Research Handbook on UN Sanctions and International Law* (Cheltenham: Edward Elgar 2017).

Weiss, Thomas G. and Sam Daws (eds.), *The Oxford Handbook on the United Nations* (2nd ed., Oxford: Oxford University Press 2018).

PART V

Towards Better Protection of Animals in Wartime

22

Key Findings and Recommendations

Jérôme de Hemptinne, Anne Peters and Robert Kolb

There can be no doubt that all types of animals – be they wild animals, livestock, companion animals, zoo animals, 'animal soldiers', animals used for medical purposes or endangered species – and their habitats may be seriously impacted by warfare.[1] Despite their vulnerability in such situations, our study has shown that animals are only incidentally protected by international humanitarian law (IHL) as mere objects (or properties). They are neither treated as 'subjects of protection' nor granted any rights. Our research has also highlighted that the few IHL provisions that could potentially apply to animals have rarely been enforced or effectively implemented by international courts and tribunals. In light of these general observations, we will first set out the key findings of the study, focusing on the main legal challenges that are raised by the protection of animals during warfare (Section 1). We will then formulate several recommendations to address these challenges and to ensure that the applicable legal framework is strengthened (Section 2).

1 KEY FINDINGS

First finding: the level, type and nature of the protection that animals receive under IHL vary widely from one animal to another, depending on a multitude of factors.[2] These factors include the roles animals play during warfare (e.g. as weapons of war, means of medical transportation and rescue, or as objects of medical experimentation); the circumstances in which they are placed (e.g. when they are targeted or 'detained'); the areas in which they live (e.g. in invaded or occupied territories, land or sea, protected or unprotected zones); and their specific nature (e.g. whether they are listed as endangered species, domestic animals or wild animals). Some safeguards – such as those protecting the environment as a whole – apply generally to the

1 See Daskin and Pringle, Chapter 3, 'Ecological Effects of Warfare on Wildlife', in this volume. For precise indications of case law, conventions, national laws and scholarship, see the references in each chapter of this volume.

2 This finding is mainly drawn from Peters and de Hemptinne, Chapter 1, 'Animals in Armed Conflicts: A Legal Research Agenda', in this volume.

entire wildlife population. That said, even if the application of IHL norms to domestic animals, to the so-called charismatic megafauna or to mammals will find wide acceptance, their applicability to other animals, such as insects or ocean animals, will frequently be beset with difficulties and raise controversies. Indeed, assessing the lawfulness of incidental damages caused to this latter category of animals may turn out to be extremely complicated. It requires environmental knowledge that even well-equipped state-armed forces often do not possess, in particular because these damages tend to manifest themselves in the long run and are often merely an indirect result of the destruction of certain habitats.

Second finding: IHL provisions governing the protection of property and objects provide minimal, direct and individual protection to animals in warfare, including in sea warfare.[3] In principle, animals enjoy a similar degree of protection in their quality as property under Article 23(g) of the Hague Regulations and in their quality as objects, under the rules on targeting as codified in Additional Protocol (AP) I. This means that animals can only be targeted when they qualify as military objectives because of their involvement in hostilities or when the harm done to them constitutes proportionate incidental damage resulting from attacks on military objectives. When calculating proportionality, reverberating and long-term effects arising from attacks on military objectives must be considered to the extent that these effects can be reasonably foreseen. This is of particular relevance for attacks that might contribute to the extinction of species indispensable for the good functioning of the ecosystem where these animals live. Before attacking animals, all necessary measures of precaution must be taken. A useful tool for the implementation of this obligation of 'due regard' is to agree on the creation of protected zones where no combat will take place, especially in marine areas containing rare or fragile ecosystems or the habitat of depleted, threatened or endangered species. Finally, under the principle of military necessity, whenever feasible in concrete situations, belligerents should consider capturing rather than killing animals used as war weapons by the enemy. But the system of protection remains imperfect: when categorising animals as mere property or objects, the mentioned IHL norms ignore the fact that animals 'are living creatures with their own interests, which can take independent actions and are capable of subjective perceptions and suffering'.[4]

Third finding: IHL provisions protecting the environment as such provide minimal, indirect and global protection to animals during warfare, including sea warfare.[5] International humanitarian law also protects animals indirectly and globally as general components of the environment in which they live. Traditionally, the notion of environment encompasses wildlife and its habitats, as well as the relationship that

[3] This finding is mainly drawn from Roscini, Chapter 5, 'Property and Objects' and Henry, Chapter 15, 'Animals in Sea Warfare', in this volume.

[4] Roscini, Chapter 5, 'Property and Objects', in this volume.

[5] This finding is mainly drawn from de Hemptinne, Chapter 7, 'Animals as Part of the Environment' and Henry, Chapter 15, 'Animals in Sea Warfare', in this volume.

these elements entertain with the ecological system in which they exist. The ICRC Environmental Guidelines specify that, for purposes of IHL, the environment encompasses not only natural elements *stricto sensu*, but also 'elements that are or may be the product of human intervention, such as foodstuffs, agricultural areas, drinking water and *livestock*.'[6] Accordingly, all animals, including farm and companion animals, are part of the environment. As a result, they are duly protected by the laws of warfare and, in particular, by three sets of rules.

First, the general principles governing the conduct of hostilities which protect civilian objects – that is the principles of distinction, proportionality and precaution – are applicable to the environment as a whole. Specific elements of the environment can become military objectives, but only under restrictive conditions set forth in Article 52(2) of AP I. In principle, no component of the natural environment is a military objective by its nature. Moreover, wildlife can never be treated as a military objective by virtue of its use or purpose, even if the trading of endangered species might contribute to sustaining military activities. Furthermore, the natural environment always remains protected against excessive collateral damage. Wildlife should thus be fully brought into the proportionality equation. Second, other IHL rules that seek to prevent or limit certain damage – such as those for specially protected objects – or that regulate the usage of specific weapons or combat techniques also play a role in this context.

Third, Articles 35(3) and 55 of AP I prohibit using means and methods of warfare that are intended, or may be excepted, to cause 'long-term, widespread and severe damage' to the environment. Today, the importance of environmental values, the progressive understanding that the environment must be protected as such, and the awareness of the dramatic consequences that wars have on the whole ecosystem – and wildlife in particular – should impact the way these provisions are interpreted. What might not have appeared to be 'widespread, long-term and severe damage' forty years ago when AP I was adopted may now be considered as such. For instance, it is increasingly accepted by scientists that destroying biodiversity spots or areas known to be populated by endangered species or by a great diversity of fauna and flora can also entail serious repercussions for the environment as a whole, even if the area concerned is relatively small. However, Articles 35(3) and 55 of AP I do not formally apply in the context of non-international armed conflicts. Reflecting the reluctance of states to accept tight constraints on the way they conduct hostilities against rebels, the non-application of the norms specifically protecting the environment is at odds with the fact that environmental concerns exceed the mere domestic affairs of individual states. This means that certain essential or rare natural resources, including species, should receive an absolute protection in all circumstances, wherever they are situated.

[6] ICRC, ICRC Environmental Guidelines, Preliminary Considerations, para. 16 (emphasis added).

Fourth finding: international environmental norms provide additional protection to animals during warfare, including sea warfare.[7] Beyond the general principles governing the conduct of hostilities that potentially apply to natural resources and animals and the few provisions that specifically protect them, IHL does not address any other environmental matters, for instance, those relating to the conservation and the preservation of wildlife. This lacuna offers much scope for international environment treaties which continue to apply during armed conflicts to fill the remaining gaps. The content and nature of the environmental norms vary widely from one convention to the other. Some conventions pursue a sectorial approach, protecting particular species or areas. Others are more holistic in nature: they focus not only on environmental protection and conservation, but more broadly on issues of common interest for humanity, such as sustainable development, biological diversity, or the impact of climate change on ecosystems. Moreover, IHL provisions and customary principles are themselves rather broad and vague. They leave wide discretion on how to read and apply them concretely. In this respect, international environmental law can play a complementary role by giving a meaning and substance to the norms of IHL. Indeed, IHL provisions and principles must be construed in conformity with fundamental environmental standards that have progressively emerged from the numerous international conventions and soft law instruments during the last decades. This means that, through a harmonious interpretation, relevant IHL provisions and principles could – and should – be interpreted and applied by reference to the normative context in which they operate, a context co-shaped by international environmental law. All this should be done with a view to modernising old IHL norms and principles governing the conduct of hostilities with help of current environmental norms and to foster consistency and complementarity between these two bodies of international law. Such an approach, based on the principle of mutual supportiveness, could lead to a form of 'environmentalisation' of warfare and IHL through the application of reasonable standards drawn from international environmental law, in light of contemporary concerns expressed by most states about the protection and the conservation of the fauna and flora.

Fifth finding: weaponised animals constitute 'weapons' or 'means and methods or warfare' under IHL and are thus subject to legal reviews.[8] The usage of animals as weapons is not per se illegal. It is merely subject to legal reviews in order to determine whether weaponised animals are able to distinguish between military objectives and civilian objects or persons and whether their use could cause superfluous injury. The injury to animals themselves when employed as war weapons should be taken into account to make such an assessment. Moreover, debates on the

[7] This finding is mainly drawn from de Hemptinne, Chapter 7, 'Animals as Part of the Environment' and Henry, Chapter 15, 'Animals in Sea Warfare', in this volume.

[8] This finding is mainly drawn from Jenks, Chapter 9, 'War Weapons', in this volume.

compatibility of the employment of lethal autonomous weapons systems with IHL principles – in particular with the principle of discrimination – could inform the discussions surrounding the weaponising of animals.

Sixth finding: IHL provisions governing the protection of means of medical transportation, search and rescue provide minimal incidental protection to animals during warfare.[9] When employed to extract persons requiring medical assistance or to provide such assistance, animals fall within the category of medical transports which are protected under IHL. When used for search or rescue activities, animals constitute equipment of medical units which are also protected under IHL. In both instances, animals may not be attacked, nor harmed in any way, nor their medical functioning be impeded, even if they do not momentarily bear any wounded and sick or medical equipment. They benefit from all the rules governing precautions in attacks and against the effects of attacks. They may not be located in the vicinity of military objectives or used to commit acts harmful to the enemy. It is only if, and when, they are employed for military purposes – for instance, to transport able soldiers or munitions, to serve as 'living bombs' or to detect explosives – that they may lose such a protection. Once again it becomes obvious that this regime does not capture the essence of animals as living creatures and does not take into account their particular needs.

Seventh finding: veterinary personnel who, as member of the armed forces, take care of animals are treated as 'combatants' or 'civilians accompanying the armed forces' and, in both roles, enjoy prisoner of war status upon capture.[10] In international armed conflicts, veterinary personnel enjoy the status as prisoners of war by Geneva Convention (GC) III. When they do not belong to state armed forces, they are protected as civilians by GC IV. In non-international armed conflicts, veterinary personnel are only protected by the minimal rules which apply in this context. In principle, when providing exclusive care to animals used by armed groups, veterinarians will not lose this minimal protection under IHL, either by virtue of being members of the armed groups or by virtue of directly participating in hostilities. In contrast, military personnel who provide care to animals do not benefit from the full special protection granted to (human) medical personnel in international and non-international armed conflicts – only when they are engaged in the prevention of diseases (e.g. zoonoses) that threaten humans. This is another illustration of the unsatisfactory system of protection offered to animals during warfare.

Eighth finding: animals are protected indirectly as property, natural resources or portion of the environment in occupied territory.[11] The rules on the protection of private and public property provide minimal safeguards to animals in occupied territory. For instance, the occupying power must respect animals as property and

[9] This finding is mainly drawn from de Hemptinne, Chapter 11, 'Medical Transport, Search and Rescue', in this volume.

[10] This finding is main drawn from Fortin, Chapter 12, 'Veterinary Personnel', in this volume.

[11] This finding is mainly drawn from Longobardo, Chapter 13, 'Occupied Territory', in this volume.

cannot confiscate them or 'destroy' them unless this is rendered absolutely necessary by military operations. The occupier can requisition animals only under strict conditions. It must also compensate the seizure of animals used as means of transportation. As administrator and usufructuary of forests and agricultural estates belonging to the occupied state, the occupying forces must safeguard the capital of these properties and administer them in accordance with the rules of usufruct. This encompasses the administration of animals living in these areas. Other rules of the law of occupation – such as the prescription that the occupying power must take measure to avoid the spreading of diseases among animals and between animals and humans – grant some sort of protection to animals. The occupying power also has a general obligation of care to protect the natural environment, including wildlife, against 'widespread, long-term and severe damage'.

Ninth finding: when establishing protected zones, belligerents can take appropriate preparatory measures to support any particularly vulnerable animals.[12] These measures, which can be taken during peacetimes, include identifying the likely location of such zones or ensuring that these zones take into account the needs of animals that are located therein. Preparatory measures could be taken to support any particularly vulnerable animal species or group – for instance by ensuring the presence of sufficient food for zoo animals. Where the natural habitat of wild animals falls within a designated protected zone, measures can be taken to ensure that the sheltered persons, who will often increase significantly in number, do not encroach excessively onto those animals' habitats. This can be done through signalisation, information campaigns and monitoring.

Tenth finding: animals are safeguarded indirectly through the protection afforded to cultural heritage sites, namely when they inhabit the surrounding areas, and through the protection afforded to objects indispensable to the survival of civilian population.[13] As inhabitants of a cultural heritage site, animals benefit from the protection against military attacks, which are only allowed in exceptional situations when required by imperative military necessity. It remains unclear whether the notion of cultural heritage itself may be interpreted so as to include some categories of animals, in particular endangered and endemic species. Animals as objects indispensable to the survival of civilian population are protected by two distinct obligations. First, attacking these animals with the purpose of deliberately depriving civilians of food is banned as a method of warfare. Second, livestock is protected by the prohibition to attack, destroy, remove or otherwise rendering useless objects indispensable to the survival of civilian population. This protection is however subject to two important limitations. First, animals are not safeguarded as such, but rather as 'a means of sustenance' for the civilian population. Second, only animals that are indispensable

[12] This finding is mainly drawn from Gillett, Chapter 14, 'Protected Zones', in this volume.

[13] This finding is mainly drawn from Krähenmann, Chapter 6, 'Specially Protected Objects', in this volume.

to the survival of the population are covered. Livestock is provided as an illustrative example, but potentially other animals, such as game, could also be covered.

Eleventh finding: wildlife benefits from the general protection offered by international wildlife conventions against poaching and trafficking activities.[14] Although wildlife treaties such as the Convention on International Trade in Endangered Species (CITES) are silent on their applicability during armed conflicts, they are presumed to continue to apply in these situations to the extent that their content does not conflict with IHL rules. These treaties are generally characterised by a variety of sophisticated implementation and compliance mechanisms aiming at preventing and at combatting wildlife trafficking. However, the capacity to implement and enforce these complex mechanisms in conflict-affected countries is often significantly weakened as a result of ongoing hostilities and the inability of belligerents to exercise control over their territories.

Twelfth finding: the International Criminal Court (ICC) and other international courts and tribunals have the jurisdiction to repress international crimes that indirectly affect animals.[15] While IHL treaties contain no provisions that expressly and directly prohibit specific conduct vis-à-vis animals, many rules are indirectly applicable to them, including those protecting the natural environment or civilian objects and private or public property. Those that shield civilians from the knock-on effects of conduct that affect animals (for instance, where animals are a source of sustenance and when their looting and killing, as a military tactic, lead civilians to acute food shortage or deprivation) can also be considered. Here, the most 'fitting' war crimes are those of intentionally using starvation as a method of warfare by depriving them of objects indispensable to their survival and, where death of humans results, the crimes of wilful killing or murder. Further, because of the severe consequences on human health and well-being that the onset of starvation brings with it, a number of other war crimes can be envisaged, such as torture, inhumane treatment, or causing great suffering or serious injury to body or health. When the acts occur within the context of a massive or systematic attack against a civilian population, a number of these crimes can additionally constitute crimes against humanity. Where civilians are forcibly displaced from an area in which they are lawfully present due to coercive acts, the crimes of deportation and forcible transfers might come into play. Coercive acts can consist in the destruction and theft of property which includes cattle and other animals. Coercive acts can also lie in damage against the natural environment. As animals are part of said environment, the crimes of deportation and forcible transfers can be envisaged in that constellation, too. Where any or all of these underlying crimes are carried out in a discriminatory manner, with the specific intent to discriminate against any identifiable social group on specific grounds, then these acts can also constitute the crime of persecution.

[14] This finding is mainly drawn from Nowrot, Chapter 20, 'Wildlife Trafficking', in this volume.

[15] This finding is mainly drawn from Ventura, Chapter 18, 'International Crimes', in this volume.

Thirteenth finding: the UN Security Council can use its binding powers under Chapter VII *of the UN Charter to address wildlife protection in several manners.*[16] The UN Security Council can address gaps in the existing international legal framework for protecting wildlife against poaching and trafficking. For instance, in accordance with Articles 39 and 41 of the UN Charter, it can call for improved legislation and enforcement of national environmental and criminal laws, it can facilitate cooperation and inter-agency work, and it can investigate and prosecute high-level wildlife crime. Furthermore, the UN Security Council has the mandate to authorise military means to maintain and restore international peace by, for instance, conducting anti-poaching operations in protected areas. Finally, it can contribute to building strong institutions to address the protection of wildlife, ultimately contributing to support for local communities and ensuring alternative livelihoods.

2 CONCLUDING RECOMMENDATIONS

To meet the challenges identified throughout the book as summarised in the preceding sections, three distinct avenues could be pursued: making increased usage of existing laws and mechanisms of protection that could potentially apply to animals during warfare (Section 2.1); progressively re-interpreting certain IHL norms to take into account that animals are living beings (Section 2.2); and granting minimal fundamental rights to particularly vulnerable animals on which a consensus could potentially emerge (Section 2.3). While the first strategy should not create conceptual difficulties, the two others are not easy to reconcile with the fact that '[t]he currently dominant *lex lata* rationale for the protection of animals in wartime is essentially anthropocentric and informed by utilitarian considerations'.[17] Moreover, only a radical change of attitude towards the animal question would allow the lawmakers and law appliers to move beyond traditional distinctions on which IHL is grounded. One of them is the distinction between (military and civilian) *objects* on the one hand and combatants/prisoners of war and civilian *persons* on the other hand. That distinction would need to be eroded in order to recognise a new intermediate category of 'non-human beings' which would stand between persons and objects. This would be a novel status in the IHL framework.

2.1 *Strengthening the Existing Applicable Laws and Systems of Protection*

The following six recommendations could be implemented without altering the existing IHL legal framework.

16 This finding is mainly drawn from Sjöstedt, Chapter 21, 'Enforcement Powers of the United Nations Security Council', in this volume.

17 See Krieger and Martínez Soria, Chapter 4, 'Rationale and Challenges', in this volume.

First recommendation: the creation of protected zones to shelter animal populations should be encouraged.[18] The identification of ecocentric protected zones for particularly vulnerable areas or environmental hotspots, in which endangered species are often located, should be promoted by states and competent organisations, such as the International Committee of the Red Cross (ICRC). This would allow that, at the outset of any conflict, these areas or hotspots are already well delineated and would then prohibit belligerents from conducting military operations within their boundaries. Moreover, the establishment of a network of such zones should be achieved in a systematic manner through reliance on other pre-existing multilateral conventions, such as the World Heritage Convention or the Convention on Biological Diversity. To facilitate matters, states could also be invited to finalise and sign the Draft Convention on the Prohibition of Hostile Military Activities in Protected Areas.

Second recommendation: the ICRC and the UN should examine the existing international legal framework for protecting animals during warfare and recommend how it can be clarified, expanded and ultimately codified. As a leading body with particular expertise in the field of IHL, the ICRC should be called upon to examine the effectiveness of the legal framework applicable to animals during warfare. It should collaborate with bodies specialised on animal matters such as the World Wildlife Fund (WWF) and the United Nations Environment Programme (UNEP) to identify gaps and barriers to enforcement. The institutions should also explore possibilities for clarifying and ultimately codifying this body of law with a view to proposing guidelines that could be implemented by state armed forces and armed groups.[19] As noted by UNEP regarding the protection of the environment in armed conflicts, '[s]tates would then be in a position to adopt and reflect these guidelines in national legislation and military manuals, as well as to integrate them into the training of their armed forces'.[20] It is also expected that sophisticated armed groups will be in position to promote respect for these guidelines upon advice of certain organisations, such as the 'Geneva Call'.

Third recommendation: international legal practitioners should be trained in enforcing the existing norms that could potentially increase animal welfare during warfare. In order to reinforce the protection of particularly vulnerable animals, human rights organisations and non-governmental organisations (NGOs) should be sensitised to questions relating to animal welfare and play a more active role to ensure that animals be effectively protected during warfare. In order to enrich the corpus of case law available, international judges, prosecutors and legal practitioners should be educated about the content of norms that could potentially be used for such purposes.[21] As rightly pointed

18 This recommendation is mainly based on Gillett, Chapter 14, 'Protected Zones', in this volume.

19 See in this regard UNEP, *Protecting the Environment During Armed Conflicts: An Inventory Analysis of International Law* (Nairobi: UNEP 2009), 6.

20 Ibid., 5–6.

21 Ibid., 6.

out by UNEP regarding the protection of the environment in armed conflicts, '[t]he subsequent development of case law would help bring clarity to existing provisions and increase deterrence by adding a credible threat of prosecution for violations'.[22]

Fourth recommendation: state armed forces and armed groups should benefit from guidelines and training on how to protect the environment, including wildlife, during warfare. Guidebooks on environmental considerations, including wildlife, for military operations should be developed by armed forces around the world.[23] These guidebooks should focus on providing those who plan and conduct military operations with the necessary concrete tools to ensure respect of environmental matters.[24] Appropriate training should take place to facilitate the usage of these guidebooks and increase awareness on wildlife considerations.

Fifth recommendation: the conclusion of special agreements or the adoption of unilateral declarations designed to increase the protection of animals during warfare should be encouraged. State armed forces and armed groups should be invited to conclude special agreements in order to supplement their IHL obligations and provide increased protection to animals that would be left unprotected (or insufficiently protected) without such agreements.[25] This should also happen in situations of occupation between the occupying power and the representatives of the local population.[26] Such a solution should be promoted by international bodies (such as UNEP), other organisations (such as the ICRC) and environmentalist NGOs (such as the WWF) especially when these agreements have no direct impact on the primary military interests of belligerents. Any party to an armed conflict should also be invited to unilaterally commit to respect the environment and notably animals.[27]

Sixth recommendation: occupying powers should pay more attention to local legislation protecting animals and to their duty to implement such laws in light of their obligation to restore and ensure public order and civil life.[28] The occupying powers are bound to respect environmental treaties that they have ratified and integrated into their legal systems. Such treaties may offer general protection to the environment or specific protection to certain animals. The occupying powers should ensure the concrete implementation of these instruments. As will be explained below, occupying powers may arguably alter existing legal regimes in occupied territories to offer a better protection to the animals living therein.

22 Ibid.

23 See Susan L. Clark-Sestak, *Environmental Tools for Use During Military Exercises* (Alexandria: Institute for Defense Analysis 2019).

24 Ibid.

25 See Roscini, Chapter 5, 'Property and Objects', in this volume.

26 See Longobardo, Chapter 13, 'Occupied Territory', in this volume.

27 Anne Peters, 'Animals in International Law', *Collected Courses of The Hague Academy of International Law – Recueil des Cours* Vol. 410 (Leiden: Brill 2020), 391.

28 This recommendation is mainly drawn from Longobardo, Chapter 13, 'Occupied Territory', in this volume.

2.2 *Reinterpretation of Norms of International Humanitarian Law*

As set out in the key findings (Section 1), animals have largely been coded under IHL into the categories of 'property' and 'objects' which are the beneficiaries of minimal protective rules.[29] In previous decades, however, several states have modified the legal status of animals. They can either be pushed on the side of persons or included in an intermediate category, between objects and persons, usually called 'sentient beings'. The contributions to this study have considered both options. The first one has led some authors to examine whether animals could fit into the categories of 'protected persons' envisaged by IHL and whether this exercise could realistically increase their protection. The second option – which runs through several chapters of the study – is to examine how classical IHL norms protecting objects, means and methods of warfare, as well as the environment could be 'reinterpreted' in order to better take account of the fact that animals are living beings and be applied whenever feasible by belligerents. We will briefly set out the outcome of the research on both options.

First option: the protection of animals as combatants/prisoners of war.[30] In Chapter 10, Jérôme de Hemptinne, Tadesse Kebebew and Joshua Niyo considered whether applying the status of combatant and prisoner of war to animals could improve their fate when they are actively involved in hostilities and when they fall into the power of the enemy. We have seen, however, that fitting animals into these categories is not an easy task since they have been designed to apply to human persons. Moreover, if treated as combatants, 'animal soldiers' may be lawfully targeted at all times when belonging to armed forces. But while human beings willingly and deliberately join armed forces, perfectly cognisant that this situation could lead to lethal consequences, animals have no freedom of choice in this regard. They are not aware of the exact role that they play in the conduct of hostilities and are unable to react autonomously to any military action undertaken by adverse military forces against them. Furthermore, they do not benefit from any immunity of prosecution that is available to those human beings who have the legal right to participate in hostilities, because they are plainly not subject to the risk of criminal prosecution. Given that the animals are physically coerced to combat, lack intellectual freedom and independence of action, and are incapable of benefiting from the privilege of being a combatant, it does not seem meaningful to qualify animals as proper combatants. We have also seen that when they fall into the hands of the enemy, the application of the full regime of protection envisaged in GC III and AP I to animals would be unrealistic and unnecessary. Besides, in situations where armed forces are already unable to protect the well-being of human detainees, providing 'animal soldiers' with the guarantees contained in GC III and AP I would certainly not constitute a priority for these forces.

29 See also Peters, 'Animals' (n. 27), 400.

30 See de Hemptinne, Kebebew and Niyo, Chapter 10, 'Combatants and as Prisoners of War?' and Henry, Chapter 15, 'Sea Warfare', in this volume.

Second option: the protection of animals as 'non-humans' or as 'sentient beings'. As recalled in the key findings, several chapters contemplate a less radical solution: many IHL norms that potentially offer protection to animals during warfare could be interpreted and applied in a progressive manner to better take into account that animals are not simply objects but a *sui generis* category of 'sentient beings' deserving to be treated as sentient. It is far from clear whether this evolutionary reading of IHL norms is grounded on a general and coherent subsequent practice of states[31] or on any relevant principles of the international law[32] of animal conservation. On the other hand, 'there are increasing elements of state practice and public opinion pointing towards the need for increased respect for elementary considerations of animal welfare as a manifestation of the "dictates of public conscience"'[33] and of the considerations of humanity, as referred to in the meta-legal Martens clause.[34] And these dictates of public conscience and considerations of humanity 'both suggest construing the relevant norms, wherever they lack clarity or precision, and wherever doubt arises in their application to the facts, in the direction of outlawing acts that cause suffering'.[35] Such an interpretation is especially plausible because the contemporary, more ecological version of the Martens clause, as proposed by the ICRC and the ILC, protects not only civilians and combatants but also 'the environment' as such[36] – which comprises animals.[37] Ultimately, 'such rethinking would not require a radical reconfiguration of (...) IHL, as it is increasingly understood that the survival of humankind is also dependent on the survival of other species'.[38] The Martens clause allows an evolutionary reading of IHL norms, based on their wording, context, and telos, even in the absence of a firm subsequent state practice. Pulling together the interpretations offered in the previous chapters of the study, we can formulate eleven fundamental principles. These aim at preserving a minimum level of integrity for all vulnerable animals, be they wild or domestic, in all circumstances of warfare.

31 See Art. 31(3)(b) of the Vienna Convention on the Law of Treaties (VCLT).

32 See Art. 31(3)(c) VCLT.

33 Henry, Chapter 15, 'Sea Warfare', in this volume, 271–72.

34 The principle of humanity can be understood as encompassing concern for the humane treatment of animals. One of us has submitted 'that the principle of humanity does not *only* prohibit things which humans must not do to other humans because this would run against their shared humanity. Rather, upon evolution of the public attitudes, the types of crimes which are intuitively recognised as inherently and plainly wrong by all members of the human community, and which shock the conscience of humankind, have expanded. They are no longer limited to human victims' (Peters, 'Animals' (n. 27), 369).

35 Peters, 'Animals' (n. 27), 388.

36 ICRC, Environmental Guidelines, Rule 16; ILC, Draft Principles on the Protection of the Environment in Relation to Armed Conflict (2019), reproduced in UN General Assembly, *Report of the International Law Commission: Seventy-first session (29 April–7 June and 8 July–9 August 2019)*, UN Doc. A/74/10, UN, New York, 2019, Chap. VI, draft principle 8*bis*.

37 See n. 6 with main text.

38 Fortin, Chapter 12, 'Veterinary Personnel', in this volume, 210.

First principle: animals should only be utilised for military purposes in exceptional circumstances and always be provided with adequate care for their needs.[39] Belligerents should not use animals to carry out military functions, except when absolutely necessary for essential tasks that cannot be accomplished by human beings in specific circumstances; such tasks as searching, rescuing or transporting wounded soldiers. When using animals for these medical tasks, belligerents should ensure, to the greatest practicable extent, that their dignity be respected by providing them with satisfactory conditions of nutrition, safety and health, especially when these animals are wounded on the battlefield. They should not employ animals outside these functions to perform military tasks such as carrying able-bodied soldiers or weapons. Belligerents should return animals that fall into their hands to their homeland or retain them to perform the mentioned medical duties only.

Second principle: during warfare, including sea warfare, animals should be treated as sentient beings experiencing emotion, pain and distress.[40] This principle demands that belligerents should never use means and methods of warfare that by their nature will cause superfluous injury or unnecessary suffering of identifiable animals. Moreover, in the proportionality calculation, animals should acquire an intrinsic value and, as a consequence, their interests should no longer be automatically subordinated to those of humans. This means that when evaluating collateral damage, belligerents should ensure, to the greatest practicable extent, that the consequences of an attack on animals are not only a factor of minor weight in the balancing exercise.

Third principle: when captured by the enemy, animals should be treated as sentient beings experiencing emotion, pain and distress.[41] Upon capture, belligerents should ensure, to the greatest practicable extent, that the welfare of animals which have been involved in hostilities be respected by providing them with satisfactory conditions regarding nutrition, safety and health. The physical and mental integrity of these animals should always be preserved. All forms of cruel treatment, torture or mutilation should be strictly prohibited. Animals should not be located in the vicinity of dangerous areas or installations, nor should they be placed in regions where essential resources, like water, are not available and cannot be provided. They should not be 'interned' close to warzones, where they run the risk of being killed or injured. Since captured animals will rarely represent a military threat to the security of the adversary, they should, as far as possible, be freed if they can survive by themselves, or be returned to their homeland.

39 This principle is mainly drawn from de Hemptinne, Chapter 11, 'Medical Transport, Search and Rescue', in this volume.

40 This principle is mainly drawn from Roscini, Chapter 5, 'Property and Objects' and Henry, Chapter 15, 'Sea Warfare', in this volume.

41 This principle is mainly drawn from de Hemptinne, Kebebew and Niyo, Chapter 10, 'Animals as Combatants and as Prisoners of War?' and Henry, Chapter 15, 'Sea Warfare', in this volume.

Fourth principle: during occupation, animals should be treated by the occupying power, not only as public or private property or as parts of the environment, but also as sentient beings experiencing emotion, pain and distress.[42] The occupying power should take appropriate measures to ensure, to the greatest practicable extent, that vulnerable animals are protected in the occupied territory and that their basic needs be fulfilled. To do so, occupying powers should be authorised to change the legal regime to offer a better protection to animals living in occupied territory, for instance by introducing new legislation against cruelty to animals that reflect international standards. In the same manner that an occupying power is allowed to pass legislation in order to discharge its basic international human rights obligations, the occupying power should be entitled to establish norms that comply with minimal animal welfare standards (as they emerged from regional and international conventions), while at the same time paying due respect to local cultural, legal and economic traditions.

Fifth principle: veterinary personnel who take care of animals should be protected by the same rules that apply to medical personnel during warfare.[43] Belligerents should take steps to ensure that veterinary personnel can provide care to animals without interference. When falling into the hands of the enemy, veterinary personnel should not become prisoners of war and be detained as prisoners. They should only be retained to the extent needed for the provision of medical care to wounded and sick animals. If veterinarians are retained, they should receive the benefits and protections of GC III and be given the facilities they need for the health care of animals. This protection should only cease if veterinarian personnel commit acts harmful to the enemy, but only after due warning has been given and remained unheeded.

Sixth principle: when conducting military experiments on animals, belligerents should respect national and international instruments that apply to animal testing in peacetimes (with necessary adjustments).[44] The generally accepted principles of scientific procedures on animals are the principle of humanitarian (humane) treatment, the 3Rs – the requirement of last resort (replacement), minimal use (reduction) and minimal harm to animals (refinement) – and the principle of effectiveness. These widely acknowledged principles should be complemented by concrete rules prescribing necessary qualifications for actors competent to conduct animal testing, the conditions under which this testing may take place and its supervision. Violations of these rules should entail administrative and in the extreme case criminal sanctions for individuals and trigger parallel state responsibility.

Seventh principle: the creation of protected zones to shelter animal populations should be encouraged already in peacetime.[45] The identification of ecocentric

42 This principle is mainly drawn from Longobardo, Chapter 13, 'Occupied Territory', in this volume.
43 This principle is mainly drawn from Fortin, Chapter 12, 'Veterinary Personnel', in this volume.
44 This principle is mainly drawn from Bílková, Chapter 17, 'Military Experimentation', in this volume.
45 This principle is mainly drawn from Gillett, Chapter 14, 'Protected Zones', in this volume.

protected zones for particularly vulnerable areas or environmental hotspots, in which endangered species are often located, should be promoted by states and competent organisations, such as the ICRC and the Geneva Call. Moreover, the establishment of a network of such zones should be achieved in a systematic manner through reliance on other pre-existing multilateral conventions, such as the World Heritage Convention and the Convention on Biological Diversity.

Eighth principle: the peacetime protection of 'endangered species' should be integrated into IHL and should thus provide increased safeguards to this category of animals during warfare, including sea warfare.[46] Existing IHL norms do not contain any explicit rules addressing the protection of 'endangered species'. This regime has only been developed in the context of peacetime international environmental law. To bring the concern of species conservation to bear, IHL rules should be interpreted so as to minimise events endangering or likely to endanger the survival of species. This systemic interpretation (Article 31(3)(c) VCLT) of the relevant IHL rules would also reflect the precautionary principle. The basic idea animates the following four proposals. First, endangered species should be protected, not only as civilian objects, but also as 'cultural objects' under Article 53 of AP I or as 'livestock' under Article 54(2) of AP I. Second, when evaluating collateral damage, the consequences of an attack on endangered species should carry a special weight in the balancing exercise, requiring the concrete expectation of a 'very special military advantage'. Third, a commander should refrain from launching an attack, even when it is uncertain (i.e. even when the indicia are not fully clear) whether the attack would threaten the survival of members of an of endangered species. Fourth, harm done to endangered species should generally be understood as satisfying all the cumulative criteria listed in the provisions protecting the environment (Articles 35(3) and 55 of AP I) which then leads to the rule that such harm is generally prohibited.

Ninth principle: endangered and endemic species should benefit from the protection afforded to cultural property.[47] The fairly narrow concept of cultural property in IHL could be expanded through an evolutionary interpretation in the light of other international law instruments relating to the protection of both cultural and natural heritage. This would allow to draw some forms of wildlife, namely endangered species and species endemic to particular areas, under the umbrella of cultural property.

Tenth principle: the legal tools for preventing and combatting wildlife trafficking that were conceived for peacetimes should be adapted to the specific circumstances of warfare.[48] International regimes aiming at suppressing – or at least limiting – the funding of belligerents with the revenues from transboundary trade of other

[46] This principle is mainly drawn from Böhringer and Marauhn, Chapter 8, 'Endangered Species', in this volume.

[47] This principle is mainly drawn from Krähenmann, Chapter 6, 'Specially Protected Objects', in this volume.

[48] This principle is mainly drawn from Nowrot, Chapter 20, 'Wildlife Trafficking', in this volume.

(non-living) natural resources could be model. An example is the Kimberley Process Certification Scheme, a joint initiative formally launched in 2003 between governments, civil society groups and representatives of the diamond industry.[49] All relevant schemes pursue a holistic approach to eradicate the illegal trading of minerals by focusing on the private and public segments of the supply chain besides the source countries.

Eleventh principle: states parties to the ICC Statute should consider strengthening the role of the ICC and of the national criminal judiciary to address serious violations committed against animals during warfare.[50] States parties should examine how the existing substantive and procedural rules that apply before the ICC could be modified to address criminal conduct involving animals during warfare. They should also study how to reinforce the national capacity to adopt, implement and enforce the relevant criminal rules with a view to improve animal welfare. In prosecuting crimes which may significantly and seriously affect animals, the ICC and national courts should accept that these animals are more than simple objects that require protection from looting or destruction for the benefit of human beings. They should acknowledge that unjustified killing and otherwise harming animals have effects on the animals themselves and make them suffer. The criminal law appliers should recognise that animal cruelty may, under certain extreme conditions, constitute 'other inhumane acts' and thus constitute crimes against humanity. At the very least, when criminal conduct affecting animals is only qualified as crimes against objects – such as plunder or extensive expropriation of property, wanton destruction of property or attacks against civilian objects – the suffering of animals should be duly taken into account in sentencing. The ICC and national courts should also progressively embed animal issues into their reparative frameworks.

2.3 *Progressive Recognition of Fundamental Rights for Animals during Warfare*

As set out above, a dynamic interpretation of IHL principles to properly reflect the fact that animals are particularly vulnerable sentient beings in wartimes could significantly increase their protection. That said, this approach rests on weak foundations. It does not seem currently backed by a wide and coherent state practice nor based on any general principle of international law, despite the dynamism instilled by the Martens clause which would allow to progressively affirm 'animal dignity' in armed conflict. Ultimately, we should envisage a more radical approach towards the protection of animal welfare during warfare. As emphasised by Heike Krieger and José Martínez Soria in Chapter 4:

> Any conceptual transfer of animals from the categories of property and tangible objects to combatants or civilians, or any attempt to completely ban the use of

49 www.kimberleyprocess.com/, accessed 22 February 2022.

50 This principle is mainly drawn from Ventura, Chapter 18, 'International Crimes', in this volume.

> animals in war, is eventually a political value decision *that should not be brought about incrementally through interpretative processes but should instead result from transparent and open political discussions*. Obviously one may wonder whether it is at all realistic to generate momentum for such a political act, both in general and in relation to our current conjuncture. Nevertheless, creating such a momentum should be a high priority for animal rights activists.[51]

Concurring with this assertion, we shall conclude our work by coming back to the idea of moving beyond an interpretative evolution to the promotion of a new international instrument formally conferring additional basic rights to animals.[52] This strategy raises three preliminary questions.

First, it is traditionally argued that IHL imposes obligations on states (and possibly on armed groups), while individuals are simply the beneficiaries of protective rules or objective standards, without being granted rights (entitlements).[53] It goes without saying that if IHL were not conferring direct rights upon human beings, it would certainly not provide any such rights to non-human beings. Determining the exact nature of IHL norms would go beyond the scope of this conclusion.[54] It suffices to observe that it is increasingly contended that, not the least under the influence of human rights law, IHL seems to have progressively evolved so as to provide substantive and independent individual rights (including rights to reparation) to individuals, as the counterpart to the obligations imposed on states and possibly on non-states actors.[55] In the same manner that human rights have progressively 'individualised' IHL, the development of an international body on animal protection in peacetimes – however thin and fragmented[56] – could play a similar role by contributing to a corresponding form of 'animalisation' of IHL. Along this trajectory, IHL could be understood to attribute rights to animals, and not only to embody standards of protection.

51 Krieger and Martínez Soria, Chapter 4, 'Rationale and Challenges', in this volume (emphasis added).

52 Ibid.

53 See Laurence Hill-Cawthorne, 'Rights under International Humanitarian Law', *The European Journal of International Law* 28 (2018), 1187–215, at 1189. For the traditional approach, see for example René Provost, *International Human Rights and Humanitarian Law* (Cambridge: Cambridge University Press 2002), 26–42; Silja Vöneky, 'Implementation and Enforcement of International Humanitarian Law', in Dieter Fleck (ed.), *The Handbook of International Humanitarian Law* (3rd ed., Oxford: Oxford University Press 2013), 647–88, at 684; Ziv Bohrer, 'Divisions over Distinctions in Wartime International Law', in Anne Peters and Christian Marxsen (series eds.), *Law Applicable to Armed Conflict*, Max Planck Trialogues on the Law of Peace and War vol. 2 (Cambridge: Cambridge University Press 2019), 106–96, at 175, 180–6, 189.

54 See generally Hill-Cawthorne, 'Rights' (n. 53), 1187–215.

55 Ibid. For a rights-based reading of IHL, see for example Theodor Meron, 'The Humanization of Humanitarian Law', 99 *American Journal of International Law* 94 (2000), 239–78, at 240; Christopher Greenwood, 'Rights at the Frontier: Protecting the Individual in Time of War', in B. Rider (ed.), *Law at the Centre: The Institute of Advanced Legal Studies at Fifty* (London: Kluwer Law International 1999) 277, at 281–3; Anne Peters, 'Direct Rights of Individuals in the International Law of Armed Conflict', in Dapo Akande, David Rodin and Jennifer Welsh (eds.), *The Individualisation of War* (Oxford: Oxford University Press 2022).

56 Krieger and Martínez Soria, Chapter 4, 'Rationale and Challenges', in this volume.

Once it is admitted that animals could potentially acquire rights under IHL, the second preliminary question is whether animals can be rights bearers without being concomitantly constrained by legal duties, given their general inaptitude to apprehend the reality of war, its violent consequences and the obligations imposed by IHL. In this regard, it should be recalled that probably no modern domestic legal system conditions the enjoyment of rights on the ability to fulfil legal obligations.[57] Today, infants or mentally handicapped persons have rights although they are not expected to comply with legal obligations.[58] Excluding animals from the circle of humanitarian rights bearers just because they are unable to comply with humanitarian duties would be contrary to contemporary thinking. The second challenge can thus also be met.

The third question is whether promoting rights for animals would run contrary to the preservation of humans' basic rights, which, as we know, are seriously threatened by wars and should be guaranteed as a top priority.[59] But contrary to what is often claimed, safeguarding animals does not necessarily interfere – or run against – the protection of human beings; the two often run in parallel without impacting negatively on each other.[60] Moreover, the IHL normative framework is flexible enough to guarantee that fundamental human rights be always preserved and, if necessary, prevail over the needs or interests of animals if one is forced to choose between the two.[61] If IHL norms attributed legal rights to animals – instead of only referring to their needs or interests – the animals' legal position would be reinforced, not only symbolically, but also practically.[62] On a symbolic level, IHL would contribute to the emancipation of animals from the guardianship of humans and would affirm the proper value of fundamental animal interests and needs (such as the interest in not being subjected to unnecessary suffering).[63] On a practical level, IHL often requires that belligerents undertake trade-offs when they cannot fully reach competing goals – for instance, satisfying their military imperatives and respecting humanitarian concerns, including those relating to the welfare of animals. The trade-off (which requires balancing) would look significantly different if animals were treated as distinct legal persons possessing rights, that is, when the trade-off were not just guided by mere 'needs' or 'interests' of animals.[64] Likewise, the interpretation and application of IHL norms on the conduct of hostilities or detention would be influenced by an animal rights-based approach. For instance,

57 Peters, 'Animals' (n. 27), 400.
58 Ibid.
59 Krieger and Martínez Soria, Chapter 4, 'Rationale and Challenges', in this volume.
60 Jérôme de Hemptinne, 'Challenges Regarding the Protection of Animals During Warfare', in Anne Peters (ed.), *Studies in Global Animal Law* (Heidelberg: Springer 2020), 173–83, at 175.
61 Ibid.
62 Peters, 'Animals' (n. 27), 440–52.
63 Ibid., 445.
64 Anne Peters, 'Toward International Animal Rights', in Anne Peters (ed.), *Studies in Global Animal Law* (Heidelberg: Springer 2020), 109–20, at 111.

belligerents would need to specifically justify restricting certain rights of animals when required by the circumstances of warfare.[65] To sum up:

> The main asset for animals is that rights confer a legal position which is elevated above the ordinary balancing of conflicting goods. When animals only benefit from protective rules, their welfare is but one interest among others. Balancing the animals' interests against human interests typically ends up prioritising the human interests, even trivial ones. Arguably, this type of balancing is structurally biased against animals. In contrast, animal rights would allow a fair balancing in which the proper value of fundamental interests (such as the interest to live) could be integrated.[66]

In reality, the obstacle is not so much *conceptual barriers* for the attribution of rights to animals, but the *political willingness of states* to adopt a new instrument which would further restrict their sovereign powers to conduct wars. At a time when states are faced with serious challenges to fight so-called terrorist organisations or powerful armed groups, it seems rather utopian to believe that governments would accept curtailing these powers to increase the protection of non-human beings by giving them rights, which is certainly not at the forefront of their agenda. Ultimately, any progress in this regard would depend on the nature of the rights that are conferred on animals. We believe that two types of rights could receive the immediate attention of the international community. The first right that could be granted to animals, if any, would arguably be the right not to be involved in human warfare.[67] Indeed, given the limited number of states that weaponise animals and the strong public opposition to this type of activity, it seems not unrealistic that a consensus could be reached on this point in due course. Such a legal evolution is even more likely because technological progress has reduced the need to employ animals as means and methods of warfare. The second right that could be envisaged would be the right not to be used in military experiments. We do acknowledge that experimentation on animals seem to be today widely practiced by armed forces around the world for three main reasons: to test weapons, to test military surgical techniques and to test resistance to physical assault or to adverse conditions.[68] While a general ban on all these types of experiments might not be agreeable to many states, a specific prohibition to carry out any testing of weapons on animals would certainly find some support, at least in the public opinion, given the excessive cruelty of these practices. All other military testing activities – which could be conducted under strict conditions – would definitively need to be prohibited when they cause unnecessary suffering to animals.

We hope that the formal recognition of these two basic rights – not to be involved in military activities and in military experiments – could potentially trigger a wider

65 Peters, 'Animals' (n. 27), 444–7.
66 Peters, 'Toward International Animal Rights' (n. 64), 111.
67 See Jenks, Chapter 9, 'War Weapons', in this volume.
68 See Bílková, Chapter 17, 'Military Experimentation', in this volume.

reflection on the conferment of additional fundamental rights to animals, such as the right to receive medical care when wounded or sick, the right not be submitted to any cruel and degrading treatment, the right to be preserved from military attacks of enemy forces and the right to be provided with satisfactory conditions regarding nutrition, safety and health. Only when such rights are formally recognised will the welfare of animal be truly safeguarded in warfare.

SELECT BIBLIOGRAPHY

Akande, Dapo David Rodin and Jennifer Welsh (eds.), *The Individualisation of War* (Oxford: Oxford University Press 2022).

de Hemptinne, Jérôme, 'Challenges Regarding the Protection of Animals During Warfare', in Anne Peters (ed.), *Studies in Global Animal Law* (Heidelberg: Springer 2020), 173–83.

Peters, Anne, 'Animals in International Law', *Collected Courses of The Hague Academy of International Law – Recueil des Cours* Vol. 410 (Leiden: Brill 2020), 95–544.

Peters, Anne, 'Toward International Animal Rights', in Anne Peters (ed.), *Studies in Global Animal Law* (Heidelberg: Springer 2020), 109–20.

UNEP, *Protecting the Environment During Armed Conflicts: An Inventory Analysis of International Law* (Nairobi: UNEP 2009).

Index

For EU product safety concerns, contact us at Calle de José Abascal, 56–1°,
28003 Madrid, Spain or eugpsr@cambridge.org.

www.ingramcontent.com/pod-product-compliance
Lightning Source LLC
LaVergne TN
LVHW010916300926
849194LV00025B/245
9781009060271